T0181397

Lecture Notes of the Institute for Computer Sciences, Social Informatics and Telecommunications Engineering   342

More information about this series at http://www.springer.com/series/8197

Mingxiang Guan · Zhenyu Na (Eds.)

Machine Learning and Intelligent Communications

5th International Conference, MLICOM 2020
Shenzhen, China, September 26–27, 2020
Proceedings

 Springer

Editors
Mingxiang Guan
Shenzhen Institute of Information
Technology
Shenzhen, China

Zhenyu Na
Sci & Tech, DianHang Bldg, Rm 321
Dalian Maritime Univ, Sch of Info
Dalian, Liaoning, China

ISSN 1867-8211   ISSN 1867-822X   (electronic)
Lecture Notes of the Institute for Computer Sciences, Social Informatics
and Telecommunications Engineering
ISBN 978-3-030-66784-9   ISBN 978-3-030-66785-6   (eBook)
https://doi.org/10.1007/978-3-030-66785-6

This Springer imprint is published by the registered company Springer Nature Switzerland AG
The registered company address is: Gewerbestrasse 11, 6330 Cham, Switzerland

Preface

We are delighted to introduce the proceedings of the fifth edition of the 2017 European Alliance for Innovation (EAI) International Conference on Machine Learning and Intelligent Communications (MLICOM). This conference brought together researchers, developers and practitioners around the world who are leveraging and developing machine learning and intelligent communications.

The technical program of MLICOM2020 consisted of 56 full papers in oral presentation sessions in the main conference tracks. The conference tracks were: Track 1 - Intelligent resource (e.g., spectrum, power) allocation schemes; Track 2 - Applications of Neural Network & Deep Learning; Track 3 - Intelligent communications; Track 4 - Intelligent positioning and navigation systems; Track 5 - Intelligent space and terrestrial integrated networks; Track 6 - Machine learning algorithms & Intelligent networks; Track 7 - Machine learning and information processing in wireless sensor networks; Track 8 - Smart unmanned vehicular technology.

Coordination with the steering chairs, Imrich Chlamtac, Xin Liu and Xin-Lin Huang was essential for the success of the conference. We sincerely appreciate their constant support and guidance. It was also a great pleasure to work with such an excellent organizing committee team who worked hard in organizing and supporting the conference. The Technical Program Committee, led by our TPC Co-Chairs, Dr. Dean Luo and Dr. Zhenyu Na, completed the peer-review process of technical papers and made a high-quality technical program. We are also grateful to the Conference Manager, Karolina Marcinova, for her support and to all the authors who submitted their papers to the MLICOM2020 conference and workshops.

We strongly believe that the MLICOM conference provides a good forum for all researchers, developers and practitioners to discuss all science and technology aspects that are relevant to machine learning and intelligent communications. We also expect that future MLICOM conferences will be as successful and stimulating, as indicated by the contributions presented in this volume.

Mingxiang Guan

Conference Organization

Steering Committee

Imrich Chlamtac	University of Trento, Italy
Xin Liu	Dalian University of Technology, China
Xin-Lin Huang	Tongji University, China

Organizing Committee

General Chair

Mingxiang Guan	Shenzhen Institute of Information Technology

General Co-chairs

Zhiliang Xu	Shenzhen Institute of Information Technology
Qing Guo	Harbin Institute of Technology

TPC Chair and Co-chairs

Tingting Zhang	Harbin Institute of Technology, Shenzhen
Gongliang Liu	Harbin Institute of Technology, Weihai
Nan Zhao	Dalian University of Technology

Sponsorship and Exhibit Chairs

Shaohua Wu	Harbin Institute of Technology, Shenzhen
Hui Li	Hainan University
Dean Luo	Shenzhen Institute of Information Technology

Local Chairs

Mingxiang Guan	Shenzhen Institute of Information Technology
Zhiliang Xu	Shenzhen Institute of Information Technology

Workshops Chairs

Xinlin Huang	Tongji University
Weidang Lu	Zhejiang University of Technology
Bo Li	Harbin Institute of Technology, Weihai

Publicity and Social Media Chairs

Mu Zhou	Chongqing University of Posts and Telecommunications
Zhenyu Na	Dalian Maritime University
Zhian Deng	Harbin Engineering University

Publications Chairs

Mu Zhou	Chongqing University of Posts and Telecommunications
Zhenyu Na	Dalian Maritime University
Zhian Deng	Harbin Engineering University

Web Chairs

Yingjie Cui	Shenzhen Institute of Information Technology
Lei Ning	Shenzhen Technology University
Zhou Wu	Shenzhen Institute of Information Technology

Technical Program Committee

Xuemei Cao	Shenzhen Institute of Information Technology
Liming Chen	Electric Power Research Institute. CSG
Zhang Cong	Guangdong Cantone Technology Co., Ltd.
Zhang Decheng	South China Normal University
Yajing Deng	Harbin Institute of Technology, Shenzhen
Li Dongqing	Harbin Institute of Technology, Shenzhen
Yingzhe Dou	Communication Research Center, Harbin Institute of Technology
Li Feng	Zhejiang Gongshang University
Jianxiang Feng	Harbin Engineering University
Rui Feng	Ludong University
Junqi Gao	Heilongjiang University
Shi Gou	Guangzhou Power Supply Company
Xin Guan	Harbin Institute of Technology
Guorong He	Shezhen Institute of Information Technology
Cui Heng	Liren College of Yanshan University
Boyu Hua	Nanjing University of Aeronautics and Astronautics
Bian Ji	Shandong Normal University
Baihui Jiang	Heilongjiang University
Mao Kai	Nanjing University of Aeronautics and Astronautics
Wang Le	Shenzhen Institute of Information Technology
Dan Li	Harbin Institute of Technology
Penghui Li	Nanjing University of Aeronautics and Astronautics
Yue Liu	Dalian Maritime University
Dean Luo	Shenzhen Institute of Information Technology
Yingnan Lv	Heilongjiang University

Xinxin Miao	Communication Research Center, Harbin Institute of Technology
Bao Peng	Shenzhen Institute of Information Technology
Zhang Renfeng	Jilin Institute of Architecture and Civil Engineering
Hanqin Shao	Nanjing University of Posts and Telecommunications
Jian Wang	Shenzhen Institute of Information Technology
Jun Wang	Dalian Maritime University
Xin Wang	Dalian Maritime University
Yi Wang	Dalian Maritime University
Qiuming Zhu	Nanjing University of Aeronautics and Astronautics

Contents

Intelligent Communications

Intelligent Positioning and Navigation Systems

Intelligent Space and Terrestrial Integrated Networks

Machine Learning Algorithm and Intelligent Networks

Smart Unmanned Vehicular Technology

Late Track

Intelligent Resource (e.g., Spectrum, Power) Allocation Schemes

Performance Optimization and Power Allocation of Amplify-and-Forward System with Multi-source

Junwei Bao[1], Dazhuan Xu[2], Qiuming Zhu[2]([✉]), and Kai Mao[2]

[1] College of Science, Nanjing University of Aeronautics and Astronautics, Nanjing 211106, China
`broadenway@nuaa.edu.cn`
[2] College of electronic and information engineering, Nanjing University of Aeronautics and Astronautics, Nanjing 211106, China
{`xudazhuan,zhuqiuming,maokai`}`@nuaa.edu.cn`

Abstract. In this paper, a performance optimization scheme based on the maximum signal-to-noise ratio (SNR) at destination of amplify-and-forward (AF) system with multi-source nodes and multi-relay nodes is proposed. For the underlying AF systems, the signal is transmitted from several identical source nodes to several parallel relay nodes via the wireless channel, and then transmitted by the relay nodes to the destination node. In order to recover the original signal, the SNR under limited system power constraint is modeled as a constrained optimization problem. Then, we transform the constrained optimization problem to a convex function with respect to the power allocation, and obtain the expression of maximum SNR at destination and corresponding power allocation. Simulation results show that the SNR at the destination of the proposed scheme significantly outperforms the one in which the limited power is equally allocated among all source nodes and all relay nodes.

Keywords: AF system · Multi-source · Parallel relay networks · Power allocation · Performance optimization · Constrained optimization problem

1 Introduction

AF is an important relaying strategy, in which one or more relays amplify the source signal to complete the communication between the source node and the destination node. It can extend wireless network coverage or improve communication quality and is widely used in wireless communication system, wireless sensor system and so on. Especially, in the communication networks of military, government and financial institution, where the relay node must be regarded as eavesdropper node, AF is safer than decode-and-forward (DF).

© ICST Institute for Computer Sciences, Social Informatics and Telecommunications Engineering 2021
Published by Springer Nature Switzerland AG 2021. All Rights Reserved
M. Guan and Z. Na (Eds.): MLICOM 2020, LNICST 342, pp. 3–15, 2021.
https://doi.org/10.1007/978-3-030-66785-6_1

Due to the widely application, AF strategy have gotten numerous researches in recently years. Many researches focus on outage probability (OP) [1–5] of opportunistic AF relaying. In addition, Rodriguez and Tran [6] had studied the achievable rates over Rayleigh fading channels. Singh and Gupta [7], Liu and Song [8] and Islam [9] studied the quality of service (QoS), symbol error rate (SER) and achievable rate of the AF system, respectively. While Nagendra and Vimal [10] derived further closed-expressions of the outage probability and the average channel capacity. Recently, Wang and Wang [11] proposed a scheme, in which they studied how to guarantee SNR at destination. Based on AF system, there are more researches, such as Su and Chen [12] and Chen and Fang [13], they design a robust transceiver for Multiple Input Multiple Output (MIMO) system, and so on.

As we know, power allocation of wireless communication system plays a vitally important role, so it is always a field that attracts much more attentions. Laneman and Wornell [14] studied an AF scheme with cooperative diversity. They equally divided up the total available power among one source node and all relay nodes. However, it is found that the performance of this scheme is sub-optimal. Zhao and Adve [15] studied the AF cooperative diversity system and proposed a selection scheme to choose the "best" relay node to assist the communication. The scheme can get a better outage behavior and throughput than all-participate scheme. After that, much more power allocation scheme was optimized from selecting relay node [16–20].

However, to the best of our knowledge, for an AF system composed of several identical source nodes and several parallel relay nodes in which the source node cannot directly communicate with the destination node, when the total system power is limited and must be allocated among several source nodes and several relay nodes, the optimized power allocation has not yet been studied. This paper aims to fill this research gap. The major contributions and novelties of the paper are summarized as follows:

1) An AF system model is proposed, in which several source nodes communication with a destination node with the help of all parallel relay nodes, and no direct path exist between source nodes and destination node. The power of every relay node is equally allocated, as well as the several source nodes, and the total system power of the relay nodes and source nodes is limited.
2) The criteria that assess the system performance usually are bit error rate (BER), OP or QoS. Without loss of generality, here the criterion that assesses the system performance is SNR at destination rather than BER, as we know that the maximum SNR can bring the minimum BER.
3) The expression of the SNR at destination is derived and transformed into a convex function with respect to power allocation. Then the expressions of maximum SNR at destination and corresponding optimized power allocation are obtained.

The remainder of this paper is organized as follows. In Sect. 2, the multi-relay AF system with multi-source nodes is introduced and the SNR at destination is given, and the expression of the maximum SNR at destination under system power constraints is derived. The power allocation is optimized and the SNR is maximized in Sect. 3. Calculations are conducted with corresponding parameters and numerical results are analyzed in Sect. 4. Finally, conclusions are given in Sect. 5.

2 Multi-relay AF System with Multi-source Nodes

Figure 1 depicts the proposed AF system, in which no direct link exists between the source S_m and destination D, here $m = 1, 2, \cdots, M$. The several sources communicate with destination D with the assistance of L parallel relay nodes $R_i(i = 1, 2, \cdots, L)$. The destination collects all signals that amplified and retransmitted by relays with equal weight and recovers original information.

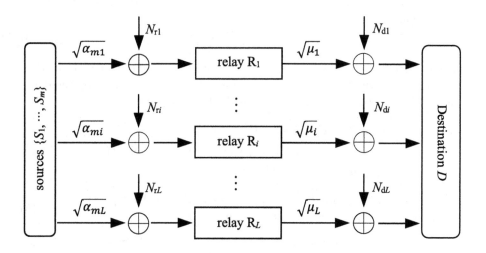

Fig. 1. Multi-relay AF system with several sources.

Assume that the power of the several source nodes are equally distributed, the original signal $X_m(t)$ generated from source S_m follows Gaussian distribution $N(0, P_x)$. The noise in every relay node and destination is independently and identically distributed (i.i.d) additive white Gaussian noise (AWGN) and obeys $N(0, \sigma_n^2)$. Meanwhile, all the wireless channels between source nodes and relay nodes, as well as that between relay nodes and destination node, are all Gaussian channels. It should be mentioned that, here what we considered is a theoretical analysis framework, encoding mechanism and access probability [21] are not taken into account. Furthermore, the numbers of source nodes and relay nodes are all more than one, while the character of the structure of the AF system make it different with the MIMO system [22]. The technologies and their relative theories of MIMO system, such as beam design [23], antenna selection and so on, are not thought about.

When the signal $X_m(t)$ that generated from the mth source reaches the ith relay node R_i, we obtain the following equations [24]

$$Y_{rmi}(t) = \sqrt{\alpha_{mi}} X_m(t) + N_{ri}(t),$$
$$m = 1, 2, \cdots, M; i = 1, 2, \cdots, L. \tag{1}$$

The power of signal $Y_{rmi}(t)$ can be represented as

$$P_{rmi} = \alpha_{mi} P_x + \sigma_n^2,$$
$$m = 1, 2, \cdots, M; i = 1, 2, \cdots, L. \tag{2}$$

where $N_{ri}(t)$ denotes the Gaussian noise at the ith relay node, α_{mi} corresponds to the channel attenuation factor between the mth source node and the ith relay node [25].

The ith relay node amplifies the power of the received signal for β times which is defined as

$$\beta = \frac{P_{ri}}{\alpha P_x + \sigma_n^2} \tag{3}$$

where P_{ri} denotes the power of the signal that the ith relay transmitted, then send it to the destination via wireless channel. The signal received by the destination and its power can be presented in the following forms

$$Y_{dmi}(t) = \sqrt{\mu_i} \sqrt{\beta} Y_{rmi}(t) + N_{di}(t)$$
$$= \sqrt{\mu_i} \sqrt{\beta} [\sqrt{\alpha_{mi}} X_m(t) + N_{ri}(t)] + N_{di}(t), \tag{4}$$
$$m = 1, 2, \cdots, M; i = 1, 2, \cdots, L.$$

$$P_{dmi} = \mu_i \beta P_{rmi} + \sigma_n^2 = \mu_i \beta (\alpha_{mi} P_x + \sigma_n^2) + \sigma_n^2,$$
$$m = 1, 2, \cdots, M; i = 1, 2, \cdots, L. \tag{5}$$

where μ_i corresponds to the channel attenuation factor between the ith relay node and destination node, $N_{di}(t)$ denotes the Gaussian noise at destination node with mean zero and power σ_n^2. For the relay nodes are parallel, all $\sqrt{\alpha_{mi}}$ are the same, as well as all $\sqrt{\mu_i}$. For simplicity, we let $\alpha_{mi} = \alpha$, $\mu_i = \mu$. For the destination received signal $Y_{di}(t)$ from the ith relay can be calculated as a coherent summation of the signals transmitted from the sources [26], we can get the following expression

$$Y_{di}(t) = \sum_{m=1}^{M} \{\sqrt{\mu} \sqrt{\beta} [\sqrt{\alpha_{mi}} X_m(t) + N_{ri}(t)] + N_{di}(t)\}. \tag{6}$$

In this case, we obtain the power of the $Y_{di}(t)$

$$P_{di} = M[\mu\beta(\alpha P_x + \sigma_n^2) + \sigma_n^2] \tag{7}$$

so the SNR of $Y_{di}(t)$ is

$$\gamma_{Ai} = \frac{M\alpha\mu\beta P_x}{M\sigma_n^2 + M\mu\beta\sigma_n^2} = \frac{\alpha\mu\beta P_x}{\sigma_n^2 + \mu\beta\sigma_n^2}. \tag{8}$$

Substituting (3) into (8) gives

$$\gamma_{Ai} = \frac{\alpha \mu P_{ri} P_x}{\sigma_n^2 [\alpha P_x + \sigma_n^2 + \mu P_{ri}]}. \tag{9}$$

where γ_{Ai} is expressed as a function of the power of every source node and relay node. In the traditional multi-relay AF system, every source-relay-destination sublink is the same. The destination node collects all signals from L relays simultaneously, and SNR of the sum of all signals at the destination node can be presented by

$$\gamma_A = \sum_{i=1}^{L} \frac{\alpha \mu P_{ri} P_x}{\sigma_n^2 [\alpha P_x + \sigma_n^2 + \mu P_{ri}]}. \tag{10}$$

For some wireless sensor networks, signal source is usually working in harsh conditions, charging and changing battery are too difficult to realize. Here we assume that the total power of all sources and all relays are limited, and the power of every relay node is equally distributed, one can finds the following expression

$$MP_x + LP_{ri} = P. \tag{11}$$

Combine the power constraint (11) into (10) to take the place of P_{ri} with independent variable P_x, we can get the expression of SNR at destination

$$\gamma_A = \frac{L\alpha \mu P_x (P - MP_x)}{\sigma_n^2 [\mu(P - MP_x) + L(\sigma_n^2 + \alpha P_x)]}. \tag{12}$$

Considering that the power of every source node P_x should lower than the total system power P, the maximum SNR at destination of the AF system can be described as an constrained optimization problem

$$\max : \gamma_A$$

$$\text{s.t.} \begin{cases} \gamma_A = \frac{L\alpha \mu P_x (P - MP_x)}{\sigma_n^2 [\mu(P - MP_x) + L(\sigma_n^2 + \alpha P_x)]}. \\ 0 \le P_x \le P \end{cases} \tag{13}$$

3 Optimizations of Power Allocation and SNR at Destination

Obviously, the value of P_x cannot take 0, for the source nodes have not enough power to transmit signal to relay nodes, nor take P, for the relay nodes will lack enough power to transmit signal to destination node. So γ_A is a convex function of variable P_x. To obtain the expression of the maximum γ_A, here we use a strict mathematical derivation.

If we make γ_A the function with respect to a variable P_x/P, the following expression can be derived from (13)

$$
\begin{aligned}
(\gamma_A)_{\max} &= \max \frac{P^2}{P^2} \cdot \frac{L\alpha\mu P_x(P - MP_x)}{\sigma_n^2[\mu(P - MP_x) + L(\sigma_n^2 + \alpha P_x)]} \\
&= \max \frac{L\alpha\mu P^2}{\sigma_n^2} \cdot \frac{P_x(P - MP_x)}{P^2[\mu(P - MP_x) + L(\sigma_n^2 + \alpha P_x)]} \\
&= \frac{L\alpha\mu P^2}{\sigma_n^2} \cdot \max \frac{\frac{P_x}{P}\left(1 - \frac{MP_x}{P}\right)}{\mu(P - MP_x) + L(\sigma_n^2 + \alpha P_x)}.
\end{aligned}
\tag{14}
$$

Obviously, the first half part of (14) $\frac{L\alpha\mu P^2}{\sigma_n^2}$ is a constant. When γ_A reaches its maximum, the second part of (14) must get its maximum, too. For further simplification, we will therefore define $\varphi\left(\frac{P_x}{P}\right)$ [27] in the following

$$
\varphi\left(\frac{P_x}{P}\right) = \frac{\mu(P - MP_x) + L(\sigma_n^2 + \alpha P_x)}{\frac{P_x}{P}\left(1 - \frac{MP_x}{P}\right)}
\tag{15}
$$

The expression given above can further be written as

$$
\left[\varphi\left(\frac{P_x}{P}\right)\right]^{-1} \triangleq \frac{\frac{P_x}{P}\left(1 - \frac{MP_x}{P}\right)}{\mu(P - MP_x) + L(\sigma_n^2 + \alpha P_x)}.
\tag{16}
$$

Putting (16) into (14), we can obtain

$$
(\gamma_A)_{\max} = \max_{\frac{P_x}{P} \in (0,1)} \frac{L\alpha\mu P^2}{\sigma_n^2}\left[\varphi\left(\frac{P_x}{P}\right)\right]^{-1} = \frac{L\alpha\mu P^2}{\sigma_n^2}\left[\min_{\frac{P_x}{P} \in (0,1)} \varphi\left(\frac{P_x}{P}\right)\right]^{-1}.
\tag{17}
$$

It can be seen that, the value of γ_A will reach the maximum when $\varphi\left(\frac{P_x}{P}\right)$ get its minimum value. Next, we will transform (15) into a sum of two equations.

$$
\begin{aligned}
\varphi\left(\frac{P_x}{P}\right) &= \frac{\mu(P - MP_x) + L(\sigma_n^2 + \alpha P_x)}{\frac{P_x}{P}\left(1 - \frac{MP_x}{P}\right)} \\
&= \frac{P(\mu P - M\mu P_x + L\sigma_n^2 + L\alpha P_x)}{\frac{P_x}{P}(P - MP_x)} \\
&= \frac{\mu P^2 - \mu MPP_x + LP\sigma_n^2 + LP\alpha P_x + (MLP_x\sigma_n^2 - MLP_x\sigma_n^2)}{\frac{P_x}{P}(P - MP_x)} \\
&= \frac{LP_x(M\sigma_n^2 + \alpha P) + (P - MP_x)(L\sigma_n^2 + \mu P)}{\frac{P_x}{P}(P - MP_x)} \\
&= \frac{L\frac{P_x}{P}\left(M\sigma_n^2 + \alpha P\right) + \left(1 - \frac{MP_x}{P}\right)\left(L\sigma_n^2 + \mu P\right)}{\frac{P_x}{P}\left(1 - \frac{MP_x}{P}\right)} \\
&= \frac{L\left(M\sigma_n^2 + \alpha P\right)}{1 - \frac{MP_x}{P}} + \frac{L\sigma_n^2 + \mu P}{\frac{MP_x}{P}}.
\end{aligned}
\tag{18}
$$

For the purpose of simplification, we set

$$u \triangleq \frac{P_x}{P},\tag{19}$$

$$A = L\left(M\sigma_n^2 + \alpha P\right),\tag{20}$$

$$B = L\sigma_n^2 + \mu P.\tag{21}$$

Applying these relationships in connection with (18) leads to

$$\varphi(u) = \frac{A}{1 - Mu} + \frac{B}{u}.\tag{22}$$

Here, we analysis that how we can get the minimum value of $\varphi(u)$. Taking the second derivative with respect to (22) results in the following inequation

$$\varphi''(u) = \frac{M^3 A}{(1 - Mu)^3} + \frac{2B}{u^3} > 0 \quad \text{for} \quad u \in (0,1),\tag{23}$$

so $\varphi(u)$ is transformed into a convex function with respect to u when $u \in (0,1)$ and the minimum value of it can be gotten from $u_0 \in (0,1)$, where the first derivative of $\varphi(u)$ should be zero

$$\varphi'(u_0) = \frac{MA}{(1 - Mu_0)^2} - \frac{B}{u_0^2} = \left(\frac{\sqrt{MA}}{1 - Mu_0} + \frac{\sqrt{B}}{u_0}\right)\left(\frac{\sqrt{MA}}{1 - Mu_0} - \frac{\sqrt{B}}{u_0}\right) = 0.\tag{24}$$

It can be seen that, this result is only valid for

$$\left(\frac{\sqrt{MA}}{1 - Mu_0} - \frac{\sqrt{B}}{u_0}\right) = 0.\tag{25}$$

By doing deformation on (25), we obtain the following expression

$$u_0 = \frac{\sqrt{B}}{\sqrt{MA} + M\sqrt{B}}.\tag{26}$$

Combining the expression of u_0 (26) and (22), it can be found that the minimum value of $\varphi(u)$ can be obtained

$$\begin{aligned}
[\varphi(u)]_{\min} = \varphi(u_0) &= \frac{A}{1 - Mu_0} + \frac{B}{u_0} \\
&= \frac{A}{1 - M\frac{\sqrt{B}}{\sqrt{MA}+M\sqrt{B}}} + \frac{B}{\frac{\sqrt{B}}{\sqrt{MA}+M\sqrt{B}}} \\
&= \left(\sqrt{A} + \sqrt{MB}\right)^2.
\end{aligned}\tag{27}$$

Combining (19), (20), (21) and (27), we can find

$$\min_{\frac{P_x}{P} \in (0,1)} \varphi\left(\frac{P_x}{P}\right) = \left[\sqrt{L\left(M\sigma_n^2 + \alpha P\right)} + \sqrt{M\left(L\sigma_n^2 + \mu P\right)}\right]^2.\tag{28}$$

Putting (28) into (17), then $(\gamma_A)_{\max}$ can be represented by

$$(\gamma_A)_{\max} = \frac{L\alpha\mu P^2}{\sigma_n^2 \left[\sqrt{L(M\sigma_n^2 + \alpha P)} + \sqrt{M\left(L\sigma_n^2 + \mu P\right)}\right]^2}. \tag{29}$$

Till now, the maximum SNR of the AF system $(\gamma_A)_{\max}$ is written as a function of several variables. The value of $(\gamma_A)_{\max}$ can be easily obtained when the working conditions of the system are determined.

Meanwhile, combining (19) and (26), we can get the corresponding power of every source node allocated

$$P_x = \frac{P\sqrt{L\sigma_n^2 + \mu P}}{\sqrt{ML(M\sigma_n^2 + \alpha P)} + M\sqrt{L\sigma_n^2 + \mu P}} \tag{30}$$

and the power of every relay node

$$P_{ri} = \frac{P - MP_x}{L} = \frac{P\sqrt{ML(M\sigma_n^2 + \alpha P)}}{L[\sqrt{ML(M\sigma_n^2 + \alpha P)} + M\sqrt{L\sigma_n^2 + \mu P}]}. \tag{31}$$

It can be seen that, both P_x and P_{ri} are expressed as the functions of the number of relay node L and that of source node M, as well as the system power P.

4   Numerical Results

From solving (29), (30) and (31), the maximum SNR at destination of the proposed AF system, the corresponding source power and every relay power can be gotten, respectively. As a contrast, we provide the SNR of the scheme that the total power is equally divided up among several source nodes and all relay nodes. For simplicity, we assume that the noise powers in every relay node and destination node are all identical, which is $\sigma_n^2 = 8.28 \times 10^{-14}$ W, here the value is gotten according to internal thermal noise. All signals are transmitted in free space and the channel attenuation factors are obtained from the free space propagation formula, carrier frequency is 2.5×10^3 MHz, the distances between source nodes and relay nodes and that between relay nodes and destination node are all 400m. The following figures are numerical results of SNRs at destination and the power allocations.

In order to demonstrate the effect taken by the number of relay node, the SNRs at destination with respect to the number of relay node are shown in Fig. 2, where the number of source node is 3. From Fig. 2 we can see that, the SNRs at destination of the two schemes grow with the increase of the number of relay node, which are consistent with the previous studies. The reason is that, more relay nodes bring more source-relay-destination sublinks and higher gain in destination. It should be pointed out that, the SNR of the proposed optimized method always outperforms that of the scheme with equal power allocation.

Due to the fact that the total system power determines the performance, the plot of SNRs at destination versus the total system power is given in Fig. 3, where the number of source node and relay node are 3 and 10, respectively. Obviously, with the increase of the system power, the SNRs at destination are improved. This is because that the noise power is a constant whatever the system power is. For this reason, the bigger the system power, the higher the SNR. Meanwhile, the SNR of the scheme with equal power allocation is similarly with the proposed one while its value is a little lower than it.

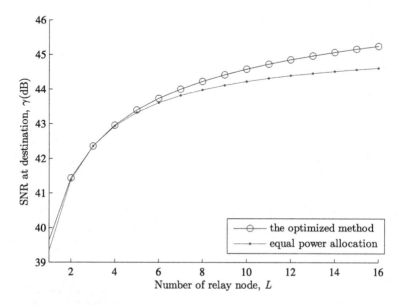

Fig. 2. SNRs at the destination of AF system versus the number of relay node ($M = 3$).

To illustrate how the distance influences the performance, the SNRs at destination with respect to the Distance are shown in Fig. 4, here the distances between the source nodes and the destination node are no longer 400 m, they range from 200 m to 1200 m and the relay nodes lie in the middle position, and the number of source node and relay node are 3 and 10, respectively. It apparently shows that both of the two values of SNR at destination decrease with the increase of the distance, which is consistent with experience and fact. For the farther distance between the source node and destination node is, the weaker the received signal is, wherever for the relay node or the destination node, so the lower the SNR at destination is. Similarly, the SNR of the optimized method outperforms that of the scheme with equal power allocation. In order to learn the power allocation among source nodes and relay nodes in the proposed AF system, and that of every node of the scheme with equal power allocation, the power allocation versus the number of relay node is given in Fig. 5, where the number of source node is 3. Obviously, for the proposed method, the power of every relay node and source node are different. When the number of relay node is more than 2, the power of every source node is bigger than that of every relay

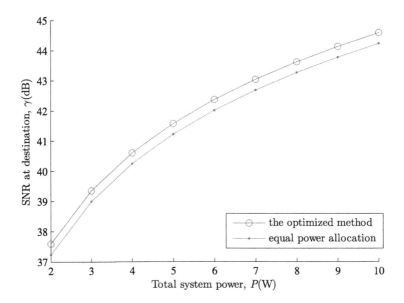

Fig. 3. SNRs at the destination of AF system versus the total system power ($M = 3$, $L = 10$).

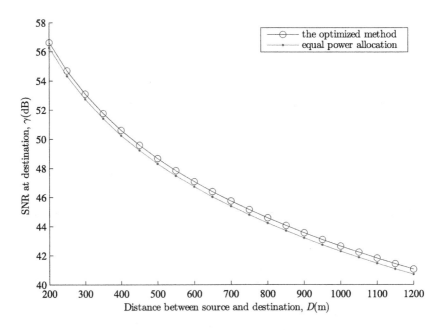

Fig. 4. SNRs at the destination of AF system versus the Distance ($M = 3$, $L = 10$).

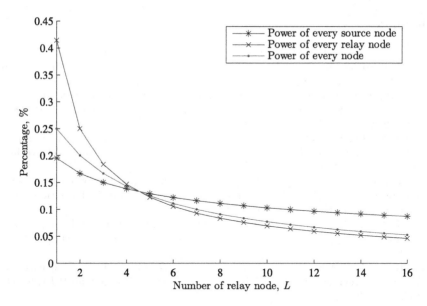

Fig. 5. Percentage of power allocation of AF system versus the number of relay node ($M = 3$).

node. This is because that, the power that the destination node received is coming from all relay nodes, while every relay node received power is only coming from several source nodes. When the relay nodes lie between the source node and the destination node, the scheme will bring higher SNR than the scheme of the latter one, in which the power of every node allocated is similar and the percentage is just the inverse of 1.

5   Conclusion

This paper has proposed an optimized transmitting scheme for the AF system which includes several source nodes and several parallel relay nodes. By an optimization procedure, we have derived the expression of the SNR and obtained the maximum SNR at the destination. Based on the expression and corresponding parameters, validations by the simulation method have been conducted. The simulation and analyze results have showed that the SNR at destination of the proposed scheme outperforms the one in which the power is equally allocated among all source and relay nodes.

Acknowledgments. This work was supported in part by the National Key Scientific Instrument and Equipment Development Project under Grant No. 61827801, and in part by the National Natural Science Foundation of China under Grant No. 61471192.

References

1. Jia, Y., Vosoughi, A.: Outage probability and power allocation of two-way amplify-and-forward relaying with channel estimation errors. IEEE Trans. Wireless Commun. **11**(6), 1985–1990 (2012)
2. Guo, H., Zhao, S.: Supplementary proof of upper and lower bounds of two-way opportunistic amplify-and-forward relaying channels. IEEE Commun. Lett. **18**(3), 401–402 (2014)
3. Liang, X., Jin, S., Wang, W., Gao, X., Wong, K.: Outage probability of amplify-and-forward two-way relay interference-limited systems. IEEE Trans. Veh. Technol. **61**(7), 3038–3049 (2012)
4. Hwang, K., Ju, M., Alouini, M.: Outage performance of opportunistic two-way amplify-and-forward relaying with outdated channel state information. IEEE Trans. Commun. **61**(9), 3635–3643 (2013)
5. Lee, I., Kim, D.: Outage performance of opportunistic cooperation in amplify-and-forward relaying systems with relay selection. IEEE Commun. Lett. **16**(2), 224–227 (2012)
6. Rodriguez, L.J., Tran, N., Le-Ngoc, T.: Achievable rates and power allocation for two-way AF relaying over Rayleigh fading channels. In: Proceedings IEEE ICC'03, Budapest, Hungary, June 2013, pp. 5914–5918 (2013)
7. Singh, K., Gupta, A., Ratnarajah, T.: Qos-driven energy-efficient resource allocation in multiuser amplify-and-forward relay networks. IEEE Trans. Signal Inf. Process. Netw. **3**(4), 771–786 (2017)
8. Liu, T., Song, L., Jiao, B., Zhang, Y.: Symbol error rate analysis and power allocation for adaptive relay selection schemes. Wireless Pers. Commun. **56**(3), 457–467 (2011)
9. Islam, S.: Achievable rate and error performance of an amplify and forward multi-way relay network in the presence of imperfect channel estimation. IET Commun. **10**(3), 272–282 (2016)
10. Kumar, N., Bhatia, V.: Outage probability and average channel capacity of amplify-and-forward in conventional cooperative communication networks over Rayleigh fading channels. Wireless Pers. Commun. **88**(4), 943–951 (2016). https://doi.org/10.1007/s11277-016-3221-0
11. Wang, J., Wang, J., Song, X.: Distributed SNR-based power allocation in wireless parallel amplify-and-forward relay transmissions using Cournot game. Wireless Pers. Commun. **70**(4), 1285–1306 (2013). https://doi.org/10.1007/s11277-012-0747-7
12. Su, J., Chen, X., Zhu, Q.: Robust transceiver design for MIMO system with amplify-and-forward relay. Int. J. Model. Optim. **6**(3), 171–176 (2016)
13. Chen, X., Fang, Z., Zhu, Q., Hu, X.: Robust transceiver design for MIMO relay systems with direct link under imperfect channel state information. Int. J. Electron. Lett. **7**(4), 377–388 (2019)
14. Laneman, J.N., Wornell, G.W.: Distributed space-time-coded protocols for exploiting cooperative diversity in wireless networks. IEEE Trans. Inf. Theory **49**(10), 2415–2425 (2003)
15. Zhao, Y., Adve, R., Lim, T.J.: Improving amplify-and-forward relay networks: optimal power allocation versus selection. IEEE Trans. Wireless Commun. **6**(8), 3114–3123 (2007)
16. Zhang, Y., Pang, L., Li, J.: Power allocation and relay selection for AF two-path successive relaying networks. Wireless Commun. Mobile Comput. **14**(4), 487–496 (2013)

17. Huang, R., Feng, C., Zhang, T.: Energy-efficient relay selection and power allocation scheme in AF relay networks with bidirectional asymmetric traffic. In: WPMC 2011, Brest, France, October 2011, pp. 1–5 (2011)
18. Qian, M., Liu, C., Fu, Y.: A relay selection and power allocation scheme for cooperative wireless sensor networks. KSII Trans. Int. Inf. Syst. **8**(4), 1390–1405 (2014)
19. Elhalawany, B.M., Elsabrouty, M., Muta, O., Abdelrahman, A., Furukawa, H.: Joint energy-efficient single relay selection and power allocation for analog network coding with three transmission phases. In: IEEE VTC Spring 2014, Seoul, South Korea (2014)
20. Cui, H., Ma, M., Song, L.: Relay selection for two-way full duplex relay networks with amplify-and-forward protocol. IEEE Trans. Wireless Commun. **13**(7), 3768–3777 (2014)
21. Tian, J., Zhang, H., Wu, D., Yuan, D.: QoS-constrained medium access probability optimization in wireless interference-limited networks. IEEE Trans. Commun. **66**(3), 1064–1077 (2018)
22. Li, J., Zhang, X., Cao, R., Zhou, M.: Reduced-dimension MUSIC for angle and array gain-phase error estimation in bistatic MIMO radar. IEEE Commun. Lett. **17**(3), 443–446 (2013)
23. Zhong, W., Xu, L., Zhu, Q., Chen, X., Zhou, J.: A novel beam design method for mmWave multi-antenna arrays with mutual coupling reduction. China Commun. **16**(10), 37–44 (2019)
24. Chen, X., Hu, X., Zhu, Q., Zhong, W., Chen, B.: Channel modeling and performance analysis for UAV relay systems. China Commun. **15**(12), 89–97 (2018)
25. Zhu, Q., Li, H., Fu, Y., Wang, C., Tan, Y., et al.: A novel 3D non-stationary wireless MIMO channel simulator and hardware emulator. IEEE Trans. Commun. **66**(9), 3865–3878 (2018)
26. Fan, W., Carton, I., Kyösti, P., Karstensen, A., Jamsa, T., et. al.: A step toward 5G in 2020: low-cost OTA performance evaluation of massive MIMO base stations. IEEE Antennas Propag. Mag. **59**(1), 38–47 (2017)
27. Bao, J., Xu, D., Luo, H., Zhang, R.: Design and SNR optimization for multi-relay compress-and-forward system based on CEO theory. IEICE Trans. Inf. Syst. **E103-D**(5), 1006–1012 (2020)

UAV-Assisted Spectrum Mapping System Based on Tensor Completion Scheme

Xiaofu Du[1,2], Qiuming Zhu[1,2(✉)], Qihui Wu[1,2], Weizhi Zhong[1,3],
Yang Huang[1,2], Neng Cheng[1,2], and Dong Liu[1,2]

[1] Key Laboratory of Dynamic Cognitive System of Electromagnetic Spectrum Space,
Ministry of Industry and Information Technology, Nanjing University of Aeronautics
and Astronautics, Nanjing 210016, China
{duxiaofu,zhuqiuming,wuqihui,zhongwz,
yang.huang.ceie,chengn1208}@nuaa.edu.cn, 1760523985@qq.com
[2] College of electronic and information engineering, Nanjing University of
Aeronautics and Astronautics, Nanjing 211106, China
[3] College of Astronautics, Nanjing University of Aeronautics and Astronautics,
Nanjing 210016, China

Abstract. Electromagnetic spectrum is an indispensable resource in the
current Information Age. Along with the rapid development of integrated
space and terrestrial communication networks, spectrum shortage is one
of the challenges faced by electromagnetic spectrum resource utilization
in both airspace and terrestrial space. In order to realize the effective
supervision and allocation of spectrum resources, a UAV-assisted spectrum mapping system based on tensor completion scheme is proposed.
By using a UAV platform, the hardware system can acquire the multi-
dimensional spectrum information, i.e., the geographical location and
spectrum power, quickly and flexibly in the 3D space. The high accuracy low rank tensor completion (HaLRTC) algorithm is adopted to process the multi-dimensional spectrum data, i.e., data completion and map
construction. The output spectrum map can display the characteristics
of electromagnetic spectrum space more intuitively, and provide a solid
basis for dynamic spectrum management. Finally, the proposed spectrum
map system is tested under campus scenario.

Keywords: Spectrum map · Spectrum visualization · Tensor
completion · UAV

1 Introduction

Spectrum resource is a scarce resource, which is not only the core of wireless communication technology but also national strategy resource [1]. With the development and wide application of integrated space and terrestrial communication
networks, spectrum resource is becoming scarcer and scarcer in both the terrestrial space and airspace. How to efficiently allocate and utilize the existing

© ICST Institute for Computer Sciences, Social Informatics and Telecommunications Engineering 2021
Published by Springer Nature Switzerland AG 2021. All Rights Reserved
M. Guan and Z. Na (Eds.): MLICOM 2020, LNICST 342, pp. 16–26, 2021.
https://doi.org/10.1007/978-3-030-66785-6_2

spectrum resource has always been an important and urgent issue. The first step of improving spectrum utilization is to cognize the current spectrum usage. However, it's difficult to cognize spectrum information from the electromagnetic environment directly or by traditional instruments. One solution is to obtain the spectrum map and display the spectrum usage of underlying region intuitively. Therefore, it is necessary and urgent to develop a spectrum mapping system that can collect and display the spectrum information in 3D space and then to improve the efficiency of spectrum utilization.

It should be mentioned that the spectrum map is also referred as radio environment map (REM) [2] and radio frequency maps [3], and the process of spectrum map construction is termed as spectrum cartography [4] or spectrum visualization. Actually, the spectrum map visually displays the spectrum information on a map and represents the distribution of different radio parameter over a geographical area, such as received signal strength, channel gain, and interference [5]. First of all, spectrum map construction needs spectrum measurements to collect original spectrum data, the mainstream method is to deploy ground spectrum sensors that can collect the spectrum data from their respective locations in the region of interest [6]. In [7], the authors builded a distributed spectrum monitoring network to collect data. In [1], the authors used spectrum detection nodes that can acquire and record received signal strength, the current GPS, temperature, humidity, and other parameters. In [8], the measurements were collected by multiple distributed radars or radio frequency sensors in the different locations. Note that the above methods can only acquire the 2D spectrum data, while the 3D spectrum map is needed for the integrated space and terrestrial communication networks.

Since the measured data are usually incomplete, spectrum completion based on measured data is necessary and crucial. In [8, 10] and [11], the Kriging spatial interpolation was adopted to estimate the spectrum information of geographical locations without measurements. In [12] and [13], the authors adopted the LIvE method and SNR-aided method, respectively, which utilized transmitter parameters and radio propagation modeling. It has better performance for the spectrum map construction than the Kriging spatial interpolation. However, all aforementioned methods are only suitable to the 2D spectrum map construction. This paper aims to fill these gaps. The major contributions and novelties of this paper are summarized as follows:

1) We develop a UAV-assisted spectrum mapping system, which mainly consists of UAV platform, spectrum monitoring module, data transmission module, and spectrum data cognition terminal. The system can acquire the multi-dimensional spectrum information including geographical location information and spectrum power quickly and flexibly in 3D space.

2) By dividing the three-dimension measurement space into serval 3D grids, we model the collected multi-dimensional spectrum data used for 3D spectrum map construction as a three-order tensor which contains aerial spectrum information. Based on the tensor completion idea, the 3D spectrum map is constructed. To our best knowledge, the existing literature hardly studies on

constructing 3D spectrum map including multi-dimensional spectrum information.

The remainder of the paper is organized as follows. Section 2 presents the hardware system structure. Section 3 introduces the spectrum map construction based on the tensor completion scheme. The experiment and tested results are provided in Sect. 4. The conclusions are drawn in Sect. 5.

2   Hardware System

The system is mainly composed of four modules: UAV platform, spectrum monitoring module, data transmission module and spectrum data cognition terminal. Spectrum monitoring module and data transmission module are mounted on UAV platform. UAV platform, spectrum monitoring module and data transmission module constitute the aerial part of the system, while the spectrum data cognition terminal constitutes the ground part of the system. The UAV platform mainly includes the GPS receiving submodule, image capturing submodule and flight control submodule; the spectrum monitoring module mainly consists of a spectrum receiver and an omnidirectional antenna; data transmission module mainly consists of a microcomputer and an airborne data link terminal; the spectrum data cognition terminal is mainly comprised of core cognition submodule, ground data receiving submodule and remote-control submodule. The hardware system structure is shown in Fig. 1 detailedly.

The UAV platform can provide the strong mobility in airspace for the system [14]. The spectrum monitoring module can collect the spectrum information around the UAV in real time when the system runs. The data transmission module can transmit the collected spectrum information and the other information such as geographical location information to the spectrum data cognition terminal and receive the flight control information from the spectrum data cognition terminal, which uses beamforming technology [15,16] and multiple-input multiple-output (MIMO) technology [17,18]. The spectrum data cognition terminal can use tensor completion algorithm to process the collected multi-dimensional spectrum data, thereby realizing 3D spectrum map construction of the measurement region. Some system performance parameters are shown in Table 1.

Table 1. System parameters.

Parameter	Value
Spectrum range	9 kHz to 8 GHz
Frequency resolution	1 Hz
Sensitivity	−155 dBm
The type of antenna	Omnidirectional
UAV's velocity	26 m/s (horizontal); 8 m/s (vertical)

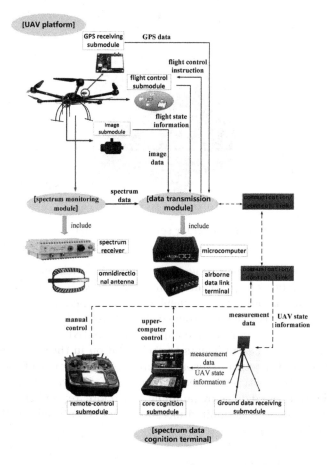

Fig. 1. Hardware structure of proposed system.

3   Spectrum Data Processing

3.1   Data Model of Spectrum Map

An n-order spectrum tensor can be defined as $\chi \in R^{I_1 \times I_2 \times \ldots \times I_n}$, and $x_{i_1,i_2,\ldots,i_n}$ denotes the n-th element of the tensor χ. As shown in Fig. 2, the real-world spectrum data that the system collects in stereoscopic space can be modeled as a three-order tensor $\chi \in R^{I_1 \times I_2 \times I_3}$. The x-axis, y-axis and z-axis corresponds to the coordinates x, y and z of the 3D stereoscopic space. Each element x_{i_1,i_2,i_3} in this spectrum tensor denotes the received signal strength in the position of the abscissa i_1, the position of the ordinate i_2 and the position of vertical coordinate i_3. In Fig. 2, different colors are used in denoting different received signal strength. Note that, the display form of three-order tensor in Fig. 2 can also be viewed as a 3D spectrum map, and what the spectrum map that our system constructs displays is the 3D spatial distribution of received signal strength in a particular area.

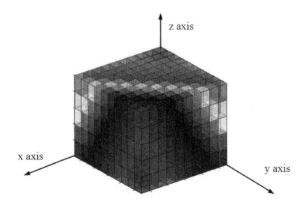

Fig. 2. Model for spectrum map data.

In practical applications, owing to these factors such as the terrain environment, the number of spectrum monitoring nodes (i.e. spectrum sensors), deployment locations, and measurement equipment performance have certain limitations, which makes the electromagnetic environment observation or spectrum measurements can only be incomplete and limited [5]. In other words, it is impractical to have measurements at each location in the measurement area. Moreover, when the spectrum tensor acquires a large amount of measurements for high accuracy of constructed spectrum map, the overhead of time or material resource will be narrowed down by sampling. Therefore, retrieving the incomplete spectrum data based on the limited measurements is essential for 3D spectrum map construction.

3.2   Spectrum Map Construction

Given a subset Ω, data in the subset Ω indicate the elements corresponding to real measurement data in χ, the other elements corresponding to unknown spectrum data of these locations without measurements would set to be "0". The subset tensor χ_Ω can be defined as:

$$\chi_\Omega = \begin{cases} \chi, (i_1, i_2, ..., i_n) \in \Omega \\ 0, \text{otherwise} \end{cases} \tag{1}$$

Because of the low-rank property of the real-world spectrum tensor [19], the spectrum tensor completion for the values of "unknown" elements in χ can be modeled as an optimization problem, which uses the known subset to complete the tensor data, specifically implemented as the following problem:

$$\min \|\chi\|_* \\ s.t. \chi_\Omega = \Gamma_\Omega \tag{2}$$

where $\|\cdot\|_*$ originally denotes the tightest convex envelop for the rank of matrices, and it extends to the tensor in this case, χ_Ω, Γ_Ω are n-mode spectrum tensors with the same size in each mode, entries of Γ from the set Ω are given by real measurement data while the remaining entries are missing and χ is the incomplete spectrum tensor to be completed. For low rank tensor completion problem, computing the rank of a tensor (mode number > 2) is an NP hard problem [20]. So, the following definition for the tensor trace norm is introduced [19],

$$\|\chi\|_* := \sum_{i=1}^{n} \alpha_i \|\chi_{(i)}\|_* \tag{3}$$

where $\chi_{(i)} \in R^{I_i \times (I_1 \times \cdots \times I_{i-1} \times I_{i+1} \times \cdots \times I_n)}$ denotes the matrix unfolded by tensor χ in the i-th mode, $\alpha_i > 0$ and $\sum_{i=1}^{n} \alpha_i = 1$, $\|\chi_{(i)}\|_*$ denotes the norm of the unfolded matrix $\chi_{(i)}$. The trace norm of a tensor is consistent with all the matrices unfolded along each mode. Under this definition, the optimization problem can be converted to the following formula,

$$\min_{\chi} \sum_{i=1}^{n} \alpha_i \|\chi_{(i)}\|_*$$
$$s.t. \chi_\Omega = \Gamma_\Omega \tag{4}$$

We adopt an efficient algorithm proposed in [21] to deal with this tensor completion problem in (4). The algorithm can work even with a small amount of samples and estimate larger missing regions of the spectrum data. Although its convergence rate is not the fastest, the convergence of the algorithm is guaranteed.

The problem in (4) is difficult to tackle due to the interdependence among the matrix trace norm terms. In order to simplify the problem in (4), additional tensors $\varphi_1, ..., \varphi_n$ are introduced [19]. Therefore, the following equivalent formulation can be obtained:

$$\min_{\chi, \varphi_i} \sum_{i=1}^{n} \alpha_i \|\varphi_{i(i)}\|_*$$
$$s.t. \chi = \varphi_i \quad for\ i = 1, ..., n$$
$$\chi_\Omega = \Gamma_\Omega \tag{5}$$

The augmented Lagrangian function is defined as follows accordingly:

$$L_\rho(\chi, \varphi_1, ..., \varphi_n, \gamma_1, ..., \gamma_n)$$
$$= \sum_{i=1}^{n} \alpha_i \|\varphi_{i(i)}\|_* + \langle \chi - \varphi_i, \gamma_i \rangle + \frac{\rho}{2} \|\varphi_i - \chi\|_F^2 \tag{6}$$

where $\langle \chi, \gamma \rangle$ is the inner product of tensor χ and tensor γ, they are two n-mode tensors with the same size in each mode, it can be also endowed with $\langle \chi, \gamma \rangle = \sum_{i_1} \sum_{i_2} \cdots \sum_{i_n} x_{i_1,...,i_n} y_{i_1,...,i_n}$; $\|\cdot\|_F$ is the Frobenius norm; ρ is the penalty parameter of the penalty function; γ_i is Lagrangian multiplier.

According to the framework of ADMM applied by the algorithm, the augmented Lagrangian function is applied to update φ_i, χ_i and γ_i iteratively.

$$\begin{aligned} &\{\varphi_1^{k+1}, ..., \varphi_n^{k+1}\} \\ &= \arg \min_{\varphi_1,...,\varphi_n} L_\rho(\chi^k, \varphi_1, ..., \varphi_n, \gamma_1^k, ... \gamma_n^k) \end{aligned} \tag{7}$$

$$\chi^{k+1} = \arg \min_{\chi \in Q} L_\rho(\chi, \varphi_1^{k+1}, ..., \varphi_n^{k+1}, \gamma_1^k, ..., \gamma_n^k) \tag{8}$$

$$\gamma_i^{k+1} = \gamma_i^k - \rho(\varphi_i^{k+1} - \chi^{k+1}) \tag{9}$$

where $Q = \{\chi \in R^{I_1 \times I_2 \times ... \times I_n} | \chi_\Omega = \Gamma_\Omega\}$ in (8), and superscript k represents the k-th iteration.

This specific algorithm is summarized in **Algorithm 1**, where $fold_i [\chi_{(i)}]$ denotes the operation of folding the matrix $\chi_{(i)}$ to the tensor χ in i-th mode; $D_\tau (\mathbf{X})$ represents the "shrinkage" operator of the matrix $\mathbf{X}$, which is defined as

$$D_\tau (\mathbf{X}) = \mathbf{U} \Sigma_\tau \mathbf{V}^\mathrm{T} \tag{10}$$

where $\mathbf{U}$ and $\mathbf{V}$ are the unitary matrices in the singular value decomposition $\mathbf{X} = \mathbf{U} \sum \mathbf{V}^\mathrm{T}$ for $\mathbf{X}$, and $\sum_\tau = diag (\max (\sigma_i - \tau, 0))$, σ's are the singular values.

4   Measurements Under Campus Scenario

4.1   Experiment Setup

The measurement campaigns were carried out in Jiangning campus of Nanjing University of Aeronautics and Astronautics. As shown in Fig. 3(a), the measurement region is divided into 20×20 grids. In order to acquire the real-world multi-dimensional spectrum data containing aerial spectrum data, we operated the aerial part of the system to fly randomly in the measurement region and measure the received signal strength in $20\,\mathrm{m}$, $25\,\mathrm{m}$ and $30\,\mathrm{m}$ high above the

---

Algorithm 1. HaLRTC: High Accuracy Low Rank Tensor Completion

---
Input: The number of iterations K, χ with $\chi_\Omega = \Gamma_\Omega$ and ρ.
Output: The completed spectrum data used for spectrum map construction χ.
1: Set $\chi_\Omega = \Gamma_\Omega$, $\chi_{\bar{\Omega}} = 0$, $\gamma_i = 0$ and $\varphi_i = 0$ $(i = 1, ..., n)$.
2: **for** $k = 0$ to K **do**
3:      **for** $i = 1$ to n **do**
4:          $\varphi_i = fold_i \left[D_{\frac{\alpha_i}{\rho}} \left(\chi_i + \frac{1}{\rho}\gamma_{i(i)} \right) \right].$
5:      **end for**
6:      $\chi_\Omega = \frac{1}{n} \left(\sum_{i=1}^{n} \left(\varphi_i - \frac{1}{\rho}\gamma_i \right) \right)_{\bar{\Omega}};$
7:      $\gamma_i = \gamma_i - \rho (\varphi_i - \chi).$
8: **end for**

---

ground respectively. The frequency band between 470 MHz and 700 MHz was chosen as the observation frequency band. For simplicity, it is assumed that the received signal strength of each grid is almost consistent during the experiment. Hence, the real-world measurement data used for spectrum map construction in the experiment can be modeled as a tensor whose size is $20 \times 20 \times 3$ by corresponding the measurement locations to the divided grids. The proposed spectrum mapping system used for measurement is shown in Fig. 3(b).

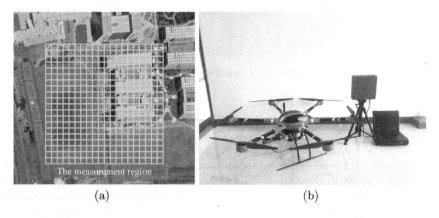

(a)   (b)

Fig. 3. (a) The measurement region under campus scenario; (b) The proposed spectrum mapping system.

4.2   Measured Results

After the real-world measured spectrum data (see Fig. 4(a)) is complemented by the adopted tensor completion algorithm, the 3D spectrum map of the measurement region is constructed (see Fig. 4(b)), where different colors denote different received signal strength. The darker the color, the lower received signal strength of the location marked with the color in the observation frequency band. The divisiory $20 \times 20 \times 3$ 3D grids in our spectrum map are the equal of the pixels of 2D spectrum map. Through the constructed spectrum map, the situation of 3D spectrum usage in the measurement region is displayed intuitively.

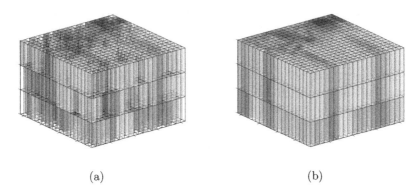

(a)   (b)

Fig. 4. The real-world measured spectrum data (a) before completion, (b) after completion.

5 Conclusions

The UAV-assisted spectrum mapping system based on tensor completion scheme has been developed in this paper. The system can collect the multi-dimensional spectrum information quickly and intelligently in 3D space. The tensor completion algorithm HaLRTC has been adopted in the multi-dimensional spectrum data completion to construct the 3D spectrum map. Thus, the invisible spectrum space can be visualized to intuitively show the usage of regional spectrum, which is convenient for discovering spectrum holes and managing spectrum dynamically. The spectrum map construction effectiveness of the system has been verified under campus scenario. For the future work, we would take the frequency and time information into the collected spectrum data and obtain the spectrum map including more information.

Acknowledgements. This work was supported in part by the National Key Scientific Instrument and Equipment Development Project under Grant No. 61827801, in part by Aeronautical Science Foundation of China No. 201901052001, and in part by the Fundamental Research Funds for the Central Universities No. NS2020026 and No. NS2020063.

References

1. Guo, X., Zhang, Y., Chen, Z., He, C., Hai, W.: Distributed electromagnetic spectrum detection system based on self-organizing network. In: 2018 12th International Symposium on Antennas, Propagation and EM Theory (ISAPE), Hangzhou, China, pp. 1–5 (2018)
2. Pesko, M., Javornik, T., et al.: Radio environment maps: the survey of construction methods. KSII Trans. Internet Inf. Syst. **81**(3), 3789–3809 (2014)

3. Vanhoy, G., Volos, H., Bastidas, C.E.C., Bose, T.: a spatial interpolation method for radio frequency maps based on the discrete cosine transform. In: MILCOM 2013–2013 IEEE Military Communications Conference, San Diego, CA, pp. 1045–1050 (2013)
4. Jayawickrama, B.A., Dutkiewicz, E., Oppermann, I., Fang, G., Ding, J.: Improved performance of spectrum cartography based on compressive sensing in cognitive radio networks. In: 2013 IEEE International Conference on Communications (ICC), Budapest, pp. 5657–5661 (2013)
5. Lu, J., Zha, S., Huang, J., Liu, P., Chen, G., Xu, S.: The iterative completion method of the spectrum map based on the difference of measurement values. In: 2018 IEEE 3rd International Conference on Signal and Image Processing (ICSIP), Shenzhen, pp. 255–259 (2018)
6. Zha, S., Huang, J., Qin, Y., Zhang, Z.: An novel non-parametric algorithm for spectrum map construction. In: 2018 International Symposium on Electromagnetic Compatibility (EMC EUROPE), Amsterdam, pp. 941–944 (2018)
7. Patino, M., Vega, F.: Model for measurement of radio environment maps and location of white spaces for cognitive radio deployment. In: 2018 IEEE-APS Topical Conference on Antennas and Propagation in Wireless Communications (APWC), Cartagena des Indias, pp. 913–915 (2018)
8. Melvasalo, M., Koivunen, V., Lundn, J.: Spectrum maps for cognition and co-existence of communication and radar systems. In: 2016 50th Asilomar Conference on Signals, Systems and Computers, Pacific Grove, CA, pp. 58–63 (2016)
9. Chaudhari, S., et al.: Spatial interpolation of cyclostationary test statistics in cognitive radio networks: methods and field measurements. IEEE Trans. Veh. Technol. **67**(2), 1113–1129 (2018)
10. Janakaraj, P., Wang, P., Chen, Z.: Towards cloud-based crowd-augmented spectrum mapping for dynamic spectrum access. In: 2016 25th International Conference on Computer Communication and Networks (ICCCN), Waikoloa, HI, pp. 1–7 (2016)
11. Mao, D., Shao, W., Qian, Z., Xue, H., Lu, X., Wu, H.: Constructing accurate radio environment maps with kriging interpolation in cognitive radio networks. In: 2018 Cross Strait Quad-Regional Radio Science and Wireless Technology Conference (CSQRWC), Xuzhou, pp. 1–3 (2018)
12. Yilmaz, H.B., Tugcu, T.: Location estimation-based radio environment map construction in fading channels. Wireless Commun. Mobile Comput. **15**(3), 561–570 (2015)
13. Sun, G., van de Beek, J.: Simple distributed interference source localization for radio environment mapping. In: 2010 IFIP Wireless Days, Venice, pp. 1–5 (2010)
14. Cui, Z., Briso-Rodrguez, C., Guan, K., Calvo-Ramrez, C., Ai, B., Zhong, Z.: Measurement-based modeling and analysis of UAV air-ground channels at 1 and 4 GHz. IEEE Antennas Wirel. Propag. Lett. **18**(9), 1804–1808 (2019)
15. Zhong, W., Xu, L., Zhu, Q., Chen, X., Zhou, J.: MmWave beamforming for UAV communications with unstable beam pointing. China Commun. **16**(1), 37–46 (2019)
16. Zhong, W., Xu, L., Liu, X., Zhu, Q., Zhou, J.: Adaptive beam design for UAV network with uniform plane array. Phys. Commun. **34**, 58–65 (2019)
17. Zhu, Q., Wang, Y., Jiang, K., Chen, X., Zhong, W., Ahmed, N.: 3D non-stationary geometry-based multi-input multi-output channel model for UAV-ground communication systems. IET Microwaves Antennas Propag. **13**(8), 1104–1112 (2019)

18. Zhu, Q., Jiang, K., Chen, X., Zhong, W., Yang, Y.: A novel 3D non-stationary UAV-MIMO channel model and its statistical properties. China Commun. **15**(12), 147–158 (2018)
19. Tang, M., Ding, G., Xue, Z., Zhang, J., Zhou, H.: Multi-dimensional spectrum map construction: a tensor perspective. In: 2016 8th International Conference on Wireless Communications & Signal Processing (WCSP), Yangzhou, pp. 1–5 (2016)
20. Hillar, C.J., Heng Lim, L.: Most tensor problems are NP hard. Computing Research Repository. http://arxiv.org/abs/0911.1393 (2009)
21. Liu, J., Musialski, P., Wonka, P., Ye, J.: Tensor completion for estimating missing values in visual data. IEEE Trans. Pattern Anal. Mach. Intell. **35**(1), 208–220 (2013)

A Two-Step Phase-Shifting Phase Retrieval Algorithm Based on Orthogonal Characteristics of Interfeograms

Jinping Fan[✉], Chunjun Li, Yingjie Cui, Xuemei Cao, and Jingdan Zhang

Electronic Communication Technology Department, Shenzhen Institute of Information Technology, Shenzhen 518172, China
fanjp@sziit.edu.cn

Abstract. A new two-step phase-shifting phase retrieval method is put forward to recover the real phase of the measured object through the orthogonal characteristics of the diamond diagonal vectors from three phase shift interference fringe patterns whose phase shifts are random and unknown. From the results of both simulation and experiment prove that the proposed method can obtain the phase to be measured with fast speed and high accuracy.

Keywords: Interferometry · Phase measurement · Phase shift · Phase retrieval

1 Introduction

As a high-precision optical measurement technology, optical phase-shifting interferometry has been used in scientific research and engineering applications broadly and deeply. Traditional phase-shifting phase retrieval method, which called N-step phase-shifting algorithm (N $\geq$ 3), is to recover the measured phase by calculating N-frame of phase-shifting interferograms whose phase shift is the same or a fixed value (mostly 90°), such as equal-step algorithm and fixed-step algorithm [1]. These methods have high requirements on the value of phase shift, in order to obtain high-precision of phase information, such algorithms usually need to calibrate the phase shifter [2]. Obviously, the phase shift error is one of the main element affecting the precision of the traditional phase-shifting phase retrieval algorithm. For the needs of practical engineering applications, it is necessary to study the phase-shifting phase measurement method when the phase shift amount is unknown or random. In recent decades, multi-step phase retrieval algorithms whose phase shifts are random and unknown have been put forward, mainly include the advanced iterative algorithm (AIA) [3], the principal component analysis (PCA) [4], the Euclidean matrix norm (EMN) [5], etc. The above mentioned algorithms or method require at least three or more interferograms to perform effective caluations.

Two-step phase-shifting interferometry, which can retrieve the phase quickly and accurately from two phase-shifting interference fringe patterns whose phase shifts are random and unknown [6–12]. In a large range, approximately $0.16\pi \sim 0.45\pi$, the results aren't influenced by the value of the phase shift. This makes the airflow changes and vibration and many more environmental factors significantly reduced so that can be

M. Guan and Z. Na (Eds.): MLICOM 2020, LNICST 342, pp. 27–35, 2021.
https://doi.org/10.1007/978-3-030-66785-6_3

applied to dynamic phase measurement. However, for most two-step phase-shifting methods, it is necessary to remove the background items of the fringe patterns in advance. For interferograms with slowly changing background intensity, the background items can be eliminated with a filter in the frequency domain. However, for interferograms with high-frequency background intensity changes, although the method of filtering in the frequency domain can filter out the background part, the high-frequency phase information has also been filtered out. In addition, the choice of filter window size has a direct and important influence on the accuracy of the two-step algorithm. These will bring certain errors to the measurement results.

To resolve such problems, interferograms subtraction method is employed to remove background item, the phase to be measured can be obtained fast and accurately [13]. In this work, combined with the interferogram subtraction and the orthogonal characteristics of three phase-shifting interferograms, a new two-step phase-shifting phase retrieval method is proposed to reconstruct the measured phase rapidly and accurately. Next we will first introduce the principle of the proposed method, and then show the effectiveness of the proposed method through the numerical simulation and experimental research.

2 Principle

Generally speaking, for the m-th pixel of the n-th phase shift interference fringe pattern, the distribution of the intensity expressed as

$$I_{mn} = A_m + B_m \cos[\phi_m + \delta_n] \tag{1}$$

where $n = 1, 2, 3$ represent the serial number of the interference fringe patterns; $m = 1, 2, \ldots, M$ denote the position of the pixel, the sum of all pixels on the interferogram is M; A_m, B_m and φ_m respectively denote the background item, modulation item and phase to be measured; δ_n represent the n-th interferogram phase shift of unknown and random. For simplicity, we define $\delta_1 = 0$. Two frames of differential interference fringe patterns can be obtained through subtraction of the 2nd and 3rd interferograms from 1st interferogram which can be expressed as

$$D_{m1} = I_{m1} - I_{m2} = 2B_m \sin\frac{\delta_2}{2} \sin \Phi_m \tag{2}$$

$$D_{m2} = I_{m1} - I_{m3} = 2B_m \sin\frac{\delta_3}{2} \sin(\Phi_m + \Delta) \tag{3}$$

where $\Phi_m = \phi_m + \frac{\delta_2}{2}$, $\Delta = \frac{\delta_3 - \delta_2}{2}$. Through the plain subtraction operation, the background item A_m has been removed thoroughly. In practical phase-shifting interferometry, due to the different interference fringe patterns have different phase shifts, expressed as $B_m \sin\frac{\delta_2}{2} \neq B_m \sin\frac{\delta_3}{2}$, which make two differential interferograms have different amplitudes. In order to remove the phase shift influence on differential interferograms amplitudes, normalization operation has been utilized. The normalized vector of u can be denoted as

$$\tilde{u} = \frac{u}{\sqrt{<u \cdot u>}} = \frac{u}{\|u\|} \tag{4}$$

where $<u \cdot u> = u^T u$, the superscript T stands for transpose operation. Normalizing Eqs. (2) and (3), we can obtain

$$\tilde{D}_{m1} = \frac{2B_m \sin \frac{\delta_2}{2} \sin \Phi_m}{2 \sin \frac{\delta_2}{2} \sqrt{\sum\limits_{m=1}^{M} B_m^2 \sin^2 \Phi_m}} = \frac{B_m \sin \Phi_m}{\sqrt{\sum\limits_{m=1}^{M} B_m^2 \sin^2 \Phi_m}} \tag{5}$$

$$\tilde{D}_{m2} = \frac{2B_m \sin \frac{\delta_3}{2} \sin(\Phi_m + \Delta)}{2 \sin \frac{\delta_3}{2} \sqrt{\sum\limits_{m=1}^{M} B_m^2 \sin^2(\Phi_m + \Delta)}} = \frac{B_m \sin(\Phi_m + \Delta)}{\sqrt{\sum\limits_{m=1}^{M} B_m^2 \sin^2(\Phi_m + \Delta)}} \tag{6}$$

If there are more than one fringe numbers in the interference fringe pattern, the following approximate expression can be obtained as

$$\sum_{m=1}^{M} B_m^2 \sin^2 \Phi_m - \sum_{m=1}^{M} B_m^2 \sin^2(\Phi_m + \Delta) = \sin(-\Delta) \sum_{m=1}^{M} B_m^2 \sin(2\Phi_m + \Delta) \approx 0 \tag{7}$$

And then we will get the following approximation

$$\sqrt{\sum_{m=1}^{M} B_m^2 \sin^2 \Phi_m} \approx \sqrt{\sum_{m=1}^{M} B_m^2 \sin^2(\Phi_m + \Delta)} \tag{8}$$

Rewrite Eqs. (5) and (6) we can get

$$\tilde{D}_{m1} = \frac{B_m \sin \Phi_m}{\sqrt{\sum\limits_{m=1}^{M} B_m^2 \sin^2 \Phi_m}} = b_m \sin \Phi_m \tag{9}$$

$$\tilde{D}_{m2} = \frac{B_m \sin(\Phi_m + \Delta)}{\sqrt{\sum\limits_{m=1}^{M} B_m^2 \sin^2(\Phi_m + \Delta)}} \approx b_m \sin(\Phi_m + \Delta) \tag{10}$$

where $b_m = \frac{B_m}{\sqrt{\sum\limits_{m=1}^{M} B_m^2 \sin^2 \Phi_m}}$. It can be seen from the above two equations that the two

differential interferograms has same amplitudes. We can obtain the following expression if the fringe number of the interferograms is more than one.

$$\left\|\tilde{D}_{m1}\right\| = \sqrt{\sum_{m=1}^{M} b_m^2 \sin^2 \Phi_m} \approx \left\|\tilde{D}_{m2}\right\| = \sqrt{\sum_{m=1}^{M} b_m^2 \sin^2 (\Phi_m + \Delta)} \qquad (11)$$

It can be seen that the lengths of $\tilde{D}_{m1}$ and $\tilde{D}_{m2}$ are approximately equal and they can be regard as equal-length vectors. According to the law of parallelograms of vectors, we can see that the sum and subtraction of the two equal-length vectors are the diagonal vectors of the diamond which formed by these two equal-length vectors, and these two diagonal vectors are orthogonal to each other. The two orthogonal diagonal vectors of the diamond can be expressed as

$$\tilde{d}_{m1} = \tilde{D}_{m2} - \tilde{D}_{m1} = 2b_m \sin \frac{\Delta}{2} \cos \psi_m \qquad (12)$$

$$\tilde{d}_{m2} = \tilde{D}_{m2} + \tilde{D}_{m1} = 2b_m \cos \frac{\Delta}{2} \sin \psi_m \qquad (13)$$

where $\psi_m = \Phi_m + \frac{\Delta}{2}$. Normalizing the two orthogonal diagonal vectors of formulas (12) and (13), we will get

$$\hat{d}_{m1} = \frac{\tilde{d}_{m1}}{\|\tilde{d}_{m1}\|} = \frac{2b_m \sin \frac{\Delta}{2} \cos \psi_m}{2 \sin \frac{\Delta}{2} \sqrt{\sum_{m=1}^{M} b_m^2 \cos^2 \psi_m}} = \frac{b_m \cos \psi_m}{\sqrt{\sum_{m=1}^{M} b_m^2 \cos^2 \psi_m}} \qquad (14)$$

$$\hat{d}_{m2} = \frac{\tilde{d}_{m2}}{\|\tilde{d}_{m2}\|} = \frac{2b_m \cos \frac{\Delta}{2} \sin \psi_m}{2 \cos \frac{\Delta}{2} \sqrt{\sum_{m=1}^{M} b_m^2 \sin^2 \psi_m}} = \frac{b_m \sin \psi_m}{\sqrt{\sum_{m=1}^{M} b_m^2 \sin^2 \psi_m}} \qquad (15)$$

Under the above assumption of more than one fringe numbers, we can get the following expression.

$$\sqrt{\sum_{m=1}^{M} b_m^2 \cos^2 \psi_m} \approx \sqrt{\sum_{m=1}^{M} b_m^2 \sin^2 \psi_m} \qquad (16)$$

Though a simple arctangent operation we can get the measured phase.

$$\psi_m = \arctan \left(\frac{\hat{d}_{m2}}{\hat{d}_{m1}} \right) \qquad (17)$$

3 Numerical Simulation

In order to prove the effectiveness of the proposed method, we conducted simulation verification. First of all, on the basis of formula (1), three simulated phase-shifting interference fringe patterns with size of 512×512 pixels are generated, the phase shifts are respectively set as $\delta_1 = 0$, $\delta_2 = 1$ and $\delta_3 = 2$. Among them, the background item is set as $A(x,y) = 10\exp[-0.2(x^2 + y^2)] = 80$, the modulation item is $B(x,y) = 80\exp[-0.25(x^2 + y^2)]$, where $-2.56 \leq x, y \leq 2.56$. The phase distribution to be measured is $\varphi(x,y) = \pi(x^2 + y^2) - <\pi(x^2 + y^2)>$ rad, where the operator $<\cdot>$ denote the average operation. In the simulated interferograms, an additive Gaussian noise with a signal-to-noise ratio of 5% has been added to achieve the actual situation.

Three simulated phase-shifting interferograms with a size of 512×512 pixels are shown in Figs. 1(a)–(c). Subtract Fig. 1(b) and 1(c) from Fig. 1(a), two differential

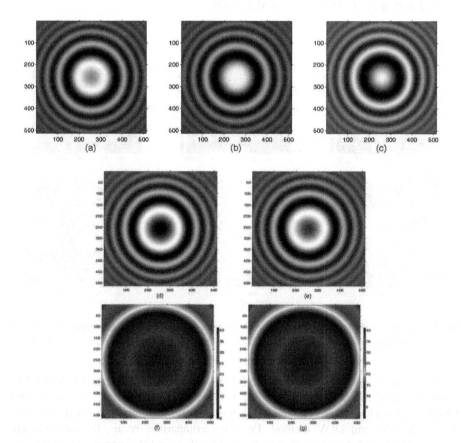

Fig. 1. Simulated phase-shifting interferograms. (a) (b) (c) three simulated phase-shifting interferograms; (d) (e) two differential interferograms; (f) the real phase; (g) the unwrapped phase of the proposed method.

interferograms shown in Fig. 1(d) and 1(e) can be obtained. Theoretical phase and unwrapped phase of the proposed method are shown in Fig. 1(f) and Fig. 1(g) respectively. Between the real phase and the measured phase, the root mean square error is measured as 0.0294 rad.

Next, AIA, PCA, GS3, DDV and GS2 have been utilized to compare with the phase measurement results of the proposed method, in which the numbers of fringe patterns are set as 32 for AIA and PCA, 3 for GS3, 2 for DDV and GS2. For AIA and PCA, the phase shift between two neighboring interferograms is set as 0.1 rad. Conventional Gaussian high-pass filter, whose transfer function expressed as $H(u, v) = 1\text{-}exp[-(u^2 + v^2)/2\sigma^2]$, where σ represents filter window width and the value is 2, has been utilized to eliminate the background item in the algorithm of GS2 and DDV. Figure 2 (a)–2(f) show phase difference between the real phase and the unwrapped phase of AIA, PCA, GS2, DDV, GS3 and the proposed algorithm. To facilitate analysis and comparison, two important parameters, root mean square error (RMSE) and processing time, have been used to compare different methods as shown in Table 1. All results are obtained with a 2.5 GHz laptop and MATLAB.

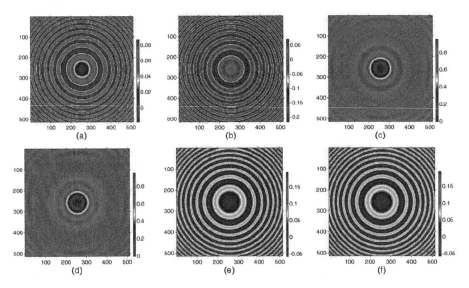

Fig. 2. The phase difference between the theoretical phase and the unwrapped phase with different algorithms: (a) AIA; (b) PCA; (c) GS2; (d) DDV; (e) GS3; (f) the proposed method

Obviously, the processing speed of the method proposed in this paper is lower than all other methods; in addition, the RMSE with the proposed method is the same with the GS3 and is close to AIA method with the longest processing time, and is far less than PCA, GS2 and DDV method. From the comparison result, the measurement accuracy of AIA is better than other methods. Therefore, in the experiment research, we use AIA measurement result as the reference phase.

Table 1. RMSE and the computing Time of different Algorithms (Simulation)

	AIA	PCA	GS2	DDV	GS3	The proposed method
RMSE (rad)	0.0281	0.0929	0.1085	0.1080	0.0294	0.0294
Time (s)	36.2890	0.4091	0.1683	0.0629	0.0258	0.0244

4 Experiment

Next, the effectiveness of the proposed method is verified by experiments research and the AIA measurement result is used as the reference phase. Three experimental interferograms selected randomly from 32-frame phase-shifting interferograms are shown in Fig. 3. Figure 4(a) shows the reference phase calculated by using AIA from 32-frame phase-shifting interferograms. Figures 4(b)–4(f) show the difference between

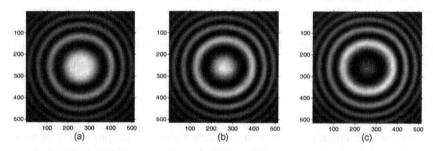

Fig. 3. Three-frame experimental phase-shifting interferograms

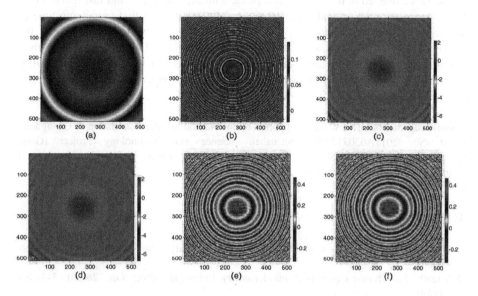

Fig. 4. The experimental results: (a) The referenced unwrapped phase of AIA; difference between the referenced AIA phase and the unwrapped phase of other methods: (b) PCA; (c) GS2; (d) DDV; (e) GS3; (f) the proposed method

the unwrapped phase maps of PCA, GS2, DDV, GS3 and the proposed method with the referenced phase map of AIA. The corresponding RMSE of the difference between referenced AIA and other methods, and the processing time are respectively shown in Table 2.

Table 2. RMSE and the processing Time of Phase Extraction with different Algorithms (Experiment)

	PCA	GS2	DDV	GS3	The proposed method
RMSE (rad)	0.0707	0.2829	0.2826	0.0625	0.0625
Time (s)	0.3450	0.0916	0.0646	0.0268	0.0252

It can be seen from the calculation results that the processing time of the proposed method in this paper is less than all other methods; in addition, the RMSE with the proposed method is the same with the GS3 and is close to the referenced AIA, and is far less than PCA, GS2 and DDV algorithm. The experimental results show that the proposed algorithm is suitable for the phase extraction with high precision and fast speed.

5   Conclusions

By using the interferogram subtraction and then normalization processing to remove the background, according to the orthogonal characteristics of the diamond diagonal vectors, only three phase-shifting interferograms whose phase shifts are unknown and randomly are needed to recover the real phase with high accuracy and fast speed. From the numerical simulation and experimental results, we can see that processing time of the method introduced in this paper is less than all other methods, in addition, the RMSE of the proposed method is the same with the GS3 and is close to AIA method with the longest processing time, and the result is far less than the PCA, GS2 and DDV algorithm. In summary, the algorithm proposed in this paper provides a very useful phase extraction tool.

Acknowledgements. This work is supported by the Natural Science Foundation of Guangdong (Grant No. 2017A030313337), Shenzhen Science and Technology Project (Grant No. JCYJ20190808093001772), the Development Program Funds of Shenzhen Institute of Technology (Grant No. ZY201704).

References

1. Malacara, D., Servín, M., Malacara, Z.: Interferogram analysis for optical testing. CRC Press (2005)
2. Creath, K.: Phase-measurement interferometry techniques. Prog. Opt. **26**(26), 349–393 (1988)

3. Wang, Z., Han, B.: Advanced iterative algorithm for phase extraction of randomly phase-shifted interferograms. Opt. Lett. **29**(14), 1671–1673 (2004)
4. Vargas, J., Quiroga, J.A., Belenguer, T.: Analysis of the principal component algorithm in phase-shifting interferometry. Opt. Lett. **36**(12), 2215–2217 (2011)
5. Deng, J., Wang, H., Zhang, D., Zhong, L., Fan, J., Lu, X.: Phase shift extraction algorithm based on euclidean matrix norm. Opt. Lett. **38**(9), 1506–1508 (2013)
6. Kreis, T.M., Jueptner, W.P.: Fourier transform evaluation of interference patterns: demodulation and sign ambiguity. In: Proceedings of Spiel the International Society for Optical Engineering, 1553 (1992)
7. Vargas, J., Quiroga, J.A., Sorzano, C.O.S., Estrada, J.C., Carazo, J.M.: Two-step interferometry by a regularized optical flow algorithm. Opt. Lett. **36**(17), 3485–3487 (2011)
8. Vargas, J., Quiroga, J.A., Sorzano, C.O.S., Estrada, J.C., Carazo, J.M.: Two-step demodulation on the Gram-Schmidt ortho normalization method. Opt. Lett. **37**(3), 443–445 (2012)
9. Muravsky, L., Ostash, O., Voronayk, T., et al.: Two-frame phase-shifting interferometry for retrieval of smoothy surface and its displacement. Opt. Lasers Eng. **49**(3), 305–132 (2011)
10. Deng, J., Wang, H., Zhang, F., et al.: Two-setp phase demodulation algorithm based on the extreme value of interference. Opt. Lett. **37**(3), 443–445 (2012)
11. Luo, C., Zhong, L., Sun, P., Wang, H., Tian, J., Lu, X.: Two-step demodulation algorithm based on the orthogonality of diamond diagonal vectors. Appl. Phys. B **119**(2), 387–391 (2015). https://doi.org/10.1007/s00340-015-6087-z
12. Niu, W., Zhong, L., Sun, P., Zhang, W.: Two-step phase retrieval algorithm based on the quotient of inner products of phase-shifting interferograms. J. Opt. **17**(8), 085703 (2015)
13. Wang, H., Luo, C., Zhong, L., Ma, S., Lu, X.: Phase retrieval approach based on the normalized difference maps induced by three interferograms with unknown phase shifts. Opt. Express **22**(5), 5147–5154 (2014)

Research on Spectrum Allocation Strategy Based on Stackelberg Game in Ultra Dense Network

Han Zhihao, Zhao Donglai, and Wang Gang[(✉)]

Harbin Institute of Technology, Communication Research Center,
Harbin 150001, Heilongjiang, China
gwang5l@hit.edu.cn

Abstract. As one of the key technologies of 5G, ultra dense network (UDN), densely distributed small base stations has brought about an increase in system capacity and transmission rate, and has become a research hotspot in recent years. In order to compensate for the severe co-layer and cross-layer interference caused by UDN, clustering small cells first and Stackelberg game is applied to spectrum allocation, and the Nash equilibrium is solved to obtain a spectrum allocation strategy with less interference. The performance of spectrum allocation algorithm based on Stackelberg game (SASG) is simulated and the simulation results verify the performance of SASG, showing that SASG can effectively improve the system throughput under limited spectrum resources.

Keywords: Ultra dense network · Game theory · Spectrum allocation · Nash equilibrium · Clustering

1 Introduction

In recent years, wireless communication network technology has been rapidly updated. User requirements of communication services and the system and architecture of communication networks have undergone tremendous changes. On the one hand, the services supported by the mobile communication network are more complex, from traditional voice and short message services to multimedia services such as mobile data Internet access and video. On the other hand, various intelligent end users pursue higher rates and higher quality wireless communication service. Therefore, increasing the system capacity of mobile communication networks, supporting more communication users, and providing more stable, faster, and more efficient data transmission has become an urgent requirement for the future development of mobile communication.

The IMT-2020 (5G) Promotion Group of China promulgated the "5G Vision and Demand White Paper" in 2014, which vividly explained the key capabilities of the 5G mobile communication system [1]. And the related technologies of the 5G mobile communication system have become research hotspots. Within the coverage of the

This work is supported in part by National Natural Science Foundation of China (No. 61671184, No. 61901137).

M. Guan and Z. Na (Eds.): MLICOM 2020, LNICST 342, pp. 36–46, 2021.
https://doi.org/10.1007/978-3-030-66785-6_4

macro base station, various types of small base stations are densely deployed, the communication distance between the small base stations and users is greatly shortened, and the transmission rate is significantly improved. However, a large number of densely deployed small base stations of different types and different service scales will cause serious cross-layer and co-layer interference, and the wireless network communication environment becomes more and more complicated. Therefore, a reasonable spectrum allocation strategy can make the most efficient use of limited spectrum resources, coordinate interference between base stations, and improve the spectrum utilization rate of the network.

A large number of scholars have conducted in-depth research on spectrum allocation strategies in ultra dense networks, and various new ideas are emerging. Combined with the idea of clustering, small cells are divided into different clusters for calculation according to different algorithms [2–5]. Combined with the idea of graph theory, cells with severe interference are assigned different colors, and each color represents a kind of spectrum resource. In this way, the interference problem between adjacent cells can be solved by allocating orthogonal spectrum resources. Paper [6] proposed a QoS graph coloring (QGC) spectrum allocation scheme. The QGC algorithm attempts to color the minimum number of colors for all vertices in each cluster, and matches the QoS requirements of the vertices by coloring each vertex once or twice. Paper [7] proposed a dynamic spectrum allocation algorithm based on interference graph (CBRA), which effectively suppressed the co-layer interference and improved the spectrum efficiency.

With the continuous improvement and development of game theory, it is increasingly used in the field of mobile communications, providing a good idea for solving resource allocation and interference coordination problems. Paper [8] proposed a macro base station power control and time-domain interference coordination algorithm based on game theory, using an adaptive configuration scheme for ABS subframes. Paper [9] allocates the spectrum resources of macro cell and small cell based on game theory, and obtains better results than the average allocation.

In this paper, Stackelberg game is applied to spectrum allocation, combined with the concept of Nash equilibrium, a spectrum allocation scheme that is satisfactory to every participant is obtained.

2 System Model of Ultra Dense Network

The issue of interference management between small base stations is an important challenge in the environment of large-scale deployment of small base stations. The system model and interference scenario of the ultra dense network are shown in Fig. 1. In this model, macro base station and small base stations co-exist, and small base stations serve their users. Within the coverage area of the macro base station, there are N_r small base stations randomly distributed, and the coverage radius of the small base stations is R_s.

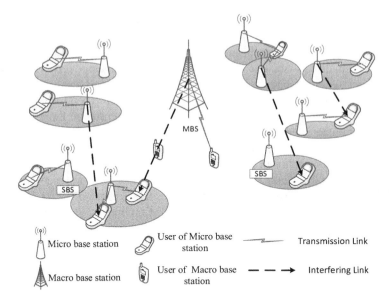

Fig. 1. System model of ultra dense network

The ultra dense network reduces the transmission delay by densely deploying small base stations to bring the transmission nodes closer to the terminal. The adding in the number of small base stations can increase system capacity, support massive user connections, and provide users with global coverage. Compared with traditional macro base station deployments, ultra dense networks have the advantages of strong blind spot coverage, low deployment costs, and flexible configuration. In response to different usage environments, different types and sizes of small base stations have been developed and put on the market, greatly accelerating the development of ultra dense networks.

3 Small Cell Clustering

Clustering is to divide the complex network topology into several small network clusters according to certain criteria (such as the location of the base station, the degree of interference in the network, etc.), and then perform intra-cluster or inter-cluster resources allocation in cluster units.

At present, domestic and international cluster-based spectrum allocation management schemes can be divided into two categories according to different optimization objectives of interference: one is to maximize intra-cluster interference; the other is contrary to the former. By dividing into the same cluster, there are base stations with very little intra-cluster interference, so that when the same frequency resources are reused in the cluster, no serious interference will occur, which greatly improves the utilization rate of resources. Therefore, adjacent base stations with severe interference to each other are divided into different clusters, and orthogonal frequency resources are allocated in the different clusters, thereby suppressing interference.

In the research of this paper, the latter optimization goal is selected, and annealing evolution algorithm (AEA) is used to cluster small base stations.

The algorithm flow can be implemented according to Algorithm 1.

Table 1. Algorithm flow

	Algorithm 1: annealing evolution clustering algorithm
Input	$MAXGEN, T_{end}, k, p_c, p_m, gen = 0, T_i = T_0$
1.	Initial clustering S, interference sum $C(S)$
2.	**for** $r = 1, 2, \ldots N_b$ **do**
3.	**for** $gen = 1, 2, \ldots MAXGEN$ **do**
4.	Perform genetic operations such as selection, crossover, and mutation to obtain new clustering results S' for small cells
5.	Get new interference sum $C(S')$
6.	$\Delta C = C(S') - C(S)$
7.	**if** $\Delta C < 0$ **then**
8.	Use new clustering results
9.	**else**
10.	Accept new clustering results with a probability of $\exp(-\Delta C / T)$
11.	**end if**
12.	$gen = gen + 1$
13.	**end for**
14.	**if** $T_i > T_{end}$ **then**
15.	$T_{i+1} = kT_i$, back to 3
16.	**else**
17.	break
18.	**end if**
19.	**end for**
Output	Clustering results

4 Spectrum Allocation Strategy Based on Stackelberg Game

The Stackelberg game is a hierarchical non-cooperative game, that is, some participants declare their own strategies before others choose strategies. When formulating a tiered strategy plan, the players who execute their strategies before other participants and dominate the game are called "leaders", who can impose their strategies on other players. And those who respond to the leaders declare strategies of gamers are called "followers".

The Stackelberg game can also be applied to a scenario containing one leader and multiple followers. At this time, for a given leader Stackelberg strategy, a set of follower joint strategy sets can be obtained by maximizing the utility. Each follower utility is a function of the leader strategy and other followers strategies. Therefore, the single-leader multi-follower non-cooperative game equilibrium solution corresponds to a situation in which the leader maximizes his utility according to the follower response set, and the followers play each other according to the leader's statement strategy until the Nash equilibrium is reached.

In the ultra dense network model, each small base station competes for available spectrum to maximize their own utility. First, the small base stations are clustered, and then the macro base station is the leader, and the small base station clusters are the followers to establish the Stackelberg game model.

Suppose a macro base station and N_r small base stations are considered in the model, and the small base stations are numbered by $1, 2, \ldots, N_r$. The available spectrum bandwidth is B, the number of sub-carriers is C, adjacent sub-carriers have similar fading characteristics, set S adjacent sub-carriers to form a channel, so the number of available spectrum resource blocks (number of frequency channels) is $M = C/S$ and the users of small base stations are random distributed in their respective coverage areas. According to Algorithm 1, the small base stations are divided into $N_g (N_g > M)$ clusters, and there are N_r/N_g small base stations in each cluster. Matrix $\mathbf{G_r} \in R^{N_g \times \frac{N_r}{N_g}}$ is used to represent the distribution of each cluster. The row vector G_m represents the number of all small base stations in the mth cluster.

$$
\mathbf{G_r} = \begin{bmatrix} G_{1,1} & \cdots & G_{1,\frac{N_r}{N_g}} \\ \vdots & \ddots & \vdots \\ G_{N_g,\frac{N_r}{N_g}} & \cdots & G_{N_g,\frac{N_r}{N_g}} \end{bmatrix} \tag{1}
$$

Firstly, according to the principle of not reusing the spectrum as much as possible, each small base station cluster is randomly assigned a spectrum resource block to obtain an initial spectrum distribution $\mathbf{S_r} \in R^{M \times N_g}$, in which time $S_{m,n} \in \{0, 1\}$. $S_{m,n} = 1$ indicates that the small base station n is allocated the spectrum resource block m, and $S_{m,n} = 0$ indicates that the spectrum resource block m is not allocated to small base station n. $Count(m)$ represents the number of small base station clusters to which spectrum blocks are allocated.

$$
\mathbf{S_r} = \begin{bmatrix} S_{1,1} & \cdots & S_{1,N_g} \\ \vdots & \ddots & \vdots \\ S_{M,1} & \cdots & S_{M,N_g} \end{bmatrix} \tag{2}
$$

$$
\sum_{m=1}^{M} S_{m,n} = 1 \tag{3}
$$

$$
\sum_{n=1}^{N_g} S_{m,n} = Count(m) \times \frac{N_r}{N_g} \tag{4}
$$

The small base station clusters at this time are classified: the first type cluster is a cluster whose allocated spectrum is not used by other clusters; the second type cluster is the allocated spectrum and other small base station clusters are used at the same time. For the first type cluster, the interference between them is small; for the second type cluster, because there is another cluster member using the same frequency spectrum at the same time, if the distance between some small base stations is close, it will cause a large co-layer interference.

The mathematical expression of Stackelberg game is:

$$G = \left\{ N, \{S^c\}, \left\{ u_j^c \right\} \right\} \tag{5}$$

Where N represents the set of small base station clusters and $\{S^c\}$ represents the set of spectrum allocation strategies of the cluster. Where S^c represents the spectrum allocated by the small base station cluster c, and u_j^c represents the utility function of the small base station j in the cluster c.

Consider that when a small cell r transmits information to user i within its coverage area, the user's signal-to-noise ratio can be defined as:

$$SINR_i^r = \frac{P_i^r (d_i^r)^{-\gamma} h_i^r}{\sum\limits_{m \in C_r, m \neq r} P_i^m (d_i^m)^{-\gamma} h_i^m + N_0} \tag{6}$$

Among them, P_i^r represents the transmission power when the small base station r transmits information to the user i. d_i^r represents the distance between the small base station r and the user i, and $(d_i^r)^{-\gamma}$ represents the path loss. C_r represents the set of all small base stations that are allocated the same spectrum resource block as the small base station r. The noise consists of two parts, the additive white Gaussian noise and co-channel interference. N_0 represents the additive white Gaussian noise and co-frequency interference is represented by $\sum\limits_{m \in C_r, m \neq r} P_i^m (d_i^m)^{-\gamma} h_i^m$, which represents the total interference caused to user i by other users using the same spectrum resource block.

Using the throughput of each cluster as the utility function, the utility function of the small base station r in the cluster c is:

$$U_r^c = \sum\limits_{i \in \{r\}} \log_2 (1 + SINR_i^r) \tag{7}$$

The utility of each small cell cluster is:

$$U^c = \sum\limits_{r \in C_r} U_r^c \tag{8}$$

Since the spectrum allocation of each cluster is controlled by the cluster head, and each cluster is independent and selfish. When the game reaches the equilibrium point, each cluster has no incentive to change its strategy, and the game reaches an equilibrium.

If formula (9) holds for any S^c, then point $(S^{1*}, S^{2*}, \ldots, S^{c*})$ is the equilibrium point of the Stackelberg game.

$$U^c(S^{c*}, S^{-c*}) \geq U^c(S^c, S^{-c*}) \tag{9}$$

The total utility function of the system can be expressed as:

$$U = \sum U^c \tag{10}$$

The flow of spectrum allocation strategy algorithm based on Stackelberg game is shown in Algorithm 2 (Table 2).

Table 2. Algorithm flow

Algorithm 2: Spectrum allocation strategy based on Stackelberg game	
Input	Small cell cluster obtained from Algorithm 1
1.	**for** $T = 1, 2, 3, \ldots$ **do**
2.	**for** $r = 1, 2, \ldots, N_g + 1$ **do**
3.	Change strategy of cluster r
4.	Calculate the utility of cluster r according to formula (7)(8)
5.	**if** satisfy (9) **then**
6.	Cluster r chooses the corresponding strategy
7.	**end if**
8.	$r = r + 1$
9.	**end for**
10.	**end for**

5   Simulation Analysis

Based on the ultra dense network model, considering Rayleigh fading and path loss, this paper simulate the throughput of macro base stations and small base station clusters. The system simulation parameters are shown in Table 1 (Table 3):

Table 3. Simulation parameters

Parameters	Value
System bandwidth	6 MHz
Carrier frequency band	2.6 GHZ
Number of subcarriers	360
Number of resource blocks	4
Transmit power of MBS	45 dBm
Transmit power of SBS	20 dBm
Coverage radius of MBS	500 m
Coverage radius of SBS	50 m
Path loss index	3.7
White Gaussian Noise	−174 dBm/Hz

The interference change when using AEA for clustering is shown in Fig. 2. It can be seen from the figure that with each change, the interference and the cluster gradually become smaller until the minimum value is reached or the termination condition is satisfied.

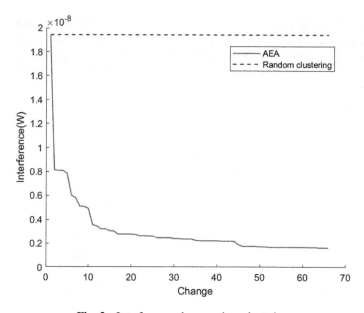

Fig. 2. Interference change when clustering

When the Stackelberg game reaches Nash equilibrium, the performance simulation of the macro base station and small base station clusters is shown in Figs. 3, 4 and 5.

As can be seen from Fig. 3, in the initial game stage, in order to optimize their utility, the small base station clusters and macro base stations continuously change their own strategies until all participants reach a stable state.

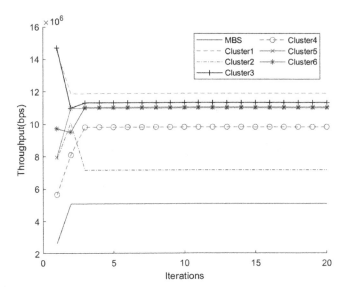

Fig. 3. Performance of small cell cluster

After reaching the equilibrium, the macro base station change the strategy independently, and the strategies of other participants remain unchanged. The throughput changes of all participants are shown in Fig. 4. It can be seen from the figure that the throughput of the macro base station decreases, which meets the definition of Nash equilibrium.

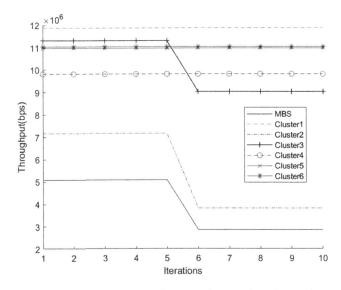

Fig. 4. Performance changes when the macro base station changes its strategy

The trend of the total throughput of the system during the game is shown in Fig. 5. It can be seen from the figure that in the initial stage, due to the players playing each other and changing their strategies, the system throughput fluctuates to a certain extent. After about 15 games, the system reaches the Nash equilibrium.

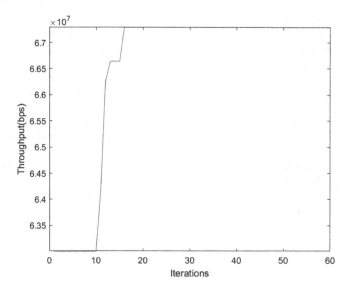

Fig. 5. Performance of system

6 Conclusion

This paper proposes a spectrum allocation strategy based on Stackelberg game. In the proposed strategy, the first goal is using AEA for clustering to minimize the intra-cluster interference. Then let the macro base station as the leader and the small base station cluster as the followers to construct the Stackelberg game model. Optimizing the spectrum allocation strategy of small base stations by solving Nash equilibrium of games. The simulation analysis of the performance is processed from the number of iterations, throughput and so on.

References

1. IMT-2020(5G) Promotion Group.: 5G Vision and Demand White Paper [EB/OL] 2015/04/17
2. Seno, R., Ohtsuki, T., Jiang, W., Takatori, Y.: A low-complexity cell clustering algorithm in dense small cell networks. EURASIP J. Wirel. Commun. Netw. **2016**(1), 1–11 (2016). https://doi.org/10.1186/s13638-016-0765-3
3. Qiu, J., Wu, Q., Xu, Y.: Demand-aware resource allocation for ultra-dense small cell networks: an interference-separation clustering-based solution. Trans. Emerg. Telecommun. Technol. **27**(8), 1071–1086 (2016)

4. Liang, L., Wang, W., Jia, Y.: A cluster-based energy-efficient resource management scheme for ultra-dense networks. IEEE Access **4**, 6823–6832 (2016)
5. Wenchao, L., Jing, Z.: Cluster-based resource allocation scheme with QoS guarantee in ultra-dense networks. IET Commun. **12**(7), 861–867 (2018)
6. Xu, Z., He, Y., Xu, X.: Qo graph coloring spectrum allocation for femto cell in macro/femto heterogeneous network. In: Communications and Networking in China (CHINACOM), pp. 374–378. IEEE Press, Guilin (2013)
7. Tang, H., Hong, P., Xue, K.: Cluster-based resource allocation for interference mitigation in LTE heterogeneous networks. In: Vehicular Technology Conference (VTC Fall), pp. 1–5. IEEE Press, Canada (2012)
8. Nai, S., Quek, T., Debbah, M.: Slow admission and power control for small cell networks via distributed optimization. In: Wireless Communications and Networking Conference (WCNC), pp. 2261–2265. IEEE Press, Shanghai (2013)
9. Lien, S., Lin, Y., Chen, K.: Cognitive and game-theoretical radio resource management for autonomous femto cells with QoS guarantees. IEEE Trans. Wirel. Commun. **10**(7), 2196–2206 (2011)
10. Duong, N., Madhukumar, A.: Niyato allocation in two-tier networks. Stackelberg Bayesian Game Power Trans. Veh. Technol. **65**(4), 2341–2354 (2016)
11. Chen, S., Fei, Q., Bo, H.: User-centric ultra-dense networks for 5G. IEEE Wirel. Commun. **23**(2), 78–85 (2018)

A D2D Resource Scheduling Algorithm Based on Position Relation in Cellular Network

Xing Su and Yanyong Su[(✉)]

Communication Research Center, Harbin Institute of Technology,
1, Harbin 50001, China
18S005050@stu.hit.edu.cn, suyanyong@hit.edu.cn

Abstract. With the development of 5G, device-to-device (D2D) and other technologies have emerged one after another, making the communication services faster and wider in coverage. Aiming at the problem of high computational complexity of traditional resource allocation algorithms, by studying the D2D communication network model and the spatial location relationship of users, ignoring parameters that have little impact on the calculation, a D2D resource scheduling algorithm based on location relationship is proposed and optimized system performance. Simulation results show that, compared with traditional algorithms, the proposed resource scheduling algorithm has greatly reduced algorithm complexity, and has good data transfer rate and high system capacity.

Keywords: D2D · Resource scheduling · Location relationship

1 Introduction

Terminal pass-through D2D technology refers to data transmission between two terminals with relatively close geographical locations using a direct link without forwarding through the base station [1]. This method can offload traffic from the core network, and has extremely high flexibility, which can greatly improve system capacity and spectrum efficiency, and reduce energy consumption. It is listed as one of the key technologies in the 5G mobile communication system [2].

D2D technology in cellular mobile networks can improve spectrum utilization and system throughput. The contradiction between numerous user equipment and limited spectrum resources cannot be ignored, and it is easy to cause co-channel interference (CCI). Common solutions include precoding algorithms and resource management algorithms. The precoding algorithm calculates the appropriate coding method by estimating the channel information, thereby facilitating the smooth recovery of the signal at the receiver [3]. Resource management algorithms are often combined with other technologies [4], to study frequency selection and power control issues of D2D [5].

The rest of this paper is organized as follows. Section 2 will analyze the research model of this paper. Section 3 will analyze the theory of the proposed algorithm in detail from the perspective of positional relationship and give the framework of the proposed method. Section 4 will provide the implementation and performance analysis. The conclusion will be drawn in Sect. 5.

© ICST Institute for Computer Sciences, Social Informatics and Telecommunications Engineering 2021
Published by Springer Nature Switzerland AG 2021. All Rights Reserved
M. Guan and Z. Na (Eds.): MLICOM 2020, LNICST 342, pp. 47–52, 2021.
https://doi.org/10.1007/978-3-030-66785-6_5

2 System Model

The D2D channel in the cellular network is different from the channel of the cellular users, because the antennas of the transmitter and receiver of the D2D user are very low (compared to the base station) and will interact with a large number of scatterers. Therefore, in most literatures, the channel model is set to large-scale path loss and Rayleigh fading channels. Considering the above model, the power received by the base station (BS) from the Cellular transmitter (CT) is $P_{BS} = P_{CT}|h|^2 d^{-\alpha}$. Where h represents the channel fading coefficient, obeys CN(0,1) distribution, α represents the path loss index, and d represents the distance between CT and BS. Similarly, the power of any transmitter in the network can be expressed similarly.

In the downlink, the base station's transmit power is much greater than the mobile user's transmit power, which means that the DR will be subject to stronger CCI. In the uplink, the base station acts as the receiver and does not interfere with other users. So, this paper studies the issue of multiplexing resources for D2D users in the uplink.

Consider the situation shown in Fig. 1.

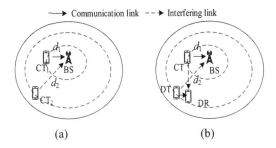

Fig. 1. Two users' CCI under a single antenna

When the same antenna of two cellular users CT_1 and CT_2 is received at the same BS, their signal-to-interference and noise ratios $SINR_1$ and $SINR_2$ are respectively:

$$SINR_1 \cdot SINR_2 = \frac{P_1 d_1^{-\alpha}|h_1|^2}{P_2 d_2^{-\alpha}|h_2|^2 + \sigma^2} \cdot \frac{P_2 d_2^{-\alpha}|h_2|^2}{P_1 d_1^{-\alpha}|h_1|^2 + \sigma^2} < 1 \qquad (1)$$

Where P_1 and P_2 are the transmission power of CT_1 and CT_2 respectively, d_1 and d_2 are the distances from CT_1 and CT_2 to the BS, h_1 and h_2 are the channel attenuation coefficients of CT_1 and CT_2 to the BS, and α represents the path loss index.

Assuming that the minimum SINR for the user to guarantee the communication quality QoS is γ_0. Usually, $\gamma_0(\text{dB}) > 0$, so it is impossible to guarantee the communication quality of two CTs at the same time. Therefore, there can only be one CT user on the same frequency under a single antenna. Assuming $P_1 = P_2$, $h_1 = h_2 = 1$, then for CT, the $SINR_1 \geq \gamma_0$ is derived to $d_1 < \gamma_0^{\frac{-1}{\alpha}} d_2 < d_2$. It can be seen that the distance from the DT to the BS needs to be greater than the distance from the CT to the BS.

3   The Proposed Method

3.1   Analysis of Positional Relationship

There are two quantities that have little effect on the algorithm. One is the transmission power. Since most users in the cellular network are smartphones, there is an approximate relationship of $P_1 = P_2$. Other is the channel attenuation coefficient, because h follows the distribution CN(0,1), then the magnitude of $|h|^2$ is around $10°$, having little effect on $P \cdot d^{-\alpha}$, so it is approximately regarded as the case of no attenuation $h_1 = h_2 = 1$.

Analyze the situation of DR being disturbed. Assuming that the minimum distance between the transmitting user in the same frequency band and the DR is d_{min}, and the distance d between the same pair of DT and DR is much smaller than d_{min}, neglecting small amounts, then the transmitting user in the same frequency band and DR are equivalent, and the case of maximum interference will be As shown in Fig. 2.

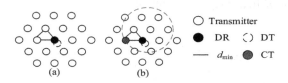

Fig. 2. Position relationship in the same frequency band

The positional relationship of the equilateral triangle is extended outward, and the distance between each pair is d_{min}. If the layer is extended outward, the radius of the occupied area increases by d_{min}. Then the SINR of DR is:

$$SINR = \frac{P_0|h_0|^2 d^{-\alpha}}{\sum P_i|h_i|^2 d_i^{-\alpha} + \sigma^2} \tag{2}$$

Where b is the distance factor, $b = \sum d_i^{-\alpha}/d_{min}^{-\alpha}$, which is determined by the location of the transmitting user in the same frequency band. Assuming $P_1 = P_2$, $h_1 = h_2 = 1$, then the constraint condition can be obtained from (2):

$$d_{min} = \left(\frac{\gamma_0 b P_0}{P_0 d^{-\alpha} - \gamma_0 \sigma^2}\right)^{\frac{1}{\alpha}} \tag{3}$$

To further discuss the situation in Fig. 2(b), suppose that there are n DTs equidistantly arranged on a circle with a radius of R_2 at a distance of d_{min}, in order to simulate the CCI situation of CT and estimate R_1 and R_2 relationship.

$$b = n = \left[\frac{2\pi R_2}{d_{min}}\right] \tag{4}$$

$$R_1 < \left(b\gamma_0 R_2^{-\alpha} + \frac{\gamma_0 \sigma^2}{P} \right)^{\frac{-1}{\alpha}} \tag{5}$$

3.2   Resource Scheduling Algorithm

Through the study of the positional relationship, it is found that when the user interval of the same frequency band is large and the number is small, the CCI is small. So consider the quantity (variance) that can measure the degree of dispersion of points as a system indicator.

Let $\omega_{m,k}$ indicate whether the mth mobile user uses the kth frequency band. Assuming the user's position is represented by (x, y). Also, a D2D user pair occupies only one frequency band, $\sum_{l=1}^{K} \omega_{m,l} = 1$. The average position of all mobile users in the kth band is expressed as $(\overline{x}_i, \overline{y}_i)$. The objective function is the maximum sum of variance of all points in the K frequency bands, that is:

$$\max \sum_{l=1}^{K} \frac{\sum_{j=1}^{M} \left(\omega_{j,k}x_j - \overline{x_k} \right)^2 + \sum_{j=1}^{M} \left(\omega_{j,k}y_j - \overline{y_k} \right)^2}{\sum_{j=1}^{M} \omega_{j,k}} \tag{6}$$

Based on the above theoretical basis, a resource scheduling algorithm based on position relationship is proposed. The specific process is as follows.

Step 1: If CT, go to **Step 2**; otherwise, go to **Step 6**.

Step 2: If there is an unused frequency band, access & end; otherwise, go to **Step 3**.

Step 3: If CT exists in any frequency band, go to **Step 7**; otherwise, go to **Step 4**.

Step 4: Iterate through the frequency bands used only by DT, select the frequency band with the least DTs that cannot work after access. If there are no DTs that cannot work, end; otherwise, use these DTs as the object of new access, go to **Step 5**.

Step 5: If there is an unused frequency band, access & end; otherwise go to **Step 6**.

Step 6: Try to access each frequency band, on the premise of not affecting the communication of the original user, select the frequency band with the largest sum of variance to access, end; otherwise, go to **Step 7**.

Step 7: Unable to connect to the network, end.

4   Simulation and Analysis

With the base station as the center and the coverage area of radius R, the distribution of cellular users and D2D users are subject to the uniform Poisson Point Process (PPP). Other simulation parameters of cellular networks are shown in Table 1.

Table 1. Simulation parameter settings

Parameter	Value
Cell radius	500 m
Transmit power	0.1 W
D2D maximum spacing	50 m
Number of frequency bands	40
Path loss index α	4
SINR threshold	16 dB
AGWN power spectrum	−174 dBm/Hz

Based on the model in Fig. 2, the cell theoretically needs to accommodate at least two densely arranged transmitting users in the same frequency band.

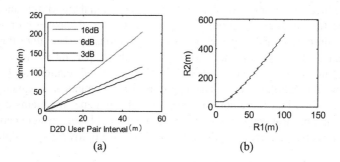

(a)   (b)

Fig. 3. Mathematical relationship of parameters

Changing the spacing d of D2D user pairs, the minimum interval d_{min} changes as shown in Fig. 3(a). When $d = 50$ m and $\gamma_0 = 16$ dB, d_{min} is about 204 m, and the cell radius is between $2d_{min}$–$3d_{min}$. That is, the two-layer dense arrangement is suitable as the analysis condition. The curve in Fig. 3(b) is the critical value of R_1 and R_2. The feasible region is the area above the curve while satisfying $R_1 > 0, R_2 < 500$. The vertices are (0, 32), (101.1, 500), (0, 500) (unit m). It means that the DT is at least 32 m away from the BS. When the distance between the CT and the BS is greater than 101.1 m, the cell will not be able to accommodate D2D communication in the same frequency band.

Then simulate and analyze the resource scheduling algorithm based on the maximum sum of variance (Algorithm 1). The algorithms used for comparison are the resource scheduling algorithm based on the maximum data transfer rate (Algorithm 2). The results of the simulation are shown in Fig. 4.

It can be seen when the frequency resources are sufficient, Algorithm 1 and Algorithm 2 have little difference in the total data transfer rate and system capacity. When the total number of users increases, Algorithm 2 has a higher data transmission rate, but Algorithm 1 has a larger system capacity. In this simulation, the system capacity of Algorithm 1 is 65, and the system capacity of Algorithm 2 is 55.

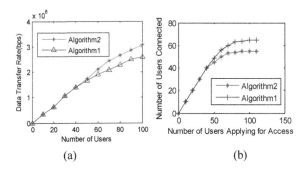

Fig. 4. Algorithm performance comparison

5   Conclusion

In order to reduce the computational complexity of traditional algorithms and make full use of the location relationship of users in cellular networks, this paper proposes a D2D resource scheduling algorithm based on location relationship. The algorithm uses the sum of variance as the performance index, pursues the dispersion in the user space to reduce CCI, and determines the constraints by the positional relationship between the D2D user and the cellular user to ensure the user's communication quality. Experimental results show that the algorithm proposed in this paper maintains a good data transfer rate, and has lower computational complexity and higher system capacity. The next step of research can be in-depth in the direction of improving system throughput.

References

1. Andreev, S., Pyattaev, A., Johnsson, K.: Cellular traffic offloading onto network-assisted device-to-device connections. IEEE Commun. Mag. **52**, 20–31 (2014)
2. Karvouna, D., Georgakopoulos, A., Tsagkaris, K.: Smart management of D2D constructs: an experiment-based approach. IEEE Commun. Mag. **52**, 82–89 (2014)
3. Li, W.: ATSC 3.0 transmitter carrier and timing offset for co-channel interference mitigation. In: IEEE International Symposium on Broadband Multimedia Systems and Broadcasting (BMSB), pp. 1–5 (2018)
4. Liu, Y., Wang, Y., Sun, R., Miao, Z.: Distributed resource allocation for D2D-assisted small cell networks with heterogeneous spectrum. IEEE Access **7**, 83900–83914 (2019)
5. Khuwaja, A.A., Zheng, G., Chen, Y., Feng, W.: Optimum deployment of multiple UAVs for coverage area maximization in the presence of co-channel interference. IEEE Access **7**, 85203–85212 (2019)

Research on Fair Scheduling Algorithm of 5G Intelligent Wireless System Based on Machine Learning

Zhou Wu$^{(\boxtimes)}$ and Mingxiang Guan

Shenzhen Institute of Information Technology, Shenzhen 518172, China
wuz@sziit.edu.cn

Abstract. In the multi-user scenario of 5G intelligent wireless system, the users can't get the fair transmission opportunity because of the different service packet length, transmission delay and channel environment of each user equipment. This paper proposes an two-stage k-means machine learning algorithm, which can select the user equipment intelligently among different user's equipment to schedule, while guaranteeing the quality of service of each user's equipment, it can also take into account fairness.

Keywords: Intelligent wireless system · Machine learning · Artificial intelligent · Fair scheduling

1 Introduction

In view of the demand for broadband wireless access in the future, the EU, China, Japan, the United States and other countries have launched the research on the demand and key technologies of the fifth generation mobile communication system [1–5]. 5g has become a research hotspot in the field of mobile communication at home and abroad.

5g network is an intelligent wireless network, which can learn the past behavior patterns, output results and the behavior of similar entities on the unified network or other networks, and the decision quality of the network will continue to improve.

Machine learning and artificial intelligence are the best candidate technologies, which can provide more powerful complex decision-making ability for 5g intelligent wireless system. In 5g intelligent wireless system, there will be a variety of standards and user devices, such as 4G, 5g, Wi-Fi or satellite communication.

At the same time, the business types of user equipment with different standards and systems are also different, such as video business, live broadcast business, game business, etc., so what kind of machine learning algorithm can be used to intelligently select user equipment among user equipment with different delays for scheduling, which can not only ensure the service quality of each user equipment business, but also take into account the fairness, which is the research goal of this paper.

In this paper, a two-stage K-means machine learning algorithm is proposed for 5g intelligent wireless system, which can intelligently select user equipment among

M. Guan and Z. Na (Eds.): MLICOM 2020, LNICST 342, pp. 53–58, 2021.
https://doi.org/10.1007/978-3-030-66785-6_6

different conditions to schedule, and while ensuring the service quality of each user's equipment business, it can also take fairness into account.

2 System Model

The 5g intelligent wireless system base station uses the mass MIMO multi antenna system. This paper assumes that the base station is equipped with M antennas, the service cell has a total of A user equipment, each user is equipped with N antennas, and all users are evenly distributed in the cell. At the same time, it is assumed that the transmitter knows the channel information of the user. The system model is shown in Fig. 1.

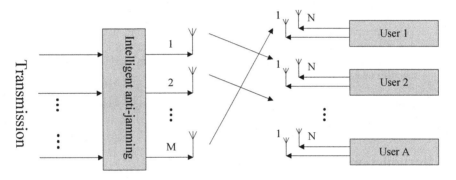

Fig. 1. System model diagram

Assuming that the transmission signal of device a in time slot t is $\mathbf{s}(t)$, the received signal can be expressed as:

$$\mathbf{r}_a(t) = \sqrt{\rho_t}\mathbf{H}_a(t) \cdot \mathbf{s}(t) + \mathbf{n}_a(t) \tag{1}$$

Where $\sqrt{\rho_t}$ is the emission power, $\mathbf{n}_a(t)$ is the complex Gaussian random variable with the mean value of independent identically distributed being 0 and the variance being N_0. $\mathbf{H}_a(t)$ is the system channel matrix. Defined h_{ij} as the channel coefficient between the receiving antenna i and the transmitting antenna j, then the channel matrix of the user a can be obtained as follows:

$$\mathbf{H}_a = \begin{bmatrix} h_{1,1} & h_{1,2} & \cdots & h_{1,An} \\ h_{2,1} & h_{2,2} & \cdots & h_{2,An} \\ \cdots & \cdots & \cdots & \cdots \\ h_{m,1} & h_{m,2} & \cdots & h_{m,An} \end{bmatrix}_{m \times An} \tag{2}$$

The channel h_{ij} can be expressed as:

$$h_{ij} = Normal(0, \sqrt{\frac{S_n}{2}}) + j \cdot Normal(0, \sqrt{\frac{S_n}{2}}) \tag{3}$$

The mean value S_n is equal to the path loss and the variance is σ_n.

As mentioned before, in 5g intelligent wireless system, there will be multiple standards and user equipment with multiple systems. The service packet transmission delay of each user's equipment will be different, which will bring fairness to user scheduling.

In this paper, a multi-user intelligent fair scheduling algorithm suitable for 5g intelligent wireless system is proposed. K-means unsupervised learning algorithm is used in machine learning algorithm.

The traditional K-means algorithm is very sensitive to the selection of initial centroid, which may lead to local optimal solution. In order to overcome this problem, we improved the traditional K-means algorithm, and proposed a two-stage k-means method. The selection of K value is not randomly selected, but pre-processing training is carried out at the beginning of scheduling. During a period of scheduling, the scheduling priority of user equipment is calculated according to the channel environment, service data length and average transmission delay of all user equipment to be scheduled in the system (the average transmission delay will be dynamically updated in the training stage), and the scheduling priority is sorted according to the priority, The first k user devices are selected as the initial clustering points, and the pre-processing training phase is over. Then the new user devices to be scheduled are clustered according to the normal k-means algorithm until convergence.

3 Intelligent Fair Scheduling Algorithm Based on Two-Stage K-Means

3.1 Pretreatment Stage

In order to overcome the problem that the traditional K-means algorithm is very sensitive to the selection of the initial centroid, which may cause the problem of the local optimal solution, using the preprocessing method, the selection of K-means algorithm is not randomly selected, but the preprocessing training is carried out at the beginning of scheduling, in a period of scheduling time, the scheduling priority of user equipment is calculated according to the channel environment, service data length and average transmission delay of all user equipment to be scheduled in the system (the average transmission delay will be dynamically updated in the training stage), and the first k user equipment are selected as the initial clustering points, and the pre-processing training stage ends.

Firstly, the equalization matrix G is defined to estimate the transmitted signal:

$$\mathbf{y} = G\mathbf{r} = \sqrt{\rho_t}\mathbf{G}\mathbf{H}_p \cdot \mathbf{s} + \mathbf{Gn} \tag{4}$$

According to Eq. (4), the user's SNR can be estimated:

$$\gamma_{n,m} = \frac{E_s \left| g_{n,m}^* h_{n,m} \right|^2}{N_0 \left\| g_{n,m}^* \right\|^2 + E_s \sum_{j \neq m} \left| g_{n,m}^* h_{n,j} \right|^2} \tag{5}$$

Where $g_{n,m}^*$ is the m-th row of matrix G and the m-th column of matrix H_P. Es is the received signal power. The equilibrium matrix G can be obtained from the following formula:

$$G = \left[H_p^* H_p + \frac{N_0}{E_s} I \right]^{-1} H_p^* \tag{6}$$

From Eq. (5), the transmission rates R_a that the user device a can achieve under the SNR can be obtained as follows:

$$R_a = \log_2 (1 + \gamma_{n,m}) \tag{7}$$

Assuming the service data length of the user device a is $F_i, (i = 1, 2, \ldots, A)$, the waiting transmission delay of a is:

$$T_i^a = \max_{i \neq j} \left(\frac{F_j}{R_j} \right) \tag{8}$$

Where F_j is the service data length and R_j is transmission rate of other user's equipment.

Then the priority of the user equipment to be dispatched is calculated according to the following formula:

$$k = \arg \min \left(\frac{T_i^a}{\overline{T_i^a}} \right) \tag{9}$$

Where $\overline{T_i^a}$ is the average transmission delay of the selected user, which can be updated adaptively and dynamically according to the following formula:

$$\overline{T_i^a}(t + \Delta t) = (1 - \frac{1}{T}) \overline{T_i^a}(t) + \frac{1}{\overline{T_i^a}} T_i^a(t + 1) \tag{10}$$

Where T is the time constant, which is the length of the sliding time window. It reflects a user's tolerance for data transmission, which will allow a long time to wait until the user's channel quality becomes better, which is conducive to the improvement of system capacity, but may lead to the increase of delay.

According to formula (9), the scheduling priority of each user is obtained, and the first k user devices are selected as the initial clustering points, and the pre-processing training phase is over.

The K initial clustering points selected after preprocessing are obtained according to the fairness criterion, which ensures that the clustering results of K-means algorithm are divided according to the fairness, and avoid the local optimal solution problem caused by random selection of initial clustering points.

3.2   K-Means Algorithm

After K initial clustering points are obtained by preprocessing, the new user devices to be scheduled are clustered according to the normal k-means algorithm until convergence. The algorithm steps are as follows:

(1) The coordinate values $c_0, c_1, \ldots, c_{k-1}$ of K initial clustering points are recorded. Here, the waiting transmission delay T_i^a and the average transmission delay $\bar{T}_i^a$ of users are used as the coordinate values $c_0(T_0, \bar{T}_0), c_1(T_1, \bar{T}_1), \ldots, c_{k-1}(T_{k-1}, \bar{T}_{k-1})$;
(2) According to the channel environment and the length of traffic data, the waiting transmission delay T_i^a and the average transmission delay $\bar{T}_i^a$ of users are calculated for the new user equipment to be scheduled, and the coordinate value $x_0(T_0, \bar{T}_0), x_1(T_1, \bar{T}_1), \ldots, x_{n-1}(T_{n-1}, \bar{T}_{n-1})$ of the new scheduling user is obtained. Then the distance between the user and each initial cluster point is calculated, and the user equipment is assigned to the cluster point with the smallest distance to form K clusters. Common distances include Euclidean distance and Manhattan distance. The project adopts the Euclidean distance:

$$D = \sqrt{(T_i - T_j)^2 + (\bar{T}_i - \bar{T}_j)^2}, (i = 0, 1, \ldots, n-1, j = 0, 1, \ldots, k-1) \qquad (11)$$

(3) Recalculate the coordinates of cluster points:

$$
\begin{aligned}
T_i' &= \sum \frac{T_m}{M} (m = 1, 2, \ldots, M) \\
\bar{T}_i' &= \sum \frac{T_m'}{M} (m = 1, 2, \ldots, M)
\end{aligned}
\qquad (12)
$$

M is the number of user devices in each cluster. The number of user devices in each cluster is different.

(4) Repeat steps (2) and (3) until the cluster does not change or the maximum number of iterations is reached.
(5) The user devices are scheduled according to the clusters.

Based on the improved k-means machine learning algorithm, the user equipment can be intelligently selected for scheduling among the user equipment with different delay, which can guarantee the service quality of each user equipment business and take into account the fairness.

At the same time, in order to overcome the problem that the traditional K-means algorithm is very sensitive to the selection of the initial center of mass, which may cause the problem of local optimal solution, using the preprocessing method, the selection of K-means algorithm is not randomly selected, but carries out the preprocessing training at the beginning of scheduling to ensure that the global optimal solution can be obtained, which makes the machine learning algorithm convergence.

4   Conclusion

In the multi-user scenario of 5g intelligent wireless system, due to the different service packet length, transmission delay and channel environment of each user's device, the user cannot get the transmission opportunity fairly. This paper proposes an improved k-means machine learning algorithm, which can intelligently select the user's device to schedule among the user's devices under different conditions. While ensuring the service quality of each user's equipment business, it can also take into account the fairness.

Acknowledgements. This paper is supported by the Guangdong Province higher vocational colleges and schools, the Pearl River scholar funding scheme (2016), a project of the Shenzhen Science and Technology Innovation Committee (JCYJ20170817114522834, JCYJ20160608151239996), Research platform and project of Department of Education of Guangdong Province(2019GGCZX009), the Key laboratory of Longgang District (LGKCZSYS2018000028), the science and technology development center of the Ministry of Education of China (2017A15009) and Engineering Applications of the Artificial Intelligence Technology Laboratory (PT201701).

References

1. METIS.Mobile and wireless communications enablers for the 2020 information society, 30 April 2015
2. Cao, Z., Zhao, X., Soares, F.M.: 38-GHz millimeter wave beam steered fiber wireless systems for 5G indoor coverage: architectures, devices, and links. IEEE J. Quantum Electron. J. **53**(1), 1–9 (2017)
3. Boccardi, F., Heath, R.W., Lozano, A.: Five disruptive technology directions for 5G. IEEE Commun. Mag. J. **52**(2), 74–80 (2014)
4. Yuan, Y., Zhao, X.: 5G: vision, scenarios and enabling technologies. ZTE Commun. J. **13**(1), 69–79 (2015)
5. Cid, E.L., Taboas, M.P., Sanchez, M.G., Alejos, A.V.: Microcellular radio channel characterization at 60 GHz for 5G communications. IEEE Antennas Wirel. Propag. Lett. J. **99**, 1–4 (2017)
6. Zhao, C., Wu, Z.: Adaptive delay fairness scheduling algorithm in MIMO systems. J. Harbin Inst. Technol. J. **12**(41), 243–246 (2009). (in Chinese)

Research on Anti-jamming Algorithm of Multi-antenna System Based on Artificial Intelligence Technology

Mingxiang Guan[✉] and Zhou Wu

Shenzhen Institute of Information Technology, Shenzhen 518029, China
gmx2020@126.com, 66827983@qq.com

Abstract. In order to solve the system interference problem caused by beam-forming technology of multi-antenna system, an anti-jamming solution based on artificial intelligence technology is proposed, and a multi antenna anti-jamming model based on artificial intelligence algorithm is constructed. PSO algorithm is adopted to train and verify the rationality, convergence ability and performance of the model. Finally, the antenna array will form a great gain in the desired direction to improve the desired signal, while it will form a zero notch at the interference direction for interference suppression. It effectively improves the SINR (signal to interference ratio) of the receiver, and then improves the system performance and increase the system capacity.

Keywords: Multi-antenna system · Artificial intelligence · Particle swarm optimization algorithm

1 Introduction

The next new communication network will be an intelligent network with multi services, multi access technology and multi-level coverage. Among them, the application of multiple antennas [1] has great prospects and even necessary directions. The influence of deep fading can be alleviated effectively by MIMO technology through spatial diversity. The reliability of the communication system can be increased. Meanwhile, space division multiple access can be realized by adaptively adjusting weighting vector of antenna array. Finally, the space multiplexing or space diversity of communication system is realized, and the capacity of wireless link is greatly improved.

Artificial intelligence to minimize human intervention has been begun to explore in the management network [2], and a research group called intelligent definition network has also been launched to study the application of machine learning in the communication network. In addition, some EU 5g PPP projects, namely selfnet [3] and cognet [4], focus on the design and implementation of 5g mobile network intelligent management. The self net framework [5] utilizes self-organizing network (son) [6] and AI to automate infrastructure management based on Software Defined Network (SDN) [7] and network function Virtualization (nfv) [8].

© ICST Institute for Computer Sciences, Social Informatics and Telecommunications Engineering 2021
Published by Springer Nature Switzerland AG 2021. All Rights Reserved
M. Guan and Z. Na (Eds.): MLICOM 2020, LNICST 342, pp. 59–64, 2021.
https://doi.org/10.1007/978-3-030-66785-6_7

In reference [9], a test-bed is established to evaluate the performance that can be achieved in the real wireless scene, and the setting, closed-loop control and enabling algorithm of a 5g test-bed compatible with mobile edge computing are adopted. Taking traffic congestion as an example, the detection accuracy of traffic congestion rate was observed. The experimental results show that the application of artificial intelligence is feasible and effective. In reference [10], the basic concept of AI is introduced, and the relationship between AI and candidate technology in 5g cellular network is discussed. The effectiveness of artificial intelligence management and arrangement of cellular network resources is demonstrated. Reference [11] introduces the advantages of machine learning in artificial intelligence assisted wireless system and discusses their applications in the context of next generation network, including large-scale array antenna, cognitive radio, heterogeneous network, Pico/small base station, D2D network, etc. The types of supervised, unsupervised and reinforcement learning tools, the corresponding modeling methods and possible future applications in 5g networks are studied.

In this paper, by studying the anti-jamming strategy of multibeam decision-making system and the coordination and cooperation between multi-user devices, a multi antenna anti-jamming model based on artificial intelligence algorithm is established, with rules set, strategies used and expected return function. After the establishment of multi antenna anti-jamming model based on artificial intelligence algorithm, the model needs to be trained to verify whether the model is reasonable, whether it meets the needs of multi antenna system anti-jamming, and whether the training results can eventually converge. PSO algorithm is adopted to train artificial intelligence model to verify the rationality, convergence ability and performance of the model. Finally, the antenna array will form a great gain in the desired direction to improve the desired signal, while it will form a zero notch at the interference direction for interference suppression. It improves the SINR (signal to interference ratio) of the receiver effectively, and then improves the system performance and increase the system capacity.

2 System Model

It is assumed that there are a A users in the multi antenna communication system, and the number of antenna arrays at the transmitter and the receiver is m. All users are evenly distributed in the cell. Figure 1 is the system model.

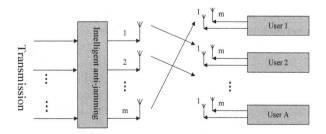

Fig. 1. Model diagram of multi antenna system

Then the received signal of the user l can be expressed as:

$$\mathbf{y} = \mathbf{H}_l \mathbf{v}_l \mathbf{x}_l + \mathbf{n} \tag{1}$$

Where $\mathbf{x}_l$ is the transmitted signal, assuming that the signal is a generalized stationary signal and $E\{x_l x_i^H\} = \begin{cases} 1 & l = i \\ 0 & l \neq i \end{cases}$. $\mathbf{H}_l$ Represents the channel matrix, assuming that the transmitter has perfectly known the channel information of the user. Indicates $\mathbf{v}_l$ the transmission weight, $\|\mathbf{v}_l\| = 1$. For white Gaussian noise vector $\mathbf{n}$, we assume $E[\mathbf{nn}^H] = \mathbf{I}$. Then the SINR of the user l can be expressed as:

$$\Gamma_l = \frac{\mathbf{v}_l^H \mathbf{R}_l \mathbf{v}_l}{\sum\limits_{i=1, i \neq l}^{L} \mathbf{v}_i^H \mathbf{R}_l \mathbf{v}_i + 1} \tag{2}$$

$\mathbf{v}_i$ represents the transmission weight of other users. $\mathbf{R}_l$ is the covariance matrix of the channel, which can be expressed as:

$$\mathbf{R}_l = E\{\mathbf{HH}^H\} \tag{3}$$

The transmission weight $\mathbf{v}_l$ consists of two parts:

$$\mathbf{v}_l = \sqrt{P_l}\mathbf{u}_l \tag{4}$$

Then the SINR of the user l is a function of the user's transmission power P_l, namely:

$$\Gamma_l(P_l) = \frac{P_l \mathbf{u}_l^H \mathbf{R}_l \mathbf{u}_l}{\sum\limits_{i=1, i \neq l}^{L} P_i \mathbf{u}_i^H \mathbf{R}_l \mathbf{u}_i + 1} \tag{5}$$

3 Multi Antenna Anti-jamming Algorithm Based on Artificial Intelligence Algorithm

3.1 Multi Antenna Anti-jamming Model Based on Artificial Intelligence Algorithm

The multi antenna anti-jamming model based on artificial intelligence algorithm consists of four parts: agents participating in decision-making, rule setting, strategies used and expected benefits. In the multi antenna anti-jamming model based on artificial intelligence algorithm in this paper, Different user devices are the agents involved in decision-making. Rule setting is the multi beam anti-jamming between multi-user devices. The set of strategies they adopt is their own transmitting power

$S_l = \{P_l, l = 1, 2, \cdots, L\}$. Each agent is independent and their strategies will affect other agent. The net utility function is:

$$U_l = U_u - U_c \tag{6}$$

U_u is the utility function of the user, which represents the benefits obtained by the user. U_c is the cost function of the user.

The utility function is defined as:

$$U_u = f(\Gamma_l) = \frac{\Gamma_l}{\Gamma_l + \alpha} \tag{7}$$

α is a constant, which is the same for all users.

The cost function U_c is:

$$U_c = \lambda P_l \tag{8}$$

λ is a constant, cost factor, which defines the user's cost when disturbed. So the net utility function is:

$$U_l = U_u - U_c = \frac{\Gamma_l}{\Gamma_l + \alpha} - \lambda P_l \tag{9}$$

From Eq. (9), it can be seen that the utility function U_l is a function expressed by the user's transmission power. The core of multi antenna anti-jamming model based on artificial intelligence algorithm in this paper is to maximize the net utility function, namely:

$$\arg \max U_l = \arg \max \left(\frac{\Gamma_l}{\Gamma_l + \alpha} - \lambda P_l \right) \tag{10}$$

3.2   Artificial Intelligence Training Model Based on Particle Swarm Optimization

After the establishment of multi antenna anti-jamming model based on artificial intelligence algorithm, the model needs to be trained to verify whether the model is reasonable, whether it meets the needs of multi antenna system anti-jamming, and whether the training results can eventually converge. In this paper, PSO algorithm is adopted to train the artificial intelligence model to verify the rationality, convergence ability and performance of the model.

The main idea is to operate according to the fitness value of individual (particle). Every user is thought as a particle without weight and volume in the n-dimensional search space, and a particle without weight and volume in the search space flies at a certain speed in the search space. Individual flight experience and group flight experience can help us to adjust the flight speed.

PSO algorithm is simple in concept, which is fast in search speed and wide in search range. At the same time, it has profound intelligent background, which is suitable for both scientific research and engineering application.

4 Results and Discussion

In this paper, a new anti-jamming algorithm based on artificial intelligence technology is proposed for multi antenna system with the aid of beamforming technology. A multi antenna anti-jamming model based on artificial intelligence algorithm is constructed. PSO algorithm is adopted to train artificial intelligence model to verify the rationality, convergence ability and performance of the model. Finally, the antenna array will form a great gain in the desired direction to improve the desired signal, while it will form a zero notch at the interference direction for interference suppression. It improves the SINR (signal to interference ratio) of the receiver effectively, and then improves the system performance and increase the system capacity.

Acknowledgements. This paper is supported by the Key laboratory of Longgang District (LGKCZSYS2018000028), the Pearl River scholar funding scheme (2016), the science and technology development center of the Ministry of Education of China (2017A15009) and a project of the Shenzhen Science and Technology Innovation Committee (JCYJ20170817114522 834, JCYJ20160608151239996), Engineering Applications of the Artificial Intelligence Technology Laboratory (PT201701) Research platform and project of Department of Education of Guangdong Province (2019GGCZX009) and the Guangdong Province higher vocational colleges and schools.

References

1. Sharawi, M.S., Ikram, M., Shamim, A.: A two concentric slot loop based connected array MIMO antenna system for 4G/5G terminals. IEEE Trans. Antennas Propag. **65**(12), 6679–6686 (2017)
2. Neves, P., et al.: The SELFNET approach for autonomic management in an NFV/SDN networking paradigm. Int. J. Distrib. Sens. Netw. **16**(2), 1–17 (2016)
3. EU H2020 5G-PPP SELFNET project. https://selfnet-5g.eu/
4. EU H2020 5G-PPP CogNet project. http://www.cognet.5g-ppp.eu/
5. Jiang, W., Strufe, M., Schotten, H.D.: Intelligent network management for 5G systems: the SELFNET approach. In: IEEE European Conference on Networks and Communications (EUCNC), Oulu, Finland, pp. 109–113, June 2017
6. Klein, A., et al.: A novel approach for combined joint call admission control and dynamic bandwidth adaptation in heterogeneous wireless networks. In: The 7th Conference on Next Generation Internet, EURO-NGI, Kaiserslautern, Germany, pp. 1–8, June 2011
7. Nunes, B.A.A., et al.: A survey of software-defined networking: past, present, and future of programmable networks. IEEE Commun. Surv. Tutor. **16**(3), 1617–1634 (2014)
8. Mijumbi, R., et al.: Network function virtualization: state-of-the-art and research challenges. IEEE Commun. Surv. Tutor. **18**(1), 236–262 (2016)

9. Jiang, W., Strufe, M., Schotten, H.D.: Experimental results for artificial intelligence-based self-organized 5G networks. In: IEEE 28th Annual International Symposium on Personal, Indoor, and Mobile Radio Communications (PIMRC), pp. 1–6 (2017)
10. Li, R., et al.: Intelligent 5G: when cellular networks meet artificial intelligence. IEEE Trans. Wireless Commun. **24**(5), 175–183 (2017)
11. Zhang, H., Ren, Y., Han, Z., Chen, K.-C., Hanzo, L.: Machine learning paradigms for next-generation wireless networks. IEEE Trans. Wireless Commun. **24**(2), 98–105 (2017)

A Radar-Communication Integrated Signal of OFDM Based on Four-Phase Code

Jiaqi Sun, Yongkui Ma, Chengzhao Shan, and Honglin Zhao[✉]

Institute of Electronics and Information Engineering,
Harbin Institute of Technology, Harbin, China
19S005047@stu.hit.edu.cn, hlzhao@hit.edu.cn

Abstract. Traditional radar signal has only detection function. With the advent of technologies such as Internet of Vehicles and driverless cars, radar-communication integrated signal has got more attention, which can realize communication and radar detection using the same signal. However, the uncertainty of communication information such as transmitting the same information continuously can influence radar detection performance. In this paper, a radar-communication integrated signal of OFDM based on four-phase code is proposed. This signal combines radar-communication integrated signal of OFDM with orthogonal four-phase-coded sequences optimized by genetic algorithm in MIMO radar, these four-phase-coded sequences form a set and the radar-communication integrated signal of OFDM can carry communication information by different permutations of these sequences without damaging radar detection performance. The simulation results show that the four-phase-coded sequences have good autocorrelation and cross-correlation properties, and the radar-communication integrated signal of OFDM using these sequences has good detection performance, which can meet the practical requirements.

Keywords: Radar-communication integration · OFDM · Four-phase code

1 Introduction

Radar-communication integrated signal can improve spectrum utilization ratio and reduce interference between devices, so it is significant to research radar-communication integrated signal. In the design of radar-communication integrated signal, OFDM which is widely used in communication system has many advantages [1], for instance, it is easy to synchronize and equalized and it has high spectral efficiency. As a radar signal, OFDM has good detection performance [2–4].

As for polyphase code, it is widely used in MIMO radar. To avoid interference between different signal channels, polyphase code is optimized to be more orthogonal [5, 6]. However, the polyphase code used in MIMO radar does not carry communication information generally.

This work was supported by the Fundamental Research Funds for the Central Universities [grant numbers HIT. MKSTISP. 2016 13].

M. Guan and Z. Na (Eds.): MLICOM 2020, LNICST 342, pp. 65–72, 2021.
https://doi.org/10.1007/978-3-030-66785-6_8

In this paper, we design a radar-communication signal of OFDM based on four-phase code. By constructing four-phase-coded sequence set optimized by genetic algorithm, the radar-communication integrated signal can carry communication information and the detection performance can not be affected. The remainder of this paper is organized as follows. Section 2 introduces radar-communication integrated signal model and genetic algorithm, and analyzes the ambiguity function. Section 3 introduces four-phase-coded sequence set optimized by genetic algorithm, explains how to combine the sequence set with radar-communication integrated signal. Section 4 gives the simulation results and Sect. 5 gets conclusion.

2 Signal Model and Genetic Algorithm

2.1 Signal Model

Traditional OFDM radar emits only one OFDM signal in a pulse, if we use traditional OFDM radar for communication, it will be processed in multiple pulses and be not convenient to synchronize. In this paper, a kind of radar-communication integrated signal is used. In this signal, there are multiple subpulses in a pulse and each subpulse is an OFDM signal. In this way, communication can be realized in one pulse, and the receiver is easier to synchronize.

Suppose that each pulse consists of N OFDM symbols, each OFDM symbol has M subcarriers, the baseband signal can be expressed in the following form:

$$s(t) = \sum_{n=0}^{N-1} \sum_{m=0}^{M-1} a(m,n) \exp\{j2\pi m\Delta f(t-nT)\} rect\left[\frac{t-nT}{T}\right] \qquad (1)$$

In the formula, T is an OFDM symbol period, $\Delta f = 1/T$ is the frequency interval of the carrier, $a(m,n)$ is the communication information modulated on the mth subcarrier of the nth OFDM symbol, $rect$ is a step function for symbol duration. Figure 1 shows the time-frequency domain representation of this radar-communication signal.

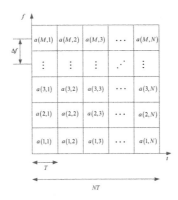

Fig. 1. Time-frequency domain representation of radar-communication integrated signal

2.2   Analysis of Ambiguity Function

The ambiguity function of Radar, which is related to the transmitted waveform, is an effective tool for radar signal analysis and waveform design. It can reflect the distance and speed resolution, ambiguity and measurement accuracy. To get high resolution of distance and Doppler, an ideal ambiguity function should be a shape of pushpin. In other words, it has a single central peak and the rest of the energy is evenly distributed across the distance and Doppler plan.

The definition of the ambiguity function is:

$$\chi(\tau, f_d) = \int_{-\infty}^{+\infty} s(t)s^*(t - \tau) \exp\{j2\pi f_d t\} dt \tag{2}$$

Where $s(t)$ is the signal function, * is conjugation of the signal, τ is the time delay of the echo received by radar after the signal reaches the target and f_d is the Doppler frequency offset generated by the target motion.

Bring Eq. (1) to Eq. (2). Without loss of generality, we simplify the equation in the condition of $-NT < \tau < 0$. Let $\lfloor t/T \rfloor = k$, $\tau' = \tau + (1 + |k|)T$, $\tau'' = \tau + |k|T$, so $\tau' = \tau'' + T$, $-T < \tau'' \leq 0$, $0 < \tau' \leq T$. We can get the following [7]:

$$\chi(\tau, f_d) = \sum_{n=1}^{N-1-|k|} \exp\{j2\pi(n-1)f_d T\} \chi_{n-1,n+|k|}^+ (\tau', f_d)$$
$$+ \sum_{n=0}^{N-1-|k|} \exp\{j2\pi n f_d T\} \chi_{n,n+|k|}^- (\tau'', f_d) \tag{3}$$

Where $\chi_{n,q}^-(\tau, f_d)$ and $\chi_{n,q}^+(\tau, f_d)$ represent the ambiguity function of the nth OFDM symbol and qth OFDM symbol, $^-$ represents $-T \leq \tau \leq 0$ and $^+$ represents $0 < \tau < T$. Without loss of generality, let $f_d = 0$, we get:

$$\chi(\tau, 0) = \sum_{n=1}^{N-1-|k|} \chi_{n-1,n+|k|}^+ (\tau', 0) + \sum_{n=0}^{N-1-|k|} \chi_{n,n+|k|}^- (\tau'', 0) \tag{4}$$

When $(T + \tau'')\Delta f/2$ can be ignored, we get:

$$\chi_{n,n+|k|}^- (\tau'', 0) = (T + \tau'') \sum_{i=-N+1}^{0} \sum_{p=-i}^{M-1} a(p+i, n)a^*(p, n+|k|)$$
$$\exp\{j2\pi p \Delta f \tau''\} \exp\left\{j2\pi i \Delta f \frac{T + \tau''}{2}\right\}$$
$$+ (T + \tau'') \sum_{i=1}^{N-1} \sum_{p=0}^{M-i-1} a(p+i, n)a^*(p, n+|k|)$$
$$\exp\{j2\pi p \Delta f \tau''\} \exp\left\{j2\pi i \Delta f \frac{T + \tau''}{2}\right\} \tag{5}$$

$$\chi_{n-1,n+|k|}^{+}(\tau',0) = (T-\tau') \sum_{i=-N+1}^{0} \sum_{p=-i}^{M-1} a(p+i,n-1)a^*(p,n+|k|)$$

$$\exp\{j2\pi p\Delta f\tau'\} \exp\left\{j2\pi i\Delta f\frac{T+\tau'}{2}\right\}$$

$$+ (T-\tau') \sum_{i=1}^{N-1} \sum_{p=0}^{M-i-1} a(p+i,n-1)a^*(p,n+|k|) \tag{6}$$

$$\exp\{j2\pi p\Delta f\tau''\} \exp\left\{j2\pi i\Delta f\frac{T+\tau'}{2}\right\}$$

In order to get high resolution of distance and Doppler, the value of Eq. (4) sidelobe should be small. As we can see in Eq. (5) and Eq. (6), adjusting $a(m,n)$ can change the value of Eq. (4). For convenience of expression, we let $\mathbf{a}(n) = [a(1,n),\ldots,a(M,n)]^T$. The specific requirements are that the value of aperiodic cross-correlation function of $\mathbf{a}(n_1)$ and $\mathbf{a}(n_2)$ should be small, and the value of sidelobe of the aperiodic autocorrelation function of $\mathbf{a}(n)$ should be small, where n_1 and n_2 represent different OFDM symbol. In other words, the communication information modulated on different OFDM symbol should have good autocorrelation and cross-correlation properties for good ambiguity function.

2.3 Genetic Algorithm

Genetic algorithm (GA) is an analogy of biological evolution, it can solve optimization problem by robust and adaptive searching. The main step of GA is encoding the results to population and optimizing the results by selection, crossover and mutation. The specific steps of GA are listed as follows:

Step 1: Code the actual problem, and generate the initial population randomly. The initial population represents initial solutions.
Step 2: Define the fitness function. Each individual in population has a value of fitness function. Initialize the probability of crossover and mutation.
Step 3: Select a part of the population to do crossover and mutation, then get new population.
Step 4: Calculate the fitness function value of the new population, if the new population meets the requirements, output the results, or else, jump to step 3.

3 Design of Radar-Communication Signal Based on Four-Phase Code

Through the above analysis, we know the communication information modulated on different OFDM symbols should have good autocorrelation and cross-correlation properties for good shape of ambiguity function. For traditional radar, the information modulated on OFDM is fixed. For radar-communication integrated signal, however, the communication information is uncertain, which can damage the radar detection performance. A typical example is transmitting the same information continuously.

In order to ensure the performance of radar detection, we construct polyphase code sequence set. Four-phase-coded sequence is selected in this paper, the reason is that random four-phase-coded sequences have good autocorrelation and cross-correlation properties, then using genetic algorithm to optimize them, the sequences can have better autocorrelation and cross-correlation properties. Suppose the sequence set has L sequences, the length of each one is M, the sequence set can be expressed as:

$$
S(L, M) = \begin{bmatrix} \phi_1(1) & \phi_1(2) & \cdots & \phi_1(M) \\ \phi_2(1) & \phi_2(2) & \cdots & \phi_2(M) \\ \vdots & \vdots & \ddots & \vdots \\ \phi_L(1) & \phi_L(2) & \cdots & \phi_L(M) \end{bmatrix}
\tag{7}
$$

Where $\phi_l(m) \in \{0, \pi/2, \pi, 3\pi/2\}$, $1 \leq l \leq L$. $[\phi_l(1)\ \phi_l(2)\ \dots\ \phi_l(M)]^T$ is the information carried on radar-communication integrated signal, that is to say, it should replace $\mathbf{a}(n)$. The autocorrelation and cross-correlation of four-phase-coded sequences can be expressed as:

$$
A(\phi_l, k) = \begin{cases} \frac{1}{M} \sum_{m=1}^{M-k} \exp\{j[\phi_l(m) - \phi_l(m+k)]\} & 0 \leq k < M \\ \frac{1}{M} \sum_{m=-k+1}^{M} \exp\{j[\phi_l(m) - \phi_l(m+k)]\} & -M < k < 0 \end{cases}
\tag{8}
$$

$$
C(\phi_p, \phi_q, k) = \begin{cases} \frac{1}{M} \sum_{m=1}^{M-k} \exp\{j[\phi_q(m) - \phi_p(m+k)]\} & 0 \leq k < M \\ \frac{1}{M} \sum_{m=-k+1}^{M} \exp\{j[\phi_q(m) - \phi_p(m+k)]\} & -M < k < 0 \end{cases}
\tag{9}
$$

GA is used to optimize $A(\phi_l, k)$ and $C(\phi_p, \phi_q, k)$. When we use genetic algorithm, we should define cost function. In order to make different sequences have great autocorrelation and cross-correlation properties, we define cost function as:

$$
E = \sum_{l=1}^{L} \sum_{k=1}^{M-1} |A(\phi_l, k)|^2 + \sum_{p=1}^{L-1} \sum_{q=p+1}^{L} \sum_{k=-(M-1)}^{M-1} |C(\phi_p, \phi_q, k)|^2
\tag{10}
$$

In order to use GA [8], we should expand out the sequence set. In particular, each individual of GA can be expressed as $\phi_1(1) \dots \phi_1(M) \dots \phi_L(1) \dots \phi_L(M)$, then we should initialize crossover probability and mutation probability. Let $F = 1/E$ be the adaptability function, then go into the loop. After GA processing, more orthogonal sequence set can be got.

The processed sequence set does not carry information itself, but we can map information to the sequences. Different permutations of sequences can map different information. In this way, the same information can be mapped to different sequences and the performance of radar detection is guaranteed.

It is worth noting that the permutation of L sequences will be used to transmit information, which can reduce communication rate compared with transmitting information directly using the same signal model. For convenience of expression, we let $\psi = [\phi(1), \cdots, \phi(M)]^T$. For example, When $L = 3$, the information bit 00 can be mapped to $[\psi_1\ \psi_2\ \psi_3]$, and 01 can be mapped to $[\psi_1\ \psi_3\ \psi_2]$. Assume that the communication rate in this way is r_1 and the communication rate by transmitting information directly is r_2, the ratio of r_1 and r_2 is:

$$\frac{r_1}{r_2} = \frac{\log_2(L \times (L-1) \times \cdots \times (L-M+1))}{2MN} \tag{11}$$

The actual communication rate r_1 can be expended by expending the size of the sequence set $S(L,N)$, the number of subcarrier in an OFDM symbol and the number of OFDM in a pulse. Reducing the period of OFDM symbol is also a choice.

4 Simulation Results

In the simulation, we set an OFDM symbol period to 0.1 μs, one OFDM symbol has 40 subcarrier and one pulse has 40 OFDM symbol. The size of the four-phase-coded sequence set is 80×40. Two sequences are randomly selected in the set and Fig. 2 shows their aperiodic cross-correlation and aperiodic autocorrelation.

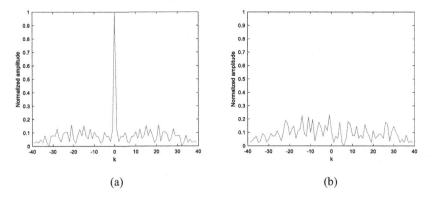

(a)   (b)

Fig. 2. (a) Aperiodic autocorrelation (b) Aperiodic cross-correlation

As can be seen from Fig. 2, the four-phase-coded sequences have good autocorrelation and cross-correlation properties. By the previous analysis, we know these sequences meet the requirement of radar-communication integrated signal. Then we select 40 sequences from the sequences set randomly, Fig. 3 and Fig. 4 show the ambiguity function.

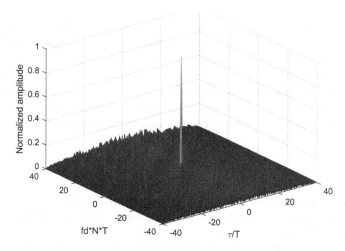

Fig. 3. Ambiguity function of radar-communication integrated signal

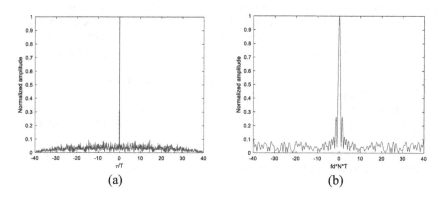

Fig. 4. (a) Section of distance of the ambiguity function (b) Section of speed of the ambiguity function

As can be seen from Fig. 3 and Fig. 4, the ambiguity function has a single central peak and the rest of the energy is evenly distributed across the distance and Doppler plan. It shows that the radar-communication integrated signal of OFDM using four-phase-coded sequences has good detection performance.

In this simulation, we choose 40 subcarriers in an OFDM symbol and 40 OFDM symbols in a pulse. In actual practice, the size of radar-communication integrated signal can be changed, such as 16 and 64 subcarriers in an OFDM symbol, which is convenient to FFT. And according to the hardware performance, different OFDM periods can be selected to meet practical requirements.

5   Conclusion

In this paper, a radar-communication integrated signal of OFDM based on four-phase code is proposed. The simulation results show that the four-phase-coded sequences optimized by GA have good autocorrelation and cross-correlation properties, and the radar-communication integrated signal using these sequences has good radar detection capability. Although compared with direct transmitting information the rate of communication is lower, it ensures radar performance. And the rate of communication can be increased by changing the parameters. The radar-communication integrated signal designed in this paper can be applied to driverless operation system, which requires good radar detection performance and stable communication rates.

References

1. Manosueb, A., Kosseyaporn, J., Wardkein, P.: An adaptive demodulation for OFDM signal. In: 2016 International Symposium on Intelligent Signal Processing and Communication Systems (ISPACS), pp. 1–6 (2016)
2. Levanon, N.: Multifrequency complementary phase-coded radar signal. Proc. Radar Sonar Navig. **147**(6), 276–284 (2000)
3. Tigrek, R.F., Heij, W.J.A.D., Genderen, P.V.: Multi-carrier radar waveform schemes for range and doppler processing. In: 2009 IEEE Radar Conference, pp. 1–5 (2009)
4. Sturm, C., Wiesbeck, W.: Waveform design and signal processing aspects for fusion of wireless communications and radar sensing. Proc. IEEE **99**(7), 1236–1259 (2011)
5. Deng, H.: Polyphase code design for orthogonal netted radar systems. IEEE Trans. Signal Process. **52**(11), 3126–3135 (2004)
6. Khan, H.A., Edwards, D.J.: Doppler problems in orthogonal MIMO radars. In: 2006 IEEE Conference on Radar, pp. 24–27 (2006)
7. Liu, Y.J., Liao, G.S., Yang, Z.W.: Ambiguity function analysis of integrated radar and communication waveform based on OFDM (in Chinese). Syst. Eng. Electron. **38**(9), 2008–2018 (2016)
8. Liu, B., He, Z., Zeng J., Liu B.: Polyphase orthogonal code design for MIMO radar systems. In: 2006 CIE International Conference on Radar, pp. 1–4 (2006)

An Empirical Comparison of Implementation Efficiency of Iterative and Recursive Algorithms of Fast Fourier Transform

Lin Lin[ID], Zeng Xu, He Huan, Zhao Jian, and Liang Li-Xin[✉]

College of Big Data and Internet,
Shenzhen Technology University, Shenzhen 518118, China
lianglixin@sztu.edu.cn

Abstract. Fourier Transform is the basis of modern signal processing technology, and Fast Fourier Transform reduces the time complexity of Fourier Transform. Iterative algorithm and recursive algorithm are two basic methods to implement Fast Fourier Transform on the computer. This paper uses Java, C#, C++, and Python to implement iterative algorithm and recursive algorithms of Fast Fourier Transform, and tests the runtime of these two algorithms on Windows, Mac, and Linux platforms. The experimental results show that program written in Python has the longest runtime no matter iterative or recursive algorithm, and iterative algorithm written in C++ runs most efficiently; iterative program written in C++, C# and Python is more efficient than recursive algorithm, and Java's recursive algorithm is more efficient than iterative algorithm.

Keywords: Fast Fourier Transform · Recursive algorithm · Iterative algorithm · Runtime efficiency

1 Introduction

In 1807, French scientist Fourier took the lead in using sine curves to carry out research on thermal theory. In 1822, he published his research results in the landmark work "Analytical Theory of Heat", which detailed the Fourier series and Fourier integral theory [1]. Fourier Transform (FT) occupies an extremely important position in the field of basic mathematical physics, and also lays the foundation for modern signal analysis. In the field of signal processing, Fourier Transform (FT) is a method of signal analysis, which can realize the conversion of signals between time domain and frequency domain. However, for a long time since the establishment of Fourier Transform, it made sense for the theoretical analysis, but it was difficult to apply in engineering practice because of the limitation in its huge computational complexity. A great breakthrough was made in 1965, when Cooley and Turkey proposed the famous Fast Fourier Transform (FFT) [2] ,which significantly reduced the time complexity of the algorithm,leading to a great advance on the application of FT in engineering fields, such as communication system, data compression, signal processing, nonlinear science and laser engineering etc. [3].

© ICST Institute for Computer Sciences, Social Informatics and Telecommunications Engineering 2021
Published by Springer Nature Switzerland AG 2021. All Rights Reserved
M. Guan and Z. Na (Eds.): MLICOM 2020, LNICST 342, pp. 73–81, 2021.
https://doi.org/10.1007/978-3-030-66785-6_9

There are two ways to implement Fast Fourier Transform on the computer: iterative algorithm and recursive algorithm [4]. It is generally believed that the iterative algorithm has a large amount of code, and the algorithm implementation process is complicated and difficult to understand, but the program can run at high efficiency. On the contrary, the recursive algorithm has a clear code structure, and is easy to understand because of its better readability. The disadvantage is that the recursive program takes more time to run, and the code efficiency will drop sharply as the scale of the problem increases [5]. However, in real programming environment, there is no more in-depth research on the actual effect of iterative and recursive algorithms of FFT.

Regarding the above issue, in this paper we attempt to implement iterative and recursive algorithms of FFT using four mainstream object-oriented languages: Java, C#, C++ and Python, test the runtime of these two algorithms on Windows, Mac and Linux operating systems, study the performance of these two algorithms in different platforms and different compilation environments using statistical methods, and conduct a reasonable analysis and discussion.

2   The Implementation Method of Fast Fourier Transform

The Fourier Transform of discrete sequences is called Discrete Fourier transform (DFT). If a N-point discrete signal sequence (x[n], n = 0, 1, ..., N − 1) is given, then the kth Fourier coefficient can be calculated as:

$$X[k] = \sum_{n=0}^{N-1} x[n] W_N^{nk} \qquad n, k \in [0, N-1] \tag{1}$$

where twiddle factor $W_N^{nk} = e^{-i\frac{2\pi}{N}nk}$ where $i = \sqrt{-1}$. The algorithm has a time complexity of O(N2).

The Fast Fourier Transform in the case of radix 2 is split into odd and even subsequences, and the DFT of N-point sequence can be synthesized by the DFT of the two N/2-point subsequences [6]. In the same way, the DFT of each subsequence can be calculated by the DFT of the smaller subsequences. The procedure is so called butterfly operation as its butterfly-shaped. The Fast Fourier Transform algorithm can reduce the time complexity to O($Nlog_2N$).

Radix 2 FFT has a strong regularity. The DFT of N-point sequence depends only on the N/2-point subsequences, so the FFT of the entire sequence can be obtained by iterative calculation. That is so-called iterative algorithm of FFT. In computer programming, iteration can be realized by loop nesting. The flow chart is shown in Fig. 1 (a). From another prospective, each sequence in FFT butterfly operation calculates and divides subsequences in the same way. If this process is encapsulated into a function, the operations at each layer can be implemented by this function. When calling a function, there is a direct call to the function itself until the sequence becomes only one data. That is a typical recursive problem, and this calculation method is so-called recursive algorithm of FFT which is showed in Fig. 1(b).

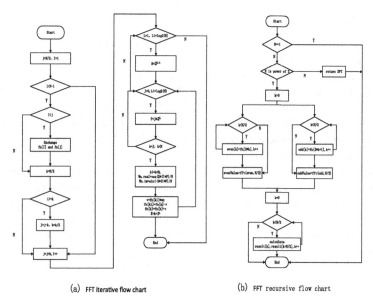

(a) FFT iterative flow chart   (b) FFT recursive flow chart

Fig. 1. Schematic of iterative (a) and recursive (b) algorithms of FFT

3 The Experiment Study

3.1 The Test Platform

In this paper, the performances of iterative and recursive algorithms of FFT with C++, C#, Java and Python languages on Windows, Mac and Linux operating system are studied. For the better accuracy of the experiment, computers with similar hardware configuration are used. Table 1 shows the information about the hardware and operating system of experimental computers, and Table 2 shows the compilers of four programming languages in three platforms.

Table 1. Hardware and operating system of experimental computers

	CPU	RAM	OS
Windows	Intel Core i7 @3.6 GHz	8G	Windows 10
Mac	Intel Core i7 @2.7 GHz	16G	MacOs Mojave
Linux	Intel Core i7 @3.6 GHz	8G	Ubuntu 18.04.2

Table 2. Compilers used in the experiment

	Java	C#	C++	Python
Windows	JRE 8u211	CSC15.0	CL 14.16	Python 3.7
Mac	JRE 8u211	CSC15.0	LLVM 10.0.1	Python 3.7
Linux	JRE 8u211	Net Core 2.2.203	GNU g++7.3.0	Python 3.7

3.2   Experiment Description

The purpose of this study is to analyze the actual performances of iterative and recursive algorithms of FFT through experiments. Considering that the hardware platform, operating system and compiler may have an impact on the performance of the algorithm, the experimental design is as follows: use Java, Python, C++, and C# to implement iterative and recursive algorithms of Fast Fourier Transform on Windows, Linux, and Mac platforms respectively, run each program ten times with an input data of a random sequence of length N = 2 M (where M = 1, 2, ..., 14), and record the experiment results in milliseconds for data analysis.

In order to ensure the consistency of the code complexity as much as possible, all programming languages rewrite the complex class and the four operations in the same way to avoid using the library functions provided by the platform or third parties to implement complex operations. Similar operations, such as the definition of data structures, use consistent processing in programming to minimize the impact of different code quality on runtime efficiency.

3.3   Data Processing Methods

1. Statistical method: Paired t-test is performed on the data measured by each set of the iterative algorithm and the recursive algorithm to check whether the runtime of the two algorithms of FFT is statistically different.
2. Analysis method: If there is a statistical difference between the runtime of the iterative algorithm and the recursive algorithm, then the difference between the efficiency of these two algorithms is further studied. In this paper, the Rate of Runtime (RORT) of the two algorithms is used as an indicator to measure the time efficiency, defined as RORT = T_i/T_r, where T_i represents the runtime of the iterative algorithm and T_r represents the runtime of the recursive algorithm.

4   Experimental Results

Figure 2 shows the runtime of the Fast Fourier Transform algorithm written in four mainstream languages on three platforms. The three subgraphs all use a base-2 logarithmic coordinate system, where the abscissa is the sequence number of the FFT, the ordinate is the runtime of algorithm in ms, and the data points in the graph represent the average time of running 10 times. Figure 2(a) (b) (c) shows experimental data on Windows, Linux and Mac platforms, respectively, where the black, blue, green and red color represent C#, C++, Java and Python languages, and the solid and dashed lines represent the runtime of iterative and recursive algorithms of FFT, respectively.

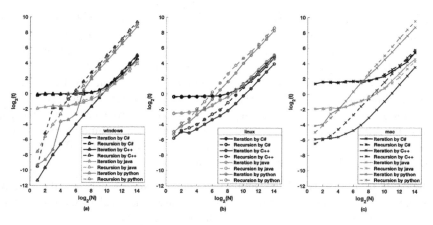

Fig. 2. Runtime of FFT algorithm

It can be seen from Fig. 2 that the runtime of algorithm has the following characteristics:

1. The curves under all platforms show that as the length of the sequence increases, whether it is the iterative algorithm or the recursive algorithm, the runtime increases accordingly. Such relationship approaches to strictly linear for adequate long sequence. When the sequence length is less than 256, C++ and Python generally maintain linear increment, while C# and Java show nonlinear characteristics. This shows that the increase in sequence length does not result in a significant increase in the runtime of the FFT transform when the sequence is short.

2. In overall, when the sequence is short, the runtime of C++ programs is the shortest, followed by Python and Java, while that of C# is the longest; when the sequence is long, the runtime of C++, C#, and Java is close while that of Python is much longer. This phenomenon is related to the mechanism of the four programming languages. C++ is a compiled language. After compiling, C++ code is a binary file that can be recognized by the machine and run directly on the operating system. Therefore, C++ is the most efficient programming language. However, C++ is not cross-platform. C++ programs that use the API under Windows cannot generally be compiled on Unix and Mac,and different compilers have different interpretations of language specifications, therefore C++ is not as compatible as the other three languages. Although C++ has advantages in terms of efficiency, it cannot be applied to various application scenarios. This study also noticed that on Windows platform, the recursive algorithm written in C++ is quite special, and its runtime even exceeds Python. This phenomenon is probably related to the C++ compiler on Windows system which will perform automatic optimization of the recursive code. Java is a compiled and interpreted language, the source code is first compiled into a bytecode file by javac, and then interpreted and run by a Java virtual machine installed on different operating systems [7]. This mechanism is also the reason why Java can run across platforms and explains why Java's runtime under three operating system platforms is almost the same. C# is a compiled and recompiled language, the code is

first compiled into a low-level intermediate language by the C# compiler, then compiled into machine code by the C# virtual machine, and finally run by the CPU. This is the mechanism for two-time compilation [8]. Python is an interpreted language that dynamically changes its structure at runtime. In each process of running the code, the Python parser first converts it into bytecode, which is then converted to machine language by the virtual machine [9]. Compared with Java and C# languages, the process is more complicated. In the environment with small data size, the difference between the three is not big, but when the amount of data being processed is large, the performance of Python will be significantly affected, and the runtime is significantly larger than Java and C#.

In order to further study the similarities and differences between the iterative algorithm and the recursive algorithm, this paper uses statistical method to perform paired t-test on the measured data to verify whether the runtime of these two algorithms is statistically different. The results are shown in Fig. 3. The logarithmic coordinates of the abscissa with the base of 2 show the number of points of the FFT sequence. The thick black line in the figure indicates that there is a statistically significant difference between the runtime of the iterative algorithm and the recursive algorithm, while the blank interval indicates that there is no significant difference.

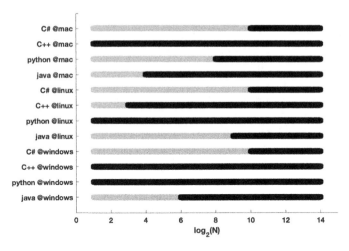

Fig. 3. Difference analysis of the runtime of the iterative algorithm and the recursive algorithm

As can be seen from Fig. 3, when the sequence length is greater than 1024, the runtime between iterative and recursive algorithms of FFT written in the four languages of Java, C#, C++ and Python is significant different on Windows, Linux or Mac operating systems. When the sequence length is small, the efficiency of the iterative algorithm and the recursive algorithm is related to the programming language and operating system. Among them, for C# and Python on Mac operating system, C# and Java on Linux operating system, C# and Java on Windows operating system, the runtime of the iterative algorithm and the recursive algorithm is not significantly different. This phenomenon suggests that when the sequence is short, the execution efficiency of the two algorithms is not much different. Considering the clear and easy-to-understand structure of the recursive algorithm, the use of the recursive algorithm in engineering practice is beneficial to improve the efficiency of writing code.

Figure 4 shows the rate of runtime of the iterative algorithm and the recursive algorithm over different sequence lengths. When the RORT is less than 1, the runtime of the iterative algorithm is smaller than that of the recursive algorithm. The running efficiency of the iterative algorithm is better than that of the recursive algorithm. On the contrary, when the RORT is greater than 1, the runtime of the iterative algorithm is greater than that of the recursive algorithm. The running efficiency of the recursive algorithm is better than that of the iterative algorithm.

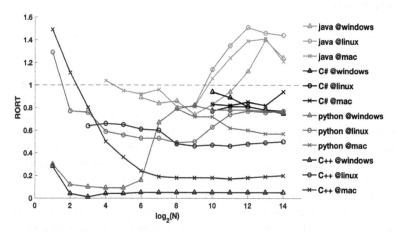

Fig. 4. Rate of runtime of the iterative algorithm and the recursive algorithm

As can be seen from Fig. 4, in the FFT calculation of the long sequence, the programming language has a greater influence on the efficiency of the algorithm than the operating system. The iterative algorithm written in C#, Python and C++ is more efficient than the recursive algorithm. C++ on Window is the most efficient, and the runtime of the iterative algorithm is about 5% of the recursive algorithm. This phenomenon is related to the recursive mechanism. In the process of program execution, recursive calculation includes two phases. The first is the extension phase, which breaks down the problem into smaller problems. In this process, the compiler constructs a recursive work stack to hold the deferred operation. The second is the shrinking phase, which is executed back and forth in the recursive work stack. Throughout this process, it is necessary to complete the repeated calls to itself. As the sequence increases, the number of steps increases dramatically, resulting in greater additional time overhead. The measured data in C#, Python, and C++ supports this view. It also suggests that when using C#, Python, and C++ to implement Fast Fourier Transform in engineering practice, the iterative algorithm should be preferred.

Figure 4 also shows that Java is inconsistent with the measured performance of the other three languages. When the sequence length is less than 1024, the runtime of the iterative algorithm is smaller than that of the recursive algorithm; when the sequence length is greater than 1024, the running efficiency of the recursive algorithm is better than that of the iterative algorithm. This phenomenon is related to Java's JIT compiler. When the same function is called repeatedly in a program, the JIT compiler dynamically optimizes the recursive code [10]. The measured data of the Java code suggests that the running efficiency of the program is related to the length of the sequence. When the sequence is long, the running efficiency of the recursive algorithm is higher than that of the iterative algorithm.

5   Conclusions

In engineering practice, it is often necessary to use the Fast Fourier Transform to perform time-frequency conversion on the signal, and perform FFT calculations on the computer. There are two ways to implement Fast Fourier Transform: the iterative algorithm and the recursive algorithm. These two algorithms have their own advantages and disadvantages. It is generally believed that the iterative algorithm is more efficient than the recursive algorithm. This study uses iterative and recursive algorithms of FFT in Java, C#, C++ and Python, and tests the runtime of the iterative algorithm and the recursive algorithm on Windows, Mac and Linux platforms. The experimental results show that the program written in Python has the longest runtime, whether it is the iterative or recursive algorithm. The iterative algorithm written in C++ has the highest running efficiency, and this phenomenon has little relationship with the operating system. The paired t-test is performed on the experimental data of iterative and recursive algorithms. The results show that the sequence length has an impact on the runtime. In the case of a long sequence, iterative and recursive algorithms have statistically significant differences. Further calculating the rate of runtime of iterative and recursive algorithms for different sequence lengths shows that the iterative program written by C++, C# and Python is better than the recursive algorithm, while Java is the opposite where the efficiency of the recursive algorithm is better than that of the iterative algorithm. The research conclusions of this paper have certain guiding significance for engineering practice, and provide a reference basis for engineers to select programming language and implementation algorithm for FFT.

References

1. Fourier, J.: The Analytical Theory of Heat. Translated with notes by Alexander Freeman. Dover Publication, New York 1-209, pp. 333–464 (1955)
2. Cooley, J.W., Tukey, J.W.: An algorithm for the machine calculation of complex Fourier series. Math. Comput. **19**(90), 297–301 (1965)
3. Kovács, M., Kollár, Z.: Software implementation of the recursive discrete Fourier transform. IEEE Radioelektronika (2017)

4. Hammes, J., Sur, S., Böhm, W.: On the effectiveness of functional language features: NAS benchmark FT. J. Funct. Programm. **7**(1), 103–123 (1997)
5. Zhenyuan, Z., Cheng, Z.: Non-recursive implementation of recursive algorithm. Small Comput. Syst. **3**, 567–570 (2003)
6. Houjin, C., Jian, X., Jian, H.: Digital Signal Processing. Higher Education Press, Beijing (2004)
7. Lindholm, T., Yellin, F.: The Java virtual machine specification. Pearson Schweiz Ag **15**(2), 27–59 (1996)
8. Xu, P.: Analysis on the Features and Functions of C# Programming Language. Digital World, p. 12 (2017)
9. Downey, A.: Think Python.: An Introduction to Software Design. CreateSpace Independent Publishing Platform, Scotts Valley (2011)
10. Nikishkov, G.P., Nikishkov, Y.G., Savchenko, V.V.: Comparison of C and Java performance in finite element computations. Comput. Struct. **81**(24), 2401–2408 (2003)

Resource Optimization for UAV-Enabled Multichannel Internet of Things

Xin Liu$^{(\boxtimes)}$ and Biaojun Lai

School of Information and Communication Engineering,
Dalian University of Technology, Dalian 116024, China
`liuxinstar1984@dlut.edu.cn, 1214429036@qq.com`

Abstract. In this paper, the UAV as a relay forwards the information of multichannel IoT to the data center in the case of terrestrial channel fading. Throughput maximization for the multichannel IoT is studied, respectively, subject to the constraints of information-causality as well as total power and maximum rate of UAV. An iterative joint optimization algorithm is proposed to optimize the subcarrier, power and UAV trajectory alternatively, to achieve the optimal solution. The simulations show that the dynamic subcarrier allocation outperforms the fixed subcarrier allocation, and the joint optimization algorithm can improve the transmission performance of the UAV-enabled multichannel IoT effectively.

Keywords: UAV-enabled Multichannel IoT · Joint optimization · Transmit rate

1 Introduction

Internet of Things (IoT) has been widely used in transportation, agriculture, industry, logistics etc., which can realize the interconnections of all things based on the Internet, traditional telecommunication network and other information carriers [1]. However, relying on fixed communication facilities limits the mobility and deployment of the IoT. Recently, unmanned aerial vehicle (UAV) has been used as an ideal relay to assist the ground communications, due to the characteristics of agility, low cost and easy-to-deploy [2–4].

In [5], the optimal placement of an UAV in cooperative communications had been studied, which focused on the reliability by optimizing the UAV altitude. In [6], A system of multiple communication pairs had considered, which improved the cooperative performance by joint optimizing the position of UAV and resource allocation. In [7], Zeng et al. proposed an UAV-enabled mobile relaying system, whose throughput was maximized by optimizing the source/relay power allocation and the trajectory of the UAV by successive convex approximation (SCA). In [8], Jiang et al. considered an UAV-relayed system in the amplify-and-forward (AF) scenario, whose throughput was maximized by jointly optimizing the transmission power and UAV trajectory. As the mobility

© ICST Institute for Computer Sciences, Social Informatics and Telecommunications Engineering 2021
Published by Springer Nature Switzerland AG 2021. All Rights Reserved
M. Guan and Z. Na (Eds.): MLICOM 2020, LNICST 342, pp. 82–92, 2021.
https://doi.org/10.1007/978-3-030-66785-6_10

of the UAV may generate great transmission performance difference, the fairness problem for UAV-assisted communication system should be considered. In [9,10], the authors maximized the minimum user rate for an UAV-relayed system by joint power and UAV trajectory optimization.

Currently, there are fewer works on the UVA-enabled IoT, where the UAV can relay the information for multiple nodes. In this paper, An UAV-assisted multichannel IoT consisting of multiple nodes, one UAV relay and one data center is considered. Each node uses a single subcarrier to transmit its information to an mobile UAV, which then relays the information of all the nodes to and the data center.

2   System Model

We consider an UAV-assisted IoT constituting of K nodes and one data center. Assuming that the power for each node is constrained and the ground channel is in severe fading, the direct links from the nodes to the data center are ignored. Hence, the UAV is deployed to facilitate one-way communication from the node to the data center, which can forward the data previously received from the IoT node to the data center, as shown in Fig. 1.

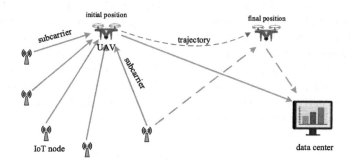

Fig. 1. A UAV-assisted IoT

Consider a Cartesian coordinate system, where the IoT nodes and the data center are located at $(x_1, y_1, 0), \cdots, (x_K, y_K, 0)$ and $(L, 0, 0)$. Assume that the UAV is deployed at a stable height H, and there is no obstacle or building that makes the UAV rise or fall frequently. The flight trajectory of the UAV is denoted as $(x(t), y(t), H)$ for $0 \le t \le T$, where T is the flight time and $x(t), y(t)$ represent the plane coordinates. The initial position and the final position of the UAV are located at (x_o, y_o, H) and (x_F, y_F, H), respctively. Hence, the minimum distance between the initial position and the final position of the UAV is $d_{min} = \sqrt{(x_F - x_o)^2 + (y_F - y_o)^2}$. Considering that the maximum speed of the UAV is V_{max}, let $V_{max} \ge d_{max}/T$ ensure that at least one feasible trajectory exists from the initial position to the final position. With the maximum UAV speed, we have $\sqrt{(\nabla x(t))^2 + (\nabla y(t))^2} \leq V_{max}$ for $0 \leq t \leq T$, where $\nabla x(t)$ and $\nabla y(t)$ denote the derivatives of $x(t)$ and $y(t)$ in t, respectively.

Note that T is divided into U time slots, i.e., $T = U\delta_t$, where δ_t is so small that the position and speed of the UAV in each time slot is constant. The UAV trajectory in the uth slot can be described as $(x(u), y(u))$ for $1 \leq u \leq U$. Therefore, the constraints on the UAV trajectory and speed are given by

$$(x(1) - x_o)^2 + (y(1) - y_o)^2 \leq \varepsilon^2 \tag{1}$$

$$(x(u + 1) - x(u))^2 + (y(u + 1) - y(u))^2 \leq \varepsilon^2 \tag{2}$$

$$u = 1, 2, ..., U - 1$$

$$(x_F - x(U))^2 + (y_F - y(U))^2 \leq \varepsilon^2 \tag{3}$$

where $\varepsilon = V_{max}\delta_t$ is the maximum displacement of UAV within one time slot.

In this paper, the transmit channel is divided into M narrow-band subchannels. $\omega = \{\omega_{m,k}(u), \forall k, m, u\}$, where $\omega_{m,k}(u) = \{0, 1\}$, represents the subcarrier assignment indicator in slot u. $\omega_{m,k}(u) = 1$ represents mth subcarrier is assigned to user k, otherwise, $\omega_{m,k}(u) = 0$. We assume that the communication channels from the IoT nodes to the relay and the relay to the data center are line-of-sight (LoS) links. Therefore, the Doppler effect can be ignored. The distances from each IoT node to the relay and the relay to the data center at slot u are given by $d_{sr,k} = \sqrt{H^2 + (x(u) - x_k)^2 + (y(u) - y_k)^2}, \forall k$ and $d_{rd} = \sqrt{H^2 + (L - x(u))^2 + y(u)^2}$, respectively. For simplicity, $q(u) = [x(u), y(u)]^T$, $z_d = [L, 0]^T$ and $z_k = [x_k, y_k]^T$ indicate the positions of UAV, data center and IoT node, respectively. In the free-space path loss model, the channel gain from the IoT nodes to the relay can be described as

$$h_{sr,k}(u) = \frac{\rho_k}{H^2 + ||q(u) - z(k)||^2}, \quad \forall k, u \tag{4}$$

where ρ_k denotes the channel gain at unit distance $d_0 = 1$. We use $p_{s,k}^m(u)$ to denote the transmit power of kth node at slot u in subcarrier m. The maximum transmit rate from the nodes to the relay in slot u can be given by

$$R_s(u) = \sum_{k=1}^{K} \sum_{m=1}^{M} \omega_{m,k}(u) \log_2 \left(1 + p_{s,k}^m(u)\gamma_{sr,k}(u)\right), \quad \forall u \tag{5}$$

where $\gamma_k = \rho_k/\sigma^2$ is the reference signal-to-noise ratio (SNR), and $\gamma_{sr,k}(u)$ is defined as

$$\gamma_{sr,k}(u) = \frac{\gamma_k}{H^2 + ||q(u) - z(u)||^2}, \quad \forall k, u \tag{6}$$

Similarly, the channel gain from the relay to the data center can be described as

$$h_{rd}(u) = \frac{\rho_k}{H^2 + ||z_d - q(u)||^2}, \quad \forall k, u \tag{7}$$

and the maximum transmit rate from the relay to the center is given by

$$R_r(u) = \sum_{k=1}^{K} \sum_{m=1}^{M} \omega_{m,k}(u) \log_2 \left(1 + p_{r,k}^m(u) \gamma_{rd,k}(u) \right), \ \forall u \tag{8}$$

where $p_{r,k}^m(u)$ denotes the transmit power of the relay at slot u in subcarrier m, and $\gamma_{rd,k}(u) = \frac{\gamma_k}{H^2 + ||z_d - q(u)||^2}$. Our goal is to maximize the total throughput from the IoT to the data center by jointly optimizing ω, $\mathbf{p} = \{p_{s,k}^m(u), p_{r,k}^m(u), \forall k, m, u\}$ and $\mathbf{q} = \{(x(u), y(u)), \forall u\}$ as follows

$$\text{(P1): } \max_{\mathbf{q,p},\omega} \sum_{u=2}^{U} R_r(u)$$

$$\text{s.t. } \sum_{i=2}^{u} R_r(i) \leq \sum_{i=1}^{u-1} R_s(i), \quad u = 2, 3, ..., U \tag{9}$$

$$\sum_{k=1}^{K} \sum_{m=1}^{M} \sum_{u=1}^{U-1} \omega_{m,k}(u) p_{s,k}^m(u) \leq P_s \tag{10}$$

$$\sum_{k=1}^{K} \sum_{m=1}^{M} \sum_{u=2}^{U} \omega_{m,k}(u) p_{r,k}^m(u) \leq P_r \tag{11}$$

$$p_{s,k}^m(u) \geq 0, \quad u = 1, 2, ..., U - 1 \tag{12}$$

$$p_{r,k}^m(u) \geq 0, \quad u = 2, 3, ..., U \tag{13}$$

$$\sum_{k=1}^{K} \omega_{m,k}(u) = 1, \quad m = 1, 2, ..., M \tag{14}$$

$$(x(1) - x_o)^2 + (y(1) - y_o)^2 \leq \varepsilon^2 \tag{15}$$

$$(x(u+1) - x(u))^2 + (y(u+1) - y(u))^2 \leq \varepsilon^2 \tag{16}$$

$$(x_F - x(U))^2 + (y_F - y(U))^2 \leq \varepsilon^2 \tag{17}$$

where (9) represents information causality constraint, i.e., the data capacity forwarded from the relay cannot exceed that received from the IoT nodes, P_s and P_r are total transmit power of IoT and relay, respectively, (14) represents one user occupies one subcarrier within one time slot.

3   Optimal Solution to P1

(P1) is non-convex and hard to solve directly. Therefore, we divide it into three suboptimization problems, including subcarrier allocation optimization, power optimization and UAV trajectory optimization. Then (P1) can be solved by an iterative algorithm for jointly optimizing subcarrier, power and trajectory. The subcarriers can be allocated to the nodes according to the channel gains, which are constant within one time slot. To guarantee transmission performance, one subcarrier is allocated to the node with the best channel gain on it, and the subcarrier cannot be occupied by the other users in this time slot.

3.1   Power Optimization

Assume the UAV trajectory is fixed, and the power optimization with fixed trajectory is considered. By ignoring the UAV's mobility constraints (15)–(17), (P1) can be converted into the power optimization problem with fixed UAV trajectory. However, it is still a non-convex optimization problem, which is difficult to solve directly. Hence, we introduce the slack variables $R_{r,k}(u), u = 2, ..., U$ to solve (P1), and (P1) is rewritten as follows

$$(\text{P1.1}): \quad \max_{\mathbf{p}, \mathbf{w}, R_{r,k}(u)} \sum_{k=1}^{K} \sum_{m=1}^{M} \sum_{u=2}^{U} \omega_{m,k}(u) R_{r,k}(u) \tag{18}$$

$$\text{s.t.} \sum_{k=1}^{K} \sum_{m=1}^{M} \sum_{i=2}^{u} \omega_{m,k}(i) R_{r,k}(i) \leq \sum_{i=1}^{u-1} R_s(i) \tag{19}$$

$$\sum_{m=1}^{M} \omega_{m,k}(u) R_{r,k}(u) \leq \sum_{m=1}^{M} \omega_{m,k}(u) \bar{R}_{r,k}(u) \tag{20}$$

$$\sum_{k=1}^{K} \sum_{m=1}^{M} \sum_{u=1}^{U-1} \omega_{m,k}(u) p_{s,k}^{m}(u) \leq P_s \tag{21}$$

$$\sum_{k=1}^{K} \sum_{m=1}^{M} \sum_{u=2}^{U} \omega_{m,k}(u) p_{r,k}^{m}(u) \leq P_r \tag{22}$$

$$p_{s,k}^{m}(u) \geq 0, \quad u = 1, 2, ..., U - 1, \ \forall k \tag{23}$$

$$p_{r,k}^{m}(u) \geq 0, \quad u = 2, 3, ..., U, \ \forall k \tag{24}$$

$$\sum_{k=1}^{K} \omega_{m,k}(u) = 1, \quad \forall m \tag{25}$$

where $\bar{R}_{r,k}(u) = \log_2(1 + p_{r,k}^{m}(u)\gamma_{rd,k}(u))$, and $R_s(u) = \sum_{k=1}^{K} \sum_{m=1}^{M} \omega_{m,k}(u)$ $\bar{R}_{s,k}(u)$, where $\bar{R}_{s,k}(u) = \log_2(1 + p_{s,k}^{m}(u)\gamma_{sr,k}(u))$. The optimal power can be achieved by the water-filling algorithm. The Slater's condition is satisfied for (P1.1), where the Lagrangian function is given by

$$L\left(\mathbf{p}, \mathbf{w}, \{\lambda_u\}, R_{r,k}(u)\right)$$

$$= \sum_{k=1}^{K} \sum_{m=1}^{M} \sum_{u=2}^{U} \omega_{m,k}(u) R_{r,k}(u) + \sum_{u=2}^{U} \lambda_u \left(\sum_{i=1}^{u-1} R_s(i) - \sum_{k=1}^{K} \sum_{m=1}^{M} \sum_{i=2}^{u} \omega_{m,k}(i) R_{r,k}(i) \right) \quad (26)$$

where $\lambda_u \geq 0, u = 2, 3, ..., U$ are the Lagrange dual variables. By introducing $\theta_u = \sum_{i=u+1}^{U} \lambda_i, u = 1, 2, ..., U - 1$ and $\mu_u = 1 - \sum_{i=u}^{U} \lambda_i, u = 2, 3, ..., U$, the function L can be rewritten as follows

$$L\left(\mathbf{p}, \mathbf{w}, \{\lambda_u\}, R_{r,k}(u)\right)$$

$$= \sum_{k=1}^{K} \sum_{m=1}^{M} \sum_{u=2}^{U} \mu_u \omega_{m,k}(u) R_{r,k}(u) + \sum_{k=1}^{K} \sum_{m=1}^{M} \sum_{u=1}^{U-1} \theta_u \omega_{m,k}(u) \bar{R}_{s,k}(u) \quad (27)$$

The optimal solution can be obtained by solving the Lagrangian dual problem as follows

$$\min_{\lambda_u} \quad f(\lambda_u) \qquad (28)$$

$$\text{s.t.} \quad \lambda_u \geq 0, \; \forall u$$

where $f(\lambda_u) = \max_{\mathbf{p}, \mathbf{w}, R_{r,k}(u)} L\left(\mathbf{p}, \mathbf{w}, \lambda_u, R_{r,k}(u)\right)$, s.t. (20)–(26)

The dual function $f(\lambda_u)$ can be obtained with fixed λ_u by maximizing L and then we minimize $f(\lambda_u)$ by finding the optimal dual solutions λ_u^*. Then the optimal power values can be obtained by substituting λ_u^*. By applying the Karush-Kuhn-Tucker (KKT) conditions and taking the derivatives of the objective function with respect to $p_{s,k}^m(u)$ and $p_{r,k}^m(u)$, respectively, the optimal power values of IoT nodes and UAV can be obtained as follows

$$p_{s,k}^{m\star}(u) = \left[\frac{\theta_u}{\eta \ln 2} - \frac{1}{\gamma_{sr,k}(u)} \right]^+, \; \forall u, k \qquad (29)$$

$$p_{r,k}^{m\star}(u) = \left[\frac{\mu_u}{\nu \ln 2} - \frac{1}{\gamma_{rd,k}(u)} \right]^+, \; \forall u, k \qquad (30)$$

where η and ν are the non-negative Lagrange multipliers associated with the constraints (21) and (22), respectively, and $[x]^+ = \max\{x, 0\}$. Then we can get $R_{r,k}^\star(u) = \left[\log_2 \left(\frac{\mu_u}{\nu \ln 2} \gamma_{rd,k}(u) \right) \right]^+$.

3.2 Trajectory Optimization

Then the UAV trajectory will be optimized with the fixed power allocation. (P1) can be described as follows

$$(\text{P1.2}): \quad \max_{\mathbf{q}, \mathbf{w}, R_{r,k}(u)} \sum_{k=1}^{K} \sum_{m=1}^{M} \sum_{u=2}^{U} \omega_{m,k}(u) R_{r,k}(u)$$

$$\text{s.t.} \sum_{k=1}^{K} \sum_{m=1}^{M} \sum_{i=2}^{u} \omega_{m,k}(i) R_{r,k}(i) \leq \sum_{i=1}^{u-1} R_s(i) \qquad (31)$$

$$\sum_{m=1}^{M} \omega_{m,k}(u) R_{r,k}(u) \leq \sum_{m=1}^{M} \omega_{m,k}(u) \bar{R}_{r,k}(u) \qquad (32)$$

$$(x(1) - x_o)^2 + (y(1) - y_o)^2 \leq \varepsilon^2 \qquad (33)$$

$$(x(u+1) - x(u))^2 + (y(u+1) - y(u))^2 \leq \varepsilon^2 \qquad (34)$$

$$(x_F - x(U))^2 + (y_F - y(U))^2 \leq \varepsilon^2 \qquad (35)$$

where $R_s(u) = \sum_{k=1}^{K} \sum_{m=1}^{M} \log_2\left(1 + \frac{\gamma_{s,k}(u)}{H^2+||q(u)-z(u)||^2}\right)$ and $\bar{R}_{r,k}(u) = \log_2\left(1 + \frac{\gamma_{r,k}(u)}{H^2+||z_d-q(u)||^2}\right)$, where $\gamma_{s,k}(u) \triangleq p^m_{s,k}(u)\gamma_k$ and $\gamma_{r,k}(u) \triangleq p^m_{r,k}(u)\gamma_k$.

(P1.2) is a non-convex optimization problem, which can be solved using the successive convex optimization method to optimize the trajectory increment of the UAV at each iteration. Assume $(x_j(u), y_j(u))$ is the UAV trajectory after the jth iteration, and $R_{sk,j}(u) \triangleq \log_2\left(1 + \frac{\gamma_{s,k}(u)}{H^2+(x_j(u)-x_k)^2+(y_j(u)-y_k)^2}\right)$ and $R_{rk,j}(u) \triangleq \log_2\left(1 + \frac{\gamma_{r,k}(u)}{H^2+(L-x_j(u))^2+y_j^2(u)}\right)$ are the corresponding transmission rates from the IoT nodes to the UAV and the UAV to the data center, respectively. Furthermore, $(\delta_j(u), \zeta_j(u))$ is denoted as the trajectory incremental from the jth to the $(j+1)$th iteration. Then we can obtain [7].

$$R_{sk,j+1}(u) \geq R^{lb}_{sk,j+1}(u) = R_{sk,j}(u) - a_{sk,j}(u)\left(\delta_j^2(u) + \zeta_j^2(u)\right)$$
$$- b_{sk,j}(u)\delta_j(u) - c_{sk,j}(u)\zeta_j(u), \forall k. \qquad (36)$$

$$R_{rk,j+1}(u) \geq R^{lb}_{rk,j+1}(u) = R_{rk,j}(u) - a_{rk,j}(u)\left(\delta_j^2(u) + \zeta_j^2(u)\right)$$
$$- b_{rk,j}(u)\delta_j(u) - c_{rk,j}(u)\zeta_j(u), \forall k. \qquad (37)$$

where $\{a_{sk,j}(u), b_{sk,j}(u), c_{sk,j}(u)\}$ and $\{a_{rk,j}(u), b_{rk,j}(u), c_{rk,j}(u)\}$ are the coefficients of the links from the IoT nodes to the UAV and the UAV to the data center, respectively, which are describe as follows

$$\begin{cases} a_{sk,j}(u) = \frac{\gamma_{s,k}(u)\log_2 e}{d^2_{sr,j}(u)\left(\gamma_{s,k}(u)+d^2_{sr,j}(u)\right)}, \\ b_{sk,j}(u) = 2\left(x_j(u) - x_k\right)a_{sk,j}(u), \forall u, k \\ c_{sk,j}(u) = 2\left(y_j(u) - y_k\right)a_{sk,j}(u) \end{cases} \qquad (38)$$

and

$$\begin{cases} a_{rk,j}(u) = \dfrac{\gamma_{r,k}(u)\log_2 e}{d_{rd,j}^2(u)\left(\gamma_{r,k}(u)+d_{rd,j}^2(u)\right)} \\ b_{rk,j}(u) = -2\left(L - x_j(u)\right)a_{rk,j}(u), \forall u, k \\ c_{rk,j}(u) = 2y_j(u)a_{r,j}(u) \end{cases} \tag{39}$$

(36) and (37) represent the lower bounds of channel capacities with given trajectory increment. Then (P1.2) can be reformulated as follows

$$\text{(P1.3):} \quad \max_{\delta_j(u),\zeta_j(u),\mathbf{w},R_{r,k}(u)} \sum_{k=1}^{K}\sum_{m=1}^{M}\sum_{u=2}^{U} \omega_{m,k}(u)R_{r,k}(u)$$

$$\text{s.t.} \sum_{k=1}^{K}\sum_{m=1}^{M}\sum_{i=2}^{u} \omega_{m,k}(i)R_{r,k}(i) \le \sum_{k=1}^{K}\sum_{m=1}^{M}\sum_{i=1}^{u-1} \omega_{m,k}(i)R_{sk,j+1}^{lb}(i) \tag{40}$$

$$\sum_{m=1}^{M} \omega_{m,k}(u)R_{r,k}(u) \le \sum_{m=1}^{M} \omega_{m,k}(u)R_{rk,j+1}^{lb}(u) \tag{41}$$

$$\left(x_j(1) + \delta_j(1) - x_o\right)^2 + \left(y_j(1) + \zeta_j(1) - y_o\right)^2 \le \varepsilon^2 \tag{42}$$

$$\begin{aligned} &\left(x_j(u+1) + \delta_j(u+1) - x_j(u) - \delta_j(u)\right)^2 + \\ &\left(y_j(u+1) + \zeta_j(u+1) - y_j(u) - \zeta_j(u)\right)^2 \le \varepsilon^2, \forall u \end{aligned} \tag{43}$$

$$\left(x_F - x_j(U) - \delta_j(U)\right)^2 + \left(y_F - y_j(U) - \zeta_j(U)\right)^2 \le \varepsilon^2 \tag{44}$$

which is a standard convex optimization problem and can be solved by the optimization tool CVX. Hence, the optimal solution to (P1.2) can be achieved by solving (P1.3).

3.3 Joint Optimization

An joint power, subcarrier and trajectory optimization algorithm is proposed to solve (P1) by alternatively optimizing (P1.1) and (P1.2). The joint optimization algorithm is described in Algorithm 1.

4 Numerical Results

We consider an IoT with $K = 8$ nodes randomly distributed in $2000\,\text{m} \times 500\,\text{m}$ regions, and $M = 8$ subcarriers with the bandwidth of $20\,\text{MHz}$ and the

Algorithm 1. Joint power, subcarrier and trajectory optimization.
***
Require: the initial and final locations of the UAV, the power of IoT nodes and UAV, and the UAV trajectory;
  1: **while** trajectory is not convergent or the maximum number of iterations has not been reached **do**
  2:     with given UAV trajectory, optimize the subcarrier allocation according to the channel gain;
  3:     with given power, optimize the UAV's trajectory by solving (P1.2);
  4:     with given UAV trajectory, optimize the power allocation by solving (P1.1);
  5: **end while**
Ensure: subcarrier allocation, power of IoT nodes and UAV, and UAV trajectory.
***

carrier frequency of $4.9\,\text{GHz}{\sim}5.04\,\text{GHz}$. The noise power spectrum density is $-169\,\text{dBm/Hz}$. The altitude of the UAV is fixed to $H = 100\,\text{m}$, which can avoid most obstacles. The maximum speed of the UAV is set as $V_{max} = 60\,\text{m/s}$. The maximum average transmit power for each node and UAV is assumed to be $p_{s,k}^m(u) = p_{r,k}^m(u) = 20\,\text{mW}$, respectively.

To verify the effect of mobile UAV on the IoT with the fixed UAV trajectory, two UAV trajectories are considered: (a) UAV is static at the location (1000, 0); (b) UAV flies from the initial location (750, 500) to the final location (1500, 500) with the maximum speed towards the data center. Then we consider two subcarrier allocation strategies: one is the subcarriers are dynamically allocated at each slot according to the channel gain, and the other is the subcarrier allocation is fixed in the first slot and remain unchanged until the end of the flight. The total transmit rate of IoT R_r versus the transmit time T is plotted in Fig. 2. It is observed that the transmit rate under the mobile UAV is higher than that

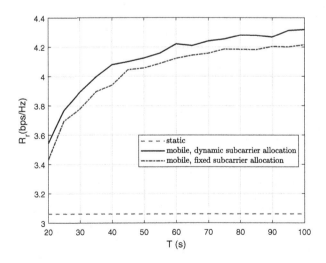

Fig. 2. Throughput in different subcarrier allocation and relay states.

in the static UAV. In addition, the transmission under the dynamic subcarrier allocation is higher than that under the fixed subcarrier allocation.

The UAV trajectory by the joint optimization algorithm is shown in Fig. 3. It is seen that the UAV first moves toward the IoT nodes and then closer to the data center instead of the direct flight. Such a trajectory can guarantee the UAV to receive enough data from the IoT.

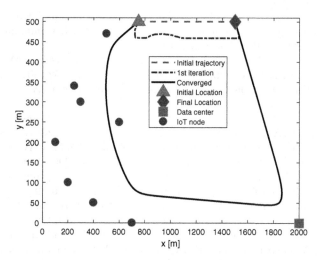

Fig. 3. UAV trajectory evolution by Algorithm 1; the circle, square, triangle, and diamond represent IoT node, data center, initial and final UAV locations, respectively.

5   Conclusions

In this paper, we propose resource optimization for an UVA-enable multichannel IoT, which seeks to maximize the throughput of the IoT by jointly optimizing subcarrier, power and UAV trajectory. The proposed optimization problems are divided into two sub-optimization problems, i.e., the power optimization under the fixed trajectory can be solved by the water filling algorithm, and the trajectory optimization under the fixed power can be achieved by the successive convex optimization. A joint optimization algorithm is given to obtain the optimal resource allocation. Numerical results show that the proposed resource optimization algorithm can improve the transmission performance of the UAV-enabled multichannel IoT effectively.

Acknowledgment. This work was supported by the Joint Foundations of the National Natural Science Foundations of China and the Civil Aviation of China under Grant U1833102 and the Natural Science Foundation of Liaoning Province under Grant 2019-ZD-0014 and 2020-HYLH-13.

References

1. Chaudhary, S., Johari, R., Bhatia, R., Gupta, K., Bhatnagar, A.: CRAIoT: concept, review and application(s) of IoT. In: 4th International Conference on Internet of Things: Smart Innovation and Usages (IoT-SIU), Ghaziabad, India, pp. 1–4 (2019)
2. Wang, H., Zhao, H., Zhang, J., Ma, D., Li, J., Wei, J.: Survey on unmanned aerial vehicle networks: a cyber physical system perspective. IEEE Commun. Surv. Tutor. **22**, 1027–1070 (2020)
3. Hayat, S., Yanmaz, E., Muzaffar, R.: Survey on unmanned aerial vehicle networks for civil applications: a communications viewpoint. IEEE Commun. Surv. Tuts. **18**(4), 2624–2661 (2016). Fourthquarter
4. Gupta, L., Jain, R., Vaszkun, G.: Survey of important issues in UAV communication networks. IEEE Commun. Surv. Tuts. **18**(2), 1123–1152 (2015). 2nd Quarter
5. Chen, Y., Feng, W., Zheng, G.: Optimum placement of UAV as relays. IEEE Commun. Lett. **22**(2), 248–251 (2018)
6. Fan, R., Cui, J., Jin, S., Yang, K., An, J.: Optimal node placement and resource allocation for UAV relaying network. IEEE Commun. Lett. **22**(4), 808–811 (2018)
7. Zeng, Y., Zhang, R., Lim, T.J.: Throughput maximization for UAV-enabled mobile relaying systems. IEEE Trans. Commun. **64**(12), 4983–4996 (2016)
8. Jiang, X., Wu, Z., Yin, Z., Yang, Z.: Power and trajectory optimization for UAV-enabled amplify-and-forward relay networks. IEEE Access **6**, 48688–48696 (2018)
9. Jiang, X., Wu, Z., Yin, Z., Yang, Z.: Joint power and trajectory design for UAV-relayed wireless systems. IEEE Wirel. Commun. Lett. **8**(3), 697–700 (2019)
10. Hu, Q., Cai, Y., Liu, A., Yu, G.: Joint resource allocation and trajectory optimization for UAV-aided relay networks. In: IEEE Global Communications Conference (GLOBECOM), Waikoloa, HI, USA, pp. 1–6 (2019)

Applications of Neural Network and Deep Learning

Hardware Design and Development of Intelligent Meter Data Acquisition Module Based on WIFI

Ming Tang[(✉)]

University of Electronic Science and Technology of China,
Zhongshan Institute, Zhongshan 528400, China
tangml21@163.com

Abstract. The purpose of this design is to design a WIFI based intelligent meter data acquisition module; it is mainly composed of HT6015 chip, WIFI module, etc. The voltage and current signals are first entered into the relevant resistive and capacitance filter processing signal, filter clutter and so on, and then transmitted to the RN8027C metering chip to realize the conversion of electric energy into pulse signal, then transmitted to the HT6015 chip to complete the statistics of pulse signal and then to complete the statistics of electric energy. Finally, the power information is transmitted by the WIFI module. The electrical signals in this system are first passed through the capacitance resistor to divide the voltage to produce the equal proportion signal, and are easily adjusted to the input range of the sampling port of the metering chip. The low pass filter is used to filter out the interference signal containing the useful signal, so as to obtain the real power consumption and other information more accurately. After RN8027C the chip, the electrical signal to the pulse signal is transformed, and then the electrical information can be obtained by processing the statistical change of the HT6015 chip, and the WIFI module can be transmitted. As a result, the electronic signal is collected, processed and transmitted quickly, which is the design of the intelligent meter data acquisition module based on WIFI.

Keywords: WIFI · Smart meters · Smart grid · IOT

1 Introduction

On the basis of the electronic watt-hour meter, the design of electronic integrated circuit is more optimized, both in the performance and in the operation of the first than the original electronic watt-hour meter has a great advantage. Compared with ordinary electronic watt-hour meters, it has the following advantages:

1. Power consumption. The power consumption of a single meter is only about 0.6–0.7 w because of the design of electronic components used in smart meters. If you need less power, you can make a multi-family centralized watt-hour meter so that the average power to the home can be smaller

2. Accuracy. Because the mechanical wear of mechanical watt-hour meter, such an insurmountable congenital defect, will lead to mechanical watt-hour meter walking more and more slowly, the final reading of the meter will be more and more errors; electronic intelligent watt-hour meter does not have such defects.
3. Overload and power frequency range. The overload multiples of smart meters can generally reach 6 to 8 times, with a large range; the frequency at work is also relatively wide, can reach 40 Hz to 1000 Hz; while the overload multiples of ordinary inductive meters are generally 4 times, far smaller than that of smart meters, and the working frequency is also relatively small, 45 Hz to 55 Hz, which is much smaller than that of smart meters, so the working environment is not as good as smart meters.
4. Functional aspects. The reason that the function of intelligent electric meter is more abundant than electronic electric energy meter is that the electronic technology of intelligent electric meter is adopted. Through the related communication protocol and programming software, intelligent electric meter can connect with computer, realize human-computer interaction, at the same time, we can also better and more convenient and timely monitoring and management of hardware. Its safety, correctness and so on have the positive influence to the supply and demand both sides. Therefore, because the intelligent meter has different functions from ordinary electronic watt-hour meter, such as small size, remote control, human-computer interaction, anti-theft, prepaid electricity and so on. Further, in order to meet the requirements of control functions in different situations, we implement by modifying the software. All kinds of functions are difficult to realize for traditional mechanical watt-hour meter and common electronic watt-hour meter (Fig. 1).

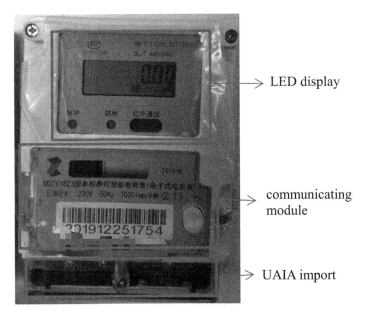

Fig. 1. Physical diagram of smart meter

This paper designs and develops the hardware of data acquisition module of WIFI intelligent meter, mainly using HT6015 chip to collect electricity data, and using ESP-7 WIFI module as communication tool. The specific process of this project is as follows: first, the filter filters the electric signal and imports it into the metering chip through the electric signal after the current transformer and the resistance network partial voltage, then completes the conversion of the electric signal to the pulse signal, then imports it into the HT6015, processes and statistics the pulse signal through the HT6015 chip, and feedback the processed electric information through the WIFI signal.

2   System Design

2.1   Overall Design Scheme

This design is mainly aimed at the meter system, a total of 8 main modules. How it works is that the metering module transmits the metering data to the CPU. through the communication mode of serial port bus different modules are used by providing different levels by the power module. LCD display module is used to display all kinds of electricity information of users. Data storage module is used to manage events, electricity and other data. WIFI module is used to realize the interaction between device communication and user information (Fig. 2).

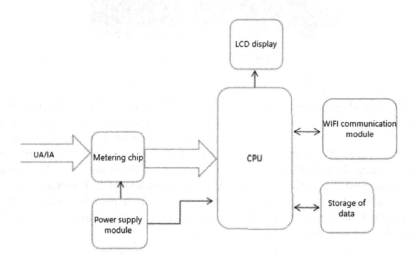

Fig. 2. Hardware design block diagram

2.2   Selection of Major Devices

(1) Selection of main chips

HT6015 is the main chip selected for this design HT6015. HT6x1x series of MCU, for the new generation of smart meter applications; The kernel uses a Cortex-M0 processor with 128 k flash, 8 k SRAM, power supply and reset management, clock management, temperature sensors, hardware automatic temperature compensation RTC, PLL, high frequency RC, low frequency RC, LCD driver and other rich IP. The 32.768 kHz crystal oscillator external RTC clock source scheme, with 70 GPIO, 6 channels UART, 7 external interrupts, LCD support 4 segments, all adopt lqfp80 package.

(2) **Choose WIFI module**

Fig. 3. ESP-07 physical

The WIFI module selected for this design is ESP-07, ESP-7 physical object as shown in Fig. 3. the core processor of the ESP-07 WIFI module ESP8266; it integrates the industry-leading ten silica 1106 ultra-low power 32 micro MCU in smaller sizes with 16-bit lean mode. the main frequency part supports both 80 MHz and 160 MHz, support integrated WIFI MAC/BB/RF/PA/LNA and on-board antennas. This module supports standard IEEE802.11b/g/n protocol with complete TCP/IP protocol line, can add networking function for user's existing device, is a complete WIFI network solution. By ESP8266, only need simple serial port configuration to achieve data transmission through the network.

3 System Hardware Design

For the hardware design circuit part of the equipment, look up the literature and read the data, determine the overall idea. Then by selecting whether the relevant hardware can meet the requirements of the whole system design, see whether to achieve the overall goal to sort out the confirmation ideas. Then complete the circuit diagram design, device purchase, welding and other overall work.

3.1   Sampling Unit of Smart Meter

Since the actual requirements for users to provide basic electricity information, then the use of electricity users are essential. this design, after the voltage, current signal is converted into pulse signal input to the main chip after the sampling circuit composed of the metering chip RN8027C HT6015, the desired electricity information (such as current, frequency, power factor, power consumption, voltage, etc.) can be obtained after re-calculation, and the external communication and interactive data can be obtained through the WIFI module interface; at the same time, the event recording and data can be carried out for human-computer interaction. The function of the sampling circuit is described below.

(1) **Current Sampling Circuit**

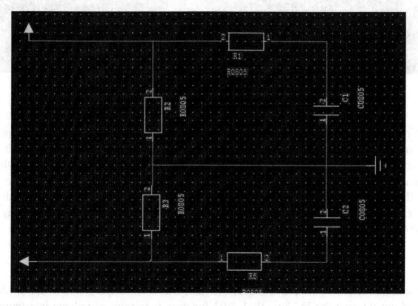

Fig. 4. Current sampling circuit

From Fig. 4, we can see that the a current in the circuit is filtered out by the low-pass filter and the current transformer, and enters into the chip RN8027C. the larger current signal is induced into a smaller mV voltage signal through the current transformer into the current sampling signal. the load resistance is used to convert the larger current signal in the transformer into a smaller voltage signal R2, R3, and the smaller voltage signal is mV adjusted to the input range that the analog-to-digital sampling port of the RN8027C chip can withstand. and so can get mV small signal. The current sampling signal of the small mV can be input into the differential signal pin RN8027C the chip after processing by the low cylinder filter.

(2) **Voltage Sampling Circuit**

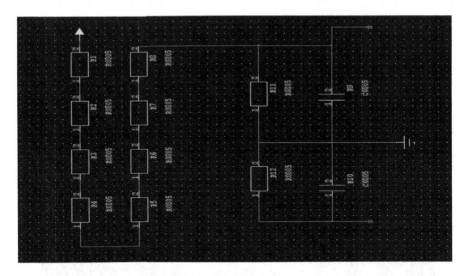

Fig. 5. Voltage sampling circuit

From Fig. 5, we can see that the a voltage in the circuit is input to the ad sampling port of the chip through a number of resistance partial voltages, and then through the low-tube filter. The voltage sampling circuit R1-R8 a voltage voltage divider, which generates a mV signal proportional to the input external voltage at both ends of the r11 and R12. The signal is removed from the useless signal by a low-pass filter made of r11, r12 and two inducement a useful signal and then input to the HT6010 through a RN8027C serial port.

3.2 Display Unit of Smart Meter

The communication between the HT6015 and the LCD display unit BL55077A is carried out through the FC bus. R92, R93 function is to prevent voltage interference. where the LCD drive circuit diagram is shown in figure; where seg0-sef33 is the segment output, como-com3 is the common output, connected to the LCD back pole. LCD display unit schematic as shown in (Fig. 6).

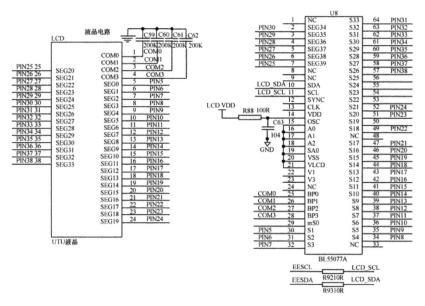

Fig. 6. LCD drive line

3.3 Clock Unit of Smart Meter

The HT6015 integrated hardware RTC module has already mentioned above that the self-contained temperature compensation does not require user software residue in the operating temperature range; the RTC unit provides various functions, including the implementation of clocks, calendars, leap year adjustments, etc., and remains operational at low power consumption with high accuracy.

4   System Hardware Testing

We know from Figs. 7 and 8 that our WIFI module is set up successfully, can send NIHAO to WIFI module from serial port end, WIFI module sends out the data through hot spot way, and then receives the NIHAO. through network debugging assistant. i.e. WIFI module works properly.

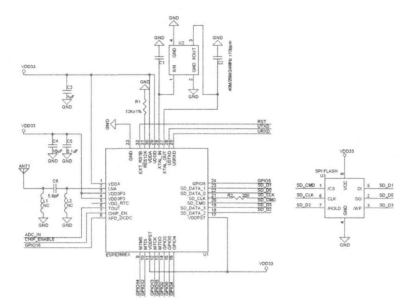

Fig. 7. ESP-07 schematic

Fig. 8. LCD display screen

5 Conclusions

A data acquisition module of intelligent meter based on WIFI is designed in this paper. Through analyzing the detailed data of HT6015 chip and ESP-7 WIFI module, the circuit schematic diagram of this module is designed and the code of related hardware is written, and the design and development of intelligent meter data acquisition module based on WIFI is realized.

References

1. Chen, S.Y., Song, S.F., Lan-Xin, L.I., et al.: Survey on smart grid technology. Power Syst. Technol. **33**(8), 2–5 (2009)
2. Zhe, Yu.: Construction and Evaluation Method of Comprehensive Evaluation Index System of Intelligent Power Cell. North China Electric Power University, Beijing (2012)
3. Yang, Y.: Research on Transmission Network Scheduling Mode Based on Safety Evaluation. North China Electric Power University, Beijing (2012)
4. Fang, X., Misra, S., Xue, G., et al.: Smart grid-the new and Improved power grid; a survey. IEEE Commun. Surv. Tutorials **14**(4), 944–980 (2012)
5. Tian, Rang: Design and Application of Electric Energy Acquisition System. Tianjin University, Tianjin (2014)
6. Ajay Kumar, V.: Overcoming data corruption in RS485 communication. In: International Conference on Electromagnetic Interference and Compatibility. (26), pp. 9–12. IEEE (1995)

Attention-Based Bidirectional Long Short-Term Memory Neural Network for Short Answer Scoring

Linzhong Xia[✉], Mingxiang Guan, Jun Liu, Xuemei Cao, and Dean Luo

Shenzhen Institute of Information Technology, Shenzhen 518172, China
xialz@sziit.edu.cn

Abstract. The automatic short answer scoring by using computational approaches has been considered the best way to release the workload of human answer raters. In this paper, we designed a novel neural network architecture which is attention-based bidirectional long short-term memory to implement the task of automatic short answer scoring. We evaluate our approach on the Kaggle Short Answer dataset (ASAP-SAS). Our experiment results indicate that our model can scoring short answers more accurately in terms of the quality of the results. Meanwhile, our experiment results demonstrate that our model is more effective and efficient than other baseline methods in most cases.

Keywords: Natural language processing · Short answer scoring · Long Short-Term memory · Attention mechanism · Quadratic Weighted Kappa

1 Introduction

The short answer examinations are considered as an essential part in the educational processes. It can help students to check the mastery of problem. But now, there are a large of short answers which are produced by students need to be examined. It is a large workload for human answer raters [1].

To solve above problem, many answer examination computational approaches have been invented. Those approaches are regarded as a machine learning approach, such as classification, or linear regression. Most of machine learning approaches make use of various statistical features, such as total words number, different words number, words spelling errors, average of words syllables, sentences frequency, essay's length, term frequency-inverse document frequency (TF-IDF), and so on. Short answer correction by this type of methods are usually seen as a linear regression problem. The commercial correction systems such as Project Essay Grader (PEG) [2] and E-rater [3] are the typical Representatives. However, the obvious drawback of the PEG and E-rater is that they both can't extract the semantic features of answers.

In order to extract the semantic features from answers, latent semantic analysis (LSA) [4] had been invented. The key idea of LSA is the analysis of the underlying semantic of answers. LSA solves the problem of synonymy or polysemy by mapping the same answers or words into a different space and doing the comparison in the space

M. Guan and Z. Na (Eds.): MLICOM 2020, LNICST 342, pp. 104–112, 2021.
https://doi.org/10.1007/978-3-030-66785-6_12

with the method of Singular Value Decomposition (SVD) of term-essay matrix. In the process of mapping, the high dimensional answer vector will be transformed to low dimensional vector. The commercial correction systems such as intelligent essay assessor (IEA) [5] is the typical Representatives. However, there are some limitations for LSA. First, the computational cost of the SVD is expensive. Second, word order is not taken into consideration in the space representation.

The limitations of LSA had been solved by the approach of probabilistic LSA (pLSA) [6] or latent Dirichlet allocation (LDA) [7]. The different with LSA is that the LDA can capture the exchangeability of both words and answers. LDA is a generative probabilistic model of a corpus. The answers of corpus are represented as random mixtures over latent topics. Each latent topic of answers is characterized by a probabilistic distribution over words and the word distributions of topics share a common Dirichlet prior as well.

In a word, the final representation of an answer consists of a features vector that have been selected and tuned by human experts to assess a score in a marking scale [8]. Although those approaches have achieved performance comparable to human raters, there is essential manual effort involved in obtaining these results on different fields. It is hard to select or tune suitable linguistic features by human experts in specific fields. In order to perform well on specific data, separate models with distinct feature sets are needed.

But now, the most effective approach to solve the problems mentioned above paragraph is the technology of deep neural network (DNN) [9]. And DNN has achieved remarkable advances in the field of automatic answer scoring (AAS). The ability of AAS systems which based on DNN have surpass state-of-the-art models in similar areas [10]. In a sense, answer scoring is like answer classification. In answer classification field, most of the studies are focus on how to learn word vector representations by neural language models [11] and how to classify the answers based on the learned word vectors [12]. Therefore, the basic of answer classification is find a highly efficient word vector representations. At present, the most popular word vector representation models are Word2Vec [13], C&W [14], GloVe [15], and so on. Before starting answer classification, we can use the word vectors which trained on external big dataset [16, 17] or trained on local [18] dataset to represent answers. Then taking the word vectors as the input of DNN models which are used to execute the task of answer classification. There are two types of DNN models for answer classification: recurrent neural network (RNN) and convolutional neural networks (CNN). In recent years, much great results have been achieved in text classification by using RNNs or CNNs [19–22]. CNN is good at handling spatial data but not good at handling sequence data. In contrast of CNN, RNN is good at handling sequence data which makes it a more 'natural' approach when dealing with textual data since answer is naturally sequential. The answer classification can be considered as a sequential modelling problem. Due to the characteristic of RNN, we usually use RNN to process the task of answer classification. However, RNN can capture the correlations of short-term dependencies but the ability to learn the long-term dependencies is weakly. Long short-term memory (LSTM) [23] is a special kind of RNN and it is powerful to learn the correlations of long-term dependencies. Now, LSTM has been widely used in text classification field [24, 25]. Moreover, bidirectional long short-term memory (BiLSTM) [26] can run inputs in two ways, one from past to future and one from future to past. Therefore, you are able in any point in time to preserve information from both past and future by combining the two hidden states [27].

Ideally, we hope to obtain the word vectors which can retain all contextual information of answer. In fact, represent ability of different word vectors which are obtained by training in different datasets is different. Therefore, well-suited dataset is the key point to obtain the powerful word vectors. Google word vector (GWV) which pretrained on roughly 100 billion words from a Google News dataset includes a vocabulary of 3 million words and phrases has advantages over local-trained word vector (LWV) which trained on local dataset in most cases. Although GWV can obtain powerful representation of the contextual information of the essay, it is not possible to focus on the important information in the obtained contextual information. Therefore, attention mechanism (AM) [28, 29] which is used to focus on the important information of the contextual information has been recommended. The combination of GWV and AM can further improve the ability of answer classification.

In this paper, we propose a novel DNN architecture for short answer scoring. This new architecture is an enhanced BiLSTM by using GWV and AM, referred to as attention-based BiLSTM Neural Network with GWV as the input layer (GA-BiLSTM). The rest of this paper is organized as follows. Section 2 presents the related work. Section 3 introduces the propose approach in detail. Section 4 shows the result of the experiment. Section 5 is conclusions.

2   Related Work

The AAS has been pushed into a new stage by the invention of DNN. In recent years, there are many researchers have proposed many approaches to improve DNN. Zhang et al. [30] proposed a deep belief networks (DBN) to tackle the task of AAS. Their experimental results show that DBN is the best model than other models which mentioned in the article. Xiang et al. [31] apply a temporal convolutional network to various large-scale datasets, including ontology classification, sentiment analysis, and text categorization. Their model can achieve astonishing performance without the knowledge of words, phrases, sentences and any other syntactic or semantic. Walia et al. [32] proposed a BiLSTM to achieve an efficient AAS for Punjabi language. Surya K et al. [33] compared some DNN techniques for AAS task. The results show that BERT (bidirectional encoder representations from transformers) performs better than CNN and LSTM.

3   Automatic Short Answer Scoring Model

In this section, we introduce our AAS model as shown in Fig. 1. The designed novel architecture is named attention-based BiLSTM with GWV as the input layer (GA-BiLSTM). The model consists of four components, word embedding layer, BiLSTM, attention layer, as well as Softmax layer.

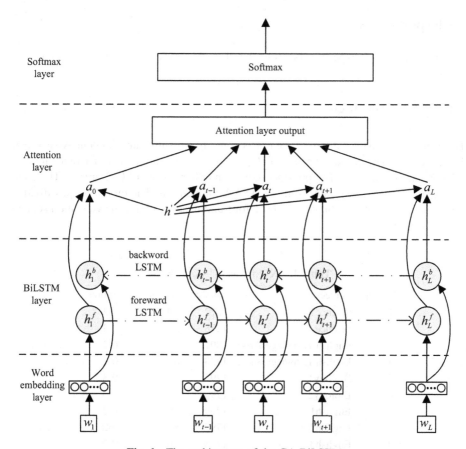

Fig. 1. The architecture of the GA-BiLSTM

The word embedding layer converts words of answer to word vectors and takes them as the input of the BiLSTM layer. In natural language processing field, how to represent words of text is important. Usually, there are two ways to represent words: one-hot representation and distributed representation. Compared to one-hot representation, distributed representation of word embedding not only reflect the characteristics of low dimension but also reflect the orderly relationship between words of text. In this paper, we use the word vector which trained on Google News dataset in experiments.

The BiLSTM layer accesses the contextual features. The contextual features extraction capability of BiLSTM is more powerful than LSTM. Because the BiLSTM can access to both history and future of the given time frame throughout backward and forward layers together.

The Attention layer has been used to pay more attention to information units which strongly related to the score of the answer. Because AM can focus on the important words to reduce the impact of unimportant words. In this paper, we provide an AM layer after the output of BiLSTM to learn a weight combination of hidden states across all time steps and produce a global feature vector.

The Softmax layer is to classify the output of the AM layer.

4 Experiments

In this section, the experiments setup, baseline methods and experiment results are described.

4.1 Experiments Setup

Dataset. In this paper, the used dataset is come from Automated Student Assessment Prize (ASAP). The dataset consists of 10 prompts as listed in Table 1. There are total of 17207 training answers. The prompts scored on either a scale of 0–2 or 0–3. There are no released labeled test data from the ASAP competition. Therefore, we just divided the released dataset into three parts: 60% for training set, 20% for the validation set and 20% for the test set.

Table 1. Description of ASAP dataset

Prompt	Subject	Answers	Avg length	Scores
1	Science1	1672	50	0-3
2	Science2	1278	50	0-3
3	English Language Arts1	1891	50	0-2
4	English Language Arts2	1738	50	0-2
5	Biology1	1795	60	0-3
6	Biology2	1797	50	0-3
7	English1	1799	50	0-2
8	English2	1799	50	0-2
9	English3	1798	40	0-2
10	Science3	1640	60	0-2

Evaluation Metrics. In our experiment, we use Quadratic Weighted (QW) Kappa to evaluate our results. At the same, the QW Kappa is also used in ASAP competition. The QW Kappa is an index to measure the agreement between the raters. The result of QW Kappa equal to 1 when the scores of raters are identical. The result of QW Kappa equal to 0 when the scores of raters are totally inconsistent.

Parameter Settings. We adopt the Adam optimizer as the optimization algorithm. The best hyper-parameters obtained through multiple experiments are shown in Table 2. The initial learning rate is set to 0.01. The learning rate is reduced by 0.05 times once every 1 epoch.

Table 2. The hyper-parameter settings

Layer	Parameter Name	Value
Word Embedding	GWV dimension	300
BiLSTM layer	Hidden units	128
Dropout	Dropout rate	0.5
Others	Epochs	30–100
	Batch size	32
	Initial learning rate	0.01

4.2 Baselines

We use several baseline methods as the benchmarks, they are effective methods for AAS. CNN: the approach uses a CNN to score the student answers [33]. BiLSTM: the approach uses a BiLSTM to score the student answers [33]. BERT: the approach uses a BERT to score the student answers [33]. We name our model described in Sect. 3 as GA-BiLSTM. The results of those baseline models are listed in Table 3.

Table 3. Experiment results of all compared models on the ASAP dataset. Best result is in bold.

Model	Prompts										Aver.
	1	2	3	4	5	6	7	8	9	10	
CNN	0.68	0.67	0.27	0.55	0.75	0.74	0.58	0.50	0.64	0.67	0.61
BiLSTM	0.70	0.66	0.28	0.59	0.78	0.74	0.60	0.54	0.70	0.71	0.63
BERT	0.79	0.70	0.37	0.69	0.75	0.84	0.66	0.60	0.80	0.74	0.69
GA-BiLSTM	0.81	0.71	0.47	0.67	0.79	0.85	0.61	0.58	0.78	0.76	0.70

4.3 Results

The comparison results are presented in Table 3. The experiment results are evaluated by QWK. The font which is bold presents the best experiment results as the Table 3 shown. All approaches, including our approach, are deep neural network approaches. In Table 3, we can find that our approach of GA-BiLSTM has achieved the best result than other approaches on the average QWK value. Among the four approaches mentioned in Table 3, our approach outperforms other baseline models on all prompts except prompt4, prompt7, prompt8, and prompt9. The results of GA-BiLSTM are 0.81, 0.71, 0.47, 0.79, 0.85, and 0.76 for prompt1, prompt2, prompt3, prompt5, prompt6, and prompt10. Compared to BERT, the QWK value of GA-BiLSTM obtains the relative improvements of 2.5%, 1%, 27%, 5.3%, 1.2%, 2.7%, respectively. In a word, the results of our model outperform most of the published baseline models. In Table 3, we can conclude that the overall performance of GA-BiLSTM is better than other approaches in term of the average QWK value.

As the results show, the combination of GWV, BiLSTM architecture and attention mechanism has remarkably improved the performance of AAS. For most of the benchmark prompts, GA-BiLSTM can obtain better results than other baseline models. And GA-BiLSTM obtains the best result for the average QWK value.

5   Conclusions

In this paper, we augmented the input by using GWV as the representation of the contextual information of answers. It is expected to learn more key information of answers by using BiLSTM which can in any point in time to preserve information from both past and future by combining two hidden states. The themes of some prompts of ASAP dataset are clear. To this kind of short answers, the technique of AM is an efficient choice to extract the key themes information. Therefore, word vector, neural network architecture, and the design of classifier are the key point for AAS. Our experiment results indicate that our model can scoring short answers more accurately in terms of the quality of the results. Meanwhile, GA-BiLSTM demonstrates that our model is more effective and efficient than other baseline methods in most cases.

Acknowledgement. This work is supported by Engineering Applications of Artificial Intelligence Technology Laboratory of Shenzhen Institute of Information Technology (Number: PT201701), the Guangdong Province higher vocational colleges & schools Pearl River scholar funded scheme (2016), and The Scientific and Technological Projects of Shenzhen (No. JCYJ20190808093001772).

References

1. Dikli, S.: An overview of automated scoring of essays. J. Technol. Learn. Assess. **5**(1), 1–35 (2006)
2. Page, E.B.: The imminence of grading essays by computer. Phi Delta Kappan **48**, 238–243 (1966)
3. Claudia, L., Martin, C.: C-rater: Automated scoring of short-answer questions. Comput. Humanit. **37**(4), 389–405 (2003)
4. Deerwester, S., Dumais, S.T., Furnas, G.W., Landauer, T.K., Harshman, R.: Indexing by latent semantic analysis. J. Am. Soc. Inf. Sci. **41**(6), 391–407 (1990)
5. Landauer, T., Laham, D., Foltz, P.: Automated scoring and annotation of essays with the intelligent essay assessor. In: Automated Essay Scoring: A Cross-Disciplinary Perspective, pp. 87–112 (2003)
6. Hofmann T.: Probabilistic latent semantic indexing. In: Proceedings of the 22nd Annual International ACM SIGIR Conference on Research and Development in Information Retrieval, pp. 50–57. Association for Computing Machinery ACM, Berkeley (1999)
7. Blei, D.M., Ng, A.Y., Jordan, M.I.: Latent Dirichlet allocation. J. Mach. Learn. Res. **3**, 993–1022 (2003)
8. McNamara, D., Crossley, S.A., Mccarthy, P.M.: Linguistic features of writing quality. Written Commun. **27**(1), 57–86 (2010)

9. Gomaa, W.H., Fahmy, A.A., Ans2vec: a scoring system for short answers. In: Hassanien, A., Azar, A., Gaber, T., Bhatnagar, R., F. Tolba, M. (eds) AMLTA 2019, vol. 821, pp. 586–595. Springer, Cham (2020). https://doi.org/10.1007/978-3-030-14118-9_59

10. Tang, D.: Sentiment-specific representation learning for document-level sentiment analysis. In: Proceedings of the Eighth ACM International Conference on Web Search and Data Mining, pp. 447–452. Association for Computing Machinery (ACM), Shanghai (2015)

11. Pang, B., Lee, L.: Seeing stars: exploiting class relationships for sentiment categorization with respect to rating scales. In: Proceedings of the 43rd Annual Meeting of the Association for Computational Linguistics, pp. 115–124. Association for Computational Linguistics (ACL), Ann Arbor (2005)

12. Lee, K., Han, S., Myaeng, S.-H.: A discourse-aware neural network-based text model for document-level text classification. J. Inf. Sci. **44**(6), 715–735 (2018)

13. Mikolov T., Chen K., Corrado G., Dean J.: Efficient estimation of word representations in vector space. arXiv:1301.3781[cs.CL], 1–12 (2013)

14. Collobert, R., Weston, J., Bottou, L., Karlen, M., Kavukcuoglu, K., Kuksa, P.: Natural language processing (almost) from scratch. J. Mach. Learn. Res. **12**, 2493–2537 (2011)

15. Pennington, J., Socher, R., Manning, C.D.: Glove: global vectors for word representation. In: Proceedings of the 2014 Conference on Empirical Methods in Natural Language Processing, pp. 1532–1543. Association for Computational Linguistics (ACL), Doha (2014)

16. Zhang, H., Litman, D.: Co-attention based neural network for source-dependent essay scoring. In: Proceedings of the Thirteenth Workshop on Innovative Use of NLP for Building Educational Applications, pp. 399–409. Association for Computational Linguistics (ACL), New Orleans (2018)

17. Ali, M.N.A., Tan, G.Z., Hussain, A.: Bidirectional recurrent neural network approach for Arabic named entity recognition. Future Internet **10**(12), 123 (2018)

18. Alikaniotis, D., Yannakoudakis, H., Rei, M.: Automatic text scoring using neural networks. In: Proceedings of the 54th Annual Meeting of the Association for Computational Linguistics, pp. 7–12. Association for Computational Linguistics (ACL), Berlin (2016)

19. Kim, Y.: Convolutional neural networks for sentence classification. In: Proceedings of the Conference on Empirical Methods in Natural Language Processing, pp. 1746–1751. Association for Computational Linguistics (ACL), Doha (2014)

20. Liao, S., Wang, J., Yu, R., Sato, K., Cheng, Z.: CNN for situations understanding based on sentiment analysis of twitter data. In: Proceedings of the 8th International Conference on Advances in Information Technology, Elsevier B.V., pp. 376–381. Macau (2016)

21. Zhang, Y., Wallace, B.C.: A sensitivity analysis of (and practitioners' guide to) convolutional neural networks for sentence classification. arXiv:1510.03820[cs.CL], pp. 1–18 (2016)

22. Zhang, Y., Er, M.J., Venkatesan, R., Wang, N., Pratama, M.: Sentiment classification using comprehensive attention recurrent models. In: Proceedings of the International Joint Conference on Neural Networks, pp. 1562–1569. IEEE, Vancouver (2016)

23. Hochreiter, S., Schmidhuber, J.: Long short-term memory. Neural Comput. **9**(8), 1735–1780 (1997)

24. Ran, X., Shan, Z., Fang, Y., Lin, C.: An LSTM-based method with attention mechanism for travel time prediction. Sensors **19**(4), 861 (2019)

25. Nowak, J., Taspinar, A., Scherer, R.: LSTM recurrent neural networks for short text and sentiment classification. In: Proceedings of the 16th International Conference on Artificial Intelligence and Soft Computing, pp. 553–562. Springer Verlag, Zakopane (2017)

26. Graves, A., Schmidhuber, J.: Framewise phoneme classification with bidirectional LSTM and other neural network architectures. Neural Netw. **18**(5–6), 602–610 (2005)

27. Bin, Y., Yang, Y., Shen, F., Xie, N., Shen, T., Li, X.: Describing video with attention-based bidirectional LSTM. IEEE Trans. Cybern. **49**(7), 2631–2641 (2019)
28. Luong, M.-T., Pham, H., Manning, C.D.: Effective approaches to attention-based neural machine translation. In: Proceedings of Conference on Empirical Methods in Natural Language Processing, pp. 1412–1421. Association for Computational Linguistics (ACL), Lisbon (2015)
29. Yin, W., Ebert, S., Schütze, H.: Attention-based convolutional neural network for machine comprehension. In: Proceedings of the Workshop on Human-Computer Question Answering, pp. 15–21. Association for Computational Linguistics (ACL), San Diego (2016)
30. Zhang, Y., Shah, R., Chi, M.: Deep learning + student modeling + clustering: a recipe for effective automatic short answer grading. In: Proceedings of the 9th International Conference on Educational Data Mining, pp. 562–567. International Educational Data Mining Society (IEDMS), Raleigh (2016)
31. Zhang, X., LeCun, Y.: Text Understanding from Scratch. arXiv:1502.01710 [cs.LG] (2016)
32. Walia, T.S., Josan, G.S., Singh, A.: An efficient automated answer scoring system for Punjabi language. Egyptian Inf. J. **20**, 89–96 (2019)
33. Surya, K., Ekansh, G., Nallakaruppan, K.: Deep learning for short answer scoring. Int. J. Recent Technol. Eng. **7**(6), 1712–1715 (2019)

Automatic Scoring of L2 English Speech Based on DNN Acoustic Models with Lattice-Free MMI

Dean Luo$^{(\boxtimes)}$, Mingxiang Guan, and Linzhong Xia

Shenzhen Institute of Information Technology, Shenzhen, China
luoda@sziit.edu.cn

Abstract. This paper proposed improved automatic scoring methods for L2 English speaking tests based on acoustic models with lattice-free Maximum Mutual Information (MMI). Deep Neural Network (DNN) acoustic modeling with lattice-free MMI is the state-of-the-art technology in speech recognition because of its effectiveness in sequential discriminative training. Novel Goodness of Pronunciation (GOP) implementations based on lattice free MMI were proposed to improve the performance of automatic scoring for L2 English speech tests. Sequential acoustic weights during forced-alignment and posteriors based on Forward-Backward Algorithm with lattice free MMI acoustic models were used to improved GOP based automatic scoring. Experimental results show that our proposed lattice free MMI based methods outperform conventional regular DNN based automatic scoring methods.

Keywords: Automatic scoring · L2 speech evaluation · Goodness of pronunciation · Lattice free MMI · DNN acoustic models

1 Introduction

English speaking tests have been incorporated in high-stake tests such as National College English Test (CET), College Entrance Examination and senior high school entrance examination. It is very time-consuming and labor intense to evaluate L2 speech manually in large-scale tests such as CET. Human raters are usually required to have some expertise in both phonetics and language education. Therefore, it is not practical to assess L2 speech manually for large-scale tests.

Computer-Aided Language Learning (CALL) based on automatic speech recognition (ASR) has been very active for the past two decades. One application of CALL is automatic scoring based on ASR which uses machine learning algorithms to learn human experts' scoring strategies from features extracted with speech processing [1–5].

Dramatic improvements have been reported with ASR based on Deep Neural Networks (DNN) in recent years [6, 7]. Since 2011, we have been working on improvements of automatic scoring methods for English speaking tests [8–10]. In this paper, we proposed two novel implementations of Goodness of Pronunciation scores to better utilize criminative training power of lattice free MMI based DNN acoustic

M. Guan and Z. Na (Eds.): MLICOM 2020, LNICST 342, pp. 113–122, 2021.
https://doi.org/10.1007/978-3-030-66785-6_13

models. Experimental results show that our proposed methods outperform conventional DNN approaches for automatic scoring in high-state English speaking tests.

2 Automatic Scoring for L2 Speech

2.1 Goodness of Pronunciation

The Goodness of Pronunciation (GOP), which is defined as phone level confident sore extracted for ASR, is often used for evaluate learners' pronunciation and often used for automatic scoring [11]. The GOP score can be defined as the following,

$$
\begin{aligned}
\text{GOP}(p) &= \log(\text{p}(p|\mathbf{o})) \\
&\approx \log \frac{\text{p}(\mathbf{o}|p)\text{p}(p)}{\max\{q \in Q\}p(\mathbf{o}|q)p(q)} \\
&\approx \log \frac{\text{p}(\mathbf{o}|p)}{\max\{q \in Q\}\text{p}(\mathbf{o}|q)}
\end{aligned}
\tag{1}
$$

where the probability $\text{p}(p|\mathbf{o})$ is the posterior of phoneme p given speech segment feature $\mathbf{o}$, Q represents the whole set of all phonemes. The numerator of Eq. (1) is a likelihood that can be attained with phone-level GMM- HMM forced alignment, and the denominator is the maximum likelihood of any phonemes recognized by HMM with a grammar model generated through a phone-loop grammar network.

2.2 DNN Based GOP Implementation

The most popular DNN based ASR engines usually train a neural network to output HMM state-level probabilities [12]. For state likelihoods, the outputs of DNN are divided by the priors attained through acoustic model training.

For DNN based acoustic models, GOP can be calculated using the average state posteriors, which is usually the softmap output of DNN models [7]:

$$
\text{GOP}(p) = \text{p}(p|t_s, t_e; \mathbf{O}) = \frac{1}{t_e - t_s} \sum_{t_s}^{t_e} \text{p}(s_t|\mathbf{o}_t),
\tag{2}
$$

where $p(s_t|\mathbf{o}_t)$ is the state-level posterior that is attained from the output of DNN, $\mathbf{o}_t$ is the segment of acoustic feature at time t, t_s is the start and t_e are the end time of the acoustic feature of phoneme p, which can be obtained with forced alignment. We refer this baseline definition of DNN based GOP as GOP1.

As mentioned above, with DNN-HMM hybrid acoustic models, the state-level posteriors are converted to state-level quasi-likelihoods by dividing with the priors of the HMM states. Therefore, the numerator and denominator of Eq. (1) can be calculated with forced alignment:

$$P(o|p) \approx \frac{1}{t_e - t_s} \sum_{t_s}^{t_e} p(s_t|o_t)/p(s_t), \tag{4}$$

$$p(o|q) \approx \frac{1}{t_e - t_s} \sum_{t_s}^{t_e} \max\{s_t^* \in S\}(P(s_t^*|o_t)/p(s_t^*)), \tag{5}$$

where S represents the full set of all HMM states also called "senones", $p(s_t)$ the state-level prior of the state at time t with is attained during DNN-HMM acoustic model training. If we apply Eqs. (4) and (5) to Eq. (1), we get another GOP score, and we call it GOP2 hear after. GOP2 is more robust than GOP1, since noises due to acoustic mismatches appear in the numerator and denominator of Eq. (1) . GOP1 and GOP2 are used as baseline automatic scores in this study.

3 Automatic Scoring Based on Lattice Free MMI

3.1 Lattice Free MMI Acoustic Modeling

The objective function for estimating HMM parameters of GMM-HMM or DNN-HMM in speech recognition is define as:

$$F_{ML} = \sum_{r=1}^{R} \log P_\theta(O_r|W_r)P(W_r) \tag{6}$$

$$= \sum_{r=1}^{R} \log \sum_{s \in w_r} \prod_{t=0}^{T_r-1} P(s_{t+1}|s_t)P(O_r(t)|s_t) \tag{7}$$

where θ is the set of HMM parameters, R is the number of all training utterances, O_r is the rth utterance with length T_r, and W_r is all the possible sequences given the transcription.

Maximum Mutual Information (MMI) is can be considered as a discriminative objective function which is used to maximize the probability of the reference transcriptions, while minimizing the probability of all other alternatives:

$$F_{MMI} = \sum_{r=1}^{R} \log \frac{P_\theta(O_r|W_r)P(W_r)}{\sum_{\widehat{W}} P_\theta(O_r|\widehat{W})P(\widehat{W})} \tag{8}$$

$$= \sum_{r=1}^{R} \left[\log P_\theta(O_r|W_r) + logP(W_r) - \log \sum_{\widehat{W}} P_\theta(O_r|\widehat{W})P(\widehat{W}) \right] \tag{9}$$

If we take the gradient with respect to parameter θ:

$$\nabla_\theta F_{MMI}[\theta] = \nabla_\theta \sum_{r=1}^{R} \left[\log P_\theta(O_r|W_r) + log P(W_r) - \log \sum_{\widehat{W}} P_\theta\left(O_r|\widehat{W}\right) P\left(\widehat{W}\right) \right]$$

(10)

Since $log P(W_r)$ is independent of θ, we use $\nabla_\theta log P(W_r) = 0$,

$$\nabla_\theta F_{MMI}[\theta] = \sum_{r=1}^{R} \left[\nabla_\theta \log P_\theta(O_r|W_r) - \nabla_\theta \log \sum_{\widehat{W}} P_\theta\left(O_r|\widehat{W}\right) P\left(\widehat{W}\right) \right]$$ (11)

$$= \sum_{r=1}^{R} \left[\nabla_\theta \log P_\theta(O_r|W_r) - \frac{\sum_{\widehat{W}} P\left(\widehat{W}\right) P_\theta\left(O_r|\widehat{W}\right) \nabla_\theta \log P_\theta\left(O_r|\widehat{W}\right)}{\sum_{\widehat{W}} P_\theta\left(O_r|\widehat{W}\right) P\left(\widehat{W}\right)} \right]$$ (12)

If we define state occupancy probability (word sequence conditioned state posterior) as:

$$\gamma_{rt}(s|W) = \frac{\sum_{s' \in s} P_\theta(O_r, s'|W)}{P_\theta(O_r|W)} = P_{\theta,t}(s|O_r, W)$$ (13)

where s is the state sequence and W is word sequence, our gradient equation becomes,

$$\nabla_\theta F_{MMI}[\theta] = \sum_{r=1}^{R} \sum_{t=1}^{T} \sum_s \nabla_\theta \log P_\theta(O_t|s_t)(\gamma_{rt}(s|W_r)$$

$$- \frac{\sum_{\widehat{W}} P\left(\widehat{W}\right) P_\theta\left(O_r|\widehat{W}\right) \gamma_{rt}\left(s|\widehat{W}\right)}{\sum_{\widehat{W}} P_\theta\left(O_r|\widehat{W}\right) P\left(\widehat{W}\right)} \right)$$ (14)

$$= \sum_{r=1}^{R} \sum_{t=1}^{T} \sum_s \nabla_\theta \log P_\theta(O_t|s_t)(\gamma_{rt}(s|W_r) - \gamma_{rt}(s))$$ (15)

where $\gamma_{rt}(s)$ is the general state posterior and computed by Forward-Backward algorithm with denominator graph of the lattice free MMI models, $\log P_\theta(O_t|s_t)$ can be obtain through neural network output, and $\gamma_{rt}(s|W_r)$ can be calculate with numerator graph of LF-MMI models.

Povey et al. [13] used MMI training for lattice free MMI models using a full denominator graph using a phone-level language model instead of a word-level language model for the denominator graph. The conducted the denominator computation on GPU instead of CPU. The phone-level language model for the denominator graph was a pruned n-gram language model trained with the phone-level alignments of the training transcription. Also, the numerator graph doesn't use the composite HMM and instead uses a special acyclic which could better utilize the alignment information from previous acoustic models. The numerator graph of the regular Lattice-free MMI method can be considered as an expanded version of the composite HMM. The amount of the self-loops expansion for each utterance is determined by the alignment (i.e. there are no self-loops).

3.2   Forward-Backward Algorithm

Forward-Backward (FB) algorithm is widely used to calculate state occupancy probabilities for HMM parameter estimation. $\gamma_{rt}(s|W_r)$ and are calculated through Forward-Backward algorithm with numerator and denominator graphs.

The forward probability of FB algorithm is the joint probability of observing first t speech vectors and being in state j at time t, given some model M:

$$\alpha_j(t) = P(o_1, \ldots, o_t, s_t = j|M). \tag{16}$$

It can be efficiently calculated by the following recursion

$$\alpha_j(t) = \left[\sum_{i=2}^{N-1} \alpha_i(t-1)a_{ij} \right] b_j(b_j(o_t)) \tag{17}$$

where a_{ij} is transition probability from state i to j, $b_j(o_t)$ is the probability density of speech vector o_t being generated from state j, and N is the total number of states.

The initial conditions for the above recursion are

$$\alpha_1(1) = 1 \tag{18}$$

$$\alpha_j(1) = a_{1j}b_j(o_1) \tag{19}$$

for $1 < j < N$ and the final condition is given by

$$\alpha_N(T) = \sum_{i=2}^{N-1} \alpha_i(T)a_{iN}. \tag{20}$$

From the definition of forward probability, $\alpha_N(T)$ is the total likelihood P(O|M), i.e.,

$$P(O|M) = \alpha_N(T) \tag{21}$$

The backward probability is defined as

$$\beta_j(t) = P(o_{t+1}, \ldots, o_T|s_t = j, M), \tag{22}$$

and can be computed with the following recursion

$$\beta_j(t) = \sum_{i=2}^{N-1} a_{ij}b_j(o_{t+1})\beta_j(t+1) \tag{23}$$

The initial condition is given by

$$\beta_j(T) = a_{iN} \tag{24}$$

and for $1 < j < N$ and the final condition is given by

$$\beta_1(1) = \sum_{i=2}^{N-1} a_{1j}b_j(o_1)\beta_j(1). \tag{25}$$

By the definitions of the forward and backward probabilities, if we take the product of the two,

$$\alpha_j(t)\beta_j(t) = P(O, s_t = j|M) \tag{26}$$

The state occupation probability in Eq. (13) becomes,

$$P_{\theta,t}(s|O_r, W) = P(s_t = j|O_r, M) \tag{27}$$

$$= \frac{P(O, s_t = j|M)}{P(O|M)} \tag{28}$$

Substituting Eq. (26) and (21) into Eq. (28) gives:

$$P_{\theta,t}(s|O_r, W) = \frac{\alpha_j(t)\beta_j(t)}{\alpha_N(T)} \tag{29}$$

This demonstrates that state occupation probabilities used for lattice free MMI training can be computed through Forward-Backward algorithm with numerator and denominator graphs.

3.3   GOP Scores Based on Lattice Free MMI

As described in Sects. 3.1 and 3.2, the LF MMI training of DNN-HMM models is compute word conditioned probability which is defined as state occupancy probability given the word sequences using numerator graph, and general state prior calculated though denominator graph with all possible sequences in training data.

To fully utilize the discriminative power of LF-MMI, we implemented two novel GOP scores that can corporate sequential information through LF-MMI. First use word conditioned probability $P_{\theta,t}(s|O_r, W)$ at frame level through forced alignment to substitute DNN out puts $p(s_t|o_t)$ as used in Eq. (2). Capered with the no-linearity characteristics of DNN outputs, conditioned probability $P_{\theta,t}(s|O_r, W)$ incorporates transition probabilities a_{ij} and sequential information W pertaining to transcription which is very suitable for pronunciation assessment of reading-aloud. Therefore, our first implementation of LF-MMI GOP score is given by

$$\text{GOP\_weight}(p) = \text{p}(\text{p}|t_s, t_e; \boldsymbol{O}, \boldsymbol{W}) = \frac{1}{t_e - t_s} \sum_{t_s}^{t_e} P_{\theta,t}(s|O_r, W) \tag{30}$$

Where W can be viewed as the word sequence from transcription. We call this implementation GOP weight, because the word sequenced conditioned probability $P_{\theta,t}(s|O_r, W)$ can be interpreted as state posterior weights during forced alignment.

During the LF-MMI training, the gradient of the denominator of objective function is given by general state posterior $\gamma_{rt}(s)$ which is not dependent of the transcription of a specific utterance. However, $\gamma_{rt}(s)$ is computed with denominator graphs that incorporates all possible sequences in training data. With the success of LF-MMI models in speech recognition, we considered that $\gamma_{rt}(s)$ computed with denominator graph of a LF-MMI model can effectively general sequential information and thus $\gamma_{rt}(s)$ is a reliable state posterior to evaluate pronunciation. As the same with GOP-weight, we substitute $p(s_t|o_t)$ used in Eq. (2) with $\gamma_{rt}(s)$. We call this implementation of GOP as GOP_FB, as it is computed through Forward-Backward algorithm with denominator graph of LF-MMI acoustic models.

$$\text{GOP\_FB}(p) = \text{p}(\text{p}|t_s, t_e; \boldsymbol{O}, \boldsymbol{W}) = \frac{1}{t_e - t_s} \sum_{t_s}^{t_e} \gamma_{rt}(s) \tag{31}$$

As $\gamma_{rt}(s)$ is independent of specific transcripts of a given utterance, GOP-FB can be used for general pronunciation evaluation purposes, not only for reading-aloud, but also other more open task such as retelling or spontaneous conversations.

4 Experiments

4.1 Speech Data and Reference Scores

For our evaluation experiments, we used the L2 speech corpus of Shenzhen High Schools English Speaking Test. We only used the reading-aloud part of the test, in with students are presented with a one-minute long video and required to read out the subtitle of the video. The recordings of this reading-aloud speech used for our automatic scoring experiments.

All together we used 600 senteces uttered by 600 students, including 300 male and 300 female students with various levels of overall proficiency (beginners, intermedium learners and advanced learners). There are 200 learners in each proficiency group.

Three experts were recruited to manually evaluate students' speech and give an overall proficiency score for each utterance. The assessment standard is shown in Table 1.

Table 1. Assessment standard

Score	Scoring standards
5	Fluent and native-like in pronunciation and intonation without any mistakes
4	Fluent and intelligible with minor unnaturalness in pronunciation or intonation. Very few linguistic or phonetic mistakes
3	Have some errors in pronunciation or unnaturalness in intonation, but most part of the speech is intelligible
2	Large amount of pronunciation errors and unnatural intonation, but parts of the speech is still intelligible
1	Severe errors in pronunciation and most part of the speech is unintelligible
0	Completely unintelligible, silence or speaking something unrelated to presented subtitle text

4.2   Acoustic Models

Both conventional DNN-HMM and lattice free MMI models were used for computing different GOP scores. The acoustic models are trained using the Kaldi toolkit [14]. The DNN based models were trained on Librispeech corpus [15].

The acoustic features we used for training monophone and triphone models is mel-frequency cepstral coefficients or MFCCs and their delta and double deltas. The 40-dimensional features are then transformed with Linear Discriminant Analysis (LDA) and Maximum Likelihood Linear Transform (MLLT). For DNN training, we used time-delay feedforward neural networks with 6 layers. The p of p-norm activations is set to be 2 and the dimensions of the input and output are set to be 2000 and 250 respectively. The initial learning rate is set to 0.005, which was the reduced exponentially to a tenth of the original rate. The number of epochs is set to be 8. The lattice free MMI setups are the same as in [13].

4.3   Experimental Results and Analysis

As mentioned in Sect. 3.2, GOP-weight and GOP-FB were computed based on lattice free MII models. For comparison, we also calculated baseline GOP scores, GOP1 and GOP2 based on conventional DNN-HMM models as described in Sect. 3.1.

The correlations between different automatic scores are shown in Table 2. GOP-weight and GOP-FB show significant improvements over baseline GOP1 and GOP2.

Table 2. Correlations between automatic scores and reference scores

GOP1	GOP2	GOP-weight	GOP-FB
0.72	0.75	0.82	0.81

We further investigate the performances of these scores on different groups of students with beginner, intermediate and advanced proficiency levels. As shown in Table 3, the proposed GOP-weight and GOP-FB outperform GOP1 and GOP2 on data in every proficiency group. GOP-weight shows higher performance with advanced intermediate learners than GOP-FB while GOP-FB performs better with beginners. We used linear regression models to combine to combine GOP-FB and GOP-weight with leave-one-out cross verification and yielded the best performance of 0.85 over all the data.

Table 3. Correlations between automatic scores and reference scores with different groups of learners

Proficiency	GOP1	GOP2	GOP-weight	GOP-FB
Beginner	0.51	0.58	0.62	**0.65**
Intermediate	0.43	0.49	**0.54**	0.52
Advanced	0.42	0.50	**0.59**	0.56

5 Conclusion

Two novel implementations of Goodness of Pronunciation (GOP) based on lattice free MMI were proposed to improve automatic scoring of L2 English speech. Experimental results show that by incorporating sequential information of speech, significant improvements have been found over the conventional GOP based automatic scoring methods based on DNN-HMM acoustic models within the Maximum Likelihood criterion. Future work includes combine different features to further improve robustness of automatic scoring.

References

1. Tsubota, Y., et al.: Practical use of english pronunciation system for Japanese students in the CALL classroom. In: Proceedings of ICSLP 2004, pp. 1689–1692 (2004)
2. Zhang, et al.: Generalized segment posterior probability for automatic Mandarin pronunciation evaluation. In: Proceedings of the ICASSP, pp. 201–204 (2007)
3. Neri, A., et al.: Automatic Speech Recognition for second language learning: How and why it actually works. In: Proceedings of International Congresses of Phonetic Sciences, pp. 1157–1160 (2003)
4. Cardenoso-Payo, V., et al.: Assessment of Non-native Prosody for Spanish as L2 using quantitative scores. In: Proceedings of LREC, pp. 3967–3972 (2014)
5. Luo, D., et al.: Automatic pronunciation evaluation of lan-guage learners' utterances generated through shadowing. In: Proceedings of the INTERSPEECH, pp. 2807–2810 (2008)
6. Dahl, G.E.,. et al.: Large-vocabulary continuous speech recognition with context-dependent DBN-HMMs. In: Proceedings of the ICASSP (2011)
7. Hu, W., et al.: A new DNN-based high quality pronunciation evaluation for computer-aided language learning (CALL). In: Proceedings of the INTERSPEECH 2012, pp. 1886–1890 (2012)

8. Luo, D., et al.: Improvement of segmental mispronunciation detection with prior knowledge extracted from large L2 speech corpus. In: Proceedings of the INTERSPEECH 2011, pp. 1593–1596 (2011)
9. Luo, D., et al.: Naturalness judgement of L2 english through dubbing practice. In: Proceedings of the INTERSPEECH (2016)
10. Luo, D., et al.: Factorized deep neural network adaptation for automatic scoring of L2 speech in english speaking tests. In: Proceedings of INTERSPEECH 2018, pp. 1656–1660 (2018)
11. Witt, S.M., Young, S.J.: Phone-level pronunciation scoring and assessment for interactive language learning. Speech Commun. **30**(2–3), 95–108 (2000)
12. Dahl, G.E., et al.: Context-Dependent pre-trained deep neural networks for large-vocabulary speech recognition. IEE Trans. Audio, Speech Lang. Process. **20**(1), 30–42 (2012)
13. Hadian, H., Sameti, H., Povey, D., et al.: End-to-end speech recognition using lattice-free MMI. In:. Conference of the International Speech Communication Association, pp. 12–16 (2018)
14. Povey, D., et al.: The Kaldi speech recognition toolkit. In: Proceedings of the ASRU (2011)
15. Panayotov, V., Chen, G., Povey, D., Khudanpur, S.: Librispeech: an ASR corpus based on public domain audio books. In: 2015 IEEE International Conference on Acoustics, Speech and Signal Processing (ICASSP), pp. 5206–5210 (2015)

Self-organizing Map for Blood Vessel Segmentation of Fundus Images

Jingdan Zhang[1]([✉]), Le Wang[1], Yingjie Cui[1], Lili Guo[1], and Wuhan Jiang[2]

[1] Department of Electronics and Communication, Shenzhen Institute
of Information Technology, Shenzhen 518172, China
zhangjd358@163.com, wangleathit@126.com,
cuiyj@sziit.edu.cn, 723722242@qq.com
[2] Yangyi Road, Longgang District, Shenzhen 518129, China

Abstract. Blood vessel segmentation is a topic of high interest in fundus image analysis. This paper presents a clustering method to segment the blood vessels automatically from the fundus images. Our proposed method integrates with the wavelet transform, the morphological transformation and self-organizing map (SOM). Firstly, we extract a multi-dimensional feature vector of every pixel in the fundus image by wavelet transform and morphological operation. Then, the SOM network is integrated with K-mean method to cluster pixels. Finally, we validate the accuracy of our proposed method on DRIVE database, and compare our proposed method with other methods.

Keywords: Wavelet transform · Fundus images · Self-organizing map

1 Introduction

Detecting, diagnosis and controlling eyes diseases require the precise and real information of the fundus blood vessels structure [1]. Manual detection of the fundus blood vessels is time consuming and difficult, because the fundus image shows low contrast and noise [2]. Automatic segmentation of blood vessels from fundus images can reduce the work of doctors and provide more useful information for the retinal disease diagnosis.

Many methods have been proposed for fundus vessel segmentation, including rule-based method and machine learning methods. The rule-based methods include model-based methods [3–5], kernel-based methods [6, 7], and adaptive thresholding methods [8, 9]. The machine learning method is divided into supervised and unsupervised method. The supervised methods train the classifier with the prior knowledge, including support vector machine, Bayesian classifier and K-nearest neighbor classifier [4, 10, 11]. The unsupervised methods segment blood vessels without any prior knowledge, including fuzzy C-mean method, K-mean algorithm and self-organizing map [12, 13].

M. Guan and Z. Na (Eds.): MLICOM 2020, LNICST 342, pp. 123–128, 2021.
https://doi.org/10.1007/978-3-030-66785-6_14

This paper presents an unsupervised method to segment blood vessels from the fundus images automatically without any prior knowledge. Firstly, we extract a three-dimensional feature vector with wavelet transform and morphological operation in order to improve the accuracy of segmentation. Then, we exploit SOM as our classifier, and cluster the output neurons of SOM with K-mean algorithm.

The rest of our paper is organized as follows. In Sect. 2, we propose our automatic unsupervised method for fundus image segmentation. In Sect. 3, we presents the experimental results, and we give the conclusions in Sect. 4.

2   Our Proposed Unsupervised Segmentation Method

2.1   Multi-dimensional Feature Extraction

Because there are some problems in fundus image acquisition, such as poor contrast and high variability [14], the segmentation results based on simple pixel intensities are not accurate. Therefore, a three-dimensional feature vector of each pixel is constructed from the fundus image to improve the accuracy of segmentation.

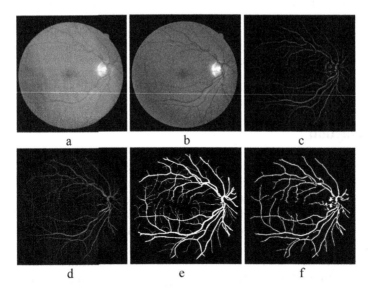

Fig. 1. The feature extraction from a fundus image. (a) The RGB fundus image. (b) The image in the green channel. (c) The high-frequency db4 wavelet image with scale two, three and four. (d) The enhancement image with morphological transformation. (e) The ground truth segmented by the first specialist. (f) Our segmentation result with the unsupervised method.

The image in the green channel of RGB fundus image has better vascular-background contrast than the images in the red channel and blue channel [10, 14]. Therefore, the intensity of green channel is taken as the intensity feature of each pixel. Figure 1(a) is a RGB fundus image from DRIVE database, and Fig. 1(b) is the image in the green channel of Fig. 1(a).

Fundus images often show noise and poor contrast [14]. Wavelet method can decompose the fundus image into different orientations and scales. We extract the wavelet feature from the high-frequency subbands of db4 wavelet transform with scale two, three and four. The high-frequency wavelet image with scale two, three and four of Fig. 1(b) is shown in Fig. 1(c).

For removing the background lightening variations in the fundus image, we exploit the shade-correction method [13] in our paper. But the shade-correction processing deteriorates the contrast between background and blood vessels. Therefore, we apply the morphological top-hat transformation on the complementary image after the shade-correction processing. Figure 1(d) is the enhancement image with morphological top-hat transformation.

Therefore, we extract a three-dimensional feature vector for the fundus image pixels with the image in the green channel, the high-frequency features of the wavelet transform and vessel enhancement feature by morphological transformation.

2.2 Segmentation Method Based on Unsupervised Neutral Network

Self-organizing map proposed by Kohonen [15] is a two-layer feedforward competitive learning neural network. During training process, it can cluster the training data to the same neuron or neighboring neuron in one or two dimensional space without any prior knowledge. Therefore, SOM is widely used as an unsupervised neural network in automatic medical image segmentation [10]. In this paper, we use SOM network for pixel clustering.

In our experiment, SOM has one input layer and one output layer. The SOM with only two neurons in the output layer can't accurately segment the small and thin blood vessels from the fundus image. So, the output layer is a 4×4 array consisted by 16 neurons in our experiments, where every output neuron i has a weight vector w_i.

In the training step t, we randomly select the input pixel p from the fundus image I, and calculate the distance $d_{v_p,i}(t)$ between the weight of output neuron i and the input feature vector v_p. The neuron c whose weight vector is closest to the input feature vector v_p is selected as the winning neuron.

Then, we update the neurons' weight in the neighborhood of neuron c with the equation $w_i(t+1) = w_i(t) + \alpha(t)N_t(c,i)(v_p(t) - w_i) \forall i \in N_c, p \in I$, where

- N_c is the set of neighboring neurons of neuron c, and its neighborhood radius decreases with time t.
- $N_t(c,i)$ is the activation function in the neighborhood of winning neuron c at time t, representing the activation degree of neuron i. In our experiment, we exploit Gaussian function as the neighborhood activation function

$$N_t(c,i) = \exp(-\frac{\|r_i - r_c\|^2}{2N_c^2(t)})$$

where r_i is the coordinate of neuron i in the output layer, and $N_c(t)$ is the neighborhood radius of winning neuron c at time t.

- The parameter $\alpha(t)$ is the learning rate, and it monotonically decreases with time [15, 16].

After the training process of SOM, K-mean method is exploited to determine the class of output neurons, which labels the neurons' class according to the distance from each other. At last, we input the pixel feature vector of the testing fundus image into the trained SOM and get the final segmentation result. Our segmentation result of Fig. 1(a) is shown in Fig. 1(f), and the ground truth shown in Fig. 1(e).

3   Experimental Results

The DRIVE database [17] is a public database with the color fundus images with size 565×584. Researchers often use it to verify their segmentation methods. In addition, the DRIVE database has also provided two sets of results manually partitioned by two specialists as the ground truth. In our experiments, the DRIVE database is used and the segmentation results by the first specialist are exploited as the ground truth. Accuracy index is exploited in our experiments to quantify the overlap between the ground truth and our segmentation results.

Table 1. Comparing the segmentation results of our proposed method with the other methods on the DRIVE database in terms of the average accuracy value.

Method type	Method	DRIVE
Rule-based method	Martinez Perez et al. [18]	0.934
Model-based method	Jiang X. et al. [8]	0.891
Matched filter	Chaudhuri S. et al. [19]	0.877
	Cinsdikici M. G. et al. [20]	0.929
Supervised method	Niemeijer M. et al. [21]	0.941
Unsupervised method	Our proposed method	0.935

For comparing our proposed method with other segmentation methods, we use the average accuracy value as a measure of method performance. In our experiments, the average accuracy value of our proposed unsupervised method is 0.935. The DRIVE database has provided the segmentation results with the methods proposed by Jiang X. et al. [8], Martinez Parez et al. [18], Cinsdikici M. G. et al. [20], Chaudhuri S. et al. [19] and Niemeijer M. et al. [21]. We compare the segmentation results of our proposed method with other methods mentioned above, and list the comparison results in Table 1. Table 1 shows that our proposed method is superior to most other methods.

4 Conclusions

Our study proposes a blood vessel segmentation method based on the unsupervised neural network. Firstly, we extract the input feature vector with the wavelet transform and the morphological operation, which improves the segmentation results. Then, we cluster the pixels in the fundus image with SOM method, and classify the output neurons as vessel class or non-vessel class with K-mean method. All the processing mentioned above is automatic, and does not need any prior knowledge.

We validate the accuracy of our proposed method on DRIVE database. The experimental results indicate that our proposed method achieves good results in fundus image segmentation. Moreover, we also compare the segmentation results of our proposed method with other segmentation methods, and the experimental results show that our proposed method is superior to most other methods.

References

1. Hajabdollahi, M., Esfandiarpoor, R., Soroushmehr, S.M.R., Karimi, N., Samavi, S., Najarian, K.: Low complexity convolutional neural network for vessel segmentation in portable retinal diagnostic devices. Comput. Vis. Pattern Recogn. **2**, 1–5 (2018)
2. Bekkers, E., Duits, R., Berendschot, T., Terhaarromeny, B.: A multi-orientation analysis approach to retinal vessel tracking. J. Math. Imaging Vis. **49**, 583–610 (2014)
3. Lam, B., Yan, H.: A novel vessel segmentation algorithm for pathological retina images based on the divergence of vector fields. IEEE Trans. Med. Imaging **27**(2), 237–246 (2008)
4. Al-Diri, B., Hunter, A., Steel, D.: An active contour model for segmenting and measuring retinal vessels. IEEE Trans. Med. Imaging **28**, 1488–1497 (2009)
5. Dizdaroglu, B., Ataer-cansizoglu, E., Kalpathy-cramer, J., Keck, K., Chiang, M.F., Erdogmus, D.: Level sets for retinal vasculature segmentation using seeds from ridges and edges from phase maps. In: IEEE International Workshop on Machine Learning for Signal Processing (2012)
6. Zhang, Y., Hsu, W., Lee, M.L.: Detection of retinal blood vessels based on nonlinear projections. J. Signal Process. Syst. **55**, 103 (2008)
7. Zhang, B., Lin, Z., Lei, Z., Karray, F.: Retinal vessel extraction by matched filter with first-order Derivative of Gaussian. Comput. Biol. Med. **40**(4), 438–445 (2010)
8. Jiang, X., Mojon, D.: Adaptive local thresholding by Verification-based multithreshold Probing with application to Vessel detection in retinal images. IEEE Trans. Pattern Anal. Mach. Intell. **25**(1), 131–137 (2003)
9. Christodoulidis, A., Hurtut, T., Tahar, H.B., Cheriet, F.: A multi-scale tensor voting approach for small retinal vessel segmentation in high resolution fundus images. Comput. Med. Imaging Graph. **52**, 28–43 (2016)
10. Marin, D., Aquino, A., Gegundez-Arias, M.E., Bravo, J.M.: A new supervised method for blood vessel segmentation in retinal images by using gray-level and moment invariants-based features. IEEE Trans. Med. Imaging **30**, 146–158 (2011)
11. Soares, J.V.B., Leandro, J.J.G., Cesar, R.M., Jelinek, H.F., Cree, M.J.: Retinal vessel segmentation using the 2-D gabor wavelet and supervised classification. IEEE Trans. Med. Imaging **25**(9), 1214–1222 (2006)

12. Kande, G.B., Savithri, T.S., Subbaiah, P.V.: Segmentation of vessels in fundus images using spatially weighted fuzzy C-means clustering algorithm. Int. J. Comput. Sci. Network Secur. **7**, 102–109 (2007)

13. Niemeijer, M., van Ginneken, B., Staal, J.J., Suttorp-Schulten, M.S.A., Abramoff, M.D.: Automatic detection of red lesions in digital color fundus photographs. IEEE Trans. Med. Imaging **24**, 584–592 (2005)

14. Roychowdhury, S., Koozekanani, D.D., Parhi, K.K.: Blood vessel segmentation of fundus images by major vessel extraction and sub-image classification. IEEE J. Biomed. Health Inf. **99** (2014). https://doi.org/10.1109/jbhi.2014.2335617

15. Kohonen, T.: The self-organizing maps. Proc. IEEE **78**, 1464–1480 (1990)

16. Kohonen, T.: Self-Organizing Maps. Springer, New York (1995)

17. Staal, J., Abramoff, M.D., Niemeijer, M., Viergever, M.A., Ginneken, B.: Ridge-based vessel segmentation in color images of the retina. IEEE Trans. Med. Imaging **23**, 501–509 (2004)

18. Marinez Perez, M.E., Hughes, A.D., Thom, S.A., Bharath, A.A., Parker, K.H.: Segmentation of blood vessels from red-free and fluorescein retinal images. Med. Imaging Anal. **11**, 47–61 (2007)

19. Chaudhuri, S., Chatterjee, S., Katz, N., Nelson, M., Goldbaum, M.: Detection of blood vessels in retinal images using two-dimensional matched filters. IEEE Trans. Med. Imaging **8**(3), 263–269 (1989)

20. Cinsdikici, M.G., Aydin, D.: Detection of blood vessels in ophthalmoscope images using MF/ant (matched filter/ant colony) algorithm. Comput. Methods Programs Biomed. **96**, 85–95 (2009)

21. Niemeijer, M., Staal, J., Ginneken, B.V., Loog, M., Abramoff, M.D.: Comparative study of retinal vessel segmentation methods on a new publicly available database. SPIE Med. Imag. **5370**, 648–656 (2004)

Seizure Detection Using Deep Discriminative Multi-set Canonical Correlation Analysis

Xuefeng Bai$^{(\boxtimes)}$, Lijun Yan, and Yang Li

School of Computer, Shenzhen Institute of Information Technology, Shenzhen, China
xuefeng.bai@outlook.com, yanlj@sziit.edu.cn, yangzai1529@163.com

Abstract. Due to the nonlinear and nonstationary properties in EEG signals, some seizure detection methods tried to decompose EEG signal into nonlinear and nonstationary components and use them for feature extraction. Seizure detection results showed a certain degree of improvement in these approaches. Based on this idea, more signal decomposition methods have been explored. Signal decomposition methods are designed according to different principles, which show different properties of signals. So, it can be more effective using features extracted from different signal decomposition methods. Based on this consideration, a novel method for seizure detection based on feature combination exploiting deep neural network is proposed in this paper. We introduced a discriminative extension of Deep Multi-set Canonical Correlation Analysis (DMCCA) for seizure detection. Features extracted from different decomposed signals are combined by a joint optimization target of discriminative loss and multi-set canonical correlation loss, which is both discriminative and canonical correlated. Preliminary experiments show the proposed method improves seizure detection results in terms of accuracy and AUC.

Keywords: Seizure detection · Deep linear discriminative analysis · Deep Multi-set Canonical Correlation Analysis

1 Introduction

Epilepsy is one of the most common neurological diseases in the world. To recognize a seizure, it is typically necessary for physicians to observe EEG signal of the patient carefully, which is a time consuming process. What's more, it is not realistic for long time duration EEG signals [1]. Thus, there is an urgent need for automatic detection of seizure.

Thanks to the development of signal processing and machine learning, various seizure detection methods have been proposed [2,3]. In the early, Fourier

This research is supported by Young Innovative Talents Project of 2018 Guangdong University's key scientific research platform and scientific research project, project number: 2018GkQNCX087.

M. Guan and Z. Na (Eds.): MLICOM 2020, LNICST 342, pp. 129–136, 2021.
https://doi.org/10.1007/978-3-030-66785-6_15

transform based spectral features are introduced to classify seizures and positive results are obtained [4]. As there is not any time-domain characteristic can be obtained using Fourier transform, time-frequency domain features based on short time Fourier transform (STFT) have been exploited [5]. What's more, in order to analyze multi-resolution time-frequency characteristics, wavelet analysis is used to extract features from EEG signal [6]. Wavelet analysis is suitable for stationary signal. However, some researchers have pointed out that frequency of EEG signals may change over a period of time, which indicates it is nonstationary [7]. Thus, new signal processing tool is desired for EEG based seizure detection.

Recently, Empirical Mode Decomposition (EMD) [8] is proposed to decompose EEG signal into intrinsic mode functions (IMFs) and then extracted feature for seizure detection [9]. EMD is an adaptive signal decomposition method that is able to decompose signal into IMFs, which can be handled by Hilbert Transforms [8]. EMD based feature extraction has been applied in lots of seizure detection methods [9–13].

Another adaptive signal decomposition method is Empirical Wavelet Transform (EWT) [14]. In EWT, signal will be decomposed into a fix number of predetermined modes. Compared with EMD, IMFs decomposed by EWT are more consistent. Some researchers have proposed to use EWT for EEG based seizure detection [15,16].

More recently, a new type of adaptive signal decomposition method called Variational Mode Decomposition (VMD) is proposed [17]. In VMD, a signal is decomposed into an ensemble of band-limited intrinsic mode functions. Thanks to the Wiener filtering in the decomposition process, it is more robust to noise. There are also some work using VMD to detect seizure [18,19].

After decomposed by signal process tools mentioned above, various features can be extracted. Although these adaptive decomposition methods are different in principle, the decomposed IMFs are all compact around specific center frequencies and have well-behaved Hilbert transforms [20]. Thus, features related to amplitude, bandwidth modulation, as well as instantaneous phase and amplitude can be calculated.

In addition to exploring new signal process techniques or feature extract methods, making full usage of existing methods may improve classification results. As different signal decomposition methods reflect different aspects of the signal, it can be more effective using features extracted from different signal decomposition methods. According to this consideration, a deep neural network based feature fusion method is proposed in this paper.

The rest of this paper is organized as follows. In Sect. 2, details of the proposed method is presented. In Sect. 3, experimental results are shown and discussed. We conclude this paper at last.

2   Methodology

2.1   Deep Linear Discriminant Analysis (Deep LDA)

As shown in Eq. 1, LDA tries to find a projection matrix $\mathbf{A}$ that maximizes the ratio of between class scatter Σ_{X_b} and within class scatter Σ_{X_w}.

$$\underset{A}{\arg\max} \frac{|\mathbf{A}\Sigma_{X_b}\mathbf{A}^T|}{|\mathbf{A}\Sigma_{X_w}\mathbf{A}^T|} \tag{1}$$

$\mathbf{A}$ is determined by solving a eigenvalue problem $\Sigma_{X_b}\mathbf{e} = \mathbf{v}\Sigma_{X_w}\mathbf{e}$, where $\mathbf{v}$ are eigenvalues. What's more, $\mathbf{v}$ quantifies the interval in direction of eigenvectors and the projection matrix A is the corresponding eigenvector $\mathbf{e}$ of this group.

A drawback of LDA is lack of ability to handle non-linear projection. Although non-linear method such as kernel LDA [21] is proposed, it is still difficult to design a well-adaptive kernel.

DeepLDA is a non-linear extension of LDA using deep neural network [22]. As shown in Fig. 1(a), a LDA loss function is put on top of a deep neural network in DeepLDA, which is able to learn latent representations. With the constrain of LDA loss function, DeepLDA maximize the separation between classes. Optimization target of DeepLDA is set as maximizing k smallest eigenvalues $\{v_1, \ldots, v_k\}$:

$$\underset{\Theta}{\arg\max} \frac{1}{k} \sum_{i=1}^{k} v_i \tag{2}$$

With objective function set as Eq. 2, deep neural network in DeepLDA is optimized to transform features into more discriminative form.

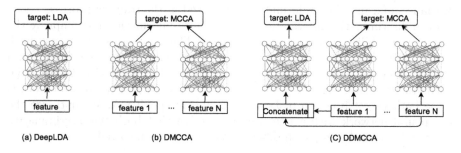

(a) DeepLDA   (b) DMCCA   (C) DDMCCA

Fig. 1. Schematic sketches of nonlinear extension methods based on deep neural network

2.2   Deep Multi-set Canonical Correlation Analysis (DMCCA)

The goal of MCCA is trying to maximize the correlation between multiple data sets, as shown in Eq. 3.

$$\underset{\mathbf{v}_d}{\arg\max} \frac{\mathbf{v}_d^\top \mathbf{R}_B \mathbf{v}_d}{\mathbf{v}_d^\top \mathbf{R}_W \mathbf{v}_d} \tag{3}$$

where $\mathbf{R}_B$ and $\mathbf{R}_w$ is between-set and within-set covariance matrices. MCCA finds projection vectors $\mathbf{v}_d$ by solving a generalized eigenvalue problem:

$$\mathbf{R}_B \mathbf{V} = \mathbf{R}_W \mathbf{V} \mathbf{\Lambda} \tag{4}$$

Generally speaking, nonlinear information in the data sets is not handled. In order to handle these nonlinear information, Deep MCCA is proposed. Deep MCCA is an extension of MCCA [23], which is able to learn nonlinear relationship from features.

As shown in Fig. 1(b), main idea of DMCCA is set multi-set CCA as target function on the top of several deep neural networks, each network deal with a specific modality. Target of DMCCA optimization is shown in Eq. 6

$$\arg\max_{\Theta} \frac{1}{D} \Sigma_{d=1}^{D} \rho_d \tag{5}$$

where ρ_d is the inter-set correlation of N modalities.

With the constrain of this target function, DMCCA handles nonlinear transformations from different modalities when maximizing the ratio of between-modality and within-modality covariance of the input data.

2.3 Deep Discriminative Canonical Correlation Analysis (DDMCCA)

As described above, target of Deep LDA is designed for maximizing the ratio of between class scatter and within class scatter, and discriminative information is involved in the training process. While target of Deep MCCA is designed for maximizing the ratio of between modality covariance and within modality covariance, and modality information is involved in the training process.

Both discriminative information and modality information may improve the classification ability of transformed features. Thus, we proposed to use both discriminative information and modality information when training deep neural network, which is named as Deep Discriminative Multi-set CCA (DDMCCA). Schematic of DDMCCA is shown in Fig. 1(c). Main idea of the present work is to use both target function of Deep LDA and Deep MCCA. We optimize the deep neural network with a joint target function that both the discriminative power and correlation between different modalities are involved:

$$\arg\max_{\Theta} \left\{ \lambda_{LDA} \frac{1}{k} \sum_{i=1}^{k} v_i + \lambda_{MCCA} \frac{1}{D} \Sigma_{d=1}^{D} \rho_d \right\} \tag{6}$$

λ_{LDA} and λ_{MCCA} are weight factors of two target function respectively.

2.4 Feature Extraction and Feature Selection

In order to perform seizure detection using deep neural network based method mentioned above, features should be extracted from IMFs. We extract features from both spectral domain and time domain.

The first extracted feature is Spectral Energy (SE), given by Eq. 7

$$SE = \frac{1}{N} \sum_{f=0}^{\frac{f_s}{2}} P_{XX}(f) \tag{7}$$

where N is the total number of spectral coefficients, P_{XX} is the PSD estimated by Welch's method.

Then Spectral Entropy(SEP) is calculated as in 8

$$SEP = - \sum_{f=0}^{\frac{f_s}{2}} \bar{P}_{XX}(f) \log\left[\bar{P}_{XX}(f)\right] \tag{8}$$

where $\bar{P}_{XX}$ is the normalized PSD.

Main frequency is an important characteristic of signal. Thus, Spectral Peak (SP) of PSD is exploited. Beside this, Spectral Centroid (SC) is also extracted as in Eq. 9

$$SC = \frac{\sum_{f=0}^{\frac{f_s}{2}} \omega(f) M(f)}{\sum_{f=0}^{\frac{f_s}{2}} M(f)} \tag{9}$$

Bandwidth of AM and FM are also extracted as in Eq. 10, where A is the amplitude of the analytic signal, E is the Energy.

$$
\begin{aligned}
B_{AM}^2 &= \frac{1}{E} \int \left(\frac{dA(t)}{dt}\right)^2 dt \\
\langle \omega \rangle &= \frac{1}{E} \int \frac{d\phi(t)}{dt} A^2(t) dt \\
B_{FM}^2 &= \frac{1}{E} \int \left(\frac{d\phi(t)}{dt} - \langle \omega \rangle\right)^2 A^2(t) dt
\end{aligned}
\tag{10}
$$

After that, several time-domain features are extracted such as Hjorth parameters and statistical moments, which are defined as:

$$Mob(x) = \sqrt{\frac{Var\left(\frac{dx(t)}{dt}\right)}{Var(x(t))}} \tag{11}$$

$$Comp(x) = \frac{Mob\left(\frac{dx(t)}{dt}\right)}{Mob(x(t))} \tag{12}$$

$$SK(x) = E\left[\left(\frac{x(t) - \mu}{\sigma}\right)^3\right] \tag{13}$$

$$Std(x) = E\left[\left(\frac{x(t) - \mu}{\sigma}\right)^3\right] \tag{14}$$

3   Experimental Results

We use a publicly available database offered by the University of Bonn [24] to perform experiments. There are 5 subsets in this database: Z, O, N, F, S. In each subset, there are 100 temporal series that is sampled with a frequency of 173.6 Hz and a duration of 23.6 s. The Z and O are collected from 5 health volunteers with eyes open and closed. The N, F, S are collected from epileptic patients. In particular, Set S is sampled during the seizure activity, set F and N are sampled during the seizure-free interval with electrodes placed on the epileptogenic zone and opposite hippocampus. We focus on dealing with the S, F, Z sets, which are corresponding to ictal, interictal and normal category.

Samples of each category is decomposed by EMD, EWT and VMD into 6, 6 and 5 modes respectively, which is the best parameters according to [20]. Then, Deep Multi-set CCA, Deep LDA and Deep Discriminative Multi-set CCA are used to obtain the fused features.

Table 1. Classification AUC of different classification methods.

Methods	KNN	Linear SVM	RBF SVM	GP	NN
EEG	98.05	97.92	99.16	98.97	99.10
EMD	96.60	99.20	99.07	99.20	99.03
VMD	97.93	99.50	99.28	95.72	99.50
EWT	96.80	99.26	99.04	99.33	99.61
DMCCA	99.09	99.84	99.79	99.71	99.80
DeepLDA	97.55	98.00	98.67	95.97	98.53
DDMCCA	99.65	99.95	99.97	99.94	99.94

To evaluate performance of the obtained features, AUC and accuracy are computed using K nearest neighbors (KNN), Linear and RBF SVM, Gaussian Process classification (GP) and neural network classifier (NN). Classification results of AUC are shown in Table 1. With the help of the discriminative loss function, the highest AUC value is obtained by Deep Discriminative MCCA, with slight superior values for other methods.

Accuracy value of these methods are show in Table 2. All of the classification methods provide an accuracy above 90%. In these method, Deep Discriminative MCCA got the best performance.

Table 2. Accuracy of different classification methods.

Methods	KNN	Linear SVM	RBF SVM	GP	NN
EEG	94.67	90.33	92.67	96.00	92.67
EMD	90.00	95.00	94.00	95.33	94.67
VMD	94.00	95.67	96.33	83.00	95.33
EWT	89.00	94.67	93.67	94.67	94.67
DMCCA	95.67	97.33	97.00	96.33	96.00
DeepLDA	92.00	91.00	91.67	34.33	93.67
DDMCCA	97.67	97.67	98.67	98.33	98.00

4   Conclusion

We presented a discriminative extension of Deep MCCA, which is named as Deep Discriminative MCCA (DDMCCA). In this work, we maximize multi-set canonical correlation with a discriminative loss. A public available seizure dataset is used to verify the feasibility of DDMCCA. Features extracted from IMFs of EMD, EWT and VMD are used as the training features of the deep neural networks. Preliminary experiments indicate this method has the potential to improve seizure classification performance.

References

1. Mohseni, H., Maghsoudi, A., Shamsollahi, M.B.: Seizure detection in EEG signals: a comparison of different approaches. In: International Conference of the IEEE Engineering in Medicine and Biology Society, New York, USA, August 2006, pp. 6724–6727 (2006)
2. Sharmila, A., Geethanjali, P.: A review on the pattern detection methods for epilepsy seizure detection from EEG signals. Biomed. Eng. **64**(5), 507–517 (2019)
3. Sharmila, A.: Epilepsy detection from EEG signals: a review. J. Med. Eng. Technol. **42**(5), 368–380 (2018)
4. Srinivasan, V., Eswaran, C., Sriraam, N.: Artificial neural network based epileptic detection using time-domain and frequency-domain features. J. Med. Syst. **29**(6), 647–660 (2005). https://doi.org/10.1007/s10916-005-6133-1
5. Tzallas, A.T., Tsipouras, M.G., Fotiadis, D.I.: Epileptic seizure detection in EEGs using time-frequency analysis. IEEE Trans. Inf. Technol. Biomed. **13**(5), 703–710 (2009)
6. Robinson, N., Vinod, A.P., Ang, K.K., Tee, K.P., Guan, C.: EEG-based classification of fast and slow hand movements using wavelet-CSP algorithm. IEEE Trans. Biomed. Eng. **60**(8), 2123–2132 (2013)
7. Pachori, R.B., Sircar, P.: EEG signal analysis using FB expansion and second-order linear TVAR process. Sig. Process. **88**(2), 415–420 (2008)
8. Long, S.R., et al.: The empirical mode decomposition and the Hilbert spectrum for nonlinear and non-stationary time series analysis. Proc. R. Soc. A Math. Phys. Eng. Sci. **454**(1971), 903–995 (1998)

9. Oweis, R.J., Abdulhay, E.: Seizure classification in EEG signals utilizing Hilbert-Huang transform. Biomed. Eng. Online **10**(1), 38 (2011)

10. Pachori, R.B.: Discrimination between ictal and seizure-free EEG signals using empirical mode decomposition. Res. Lett. Signal Process. **2008**, 14 (2008)

11. Bajaj, V., Pachori, R.B.: Classification of seizure and nonseizure EEG signals using empirical mode decomposition. IEEE Trans. Inf Technol. Biomed. **16**(6), 1135–1142 (2012)

12. Alam, S.M.S., Bhuiyan, M.I.H.: Detection of seizure and epilepsy using higher order statistics in the EMD domain. IEEE J. Biomed. Health Inform. **17**(2), 312–318 (2013)

13. Alickovic, E., Kevric, J., Subasi, A.: Performance evaluation of empirical mode decomposition, discrete wavelet transform, and wavelet packed decomposition for automated epileptic seizure detection and prediction. Biomed. Signal Process. Control **39**, 94–102 (2018)

14. Gilles, J.: Empirical wavelet transform. IEEE Trans. Signal Process. **61**(16), 3999–4010 (2013)

15. Bhattacharyya, A., Sharma, M., Pachori, R.B., Sircar, P., Acharya, U.R.: A novel approach for automated detection of focal EEG signals using empirical wavelet transform. Neural Comput. Appl. **29**(8), 47–57 (2016). https://doi.org/10.1007/s00521-016-2646-4

16. Saxena, S., Hemanth, C., Sangeetha, R.G.: Classification of normal, seizure and seizure-free EEG signals using EMD and EWT. In: 2017 International Conference on Nextgen Electronic Technologies: Silicon to Software, pp. 360–366, March 2017

17. Dragomiretskiy, K., Zosso, D.: Variational mode decomposition. IEEE Trans. Signal Process. **62**(3), 531–544 (2014)

18. Taran, S., Bajaj, V.: Clustering variational mode decomposition for identification of focal EEG signals. IEEE Sens. Lett. **2**(4), 1–4 (2018)

19. Ravi Kumar, M., Srinivasa Rao, Y.: Epileptic seizures classification in EEG signal based on semantic features and variational mode decomposition. Cluster Comput. **22**(6), 13521–13531 (2019)

20. Carvalho, V.R., Moraes, M.F.D., Braga, A.P., Mendes, E.M.A.M.: Evaluating three different adaptive decomposition methods for EEG signal seizure detection and classification. BioRxiv, p. 691055 (2019)

21. Roth, V., Steinhage, V.: Nonlinear discriminant analysis using kernel functions. In: Advances in Neural Information Processing Systems 12, pp. 568–574. MIT Press (2000)

22. Dorfer, M., Kelz, R., Widmer, G.: Deep linear discriminant analysis. In: 4th International Conference on Learning Representations, San Juan, Puerto Rico, 2–4 May 2016 (2016)

23. Somandepalli, K., Kumar, N., Travadi, R., Narayanan, S.: Multimodal representation learning using deep multiset canonical correlation (2019)

24. Andrzejak, R.G., Lehnertz, K., Mormann, F., Rieke, C., David, P., Elger, C.E.: Indications of nonlinear deterministic and finite-dimensional structures in time series of brain electrical activity: dependence on recording region and brain state. Phys. Rev. E **64**(6), 061907 (2001)

The Generation of Virtual Immunohistochemical Staining Images Based on an Improved Cycle-GAN

Shuting Liu[1], Xi Li[2], Aiping Zheng[3], Fan Yang[2], Yiqing Liu[1],
Tian Guan[1(✉)], and Yonghong He[1(✉)]

[1] Graduate School at Shenzhen, Tsinghua University, Beijing, China
{guantian,heyh}@sz.tsinghua.edu.cn
[2] Gastroenterology Department, Peking University Shenzhen Hospital,
Shenzhen, China
[3] Pathology Department, Peking University Shenzhen Hospital,
Shenzhen, China

Abstract. Pathological examination is the gold standard for the diagnosis of cancer. In general, common pathological examinations include hematoxylin-eosin (H&E) staining and immunohistochemistry. H&E staining examination has the advantages of short dyeing duration and low cost, which is the most common one in the clinical practice. However, in some cases, the pathologist is hard to conduct an accurate diagnosis of cancer only according to the H&E staining images. Whereas, the immunohistochemistry examination can further provide enough evidence for the diagnosis process. Hence, the generation of virtual Ki-67 staining sections from H&E staining sections by computer assisted technology will be a good creative solution. Currently, this is still a challenge due to the lack of pixel-level paired data. In this paper, we propose a new method based on Cycle-GAN to generate Ki-67 staining images from the available H&E images, and our method is validated on a neuroendocrine tumor dataset. Massive experiment results show that the addition of skip connection and structural consistency constraint can further improve the performance of Cycle-GAN in unpaired pathological image-to-image transfer tasks. The quantification evaluation demonstrates that our proposed method achieves the state of art and reveals significant potential in clinical virtual staining.

Keywords: Virtual staining · Immunohistochemistry · Cycle-GAN

1 Introduction

As the gold standard for pathological diagnosis, pathological slices have significant application value in clinical and scientific research. The pathologists perform the pathological diagnosis and evaluation through microscopic examination of the pathological section, which is time-consuming and laborious. The digitization of pathological slices is considered to be an important turning point in the development of pathology [1]. The stained slices can be obtained with a full-scale digital image (WSI) through a professional scanner, making the transmission and storage of pathological slices safer and more convenient.

M. Guan and Z. Na (Eds.): MLICOM 2020, LNICST 342, pp. 137–147, 2021.
https://doi.org/10.1007/978-3-030-66785-6_16

Hematoxylin-eosin staining (H&E) is a common pathological examination and is widely used in clinic [2]. It has the advantages of high efficiency and low cost. The cells and tissues components can be clearly identified by the pathologists, and the cancer can be initially diagnosed and graded. However, there still need enough contrast to differentiate some low-grade cancer areas, which can be diagnosed with immuno-histochemistry staining (IHC). IHC is a molecular-level staining [3]. It uses the principle of antigen-antibody binding, and the chemical reaction can bind the chromogen with labeled antibody to intracellular antigen. Meanwhile, the Ki-67 protein is a cellular marker and can be used in IHC, which is a proliferating cell-associated antigen, and can be used for qualitative and quantitative studies of cancer based on its staining results. However, Ki-67 IHC examination takes a long time and has a high cost. Hence, the generation of virtual Ki-67 staining sections from H&E staining sections by computer assisted technology will be a good creative solution.

In recent years, the deep convolution neural networks (DCNN) have received more and more attention in many aspects of medical image analysis, such as X-ray [4], CT [5], PET [6] and MRI [7, 8], which makes better use of contextual information and extracts powerful high-level features. Furthermore, it is also suitable for the analysis and mining of pathological data with large data volume. At present, the application of deep learning in the analysis of pathological slices mainly focuses on three aspects: the segmentation and detection of cells or tissues, the classification of tissue levels, and the classification of cancer grades. However, the most current DCNNs belong to supervised learning, which requires a lot of annotation information. Therefore, artificial intelligence pathological slices analysis has not been applied in clinical practice, and further research is needed.

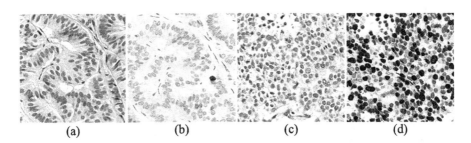

(a)   (b)   (c)   (d)

Fig. 1. Examples of H&E and Ki-67 staining image. (a) and (c) are the H&E staining patches; (b) and (d) are the corresponding Ki-67 staining patches.

Generating virtual Ki-67 staining images from H&E staining images is a challenging task due to three reasons: first, most of the DCNN-based image synthesis methods require a large number of registered image pairs, like Pix2pix, which is infeasible to obtain paired H&E/Ki-67 staining images in clinical practice; second, the image appearance between two different image modalities can be significantly different. For instance, hematoxylin principally stains cell nuclei blue or dark-purple, and eosin stains the extracellular matrix and cytoplasm pink, however, in Ki-67 staining image, Ki-67-positive tumor cells will be stained to be brown, and the Ki-67-negative ones will be colored blue, as shown in Fig. 1; third, the field of view between two different modalities can be different, and some voxels in one modality might not have correspondences in the other modality. At present, most of the available rough paired pathological images stained from two adjacent slices in the same part. In addition, currently there are few rigidly paired HE and IHC images, because the processes of de-staining and re-staining will destroy the original tissue structure of the slice.

In this paper, we explored the potential of deep learning in unpaired image-to-image transformation in the field of histopathological analysis. We propose a new method to generate virtual Ki-67 staining images from H&E staining images. First, we employ the combination of structural similarity constraint and mean squared error constraint as cycle loss to improve the synthesis quality of virtual staining images. Second, the skip connections are added between the encoder and decoder of generators, which provide more texture information under different resolutions for the stain transformation process. In addition, the experimental results demonstrate that our method can achieve better virtual Ki-67 staining image synthesis results both qualitatively and quantitatively compared with Cycle-GAN.

2 Related Work

The generation of virtual Ki-67 staining images is similar to some natural image related tasks like style transfer, image synthesis, image super-resolution. For these tasks, generative adversarial networks (GANs) [9], has gained more and more attention from the researchers. The GAN contains two sub-networks, one is generator and the other is discriminator. Under the specific constraint, the generator is employed to generate fake similar data which then is used to fool the discriminator; the discriminator is trained by both real data and fake similar data, which is employed to differentiate the fake similar data from the real data. The generator and the discriminator compete against each other. Once the discriminator cannot distinguish the authenticity of the image, it means that the generator has learned to model the distribution of the input data appropriately. Not only natural image processing, but GAN is also a pretty hopeful approach for pathological image analysis.

At present, the common GANs include conditional generation adversarial Network (CGAN), Pix2pix and cyclic adversarial network (Cycle-GAN), etc. CGAN is based on the GAN network and adds conditional constraints to the generator and discriminator. The condition can be labels or other modal information [10]. The Pix2pix network can be used to translate pixel-level paired images, which can convert the image's expression while ensuring semantics [11]. The Cycle-GAN can be used to do style transfer between unpaired images, such as horses to zebras, and apples to oranges [12].

In general, most available clinical data is lack of the semantic annotations, and different modality data are not rigidly registered. Hence, Cycle-GAN shows significant potential in clinical pathological image analysis. Currently, stain normalization is the most common uses of Cycle-GAN in pathological image processing. Stain normalization can be also regarded as a basic simple form of staining transfer, which mainly focuses on reducing the staining variance among slides caused by different staining protocols and scanners.

3   Method

Generally, the design idea of GAN is one-way from the perspective of information flow. In the absence of unpaired images, GAN may cause different H&E staining images to be mapped to the same KI-67 staining image. Compared with GAN, Cycle-GAN is one of the state-of-the-art unpaired image synthesis algorithms, which introduces two cycle consistency losses. It contains two generators $G_{HE\text{-}to\text{-}Ki67}$ and $G_{Ki67\text{-}to\text{-}HE}$ and two associated adversarial discriminators D_{HE} and D_{Ki67}.

3.1   Overview

Based on the Cycle-GAN basic concept, our framework, as depicted in Fig. 2, transfer the H&E staining domain to the Ki-67 staining domain, without the need of paired images from both domains. It consists of two generator and discriminator pairs: the first pair ($G_{HE\text{-}to\text{-}Ki67}$ and D_{Ki67}) and the second pair ($G_{Ki67\text{-}to\text{-}HE}$ and D_{HE}). The generator $G_{HE\text{-}to\text{-}Ki67}$ tries to map images from domain H&E to domain Ki-67,

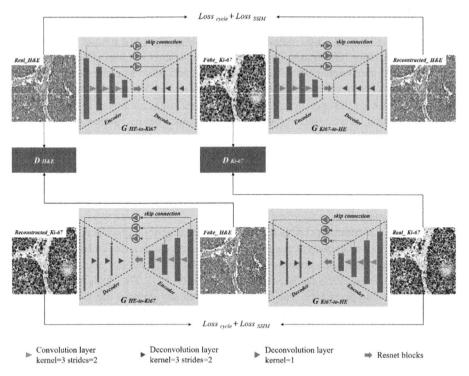

Fig. 2. An overview of our framework. Real H&E gets fake Ki-67 through $G_{HE\text{-}to\text{-}Ki67}$, and then gets reconstructed H&E through $G_{Ki67\text{-}to\text{-}HE}$. Similarly, real Ki-67 gets fake H&E through $G_{Ki67\text{-}to\text{-}HE}$, and then gets reconstructed Ki-67 through $G_{HE\text{-}to\text{-}Ki67}$. There are two discriminators, among which $D_{H\&E}$ can discriminate the authenticity of H&E; D_{Ki67} can discriminate the authenticity of Ki-67.

$G_{HE\text{-}to\text{-}Ki67}$: $S_{HE} \rightarrow S_{Ki67}$; while the generator $G_{Ki67\text{-}to\text{-}HE}$ tries to map images from domain Ki-67 to domain H&E, $G_{Ki67\text{-}to\text{-}HE}$: $S_{Ki67} \rightarrow S_{HE}$. The discriminator D_{Ki67} tries to verify if images come from the real domain Ki-67 or the fake generated ones. Similarly, the discriminator D_{HE} tries to verify if images come from the real domain H&E or the fake generated ones.

In the encoder part of each generator, the staining images with the size of 288 × 288 × 3 is cropped from whole slice image as input. The encoder starts with a convolution with a kernel size of 7 × 7 and stride of 1. In order to maintain the spatial continuity of features, there does not exist any pooling operation, which is instead by the convolution with a stride of 2. It is worth to note that each convolution layer, as shown in Fig. 2, is a series of operations, i.e. convolution with a kernel of 3 × 3, instance normalization, and 'Leaky ReLU' activation layer. Thus, the input image is down-sampled from 288 × 288 to 36 × 36 after three convolutions with the stride of 2. The following part architecture is feature extractor which consists of ten residual convolution blocks, as shown by red arrow in Fig. 2. In the decoder part, it aims to recover the resolution of the feature map from 36 × 36 to 288 × 288, deconvolution with the kernel of 3 × 3 and strider of 2 is adopted to up-sample the feature map. Finally, the virtual staining image is obtained by a 7 × 7 convolution and a 'tanh' activation function. In addition, the skip connections are added between the encoder and decoder at the same resolution, thus more low-level features are integrated into the finally recovered feature map, and the fusion of features of different scales is also achieved in this process.

3.2 Loss Function

The overall optimization function used to train the designed framework includes a combination of adversarial loss, cycle consistency loss and structural cycle consistency loss based on the structural similarity index (SSIM), which is as followed:

$$\mathcal{L} = \mathcal{L}_{adv} + \lambda \mathcal{L}_{cycle} + \beta \mathcal{L}_{ssim}$$

where $\mathcal{L}_{adv}$ is the adversarial loss; $\mathcal{L}_{cycle}$ is the cycle consistency loss, and λ is a regularization parameter for consistency loss; $\mathcal{L}_{ssim}$ is the structural cycle consistency loss, and β is the associated regularization parameter.

Adversarial Loss, is employed to match the distribution of the generated images to that of the target domain, and match the distribution of the generated target domain back to the source domain as $\mathcal{L}_{adv} = \mathcal{L}_{GAN}^{H\&E} + \mathcal{L}_{GAN}^{Ki67}$, where $\mathcal{L}_{GAN}^{H\&E}$ and $\mathcal{L}_{GAN}^{Ki67}$ are defined as

$$\mathcal{L}_{GAN}^{H\&E} = \mathbb{E}_{S_{H\&E} \sim p(S_{H\&E})} [\log D_{H\&E}(S_{H\&E})]$$
$$+ \mathbb{E}_{S_{Ki67} \sim p(S_{Ki67})} [\log (1 - D_{H\&E}(G_{Ki67\text{-}to\text{-}HE}(S_{Ki67})))]$$

and,

$$\mathcal{L}_{GAN}^{Ki67} = \mathbb{E}_{S_{Ki67} \sim p(S_{Ki67})}[\log D_{Ki67}(S_{Ki67})]$$
$$+ \mathbb{E}_{S_{H\&E} \sim p(S_{H\&E})}[\log (1 - D_{Ki67}(G_{HE-to-Ki67}(S_{H\&E})))]$$

Cycle Consistency Loss. To alleviate the lack of ground truth images for the fake images generated in a particular domain, the image is mapped back to its source domain using the reverse mapping function. This loss component ensures that the reconstructed images preserve similar structure as in the source domain. In addition, this loss goes in both directions forward and backward cycles to assure stability, which is given as

$$\mathcal{L}_{cycle} = \mathbb{E}_{S_{Ki67} \sim p(S_{Ki67})}\left[\|G_{HE-to-Ki67}(G_{Ki67-to-HE}(S_{Ki67})) - S_{Ki67}\|_1\right]$$
$$+ \mathbb{E}_{S_{H\&E} \sim p(S_{H\&E})}\left[\|G_{Ki67-to-HE}(G_{HE-to-Ki67}(S_{H\&E})) - S_{H\&E}\|_1\right]$$

Structural Cycle Consistency Loss. In some cases, the reconstructed images are likely to have a distinct color distribution than any of the sub-domains. Therefore, minimizing the L1 distance between the source and the reconstructed images alone is not an effective way to ensure cycle consistency. We introduce the structural cycle consistency loss to our model to regulate the structural changes between the input and output images. This loss is calculated based on the SSIM which has been used for assessing the image quality in many related studies [13]. The SSIM is defined as followed,

$$SSIM(x, y) = \frac{\left(2\mu_x\mu_y + c_1\right)\left(2\sigma_{xy} + c_2\right)}{\left(\mu_x^2 + \mu_y^2 + c_1\right)\left(\sigma_x^2 + \sigma_y^2 + c_2\right)}$$

where μ_x, μ_y are the mean of a fixed window ($N \times N$) centered as the pixel, σ_x, σ_y are the standard derivations, σ_{xy} is the covariance. c_1 and c_2 are stabilizing factors that prevent the denominator from being zero. Hence, the structural cycle consistency loss can be formulated as:

$$\mathcal{L}_{ssim} = 2 - SSIM(G_{HE-to-Ki67}(G_{Ki67-to-HE}(S_{Ki67})), S_{Ki67})$$
$$- SSIM(G_{Ki67-to-HE}(G_{HE-to-Ki67}(S_{H\&E})), S_{H\&E})$$

4   Dataset and Implementation

4.1   Dataset

In this work, our model is validated on a neuroendocrine tumor dataset which is collected from Peking University Shenzhen Hospital. During data collection, two slices were consecutively cut at the same site of each patient for pathological examination, one of which was stained with H&E dyes, and the other was processed with Ki-67 antibody. These slices were saved in the archives of the Department of Pathology, Peking University Shenzhen Hospital. The head of the Department of Pathology approved the use of the samples in this study. The samples were anonymous, and all patient-related data and unique identifiers were deleted. These procedures are carried out under the supervision and approval of the Ethics Committee of Peking University Shenzhen Hospital.

Our experiment dataset consists of 180 pairs H&E and Ki-67 staining images with the size of 6000 × 6000, which are basically similar in tissue structure but not pixel-level matched. All of the images were scanned at 40× with Slide Scanner Systems. We divide the total of the 180 pairs images into training and test set with 150 pairs and 30 pairs respectively. For the testing sets, the consecutive slide images are registered to each other using an alignment technique that constructs a coarse pose transformation matrix to perform an initial alignment of the tissue, then dynamically warps the Ki-67 to the respective H&E staining image. Due to memory limitations, all high-resolution training images were split into 288 × 288 tiles with 144 overlap at 20× magnification factor. After tiling, our training dataset contains about 60000 H&E 288 × 288 RGB tiles and 60000 Ki-67 288 × 288 RGB tiles.

4.2 Implementation Details

All the parameters in the convolutional layers are initialized according to Xavier et al.'s work [14]. The parameter values of $\lambda = 5$, $\beta = 5$ are chosen for the model, and Adam optimizer [15] is utilized to minimize the loss. Meanwhile, the batch size is set to 4, and the learning rate is set as 0.0002 initially and decreases using exponential decay with the decay rate of 0.9 and the decay epoch of 2. The network is trained on a computer with Intel Core i7-6850 k CPU, 128 GB RAM, and three NVidia GTX 1080-Ti GPUs.

5 Results and Evaluation

5.1 Improvement of Details Expression

We evaluate and compare our method to several variants of Cycle-GAN architecture by measuring four different evaluation metrics, i.e. SSIM [13], multi-scale structural similarity index (MS-SSIM) [16], Peak Signal to Noise Ratio (PSNR) and Mean Absolute Error (MAE), between the reconstructed H&E staining images and source H&E staining images.

Four evaluation metrics value of different methods that are calculated at different epochs are presented in Fig. 3. Compared with the other three Cycle-GAN variants, our proposed method shows a significant improvement. Meanwhile, the variant, Cycle-GAN with skip connection, and the variant, Cycle-GAN with structural cycle consistency loss, also achieve a relatively equal improvement, which means that both the skip connection and structural cycle consistency loss can further improve the quality of generated images on detail expression. In addition, more intuitive results are shown in Fig. 4.

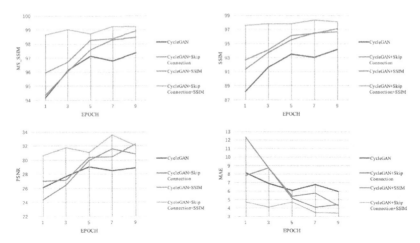

Fig. 3. Four evaluation metrics value of different methods at different epochs. CycleGAN + skip connection: Cycle-GAN with skip connection; CycleGAN + SSIM: CycleGAN with structural cycle consistency loss; CycleGAN + skip connection + SSIM: CycleGAN with skip connection and structural cycle consistency loss (our proposed).

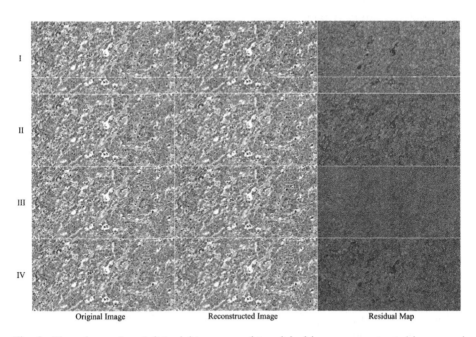

Fig. 4. The columns from left to right correspond to original image, reconstructed image, and residual map; the rows from I to IV correspond to CycleGAN, CycleGAN + skip connection, CycleGAN + SSIM, and CycleGAN + skip connection + SSIM (our proposed).

5.2   Generation of Virtual Ki-67 Staining Image

Since our original data is not pixel-level paired, the spatial structure and pixel-level evaluation strategy are not suitable for this task. Several mainly correlated features are selected from the second layer of resnet18, then the average value of each channel feature is calculated, so that the generated staining image can be expressed by a channel-level vector. Then the perceptual hash algorithm [17] is employed to calculate the correlation between the generated staining image and the referenced staining image. The visual comparison is shown in Fig. 5, where the image generated by our proposed method is obviously superior to the others' results. Furthermore, the quantification evaluation result is presented in Table 1. Our proposed method achieves the state of art with the P-hash performance of 0.7767.

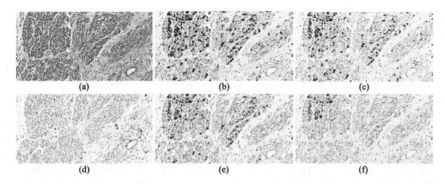

Fig. 5. Experiment results with different methods. (a) original H&E image; (d) referenced Ki-67 image; (b) generated Ki-67 image by CycleGAN; (c) generated Ki-67 from CycleGAN + skip connection; (e) generated Ki-67 from CycleGAN + SSIM; (f) generated Ki-67 from CycleGAN + skip connection + SIM (our proposed).

Table 1. Perceptual hash based on resenet18 of different methods.

Methods	P-hash
CycleGAN	0.7366 ± 0.2015
CycleGAN + Skip connection	0.7544 ± 0.2097
CycleGAN + SSIM	0.7545 ± 0.1939
CycleGAN + Skip connection + SSIM	0.7767 ± 0.1870

6   Conclusion

In the paper, we presented a method for the virtual staining task based on an improved Cycle-GAN. Our experiments revealed that our method significantly outperforms the state of the art. The visual appearance of different methods can be seen in Fig. 5. It clearly shows that the generated staining images are very similar to the referenced staining image. However, due to the lack of pixel-level paired data, we cannot guarantee that each pixel in the H&E staining images is correctly mapped to the real Ki-67 staining domain, and there is still more room for improvement, for example, the generated Ki-67 staining image should keep same pathological presentation with the source H&E staining image. Hence, there are still certain challenges in clinical application and popularization.

Acknowledgment. This research was made possible with the financial support from National Science Foundation of China (NSFC) (61875102, 81871395, 61675113), Science and Technology Research Program of Shenzhen City (JCYJ20170816161836562, JCYJ20170817111 912585, JCYJ20160427183803458, JCYJ20170412171856582, JCY20180508152528735), Oversea cooperation foundation, Graduate School at Shenzhen, Tsinghua University (HW2018007).

References

1. Weinstein, R.S., et al.: Overview of telepathology, virtual microscopy, and whole slide imaging: prospects for the future. Human Pathol. **40**(8), 1057–1069 (2009)
2. Soares, C.T., Frederigue-Junior, U., de Luca, L.A.: Anatomopathological analysis of sentinel and nonsentinel lymph nodes in breast cancer: hematoxylin-eosin versus immunohistochemistry. Int. J. Surg. Pathol. **15**(4), 358–368 (2007)
3. Sheikh, R.A., et al.: Correlation of Ki-67, p53, and Adnab-9 immunohistochemical staining and ploidy with clinical and histopathologic features of severely dysplastic colorectal adenomas. Dig. Dis. Sci. **48**(1), 223–229 (2003). https://doi.org/10.1023/A:1021727608133
4. Wang, Y., Sun, L.L., Jin, Q.: Enhanced diagnosis of pneumothorax with an improved real-time augmentation for imbalanced chest x-rays data based on DCNN. In: IEEE/ACM Transactions on Computational Biology and Bioinformatics (2019)
5. Tang, Z., et al.: An augmentation strategy for medical image processing based on statistical shape model and 3D thin plate spline for deep learning. IEEE Access **7**, 133111–133121 (2019)
6. Yang, J., et al.: Joint correction of attenuation and scatter in image space using deep convolutional neural networks for dedicated brain 18F-FDG PET. Phys. Med. Biol. **64**(7), 075019 (2019)
7. Tang, Z., Wang, M., Song, Z.: Rotationally resliced 3D prostate segmentation of MR images using Bhattacharyya similarity and active band theory. Physica Med. **54**, 56–65 (2018)
8. Zhang, B., et al.: Cerebrovascular segmentation from TOF-MRA using model-and data-driven method via sparse labels. Neurocomputing **380**, 162–179 (2020)
9. Goodfellow, I., et al.: Generative adversarial nets. Adv. Neural. Inf. Process. Syst. **27**, 2672–2680 (2014)
10. Mirza, M., Osindero, S.: Conditional generative adversarial nets. arXiv preprint arXiv:1411. 1784 (2014)
11. Isola, P., et al.: Image-to-image translation with conditional adversarial networks. In: Proceedings of the IEEE Conference on Computer Vision and Pattern Recognition (2017)
12. Zhu, J.-Y., et al.: Unpaired image-to-image translation using cycle-consistent adversarial networks. In: Proceedings of the IEEE International Conference on Computer Vision. (2017)
13. Wang, Z., et al.: Image quality assessment: from error visibility to structural similarity. IEEE Trans. Image Process. **13**(4), 600–612 (2004)

14. Liu, L., et al.: Understanding the Difficulty of Training Transformers. arXiv preprint arXiv: 2004.08249 (2020)
15. Kingma, D.P., Ba, J.: Adam: A method for stochastic optimization. arXiv preprint arXiv: 1412.6980 (2014)
16. Wang, Z., Simoncelli, E.P., Bovik, A.C.: Multiscale structural similarity for image quality assessment. In: The Thirty-Seventh Asilomar Conference on Signals, Systems and Computers, vol. 2. IEEE (2003)
17. Weng, L., Preneel, B.: A secure perceptual hash algorithm for image content authentication. In: De Decker, B., Lapon, J., Naessens, V., Uhl, A. (eds.) CMS 2011. LNCS, vol. 7025, pp. 108–121. Springer, Heidelberg (2011). https://doi.org/10.1007/978-3-642-24712-5_9

An Optimized SSD Target Detection Algorithm Based on K-Means Clustering

Yonggang Chi$^{(\boxtimes)}$ ⓘ, Jialin Fan ⓘ, Bo Pang ⓘ, and Yuelong Xia ⓘ

Harbin Institute of Technology, Harbin 150000, China
chiyg@hit.edu.cn

Abstract. In response to the problem that the default box size and shape of the SSD network model need to be manually set based on experience and the lack of specificity for different data, this paper uses the k-means clustering method to optimize the default box setting method of the SSD network to make the default box more consistent with the data, enhancing the self-adaptive ability of SSD default box positioning regression, thereby improving detection accuracy and detection speed. The algorithm is applied to actual aluminum defect detection, the defect detection accuracy reaches 77.6% mAP, which is 2.86% higher than the original SSD512 model, and the detection speed is increased from 37 FPS to 39 FPS.

Keywords: SSD network · Target detection · K-means · Deep learning

1 Introduction

Artificial naked eye recognition is a commonly used target detection method. This method has the problems of low work efficiency, and high product cost, and is easily affected by many factors such as the quality of the inspection personnel, the naked eye resolution, and the eye fatigue [1, 2]. With the gradual maturity of machine learning, detection methods based on machine vision have developed rapidly [3]. When using this type of method for detection, not only a series of pre-processing such as denoising of the image but also feature extraction of the image, such as Haar [4], HOG [5], SHIFT [6] and other features extraction have to be done. In addition, in the face of the increasingly complex detection environment, such methods have the problems of single detection target, poor robustness, low efficiency.

In recent years, deep learning algorithms based on convolutional neural networks have performed well in computer vision such as target detection [7], avoiding the difficulty of manually extracting features based on machine learning detection methods. At present, target detection methods based on convolutional neural networks can be divided into two categories: the first two-stage scheme is based on candidate region algorithms, such as RCNN [8], Fast-RCNN [9], Faster-RCNN [10] and other models, to perform target detection through two steps, region proposal and region classification. The second scheme is one-stage scheme which is based on regression algorithms, such as YOLO [11], SSD [12] and so on. Unlike the two-step working mode of the R-CNN series network, one-stage can complete the above two steps in a single step. And the

© ICST Institute for Computer Sciences, Social Informatics and Telecommunications Engineering 2021
Published by Springer Nature Switzerland AG 2021. All Rights Reserved
M. Guan and Z. Na (Eds.): MLICOM 2020, LNICST 342, pp. 148–156, 2021.
https://doi.org/10.1007/978-3-030-66785-6_17

SSD network shows better detection accuracy and detection speed compared with the YOLO network. The SSD network unifies the area selection, image feature extraction and classification into a deep convolutional neural network, which realizes the automatic selection and automatic extraction of the target detection area. This method effectively improves the detection speed and detection accuracy of the detection network. But the default box size and shape of the SSD network model need to be manually set according to experience, and this setting lacks adaptability to different data objects, which may cause to some default boxes not match the real boxes and thus miss the target. To solve this problem, this paper uses the k-means clustering method to improve the setting of the default box. By clustering the calibration box size of the data set, the default box setting that more closely matches the calibration box in the data set is obtained, so that the default box is more precise and streamlined, and this method optimizes the regression positioning process of the SSD default box. The experimental results show that the improved SSD model has obviously improved in accuracy and speed.

2   SSD (Single Shot Multibox Detector)

Unlike the Faster RCNN network that first extracts candidate regions and then extracts candidate region features for classification, the SSD network uses independent convolution kernels to predict target position offsets and target categories on multi-scale feature maps. And unlike each cell in the YOLO network that only predicts two candidate boxes, the SSD network extracts a total of 30 or 36 types of candidate boxes in the multi-scale feature layer.

The structure of the SSD model can be divided into two parts: the basic network and the auxiliary network structure according to the network implementation function, as shown in Fig. 1. The basic network is a standard architecture for image classification. The basic network of the SSD model uses the truncated VGG-16 [13]. The main auxiliary structures include: (a) Multi-scale feature map layer; (b) Convolutional filters; (c) Default box; (d) Non-maximum Suppression (NMS).

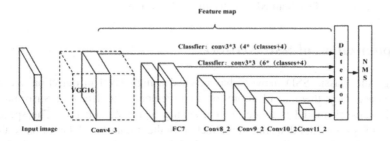

Fig. 1. SSD network structure diagram

For the target detection algorithm such as SSD, the loss function is more complicated than the general convolutional neural network, because in addition to identifying the target category, it also optimizes the position information of the target in the image. The loss function of SSD is composed of two parts: default box positioning loss (L_{loc}) and confidence loss (L_{conf}). The loss function of SSD is

$$L(x,c,l,g) = \frac{1}{N}\left(L_{conf}f(x,c) + \alpha L_{loc}(x,l,g)\right) \tag{1}$$

In the formulation: N is the number of default boxes that meet the IOU greater than a certain threshold, c is the predicted value of category confidence, and α is the weight parameter.

Positioning loss is

$$L_{loc}(x,l,g) = \sum_{i \in pos}^{N} \sum_{m \in \{cx,cy,w,h\}} x_{ij}^k smooth_{L1}(l_i^m - \hat{g}_j^m) \tag{2}$$

$$smooth_{L1}(x) = \begin{cases} 0.5x^2 & \text{if } |x| < 1 \\ |x| - 0.5 & \text{otherwise} \end{cases} \tag{3}$$

In the formulation: the g of the real box needs to be encoded to obtain $\hat{g}$ (offset), because the predicted value l is also the encoded value.

The confidence loss is

$$L_{conf}(x,c) = - \sum_{i \in Pos}^{N} x_{ij}^p \log(\hat{c}_i^p) - \sum_{i \in Neg} \log(\hat{c}_i^0) \tag{4}$$

$$\hat{c}_i^p = \frac{\exp(c_i^p)}{\sum_p \exp(c_i^p)} \tag{5}$$

SSD networks have great advantages in accuracy and real-time, but SSD networks also have some disadvantages. For example, the very important default box in the SSD network needs to be set according to human experience, the size and shape of the default box can not be obtained directly through learning.

3   Optimization of SSD Network

Although the classic SSD network has reached a high level in detection speed and detection accuracy, there is still room for improvement. The detection performance of the SSD network model is related to the setting of the default box. The speed and accuracy of SSD model detection are affected by the number of default boxes. On the one hand, selecting a smaller number of default boxes can increase the speed of model detection but will reduce the detection accuracy, while selecting a larger number of default boxes will increase the accuracy of the model but will reduce the detection speed. On the other hand, the default box size and shape of the SSD network model are manually set based on experience and lack specificity for different data objects. If the initial default box size and number are more in line with the characteristics of the marked box in the data set, then the model can accelerate convergence while improving the speed and accuracy of the detection algorithm.

In view of the above problems, in order to obtain a more reasonable default box setting, this paper provides a new idea for the selection of the default box by performing k-means clustering on the calibration box of the training set, making the default box generated during training and prediction more accurate, and training also converges better.

3.1 K-Means Algorithm

k-means [14] belongs to a clustering algorithm. The algorithm accepts an unlabeled data set and then clusters the data into different groups. The k-means algorithm can be defined abstractly: given a series of data$(x_1, x_2,..., x_n)$, each data is d-dimensional, the k-means algorithm divides the n data into k clusters $S = \{S_1, S_2, ..., S_n\}$,$\mu_i$ is the cluster center of each cluster, so that the internal mean square sum of the cluster is minimum, the objective function can be expressed as

$$\arg\min \sum_{i=1}^{k} \sum_{x \in S_i} ||x - \mu_i||^2 = \arg\min \sum_{i=1}^{k} VarS_i \qquad (6)$$

3.2 The Optimization Method of Default Box Setting

The original SSD network default box generation rules are as follows:

For each cell in each feature map, multiple default boxes are generated in the center of the default box in the original image. Each feature map has a minimum value min_size and a maximum value max_size. The maximum value is the minimum value of the next layer feature map and defines the aspect ratio $\alpha \in \{1, 2, 3, 1/2, 1/3\}$. For the case where the aspect ratio is 1, square default boxes with side lengths of min_size and max_size are generated, and for the case where the aspect ratio is not 1, the width w and height h of the default box are generated as follows

$$\begin{cases} w = \sqrt{\alpha} \times min\_size \\ h = \dfrac{1}{\sqrt{\alpha}} \times min\_size \end{cases} \qquad (7)$$

For the original SSD network model, each cell of feature map generates 4 or 6 default boxes. These parameters are selected manually. A major advantage of neural networks is that it can reduce the experience requirements for non-professionals. Therefore, k-means clustering method is used to cluster the calibration box of the training data, which provides new ideas for the selection of the default box. At the same time, by choosing a more accurate default box, it helps to improve the accuracy of network detection.

The original k-means algorithm uses Euclidean distance to find the closest center point, minimizing the distance from each point to any center point. In the SSD network, the clustering dimension of the calibration data is based on the width and height of the calibration box. If use Euclidean distance as k-means distance function, a large calibration box will produce a larger loss than a small calibration box. But in target detection we want to generate a default box with a higher overlap rate with the real box, that is, We hope that the IOU score is higher. The IOU here is the parallel ratio of the default box (DB) and the calibration true box (GT), which can be expressed as

$$IOU = \frac{DB \bigcap GT}{DB \bigcup GT} \tag{8}$$

In order to reduce the influence of the size of the calibration box, the improved k-means distance function is

$$d(box, centroid) = 1 - IOU(box, centroid) \tag{9}$$

Using the improved k-means to cluster the calibrate box of aluminum defect data, SSD512 has 7 feature layers, so k takes 7, and the clustering result is shown in Fig. 2. It can be seen from the figure that the cluster center 1 is a small size box, so the min _size of the first layer feature map is set to the abscissa of the cluster center 1. Since the size and shape change of the small target is small, the aspect ratio of 2 and 1/2 of the first feature layer are removed to reduces model complexity. The min_size of the second feature layer is set to the abscissa of cluster center 2, and the aspect ratio of 3 and 1/3 of the second feature layer are removed. Since the widths of the other five clustering centers are all 512, and these clustering centers detecting large-sized targets, and the calibration box of these clustering center vary greatly in width and height, so the min_size of the last one feature layer is set to 512, and an aspect ratio of 15 is added. The default box of the remaining feature layers are set according to the original model. The average IOU of the original network default box and the aluminum defect calibration box is 36.54%. After the optimized k-means clustering algorithm, the average IOU is 40.05%, and the default box number is reduced from 36 to 33.

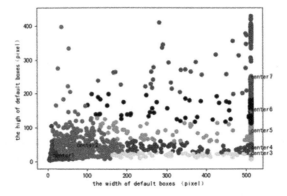

Fig. 2. K-means clustering result

4   Experimental Results and Analysis

4.1   Experimental Data

The aluminum defect detection images used in this article are from the Alibaba Cloud Tianchi platform. In the actual production process of aluminum, due to the influence of many factors, defects such as scratches, dirty spots, and paint bubbles will occur, and these defects will seriously affect the quality of aluminum. The data is derived from the actual production data of the enterprise, and each picture contains one or more defects. The pixel of the aluminum material defect image is 2560 * 1920. There are the following ten types of defects. Table 1 shows the number of various types of defective samples, and divides the data in Table 1 into a training verification set and a test set according to 9:1. It can be seen from the table that the number of each type of defects is very uneven, such as the number of samples in jet flow is very few, and the number of sample defects such as bottom leakage is much more than other categories. The scale of the defect vary largely, the size of some defect is very small, which means that the defects only occupy a small part of an image, and the size of some defect is large. These all increase the difficulty of designing the flaw detection algorithm.

Table 1. The number of various types of defects

Category	Non-conductive	Scratch	Corner bottom	Orange peel	Bottom	Jet	Paint bubble	Pit	Variegated	Dirty spots	Total
Number	360	128	346	173	538	86	82	407	365	251	2736

4.2   Model Training

The experimental platform configuration is shown in Table 2. The size of the model input picture is 512 * 512. The batch size is set to 32. The non-uniform learning rate decay strategy of multistep is used to train the SSD model. Through multiple experiments, the basic learning rate was finally selected to be 0.0001, and the step value of multi-step learning was 40,000 and 80,000, and the attenuation coefficient was 0.1. In order to increase the amount of data and prevent overfitting during training, data enhancement methods such as random mirroring, random cropping, rotation, translation, and grayscale transformation are used for the training data.

Table 2. Experimental platform configuration

Name	Configuration
Deep learning framework	Pytorch1.4
CPU	Intel Core i9-7900X, 3.3 GHz
GPU	NVIDIA GeForce GTX2080Ti, 11G
RAM	64 GB

Use the above parameters to train the SSD network and the optimized SSD network, and record the network loss value every 20 steps. Figure 3 is the original SSD training loss curve, and Fig. 4 is the optimized SSD training loss curve. From the figure, the loss curves show a downward trend with the increase of the number of iterations, and the loss value decreases greatly at the beginning of training, indicating that the learning rate is appropriate. And the loss curve tends to be stable after training to a certain stage, indicating that the model begins to converge and meets the expected requirements. It can be seen from Figs. 3 and 4 that the optimized SSD network has a smaller loss value and faster training convergence.

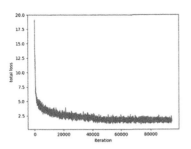

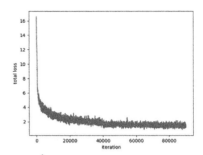

Fig. 3. Original SSD training loss   **Fig. 4.** Optimized SSD training loss

4.3   Experimental Results and Discussion

On the actual aluminum data set, the SSD network before and after optimization was tested and compared, using average precision (AP) and mean average precision (mAP) as comparison indicators.

Figure 5 compares the AP of each category before and after optimization. Table 3 shows the improvement ratio of AP in each category. It can be seen from Fig. 5 and Table 3 that the optimized SSD network greatly improves the detection average precision of the category with lower original detection average precision, among them, the improvement ratio of the "scratch" category has reached 37.8%. It is of great significance to improve the detection AP of category with original low AP. The improved default box of the SSD network model is more in line with defect calibration box, the regression positioning process of the network default box for defects is optimized, and many defect categories that are difficult to detect by the original network can be detected.

Judging from the mean average precision of all categories, the optimized SSD network mAP increased from 74.82% of the original SSD to 77.68%, and the detection speed was increased from 37fps to 39fps. In addition, using the optimized SSD network for detection, the position regression is more accurate compared to the original network. The overall performance of the algorithm is shown in Table 4.

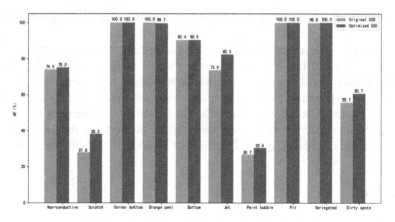

Fig. 5. Average precision

Table 3. Average precision and improvement ratio

Category	AP(%)		
	Original SSD	Optimized SSD	Improvement ratio
Non-conductive	74.0	75.0	+1.3%
Scratch	27.8	38.3	+37.8%
Corner bottom	100.0	100	0
Orange peel	100.0	99.7	−0.3%
Bottom	90.4	90.4	0
Jet	73.6	82.3	+11.8%
Paint bubble	26.7	30.4	+13.9%
Pit	100	100	0
Variegated	99.8	100	0.2%
Dirty spots	55.7	60.7	+9%

Table 4. SSD performance comparison before and after optimization

Algorithm	mAP(%)	FPS
Original SSD	74.82	37
Optimized SSD	77.68	39

5   Conclusion

This article first describes the advantages of target detection methods based on convolutional neural networks, and introduces several classic target detection models. Among them, SSD network is an algorithm with relatively good detection performance, and it is superior in speed and accuracy. Then, in response to the lack of adaptability of the default box settings of the SSD network model to different data objects, this paper uses the k-means clustering method to cluster the calibration box of the training data set, getting more accurate and simplify default box settings. In this way, the regression positioning process of the network default box to the target is optimized, so that the generated default box is more accurate and the training is better converged. By using actual data for experimental comparison, the optimized SSD model is superior to the original SSD network in AP, mAP and FPS. The optimized SSD network mAP reaches 77.68%, which is 2.86% higher than the original network, at the same time, the detection speed is increased from 37 frames per second to 39 frames per second.

References

1. Li, S., Yang, J., Wang, Z.: Review of development and application of defect detection technology. Acta Automatica Sinica (2020). https://doi.org/10.16383/j.aas.c180538
2. Zhou, L.: Present situation and development of modern precision measurement technology. Chin. J. Sci. Inst. **38**(8), 1869–1878 (2017)
3. Tang, B., Kong, J., Wu, S.: Review of surface defect detection based on machine vision. J. Image Graph. **22**(12), 1640–1663 (2017)
4. Panning, A., Al-Hamadi, A.K., Niese, R., et al.: Facial expression recognition based on haar-like feature detection. Pattern Recogn. Image Anal. **18**(3), 447–452 (2008). https://doi.org/10.1134/S1054661808030139
5. Dalal, N.: Histograms of oriented gradients for human detection. In: IEEE Proceedings of CONFERENCE 2015, CVPR, vol. 9999, pp 1640–1663. IEEE, California (2005)
6. Lowr, D.G.: Distinctive image features from scale-invariant keypoints. Int. J. Comput. Vis. **60**(2), 91–110 (2004). https://doi.org/10.1023/B:VISI.0000029664.99615.94
7. Yang, J., Li, S., Gao, Z., et al.: Real-time recognition method for 0.8 cm darning needles and bearings based on convolution neural networks and data increase. Appl. Sci. **8**(10), 1857 (2018). https://doi.org/10.3390/app8101857
8. Girshick, R., Donahue, J., Dare, T., et al.: Rich feature hierarchies for accurate object detection and semantic segmentation. In: IEEE CONFERENCE 2014, CVPR, pp. 580–587. IEEE, Columbus (2014)
9. Girshick, R.: Fast R-CNN. In: IEEE CONFERENCE 2015, CVPR, pp. 1440–1448. IEEE, Boston (2015)
10. Ren, S., He, K., Girshick, R., et al.: Faster R-CNN: towards real- time object detection with region proposal networks. In: Cortes, C., Lawrence, N.D., Lee, D.D., et al. (eds.) CONFERENCE 2015, NIPS, vol. 28, pp. 91–99. NIPS, Montreal (2015)
11. Redmon, J., Divvala, S., Girshick, R., et al.: You only look once: Unified, real-time object detection. In: IEEE CONFERENCE 2016, CVPR, pp. 779–788. IEEE, Seattle (2016)
12. Liu, W., Anguelov, D., Erhan, D., et al.: Single shot multi-box detector: towards real- time object detection with region proposal networks. In: Cortes, C., Lawrence, N.D. (eds.) CONFERENCE 2016, LNCS, vol. 9905, pp. 21–37. Springer, Amsterdam (2016)
13. Simonyan, K., Ziserman, A.: Very deep convolutional networks for large-scale image recognition. In: CONFERENCE 2015, ICLR, pp. 1440–1448. Hilton (2015)
14. Ding, C., He, X.: Cluster structure of K-means clustering via principal component analysis. In: Dai, H., Srikant, R., Zhang, C. (eds.) PAKDD 2004. LNCS (LNAI), vol. 3056, pp. 414–418. Springer, Heidelberg (2004). https://doi.org/10.1007/978-3-540-24775-3_50

Decentralized Learning for Wireless Communication Systems

Outage Probability Performance of Adaptive Cooperative Scheme with Delayed-Feedback

Lili Guo[1(✉)], Ming Xiang Guan[1], and Yang Wang[2]

[1] Department of Electronics Communication Engineering, Shenzhen Institute
of Information Technology, Shenzhen 518172, China
{guoll, guanmx}@sziit.edu.cn
[2] Departments of Sino-German, Shenzhen Institute of Information Technology,
Shenzhen 518172, China
wangy@sziit.edu.cn

Abstract. In the paper, the Adaptive all Cooperative (AAC) scheme is raised to bring significant improvements in cooperative system property, which is combined self-adaption signal modulation with automatic repeat request. Then we develop the Adaptive scheme to the Adaptive Greedy Cooperative (AGC) scheme using greedy strategy selection, which can obtain the characteristics of cooperative system significantly enhanced with the same cooperative nodes. However, the Adaptive greedy cooperative (AGC) is more sensitive than the AAC under the delayed feedback. We calculated the closed relationship expression between the probability of abnormal outage for AAC and AGC. Considering delayed feedback, we also analyze outage probability of AAC and AGC frames with different retransmission times, delayed time and cooperative users.

Keywords: Cooperation frame · Adaptive modulation · MIMO · Automatic repeat request

1 Introduction

MIMO technology is very well-known, and it can get effective diversity gain with installing several wireless antennas at the signal transmitting terminal and signal receiving terminal. Recently, a reasonable technique to improve the high efficiency of the frequency spectrum has been clearly raised to obtain diversity gain based on the application connection relay cooperation, named cooperative diversity [1–5].

Laneman developed and designed Amplify-Forward cooperative frame, Decoded-Forward cooperative frame, Select wireless Relay cooperative frame and space time coding cooperative frame in [1]. Hunter clearly proposed the code collaboration [5].

Other key work includes the characteristic analysis of cooperative transmission. For example, Hasna analyzed the mean symbol error rate [6, 7] of the cooperative network in the wireless channel of Rayleigh and Nakagami. Reference [8], the closed relationship expression of the interruption probability of the DF system is obtained. Another way to alleviate the adverse effects of the decline of the wireless channels is to use the fully automatic retransmission request on link layer. In other words, transmitter

© ICST Institute for Computer Sciences, Social Informatics and Telecommunications Engineering 2021
Published by Springer Nature Switzerland AG 2021. All Rights Reserved
M. Guan and Z. Na (Eds.): MLICOM 2020, LNICST 342, pp. 159–169, 2021.
https://doi.org/10.1007/978-3-030-66785-6_18

must deal with the incorrectly accepted data. Based on the actual situation, in order to decrease the minimum delayed time and buffer area measure, the ARQ protocol has been generally selected to limit the larger retransmission count. Aiming at cooperative transmitting, Dai suggested combining ARQ system and cooperative transmission; also he proposed a cross layer model based on the MIMO that constitutes PHY and the ARQ of link layer [9]. Le further scientifically studied the property of the ARQ cooperative transmission model in the multi-hop network [10].

None of the above-mentioned thesis considers the transmission of variable rates and powers. Recently, the cross-layer design has caused great interest among everyone. The design has mutually improved the actual operation of several protocol layers to achieve significant feature enhancements. Liu clearly proposed the SISO cross-layer model which integrates adapt modulation and auto repeat request using the extreme wireless channel information [11]. The results that cross layered model can obtain stronger characteristics than the layered model are verified by system simulation.

In the paper, we used the cross-layer design principle and applied the shortened ARQ to the adapt MIMO cooperation model, resulting in the adaptive all cooperative frame (AAC). It integrates AM and ARQ based on the feedback of the adapt modulation. In order to further improve the characteristics, we clearly proposed the adaptive greedy cooperative frame (AGC) [12, 13] based on the basic theory of "greed scheduling". The theory only selects one wireless channel standard as the best the wireless relay node is pushed together with the source node. Taking full consideration of the feedback on the delay time in the specific communication environment, we calculated the closed expression of the outage probability of the AAC frame and the AGC frame, and analyzed the effect of the time delay, retransmission count and the cooperative nodes on the system characteristics. It also compares the system capability between the AAC and AGC frames.

Part of this paper is allocated as follows. The second section introduces the system entity model. In the third section, the system characteristics based on the outage probability are analyzed, the fourth section shows the numerical results, and the fifth section gives the conclusions.

2 System Model

There is immediate connection which is combined the source Sn with the target Dn, and there are K reserved connections according to the K wireless relays R_i. The source connection node, the wireless relay connection node and the destination connection node each have only one wireless antenna. The entire transmission must have 2 time ranges: in 1st time range, the data signal x is transmitted to the target Dn, and the data is amplified by the relay Ri in the 2nd time range, and is shared to target node Dn. In the 1st time range, the received data of overall target node Dn and i-th relay node obtained as:

$$r_1 = h_{s,d}x + N_{s,d} \tag{1}$$

$$r_2 = h_{s,i}x + N_{s,i} \tag{2}$$

Among them, $h_{s,i}$ indicates wireless channels between Sn and i-th wireless relay, and $h_{s,d}$ indicates wireless channel between Sn and the target Dn. $N_{s,i}$, $N_{s,d}$ are the noise vector values between Sn and the i-th wireless relay node, between Sn and target Dn, and $e \sim CN(0, \sigma^2)$. In the 2nd time range, i-th wireless relay connection will receive the data r2 to increase the magnification using M_i, where $M_i^2 = \frac{P}{P|h_{s,i}|^2 + \sigma^2}$, P is the mean sign energy, and σ^2 is noise standard variance, severally. The second time range must be K time slots for transmission. The signal data received in the target node is indicated as

$$r_3 = M_i h_{i,d} r_2 + e_{i,d} \tag{3}$$

Among them, $h_{i,d}$ indicate the wireless channels between the cooperative user and the target Dn, and $e_{i,d}$ is noise value between the i-th wireless cooperative user and the target node Dn.

To carry out the comparison, we also considered the limit of the overall SNR, as

$$\gamma_{ov} \le \gamma_{s,d} + \sum_{i=1}^{K} \gamma_i = \gamma_u \tag{4}$$

Among them, $\gamma_i = \min(\gamma_{s,i}, \gamma_{i,d})$, and its basis have been proved to be very accurate in [7].

Unlike [14], we considered two cooperative transmission conditions: AAC frame and AGC frame. The first stipulates that all wireless relay connection nodes transmit data signals together with the source, while the second allows only one wireless relay connection node with the best wireless channel condition to transmit signal. We consider the two mentioned above responsive transmission frames. The overall goal is to receive data signals from the source of the AAC frame and all K cooperative wireless relays. However, for the AGC frame, only one wireless relay user is chose from K cooperative users.

Subsequently, the destination connection node can select the modulation mode according to the channels state information, and feedback the deployment mode to the source Sn. If receiving signals are found incorrectly, the automatic repeat request maker can produce a repeat request based on the feedback to the Sn. Otherwise; retransmission is not required. Similar to [15], it is assumed that the slow transition of the wireless channel and the extreme incorrect check based on the CRC. In order to maintain the simplicity of hardware configuration, it is assumed that the responsive deployment is selected on account of the channel state information of all routing paths, but deployment method of every wireless cooperative routing protocol is not adapted.

Here, considering the AAC frame and the AGC frame under the fading wireless channel condition of IID.

1) AAC frame:

It is assumed that the wireless channel arguments of all cooperative transmission routing paths are all the same and separate.

For the AAC frame in the IID fading channel, the function of probability density with γ_{ub} can be showed as

$$p_{\gamma_{ub}}(\gamma) = \frac{b_0}{\bar{\gamma}_{s,d}} e^{-\frac{\gamma}{\bar{\gamma}_{s,d}}} + \sum_{i=1}^{k} (\frac{2}{\bar{\gamma}})^i b_i \gamma^{i-1} e^{-\frac{2\gamma}{\bar{\gamma}}} / (i-1)! \tag{5}$$

Among them, $b_0 = 1/(1 - \frac{\bar{\gamma}}{2\bar{\gamma}_{s,d}})^k$, $b_i = \frac{(\frac{2}{\bar{\gamma}})^{(k-i)}}{(k-i)!} \frac{\partial^{(k-i)}[(1+\bar{\gamma}_{s,d}s)^{-1}]_{s=-\frac{2}{\bar{\gamma}}}}{\partial s^{(k-i)}}$, the detailed calculation can be found in [16].

2) AGC frame: In order to obtain stronger system characteristics, the AGC frame is considered that, in which the best connection user is selected among K cooperative users, and the signal data is transmitted using the chose relay together with the source node. Let $\gamma_{\max}$ indicate the transmission routing path SNR of the selected wireless relay connection node, and be able to calculate cumulative distribution function of $\gamma_{\max}$ from the c.d.f of the cooperative routing path SNR $\gamma_i = \min(\gamma_{s,i}, \gamma_{i,d})$.

Since there are K replacement cooperative connection nodes, c.d.f can be calculated as

$$F(\gamma_{\max}) = (1 - e^{-\frac{2\gamma}{\bar{\gamma}}})^k \tag{6}$$

Since the random variables $\gamma_{\max}$ and $\gamma_{s,d}$ are separate, the MGF of the overall SNR received at target user can be calculated as.

$$MGF_{\gamma_{tot}}(s) = MGF_{\gamma_{\max}}(s) \cdot MGF_{\gamma_{s,d}}(s) = (\sum_{nn=0}^{k-1} C_{k-1}^{nn} \frac{2k(-1)^{nn}}{nn+1} \cdot \frac{1}{2 + \frac{\bar{\gamma}}{nn+1}s}) \cdot (\frac{1}{1 + \bar{\gamma}_{s,d} \cdot s})$$

$$= \sum_{nn=0}^{k-1} C_{k-1}^{nn} \frac{2k(-1)^{nn}}{nn+1} \frac{1}{2(nn+1)\bar{\gamma}_{s,d} - \bar{\gamma}} \cdot [\frac{(nn+1)\bar{\gamma}_{s,d}}{1 + \bar{\gamma}_{s,d} \cdot s} - \frac{\bar{\gamma}}{2 + \frac{\bar{\gamma}}{nn+1}s}] \tag{7}$$

For the optional cooperation frame, the p.d.f of γ_{ub} is expressed as

$$\tilde{p}_{\gamma_{ub}}(\gamma) = \sum_{n=0}^{k-1} \frac{2kC_{k-1}^{nn}(-1)^{nn}}{2(nn+1)\bar{\gamma}_{s,d} - \bar{\gamma}} [e^{-\frac{\gamma}{\bar{\gamma}_{s,d}}} - e^{-\frac{2(nn+1)\gamma}{\bar{\gamma}}}] \tag{8}$$

Where, $C_{k-1}^{nn} = \frac{(k-1)(k-2)\cdots(k-nn)}{nn!}$. Note that k indicates the total number of replacement wireless relay nodes.

3 Performance Analysis

Based on the cooperation frame and cross-layer basic theories considered above, this section clearly proposes a responsive full cooperation frame (AAC) with all wireless relay connection nodes and a response greed cooperation frame (AGC) only with selected wireless relay connection node. The AGC frame based on "greed productive scheduling" saves a lot of network bandwidth than the AAC frame. And the closing expression of the AAC frame and the AGC frame with the delay time of the feedback is obtained. Because of the delayed feedback, the delayed CSI and the practical CSI have a correlation coefficient $\rho^2 = J_0(2\pi f_d \tau)$, in which J_0 (.) is the first kind of zero-order bessel, and f_d is the largest doppler frequency [17].

1) AAC frame
For the AAC frame with the IID fading wireless channel, the probability analysis of selecting the constellation diagram size $M_n = 2^n$ is expressed as

$$P_n = \int_{\gamma_n}^{\gamma_{n+1}} p_{\gamma_{ub}}(\gamma)d\gamma = b_0(e^{-\frac{\gamma_n}{\bar{\gamma}_{s,d}}} - e^{-\frac{\gamma_{n+1}}{\bar{\gamma}_{s,d}}}) + \sum_{i=1}^{k} b_i(P_i(\frac{2\gamma_n}{\bar{\gamma}}) - P_i(\frac{2\gamma_{n+1}}{\bar{\gamma}})) \quad (9)$$

$P_i(\mu) = e^{-\mu}\sum_{c=1}^{i-1}\frac{\mu^c}{c!}$ is poisson distribution and $p_{\gamma_{ub}}(\gamma)$ is calculated as (5).

Regarding the outdated feedback wireless channel, time delay will endanger the probability of mean incorrect signal. Because only one wireless antenna is configured for each cooperative connection node in the cooperation frame, and thus the MIMO space diversity is obtained, and $k + 1$ routing paths are regarded as $k + 1$ wireless antennas. Here instant packet incorrect ratio Per_n under delayed channel condition is resembled to PER in space diversity and Per_n can be shown that:

$$Per_n^{\tau}(\gamma) = A_n(\frac{1}{1 + g_n\bar{\gamma}(1 - \rho^2)})^{k+1}\exp(-\frac{g_n\rho^2\gamma}{1 + g_n\bar{\gamma}(1 - \rho^2)}) \quad (10)$$

Considering the AAC frame with IID the wireless channel, the mean error rate of packet $\overline{PE^{\tau}}$ in PHY is calculated as

$$\overline{PE^{\tau}} = 1/\sum_{n=1}^{N}R_n \cdot \{b_0(e^{-\frac{\gamma_n}{\bar{\gamma}_{s,d}}} - e^{-\frac{\gamma_{n+1}}{\bar{\gamma}_{s,d}}}) + \sum_{i=1}^{k}b_i(P_i(2\gamma_n/\bar{\gamma}) - P_i(2\gamma_{n+1}/\bar{\gamma}))\}$$

$$\times \{\sum_{n=1}^{N}R_n \times (\frac{C(n)b_0}{1 + \bar{\gamma}_{s,d}CC(n)}(e^{-\gamma_n(\frac{1}{\bar{\gamma}_{s,d}} + 1)CC(n)} - e^{-\gamma_{n+1}(\frac{1}{\bar{\gamma}_{s,d}} + 1)CC(n)}) \quad (11)$$

$$+ \sum_{i=1}^{k}\frac{C(n)b_i}{(1 + \bar{\gamma}/2CC(n))^i}(P_i(2\gamma_n/\bar{\gamma} + \gamma_nCC(n)) - P_i(2\gamma_{n+1}/\bar{\gamma} + \gamma_{n+1}CC(n))))\}$$

Among them, $C(n) = A_n(\frac{1}{1 + g_n\bar{\gamma}(1 - \rho^2)})^{k+1}$ $CC(n) = \frac{g_n\rho^2}{1 + g_n\bar{\gamma}(1 - \rho^2)}$.

Among them, R_n indicates the information content speed of the data signal, using bits per wireless channel, and $R_n = R_c\log_2(M_n) = T_sB$, where T_s is the fixed marked signal transmission time, and B indicates the signaling network bandwidth. It is assumed that the idealized Nyquist data information pulse $B = 1/Ts$ for each constellation mode. For no modulation without forward error correction, $R_c = 1$, so $R_n = \log_2(M_n)$. Taking into account the Nr-automatic repeat request in link layer, data packets that are incorrectly received are likely to be pushed for retransmission, and the largest retransmission frequency is set to Nr. Let $q^\tau = \overline{PE^\tau}$, so the average transmission frequency $\overline{N^\tau}$ is obtained by [12]:

$$\overline{N^\tau} = 1 - (q^\tau)^{N_r+1}/1 - (q^\tau) \tag{12}$$

Because there is no data transmission when the received signal noise ratio is less than the threshold value, and considering the ACC frame, the outage probability analysis is

$$P^\tau_{out}\_N_r = \overline{N^\tau} \bullet \int_0^{\gamma_1} p_{\gamma_{ub}}(\gamma)d\gamma = \overline{N^\tau} \bullet \left\{1 - \left[b_0e^{-\frac{\gamma_1}{\bar{\gamma}_{s,d}}} + e^{-\frac{2\gamma}{\bar{\gamma}}}\sum_{i=1}^{k}b_i\sum_{j=0}^{i-1}\frac{1}{j!}(\frac{2\gamma_1}{\bar{\gamma}})^j\right]\right\} \tag{13}$$

2) AGC frame
    Considering IID wireless channel, the probability of selecting method n for AGC could be indicated as

$$\tilde{P}_n = \int_{\gamma_n}^{\gamma_{n+1}} \tilde{p}_{ub}(\gamma)d\gamma$$

$$= \sum_{nn=0}^{k-1}\frac{2k_{k-1}^{nn}(-1)^{nn}}{2(nn+1)\bar{\gamma}_{s,d} - \bar{\gamma}}\{\bar{\gamma}_{s,d}(e^{-\frac{\gamma_n}{\bar{\gamma}_{s,d}}} - e^{-\frac{\gamma_{n+1}}{\bar{\gamma}_{s,d}}}) + \frac{\bar{\gamma}}{2(nn+1)}(e^{-\frac{2(nn+1)\gamma_{n+1}}{\bar{\gamma}}} - e^{-\frac{2(nn+1)\gamma_n}{\bar{\gamma}}})\} \tag{14}$$

The p.d.f. $\tilde{p}_{ub}(\gamma)$ of the optional cooperation frame is obtained in (8).

Able to obtain the average packet incorrect ratio $\overline{\tilde{PE}^\tau}$ and average ARQ count $\overline{\tilde{N}}$ of the AGC frame, and that is follow as.

$$\overline{\tilde{PE}^\tau} = 1/\{\sum_{n=1}^{N} R_n \cdot \sum_{nn=0}^{k-1} \frac{2B(n)kC_{k-1}^{nn}(-1)^{nn}}{2(nn+1)\bar{\gamma}_{s,d} - \bar{\gamma}}[\bar{\gamma}_{s,d}(e^{-\gamma_n/\bar{\gamma}_{s,d}} - e^{-\gamma_{n+1}/\bar{\gamma}_{s,d}})$$

$$+ \bar{\gamma}/(2nn+2) * (e^{-2(nn+1)\gamma_{n+1}/\bar{\gamma}} - e^{-2(nn+1)\gamma_n/\bar{\gamma}})]\}$$

$$\times \left\{ \sum_{n=1}^{N} R_n \times \sum_{nn=0}^{k-1} \frac{2B(n)kC_{k-1}^{nn}(-1)^{nn}}{2(nn+1)\bar{\gamma}_{s,d} - \bar{\gamma}} \right. \tag{15}$$

$$\times \left(\frac{e^{-(BB(n)+\bar{\gamma}_{s,d}^{-1})\gamma_n} - e^{-(BB(n)+\bar{\gamma}_{s,d}^{-1})\gamma_{n+1}}}{BB(n)+\bar{\gamma}_{s,d}^{-1}} \right.$$

$$+ \left. \left. \frac{e^{-(BB(n)+2(nn+1)\bar{\gamma}^{-1})\gamma_{n+1}} - e^{-(BB(n)+2(nn+1)\bar{\gamma}^{-1})\gamma_n}}{BB(n)+2(nn+1)\bar{\gamma}^{-1}} \right) \right\}$$

$$\bar{\tilde{N}} = 1 - (\tilde{q}^\tau)^{N_r+1}/(1 - (\tilde{q}^\tau)) \tag{16}$$

Where $B(n) = A_n(\frac{1}{1+g_n\bar{\gamma}(1-\rho^2)})^2$, $BB(n) = \frac{g_n\rho^2}{1+g_n\bar{\gamma}(1-\rho^2)}$.
The outage probability of the AGC frame is

$$\tilde{P}_{out}^\tau(N_r) = (\bar{\tilde{N}}) \cdot \int_0^{\gamma_1} \tilde{P}_{\gamma_{ub}}(\gamma)d\gamma$$

$$= \{ \sum_{nn=0}^{k-1} \frac{2kC_{K-1}^{nn}(-1)^{nn}}{2(nn+1)\bar{\gamma}_{s,d} - \bar{\gamma}}(\bar{\gamma}_{s,d}e^{-\frac{\gamma_1}{\bar{\gamma}_{s,d}}} - \frac{\bar{\gamma}}{2(nn+1)}e^{-\frac{2(nn+1)\gamma_1}{\bar{\gamma}}}) \tag{17}$$

$$- \sum_{nn=0}^{k-1} \frac{2kC_{k-1}^{nn}(-1)^{nn}}{2(nn+1)\bar{\gamma}_{s,d} - \bar{\gamma}}(\bar{\gamma}_{s,d} - \frac{\bar{\gamma}}{2(nn+1)})\} \cdot \bar{\tilde{N}}$$

It must be noted that when the time delay is 0, the characteristics of the clearly proposed AAC and AGC frames can be obtained again by incorporating the formula calculations without the feedback delay time.

4 Numerical Results

In the section, we get simulation results for AAC frame and AGC frame on the Rayleigh fading wireless channel. The marked value result shows the characteristics of the ACC frame and AGC frame with IID wireless channel. It is considered that $P_{loss} = 0.0001$, the largest count of ARQ can be used is $N_r = 2$, and the count of collaborative users k = {1, 2, 3, 5}. For the specific communication environment, the data file the length is $N_p = 4096bits$ [18]. Let $\bar{\gamma}_{sd} = \bar{\gamma}$.

Figure 1 compares the probability of outage of the ACC frame IID and the ACC frame no IID accompanying the change with the delay time of feedback. We can observe that when K = 2, the outage characteristics of ACC (IID) are better than ACC (Non-IID), but the delay threshold of ACC (IID) is smaller, in other words, the ACC (IID) is more vulnerable to delay time.

Figure 2-Fig. 3 describes the outage probability of the AGC frame with different K and Nr and no delay time and delay time feedback. It can be seen from Fig. 2 that the AGC frame with K = 5 has a better probability of outage than the AGC frame with

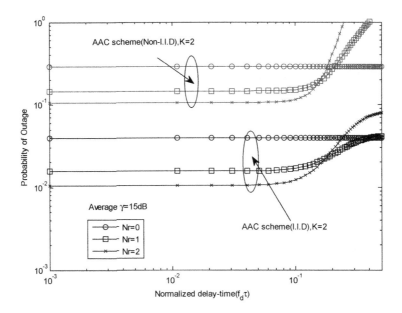

Fig. 1. Influence of delayed time on outage probability for AAC frame

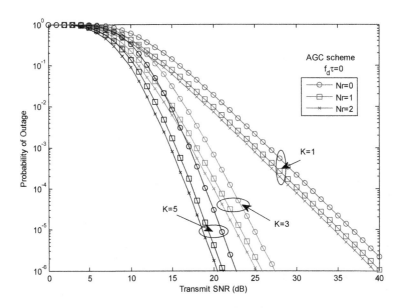

Fig. 2. Probability of outage for AGC frame with k and N_r under no delayed

K = 1 and K = 3. And with the increase of retransmission time, the AGC frame can get stronger probability of outage when N_r is 2.

Figure 3 compares the AGC frame and the ACC frame. It can be observed that the ACC frame with K = 3 has a stronger probability feature of outage. It is better than the K = 3 AGC frame. However, the probability of outage for the AGC frame with K = 5 is better than that for the ACC frame with K = 3. Therefore, we can choose the AGC frame with K = 5 to get a stronger performance of delay time feedback.

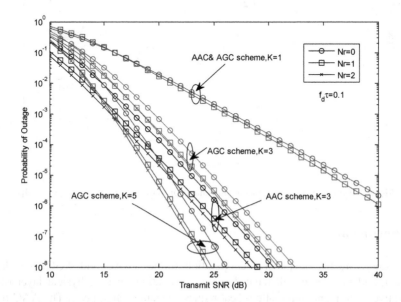

Fig. 3. Probability of outage for ACC and AGC with different k and N_r at $f_d\tau = 0.1$

Figure 4 illustrates that the probability of outage for the AGC frame when k = 1, 3, 5 is compromised under outdated channel time. In Fig. 4, we can observe that when the delayed time is large, automatic repeat request can reduce outage probability of AGC frame by a large number of cooperative nodes. Similarly, when there are a large number of collaborative nodes, the AGC probability of outage will also decrease. From Fig. 4, it is found that the AGC system with K = 5 is almost immune to the time delay.

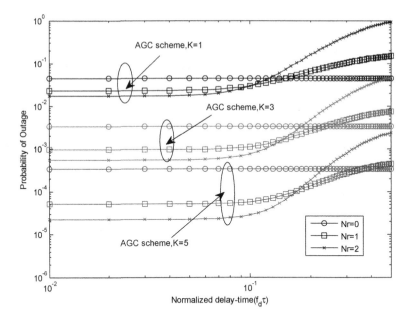

Fig. 4. Influence of delayed time on outage probability for AGC at $\bar{\gamma} = 15$ dB

5   Conclusion

In the paper, the two responsive cooperation frames (AAC and AGC) are clearly proposed; and they both will have the AM application on the physical layer of the cooperative system and automatic repeat request system on link layer. The AAC frame stipulates that all wireless relay connection nodes participate in transmission, while the AGC frame only selects a wireless relay with the best wireless channel condition because of "greed for production scheduling". We calculated the closed relationship expression between the probability of abnormal outage for AAC and AGC. The marked value results show that the characteristics of cooperative system can be significantly enhanced by ARQ. For the same collaborative nodes, AGC has a greater probability of outage; however, it is not particularly sensitive to the time delay under the feedback of the delay time. Compared with other frames, the AGC frame with K = 5 has stronger outage probability. In fact, we can choose suitable transmission frames with different requirements in different natural environments.

Acknowledgment. This work was supported by the Scientific and Technological Projects of Shenzhen (No. JCYJ20190808093001772), Guangdong Province higher vocational colleges & schools Pearl River scholar funded scheme (2016), Project of Shenzhen Science and Technology Innovation Committee (JCYJ20170817114522834), Research platform and project of Department of Education of Guangdong Province (2019GGCZX009).

References

1. Kong, C., Zhong, C., Jin, S., Yang, S. Lin, H., Zhang, Z.: Multipair fullduplex massive MIMO relaying with low-resolution ADCs and imperfect CSI. In: Proceedings of the IEEE ICC, Pairs, France, May 2017, pp. 1–6 (2017)
2. Kong, C., Zhong, C., Jin, S., Yang, S., Lin, H., Zhang, Z.: Full-duplex massive MIMO relaying systems with low-resolution ADCs. IEEE Trans. Wirel. Commun. **16**(8), 5033–5047 (2017)
3. Jin, S.-N., et al.: Power Scaling Laws of Massive MIMO FDR with Hardware Impairments, vol. 6, p. 40881 (2018)
4. Feng, J., Ma, S., Yang, G., Xia, B.: Power scaling of full-duplex two-way massive MIMO relay systems with correlated antennas and MRC/MRT processing. IEEE Trans. Wirel. Commun. **16**(7), 4738–4753 (2017)
5. Wang, S., Liu, Y., Zhang, W., Zhang, H.: Achievable rates of full-duplex massive MIMO relay systems over rician fading channels. IEEE Trans. Veh. Technol. **66**(11), 9825–9837 (2017)
6. Stefanov, A., Erkip, E.: Cooperative space-time coding for wireless networks. IEEE Trans. Commun. **53**(11), 1804–1809 (2005)
7. Hasna, M., Alouini, M.: End-to-end performance of transmission systems with relays over Rayleigh-fading channels. IEEE Trans. Wirel. Commun. **2**(6), 1126–1131 (2003)
8. Ikki, S., Ahmed, M.: Performance analysis of cooperative diversity wireless networks over Nakagami-m fading channel. IEEE Commun. Lett. **11**(4), 334–336 (2007)
9. Dai, L., Letaief, K.: Throughput maximization of ad-hoc wireless networks using adaptive cooperative diversity and truncated ARQ. IEEE Trans. Commun. **56**(11), 1907–1918 (2008)
10. Le, L., Hossain, E.: An analytical model for ARQ cooperative diversity in multi-hop wireless networks. IEEE Trans. Wirel. Commun. **7**(5), 1786–1791 (2008)
11. Liu, Q., Zhou, S., Giannakis, G.: Cross-layer combining of adaptive modulation and coding with truncated ARQ over wireless links. IEEE Trans. Wirel. Commun. **3**(5), 1746–1755 (2004)
12. Maaref, A., Aissa, S.: A cross-layer design for MIMO Rayleigh fading channels. In: 2004 Canadian Conference on Electrical and Computer Engineering, vol. 4 (2004)
13. Viswanath, P., Tse, D., Laroia, R.: Opportunistic beamforming using dumb antennas. IEEE Trans. Inf. Theory **48**(6), 1277–1294 (2002)
14. Ko, Y., Ma, Q., Tepedelenlioglu, C.: Comparison of adaptive beamforming and orthogonal STBC with outdated feedback. IEEE Trans. Wirel. Commun. **6**(1), 20–25 (2007)
15. Nechiporenko, T., Phan, K., Telllambura, C., Nguyen, H.: Capacity of Rayleigh fading cooperative systems under adaptive transmission. IEEE Trans. Wireless Commun. (submitted to)
16. Malkamaki, E., Leib, H.: Performance of truncated type-II hybrid ARQ schemes with noisy feedback over block fading channels. IEEE Trans. Commun. **48**(9), 1477–1487 (2000)
17. Cho, K., Yoon, D.: On the general BER expression of one-and two-dimensional amplitude modulations. IEEE Trans. Commun. **50**(7), 1074–1080 (2002)
18. Doufexi, A., et al.: A comparison of the HIPERLAN/2 and IEEE 802.11 a wireless LAN standards. IEEE Commun. Mag. **40**(5), 172–180 (2002)

Dynamic Resource Allocation and Streaming in Mobile Edges: A Deep Reinforcement Learning Approach

Daud Khan[1] and Zeeshan Pervaiz[2(✉)]

[1] School of Electronic Information and Electrical Engineering,
Shanghai Jiao Tong University, Shanghai, China
Daud95@sjtu.edu.cn
[2] School of Computer Science, Bahria University, Islamabad, Pakistan
ZeeshanPervaiz332@gmail.com

Abstract. Real-Time wireless communication devices with restricted assets face more extreme limit limitations than at any other time expansion of various sophisticated and calculation severe, versatile applications. In this paper, we explore the issue of resource allocation and also use real-time devices in mobile edge networks, efficient streaming with Double Deep Q Reinforcement Learning. The ideal arrangement considering the elements the system is strict about accomplishing. We aim to develop a smart agent to improve the allocation of resources in the decision-making process. We present a new combination of double Q-learning and DQN dueling algorithms and design suggested a solution to this issue based on the Double Deep Reinforcement Learning. We implement Double Deep Q Reinforcement Learning that can take into consideration a long-term task and learn from experience. The current proposal also measures the time-varying tasks of MEC servers and discusses the strategy of transferring tasks from one to another MEC server, better optimizing the value of the task by reducing unnecessary waiting times for queue. Results from the simulation show that our proposed approach significantly decreases system costs relative to the other parameters.

Keywords: Mobile Edge Computing · Resource allocation · Deep Reinforcement Learning · Real-time · Double Deep Q-network

1 Introduction

5th generation wireless systems (5-G) is one of the notable modern-day innovations. This is the case that the 5-G era was considered on advancement in networking technology, several new communication computing and models are implemented, such as hyper-dense networks, millimeter-wave communications, and adjacent device-to-device networks [1–3]. Overall techniques, Mobile Edge Computing (MEC), is one of the vital computer/data delivery technologies for

© ICST Institute for Computer Sciences, Social Informatics and Telecommunications Engineering 2021
Published by Springer Nature Switzerland AG 2021. All Rights Reserved
M. Guan and Z. Na (Eds.): MLICOM 2020, LNICST 342, pp. 170–183, 2021.
https://doi.org/10.1007/978-3-030-66785-6_19

improving the performance of cellular networks [4]. With the advantages of MEC wireless mobile users technologies, high-speed, efficient, and real-time wireless communication services can be enjoyed, including data rate enhancements and efficiency improvements. Gathering with MEC technologies, numerous networked fundamentals are also concerned, such as connected devices and cloud servers. The number of linked devices is also expeditiously rising the volume of data transmission to the MEC. This potentially introduces significant constraints on the system, such as data transfer speed limits, restrictions on storage space, battery latency, and terminal device usage energy. Because of these drawbacks and challenges, it is more efficient to use a cloud computing network when dealing with big data than with local terminal computing. While MEC systems should be able to access or process data from connected devices in cases where data can not be managed in the cloud storage due to latency conditions and security reasons, so the trade can be observed between cloud computing services and MEC services. Overall, cloud servers have much more power and central processing advantages than MEC servers, while latency constraints and security constraints/regulations may have drawbacks.

Transmission from connected devices is delayed, which is much convenient for real-time processing; this allows data collection and real-time transmission using high-quality data for streaming in real-time or streaming videos. It is, therefore, necessary to develop a methodology that can handle the scheduling of data transmission. Notice that when a decision is taken to offload data from linked devices, cloud storage servers can handle this while MEC servers manage data when requested to offload it.

Besides, these drawbacks open the new era for the MEC field in different except, but they have some standard conditions. The MEC environment's randomness and complexity are not addressed. Instead of the binary offloading feature, these programs are usually shown as a mixed-integer program. To solve MIP problems, branch and bound Algorithms, and Dynamic Programming [5,6] have been implemented. The computational complexity, however, is incredibly high, particularly for large MEC networks. Local search heuristic [7] and convex relaxation method [8] are suggested to reduce the complexity of computations. As a consequence, several methods have emerged for applying machine learning to solve the resource allocation issue with cloud computing. In this paper, we present a new dynamic distribution of resources and wireless communication devices within a Real-time approach based on Double Deep Reinforcement Learning using double Q-learning, which can balance computation and system resources under various MEC conditions dramatically reduce total system costs and optimize system resources.

- In the Software Defined Network (SDN) controller, an intelligent model the Het-Nets to establish an adaptive resource allocation, a strategy that takes taking the offload tasks into account and considering the video streaming for multiple users.
- We are implementing the SDN controller software in our MEC architecture. The benefit of the SDN controller is that it logically centralizes the distributed

network infrastructure and improves the QoS. The joint optimal task, computing allocation, and streaming problem are developed and implemented to minimize system costs under constraints of limited and dynamic storage capacity and computing resources on devices and servers, as well as limitations on a device and hard deadline delay.

- We construct a double-deep Q-learning algorithm with a multi-time system to configure the variable function and measure resource allocation, as well as to determine the set of feasible connecting server and neighboring devices.
- We showed, Results of simulation to illustrate the performance of the proposed algorithms using the optimal variable configuration for a task, computing and streaming of the device. It studied the impact on system performance of device mobility, data size, back haul capabilities, and cloud resources.

2   Related Work

In [9] proposed a joint adaptive video streaming and an intelligent offloading approach based on deep Q-networks in mobile edge computing systems. Efficient streaming and offloading algorithms are essential to the utilization of video services in mobile edge networks. In [6], Reinforcement learning is studied in which agents learn by interaction with the environment and then make better experiential decisions. An agent acts, the reward is given on a scalar reward. The agent receives an overall accumulated reward in learning the technique. Adapting deep learning has helped RL to overcome issues in decision-making rapidly. Deep Reinforcement Learning-based algorithms are implemented in a broad variety of MEC issues. Q-learning is one of the well-known methods of reinforcement learning. The authors in [10,11] presented a dynamic resource allocation model based on the DRL in the MEC process. In [12], a Q-learning-based model was developed to reduce energy consumption during run time by dynamically adjusting the operating frequency. Approaches build the capacity to optimize dynamic power by learning optimal frequency management policies. But applying Q-learning has not always been able to get the desired results. Notably, In some stochastic and uncertain environments, the accuracy of selecting the optimal actions in Q-learning can not be ensured because a large number of overestimated Q-values are generated during the learning phase [6]. In [15] have shown that the overestimation of Q-learning is possible and has suggested a Double-Q learning method that illustrates its effectiveness in the Atari 2600 domain. In [13], proposed Double Deep Q-Network architecture for collaborative edge caching in mobile networks aims to reduce the long-term average content of mobile users. In [14], the problem of task scheduling in fog-based IoT applications has been studied to achieve an efficient time-and cost-saving approach within the resource and time constraint.

2.1   Motivation

Compared to current works, the primary benefit of this manuscript. We consider further steps to enhance the efficiency of resource allocation and offloading using streaming devices for Real-Time Wireless communication. We make resource allocation and offload more effectively. We are proposing a new novel method considering the resource allocation task offload and streaming. Using Double Deep Reinforcement Learning using a recent new algorithm Double Q-Learning more specifically, When the task is offloaded the system allocates resources to terminal devices, including MEC servers, and ensures that the task is offloaded using the same servers. When the TD transfers the task to any other server. Moreover, If during the implementation of the MEC, specific existing computation resources were distributed, those resources could also be used to speed up computing. Hence, a systematic study to tackle the complexities of the MEC systems needs to be carried out to facilitate efficient resource management in a dynamic environment.

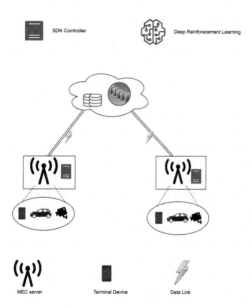

Fig. 1. MEC architecture.

2.2   Network Architecture

We design our Multi-server MEC server $M = 1, 2, 3, \ldots \ldots, M$ connected with our SDN and Terminal device $T = 1, 2, 3 \ldots \ldots, T$ are shown in Fig. 1. In which our SDN controller is considered with a MEC server to provide computation offloading service to the resources constrained users such as Augmented Reality (AR) and Virtual Reality (VR), drones, and smart phones. When delivering real-time video services to individual users such as video streaming and AR/VR, it is necessary to (i) preserve the high quality of video streaming under the tolerance latency constraint, and (ii) reduce the total execution time and total device energy consumption. In General, all MEC servers can be the physical or virtual machine with specific computing capabilities provided by the network operator and can communicate with the devices through channels. Each user can choose to offload computation tasks to the MEC server for one of the nearby servers it can connect. The modeling of user computation tasks, task uploading transmissions, and offloading utility is shown here below.

2.3   Task and Computation Model

We assume v a computational task for each TD. The η_v task is described as the (B_v, D_v, L_v) tuple, which can be executed on the local CPU of TD or the MEC server via computation offloading [16].

The B_v length of the data required for the computation the D_v length of each of the CPU cycles necessary to accomplish the task, and the L_v task length is the maximum tolerable period of time, which ensures that the task does not exceed, L_v length to satisfy the QoS requirement. We're showing $\alpha_\eta^v(t) = \alpha_{\eta(t)}^v = \alpha_\eta^v(t) \in 1, 2$ to the time slot t for TD v of the offloading decision. We've got a $\alpha_\eta^v(t) = \alpha_\eta^v(t) = \alpha_\eta^v(t)$. If v complete local computing task, $\alpha_\eta^v(t) = 1$. If v offloads the function to the nearby MEC server, we will define the $A = [\alpha_\eta^1, \alpha_\eta^2, \ldots, \alpha_\eta^n]$ offload decision matrix. Requests generated by TD are allocated to MEC servers. A task that has been achieved but has not yet been completed will be sent to the first-in-first-out (FIFO) task queue q_m of MEC server m, with the accessibility of Q. Our SDN controller uses a DRL agent to track and interact with a region with time centrally, and an agent will receive the entry-level $x(t)$ and decide which action the policy will require at each point, a profit of each operation is a reward, and the agent seeks to optimize each Device State's cumulative reward.

If TD v chooses to full the η_v task by executing it's locally, T_η^l could be described as the local execution time of the η task, and we indicate f_v^l (CPU cycles per second) as the TD v computation efficiency. Therefore the local execution delay, T_η^l of the η_v task is $T_\eta^l = \frac{D_\eta}{f_v^l}$ and the energy needed to complete the η_v task is called $E_\eta^l = \varphi D_\eta$. φ represents the energy needed to complete the task per CPU cycle. The overall costs of η_v local task execution can be expressed as $C_\eta^l = \delta^t T \eta^l + \delta^e E \eta^l$. Where δ^t and δ^e are the values, allow time and energy use to be prioritized and the value total is always equal to 1, where $\delta^t + \delta^e = 1$. If the TD v wants to offload the computational task to represent edge server m at a time of t slot, the task input data must first be shifted to the servers edge. Data rate reachable is $r_t = \frac{W}{N} \log\left(1 + \frac{P_t}{\frac{W}{N}} \frac{h_t}{N_0}\right)$. N is the number of offloading TDs, P_t is the transmission power for uploading data, h_t is channel gain of TD v in the wireless channel, N_0 is the variance of the complex white gaussian channel noise. Transmission delay can be $T_\eta^t = \frac{B_\eta}{r_t}$ and the energy consumption is $E_\eta^t = P_v T_\eta^o = \frac{P_v B_\eta}{r_t}$. Where P_v is the TD v power unit needed transition of the data.

Completion time of a task can be estimated at a serving node as $T_\eta^o = \frac{L_\eta}{f_m^o}$. Where to complete the task, f_m^o can be defined as the allocated computational resource (CPU cycles/second). Considering that the cumulative amount of over-all resources will not exceed the total computing power on the MEC server. $\sum_{m=1}^{M} f_m^o \leq F$ the corresponding energy consumption is $E_\eta^o = P_v T_\eta^o$. The $W_{v,m}$ queuing time on the m MEC server is equal to the execution time for all tasks during the execution $\sum_{n=1}^{index(W_{v,m})} \emptyset(n)$ and $\emptyset(n)$ in the queue index stand for the execution time of the task n. Then the total execution time and energy consumption resulting from the discharge of tasks is η. $T_\eta = \frac{B_\eta}{r_t} + \frac{D_\eta}{f_m^o} + T_\eta^q$ and $E_\eta = \frac{P_v B_\eta}{r_t} + \frac{P_v^i L_\eta}{f_m^o}$. Where P_v^i the stationary TD v is power unit.

The cumulative cost of offloading computation can be determined as follows by comparing the execution delay and energy consumption.

$$C_\eta^l = \delta^t T_\eta + \delta^e E_\eta \tag{1}$$

and the total overall system cost of all users in the MEC offloading system is expressed as

$$C_{total} = \sum_{v=1}^{U} \sum_{\eta=1}^{W} (1 - \alpha_\eta^v) C_\eta^l + \alpha_\eta^v C_\eta^o \tag{2}$$

Where $\alpha_\eta^v \in 0, 1$ shows the TD v offloading decision. If TD v wants to perform the task locally then $\alpha_\eta^v = 0$ otherwise $\alpha_\eta^v = 1$. Also, the output size for edge servers is much smaller compared to the input data size. The task time from the server to the TDs is, therefore, being fairly overlooked.

2.4 Video Streaming

Video streaming is the increasing usage of today's bandwidth and absorbs about 70% of Internet traffic—Cisco's video steaming projection for 2020 amounts to about 82% of total Internet traffic [17]. In 2013, on average, there had been one 11-person surveillance camera in UK [18]. It can be seen that soon rising amounts of data will be sent to the Internet from devices. Given the higher demands for bandwidth, storage, and processing, managing these gigantic amounts of data will be difficult. Edge computing provides a feasible method for storing and filtering data before they are sent to the cloud.

Massive volumes of data can be stored, and required information or data can only be sent to the cloud for further processing or research storage, saving multi terabits per second of data. In addition to reducing bandwidth consumption from devices to the Internet, some of the applications, such as target monitoring, object assessment, surveillance, etc., are mission-critical real-time demand and aggregate contact from multiple sensors or locations, which is also 2017 2017Second International Fog and Mobile Edge Computing Conference (FMEC) 70 unfeasible in current cloud scenarios. Edge technologies can be used to integrate information from several sensors for real-time analysis and communication.

3 Problem Formulation

We formulate the quality of service and better support for Terminal Devices (TDs) specialized functionality; we aim to minimize the overall costs of all offloaded tasks generated by Terminal Devices (TDs), distributed across the MEC region, within the limitation of maximum tolerable delay and computational power, the issue is formulated as follows.

$$min_{\mathcal{A},\mathcal{F},\mathcal{V}} \sum_{v=1}^{U} \sum_{\eta=1}^{W} (1 - \alpha_\beta^v)C_\eta^l + \alpha_\eta^v C_\eta^o. \tag{3}$$

$$C1 : \alpha_\eta^v(t)\epsilon 0, 1, \forall v U \forall \eta.\epsilon W \tag{4}$$

$$C2 : (1 - \alpha_\beta^v)T_\eta^l + \alpha_\eta^v(t)T_\eta^q \leq L_\eta. \tag{5}$$

$$C3 : \sum_{m=1}^{M} f_m^o \leq F, \forall \epsilon M. \tag{6}$$

The problem (3) is solved by detecting the optimal value $\mathcal{A}$ of which the decision vector is offloaded, the resource allocation vector $\mathcal{F}$, and the vector $\mathcal{V}$ Of the TD's streaming information the difference between the node and TD is described. $C1$ Is TD's decision to access or offload the task using local computing. $C2$ ensured the task's execution time could not surpass the maximum tolerable task delay. $C3$ reflects that the overall size of the computing resources allocated can not surpass the MEC server capacity as the number of TDs increases; the complexity of the problem can be increased. Rather than using the traditional methodology of optimization, we are implementing a new method of Deep Reinforcement Learning to evaluate the alternate solution.

We have introduced these problems in Markov Decision Process (MDP), time-space is subdivided into the slots of the same length is $\{t = 0, 1, 2, \ldots, \infty\}$. A be an action space and S be a State space. Then status of the MDP process for each t time is specified as $s_t \in s$, and $a_t \in A$ would be any action necessary in s_t state. Unless the a_t action is taken, which is available at s_t based on any policy, then the $r_t(s_t, a_t)$ and s_t reward is transformed to s_{t+1}, reward is a scalar quantity, and represents the efficacy of the executed action and vector for system operating would be represented by $(s_1, a_1, s_2, a_2, \ldots, s_n, a_n)$ sequence which could be described as the Markov Decision Process. The problems with the MDP can be defined as we can find an optimal control strategy, which in our case gives the highest cumulative reward, which is equal to the total system cost.

4   Dynamic Resource Allocation and Streaming in Mobile Edges: A Deep Reinforcement Learning Approach

The MDP is a policy, which maps for each State the best action in the MDP. This optimal policy can be found through a range of techniques, but we offer a Deep Reinforcement (DRL) approach due to the high complexity of our system. We claim that an SDN Controller integrates DRL Agents through edge computing.

The agent communicates with the system at all times and receives from the environment the corresponding input state.

$$x_t\{E_t, v_t, q_t, s_t\}. \tag{7}$$

where E_t = accumulate device costs at t, $v_t = [f_{m,1}^t, \ f_{m,2}^t, \ f_{m,N}^t]$ is a linear vector N consisting of available MEC server computing resources, which can be determined the following way. f_m^t At the time slot t, MEC server computing resources m are available. s_t = video streaming is considering time t.

$$f_m^t = F - \sum_{n=1}^{N} \alpha_\eta^v f_n^o. \tag{8}$$

$q_t = [q_{m,1}^t, \ q_{m,2}^t, \ q_{m,N}^t]$ is a N linear vector consisting of the queue data for each MEC. MD v is linked to one of the $m \ \in M$ serving MEC servers at each time step.

4.1   Action

Agent will decides to take action $a_t \in A$ from available actions at any time step t. The agent must decide which computing feature to offload, and which MEC server to allocate to the TD. Our action consists of the components which follow.

$$a_t = \{A_t, F_{t,}, T_t\}. \tag{9}$$

Where $A_t = [\alpha_{\eta,1}^v(t), \ \alpha_{\eta,2}^v(t), \dots, \ \alpha_{\eta,n}^v(t)]$. $\alpha_\eta^v(t) = \alpha_\eta^v(t)$ and $\alpha_\eta^v(t) \in \{0,1\}$ indicates that terminal device decision v at the time step t is offloaded. If TD v decides to execute the task locally $\alpha_\eta^v = 0$ otherwise $\alpha_\eta^v = 1$. $F_t = [f_{m,1}^v, \ f_{m,2}^v, \dots, f_{m,n}^v]$. Where $f_m^v = f_m^t$ Indicates the allocated computational resources for the tasks offloaded by TD v waiting in the task queue. Vector $T_t = [T_{m_1,m_2,1}^\eta(t), T_{m_1,m_2,2}^\eta(t), \dots, T_{m_1,m_2,n}^\eta(t)]$. Where $T_{m_1,m_2}^\eta(t)$ denotes the η task allocation action, at the time slot t waiting in the execution for task queue for $T_{m_1,m_2}^\eta(t) = 0$, implies the task will be performed by the same server $T_{m_1,m_2}^\eta(t) = 1$ which implies agent must decide to η transfer task from MEC server m_1 to m_2.

4.2   Reward

It includes evaluative feedback to a decision-making agent. The user adopt an action for each state and gets reward $r_t(s_t, a_t)$. In general, the reward feature is combined with the aim feature of the problem. Thus, the distribution of resources is aimed at minimizing cumulative device costs and meeting consumer demands, making our goal comes true. The reward feature is first designed to increase a negative cost during a choice to offload the task or perform the locally generated tasks. Instead, the DRL-based approach discovers a method for offloading with the highest overall reward. The best strategy in our framework will be the one that will result in the lowest cost of execution and will reduce the overall cost of the system. The optimization reward is described by

$$max_{at}\mathbb{E}\left[\sum_{t=0}^{T}r_t(s_t,a_t)\right].\tag{10}$$

The agent receives a r_t reward when engaging with the MEC system and agent seeks to obtain the highest possible R_t discount reward

$$R_t = r_t + \gamma R_{t+1}.\tag{11}$$

The discounted factor is γ, and the $0 \leq \gamma \leq 1$.

4.3   Deep Reinforcement Learning

Reinforcement Learning is a form of machine learning and works on enabling the agent to accurately determine the optimal behavior within a given context to maximize the cumulative return it predicts. Reinforcement Learning issues can be described as the MDP problem for optimal control decisions. Q-Learning, one of practical model-free. The agent has belonged in our architecture and obtains its currents state s_t. The agent then selects and operates a_t. Meanwhile, the environment undergoes a transition from s_t to a new s_{t+1} state and receives a $Q(s_t, a_t)$ reward The optimal state-value function $V(s)$ of Bellman Equation can be expressed as (12), where $s = s_t$ is the state at current decision epoch i, and the next state is $\acute{s} = s_{t+1}$ after take the action $a = a_t$.

$$V(s) = \max R(s,a) + \gamma \sum_{\acute{s}} P(\acute{s}|s,a).V(\acute{s}).\tag{12}$$

right hand side of (12) can be further expressed as

$$Q(s,a) = R(s,a) + \gamma \sum_{\acute{s}} P(\acute{s}|s,a).V(\acute{s}).\tag{13}$$

to obtained a optimal state value function $V(s) =$ would be expressed as

$$V(s) = \max Q(s,a).\tag{14}$$

Comparing (12), (13) can be expressed as

$$Q(s,a) = R(s,a) + \gamma \sum_{\acute{s}} P(\acute{s}|s,a).V(\acute{s}). \max \acute{a}Q(\acute{s},\acute{a}).\tag{15}$$

Q-function formula can be written as

$$Q^{i+1}(s,a) = Q^i(s,a) + \alpha^i(R(s,a) + \gamma. \max \acute{a}Q^i(\acute{s},\acute{a}) - Q^i(s,a)\tag{16}$$

Where $\alpha_i \in [0,1]$ is the learning rate, and the s_t state turns to the s_{t+1} state when the agent choose action along with the corresponding $R(s_t, r_t)$ reward based on (16), the Q table is used to store the Q value for each state-action pair when the dimensions of the state, as well as action space, are not high in the Q-Learning algorithm. Q-Learning process of learning is becoming relatively slow when the scenarios are with vast network states and action spaces. Deep learning techniques are then used as a possible method to approximate the value function (Fig. 2).

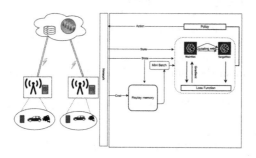

Fig. 2. Training process of double deep Q-network.

4.4   Double Deep Q-Network Method

Deep Q-Learning helps solve complicated and large-dimensional Reinforcement Learning problems and the multi-layer perceptron (MLP) structure implemented in it and can be used to estimate the optimal state-action of Q-functions. In our prototype, we use a full version of DQN to train our DRL agents, namely Double DQN [15]. The Q-function could be estimated by updating the variable θ of MLP to the optimal Q value as follows.

$$Q(s_t, a_t) = Q(s_t, a_t; \theta). \tag{17}$$

In fact, about the Double DQN characteristic, every DRL agent has two Q networks. $Q(s_t, a_t; \theta)$ and $\hat{Q}(s_t, a_t; \theta')$, with the Q network to select action, and the $\hat{Q}$ network to determine action. Remember those weight parameters of networkθ' $\hat{Q}$ are updated periodically by counterpart θ network Q. Algorithm-1 utilize Z of a N memory replay capability to save $Q(s_t, a_t, r_t, s_{t+1})$ transformation for each episode. Then sample a Z mini-batch transformation to train the Deep Neural Network (DNN) to a reduced loss feature; the estimated values are modified in each episode that follows.

A resource allocation framework based on Double Deep Q Network (DDQN) for the TDs within a MEC framework. Our DDQN uses a DNN with the values θ to estimate the Q-function. The agent will select an action that raises the Q-value at the state s_t and receives the reward r_t after the action is applied, then transitions to s_{t+1}.

Algorithm 1. Double Deep Q-Network (DDQN)

1: Initialize replay memory Z to Capacity N;
   Initialize main Q network with random weightθ;
   Initialize main Q' network with $\theta'=\theta$;
2: **for** $e = 1 to E$ **do**
3:    Initialize state $s_1 = x_1$ and pre processed sequence $\phi_1 = \phi(s_1)$;
4:    **for** $i = 1 to I$ **do**
5:        with probability ϵ choose random action a_i;
6:        Otherwise set $a_i = s_1, argmax_a Q(s_1; a_t; \theta)$;
7:        Execute the action a_i, observe reward r_1 and state $x_{(i+1)}$;
8:        set $s_{(i+1)} = s_i, a_i, x_{(i+1)}$;
9:        save transition $(s_i; a_i; r_i; s_{(i+1)})$ in Z;
10:      sample random the mini-batch of transitions $(s_i; a_i; r_i; s_{(i+1)})$
        from Z;
11:      **if** (e finishes at k + 1) **then**
12:        assign $y_k = r_k$;
13:      **else if** **then**
14:        assign $y_k = r_k + (\gamma Q(s)_1, (argmax)_a Q(s_1; a_t; \theta))$.
15:      **end if**
16:      Compute gradient descent on $(y_k - Q(s_1; a_t; \theta))^2$
17:      Update the main Q network parameters θ;
18:      Update the main Q' network parameters θ';
19:    **end for**
20: **end for**

$$L(\theta_i) = E_{(s,a,R(s,a),\acute{s}) \in minibatch} \left[\left(R(s,a) + \right. \right.$$
$$\left. \left. [\gamma.\hat{Q}(\acute{s}\ arg \max \acute{a} Q(\acute{s}, a\acute{;}\theta) : \acute{\theta}) - Q(s,a;\theta) \right)^2 \right] \tag{18}$$

In (18), the gradient guiding update. Therefore, Stochastic Gradient Descent (SGD) is conducted before Q networks converge to approximate optimum Q-function state-action. The Double DQN training algorithm is in Algorithm 1.

5 Simulation

We have performed multiple experiments to test our proposed system. It includes several edge servers and various TDs scattered around the zone. We take into consideration a scenario. The MEC server can be measured from 4 GHz second to 6 GHz s, and each MD has a CPU frequency of 1 GHz. We assume that the capacity of the transmission is 500 mW, and the idle power is 100 mW [19]. Data size B_η (in Kbits) for A task of [300, 500] is produced by the random means of W and the required computer resources are between [700; 1100] D_η (in Megacycles).

We compare our proposed DDQN with the other techniques to measure the efficacy of our proposed strategies Full Local, Full offload, greedy method [20]. All TDs which perform tasks locally can be defined as full local. Both TDs must load their tasks entirely off to MEC servers rather than run them locally. Once MEC follows the greedy method and is unable to fulfill the application, the function is carried out locally to accomplish the minimum cost. The MEC server across all TDs will spread equal computing resources.

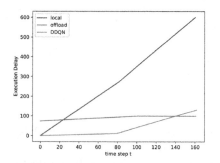 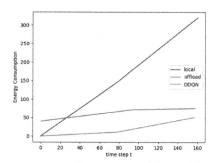

Fig. 3. Execution delay and energy consumption.

As shown in Fig. 3, the simulation performed with the results of full local computing (no offloading) and edge computing; we evaluate the effects of DDQN approach tasks, If tasks are not completed in time step t due to efficiency limit, all tasks are calculated as the tasks to be performed out in the next step. Hence, local computing increases the execution delay values and the energy consumption factor. When there are tasks that are not completed due to the ability limit at the time step t, all tasks are determined as the tasks to be taken out in the next stage. Local computing thus increases the execution delay values and the energy consumption factor. Besides, the time to perform tasks is the longest from time step 80, and it decreases the energy of TD as maximum.

The proposed DDQN approach has significantly better efficiency than TD's local computing. The achievement of the proposed DDQN approach is the lowest in terms of execution delay until time step 140. Indeed, when the time phase moves by and the task size increases, the outcomes of the recommended DDQN method are more significant than the maximum offload performance. The recommended DDQN-based approach also has the least values on the energy consumption side. These results reveal the DDQN algorithm proposed is the most relevant to real-time wireless communication devices.

Finally, as opposed to the other methods, we demonstrate the feasibility of the DDQN-based algorithm. There are one offloading action algorithms constructed using a well known greedy approach, as described in [20]. Remember that our recommended approach will be made based on the DDQN-based method, because of our rewards (Sum of delay, energy, and capacity). While depending on the data sizes transmitted (i.e., delays related), the greedy approach can be used to offload decision-making. We remind you that our proposed algorithm will be made based on the DDQN-based method because of our rewards.

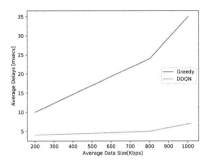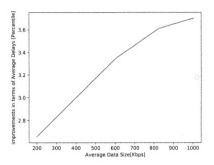

Fig. 4. Average delays and performance gap.

The delays increase the average data size for offloading increases. Our DDQN, the efficient policy will be taken during offloading decisions that consider delay, energy, and capacity, and the delays are lower than the greedy based decision making. Our proposed decision-making approach based on DDQN, as shown in Fig. 4, outperforms the greedy; and the gaps are increasing increasingly as the average data sizes increase.

6 Conclusion

We studied the issue of the allocation of resources and loaded balancing strategy in a dynamical system in mobile edge computing. While using high-quality, real-time communications in mobile edge networks. The problem is formulated under the minimal feasible delay and computational capability as the optimization problem. We used a DRL-based approach to find the optimum solution to deal with this issue. In the SDN controller, we have developed a smart agent to build an adaptive strategy for dynamic offloading and allocation of computing resources for multiple users as well as dynamic Video streaming information. The new DDQN-based agent requires the state system to determine the best strategy through interactions with the environment after the new MEC system framework. We have checked out a variety of experiments to show that the proposed research is realistic. The results of our simulation can be modified for performance evaluation due to environmental conditions or reward decision parameters. The results of the experiment show that the recommended system substantially decreases the cost of the system compared to the local, offloading, and greedy reference points.

References

1. Kim, J., Molisch, A.F.: Fast millimeter-wave beam training with receive beamforming. J. Commun. Netw. **16**(5), 512–522 (2014)
2. Kwon, D., Kim, S.W., Kim, J., Mohaisen, A.: Interference-aware adaptive beam alignment for hyper-dense IEEE 802.11 ax Internet-of-Things networks. Sensors **18**(10), 3364 (2018)

3. Kim, J., Caire, G., Molisch, A.F.: Quality-aware streaming and scheduling for device-to-device video delivery. IEEE/ACM Trans. Netw. **24**(4), 2319–2331 (2015)
4. Dao, N.N., Vu, D.N., Na, W., Kim, J., Cho, S.: SDCO: stabilized green crosshaul orchestration for dense IOT offloading services. IEEE J. Sel. Areas Commun. **36**(11), 2538–2548 (2018)
5. Tran, T.X., Pompili, D.: Joint task offloading and resource allocation for multi-server mobile-edge computing networks. IEEE Trans. Veh. Technol. **68**(1), 856–868 (2018)
6. Narendra, P.M., Fukunaga, K.: A branch and bound algorithm for feature subset selection. IEEE Trans. Comput. C **26**(9), 917–922 (1977)
7. Wang, T., Zhang, G., Liu, A., Bhuiyan, M.Z.A., Jin, Q.: A secure IoT service architecture with an efficient balance dynamics based on cloud and edge computing. IEEE Internet Things J. **6**(3), 4831–4843 (2018)
8. Bertsekas, D.P., Bertsekas, D.P., Bertsekas, D.P., Bertsekas, D.P.: Dynamic Programming and Optimal Control, vol. 1. Athena Scientific, Belmont (1995)
9. Park, S., Kim, J., Kwon, D., Shin, M., Kim, J.: Joint offloading and streaming in mobile edges: a deep reinforcement learning approach. In: 2019 IEEE VTS Asia Pacific Wireless Communications Symposium (APWCS), Singapore, pp. 1–4. IEEE (2015)
10. Mnih, V., et al.: Human-level control through deep reinforcement learning. Nature **518**(7540), 529–533 (2015)
11. Xu, Z., Wang, Y., Tang, J., Wang, J., Gursoy, M.C.: A deep reinforcement learning based framework for power-efficient resource allocation in cloud RANs. In: 2017 IEEE International Conference on Communications (ICC), Paris, pp. 1–6. IEEE (2017)
12. Tang, F., Fadlullah, Z.M., Mao, B., Kato, N.: An intelligent traffic load prediction based adaptive channel assignment algorithm in SDN-IoT: a deep learning approach. IEEE Internet Things J. **5**(6), 5141–5154 (2018)
13. Li, D., et al.: Deep reinforcement learning for cooperative edge caching in future mobile networks. In: 2019 IEEE Wireless Communications and Networking Conference (WCNC), Marrakesh, pp. 1–6. IEEE (2019)
14. Gazori, P., Rahbari, D., Nickray, M.: Saving time and cost on the scheduling of fog-based IoT applications using deep reinforcement learning approach. Future Gener. Comput. Syst. **110**, 1098–1115 (2019)
15. Hasselt, H.V.: Double q-learning. In: Advances in Neural Information Processing Systems 23, pp. 2613–2621. Curran Associates Inc. (2010)
16. Wang, C., Yu, F.R., Liang, C., Chen, Q., Tang, L.: Joint computation offloading and interference management in wireless cellular networks with mobile edge computing. IEEE Trans. Veh. Technol. **668**, 7432–7445 (2017)
17. Index, C.V.N.: Cisco visual networking index: Forecast and methodology 2015–2020. White paper, CISCO (2015)
18. Satyanarayanan, M., et al.: Edge analytics in the Internet of Things. IEEE Pervasive Comput. **142**, 24–31 (2015)
19. Cao, Y., Jiang, T., Wang, C.: Optimal radio resource allocation for mobile task offloading in cellular networks. IEEE Netw. **285**, 68–73 (2014)
20. Feng, W.J., Yang, C.H., Zhou, X.S.: Multi-user and multi-task offloading decision algorithms based on imbalanced edge cloud. IEEE Access **7**, 95970–95977 (2019)

Intelligent Antennas Design and Dynamic Configuration

Light Intensity Data Collector Based on 51 Single Chip Microcomputer

Qun Liu[1]([⊠]) and Ming Tang[2]

[1] Division of Science and Technology,
Harbin University, Harbin 150080, China
qunliu@126.com
[2] Zhongshan Institute, University of Electronic Science and Technology
of China, Zhongshan 528400, China

Abstract. This design mainly includes a brief introduction of the system background and design significance, and then describes the overall scheme of the system, through the selection of devices to achieve the optimal device selection, circuit hardware design, and finally complete the system software writing part to complete the overall function of the system.

Keywords: Single chip microcomputer · Data processing · Sensor

1 Introduction

With the rapid development of sensor technology, the application of the digital circuit technology into every aspect of life, for some of the original nature environment parameters for digital detection, such as temperature, humidity, illumination and so on the natural environment digitize measurement, in primitive society, people usually use their estimates for these natural parameters some production work, such as economic crops, poultry breeding and so on. With the progress of the society, large-scale planting industry and breeding industry have flourished and developed. Relying on primitive environmental technology, they have been unable to keep pace with The Times. For example, how to use reasonable light intensity and light time to maximize economic benefits. The digital light intensity collector is designed for this problem.

Acquisition unit is mainly used in the design of digital light intensity planting and breeding center, modern economy for both industry is extremely strict to illumination, light in the center of the plant directly affects the production of cash crops, control of light intensity and time will greatly improve the economic benefit, aquaculture centre illumination application generally applied to hatch environment, different will directly affect the hatchability of illumination, so the design of the light intensity of the collector has a simple structure, application effect is ideal, will have a great economic and social benefits.

In this design, a light sensor is used to detect the illumination of the environment. The collected data is read by a single chip microcomputer and displayed through the display screen. The parameter setting of limit value is completed by pressing the button. The main research contents are as follows:

M. Guan and Z. Na (Eds.): MLICOM 2020, LNICST 342, pp. 187–194, 2021.
https://doi.org/10.1007/978-3-030-66785-6_20

1) Completed the circuit design and software program design of the light sensor, and collected the data to the single chip microcomputer;
2) Complete the circuit design of analog-to-digital conversion, software programming, and convert analog to digital;
3) Complete the circuit design and software program design of the display, and display the data of single chip microcomputer;
4) Light supplement function;
5) It can set parameters by pressing the button.

2   System Design

The equipment mainly relies on the single-chip microcomputer for overall coordination and calculation. The single-chip microcomputer is responsible for sensor information data acquisition, control output, data calculation and other functions, and realizes the overall function through peripheral auxiliary circuit, sensor and other devices. The overall block diagram of the device is shown in Fig. 1 below.

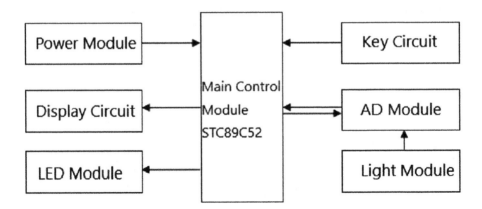

Fig. 1. Diagram of the equipment

PIC MICROcontroller is produced by an American company. From low to high end, there are many models to choose from, including conventional 8-bit microcontroller, 16-bit microcontroller and 32-bit microcontroller with higher performance.PIC microcontroller is mainly used in industrial control equipment applications, industrial applications of microcontroller performance is also required, the temperature range is relatively broad, can adapt to high and low temperature applications.

STC series MCU is a kind of domestic MCU, STC MCU development data is very much, very suitable for relatively simple device control system, SCM debugging as long as the use of USB TTL module can be debugging, download the program.

3   System Software Design and Actualize

3.1   System Main Program

The Main function is the system of the Main program, the program is the Main opening each program executed in sequence, by performing the action of each program to achieve the anticipated goal of system, the programming here need a logical, know the specific implementation process system, gradually in the process to achieve the goal of every little function, concrete process of the Main program as shown in Fig. 2, initialized Main function, the last in the Main loop repeatedly execute a program.

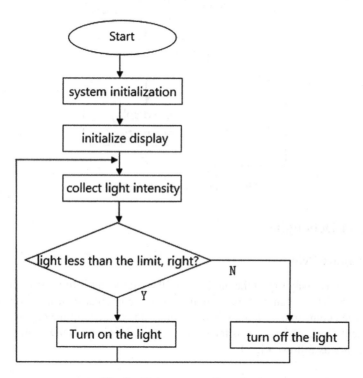

Fig. 2. Main program flow chart

3.2   Liquid Crystal Display Subroutine

LCD as human-computer interaction interface main equipment parameters input and data display on the LCD display flow chart shown in Fig. 3 after electric initialized LCD display program will be set up, mainly including the pin and the design of the data register, and then according to the write command function and write data function of the overall parameters and data display.

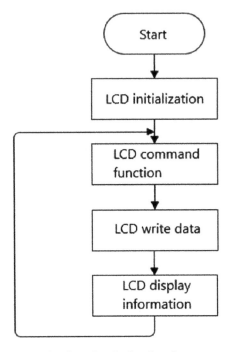

Fig. 3. LCD display flowchart

4 System Debugging

4.1 Hardware Debug

The most effective way to test the hardware of the equipment is to use a multimeter for overall testing. The welding of the equipment is not particularly clear, so it is not very intuitive when compared with the schematic diagram, so the multimeter is used for line measurement. Test, the first test is the power supply, VCC and GND short circuit. The test results are as follows Fig. 4.

Fig. 4. VCC and GND measurement results

The measurement found that the WELDING between VCC and GND was normal, proving that there was no problem with the source of the system. Then test the circuit conduction in turn, and test whether the two circuits are open according to the schematic diagram, as shown in Fig. 5, the buzzer beeps.

Fig. 5. Connected line measurement results

When testing the connecting line, it was found that the crystal vibration welding was not firmly welded, resulting in a state of circuit break, as shown in Fig. 6.

Fig. 6. Crystal resonance circuit

After correction, the solder of crystal vibration should be added to the correction welding of the system, as shown in Fig. 7.

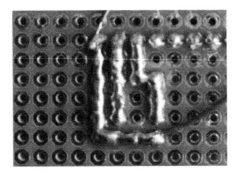

Fig. 7. Problem solving picture

Complete the overall test search of the system, the electrical test results of the equipment are normal, and the overall test effect of the system is shown in Fig. 8.

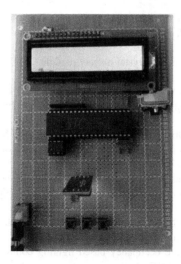

Fig. 8. Normal operation diagram of equipment

5   Conclusions

After the completion of the system, there will be many deficiencies in the system. At this time, the equipment can only be repeatedly debugged, the lick block is perfected in the whole program, the logic is rewritten, and the logic is restricted. Finally, a satisfactory device is completed by this means.

References

1. Rujian, S.: Single-chip microcomputer extension method for multi- channel illumination intensity acquisition. Autom. Instrum. **1**, 51–52 (2016)
2. Guojin, X., et al.: Application of RS422 interface chip in single-chip microcomputer system. Instrum. Technol. **3**, 14–16 (2015)
3. Changsong, Y.: Interference and anti-interference measures of SCM measurement and control system. Autom. Instrum. **6**, 153–156 (2016)
4. Hongyan, Z., Xiong, R.: Method of illumination acquisition based on single chip microcomputer. Microcomput. Inf. **11**, 126–127 (2014)
5. Ping, Z., Zhijun, X.: Design based on light intensity sensor. Electric Age **5**, 52–54 (2015)
6. Yanping, L., Wang, T.: Development of family lighting control system in residential area. Microcompu. Appl. **5**, 600–604 (2015)
7. Feng, X.: Multi-machine communication of illumination data acquisition system. Electr. Autom. **1**, 39–40 (2016)
8. Tie, L.: On the design of intelligent system for residential district. Intell. Build. Urban Inf. **1**, 30–31 (2017)
9. Yingjun, Z., Dong, K.: On the design of intelligent residential lighting system. Resid. Sci. Technol. **4**, 32–34 (2017)

10. Hennessy, J.L., Patterson, D.A.: Computer Organization and Design: The Hardware/Software Interface, pp. 78–82. Morgan Kaufman Publisher Inc., San Francisco (2017)

11. Liang, Z.: Application of liquid crystal display module LCD1602. Electronic production **17** (3), 1256–1274 (2017)

12. Yang, Y., Yi., J., Woo, Y.Y., Kim, B.: Optimum design for linearity and efficiency of microwave Doherty amplifier using a new load matching technique. Microw. J. **44**(12), 20–36 (2017)

13. Dye, R.: Visual Object-Orientated Programming. Dr. Dobbs Macintosh J. 201–306 (2016)

14. Yang, Yu.: New progress in research on automatic illumination monitoring system at home and abroad. Environ. Res. Monit. **3**, 69–72 (2017)

15. Jialin, L., Xu, Q.: Preliminary study on monitoring point placement method of Beijing urban acoustic and optical environment automatic monitoring system. China Environ. Monit. **2**, 17–20 (2008)

16. Yapeng, S., Hengyin, Z.: Lighting detection and control methods for livestock and poultry farms. Fujian Agric. Mach. **4**, 5–6 (2016)

17. Lephakpreeda, T.: Adaptive occupancy based lighting control via grey prediction. Build. Environ. **7**(40), 881–886 (2016)

18. Jia-hong, X.: Application and research of intelligent lighting system in modern building lighting. Archit. Forum Archit. Des. **27**(4), 74–77 (2017)

19. Krarti, M., Erickson, P., Hillman, T.A.: Simplified method to estimate energy savings of artificial lighting use from daylighting. Build. Environ. **13**(40), 747–754 (2015)

20. Peiliang, R., Hongyan, V.: Introduction of EIB lighting intelligent control system in airport departure hall. Smart Build. Urban Inf.

Back End Development of Classroom Management System Based on .Net

Ying Jin[1(✉)] and Chunwang Zhang[2]

[1] Fushun No.1 High School, Fushun 113001, China
jinying2006@126.com
[2] University of Electronic Science and Technology of China, Zhongshan Institute, Zhongshan 528400, China

Abstract. This system is developed to provide teachers and students with high-quality communication platform under the background of the widespread application of the Internet. It is an independent classroom management system module applied in the school's educational administration system.

Keywords: Curriculum management system · ASP.NET · Visual Studio 2015 · SQLITE · C#

1 Introduction

According to the actual needs of teachers and students, a single classroom management system module with educational administration system as the main body is established under the environment of front-end interface, and a database is created. The whole management system is designed for the purpose of safety, stability, convenience and practical and good operation. The implementation of this management system takes ASP.NET as the main body, C# language, VS2015, SQLITE as the core development tool, and DataAdapter as the means to connect to the database for development. Administrators, teachers, students as the core, for the connection of finish school with students in the system, the administrator, and teacher for students to upload information and management functions, purpose lies in the use of classroom management system to improve students' learning efficiency, strengthen the supervision of a teacher to the students, for teachers and students set up a bridge of communication before.

2 System Design

The main purpose of classroom management system is to realize the different roles, permissions and real-time management of various objects in the system. The classroom management system module is managed uniformly by the main module of the original educational administration system. After login, different operations are implemented according to different login roles. The role modules in the whole classroom management system are independent of each other, but all the data in the back end comes from the same database, and the data of each role module is interoperable, which facilitates

M. Guan and Z. Na (Eds.): MLICOM 2020, LNICST 342, pp. 195–200, 2021.
https://doi.org/10.1007/978-3-030-66785-6_21

the maintenance and optimization of the system in the later period. The following Fig. 1 shows the functional modules of the system.

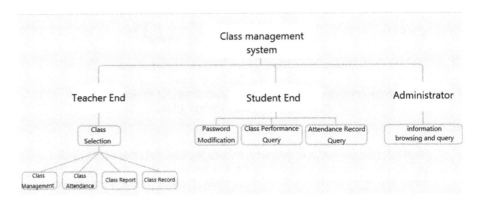

Fig. 1. The function module diagram of the system

3   Database Design of Classroom Management System

3.1   Database Design

System database design directly decides the overall efficiency of the system, in the design of database of time must be different specific naming, classification and separate the data to avoid when more data classification is not clear, repeat after, otherwise it will increase the working pressure of the developer, after completion of the system development maintenance workload also increased substantially, reduce the performance of the system and developer productivity. The design of the database should also be a comprehensive analysis of performance problems, to avoid system crash system failure and other security risks, but also conducive to saving resources and costs.

3.2   Database Logic Design ER Diagram

The logic of database is usually represented by ER design drawing, which is mainly composed of entity, attribute and relationship. Entities are objects, such as teachers, students, etc. Attributes are attributes that are owned by individual entities, such as student names, scores, and so on. Relationships are the connections between entities. Fig. 2 shows the ER design drawing for the database.

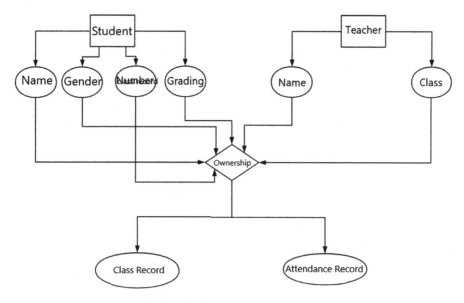

Fig. 2. ER blueprints for the database

4 System Debugging

4.1 Hardware Debug

1) Open Visual Studio 2015, load the system engineering file, generate WebApplication2, use Google Chrome browser by default to display and test the front page, enter the classroom management system, click on all returnable items, and dynamically operate the front page.

2) Click on the front page of the front-end classroom management system to enter any class, and select Class 2, Grade 3 for the test. After entering the classroom management interface of the class management interface, a student was randomly selected. During the test, student No. 23 was selected and graded. During the test, select "easy to pass", "emotional stability" and "Quiet after class" from the "praise" list, and record the time as: 2020/4/27 7:47 PM, as shown in Fig. 3 below. In the list of "to be improved", select "Distracted in class", "disruptive in class", and record the time as: 2020/4/27 7:49 PM, as shown in Fig. 4 below. Enter the classroom attendance system, select a student at random, select No. 16 Zhang Xiaolong for the test, select "late" in the "attendance" list, and record the time: 2020/4/27 7:50 PM, as shown in Fig. 5 below. Check the "Praise" screen of the scoring chart, as shown in Fig. 6 below. The "To be improved" interface of the scoring record table is shown in Fig. 7 and the attendance record table is shown in Fig. 8. Check to see if the previous action is displayed in the various tables as required.

3) Click the button in the upper right corner to select randomly, select 3 people, and click "Start to select" to see the selection results as shown in Fig. 9 below. Click "Reselect number" to select number 5, and click "Start to select", as shown in

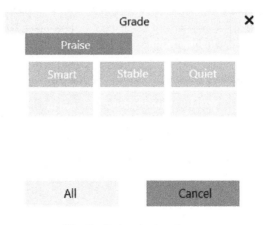

Fig. 3. Praise the interface

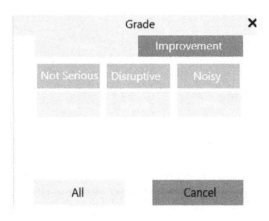

Fig. 4. Interface to be improved

Fig. 10 below. Close the random selection window, click the timer button, click "Start" on the "Timing" page, observe the timing situation, click pause, continue and start again during the start process, and record the test situation. Repeat this three times. Click the countdown function, set the countdown time to 3 min, and click Start. Click pause, continue, restart during the test, and record the test results.

4) Run the back-end database as an administrator, click "Browse data", open the "CLASSTU" table, change the name of student No. 136 to Lili, and delete the information of student No. 138, as shown in Fig. 11. Add a new student: Li Si, parameters are set as gender: female, no.: 150, class No.: 10 (Class 10, three years), as shown in Fig. 12. Save the database. Refresh the front end Web page to see if the information just recorded was uploaded to the front end. Fig. 13 shows the front-end results after modifying the name of student No. 136, deleting the information of student No. 8, and adding the information of student No. 150 "Li Si".

5 Conclusions

In the preliminary test, the dynamic jump of the front page could not be completed. After checking, it was found that the name of the back-end interface was entered incorrectly. Now it has been modified and the normal dynamic jump can be completed, achieving the expected effect. Simulate students' classroom management, attendance rating and other operations of the system through real data, and complete the expected requirements of the system.

References

1. Gan, K.: Exploration of building campus computer network. J. Chengdu Norm. Coll. (03), 11–15 (1996)
2. Gao, H., Liu, C., Jia, J.: Problems and countermeasures in campus LAN construction. Teach. Manag. (18), 38–41 (2001)
3. Liu, M.: Design and implementation of data integrity in SQL server database application system. Aeronaut. Comput. Technol. (02), 67–68 (2002)
4. Hu, B.: Brief analysis on the construction and maintenance of library database. Digit. Technol. Appl. (01), 97 (2013)
5. Du, Y.: Design and implementation of ASP.NET based attendance management system. Inf. Comput. (03), 94–95+98 (2018)
6. Luo, Y.: Design and prospect of college personnel information management system based on ASP.NET 3.5. China New Commun. 20(12), 68–69 (2012)
7. Han, B.: SQLite Database Research and Application. Nanjing University of Posts and Telecommunications (2019)
8. Pan, T., Zhou, F.: Research on teaching reform in Asp.net website design. Comput. Telecommun. (09), 18–20 (2017)
9. Zhao, F., Ni, J.: Research and development of intelligent quilting control software system based on Visual C#.NET. Mod. Text. Technol. 26(02), 85–89 (2008)
10. Luo, F.: Design and implementation of university smart classroom management system based on .net technology. J. Chang. Univ. 28(08), 15–20+24 (2015)
11. Wang, Z.: Design and Implementation of university Student Status Management System based on .NET. Jilin University (2018)
12. Zhao, W.: Design and implementation of performance salary management system based on ASP.net. Comput. Telecommun. (08), 58–60 (2017)
13. Gu, Y.: Design and implementation of BUS information management system based on ASP. NET. Fujian Comput. 34(12), 120+152 (2008)
14. Yang, Y., Yang, Y., Zhang, T., Li, S.: Common security problems and solutions developed by .NET. Comput. Telecommun. (08), 62–65 2018
15. Wu, G.: Design and implementation of online examination system based on .net. Educ. Teach. Forum (22), 94–95 (2018)
16. Qin, X., Zhu, S.: NET framework data access structure. Comput. Syst. Appl. (09), 32–34 (2002)
17. Wan, L., Li, X., Du, K.: Research on the current situation of database use and management in Chinese university libraries. In: Library Work and Research, no. 01, pp. 76–78 (2013)
18. Liu, Z.: Cloud computing and cloud data management technology. Comput. Res. Dev. S1, 76–79 (2012)

19. Li, P., Liu, B.: WEB database interface technology and application. Comput. Syst. Appl. (05), 43–45 (2001)
20. Wang, Y.: Key technologies of distributed storage in cloud computing environment. J. Softw. **04**, 70–71 (2012)

Big Data Platform System of Students' Comprehensive Ability Software Performance Test and Analysis

Ying Jin[1(✉)] and Hantao Gu[2]

[1] Fushun No.1 high school, Fushun 113001, China
jinying2006@126.com
[2] University of Electronic Science and Technology of China,
Zhongshan Institute, Zhongshan 528400, China

Abstract. This system is mainly for classroom management system, including school situation analysis, event management, school files, daily tasks, etc., teachers upload information, students view information, in the visual studio 2015 development environment, using C language object-oriented programming, using framework 4.5 framework, SQLite database development. In the software test after coding, the students' classroom management system is more and more perfect.

Keywords: Software testing · Classroom management · C# · vs2015

1 Introduction

With the continuous development of science and technology, the position and function of computer and computer network are increasingly prominent.Network classroom management should become a very important teaching method, network classroom management system is more and more attention.This paper mainly studies the application and promotion of classroom management system.To solve the problem of multiplatform heterogeneous data integration, the content of student attendance, learning and teaching evaluation is completed through multi-system. By studying the forms of classroom management score report, attendance report, student information and related technology in the network classroom system, the original multimedia teaching technology is extended and the classroom performance of students is digitized by combining the traditional teaching mode.

Inspect and test the entire project to ensure the feasibility and normal operation of the program, including data testing for each module and each function, upon completion of the classroom management development.Through the automated test (including black box testing and white box testing) to shorten the test cycle software development, can make the product faster finish, automated testing is more efficient, make full use of hardware resources and save human resources, reduce test cost, also can enhance the stability and reliability of the test, improve the accuracy of software testing and accuracy, increase software's trust, is relatively easy to make the test software test tools work.

M. Guan and Z. Na (Eds.): MLICOM 2020, LNICST 342, pp. 201–207, 2021.
https://doi.org/10.1007/978-3-030-66785-6_22

2 Demand Analysis

Students' requirements for system functions mainly include management and modification of personal accounts and passwords, inquiry of attendance records, inquiry of class results, praise from teachers or situations requiring improvement, class records, attendance summary records and other functions.

Administrators have information management, browsing and other rights.Includes records of teacher-student operations, including checks for data additions and deletions. From the perspective of user management and classroom management, user management mainly includes viewing and modifying the information of teachers and students, while classroom management includes adding, deleting, changing, checking and attendance records of classroom data, student scores and other information.

3 System Software Design and Actualize

3.1 Module Design

The user in the front end enters the account password through jquery and regular expressions to determine whether the user input conforms to the rules, including < HTML>Code and @ in accordance with the input, and to prevent SQL injection, not of the above, under the precondition of abiding by the rules of ajax, after click the button after winning two input function of the input value, the introduction of the value, the back-end through a user name to query the user list, if there is no query to the data, the user does not exist, the query to the later, the user to enter the password, and query to the password string comparison, through the if condition statements, if equal, login is success;If not, the password is wrong.Administrator login is three parallel and independent modules of student login and teacher login.The specific login name is similar to the system login name, which can take the input label from the front end and send it to the back end using Ajax for judgment and prompting.

Information management is mainly the operation of the teachers, students' class performance for a particular class, the students of class information, ratings, reviews, fill in comments on interface options, then click on the submit button, because the information has a nullable, but after filling the jquery + regular expression to determine whether the input avoid legal input HTML code and SQL injection, legally, in the same way through ajax filling is passed to the backend data, through the SQL statement to insert data into a specific table and insert specific information.Class management is mainly to classify the majors and classes of secondary majors in order to better index students, find students' corresponding classes and view specific information.Facilitate teachers and students to find their own class and performance.

3.2   Database Design

This project is mainly divided into the users table, table, teacher table, the table class, students information table, classification of secondary school, professional classification, campus information table, users table and students watch teachers and administrators table, is mainly responsible for user login, including class table and classification table and student ID, student table associated with secondary school and the professional classification.By operating the class table, the teacher adds and modifies the data of students' classroom performance.Here is the diagram.

Main user table is divided into three categories, including teachers, students, administrators, including the user table by teacher student ID, the details of the corresponding table query student ID or job number and password, the login page by getting the front end account password after compared with back-end query the database account password, if correct, the login is successful, to enter the main page (Fig. 1).

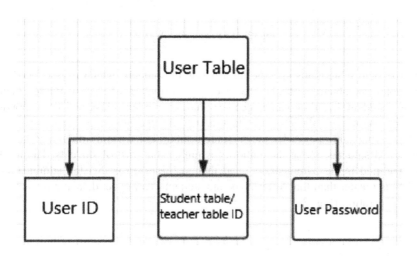

Fig. 1. The users table

The administrator is the identified teacher number. The administrator can act as the administrator as well as the teacher, adding, deleting, modifying and checking classroom records. The student only has the right to view classroom records and has no right to modify them, but the student can modify their own general information (Fig. 2).

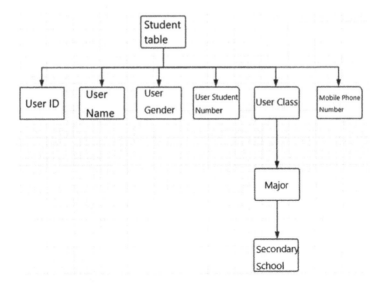

Fig. 2. The students table

The student table is the specific information of students, which is associated with other tables to obtain students' classroom performance and class rating, mainly including student ID, user name, gender, student number, class and corresponding major and secondary college of the class, and finally the mobile phone number.

The teacher table is similar to the student table, but the only difference between teachers and students is that the authority is higher than that of students. The teacher table identified is the administrator, and their relationship is that the administrator's authority is greater than that of teachers and students.To protect data and prevent data from misoperation (Fig. 3).

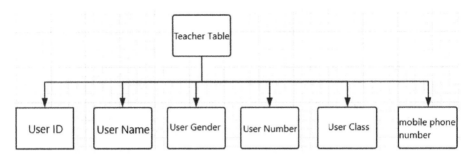

Fig. 3. The teachers table

The class table is similar to the class schedule, which records the current classroom classroom and class attending class. Each period has a teacher in charge of the current classroom. For the convenience of classification, the class table includes the class ID, class classification, teacher, classroom, class attending class, and the cellphone number of the teacher or person in charge (Fig. 4).

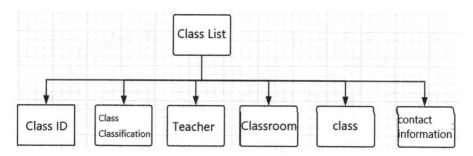

Fig. 4. The class table

Classroom performance information table is a big table, the data is also involved, mainly because the class information table and the table class, students table, table correlates to teachers, the performance of each student is a data, we can through the associated query, look at each of the students or the teacher's personal information, and each student of the teacher's classroom record, attendance, and students' classroom performance, grade class, etc.

4 System Debugging

4.1 Front-End Classroom Management Homepage Test

The implementation method of home page is relatively simple, mainly presenting class information. Click to enter the corresponding class management interface, which contains all class information and the name of the class teacher. The test here is mainly click test (Fig. 5).

Fig. 5. Classroom management homepage

Click the corresponding class on the home page and enter the class management interface, which is divided into six functions, including class grading, class attendance, class report, class record, random selection and timer, as shown in the figure below (Fig. 6).

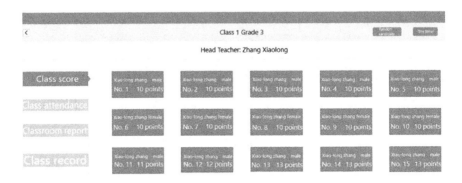

Fig. 6. Classroom grading interface

5   Conclusions

The tests should be designed for a specific purpose, and then tested for important aspects of one or more functions.Key test cases that are executed multiple times can be automated to properly evaluate the development and maintenance of automated test scripts.In general, manual testing can replace automated testing of any type and function, but automated testing is difficult to implement in situations such as multi- user concurrency.While the use of testing tools can improve the quality and efficiency of testing, the successful implementation of automated testing must follow the concepts of systematic, structured, and progressive testing.

References

1. Zhang, W.: Research on software development mode of automatic test system. Electron. World **2020**(06), 34–35 (2020)
2. Huang, Y., Xu, L.: Quality management of hospital information system based on full life cycle. China Health Qual. Manag. **27**(02), 81–83 (2020)
3. Liu, J., Wang, L., Yang, J.: Computer software testing method and application analysis. Sci. Technol. Wind **2020**(09), 119 (2020)
4. Zeng, X.: Application of ARIMA model in software test defect quantity prediction. Fujian Comput. Sci. **36**(03), 19–22 (2020)
5. Yu, Q.: Exploration of ideological and political teaching for software engineering course. Fujian Comput. Sci. **36**(03), 93–95 (2020)
6. He, W., Shen, X., Liu, B., Han, X., Tang, L.: Research on mission based ship equipment software test technology. Comput. Measur. Control **28**(03), 72–78 (2020)

7. Wu, X.: Hybrid teaching research and practice of "'software testing'" course. Wirel. Internet Technol. **17**(06), 94–95 (2020)
8. Xu, R., Jiang, F.: Application and comprehensive management of software testing technology. Electron. Qual. **2020**(03), 50–53 (2020)
9. Niu, F., Zhang, G., Su, Z., Yue, F.: Multi-stage multi- objective dynamic test resource allocation algorithm. Comput. Eng. Des. **41**(03), 656–663 (2020)
10. Baoyun, J.: Application of software automation test method. Comput. Prod. Circ. **2020**(03), 21 (2020)
11. Xu, L.X., Wu, H.Y.: Overview of software engineering methods based on swarm intelligence. Comput. Res. Dev. **57**(03), 487–512 (2020)
12. Niu, Y.: Construction and application of aerospace software test model. Software **41**(03), 268–271 (2020)
13. Zhong, R., Wang, T., Li, X., Zhang, X., Wang, J.: Heterogeneous multi-machine virtual simulation platform for aerospace control software. Microelectron. Intell. Manuf. **2**(01), 85–90 (2020)
14. Dohai, H.: Unit test case design and case analysis based on LDRA testbed. Electron. Test **2020**(06), 9–12 (2020)

Smart Beamformer Based on Artificial Intelligence

Mingxiang Guan[(✉)] and Zhou Wu

Shenzhen Institute of Information Technology, Shenzhen 518029, China
66827983@qq.com

Abstract. A decentralized smart beamformer based on artificial intelligence is proposed. Transmission weights adjustment of different users are described as a multi-users game. The existence and uniqueness of the Nash equilibrium in the adaptive beamforming algorithm based on artificial intelligence are proved. Convergent transmission weights update algorithm is designed.

Keywords: Smart beamformer · Artificial intelligence · Game theory

1 Introduction

The smart antenna [1] can focus the transmitted signal only on the desired user, making spatial nulls in the direction to the undesired users. Moreover it can adjust its transmission weight according to condition change of users. Game theory in artificial intelligence algorithm has become popular recently to analyze distributed problem. A game theoretic framework for greedy interference avoidance algorithm is presented in [2]. This model provides insight into development of algorithms that are fairer than the greedy interference avoidance algorithms. A distributed power control algorithm for wireless data systems is proposed in [3]. The QoS a wireless terminal receives is referred to as the utility and distributed power control where users maximize their utilities is a non-cooperative power control game.

In this paper we present a decentralized smart beamformer based on game theory. The main contributions of this paper are: 1) beamformer game model is constructed and transmission weights adjustment of different users are described as multi-users game; 2) the existence and uniqueness of the Nash equilibrium in the decentralized adaptive beamformer based on game theory are proved; 3) Convergent transmission weights update algorithm is designed.

2 System Model

A multiple-input multiple-output (MIMO) system using M transmit and receive antennas is characterized by:

M. Guan and Z. Na (Eds.): MLICOM 2020, LNICST 342, pp. 208–212, 2021.
https://doi.org/10.1007/978-3-030-66785-6_23

$$\mathbf{y}_l = \mathbf{H}_l \mathbf{v}_l \mathbf{x}_l + \mathbf{n}_l \tag{1}$$

where y is the M dimensional receive vector of user $l, l = 1, 2, \ldots, L$. We assume that totally L users are distributed in the system. $\mathbf{n}$ is the M dimensional white Gaussian noise vector, $\mathbf{H}_l$ describes the channel matrix and the elements of $\mathbf{H}_l$ are modeled as zero mean complex Gaussian random variables, and $\mathbf{v}_l$ is transmission weight of user l. We suppose $E[\mathbf{nn}^H] = \mathbf{I}$, $\|\mathbf{v}_l\| = 1$ and $E\{x_l x_i^H\} = \begin{cases} 1 & l = i \\ 0 & l \neq i \end{cases}$. The resulting received SINR of user l is:

$$\Gamma_l = \mathbf{v}_l^H \mathbf{R}_l \mathbf{v}_l \bigg/ \left(\sum_{i=1, i \neq l}^{L} \mathbf{v}_i^H \mathbf{R}_l \mathbf{v}_i + 1 \right) \tag{2}$$

where $\mathbf{v}_i$ is transmission weight of user i and $\mathbf{R}_l$ is the covariance of channel and $\mathbf{R}_l = E\{\mathbf{HH}^H\}$. The transmission weight vectors can be split up into [4]:

$$\mathbf{v}_l = \sqrt{P_l} \mathbf{u}_l \tag{3}$$

where P_l and $\mathbf{u}_l$ are the transmit power and the orientation of the transmission weight vector respectively. In this letter, we suppose that $\mathbf{u}_l$ is known by the transmitter. So the SINR of user l is a function of transmit power P_l.

3 Smart Beamformer Based on Game Theory

Game theory can be used to predict the outcome of these interactions and to identify optimal strategies and deleterious ones. The fundamental component of game theory is the notion of a game, expressed in normal form as $\Lambda = \{L, \{S_l\}_{l \in L}, \{U_l\}_{l \in L}\}$, where Λ is a particular game. L is a finite set of players, S_l is the set of the action available to players and U_l is the set of pure utility. In this letter we define U_l as:

$$U_l = U_u - U_{cost} = \Gamma_l / (\Gamma_l + \alpha) - \lambda P_l \tag{4}$$

where $U_u = \Gamma_l / (\Gamma_l + \alpha)$ is the whole utility function and represents the function of the SINR of user l and $U_{cost} = \lambda P_l$ is the cost function. α and λ are constant. α is an adjustable parameter and shows craggedness degree of U_u, which is set by the same value for all users. λ is the cost factor and defines the user's cost when it is interfered by other users.

We consider a best-response dynamics defined below:

$$\arg \max U_l = \arg \max (\Gamma_l / (\Gamma_l + \alpha) - \lambda P_l) \tag{5}$$

We suppose $k = \mathbf{u}_l^H \mathbf{R}_l \mathbf{u}_l \Big/ (\sum\limits_{i=1,i\neq l}^{L} P_i \mathbf{u}_i^H \mathbf{R}_l \mathbf{u}_i + 1)$, so the SINR Γ_l of user l in the Eq. (2) can also be expressed:

$$\Gamma_l = kP_l \tag{6}$$

Differentiating the Eq. (5) yields:

$$
\begin{aligned}
\frac{\partial U_l}{\partial P_l} &= \frac{\partial U_l}{\partial \Gamma_l} \cdot \frac{\partial \Gamma_l}{\partial P_l} - \lambda = \frac{\alpha}{(\Gamma + \alpha)^2} \frac{\partial \Gamma_l}{\partial P_l} - \lambda \\
&= \frac{k\alpha}{(\Gamma + \alpha)^2} - \lambda = 0
\end{aligned}
\tag{7}
$$

Through the Eq. (7) transmit power P_l can be expressed as:

$$
\begin{aligned}
\frac{k\alpha}{(\Gamma + \alpha)^2} &= \lambda \Rightarrow \frac{k\alpha}{\lambda} = (\Gamma + \alpha)^2 \\
&\Rightarrow kP_l = \sqrt{k\alpha/\lambda} - \alpha \\
&\Rightarrow P_l = \sqrt{\alpha/\lambda k} - \alpha/k
\end{aligned}
\tag{8}
$$

From the Eq. (8) we can find that the transmit power P_l of user l includes the interference of other users. So the transmit power of different users will affect each other. Next we will demonstrate that the power allocation for different users can converge to a Nash Equilibrium (NE). At a NE, given the power levels of other players, no users can improve its utility level by making individual changes in its power. In [3] the theorem of existence and uniqueness of NE is presented. According to these theorems we will prove the existence and uniqueness of NE of the proposed algorithm.

Theorem 1: The existence of NE of the proposed algorithm
① P_l is a nonempty, convex and compact subset of some Euclidean space. ② U_l is continuous in P and quasi-concave in P_l.

The first condition is satisfied because each user has a strategy space that is defined by $[0, P_l^{\max}]$ and all the power values in between.

Differentiating the Eq. (4) twice yields:

$$
\frac{\partial^2 U_l}{\partial P_l^2} = \frac{\partial \left| k\alpha \Big/ (\Gamma + \alpha)^2 - \lambda \right|}{\partial P_l} = \frac{-2k^2\alpha}{(kP_l + \alpha)^3} < 0
\tag{9}
$$

From the above equation we can know that the pure utility function U_l is concave in P_l for all l. A concave function is quasi-concave so the pure utility function U_l is quasi-concave in P_l. This completes the proof of the Theorem 1.

Theorem 2: The uniqueness of NE of the proposed algorithm
By Theorem 1, we know that there exists a NE P_l and define $r(P_l) = \sqrt{\alpha/\lambda k} - \alpha/k$. The key aspect of the uniqueness proof is that $r(P_l)$ is a standard function [5]. A function is said to be standard if it satisfied the following properties.

① *Positivity:* $r(P_l) > 0$

This property can be implied by a nonzero background receiver noise or by admission control.

② Monotonicity: If $P_l \leq P'_l$, then $r(P_l) \geq r(P'_l)$

The system is available so $U_l \geq 0$ and $k \geq k'$ for $P_l \leq P'_l$. Then we can obtain:

$$\Gamma_l/(\Gamma_l + \alpha) - \lambda P_l \geq 0 \Rightarrow \alpha/\lambda \geq \alpha^2/k \tag{10}$$

So

$$
\begin{aligned}
r(P_l) - r(P'_l) &= \left(\sqrt{\alpha/\lambda k} - \alpha/k\right) - \left(\sqrt{\alpha/\lambda k'} - \alpha/k'\right) \\
&\geq \left(\alpha k' - \alpha\sqrt{kk'} - \alpha k' + \alpha k\right)\Big/ kk' = (k - kk')\alpha/kk' \geq 0
\end{aligned}
\tag{11}
$$

So the monotonicity is satisfied.

③ *Scalability:* For all $\eta > 1$, $\eta r(P_l) \geq r(\eta P_l)$

We define $k_\eta = \mathbf{u}_l^H \mathbf{R}_l \mathbf{u}_l \Big/ (\sum\limits_{i=1,i\neq l}^{L} \eta P_i \mathbf{u}_i^H \mathbf{R}_l \mathbf{u}_i + 1)$ for all $\eta > 1$ so $k_\eta < k$. $r(\eta P_l)$ can be expressed $r(\eta P_l) = \sqrt{\alpha/\lambda k_\eta} - \alpha/k_\eta$ so

$$
\begin{aligned}
\eta r(P_l) - r(\eta P_l) &= \eta\left(\sqrt{\alpha/\lambda k} - \alpha/k\right) - \left(\sqrt{\alpha/\lambda k_\eta} - \alpha/k_\eta\right) \\
&\geq \alpha/\sqrt{k}\left(\eta/\sqrt{k} - 1/\sqrt{k_\eta}\right) - \eta\alpha/k + \alpha/k_\eta \\
&= \alpha\left(\eta/k - 1/\sqrt{kk_\eta} - \eta/k + 1/k_\eta\right) \\
&= \alpha\left((k - \sqrt{kk_\eta})/kk_\eta\right) > 0
\end{aligned}
\tag{12}
$$

So the scalability property is satisfied. Thus we prove that $r(P_l)$ is a standard function. It is shown in [5] that the NE P_l is unique for a standard function. Therefore, the NE of the proposed algorithm is unique.

According to the above conclusions we present a convergent transmission weight update algorithm to reach NE, which can be expressed as:

① Initialization: Set transmission weight $\mathbf{V} = [\mathbf{v}_1, \mathbf{v}_2, \cdots, \mathbf{v}_L]$.

② Weight update:

$$\mathbf{v}_l = \arg\max(\Gamma_l/(\Gamma_l + \alpha) - \lambda P_l)$$

$$P_l = \sqrt{\alpha/\lambda k} - \alpha/k, \ k = \mathbf{u}_l^H \mathbf{R}_l \mathbf{u}_l \Big/ (\sum\limits_{i=1,i\neq l}^{L} P_i \mathbf{u}_i^H \mathbf{R}_l \mathbf{u}_i + 1).$$

③ Iterative process:

$$|U_{n+1} - U_n| \leq \varepsilon$$

where ε is convergent precision. If the above equation is satisfied, the iteration is over.

4 Conclusions

Decentralized smart beamforming algorithm based on game theory is proposed. We construct beamforming game algorithm mathematics model. Transmission weights adjustment of different users are described as multi-users game. The existence and uniqueness of the Nash equilibrium in the smart beamforming algorithm based on game theory are proved. Convergent transmission weights update algorithm is designed.

Acknowledgements. This paper is supported by the Guangdong Province higher vocational colleges and schools, the Pearl River scholar funding scheme (2016), a project of the Shenzhen Science and Technology Innovation Committee (JCYJ20170817114522834, JCYJ2016060815 1239996), Research platform and project of Department of Education of Guangdong Province (2019GGCZX009) , the Key laboratory of Longgang District (LGKCZSYS2018000028), the science and technology development center of the Ministry of Education of China (2017A15009) and Engineering Applications of the Artificial Intelligence Technology Laboratory (PT201701).

References

1. Shahbazpanshi, S., Gershman, A.B., Luo, Z.Q., Wong, K.M.: Robust adaptive beamforming for general-rank signal models. IEEE Trans. Signal Process. **51**(9), 2257–2269 (2003)
2. Menon, R., MacKenzie, A., Buehrer, R., Reed, J.: Game theory and interference avoidance in decentralized networks. In: SDR Forum Technical Conference, 15–18 November 2004 (2004)
3. Saraydar, C.U., Mandayam, N.B., Goodman, D.J.: Efficient power control via pricing in wireless data networks. IEEE Trans. Commun. **50**, 291–303 (2002)
4. Boche, H., Schubert, M.: A new approach to power adjustment for spatial covariance based on downlink beamforming. In: ICASSP 2001, vol. 5, pp. 2957–2960 (2001)
5. Yates, R.D.: A framework for uplink power control in cellular radio systems. IEEE J. Sel. Areas Commun. **13**(9), 1341–1347 (1995)
6. Love, D.J., Health Jr., R.W., Strohmer, T.: Grassmannian beamforming for multiple-input multiple-output wireless systems. IEEE Trans. Inf. Theory **49**(10), 2735–2747 (2003)

Intelligent Communications

Blind Recognition of TT&C Signals of Satellite Based on JTFA and Fast-ICA Algorithm

Wang Le[(✉)], MingXiang Guang, and JingDan Zhang

Engineering Center of Communication Technology, College of Electrics
and Communication, Shenzhen Institute of Information Technology,
Shenzhen, China
wangleathit@126.com

Abstract. A blind sub-carrier recognition algorithm of TT&C communication is proposed based on JTFA(Joint Time-Frequency Analysis)and Fast-ICA Algorithm. In this method, we use time-frequency analysis technology to extract the features of the satellite signals, and Fast-ICA to enhance SNR (Signal Noise Ratio) effectively. As one of the best tools to analyze the non-stationary signals, it shows information in the joint time-frequency domain and makes us know about the change of frequency along with the time clearly. Before the time-frequency analysis of the satellite signal, the premise is to remove noise. This paper presents a method of Satellite TT&C signal recognition. The analysis results show that the algorithm has good effect and good convergence in the satellite TT&C signal extraction. The characteristic of this algorithm is that we need not any prior information of signals to recognize any TT&C signals of satellite.

Keywords: JTFA · ICA · TT&C signals of satellite

1 Introduction

In modern military information wars, Satellite monitoring plays an important role because satellites have important mechanics and advantages. At present, in the information reconnaissance of communication, S-band (USB) monitoring system is widely used, so it is a prominent problem to extract multiple subcarriers from a monitoring frequency band. In the identification of satellite monitoring subcarrier signals, unknown bandwidth and uncorrelated, the manual detection method is mainly used. However, this method has the disadvantages of complex operation, high cost and high false detection rate, which can not meet the needs of satellite monitoring information reconnaissance and can not adapt to the environment of information war.

The time-frequency analysis technique of signal processing is a powerful tool when it is used to analyze non-stationary signals. The number is called time-frequency distribution. Using time-frequency distribution to analyze the signal can give the

---

This paper is funded by Guangdong Province higher vocational colleges & schools Pearl River scholar funded scheme (2016).

M. Guan and Z. Na (Eds.): MLICOM 2020, LNICST 342, pp. 215–221, 2021.
https://doi.org/10.1007/978-3-030-66785-6_24

instantaneous of each moment frequency and its amplitude, and can be used for time-frequency filtering and time-varying signal research.

The so-called joint time-frequency analysis refers to mapping the time-domain signal s(t) to the time-frequency plane (phase plane), so as to analyze the local spectrum characteristics of the signal at a certain time. This method overcomes the shortcoming that the traditional Fourier transform can't describe the local characteristics of signals, so it has been widely used in signal and image analysis, seismic signal processing, speech analysis and synthesis, nondestructive testing and other non-stationary signal processing, and has achieved great success.

The advantage of independent component analysis is that it does not need instantaneous mixing parameters, and only needs a small amount of statistical information (mutual independence and Gaussian distribution) to recover the source signal from the observed signal. The signal can be extracted without statistical information.

In signal detection, this algorithm can effectively divide the signals with overlapping spectrum. ICA algorithm based on negative entropy maximization and time-frequency analysis is applied to satellite signal recognition algorithm. The analysis shows that it has a great application prospect in military communication.

1.1 Independent Component Analysis

$$\begin{bmatrix} x_1 \\ x_2 \\ \vdots \\ x_n \end{bmatrix} = \begin{pmatrix} a_{11} & \cdots & a_{1n} \\ \vdots & \ddots & \vdots \\ a_{m1} & \cdots & a_{mn} \end{pmatrix} \begin{bmatrix} s_1 \\ s_2 \\ \vdots \\ s_m \end{bmatrix} \Leftrightarrow X = AS \tag{1}$$

ICA is based on the assumption that the source signals are independent of each other. Based on this premise, the algorithm can use a linear transformation matrix to transform the variables in the case of unknown source signal and mixed matrix, so that the output variables and source signals are independent.

$$Y = W^T X = W^T AS = \widehat{S} \tag{2}$$

In this paper,a fast ICA algorithm based on negative entropy maximization combined with time-frequency analysis is adopted. The algorithm will be introduced step by step.

1.2 Algorithm Theory

The central limit theorem states that: when $X_i(i = 1, 2, \cdots)$ are independently identically distributed, $Y_n = \sum_{i=1}^{n}(X_i - n\mu_s)/\sqrt{n}\sigma_x(n = 1, 2, \cdots)$; when $n \to \infty$, $Y_n \sim N(0, 1)$.

Before this separation and extraction algorithm for satellite monitoring signals, we make the following assumptions:

(a) The influence of noise is not considered;
(b) Satellite signal is a typical stationary independent random signal.

(1) Preprocessing

Firstly, we need to preprocess the signal, including centralized processing and whitening. Hypothesis is to delete the average value of x from it, so that x becomes the zero mean vector. The meaning of whitening is to make the components independent of each other through linear transformation Q of observation vector, and they also have a unit covariance matrix (for example), whitening is realized through PCA network. $v = Qx = \ddot{E}^{-1/2}U^Tx$, where $\ddot{E} = diag(d_1, \cdots, d_n)$ is diagonal matrix of N maxima of correlation matrix $R_x = E\{xx^T\}$ on its diagonal line, and $U \in C^{m \times n}$ is a matrix consists of corresponding eigenvectors.

(2) ICA Algorithm Based on the Maximization of Negentropy

In information theory, the negative entropy of Gaussian variable is the largest among all random variables with the same variance. We can use this theory to measure the degree of non Gaussian of a variable. Negative entropy is a kind of modified entropy.. Let y_G is the combination vector of n Gauss random variables, with the same mean and variance matrix of y, then $J(y) = H_G(y) - H(y)$.

$$J(y) = \int p(y) \log p(y) dy - \int p_G(y) \log p_G(y) dy$$
$$= \int p(y) \log(\frac{p(y)}{p_G(y)}) dy + \int (p(y) - p_G(y)) \log p_G(y) dy \tag{3}$$

The parameters of the output signal can be expressed as Negentropy: $I(y) = J(y) - \sum_{i=1}^{n} J(y_i)$. So the cost function based on maximization of Negentropy is

$$\Phi_{NM}(W) = -\log|\det W| - \sum_{i=1}^{n} J(y_i) + H_G(y) - H(x)$$

$$\Delta W \propto [(W^T)^{-1} - \xi(y)x^T]W^TW = (I - \xi(y)y^T)W, \xi(Y) = -\frac{\partial}{\partial W}\sum_{i=1}^{n} J(y_i)$$

The measurement of the independence between different signals can be accomplished by the calculation of negative entropy. However, the calculation of negative entropy needs to estimate the probability density function of random variables. It is very complex to estimate the probability density function. The effectiveness of the estimation depends on the selected parameters, and the amount of calculation will become larger.

(3) The Algorithm Step

The formula of Negentropy calculation is as follows $J(y) \approx \sum_{i=1}^{p} k_i \{E[G_i(y)] - E[G_i(v)]\}^2$. G_i is a non-quadratic function,

$$G_1(u) = (1/a_1)\log\cos a_1 u, (1 \le a_1 \le 2);$$
$$G_2(u) = -(1/a_2)\exp(-a_2 u^2/2), (a_2 \approx 1); G_3(u) = 0.25u^4$$

$$J_G(\mathbf{W}) \propto \{E[G(\mathbf{w}^T\mathbf{X})] - E[G(\mathbf{v})]\}^2 \tag{4}$$

Maximizing this expression respect to $E[G(\mathbf{y})] = E[G(\mathbf{w}^T\mathbf{X})]$, namely $E'[G(\mathbf{w}^T\mathbf{X})] = E[\mathbf{X}g(\mathbf{w}^T\mathbf{X})] = 0$, where $g(x)$ is the derivative of $G(x)$.

Multiply both sides of the equation by $E[g'(\mathbf{w}^T\mathbf{X})]$, we get $\mathbf{W}'E[g'(\mathbf{w}^T\mathbf{X})] = \mathbf{W}E[g'(\mathbf{w}^T\mathbf{X})] - E[\mathbf{X}g(\mathbf{w}^T\mathbf{X})]$.

Let $\mathbf{W}^+ = -\mathbf{W}'E[g'(\mathbf{w}^T\mathbf{X})]$, after transformation we get $\mathbf{W}^+ = E[\mathbf{X}g(\mathbf{w}^T\mathbf{X})] - E[g'(\mathbf{w}^T\mathbf{X})]\mathbf{W}$.

Let $\mathbf{W}^* = \mathbf{W}^+/\|\mathbf{W}^+\|$. If the result does not converge, continue to repeat the above steps until it converges. This algorithm can be divided into five steps.

(1) Set $n = 0$, initializing the weighting vector $\mathbf{W}(0)$;
(2) Set $n = n+1$, computing $y(t) = \mathbf{w}^T(n)x(t)$;
(3) Computing $w(n+1)$, and de-correlated $w(n+1)$ from $w_1, w_2, \cdots$ w_n. $\mathbf{W}(n+1) = E[\mathbf{X}g(\mathbf{w}^T(n)\mathbf{X})] - E[g'(\mathbf{w}^T(n)\mathbf{X})]\mathbf{W}(n)$;
(4) Normalizing $\mathbf{W}(n+1) = \mathbf{W}(n+1)/\|\mathbf{W}(n+1)\|$;
    When the result of the algorithm is not convergent, jump to the second step, continue the iteration;
(5) When $|\mathbf{W}(n+1) - \mathbf{W}(n)| < \varepsilon$, the algorithm converges, we can get an independent component $y_1 = \hat{s}_1 = \mathbf{W}\mathbf{X}$.

When $\mathbf{W}_{i+1}$ is computed, we use Gram-Schmidt de-correlating algorithm, $w_1^T x, w_2^T x, \cdots w_n^T x$ will be de-correlated. $\mathbf{W}_{i+1}(n+1)$ will be After each iteration, the following formula is reused to decorrelate.

$$\mathbf{W}_{i+1}(n+1) = \mathbf{W}_{i+1}(n+1) - \sum_{j=1}^{i} \mathbf{W}_{i+1}^T(n+1)w_j w_j \tag{5}$$

$$\mathbf{W}_{i+1}(n+1) = \mathbf{W}_{i+1}(n+1)/\sqrt{\mathbf{W}_{i+1}^T(n+1)\mathbf{W}_{i+1}(n+1)} \tag{6}$$

2   Short Time-Fourier Transform

STFT(Short Time-Fourier Transform) is one solution of JTFA. The basic idea is to use window function to intercept the signal. Assuming that the signal in the window is stationary, the local frequency domain information can be obtained by Fourier transform. Corresponding to a certain moment t, STFT only analyzes the signal near the window and can roughly reflect the local spectrum information of the signal near the window. Then moving the window function along the signal, we can get the time-frequency distribution of the signal. It is defined as

$$\text{STFT}(t, \omega) = \int x(\tau)\gamma^*(\tau - t)e^{-j\omega\tau}d\tau \tag{7}$$

Where: $x(t)$-signal.
$\gamma(\tau - t)e^{-j\omega\tau}$-basic function.
t-time.
ω-frequency.

2.1 Simulation Results and Analysis

In this paper, a large number of simulation experiments are carried out to solve the problem of extracting and identifying satellite monitoring signals. In this paper, two signals randomly monitored by two satellites are selected randomly. Taking the signal of satellite downlink channel as an example, the two monitoring signals are generated by cortex monitoring terminal. Next, the two signals are extracted and separated, and the test results are verified. Firstly, the time-frequency analysis method is combined with fast ICA algorithm to separate the mixed signals. After three iterations, the first independent component is extracted. It can be seen from the figure that although there are some changes in the amplitude of the source signal, from the point of view of the signal waveform, the separation result is to achieve the desired goal (Figs. 1 and 2).

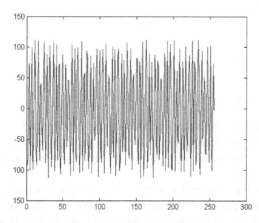

Fig. 1. Mixed signals with different parameters observed

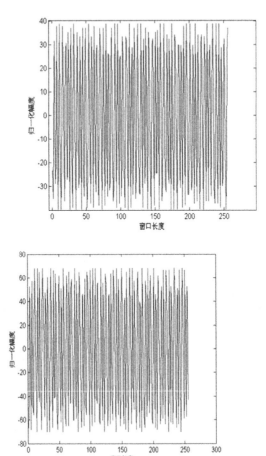

Fig. 2. Extracted signals

Simulation results show that:

(a) This method analyzes the statistical independence of the signal. Firstly, it avoids the limitation of signal complexity in the previous signal extraction algorithm, and can also identify the signal with wrong parameters, which greatly improves the recognition accuracy.

(b) Because the number of sampling points has an impact on the effect of extraction and separation, the parameters of different signals are different, so the extraction effect depends on the total number of sampling points. Generally speaking, with the increase of the number of sampling points, the higher the extraction accuracy; the greater the difference of parameters between signals, the higher the extraction accuracy. When the parameters of the signal are close, if the same number of sampling points can not be used to extract the signal properly, it can be solved by increasing the number of sampling points.

3   Conclusions

This paper presents an algorithm that combines time-frequency analysis with independent variables. As the objective function of non Gaussian random variables, this function can maximize the non Gaussian property of random variables and make the output parts independent of each other. The algorithm is applied to the extraction of satellite signals, which solves the problem of signal recognition without prior knowledge, unknown number of signals and unknown bandwidth of subcarrier signals. In this paper, the algorithm of sub carrier signal detection and acquisition is studied, and each step of the algorithm is discussed in detail. The test and simulation results show that the proposed algorithm can effectively identify the satellite signal subcarriers, and has the advantages of high extraction accuracy and fast convergence speed.

References

1. Hyvärinen, A., Karhunen, J., Oja, E.: Independent component analysis: algorithms and applications. Neural Netw. **13**(4–5), 411–430 (2000)
2. Comom, P.: Independent component analysis-a new concept. Signal Process. **36**, 287–314 (1994)
3. Jutten, C., Herault, J.: Blind separation of sources, part I an adaptive algorithm based on neuromlimetic architecture. Signal Process. **24**, 1–0 (1991)
4. Yi-long, N.I.U., Hai-yang, C.H.E.N.: Blind Signals Separate. Defense Industry University Publishing House, Beijing (2006)
5. Zhang, D., Wu, X., Shen, Q., Guo, X.: Online algorithm of independent component analysis and its application. J. Syst. Simul. **6**(1), 17–19 (2004)
6. Talwar, S., Viberg, M., Paulraj, A.: Blind separation of synchronous co-channel digital signals using an antenna array -part 1: algorithm. IEEE Trans. Signal Process. **44**(5), 1184–1197 (1996)
7. Wei-hong, Fu., Xiao-niu, Y., Xin-wen, Z., Nai-an, L.: Novel method for blind recognition communication signal based on time-frequency analysis and neural network. Signal Process. **23**(5), 775–778 (2007)

BLE Receiver with Fast DC Offset Cancellation and Carrier Frequency Offset Compensation

Cong Qiu[✉]

School of Electronic Communication Technology, Shenzhen Institute
of Information Technology, Shenzhen, Guangdong Province,
People's Republic of China
qiucong@sziit.edu.cn

Abstract. A BLE receiver with fast DC offset cancellation and carrier frequency offset (CFO) compensation is presented. The receiver employs a fully integrated RF front-end and a digital modem. The BLE SoC with embedded flash is fabricated in 55 nm RF CMOS technology, the receiver achieves sensitivity of −95 dBm and the CFO compensation in digital modem helps to extend the CFO tolerance from ± 100 kHz (BLE spec.) to ± 250 kHz with only 2 dB sensitivity degradation.

Keywords: Bluetooth low energy · DC offset cancellation · Carrier frequency offset compensation · System-on-chip

1   Introduction

Bluetooth Low-Energy (BLE) is becoming widely used in consumer IoT devices because it can communicate directly with mobile terminals (smart phones or tablets) and consumes very low average energy. In real wireless environment, the signal strength varies greatly, the receiver is required to have high gain and fast gain switching, which may lead to DC offset problem. On the other hand, due to the non-ideal reference crystals for the transmission and reception, there must be a certain carrier frequency offset between both side, which will also reduce the reception performance. In this work, a receiver with fast DC offset cancellation (DCOC) and carrier frequency offset (CFO) compensation is presented, it employs a fully integrated RF front-end and a digital modem.

2   Design of Building Blocks

As shown in Fig. 1, the proposed receiver adopts a single-conversion low-IF architecture with integrated tunable complex filter which performs image rejection and partial channel selection functionality. The down-converted IF signal is amplified by the PGA (Programable Gain Amplifier) and then digitized by the ADC for further signal processing in digital domain. The local-oscillator (LO) of RX is generated by a 4.8 GHz frequency synthesizer, the choice of a LO frequency of $2 \times$ RF solves the pulling in TX, it can also minimize the effect of LO leakage into the receiver, thereby reducing LO self-mixing induced DC offset.

M. Guan and Z. Na (Eds.): MLICOM 2020, LNICST 342, pp. 222–227, 2021.
https://doi.org/10.1007/978-3-030-66785-6_25

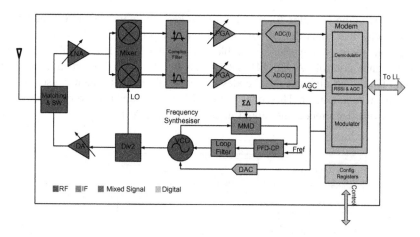

Fig. 1. Transceiver architecture

2.1 RF Front-End with On-chip Matching

The LNA input is shared with the PA output pin using an on-chip matching network and switches [1], as shown in Fig. 2, The LNA [2] is an inductor source degenerated amplifier with L-C load at the output, it is differential, requiring a transformer acts as BALUN for single-end conversion. In RX mode, switch S1 is shorted to ground and switch S2 is open, LG, CP, together with the transformer (LP, LS1, LS2) realize the desired LNA input matching network.

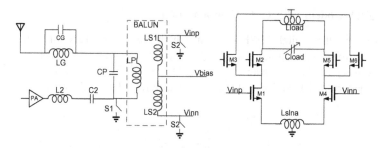

Fig. 2. RF front-end and on-chip matching

2.2 DCOC Scheme

To avoid saturating the ADC or deteriorating the RX sensitivity performance, DC offset cancellation (DCOC) is needed, especially when the gain of the PGA is large (30 dB or above) [3]. Figure 3 shows the block diagram of the proposed DCOC scheme, I-Path and Q-Path DC offset is cancelled individually, the analog comparator (COMP) compares the differential output of I-Path(Q-Path) and generates "0" or "1", the digital counter accumulates the numbers of "0" and "1" for several microseconds and then control the 8-bit DAC to cancel the DC offset at the input of RX ABB (analog baseband, including complex filter and PGA) to keep the numbers of "0" and "1" are equal to each other, thus the DC offset residual is close to zero. According to BLE specification, there is only 8 μs preamble ("01010101" or "10101010" pattern) for automatic gain control (AGC) [4], DCOC should be settled in such short time. A lookup table with different DAC codes related to different RX gain is used to meet such stringent requirement. The codes in the table will be updated every time the SoC wakes up from sleep mode and stored in the retention RAM.

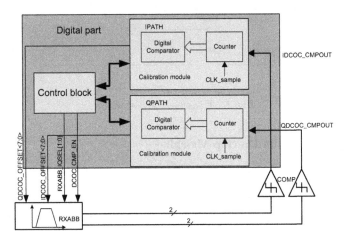

Fig. 3. DCOC scheme

2.3   Digital Modem with CFO Compensation

Figure 4 shows the digital GFSK modem, which has several functionalities such as RSSI calculation, AGC, digital down-conversion (DDC), channel-select filtering(FIR), carrier recovery etc. The Carrier Frequency Offset (CFO) is estimated based on the preamble pattern and feed-forward compensated during demodulation process.

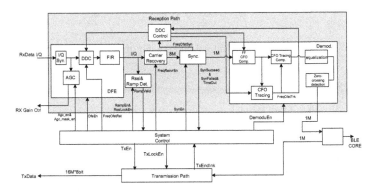

Fig. 4. Modem architecture

3   Measurement Results

The SoC is fabricated in 55 nm RF CMOS technology and the die photo is shown in Fig. 5. The radio (RF), modem, link controller, CPU, and memories (embedded flash, SRAM) are all integrated on chip, along with a PMU (Bulk DC-DC Converter and LDOs), oscillators (Crystal and RC Oscillators) and digital & analog peripheral blocks.

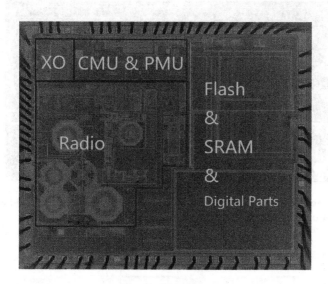

Fig. 5. Die photo

3.1   RX Input Reflection Coefficient

The input reflection coefficient in RX mode is measured by a vector network analyzer as shown in Fig. 6. It achieves good matching, less than -15 dB at 2.4 GHz.

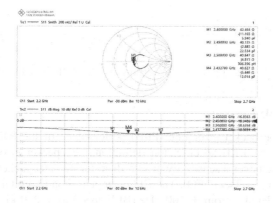

Fig. 6. RX input reflection coefficient

3.2 DCOC Settling Time

Figure 7 and Fig. 8 show the DCOC and AGC settling process respectively, the settling time is less than 3 μs while switching PGA gain from 18 dB to 42 dB, which satisfies the requirement of BLE system (less than 8 μs).

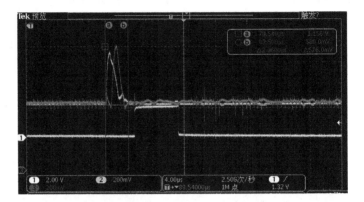

Fig. 7. DCOC settling process (The blue and pink lines represent I-Path and Q-Path DC offset respectively). (Color figure online)

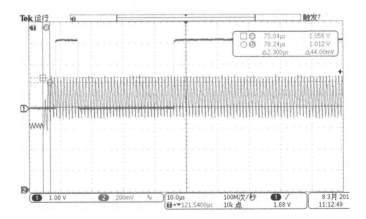

Fig. 8. AGC settling process (−70 dBm Input, RXABB gain 18 dB–42 dB)

3.3 Rx Sensitivity

Figure 9 shows the packet error rate (PER) performance of the RX. The RX measurement follows the BLE specification definition, i.e., packet error rate (PER) of 30.8% [4], and it achieves a sensitivity of −95 dBm for 37 octet packets (1 Mbps) with zero carrier-frequency offset (CFO). The CFO compensation in digital modem helps to extend the CFO tolerance from ± 100 kHz (BLE spec.) to ± 250 kHz, the sensitivity degradation is only about 2 dB.

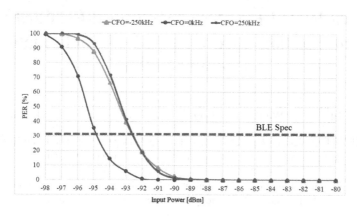

Fig. 9. RX sensitivity

4   Conclusion

A fully integrated BLE receiver with fast DCOC and CFO compensation in 55-nm RF CMOS process was presented. The DCOC settling time is less than 3 µs and the CFO tolerance is extended to ± 250 kHz with only 2 dB sensitivity degradation.

References

1. Prummel, J., Papamichail, M., Ancis, M., et al.: A 10mW bluetooth low-energy transceiver with on-chip matching. ISSCC Dig. Tech. Papers, pp. 238–239, February 2015
2. Oshiro, M., Maruyama, T., Tokairin, T., et al.: A 3.2 mA-RX 3.5 mA-TX fully integrated SoC for bluetooth low energy. In: IEEE ASSCC, November 2016
3. Sano, T., Mizokami, M., Matsui, H., et al.: A 6.3mW BLE transceiver embedded RX image rejection filter and TX harmonic-suppression filter reusing on-chip matching network. ISSCC Dig. Tech. Papers, pp. 240–241, February 2015
4. Bluetooth SIG.: Specification of the Bluetooth System, V4.2, vol. 6, December 2014. https://www.bluetooth.org

An RGB-LED Driver with Feed-Forward Equalization Used for PAM-4 Visible Light Communication

Bo Xu[1]([✉]), Li Wang[1], Jian Kang[1], Cong Qiu[2], and C. Patrick Yue[1]

[1] HKUST-Qualcomm Optical Wireless Lab, ECE Department, The Hong Kong University of Science and Technology, Hong Kong SAR, China
bxuag@connect.ust.hk
[2] School of Electronic Communication Technology, Shenzhen Institute of Information Technology, Shenzhen, Guangdong, China

Abstract. This work proposed a red-green-blue LED (RGB LED) driver based on TSMC 40 nm CMOS process with current regulator structure to drive a 5X5 RGB LED array. By adopting 4-pulse amplitude modulation (PAM-4) scheme and feed-forward equalization (FFE), the simulated driving data rate for each driver can reach 100 Mb/s.

Keywords: LED driver · Visible light communication · 4-Pulse amplitude modulation · Feed-Forward equalization

1 Introduction

With the fast development of wireless communication technology, visible light communication (VLC) has attracted increasing attention from both institute and industry as a significant direction of next generation wireless communication network. Compared with radio frequency (RF) communication, VLC is superior for its wide spectrum, easy implemented, high security, and power efficient especially when combining with extensively existing LED infrastructures. Due to the high output power intensity of LEDs, the signal to noise ratio (SNR) of LED based VLC can be higher than RF communication, which provides advantages for supporting high-order modulation such as carrierless amplitude and phase modulation (CAP) [1], discrete multi-tone modulation (DMT) [2], and pulse amplitude modulation (PAM) [3].

However, most of high-order modulation VLC prototypes are lack of implementation or just composed of discrete components. At the transmitter side, specialized high-speed LED driver is neglected. Traditional current pulse drivers are faced with large rising and falling edge problem when driving a series of LEDs at high switching frequency [4]. In addition, equalization scheme is widely adopted to extend the bandwidth of LEDs and increase SNR.

In this work, we proposed a current regulating red-green-blue LED (RGB LED) driver with feed-forward equalization (FFE) to drive a 5 × 5 RGB LED array with utilizing PAM-4 scheme. For each color LED series, the VLC driving signal is a non-return-to-zero (NRZ) signal. By combining the three different signals coming from the

M. Guan and Z. Na (Eds.): MLICOM 2020, LNICST 342, pp. 228–234, 2021.
https://doi.org/10.1007/978-3-030-66785-6_26

three-color LEDs, 4 different current levels can be formed. PAM-4 signal, therefore, is easily realized.

2   System Architecture

As shown in Fig. 1, the whole driver system is consisted of main driver, FFE driver, and light source. To simplify the system architecture, the main driver and FFE driver utilize same structure with different driving current. A 5 × 5 RGB LED array is used as light source while each color LED array equips with separate main driver and FFE driver. Input VLC data is under NRZ coding and driving red, green, and blue LEDs separately to guarantee the correct superposition in optical domain to form 4 different levels of current which produce final PAM-4 signal. The supplied voltage of LED array is 20 V and the maximum driving current for each LED branch is 60 mA.

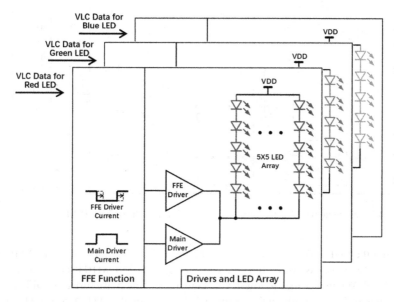

Fig. 1. System architecture of the proposed PAM-4 VLC RGB-LED driver.

2.1   Driver Architecture

Figure 2 merely presents the schematic of main driver while FFE driver employs the same structure and connects to LED array in the same way. The proposed driver is based on current regulator in [5] and simplify the function of timing controller and operational transconductance amplifier (OTA) with a dynamic gate-boosting amplifier (DGB-AMP) in [4]. The rising and falling time of current-pulse driver proposed in [6] is too long to support high speed switching. Besides, longer rising time than falling time will cause shorter high level than low level in OOK modulation, which is the origin of duty circle distortion and will decrease SNR.

In the proposed driver, I_{LED} is given by [5] which is set as 60 mA per branch:

$$I_{LED} = \frac{V_{-,DGB\,AMP}}{R_1} \tag{1}$$

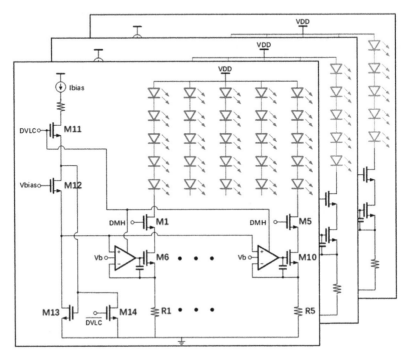

Fig. 2. Schematic of the proposed LED driver with 5X5 RGB LED array.

During the high-level stage of DVLC, the state of enable pulse in DGB-AMP is the same as DVLC which is "ON", thus the gate capacitor of M6–M10 is charged to driving voltage level. When it comes to low-level stage, the enable pulse turns to "OFF" and the charged gate is floating without discharging. The gate signal of M1–M5 (DMH) changes with DVLC synchronously but with different voltage level. At the rising edge, I_{LED} will immediately rise to high-level as the already charged gate capacitor of M6–M10 providing driving voltage to M1–M5, which immensely decreases the rising time. At the falling edge, M14 helps to discharging M13 while M1–M5 turn-off promptly. There strategies will reduce falling time. The capacitor connecting between the gate and source of M6–M10 will remove overshoot of I_{LED} at high-level.

2.2 FFE Implementation

As shown in Fig. 1, the amplitude of both FFE and main driving current is adjustable to maintain a stable output current. FFE driving current derives from main driving current with being properly inverted and delayed. After sent to corresponding FFE driver, the

FFE signal combines with main signal at the end of LED series to form final driving current I_{LED}. The function of FFE is extending the bandwidth by increasing the peak of driving current at rising and falling edges so that the quality of communication can be improved.

3 Simulation Results and Discussion

The simulation verification consists of transient analysis and eye diagram measurement which are performed in EDA tool Cadence with transient noise included. The driver is implemented in TSMC 40 nm process. R-C equivalent model is used as LED load with numerical value of 50 Ω and 200 pF separately. Since the current flowing through resistance connected in parallel with capacitance in LED model changes corresponding with LED light intensity, we utilize this resistance current to represent light signal in eye diagram analysis. Here we just applied random NRZ data as input VLC signal, and more input data pattern such as PRBS-7 could be analyzed in further research.

3.1 Verification of Driver Function

To verify the function of proposed driver, we firstly analyzed the transient waveforms under 10 Mb/s OOK modulation and the result is presented in Fig. 3(a). The maximum driving current is around 60 mA while rising and falling edges changing corresponding with input VLC data. The transient waveforms of three different random 10 Mb/s NRZ data with combined final PAM-4 driving current are shown in Fig. 3(b).

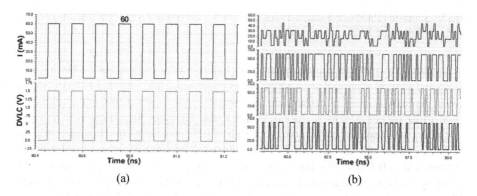

(a)   (b)

Fig. 3. Simulated transient waveforms of the LED driver with different VLC input data: (a) 10 Mb/s OOK, (b) 10 Mb/s NRZ.

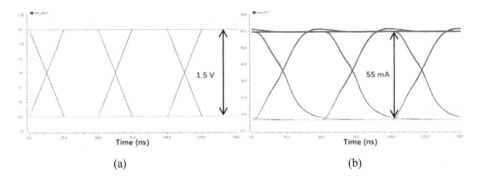

(a)   (b)

Fig. 4. Simulated eye diagrams for RGB LED single color: (a) input eye diagram of 10 Mb/s NRZ, (b) output eye diagram of 10 Mb/s NRZ.

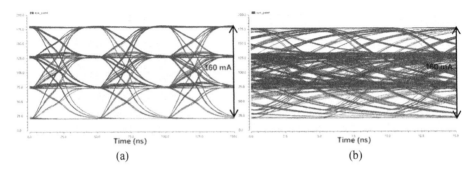

(a)   (b)

Fig. 5. Simulated PAM-4 eye diagrams for RGB LED with different VLC data rate: (a) 10 Mb/s NRZ, (b) 100 Mb/s NRZ.

Secondly, eye diagram measurement is performed for each color LEDs by analyzing input VLC data and the output current through resistance in LED equivalent model. As shown in Fig. 4(a) and (b), the height of eye diagram for input voltage is 1.5 V while output current is around 55 mA under 10 Mb/s NRZ data.

Lastly, we simulated eye diagrams of RGB LED array drove by combined driving current to verify the accuracy of PAM-4 scheme. The simulation results of random 10 Mb/s and 100 Mb/s NRZ input data are shown in Fig. 5(a) and (b) separately. The height of PAM-4 eye diagram is around 160 mA with exact superpositions of three NRZ signals in Fig. 5(a). In addition, there is no state lacking in this PAM-4 eye diagram. However, it can be noticed that there exists bandwidth limitation in Fig. 5(b) as there almost exists no open eye.

3.2   Verification of FFE

To verify the function of FFE, we simulated PAM-4 eye diagram since there exists evident bandwidth limitation in without FFE case especially for higher frequency. After adjusting both FFE and main driving current to keep 60 mA total driving current, FFE is employed to the proposed driver. The quality of eye diagram under random 10 Mb/s and 100 Mb/s NRZ data has been improved as shown in Fig. 6(a) and (b). Comparing with Fig. 5, the bandwidth has been extended obviously which is reflected in wider open eyes.

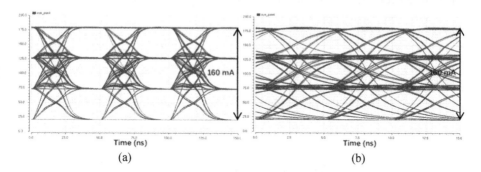

(a)   (b)

Fig. 6. Simulated PAM-4 eye diagrams with FFE under different VLC data rate: (a) 10 Mb/s NRZ, (b) 100 Mb/s NRZ.

4   Conclusion

In this work, we proposed an RGB-LED driver equipped with FFE to achieve high-speed PAM-4 visible light communication. This driver is based on traditional current regulator structure with decreasing of rising and falling time. Simulation verification utilizing TSMC 40 nm process was applied to prove the feasibility of this driver, which consisted of transient analysis and eye diagram analysis. The results shown that both PAM-4 scheme and FFE are practicable in this driver under up to 100 Mb/s random NRZ data.

Acknowledgement. This work was supported in part by the Research and Development Program in Key Areas of Guangdong Province under Grant 2019B010116002.

References

1. Chi, N., Zhou, Y., Liang, S., Wang, F., Li, J., Wang, Y.: Enabling technologies for high-speed visible light communication employing CAP modulation. J. Lightw. Technol. **36**(2), 510–518 (2018)
2. Cossu, G., Wajahat, A., Corsini, R., Ciaramella, E.: 5.6 Gbit/s downlink and 1.5 Gbit/s uplink optical wireless transmission at indoor distances (≥ 1.5 m). In: 2014 The European Conference on Optical Communication (ECOC), Cannes, pp. 1–3 (2014)
3. Li, X., Bamiedakis, N., Guo, X., et al.: Wireless visible light communications employing feed-forward pre-equalization and PAM-4 modulation. J. Lightw. Technol. **34**(8), 2049–2055 (2016)
4. Kim, J., et al.: A fast-switching current-pulse driver for LED backlight. In: 2009 IEEE International Symposium on Circuits and Systems, Taipei, pp. 1775–1778 (2009)

5. Ahn, H., Hong, S., Kwon, O.: A fast switching current regulator using slewing time reduction method for high dimming ratio of LED backlight drivers. IEEE Trans. Circuits Syst. II Express Briefs **63**(11), 1014–1018 (2016)
6. Che, F., Wu, L., Hussain, B., et al.: A fully integrated IEEE 802.15. 7 visible light communication transmitter with on-chip 8-W 85% efficiency boost LED driver. J. Lightw. Technol. **34**(10), 2419–2430 (2016)

Performance Analysis and Evaluation of Outdoor Visible Light Communication Reception

Yiru Wang[1,2(✉)], Bo Xu[1,2], Jian Kang[1,2], Cong Qiu[3], and C. Patrick Yue[1,2]

[1] HKUST Shenzhen Research Institute, Shenzhen 518057, China
ywangkf@connect.ust.hk
[2] HKUST-Qualcomm Optical Wireless Lab, ECE Department, The Hong Kong University of Science and Technology, Hong Kong, Hong Kong S.A.R., China
[3] School of Electronic Communication Technology, Shenzhen Institute of Information Technology, Shenzhen, Guangdong, People's Republic of China

Abstract. Thanks to the properties of light emitting diodes (LEDs), visible light communication (VLC) technology is very competitive in providing high-speed communication and high-precision positioning services. Compared with indoor systems, outdoor VLC faces more challenges due to the strong ambient light disturbance. In this paper, we evaluate and analyze the performance of outdoor VLC systems by conducting outdoor experiments on VLC systems with two types of receivers. For the image sensor-based VLC system, we measure the hit rate and analyze the captured rolling shutter patterns by image processing methods. For the photo detector (PD)-based VLC system, we observe the received signal by an oscilloscope and add a DC-offset to enhance the performance. The results show that when the image sensor-based VLC system is placed in the sun, it can achieve the maximum hit rate of 55% under the communication distance of about 0.3 m. Besides, the PD-based VLC system with a DC-offset can successfully identify and decode transmitted signals under much longer distance. However, PD-based receiver strictly requires the alignment between the LED and the receiver and is not readily available on mobile devices.

Keywords: Visible light communication · Photo detector and image sensor · Outdoor free space optical communication

1 Introduction

Visible light communication (VLC) systems utilize light emitting diodes (LEDs) as transmitters to transmit data at a high speed and provide illumination at the same time [1]. Due to the light-of-sight (LOS) property of visible light beam, VLC signals in different rooms are independent and private. Besides, compared with radio frequency (RF) systems, VLC systems have higher bandwidth and require lower cost. Therefore, VLC technology is very competitive in providing indoor intelligent illumination [2], communication [3] and positioning [4] services.

© ICST Institute for Computer Sciences, Social Informatics and Telecommunications Engineering 2021
Published by Springer Nature Switzerland AG 2021. All Rights Reserved
M. Guan and Z. Na (Eds.): MLICOM 2020, LNICST 342, pp. 235–241, 2021.
https://doi.org/10.1007/978-3-030-66785-6_27

VLC can also be applied to outdoor scenarios. Existing researches on outdoor VLC systems mainly focus on vehicle to vehicle (V2V) [5] and vehicle to infrastructure (V2I) [6] systems. If we enable VLC technology on mobile devices and integrate it with smart street lightings, the high-precision positioning and high-speed data rate performances of VLC technology and the wide distribution of street lightings can intensely contribute to the implement of diverse public services. However, outdoor applications face more challenges due to the strong ambient light disturbance [7] and optical defects in lens. The power of the incident parasitic light can be up to 10 mW/cm^2, compared to the power of the light containing the information which can be as low as few μW/cm^2. Addressing and solving these challenges enables VLC technology in outdoor application and leads to the perspective of fully exploiting the advantages of VLC [7].

In this paper, we conduct experiments on outdoor VLC systems with two types of receivers including photo detector (PD) and image sensor. We measure the hit rates of the image sensor-based VLC system and analyze the captured rolling shutter patterns by image processing methods. Furthermore, we evaluate the performance of PD-based VLC systems and add a DC-offset to filter the high-intensity ambient sunlight.

2 VLC Reception

For outdoor VLC systems, the main challenge is to overcome the high light intensity of ambient sunlight. We conduct outdoor experiments on image sensor-based VLC system and PD-based VLC system to evaluate their availability in outdoor environments.

2.1 Two Types of VLC Receivers

Compared with PDs, image sensors are cheaper and more widely equipped on mobile devices. Figure 1 shows an image sensor-based VLC system. The LED-based transmitter is controlled by a VLC enabled LED driver to transmit optical waveforms. The bright bars correspond to the transmitted data 1 and the dark bars correspond to the transmitted data 0. Then at the receiver side, the CMOS image sensor on the smart phone captures the pixel from top to bottom [8] ad recodes the rolling shutter patterns.

In a PD-based VLC system, the PD-based receiver converts the optical power to electrical current. Compared with an image sensor-based VLC system, a PD-based system can achieve higher data rate. The detection areas of PDs are very small. Therefore, PD-based VLC systems require precise alignment between LED and PD for signal detection [8]. The studies on PD-based VLC systems only provide simulation results [10].

Fig. 1. The image sensor-based outdoor VLC system

2.2   Experiments on the Image Sensor-Based Outdoor VLC System

We evaluate the performances of the image sensor-based outdoor VLC system in two cases. In case 1, we place the system in the sun as shown in Fig. 1 and the sunlight intensity is 67,800 lx. In case 2, we measure the hit rates in the shade with light intensity of 6,800 lx. The power of the lamp panel is 18 W.

Table 1. The results of outdoor image sensor-based VLC experiments.

Case 1	Distance (m)	1.0	0.9	0.8	0.5	0.3
	Hit rate (%)	2	4	11	40	55
Case 2	Distance (m)	1.0	0.9	0.8	0.5	0.3
	Hit rate (%)	6	60	93	97	97

The experiment results are given in Table 1. The results show that the hit rates of the VLC transmission in the sun are much lower than these in the shade. In case 1, when the distance is about 0.3 m, we can obtain the maximum hit rate of 55%. However, the transmission distance of 0.3 m is much shorter than the required minimum detection distance for outdoor communication and positioning.

When we conduct the outdoor experiment in the sun, the very low hit rate is due to the indistinct rolling shutter pattern captured by the camera as shown in Fig. 2. Then we perform image processing algorithms to analyze the performance.

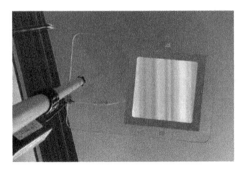

Fig. 2. The rolling shutter patterns captured in the sun

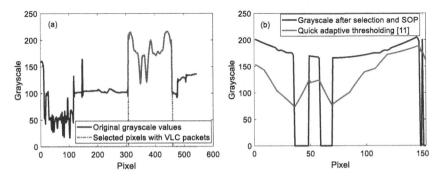

Fig. 3. The grayscale values of the rolling shutter patterns captured in the sun

Firstly, we extract the pixels with VLC pocket as shown in Fig. 3(a). Then second-order polynomial (SOP) and quick adaptive thresholding [11] are applied to reduce the extinction ratio fluctuation and identify data logic. It can be obviously observed from the Fig. 3(b) that the rolling shutter patterns cannot be decoded correctly.

Compared with the patterns captured in the sun, the rolling shutter patterns captured in the shade are much more distinct and clearer as shown in Fig. 4. Then we perform similar image processing algorithms to analyze the performance and the results are illustrated in Fig. 5. We can find that the patterns can be successfully decoded.

Fig. 4. The rolling shutter patterns captured in the shade

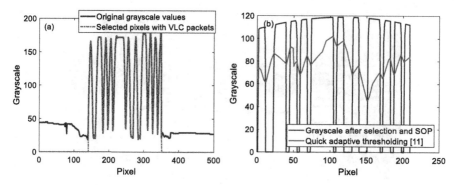

Fig. 5. The grayscale values of the rolling shutter patterns captured in the shade

2.3 Experiments on PD-Based Outdoor VLC System

To evaluate the performance of the PD-based outdoor VLC systems, we set a PD as receiver and use an oscilloscope to observe the signals as shown in Fig. 6. Since the PD is remarkably sensitive to receiving angle, we use a 1 W bulb to assure the alignment between the PD and the LED. The sunlight intensity is the same as that in case 1. The very high sunlight covers the light transmitted by the LED and the signal received by the PD is like noise. Therefore, the PD cannot recover the transmitted signals.

To filter the high-intensity ambient sunlight, a DC-offset is applied at the PD [12]. Then the pattern received by the PD is with very slight flash as shown in Fig. 7. The maximum detection distance of the PD-based VLC system is about 40 cm. Compared with an image sensor-based VLC system, a PD-based system can achieve much longer transmission distance with a lower power transmitter.

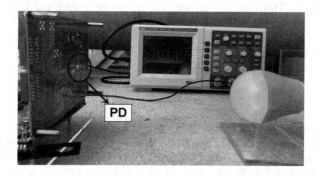

Fig. 6. The PD-based outdoor VLC system

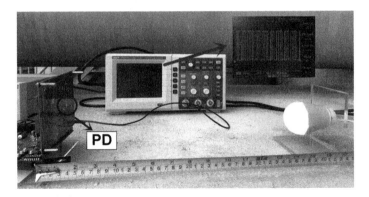

Fig. 7. The PD-based outdoor VLC system with DC-offset

3 Conclusion

In this paper, we evaluate the performances of outdoor VLC systems with two types of receivers. From the measured hit rates and captured rolling shutter patterns we can find that when the image sensor-based VLC system is in the sun, the communication distance is much shorter than the required minimum detection distance. Compared with image sensor-based systems, PD-based systems with DC-offset can successfully identify and decode transmitted signals under much longer distance of the same sunlight intensity. However, due to the strict requirement of the alignment between the LED and PD-based receiver, existing PD-based VLC systems cannot achieve angular diversity and provide communication and positioning services for mobile devices in both outdoor and indoor environments.

Acknowledgements. This work was supported in part by the Science and Technology Plan of Shenzhen under Grant JCYJ20170818113929095, in part by the Research and Development Program in Key Areas of Guangdong Province under Grant 2019B010116002 and in part by the HKUST-Qualcomm Optical Wireless Laboratory.

References

1. Wang, Y., Zhang, L.: High security orthogonal factorized channel scrambling scheme with location information embedded for MIMO-based VLC system. In: 2017 IEEE 85th Vehicular Technology Conference (VTC Spring), Sydney, NSW, pp. 1–5. IEEE (2017)
2. Boubakri, W., Abdallah, W., Boudriga, N.: A light-based communication architecture for smart city applications. In: 2015 17th International Conference on Transparent Optical Networks (ICTON), Budapest, pp. 1–6. IEEE (2015)
3. Wang, Y., Zhang, L.: Uncoordinated chaotic channel scrambling scheme for multiple-input, multiple-output-based VLC system. IET Commun. **12**(10), 1245–1252 (2018)
4. Guan, W., Chen, X., Huang, M., Liu, Z., Wu, Y., Chen, Y.: High-speed robust dynamic positioning and tracking method based on visual visible light communication using optical flow detection and Bayesian forecast. IEEE Photonics J. **10**(3), 1–22 (2018)

5. Soner, B., Ergen, S.C.: Vehicular visible light positioning with a single receiver. In: 2019 IEEE 30th Annual International Symposium on Personal, Indoor and Mobile Radio Communications (PIMRC), Istanbul, pp. 1–6. IEEE (2019)
6. Kalaiselvi, V.K.G., Sangavi, A.: Li-Fi technology in traffic light. In: 2017 2nd International Conference on Computing and Communications Technologies (ICCCT), Chennai, pp. 404–407. IEEE (2017)
7. Zhuang, Y., Hua, L., Qi, L., Yang, J., Cao, P., et al.: A survey of positioning systems using visible LED lights. IEEE Commun. Surv. Tutor. **20**(3), 1963–1988 (2018)
8. Chow, C.W., Chen, C.Y., Chen, S.H.: Enhancement of signal performance in LED visible light communications using mobile phone camera. IEEE Photonics J. **7**(5), 1–7 (2015)
9. Yeh, C.H., Chow, C.W., Chen, H.Y., Chen, J., Liu, Y.L.: Adaptive 84.44–190 Mbit/s phosphor-LED wireless communication utilizing no blue filter at practical transmission distance. Opt. Express **22**(8), 9783–9788 (2014)
10. Cai, Y., Guan, W., Wu, Y., Xie, C., Chen, Y., Fang, L.: Indoor high precision three-dimensional positioning system based on visible light communication using particle swarm optimization. IEEE Photonics J. **9**(6), 1–20 (2017)
11. Liu, Y., Chen, H.Y., Liang, K., Hsu, C.W., Chow, C.W., Yeh, C.H.: Visible light communication using receivers of camera image sensor and solar cell. IEEE Photonics J. **8**(1), 1–7 (2015)
12. Li, X., Hussain, B., Wang, L., Jiang, J., Yue, C.P.: Design of a 2.2-mW 24-Mb/s CMOS VLC receiver SoC with ambient light rejection and post-equalization for Li-Fi applications. J. Lightwave Technol. **36**(12), 2366–2375 (2018)

Simulation Study of Channel Number of Cochlear Implant in Quiet State

J. Wang and Y. S. Chen[(⌧)]

School of Electronics and Communication, Shenzhen Institute of Information
Technology, Shenzhen, Guangdong 518172, People's Republic of China
chenyoushengtsinghua@aliyun.com

Abstract. This paper studied the effect of changing channel number of cochlear implant in low, medium, and high frequency band on Mandarin Chinese tone recognition in quiet state, respectively. The input speech was filtered by a bandpass filter bank with the frequency range of 60–8000 Hz. The number of channels in low or medium frequency band was set as 2, 4, 8, 16, and 32, respectively. The number of channels in high frequency band was set as 1, 2, 4, 8, 16, and 32, respectively. In each pass band, temporal envelope was extracted by full wave rectification and low-pass filtering. The envelope was modulated with a band-limited noise of the corresponding channel. To avoid signal leakage, the modulated signal was band-pass filtered again. Then Root Mean Square equalization was performed. Then, the signals of each channel were summed to obtain a simulated composite signal for each frame. Finally, the signals of each frame were superimposed and averaged to obtain a speech signal. Tone recognition experiments found that, the number of channel in cochlear implant had a certain effect on tone recognition rate of Mandarin Chinese in quiet state. As the number of channel was increased, the tone recognition rate rose slowly. For the recognition of tone 3, the channel type (low, medium, and high) had a significant impact.

Keywords: Cochlear implant · Mandarin chinese tone recognition · Channel number

1 Introduction

Cochlear implant is a hearing recovery device. It directly stimulates auditory nerve fibers of the severe hearing impaired patients with a weak current, excites auditory nerve fibers to mimic the physiological functions of the peripheral auditory system, generates a neural release pattern similar to normal persons, and thereby partially restores the hearing of deaf patients [1]. At present, the vast majority of cochlear implant products adopt speech processing strategies based on temporal envelopes, which can effectively recognize non-tonal language. However, these strategies do not encode the tonal information of speech, making it difficult for users speaking Mandarin Chinese to perceive tonal language.

In order to enhance the tonal information of the cochlear implant, researchers studied the effect of channel number on tone recognition of Mandarin Chinese. Some

M. Guan and Z. Na (Eds.): MLICOM 2020, LNICST 342, pp. 242–249, 2021.
https://doi.org/10.1007/978-3-030-66785-6_28

researchers found that in quiet state, when the total number of channels of the cochlear implant was increased from 1 or 2 to 4, the tone recognition rate was not significantly improved [2, 3]. However, Xu *et al.* used Chinese single syllable words of the same duration to conduct simulation experiments in quiet state [4]. Xu *et al.* found that, when the total number of channels was increased from 1 to 4, the tone recognition rate increased significantly, and that the recognition rate of 3 or 4 channels was significantly higher than that of 1 channel. This phenomenon contradicts Fu's previous results. In addition, in the experiment of Xu *et al.*, when the number of channels continued to increase from 4, the tone recognition rate of 6, 8, 10, and 12 channels no longer increased significantly, but reached a platform. Besides, the recognition rates of these channels were all significantly higher than the recognition rate of only 1 channel. In addition, the recognition rates of 8 and 12 channels were significantly higher than those of 2 channels.

It is worth noting that the variable in the above studies is the total number of channels. The current paper changed the number of channels in the low, medium, and high frequency bands of the cochlear implant, respectively, and tried to explore the impact of channel number in different frequency bands on tone recognition of Mandarin Chinese.

2 Methods and Materials

2.1 Theoretical Methods

A frequency range $[f_l, f_h]$ is divided into n channels by a multiplier factor x. Then Eqs. (1) should be satisfied.

$$x = (f_h/f_l)^{1/n} \tag{1}$$

Among the n channels, the higher cutoff frequency of the i-th channel f_{ih} can be calculated by Eq. (2).

$$f_{ih} = f_l * x^i \quad (1 \le i \le n) \tag{2}$$

The lower cutoff frequency of channel $i + 1$ equals the higher cutoff frequency of channel i. Thus frequency range of each channel and the multiplication factor x can be obtained from Eqs. (1) and (2).

In this experiment, the frequency range [60, 8000] Hz was divided into three parts, including the low frequency band ([60, 1000] Hz), the medium frequency band ([1000, 4000] Hz), and the high frequency band ([4000, 8000] Hz).

Change Number of Channels in the Low Frequency Band. Keeping 2 channels for the medium frequency band (1000–2000, 2000–4000 Hz) and 1 channel for the high frequency band (4000–8000 Hz) unchanged, increase the number of channels in the low frequency band from 2 to 32 (i.e. 2, 4, 8, 16, and 32) to explore the impact of the number of the low frequency band on tone recognition rate. This situation is represented as "Low" case. The total number of channels in this case is from 5 to 35 (i.e. 5, 7, 11, 19, and 35).

Change Number of Channels in the Medium Frequency Band. Keeping 2 channels for the low frequency band (60–244.9, 244.9–1000 Hz) and 1 channel for the high frequency band (4000–8000 Hz) unchanged, increase the number of channels in the medium frequency band from 2 to 32 (i.e. 2, 4, 8, 16, and 32) to explore the impact of the number of the medium frequency band on tone recognition rate. This situation is represented as "Medium" case. The total number of channels in this case is from 5 to 35 (i.e. 5, 7, 11, 19, and 35).

Change Number of Channels in the High Frequency Band. Keeping 2 channels for the low frequency band (60–244.9, 244.9–1000 Hz) and 2 channels for the medium frequency band (1000–2000, 2000–4000 Hz) unchanged, increase the number of channels in the high frequency band from 1 to 32 (i.e. 1, 2, 4, 8, 16, and 32) to explore the impact of the number of the high frequency band on tone recognition rate. This situation is represented as "High" case. The total number of channels in this case is from 5 to 36 (i.e. 5, 6, 8, 12, 20, and 36).

2.2   Speech Processing Strategy

This paper proposed an improved continuous interleaved sampling (CIS) strategy based on the channels designed in Sect. 2.1. The voice was first enframed, added with a Hamming window, and passed through an FIR linear phase band-pass filter bank. The channels of the filter bank were designed by the method introduced in Sect. 2.1. Then, full-wave rectification and low-pass filtering was applied on the signal of each channel to obtain an envelope. The envelope was modulated with a band-limited noise of the corresponding channel. To avoid signal leakage, the modulated signal was band-pass filtered again. Then Root Mean Square (RMS) equalization was performed. Then, the signals of each channel were summed to obtain a simulated composite signal for each frame. Finally, the signals of each frame were superimposed and averaged to obtain a speech signal.

2.3   Materials

The experiment used a phonetic vocabulary of Mandarin Chinese recorded by Fu *et al.* [5], with a total of more than 1,500 female pronunciation words. The voice was processed by Matlab software, passed through the sound card (Echo Indigo IOx, 24-bit resolution and 44100 Hz sampling rate), and played through Sennheiser HD 650 headphones. The subjects were tested in double-layer soundproof rooms.

2.4   Subjects

Twelve college students (3 male and 9 female) aged between 19 and 23 years participated in the experiments. All listeners were native Mandarin speakers with normal hearing (thresholds below 15 dB HL) at octave frequencies between 125 and 8000 Hz in both ears. Each listener was trained for at least 1 h until the results became stable.

2.5   Test Content

Test contents include total tone recognition rate (Total), one tone recognition rate (T1), two tone recognition rate (T2), three tone recognition rate (T3), and four tone recognition rate (T4).

3   Results

3.1   The Result of Changing Number of Channels in Low Frequency Band

When the number of low-frequency channels was 2, 4, 8, 16, and 32, the total number of channels over the entire frequency range was 5, 7, 11, 19, and 35, respectively.

Increasing the number of low-frequency channels, Total, T1, T3, and T4 all rose slowly, but there was no significant difference. T2 showed fluctuations.

Each tone recognition rate was ranked from high to low as: T3 > T4 > T2 > T1. Total remained at 63%–70%, which is consistent with previous experimental results [2, 3].

In addition, LSD pairwise comparison found that, for T4, recognition rate for the 2 low-frequency channels was significantly lower than that for the 32 low-frequency channels ($p = 0.041 < 0.05$) (Fig. 1).

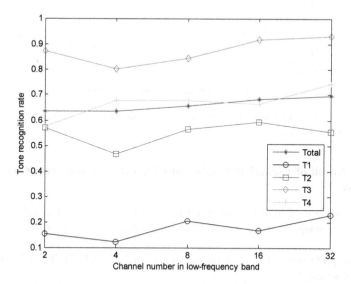

Fig. 1. The effect of changing number of channels in low frequency range on tone recognition rate in quiet state

3.2 The Result of Changing Number of Channels in Medium Frequency Band

When the number of medium-frequency channels was 2, 4, 8, 16, 32, the total number of channels over the entire frequency range was 5, 7, 11, 19, and 35, respectively.

Increasing the number of medium-frequency channels, Total, T1, and T3 all rose slowly, but there was no significant difference. T2 and T4 fluctuated.

Each tone recognition rate was ranked from high to low as: T3 > T4 > T2 > T1. The overall tone recognition rate was maintained at 60%–70%, which is consistent with the previous experimental results [2, 3] (Fig. 2).

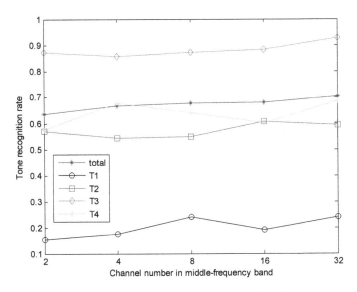

Fig. 2. The effect of changing number of channels in medium frequency range on tone recognition rate in quiet state

3.3 The Result of Changing Number of Channels in High Frequency Band

When the number of high-frequency channels was 1, 2, 4, 8, 16, and 32, the total number of channels over the entire frequency range was 5, 6, 8, 12, 20, and 36, respectively.

Increasing the number of high-frequency channels, Total, T1, T2, T3, and T4 rose slowly or fluctuated.

Each tone recognition rate was ranked from high to low as: T3 > T4 > T2 > T1. Total remained at 60%–72%, which is consistent with the previous experimental results [2, 3].

For T3, the recognition rate for 8 high-frequency channels was significantly lower than that for 32 high-frequency channels ($p = 0.042 < 0.05$).

For T1, the recognition rate for 1 high-frequency channel was significantly lower than that for 16 high-frequency channels ($p = 0.032 < 0.05$) (Fig. 3).

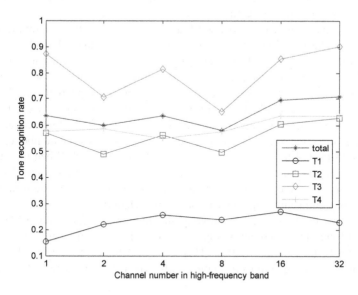

Fig. 3. The effect of changing number of channels in high frequency range on tone recognition rate in quiet state

4   Discussion

When the number of channels in the low, medium, and high frequency bands was changed respectively, Total for the three cases was maintained between 60% and 72%, which is consistent with previous results [2, 3]. Luo xin and Fu Qian-jie used noise band carrier to carry out simulation experiments, and found that the 2-channel and 4-channel tone recognition rates were about 62% in quiet state [2]. The research of Fu *et al.* found that, when the number of channels was 1 to 4, the score of Mandarin Chinese tone recognition was stable at about 60%–80% in the quiet state [3].

For the low, medium, and high cases, the recognition rates of each tone had a common phenomenon. T3 was the highest, followed by the T4 and T2 in sequence, and the lowest was T1. This indicates that tone 3 and tone 4 are easier to recognize, and the tone 1 and tone 2 are not easy to recognize. This is consistent with previous results [3]. The reason why tone 3 and tone 4 are easier to identify may be related to duration. Tone 3 has the longest length and tone 4 has the shortest length. However, the contribution of duration cue might be small [6].

When the number of channels in the low, medium, and high frequency bands was increased respectively, the tone recognition rates fluctuated or rose slowly. However, there was no significant difference. This is similar with previous results [2]. Luo xin and Fu Qian-jie used noise band carrier to carry out simulation experiments, and found that, when the total number of channels increased from 2 to 4, Mandarin Chinese tone recognition in quiet state was not affected by the total number of channels in the spectrum [2, 3]. Fu *et al.* had similar conclusions [3]. This explains from another point of view that for the CIS simulation, 4–6 channels are enough to achieve a good recognition rate of Mandarin Chinese tones in quiet state.

However, LSD pairwise comparison found that, for T4 in the low frequency band, 2-channel tone recognition rate was significantly lower than the 32-channel tone recognition rate ($p = 0.041 < 0.05$). This may be related to the easier identification of tone 4. The curve of tone 4 changes from high to low significantly with the shortest length [3, 6]. Another reason is that when the number of channels is 32, the tone recognition rate is very similar to that of the original sound. Kong and Zeng found that, when the total number of channels was increased from 1 to 2, the tone recognition rate was basically the same based on temporal envelope. When the total number of channels was increased from 4 to 12, the tone recognition rate increased. When the number of channels was 32, the tone recognition rate was similar to that of the original sound [7]. Therefore, for tone 4 recognition in the low frequency band, recognition rate with 32 channels was significantly higher than that with 2 channels.

In addition, for tone 1 recognition in the high frequency band, LSD pairwise comparison found that, recognition rate of 1 channel was significantly lower than that of 16 channels ($p = 0.032 < 0.05$). This can also be explained by the fact that recognition rate can be improved significantly when the number of channels is big enough.

Moreover, non-parametric test found that type of channel (low, medium, and high) had a significant effect on T3 ($p = 0.011 < 0.05$). LSD pairwise comparison revealed that there were significant differences between the rate for 32 channels in low frequency band and that for 8 channels in the high-frequency band ($p = 0.042 < 0.05$).

Variance analysis and non-parametric test found that type of channel had no significant effect on Total, T1, T2, or T4. However, LSD pairwise comparison found three significant differences. First, for T1, recognition rates for 4 channels in low frequency band was significantly ($p < 0.05$) lower than those for 4, 8, 16, and 32 channels in high frequency band. Second, the former was significantly ($p < 0.05$) lower than those for 8 and 32 channels in medium frequency band. Finally, for T4, recognition rates for 4 and 8 channels in the high frequency band were significantly ($p < 0.05$) lower than those for 32 channels in the low frequency band. This can also be explained by the fact that recognition rate can be improved significantly when the number of channels is big enough.

5 Conclusion

In quiet state, the number of channels has a certain effect on the tone recognition rate of Mandarin Chinese. As the number of channel increases, the tone recognition rate rises. For the recognition of tone 3, the channel type (low, medium, and high) has a significant impact. However, channel type has no significant impact on other tone recognition, except for a few local significant difference found by LSD pairwise comparison.

Acknowledgements. This paper was granted by the characteristic innovation project of Guangdong University in 2019 (Grant No. 2019GKTSCX094) and Guangdong Province higher vocational colleges & schools Pearl River scholar funded scheme (2016).

References

1. Wei, C.G., Cao, K., Zeng, F.G.: Mandarin tone recognition in cochlear-implant subjects. Hear. Res. **197**(1–2), 1–95 (2004)
2. Luo, X., Fu, Q.J.: Importance of pitch and periodicity to Chinese-speaking cochlear implant patients. In: IEEE International Conference on Acoustics. IEEE (2004)
3. Fu, Q.J., Zeng, F.G., Shannon, R.V., et al.: Importance of tonal envelope cues in Chinese speech recognition. J. Acoust. Soc. Am. **97**(1), 505–510 (1998)
4. Xu, L., Tsai, Y., Pfingst, B.E.: Features of stimulation affecting tonal speech perception: implications for cochlear prostheses. J. Acoust. Soc. Am. **112**(1), 247–258 (2002)
5. Fu, Q.J., Zhu, M., Wang, X.: Development and validation of the Mandarin speech perception test. J. Acoust. Soc. Am. **129**(6), 267–273 (2011)
6. Whalen, D.H., Xu, Y.: Information for mandarin tones in the amplitude contour and in brief segments. Phonetica **49**(1), 25–47 (1992)
7. Kong, Y.Y., Zeng, F.G.: Temporal and spectral cues in Mandarin tone recognition. J. Acoust. Soc. Am. **120**(5), 2830 (2006)

Analysis and Design of Wireless Distributed Fountain Codes with Multiplicative Network Coding

Hanqin Shao[1,2(✉)], Hongbo Zhu[1,2], and Junwei Bao[3]

[1] Jiangsu Key Laboratory of Wireless Communications, Nanjing University of Posts and Telecommunications, Nanjing 210003, China
{shaohanqin,zhuhb}@njupt.edu.cn
[2] Engineering Research Center of Health Service System Based on Ubiquitous Wireless Networks, Nanjing University of Posts and Telecommunications, Ministry of Education, Nanjing 210003, China
[3] College of Science, Nanjing University of Aeronautics and Astronautics, Nanjing 211106, China
broadenway@nuaa.edu.cn

Abstract. A novel wireless distributed fountain coding scheme is proposed for wireless distributed networks. In this scheme, a multiplicative network coding method is adopted instead of exclusive-or (XOR) network coding. Thus, the processing complexity of the relay can be reduced, and the error propagation can be avoided. Moreover, the degree distributions of the proposed coding scheme are derived and the performance is analyzed asymptotically using semi-Gaussian approximation analysis technique. Furthermore, an efficient optimization method employing linear program is presented to optimize the degree distributions of the proposed scheme. Simulation results reveal that with optimized degree distributions, the proposed scheme has good performance on additive white Gaussian noise (AWGN) channels and outperforms the scheme using alternate forwarding.

Keywords: Fountain codes · Multiplicative network coding · AWGN channels · Asymptotic analysis · Degree distributions · Linear programming

1 Introduction

Digital fountain codes [1,2] are proposed to achieve large-scale network data distribution and reliable transmission. As a novel forward error correction technology with rateless property, fountain encoders do not need to fix the code rate, and it can generate limitless number of codewords theoretically. Therefore, fountain codes can adapt to the channel state and have strong flexibility. Several examples of fountain codes are proposed and developed, such as Luby Transform (LT) codes [3], Raptor codes [2] and Batched Sparse (BATS) codes [4,5].

© ICST Institute for Computer Sciences, Social Informatics and Telecommunications Engineering 2021
Published by Springer Nature Switzerland AG 2021. All Rights Reserved
M. Guan and Z. Na (Eds.): MLICOM 2020, LNICST 342, pp. 250–264, 2021.
https://doi.org/10.1007/978-3-030-66785-6_29

Digital fountain codes are originally proposed and designed for erasure channels. With well-designed degree distributions [6–10], fountain codes can adapt to various erasure channels, and approach the channel capacity of arbitrary erasure rate. Inspired by the good performance on erasure channels, more and more researchers are working to expand the application of fountain codes from application layer to physical layer, and to study their performance on wireless channels [11–19].

Palanki and Yedidia [20] studied the performances of fountain codes on wireless channels, and concluded that there is an obvious "error floor" for LT codes on wireless noisy channels, but not for Raptor codes. Etesami and Shokrollahi [21] studied the performance of Raptor codes on binary memoryless symmetric channels, and proposed a BP decoding algorithm for fountain codes on additive white Gaussian noise (AWGN) channels. It is shown that the LT codes and Raptor codes with well-designed degree distributions for erasure channels are still with good performance on AWGN channels, but cannot approach the capacity of AWGN channels arbitrarily. Castura and Mao [22] proposed a fountain coding scheme on fading channels. The scheme has better performance than a conventional fixed-rate coding scheme while the channel state information is unknown for the receiver. Zhang [23] proposed a joint network-channel coding scheme to optimize the degree distribution on AWGN and fading channels. Nessa [24] proposed a cooperative communication scheme based on fountain codes, and applied it to Long Term Evolution-Advanced (LTE-A) network.

On wireless channels or wireless networks, a decode-and-forward (DF) scheme based on exclusive-or (XOR) network coding is usually performed at the relay nodes [4,23]. Firstly, the relay needs to decode the input symbols. Then, the relay performs XORed network coding on these decoded bits. Finally, the relay needs to re-encode and re-modulate to these bits. However, this scheme increases the coding complexity of the relay node, and brings extra processing delay. Furthermore, there is a certain decoding error probability at the relay nodes. If the error bits are re-encoded through network coding, the decoding error will further spread, which will deteriorate the decoding performance of the destination node.

This paper aims to solve the above problems. We propose a novel fountain coding scheme called wireless distributed fountain codes with multiplicative network coding [25–27] for wireless distributed networks. In the proposed scheme, a multiplicative network coding method is adopted instead of XORed network coding. The relay node can directly perform multiplicative network coding on incoming modulated symbols without the decoding and re-encoding processing, which can reduce the processing complexity greatly. Furthermore, since the relay node does not need to perform decoding, the error propagation caused by incorrect decoding can be avoided. In this paper, we further derive the degree distributions and analyze the performance of the proposed scheme using modified Gaussian approximation method. Finally, we propose an optimal design method of the degree distributions for the relay and source nodes. Simulation results reveal that the proposed fountain coding scheme has good performance on AWGN channels and the benefits are observed in comparison with the separate LT codes.

The rest of this paper is organized as follows. Section 2 gives the system model of the proposed scheme. In Sect. 3, we propose a novel fountain coding scheme with multiplicative network coding called wireless distributed fountain codes. In Sect. 4, we analyze the asymptotic performance of the proposed scheme on AWGN channels. In Sect. 5, an optimal design method of the degree distributions for the relay and source nodes is proposed. Some simulation results are given in Sect. 6 and a conclusion is made in Sect. 7.

2   System Model

Consider the wireless distributed network model in Fig. 1, where multiple source nodes transmit information to a destination node through a single relay node, which is similar to a distributed network over lossy channels with erasures. The source-relay and relay-destination channels are wireless noisy channels rather than wired erasure channels. For simplicity, we take the two-source network as an example in Fig. 1. Due to the openness of wireless channel and noise interference, each source must avoid transmitting information to the relay at the same time. Therefore, a simple time-division multiplexing method can be used. The duration of transmission can be divided into several time slots. In each time slot, only one source is allowed to send information. Thus, a complete transmission cycle needs four time slots. In a network coding scheme, less time slots are needed for transmission. Assuming that the source S_1 and S_2 send symbols to the relay R in time slot 1 and 2, respectively. The relay R performs network coding on the incoming symbols and transmits the coded symbols to the destination D in time slot 3. In this scheme, a complete transmission cycle only consumes three time slots, which is less than the above time-multiplexed scheme. Therefore, the network coding of the relay can save time slots and improve the throughput of the networks.

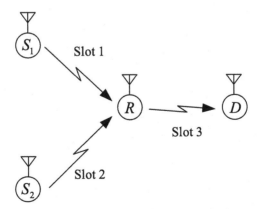

Fig. 1. Wireless distributed network model.

3   Wireless Distributed Fountain Codes with Multiplicative Network Coding

Figure 2 depicts the proposed fountain coding scheme for the wireless distributed network model in Fig. 1, named wireless distributed fountain codes (WDFC). Each source node performs LT encoding on k information bits independently. The information bit streams of source S_1 and S_2 are denoted by $\mathbf{m}_1 = (m_{1,1}, m_{1,2}, \ldots, m_{1,k})$ and $\mathbf{m}_2 = (m_{2,1}, m_{2,2}, \ldots, m_{2,k})$, respectively. The encoded bits are denoted by $\mathbf{x}_1 = (x_{1,1}, x_{1,2}, \ldots)$ and $\mathbf{x}_2 = (x_{2,1}, x_{2,2}, \ldots)$, respectively. Then, a BPSK modulator is employed to each encoded bit streams, and the modulated symbols are denoted by $\tilde{\mathbf{x}}_1 = (\tilde{x}_{1,1}, \tilde{x}_{1,2}, \ldots)$ and $\tilde{\mathbf{x}}_2 = (\tilde{x}_{2,1}, \tilde{x}_{2,2}, \ldots)$, respectively. $\tilde{\mathbf{x}}_1$ and $\tilde{\mathbf{x}}_2$ will be time-multiplexed to the relay through wireless channels. The noises of the channels are denoted by $\mathbf{n}_1$ and $\mathbf{n}_2$, respectively. Assuming that both channels between the sources and relay are AWGN channels with the same variance σ_{sr}^2.

The decoding process of the destination D is also shown in Fig. 2. The symbol stream $\mathbf{r}$ received by D can be expressed as

$$\mathbf{r} = \tilde{\mathbf{z}} + \mathbf{n}_3, \tag{1}$$

where $\mathbf{n}_3$ is Gaussian noise of the relay-destination channel with variance σ_{rd}^2. Finally, the destination D uses BP decoding and soft-decision on $\mathbf{r}$ to recover the bits stream $\hat{\mathbf{m}}$.

At the relay node, a decode-and-forward (DF) scheme is usually used. In this scheme, the relay node cannot perform bit-wise XOR on the received symbols directly. A belief propagation (BP) decoder is needed before XORed network coding. Therefore, it increases the complexity of the relay and leads to the existence of decoding error propagation. In this paper, we propose a novel network coding scheme based on multiplication rather than XORing, which is shown in Fig. 2.

The relay R receives symbols from source S_1 and S_2 alternately. Assume that the received streams of coded symbols are $\mathbf{y}_1 = (y_{1,1}, y_{1,2}, \ldots)$ and $\mathbf{y}_2 = (y_{2,1}, y_{2,2}, \ldots)$, respectively. $\mathbf{y}_i$ can be expressed as

$$\mathbf{y}_i = \tilde{\mathbf{x}}_i + \mathbf{n}_i, \quad i = 1, 2. \tag{2}$$

Unlike $\tilde{\mathbf{x}}_1$ or $\tilde{\mathbf{x}}_2$, the range of $\mathbf{y}_1$ or $\mathbf{y}_2$ is no longer restricted to binary field, but the real number field. Therefore, the network coding with XOR cannot be operated directly. The relay node uses an amplify-and-forward (AF) method, and performs network coding by multiplying two received symbols from both sources. The processing of the relay includes only two steps as follows:

- The relay R multiplies the corresponding symbols of $\mathbf{y}_1$ and $\mathbf{y}_2$, which are received in different time slots alternately. The products form a new symbol stream $\mathbf{y}$;
- The relay R amplifies $\mathbf{y}$, and then send the amplified signal $\tilde{\mathbf{z}}$ to the destination D through wireless channel or link.

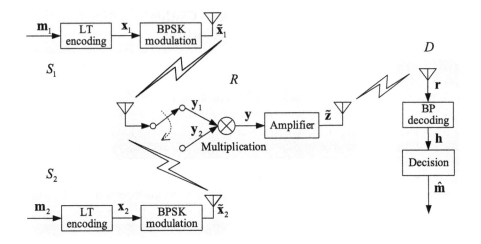

Fig. 2. The proposed coding scheme with multiplicative network coding at the relay.

Compared with XORed network coding, the proposed scheme multiplies the received symbols directly. Therefore, the decoding, re-encoding and re-modulating are not needed. As a result, the complexity of the relay can be reduced greatly. In addition, the error propagation caused by incorrect decoding can be avoided in this scheme.

Assuming that b_1 and b_2 are the information bits to be modulated, x_1 and x_2 are the BPSK-modulated symbols, where $b_1, b_2 \in \{0, 1\}$, $x_1, x_2 \in \{+1, -1\}$. We have $x_i = \exp(j\theta_i)$, $i = 1, 2$, where $\theta_i = b_i\pi$ is the phase of x_i. The product of x_1 and x_2 can be calculated as follows

$$z = x_1 x_2 = \exp[j(\theta_1 + \theta_2)] = \exp[j(b_1 + b_2)\pi]. \tag{3}$$

The product z can be seen as a modulated symbol. The corresponding bit of z is denoted by b, and the phase of z is denoted by θ. Obviously, the product z is a BPSK modulated symbol. The phase θ is consistent with the phase of a BPSK modulation, which can be expressed as $\theta = (\theta_1 + \theta_2) \bmod 2\pi$. The bit b is determined by $b_1 + b_2$, which can be expressed as $b = (b_1 + b_2) \bmod 2 = b_1 \oplus b_2$. Therefore, we can conclude that the product of two BPSK modulated symbols is equivalent to the XOR of two corresponding bits. It is indicated that multiplicative network coding is equivalent to XORed network coding. This is an important reason for performing multiplicative network coding instead of XORed network coding.

4 Asymptotic Performance Analysis of Proposed Wireless Distributed Fountain Codes

4.1 Degree Distributions

In this section, we will analyze the degree distribution of the proposed coding scheme WDFC. Assuming that each source performs LT encoding with the same degree distribution $\Phi(x)$. Let $\Phi(x) = \sum_{d=1}^{k} \Phi_d x^d$ and $\Lambda(x) = \sum_{d=1}^{D_i} \Lambda_d x^d$ be the output/input node perspective degree distribution of the source nodes, respectively. The corresponding output/input edge perspective degree distribution can be denoted by $\phi(x) = \Phi'(x)/\Phi'(1)$ and $\lambda(x) = \Lambda'(x)/\Lambda'(1)$, respectively. Let $\Gamma(x) = \Gamma_1 x + \Gamma_2 x^2$ and $\gamma(x) = \Gamma'(x)/\Gamma'(1)$ be the output node/edge perspective degree distribution of the relay node. The overall output node/edge perspective degree distribution of the received symbols by the destination node can be denoted by $\Omega(x)$ and $\omega(x) = \Omega'(x)/\Omega'(1)$. The input degree distribution $\Lambda(x)$ follows a binomial distribution, which can be expressed as

$$\Lambda_d = \binom{n\beta}{d} p^d (1 - p)^{n\beta - d}. \tag{4}$$

Where n is the number of output coded symbols, $\beta = \Phi'(1)$ is the average degree of output symbols, and $p = 1/k$ is the probability that an edge is connected to a particular input node of Tanner graph. When n goes to infinity ($n \to \infty$), the input degree distribution approaches to a Poisson distribution asymptotically as follows

$$\Lambda(x) = \lambda(x) = \exp(-\alpha(1 - x)). \tag{5}$$

where $\alpha = (1 + \varepsilon)\beta$ is the average degree of input symbols, ε is coding overhead.

Reviewing that b_1 and b_2 are the information bits to be modulated of source S_1 and S_2, respectively. x_1 and x_2 are the corresponding BPSK-modulated symbols. b_1 and b_2 can be regarded as independent random variables with the same probability generating function $\Phi(x)$. According to probability theory, $b_1 \oplus b_2$ is a random variable with probability generating function $\Omega(x) = \Phi^2(x)$. As mentioned in Sect. 3, the proposed multiplicative network coding is essentially equivalent to XORed network coding. Therefore, we can conclude that the overall degree distribution after multiplicative network coding is still $\Omega(x) = \Phi^2(x)$.

In Fig. 2, the relay performs network coding on all the received symbols, that is, the probability of network coding is 1. Thus the output degree distribution of the relay is $\Gamma(x) = x^2$. In practice, selective network coding is often used in order to ensure that the degree one symbols are still exist among the received symbols at destination node. The relay randomly selects one symbol from two received symbols with probability Γ_1, and multiplies two received symbols with probability Γ_2, where $\Gamma(x) = \Gamma_1 x + \Gamma_2 x^2$ is the output degree distribution of the relay. Therefore, the overall degree distribution $\Omega(x)$ can be expressed as a composition of $\Gamma(x)$ and $\Phi(x)$, i.e., $\Omega(x) = \Gamma(\Phi(x))$.

4.2   Asymptotic Performance Analysis

The BP decoding algorithm for wireless channel is still applicable to the proposed WDFC. According to (2), it is assumed that the relay node performs multiplicative network coding on two received symbols $y_1 = \tilde{x}_1 + n_1$ and $y_2 = \tilde{x}_2 + n_2$. The coded symbol can be expressed as

$$y = y_1 y_2 = \tilde{x}_1 \tilde{x}_2 + \tilde{x}_1 n_2 + \tilde{x}_2 n_1 + n_1 n_2. \tag{6}$$

The destination node receives the symbol after the transmission through the relay-destination channel. The received symbol can be expressed as

$$r = y + n_3 = \tilde{x}_1 \tilde{x}_2 + \underbrace{\tilde{x}_1 n_2 + \tilde{x}_2 n_1 + n_3}_{n} + n_1 n_2. \tag{7}$$

Where $\tilde{x}_1 \tilde{x}_2$ is the useful signal, $\tilde{x}_1 n_2 + \tilde{x}_2 n_1 + n_3$ can be regarded as a noise term and denoted by the equivalent noise n, $n_1 n_2$ is a small product term that can be negligible, n_1, n_2 and n_3 are independent Gaussian variables. Assuming that both n_1 and n_2 are Gaussian variables with mean 0 and variance σ_{sr}^2, n_3 is a Gaussian variable with mean 0 and variance σ_{rd}^2. Therefore, we can conclude that the overall equivalent noise n is a Gaussian variable with variance $\sigma_n^2 = 2\sigma_{sr}^2 + \sigma_{rd}^2$. The log-likelihood ratio (LLR) of the channel can be expressed as

$$
\begin{aligned}
Z_o &= \ln \frac{\Pr(r|\tilde{x}_1 \tilde{x}_2 = +1)}{\Pr(r|\tilde{x}_1 \tilde{x}_2 = -1)} = \ln \frac{\Pr(n = r - 1)}{\Pr(n = r + 1)} \\
&= \ln \frac{\exp(-(r-1)^2/2(2\sigma_{sr}^2 + \sigma_{rd}^2))}{\exp(-(r+1)^2/2(2\sigma_{sr}^2 + \sigma_{rd}^2))} \\
&= \frac{2r}{2\sigma_{sr}^2 + \sigma_{rd}^2}.
\end{aligned}
\tag{8}
$$

Z_o can be used as the initial value for LLR iteration of BP decoding algorithm.

A Gaussian approximation method is usually used to analyze the asymptotic performance of LDPC codes or fountain codes on noisy channels [21, 28]. It requires that all the LLRs of the input and output nodes passed at each iteration of the BP algorithm are Gaussian. This requirement is very strong. The LLRs of the output nodes of small degree are far from being Gaussian. Thus, the theoretical results of asymptotic performance analysis based on Gaussian approximation are far away from simulation results. In fact, according to the BP algorithm, the LLR of an input node is the sum of a set of independent random variables with the same distribution. By the central limit theorem, the LLR of an input node is close to a Gaussian variable when the number of the additions is large enough. However, the LLR of an output node does not satisfy this condition. In [21, 28], this assumption is called semi-Gaussian approximation, and is applied to analyze the performance of LDPC codes and Raptor codes. In this paper, we can improve the analytical method for WDFC by using this assumption.

Assuming that the LLRs of all input nodes are Gaussian, while the LLRs of all output nodes are not Gaussian. Let $Y^{(l)}$ be the LLR of an output node at the lth iteration. $\{X_1, X_2, \ldots, X_j, \ldots, X_d - 1\}$ represents $d - 1$ independent identically distributed random variables with symmetric Gaussian distribution, and they are corresponding to the LLRs of input nodes. $\mu^{(l)}$ is the mean of X_j at the lth iteration. According to BP decoding algorithm [21], the message sent from output node o of degree d to an input node at the lth iteration has an expectation as follows

$$
\mathrm{E}\left[Y^{(l)}|\deg(o) = d\right] = 2\mathrm{E}\left[\operatorname{atanh}\left(\tanh\left(\frac{Z_o}{2}\right)\prod_{j=1}^{d-1}\tanh\left(\frac{X_j}{2}\right)\right)\right]. \quad (9)
$$

Where $\operatorname{atanh}(\cdot)$ represents the inverse hyperbolic tangent function. It is shown in (9) that the mean of LLR of an output node with degree d can be expressed as a function of $\mu^{(l)}$. Assuming that the function is denoted by $f_d(\cdot)$, we have

$$
f_d(\mu^{(l)}) \triangleq 2\mathrm{E}\left[\operatorname{atanh}\left(\tanh\left(\frac{Z_o}{2}\right)\prod_{j=1}^{d-1}\tanh\left(\frac{X_j}{2}\right)\right)\right]. \quad (10)
$$

The right side of the equation in (10) can be wrote as the expectation of a random variable U as follows

$$
U \triangleq 2\operatorname{atanh}\left(\tanh\left(\frac{Z_o}{2}\right)\prod_{j=1}^{d-1}\tanh\left(\frac{X_j}{2}\right)\right). \quad (11)
$$

In practice, $f_d(\mu)$ can be obtained by calculating an empirical mean of U as follows:

(1) Calculating the LLR of the channel $Z_o = 2/\sigma_n^2$;
(2) Let X be a symmetric Gaussian variable with mean μ. Sampling from X for $d - 1$ times and getting $d - 1$ samples x_i, where $i = 1, 2, \ldots, d - 1$;
(3) Calculating the sample $2\operatorname{atanh}\left(\tanh\left(Z_o/2\right)\prod_{i=1}^{d-1}\tanh\left(x_i/2\right)\right)$ of U;
(4) Repeat steps (2) and (3) for q times to obtain q samples of U. Calculating the average value of q samples as the empirical mean of U. As the number of repetitions increases, the empirical mean is closer to the expectation.

The mean of the LLR of an output node at the lth iteration can be expressed as

$$
\mathrm{E}\left[Y^{(l)}\right] = \sum_{d=1}^{D_\omega}\omega_d\mathrm{E}\left[Y^{(l)}|\deg(o) = d\right] = \sum_{d=1}^{D_\omega}\omega_d f_d(\mu^{(l)}). \quad (12)
$$

Where D_ω is the maximum degree of $\omega(x)$. Let α be the average degree of an input node, we have

$$
\mu^{(l+1)} = \alpha\mathrm{E}\left[Y^{(l)}\right] = \alpha\sum_{d=1}^{D_\omega}\omega_d f_d(\mu^{(l)}). \quad (13)
$$

We can call (13) the density evolution equation based on semi-Gaussian approximation. In each iteration, we only need to calculate the mean μ of the LLR of an input node. At the beginning of the iterations, the initial value of μ is set to $\mu^{(0)} = 0$, and the LLR of the channel is $Z_o = 2/\sigma_n^2$.

5   Optimization Design of Degree Distributions for Wireless Distributed Fountain Codes

The output degree distribution is an important parameter in determining the decoding performance of fountain codes. In this section, we will discuss the design of degree distributions for the proposed WDFC. Based on the density evolution analysis, we can jointly optimize the output degree distributions of the source and relay nodes.

According to the semi-Gaussian analysis in Sect. 4, the iteration must proceed in the direction of increasing the mean $\mu^{(l)}$ of an input node to guarantee the success of density evolution. Thus, the following inequality must be satisfied

$$\mu^{(l+1)} = \alpha \sum_{d=1}^{D_\omega} \omega_d f_d(\mu^{(l)}) > \mu^{(l)}. \tag{14}$$

Assuming that the expected maximum value of $\mu^{(l)}$ is $\mu_{\max}$, then the inequality (14) holds for $\mu^{(l)} \in (0, \mu_{\max}]$. We can use (14) as the main constraint for the optimization.

When the variance σ_n^2 of the overall equivalent channel noise n is given, the optimization objective is to maximize the code rate. Assuming that the input/output average degree is α and $\Omega'(1)$, respectively. The code rate can be expressed as $R = \Omega'(1)/\alpha$. Since $1/\Omega'(1) = \sum_d \omega_d/d$, maximizing the code rate R is equivalent to minimizing $\sum_d \omega_d/d$. The optimized degree distribution is denoted by $\omega_{\mathrm{opt}}(x) = \arg \min_\omega \sum_d \omega_d/d$.

According the above objective and constraints, we can get the following linear program (LP) to optimize the degree distribution $\omega(x)$:

$$\min_\omega \alpha \sum_{d=1}^{D_\omega} \frac{\omega_d}{d}$$

$$s.t. \begin{cases} \alpha \sum_{d=1}^{D_\omega} \omega_d f_d(u_i) > u_i, & i = 1, 2, \ldots, M \\ \sum_{d=1}^{D_\omega} \omega_d = 1 \\ \omega_d \geq 0, & d = 1, 2, \ldots, D_\omega. \end{cases} \tag{15}$$

The interval $(0, \mu_{\max}]$ is divided into M equal parts and $0 < u_1 < u_2 < \cdots < u_M = \mu_{\max}$ are M equidistant points in this interval. The overall output node perspective degree distribution $\Omega(x)$ can be determined from $\omega(x)$ as follows

$$\Omega(x) = \frac{\int_0^x \omega(u) du}{\int_0^1 \omega(u) du}. \tag{16}$$

The overall output degree distribution $\Omega(x)$ can be expressed as a composition of $\Gamma(x)$ and $\Phi(x)$, i.e., $\Omega(x) = \Gamma(\Phi(x))$. So the degree distributions of the sources and the relay can be further calculated after obtaining $\Omega(x)$. Assuming that the output degree distribution of the relay is $\Gamma(x) = \Gamma_1 x + \Gamma_2 x^2$, and that of the source is $\Phi(x) = \sum_{d=1}^{D_\Phi} \Phi_d x^d$, where D_Φ is the maximum degree of $\Phi(x)$. Then, we have $\Omega(x) = \Gamma_1 \Phi(x) + \Gamma_2 (\Phi(x))^2$ and $\Omega_d = \Gamma_1 \Phi_d + \Gamma_2 (\Phi * \Phi)_d$, where $(\Phi * \Phi)_d$ denotes the dth value of the convolution of two identical sequences $\{\Phi_1, \Phi_2, \ldots, \Phi_{D_\Phi}\}$.

Considering the deviation between $\Omega(x)$ and $\Gamma(\Phi(x))$, we denote by $h_d = \Omega_d - \Gamma_1 \Phi_d - \Gamma_2 (\Phi * \Phi)_d$ the dth component of the deviation. The degree distributions $\Gamma(x)$ and $\Phi(x)$ can be optimized by the following optimization problem:

$$\min_\omega \sum_{d=1}^{D_\omega} h_d^2$$

$$s.t. \begin{cases} h_d = 0, & d = 1, 2, \ldots, D_\omega \\ \sum_{i=1}^{2} \Gamma_i = 1 \\ \sum_{i=1}^{D_\Phi} \Phi_i = 1 \\ 0 \le \Gamma_i \le 1, & i = 1, 2 \\ 0 \le \Phi_i \le 1, & i = 1, 2, \ldots, D_\Phi. \end{cases} \tag{17}$$

The objective is to minimize the sum of squared errors. Given $\Omega(x)$, the optimization problem in (17) is a least squares optimization problem with nonlinear constraints.

6   Simulation Results

In this section, we will perform simulations for the proposed WDFC and verify the asymptotic analysis. The degree distributions $\Phi(x)$ and $\Gamma(x)$ are optimized using the proposed optimization method in Sect. 5. Setting $\mu_{max} = 50$, $D_\omega = 100$ and $M = 1000$, the optimized degree distributions for $\sigma_n = 0.6$ are as follows.

$$\Phi(x) = 0.0065x + 0.8127x^2 + 0.0068x^{14} + 0.1648x^{16} + 0.0052x^{25} + 0.0034x^{39} \tag{18}$$

$$\Gamma(x) = 0.9713x + 0.0287x^2. \tag{19}$$

The overall input degree distribution $\Lambda(x)$ and the overall output degree distribution $\Omega(x)$ are shown in Fig. 3 and Fig. 4, respectively. Figure 3 shows that the input distribution $\Lambda(x)$ of the proposed WDFC approaches to a Poisson distribution with average input degree of 12.66. Figure 4 compares $\Omega(x)$ with $\Gamma(\Phi(x))$. It is shown that the values of $\Gamma(\Phi(x))$ are very close to the values of $\Omega(x)$ with small deviations. In addition, Fig. 4 compare the simulated overall output degree distribution with the corresponding theoretical degree distribution $\Omega(x)$. Simulation results show that the simulated distribution is consistent with

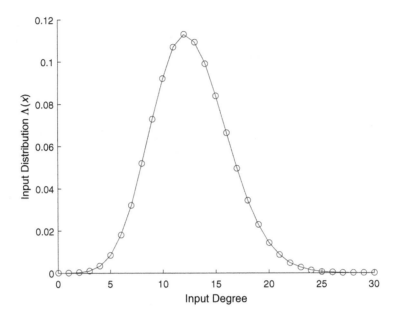

Fig. 3. The overall input degree distribution when $\sigma_n = 0.6$.

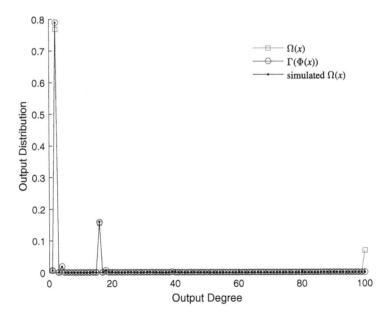

Fig. 4. The overall output degree distribution when $\sigma_n = 0.6$.

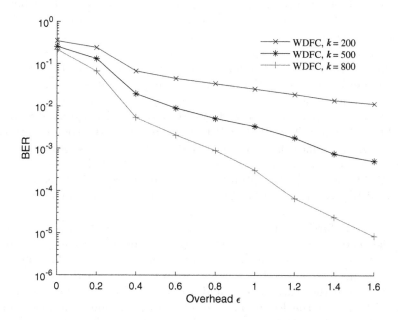

Fig. 5. The BER performance comparison of WDFC for different values of k.

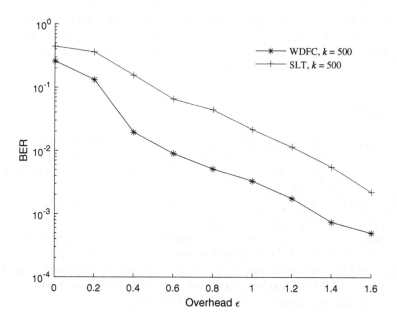

Fig. 6. The BER performance comparison of WDFC with SLT codes when $k = 500$.

the theoretical distribution. It is indicated that the overall degree distribution of the proposed WDFC based on multiplicative network coding can be expressed as a composition of $\Gamma(x)$ and $\Phi(x)$, and the correctness of the analysis for degree distributions in Sect. 4 is verified.

Figure 5 depicts the BER performance of the proposed WDFC for different lengths of information bits with optimized degree distributions in (18) and (19). The length of information bits k takes 200, 500 and 800, respectively. Simulation results show that the proposed WDFC have good performance on wireless AWGN channels. The BER of WDFC decreases as the coding overhead ε increases, which verifies the theoretical analysis. For good LT codes on AWGN channels, we can get the corresponding good degree distributions for the proposed WDFC by using the optimization method in Sect. 5. It is also shown that the BER performance of WDFC can be improved greatly by increasing the length k.

In Fig. 6, we further compare the BER performance of the proposed WDFC with other codes when $k = 500$. The optimized degree distributions in (18) and (19) are still used. A reference coding scheme is provided for comparison purpose. In this reference coding scheme, two source nodes perform LT encoding respectively, and the relay directly and alternately forwards the receiving two separate LT codes to the destination and constructs a stream of encoded symbols. We name this coding scheme as separate LT (SLT) codes. For a fair comparison, the length of information bits, the degree distribution of each source, the overall coding overhead and the channel condition of each coding scheme are with the same settings. It is shown that the BER performance of WDFC is superior to SLT codes with the same length of information bits k. This is because the overall degree distribution of WDFC has been optimized, and the multiplicative network coding is adopted at the relay. Therefore, the performance improvement can be obtained compared with SLT codes.

7   Conclusions

In this paper, we have proposed a novel wireless distributed fountain coding scheme based on multiplicative network coding and have analyzed its decoding performance asymptotically using semi-Gaussian approximation method. Based on the asymptotic performance analysis, we further proposed an optimization method for the design of degree distributions of the proposed WDFC. Due to the adoption of multiplicative network coding, the complexity of the relay node can be reduced greatly and the error propagation can be avoided. Simulation results have showed that the proposed scheme have good performance on AWGN channels, and the theoretical analysis has been verified. It also has revealed that the proposed WDFC outperform SLT codes, and its performance can be further improved by the optimization of degree distributions.

Acknowledgements. This work was supported by the Natural Science Foundation of Jiangsu Province (Grants No. BK20160900), and the NUPTSF (Grants No. NY215031,

NY217032), and the Fundamental Research Funds for the Central Universities (NO. NJ20160027).

References

1. Byers, J.W., Luby, M., Mitzenmacher, M., Rege, A.: A digital fountain approach to reliable distribution of bulk data. ACM SIGCOMM Comput. Commun. Rev. **28**(4), 56–67 (1998)
2. Shokrollahi, A.: Raptor codes. IEEE Trans. Inf. Theory **52**(6), 2551–2567 (2006)
3. Luby, M.: LT codes. In: The 43rd Annual IEEE Symposium on Foundations of Computer Science (FOCS), Vancouver, Canada, pp. 271–280. IEEE (2002)
4. Yang, S., Yeung, R.W.: Batched sparse codes. IEEE Trans. Inf. Theory **60**(9), 5322–5346 (2014)
5. Xu, X., Guan, Y.L., Zeng, Y., Chui, C.C.: Quasi-universal BATS code. IEEE Trans. Veh. Technol. **66**(4), 3497–3501 (2017)
6. Sejdinovic, D., Piechocki, R.J., Doufexi, A.: AND-OR tree analysis of distributed LT codes. In: Proceedings of 2009 IEEE Information Theory Workshop on Networking and Information Theory, Volos, Greece, pp. 261–265. IEEE (2009)
7. Abbas, R., Shirvanimoghaddam, M., Huang, T., Li, Y., Vucetic, B.: Novel design for short analog fountain codes. IEEE Commun. Lett. **23**(8), 1306–1309 (2019)
8. Xu, S., Xu, D.: Optimization design and asymptotic analysis of systematic Luby transform codes over BIAWGN channels. IEEE Trans. Commun. **64**(8), 3160–3168 (2016)
9. Shao, H., Xu, D., Zhang, X.: Asymptotic analysis and optimization for generalized distributed fountain codes. IEEE Commun. Lett. **17**(5), 988–991 (2013)
10. Shao, H., Xu, D., Zhang, X.: Distributed Luby transform coding for three-source single-relay networks based on the deconvolution of robust soliton distribution. IET Commun. **9**(2), 167–176 (2015)
11. Borkotoky, S.S., Pursley, M.B.: Fountain-coded broadcast distribution in multiple-hop packet radio networks. IEEE/ACM Trans. Network. **27**(1), 29–41 (2019)
12. Dai, J., Chen, X., Zhang, F., Kang, K.: Optimisation design of systematic fountain codes on fading channels. IET Commun. **13**(20), 3369–3376 (2019)
13. Deng, K., Yuan, L., Wan, Y., Pan, J.: Expanding window fountain codes with intermediate feedback over BIAWGN channels. IET Commun. **12**(8), 914–921 (2018)
14. Abdulkhaleq N. I., Gazi O.: A sequential coding approach for short length LT codes over AWGN channel. In: 2017 4th International Conference on Electrical and Electronic Engineering (ICEEE), Ankara, Turkey, pp. 267–271 (2017)
15. Kharel A., Cao, L.: Improved fountain codes for BIAWGN channels. In: 2017 IEEE Wireless Communications and Networking Conference (WCNC), San Francisco, USA, pp. 1–6. (2017)
16. Zhang, Z., Zhang, H., Dai, H., Chen, X., Wu, D.O.: Fountain-coded file spreading over mobile networks. IEEE Trans. Wirel. Commun. **16**(10), 6766–6778 (2017)
17. Zhong, W., Xu, L., Zhu, Q., Chen, X., Zhou, J.: A novel beam design method for mmWave multi-antenna arrays with mutual coupling reduction. China Commun. **16**(10), 37–44 (2019)
18. Zhu, Q., et al.: A novel 3D non-stationary wireless MIMO channel simulator and hardware emulator. IEEE Trans. Commun. **66**(9), 3865–3878 (2018)
19. Jiang, K., Chen, X., Zhu, Q., Chen, L., Xu, D., Chen, B.: A novel simulation model for nonstationary rice fading channels. Wireless Commun. Mobile Comput. **2018**, 1–9 (2018)

20. Palanki R., Yedidia J. S.: Rateless codes on noisy channels. In: 2004 IEEE International Symposium on Information Theory (ISIT), Chicago, USA, p. 37 (2004)
21. Etesami, O., Shokrollahi, A.: Raptor codes on binary memoryless symmetric channels. IEEE Trans. Inf. Theory **52**(5), 2033–2051 (2006)
22. Castura, J., Mao, Y.: Rateless coding over fading channels. IEEE Commun. Lett. **10**(1), 46–48 (2006)
23. Zhang, Y., Zhang, Z.: Joint network-channel coding with rateless code over multiple access relay system. IEEE Trans. Wirel. Commun. **12**(1), 320–332 (2013)
24. Nessa, A., Kadoch, M., Rong, B.: Fountain coded cooperative communications for LTE-A connected heterogeneous M2M network. IEEE Access **4**, 5280–5292 (2016)
25. Xu, S., Xu, D., Zhang, X., Shao, H.: Two-way relay networks based on product relay. Electron. Lett. **51**(5), 429–430 (2015)
26. Larsson P.: A multiplicative and constant modulus signal based network coding method applied to CB-relaying. In: VTC Spring 2008 - IEEE Vehicular Technology Conference, Singapore, pp. 61–65 (2008)
27. Manssour, J., Alyafawi, I., Slimane, S.B.: Generalized multiplicative network coding for the broadcast phase of bidirectional relaying. In: IEEE GLOBECOM Workshops (GC Wkshps), Houston, USA, pp. 1336–1341 (2011)
28. Ardakani, M., Kschischang, F.R.: A more accurate one-dimensional analysis and design of irregular LDPC codes. IEEE Trans. Commun. **52**(12), 2106–2114 (2004)

A Real-Time RGB PAM-4 Visible Light Communication System Based on a Transceiver Design with Pre- and Post-equalizations

Jian Kang[1,2], Xuanzheng Wang[3], Li Wang[1,2], Can Wang[1,2], and C. Patrick Yue[1,2(✉)]

[1] HKUST Shenzhen Research Institute, Shenzhen, China
eepatrick@ust.hk
[2] The Hong Kong University of Science and Technology,
Kowloon, Hong Kong SAR
[3] Beijing Institute of Technology, Beijing, China

Abstract. VLC is becoming a trending of next-generation communication because of its broad-spectrum range and unique application scenario. The transmission speed is limited because of the LED bandwidth. Equalization technology on analog frontend or digital baseband can broad the bandwidth of the whole system. High order modulation scheme is also an effect way to improve the data rate under a fixed bandwidth. This work presents a novel RGB PAM-4 transceiver employing digitally controlled asymmetric FFE and cascaded CTLE. The PAM-4 signal with one-tap FFE is composed of six OOK signals with different delays in the optical domain. Delay control is implemented in digital baseband and no DAC is needed in the system. The transceiver achieves 250% increase in bandwidth extension ratio in VLC links using ordinary RGB LEDs by allowing independent PAM-4 eye-height tuning.

Keywords: VLC · PAM-4 · FFE · CTLE

1 Introduction

Visible light communication (VLC) technology based on LEDs has demonstrated significant potential towards the next generation optical wireless interconnection for Internet-of-Things (IoT) devices due to its wide spectrum resources, huge bandwidth capacity, high security, and negligible electromagnetic interference. With the wide application of LEDs in every aspect of human life, VLC becomes a promising technology in various application scenarios such as illumination, display backlights and near field communication. Recent studies have demonstrated system, modulation scheme and optical link level innovations to achieve higher bandwidth efficiencies or wider bandwidth extensions. High level modulation schemes such as pulse amplitude modulation (PAM) [2, 3, 7], carrierless amplitude phase modulation (CAP) [4, 10] and orthogonal frequency division multiplexing (OFDM) combined with various bit and energy allocation algorithms [1, 8, 12] have been thoroughly investigated to

M. Guan and Z. Na (Eds.): MLICOM 2020, LNICST 342, pp. 265–270, 2021.
https://doi.org/10.1007/978-3-030-66785-6_30

significantly improve the bandwidth efficiency. Additionally, circuit and system level innovations in physical layers have been proposed to achieve real-time VLC systems by employing various pre- and post-equalization methods [5, 6, 9, 11].

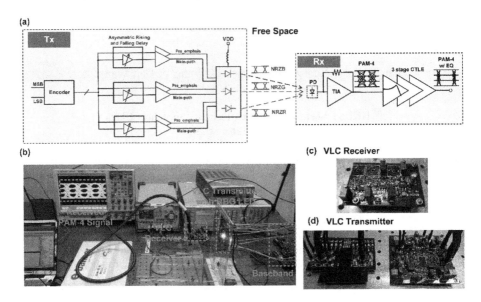

Fig. 1. (a) System architecture of the proposed PAM-4 VLC system. (b) Experimental setup. (c) VLC receiver. (d) VLC transmitter.

However, there are several physical layer challenges that severely limit the data transmission quality of real-time VLC systems, such as the nonlinearity optical responses to driving current and the limited bandwidths of LEDs, especially when a high-level modulation scheme such as PAM-4 is applied. So far, there has been a lack of investigation into the practical and compact implementation of the transceiver front-end design supporting PAM-4 modulation to serve as an electrical-to-optical and optical-to-electrical interface.

In this work, we propose a complete system-on-board RGB PAM-4 transceiver design with feed-forward equalization (FFE) and cascaded continuous-time linear equalization (CTLE). The PAM-4 optical signal is constructed by linearly combining the three serial NRZ optical signals from the red, green, and blue LEDs in the optical domain. The transceiver design can tune the three eye-heights of the PAM-4 optical signal independently to compensate for the differences in the LED optical responses. Experimental results of the RGB PAM-4 system demonstrate that PAM-4 data transmission can be achieved with high quality, and the LED bandwidth can be extended 2.5 times using pre- and post-equalization.

2   System Architecture and Operating Principle

The system architecture of the proposed RGB PAM-4 VLC system is presented in Fig. 1(a). The transmitter system consists of a baseband encoder implemented in a field programmable gate array (FPGA) and a transmitter circuit board with 1-tap FFE function as Fig. 2 shows. The baseband encoder receives two serial bits: one most significant bit (MSB) and one least significant bit (LSB). The MSB and LSB serial bits are encoded into three channels of serial data, which separately contribute to the three eyes of the PAM-4 signal. For each of the three channels, the data is duplicated into two paths, with one data path going through an inverter and a digitally controlled asymmetric rising and falling delay. On the transmitter circuit board, three serial data-pairs control the main and 1-tap FFE drivers of each of the red, green, and blue LED. The output NRZ optical signals from the red, green, and blue LEDs are linearly combined in the optical domain and generate the PAM-4 optical signal, with each NRZ optical signal contributing to one part of the PAM-4 eye. On the receiver side, the PAM-4 optical signal is converted into an electrical signal using a photo detector and a trans-impedance amplifier (TIA). The converted electrical PAM-4 signal is then equalized using a three-stage cascaded CLTE to compensate for the limited bandwidth and is delivered to the output with a unit gain buffer. The experimental setup is shown in Fig. 1(b). The receiver and transmitter circuit are shown in Fig. 1(c) and (d), respectively.

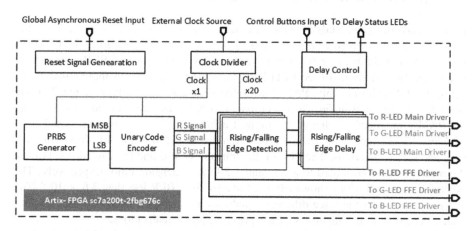

Fig. 2. Structure of digital baseband of the transmitter

The light source employed here is a commercially available RGB LED with each of the red, green, and blue LEDs capable of providing a maximum of 0.5 W output light. The optical responses and bandwidths of the three LEDs are different, which causes the eye-widths to be unequal and the eye quality to be degraded. To solve this problem, three VLC drivers with independently driving current controls and FFEs with asymmetric digitally controlled edge delays are separately implemented for the red, green, and blue LEDs. The delays for the rising and falling edges of the FFE data path can be controlled separately using digital code to compensate for the asymmetric rising and falling times of the LEDs, as shown in Fig. 3(a). The driving current of the three drivers are carefully adjusted so that the three eye heights of the PAM-4 signal are equal. On the receiver side, three-stage-cascaded CTLE with an R-C degeneration structure is implemented to compensate for the bandwidth limitation of the RGB LED and the TIA. The cascaded CTLE features variable peaking frequency, height, and slope, which can provide compensation to a wider bandwidth.

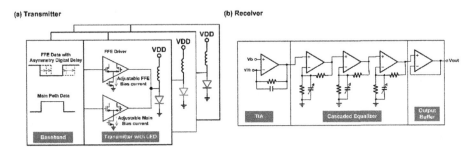

Fig. 3. (a) Transmitter implementation with 1-tap FFE. (b) Receiver implementation with three-stage cascaded CTLE.

3   Experimental Results and Discussion

Based on the designed RGB PAM-4 VLC transmission system, the data transmission performance was verified at a 5-cm transmission distance by measuring the bit-error-rates (BERs), bathtub curve (BC) and eye diagrams. The measured BERs versus data rate under the conditions of red LED NRZ transmission, PAM-4 without equalization (EQ), PAM-4 with FFE only, PAM-4 with one stage CTLE, and three stage CTLE are plotted and compared in Fig. 4(a). Compared to NRZ data transmission, by applying the PAM-4 modulation scheme, the highest achievable data rate was increased from 22 Mbps to 32 Mbps, which was further extended by 2.5 times to 80 Mbps using the FEE and CTLE functions. The FFE on the transmitter side and the cascaded CTLE on the receiver side contributed to a 2.1- and 1.2-times extension ratio, respectively. The bathtub curve at 68 Mbps shows a 0.3–UI margin for a BER less than 3.6×10^{-3}. The eye diagrams under the three different equalization conditions are shown in Fig. 4(a), which demonstrate the functions of the pre- and post-equalizations.

Due to the different optical responses of the red, green, and blue LEDs, the three eye-heights of the received PAM-4 signal were uneven and thus led to very narrow decoding margin. By tuning the driving current of the RGB LEDs independently, a much-improved PAM-4 data eye with almost equal eye-heights can be achieved, as shown in Fig. 4(c) and (d).

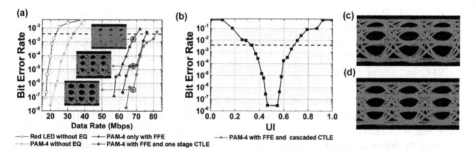

Fig. 4. (a) Measured BER versus data rate for a red LED without EQ, PAM-4 without EQ, PAM-4 with only FFE, PAM-4 with FFE and first stage CTLE, PAM-4 with cascaded CTLE, and eye diagrams at 68 Mbps for the three different equalization conditions. (b) Measured bathtub curve at 68 Mbps. (c) Measured eye diagram without independent driving current tuning. (d) Measured eye diagram with independent driving current tuning.

4 Conclusions

An RGB PAM-4 VLC transceiver system with 1-tap FFE and three-stage-cascaded CTLE was presented. The PAM-4 optical signal is constructed by linearly combining three independent NRZ signals from the RGB LEDs, respectively. The experimental results validate the independent eye-height tuning feature enables high-quality PAM-4 signal transmission resulting in 2.5-times increase in bandwidth extension ratio.

Acknowledgement. This work was supported in part by the HKUST-Qualcomm Optical Wireless Laboratory, in part by the Science and Technology Plan of Shenzhen under Grant JCYJ20170818113929095.

References

1. Bian R., Tavakkolnia I., Haas H.: 15.73 Gb/s Visible Light Communication with off-the-shelf LEDs. J Lightwave Technol. **37**, 2418–2424 (2019)
2. Chuang, C., Wei, C., Lin, T., et al.: Employing deep neural network for high speed 4-PAM optical interconnect. In: Anonymous 2017 European Conference on Optical Communication (ECOC), pp. 1–3 (2017)
3. Chi, N., Zhao, Y., Shi, M., et al.: Gaussian kernel-aided deep neural network equalizer utilized in underwater PAM8 visible light communication system. Opt. Express **26**(20), 26700–26712 (2018)
4. Khalighi, M., Long, S., Bourennane, S., et al.: PAM- and CAP-based transmission schemes for visible-light communications. Access **5**, 27002–27013 (2017)
5. Li, H., Chen, X., Guo, J., et al.: A 550 Mbit/s real-time visible light communication system based on phosphorescent white light LED for practical high-speed low-complexity application. Opt. Express **22**(22), 27203–27213 (2014)
6. Li, X., Hussain, B., Kang, J., et al.: Smart μLED display-VLC system with a PD-based/camera-based receiver for NFC applications. IEEE Photonics J. **11**(1), 1–8 (2019)

7. Zhang, M., Wang, Y., Wang, Z., et al.: A novel scalar MCMMA blind equalization utilized in 8-PAM LED based visible light communication system. In: Anonymous 2016 IEEE International Conference on Communications Workshops (ICC), pp. 321–325 (2016)

8. Tsonev, D., Chun, H., Rajbhandari, S., et al.: A 3-Gb/s single-LED OFDM-based wireless VLC link using a gallium nitride μLED. IEEE Photonics Technol. Lett. **26**(7), 637–640 (2014)

9. Xu, W., Zhang, M., Han, D., et al.: Real-time 262-Mb/s visible light communication with digital predistortion waveform shaping. IEEE Photonics J. **10**(3), 1–10 (2018)

10. Wang, X., Cui, Y., Wu, N., et al.: Performance analysis of optical carrierless amplitude and phase modulation for indoor visible light communication system. Acta Photonica Sinica **46** (5), 506001 (2017)

11. Yeh, C., Liu, Y., Chow, C.: Real-time white-light phosphor-LED visible light communication (VLC) with compact size. Opt. Express **21**(22), 26192–26197 (2013)

12. Zhu, X., Wang, F., Shi, M., et al.: 10.72 Gb/s visible light communication system based on single packaged RGBYC LED utilizing QAM-DMT modulation with hardware pre-equalization. In: Anonymous Optical Fiber Communication Conference, pp. M3K.3. Optical Society of America (2018)

Kinoform Generated Combined with the Error Diffusion Method and the Dynamic Random Phase

Xuemei Cao[(✉)], Mingxiang Guan, Linzhong Xia, Jinping Fan,
and Jian Wang

Shenzhen Institute of Information Technology, Shenzhen 518172, China
xuemei_cao88@163.com

Abstract. A computer generated kinoform combined with error diffusion and the dynamic random phase is presented. In order to compensate the error generated in the reconstructed image from the phase only hologram, the Floyd-Steinberg error diffusion technique is employed. The error can be diffused to the neighboring pixels in this method. And sequential kinoforms are generated by adding dynamic phase factor into the object domain to reduce the speckle noise. The results show that the kinoform can be achieved correctly and the representation quality of the reconstructed image can be improved compared with that obtained from the original kinoform.

Keywords: Kinoform · Error diffusion · Dynamic random phase

1 Introduction

In recent years, three-dimensional (3D) display attracts considerable attentions [1–5]. Among the three-dimensional display technologies, the digital holographic technology is recognized as the optimal and the most promising three-dimensional display technology, which can provide the most authentic 3D illusion to the naked eye. With the rapid development of digital computers, computer-generated hologram (CGH) [6–9] technology is recognized as a good way to provide content for digital holographic 3D display. Many approaches are proposed to generate CGH such as the point-based method [10], polygon-based method [11] and multiple viewpoint projection [12, 13].

Kinoform is a phase only hologram, which regards the amplitude of interference light as constant. Compared with amplitude-type holograms, the kinoform has several advantanges. It can be displayed with a phase-only device and results in higher optical diffraction efficiency as well as rejection of the conjugate image and the zero-order image. However, removing the amplitude component will result in substantial degradation on the reconstructed image. To solve this problem, some optimization approaches are presented such as the Gerberg-Saxton algorithm [14], the bidirectional error diffusion algorithm [15] and the iterative Fresnel transform method [16].

Inspired by the previous works [17, 18], kinoform generated combined with the error diffusion method and the dynamic random phase is proposed. The result show that the representation quality of the reconstructed image is improved significantly from the

M. Guan and Z. Na (Eds.): MLICOM 2020, LNICST 342, pp. 271–277, 2021.
https://doi.org/10.1007/978-3-030-66785-6_31

kinoform generated combined with error diffusion method and the random phase factor. The principle of the proposed method is demonstrated first and then the numerical simulation process is carried out. The quality of the reconstructed image are evaluated by the PSNR and the conclusions are given finally.

2 Principle

The complex amplitude $F(u, v)$ of the Fresnel hologram is generated from the object waves emitted from each point on an object in Eq. (1). Where $A(x, y)$ is the intensity of each point in the object scene. λ is the wavelength of the optical wave. $r_{x;y;u;v}$ indicates the distance between the object point and the hologram. $\varphi_t(x, y)$ represents the random phase factor, which is used to reduce the dynamic range of the object wave spectrum distribution.

$$F(u, v)\bigg|_{\substack{0 \leq u \leq X \\ 0 \leq v \leq Y}} = \sum_{x=0}^{X-1} \sum_{y=0}^{Y-1} \frac{A(x, y) \exp(j2\pi r_{x,y;u,v}/\lambda) \exp[j\varphi_t(x, y)])}{r_{x,y;u,y}} \tag{1}$$

Then, the phase only hologram $F_p(u, v)$ can be obtained from the complex amplitude of the hologram from the Eq. (2), in which the magnitude of each pixel is set to be a value of unity.

$$|F_p(u, v)| = 1, \quad and \quad \arg(F_p(u, v)) = \arg(F(u, v)) \tag{2}$$

The reconstructed image of the phase only hologram generated with Eq. (2) is poor. The large amount of error in each hologram pixel $E(u_i, v_i)$ is caused after removing the magnitude information. The error can be given by setting the magnitude to unity as Eq. (3).

$$E(u_i, v_i) = F(u_i, v_i) - F_p(u_i, v_i) \tag{3}$$

To overcome the problem, the Floyd-Steinberg error diffusion technique [15, 17] is employed to compensate the error. Figure 1 shows the error diffusion process more intuitively.

The errors generated on the odd rows are diffused to the neighborhood pixels that have not been visited according to Eqs. (4–7), from which we know the pixel on the odd rows are scanned from left to right.

$$F(u_i, v_i + 1) \leftarrow F(u_i, v_i + 1) + a_1 F(u_i, v_i), \tag{4}$$

$$F(u_i + 1, v_i - 1) \leftarrow F(u_i + 1, v_i - 1) + a_2 F(u_i, v_i), \tag{5}$$

$$F(u_i + 1, v_i) \leftarrow F(u_i + 1, v_i) + a_3 F(u_i, v_i), \tag{6}$$

$$F(u_i + 1, v_i + 1) \leftarrow F(u_i + 1, v_i + 1) + a_4 F(u_i, v_i), \tag{7}$$

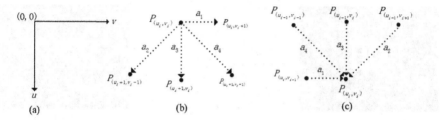

Fig. 1. a) The co-ordinate system with horizontal and vertical axes. (b) Error diffusion from the current pixel to its neighborhood, scanned from left to right. (c) An alternative representation of (a), showing the updating of a pixel from its neighborhood.

According to the Ref [17], a_1 to a_4 are set as Eq. (8).

$$a_1 = 7/16, a_2 = 3/16, a_3 = 5/16, a_4 = 1/16 \tag{8}$$

The sequential kinofroms can be obtained by setting the phase factor $\varphi_t(x, y)$ randomly assigned from $[0, 2\pi]$ in each calculation. Then the intensity information of each reconstructed image from sequential kinofroms is superimposed and normalized as the intensity information of the final reproduced image.

3 Simulation results

The numerical reconstruction image is obtained by using the convolution method. Figure 2(c) shows the image reconstructed from the original kinoform. The severe attenuation appears in the reconstructed image, which is caused by removing the magnitude information of the hologram.

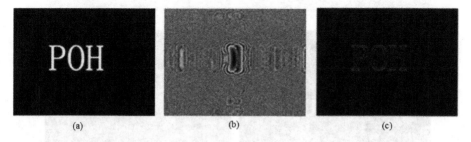

Fig. 2. a) The object plane (b) The original kinoform (c) The image reconstructed from the original kinoform

Figure 3(c) shows the image reconstructed from the error diffusion kinoform described in part 2. From which we can see the brightness of the reconstructed image is increased. However, the distortion also appears in the image.

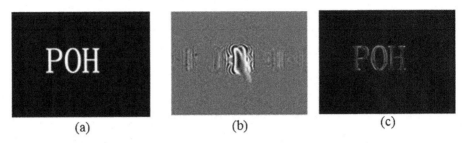

Fig. 3. a) The object plane (b) The error diffusion kinoform (c) The image reconstructed from the error diffusion kinoform

Then, based on the error diffusion method, the random phase factor is added in Eq. (1) to achieve the kinoform. Figure 4(c) represents the image reconstructed from the kinoform generated when the random phase is added only. The reconstructed image in Fig. 4(d) is obtained from the kinoform generated combined with error diffusion and the random phase factor. The results show that the representation quality of the reconstructed image is improved significantly from the kinoform generated combined with error diffusion method and the random phase factor.

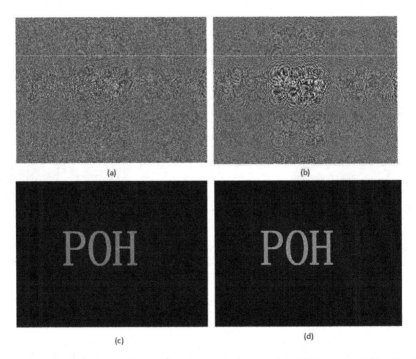

Fig. 4. a) The kinoform generated when the random phase is added only; (b) The kinoform generated by using the error diffusion method and the dynamic random phase; (c) The image reconstructed from (a); (d) The image reconstructed from (b).

Figure 5(a) shows the images reconstructed from the kinoforms using the dynamic random phase method with the 5th, 10th and 20th iteration numbers. And Fig. 5(b) represents the images reconstructed from the kinoforms generated combined with error diffusion method and the dynamic random phase with the same iteration numbers.

Peak signal to noise ratio (PSNR) is used to evaluate the quality of the reconstruction images. The results are shown in Table 1, from which we can see that the reconstruction results from the kinoforms generated combined with error diffusion and the dynamic random phase are superior to that kinoforms generated with the dynamic random phase only.

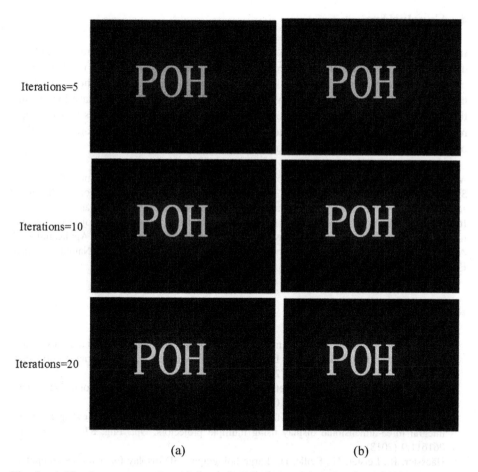

Iterations=5

Iterations=10

Iterations=20

(a)   (b)

Fig. 5. a) The images reconstructed from the kinoforms using the dynamic random phase method with the 5th, 10th and 20th iteration numbers (b) The images reconstructed from the kinoforms generated combined with error diffusion and the dynamic random phase.

Table 1. PSNRs of the reconstructed images

Iteration numbers	PSNR (dB)	
	The dynamic random phase method	The method combined with the error diffusion and the dynamic random phase
0	21.6543	23.8054
5	23.3231	25.2590
10	25.5781	28.0231
20	26.9221	30.1241

4   Conclusions

In conclusion, a computer generated kinoform combined with error diffusion and the dynamic random phase is presented. The error diffusion approach is used to compensate the error caused by removing the magnitude information of the phase only hologram. And sequential kinoforms are obtained by adding dynamic phase factor into the object domain to reduce the speckle noise. The results demonstrates that the representation quality of the reconstructed image can be improved compared with that obtained from the original kinoform.

Acknowledgment. This work was supported by the Scientific and Technological Projects of Shenzhen (No. JCYJ20190808093001772), Guangdong Province higher vocational colleges & schools Pearl River scholar funded scheme (2016), Project of Shenzhen Science and Technology Innovation Committee (JCYJ20170817114522834), Research platform and project of Department of Education of Guangdong Province (2019GGCZX009), Engineering Applications of Artificial Intelligence Technology Laboratory (No. PT201701), Provincial Natural Science Foundation of Guangdong (No. 2017A030313337).

References

1. Du, J., Sang, X., Yu, X., et al.: Demonstration of a large viewing angle and high-resolution floating three-dimensional display based on the multichannel and multivariable correction algorithm. Opt. Eng. **59**(10), 1–5 (2020)
2. Lv, G.J., Zhao, B.C., Wu, F., et al. Three-dimensional display with optimized view distribution. Opt. Eng. **58**(2), 023108.1–023108.4 (2019)
3. Okaichi, N., Miura, M., Sasaki, H., et al.: Continuous combination of viewing zones in integral three-dimensional display using multiple projectors. Opt. Eng. **57**(6), 061611.1–061611.9 (2018)
4. Häussler, R., Leister, N., Stolle, H.: Large holographic 3D display for real-time computer-generated holography. Spie Digital Optical Technologies (2017)
5. Su, Y., Cai, Z., Shi, L., et al.: A multi-plane optical see-through holographic three-dimensional display for augmented reality applications. Optik Int. J. Light Electron Opt. **157**, 190–196 (2018)
6. Pi, D., Liu, J., Han, Y., et al.: Simple and effective calculation method for computer-generated hologram based on non-uniform sampling using look-up-table. Opt. Expr. **27**(26), 37337 (2019)

7. Wen, C.: Computer-generated hologram marked by correlated photon imaging. Appl. Opt. **57**(5), 1196 (2018)
8. Anton, G., Svyatoslav, D.: Cylindrical computer-generated hologram for displaying 3D images. Opt. Expr. **26**(17), 22160 (2018)
9. Zhao, Y., Shi, C.X., Kwon, K.C., et al.: Fast calculation method of computer-generated hologram using a depth camera with point cloud gridding. Opt. Commun. **411**, 166–169 (2018)
10. Stein, A.D., et al.: Computer-generated holograms: a simplified ray-tracing approach. Comput. Phys **6**, 389 (1992)
11. Liu, Y.Z., Dong, J.W., Pu, Y.Y., et al.: High-speed full analytical holographic computations for true-life scenes. Opt. Expr. **18**(4), 3345–3351 (2010)
12. Cao, X., Guan, M., Xia, L., et al.: High efficient generation of holographic stereograms based on wavefront recording plane. Chin. Opt. Lett. **15**(12), 120901 (2017)
13. Cao, Xuemei., Sang, Xinzhu., et al.: Straightforward computer-generated fresnel hologram from multiple angular orthogonal projection images. Opt. Commun. **324**, 47–52 (2014)
14. Gerchberg, R.W., Saxton, W.O.: A practical algorithm for the determination of the phase from image and diffraction plane pictures. Optik (Stuttg.) **35**, 237–246 (1972)
15. Tsang, P.W., Poon, T.-C.: Novel method for converting digital Fresnel hologram to phase-only hologram based on bidirectional error diffusion. Opt. Express **21**(20), 23680–23686 (2013)
16. Yeom, J., Hong, J., Jung, J. -H., Hong, K., Park, J.-H., Lee, B.: Phase-only hologram generation based on integral imaging and its enhancement in depth resolution. Chin. Opt. Lett. **9**(12), 12009-1–12009-4 (2011)
17. Floyd, R.W., Steinberg, L.: An adaptive algorithm for spatial Grey scale. Proc Soc. Info. Disp. **17**, 75–77 (1976)
18. Zheng, H., Yu, Y., Wang, T., et al.: Computer-generated kinoforms of real-existing full-color 3D objects using pure-phase look-up-table method. Opt. Lasers Eng. **50**(4), 568–573 (2012)

Simulation System of Cochlear Implant

Chen Yousheng and Wang Jian[✉]

ShenZhen Institute of Information Technology, Shenzhen 518000, China
wangj01@sziit.com.cn

Abstract. Different types of hearing loss can be treated according to the etiology and degree. Commonly used methods include drug therapy, surgical treatment, wearing hearing aids and implanting electrical stimulation equipment. Among them, cochlear implant is an effective way to restore the hearing perception ability of patients with very severe deafness and total deafness, and it is the most commonly used electrical stimulation implant device. Cochlear implant is still not widely used in China because of its high price and long training period. In order to facilitate speech training and improve speech perception ability of cochlear implant, this paper designs a speech training and speech simulation system of cochlear implant. The designed software and hardware system is a simulation test platform, with low price, simple test mode, and potential huge market value and application value.

Keywords: Cochlear implant · Simulation system · Speech processing strategy

1 Introduction

Hereditary diseases, infectious diseases, delivery syndrome, chronic ear infection, improper use of drugs, excessive noise, aging and other factors can lead to hearing loss. Among them, the main cause of hearing loss of young people aged 12 to 35 is often excessive noise in entertainment environment, while one third of the elderly over 65 years old suffer from hearing loss due to disability. According to the cause and degree of hearing loss, different treatment methods can be selected. Common methods include drug therapy, surgical treatment, wearing hearing aids and implanting electrical stimulation devices. Among them, cochlear implant is an effective way to restore the hearing of patients with severe deafness. For normal people, the outer ear and the middle ear are mechanical transmission devices of external sound signals, in which the outer ear is used to collect sound and the middle ear ossicular chain is used to amplify mechanical vibration. The amplified signal from the middle ear is transmitted to the inner ear, and the sound signal is transformed into bioelectric signal through hair cells. Then, bioelectric signal is used to stimulate auditory nerve to produce auditory perception. Electrical stimulation can stimulate the residual auditory nerve in the cochlea of the deaf, and transmit it to the brain along the auditory pathway, producing the similar auditory feeling with the normal people. Therefore, as an alternative device, the

Supported by the characteristic innovation project of Guangdong University in 2019 (Grant No. 2019GKTSCX094).

M. Guan and Z. Na (Eds.): MLICOM 2020, LNICST 342, pp. 278–284, 2021.
https://doi.org/10.1007/978-3-030-66785-6_32

cochlear implant directly converts the voice signal into electrical pulse signal, which stimulates the auditory nerve to produce similar neural transmission mode and auditory perception.

At present, there are three major cochlear manufacturers in Australia, Austria and the United States. In recent years, acoustic research institutions and research universities in China have carried out research work related to cochlear implant. A company in Hangzhou has also developed a domestic cochlear implant. The clinical performance of related products are being tested and evaluated, and some products have been used in clinical.

With the development of recent decades, the performance of cochlear implant has been greatly improved, but the recognition rate is still very low in practical application. Scholars have shown that for 50% sentence recognition rate, the signal-to-noise ratio required by normal people is about −10 dB, while the signal-to-noise ratio required by cochlear users is between 5 and 15 dB. Therefore, under the noise of normal living environment, the speech recognition rate of cochlear users is still low. The factors that affect the low speech recognition rate of the cochlear implant include the interference of noise environment and the mismatch of application scenarios, which will greatly reduce the performance of the cochlear implant. Improving the speech recognition rate of cochlear implant in noisy environment is still one of the research focuses in this field. At present, the research of cochlear implant mainly focuses on the following aspects: first, improving speech processing algorithm, such as extracting and transmitting more effective information, extracting the fundamental frequency and change information for the unique tone features of Chinese; second, the improvement of device and electrode. For example, the high-resolution strategy of the cochlear implant can obtain the fine structure of the signal and improve the stimulation rate of the electrode to transmit more abundant information. At present, more research focuses on the enhancement of the front-end signal of the cochlear implant [1–6], virtual channel technology [7, 8] and the optical cochlea [9–11].

The reason why cochlear implant is not widely used in China is that the technology is not mature enough, the operation cost is expensive, and the population is large. At present, only a few research institutes and universities in the mainland have cochlear debugging platforms authorized by three major foreign cochlear companies, which are not open to the outside world or sold. This paper designs a portable cochlear implant voice simulation and speech training system. The hardware and software system is a simulation test platform, which has low price, simple test mode, large customer base and potential market value.

2 Structure and Function of Cochlear Implant

For normal people, the outer ear and middle ear are mechanical transmission devices of external sound signal, which use the auricle of the outer ear to collect sound. The sound vibrates the tympanic membrane through the external auditory canal, and the ossicular chain of the middle ear can amplify the mechanical vibration. The amplified signal from the middle ear is transmitted to the vestibular window of the inner ear, causing the fluctuation of the lymph and the vibration of the basement membrane, stimulating the spiral organ of the cochlea, converting the sound signal into bioelectrical signal through the hair cells, stimulating the auditory nerve and transmitting it to the central system of the vestibular window of the cochlea, and finally generating the auditory perception. Functional electrical stimulation can directly stimulate the residual auditory nerve in the cochlea. As an alternative device, the cochlea replaces some functions of the ear. The main part of the cochlea is shown in Fig. 1.

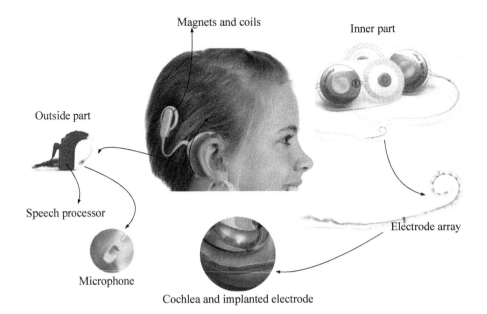

Fig. 1. Structure of cochlear implant.

The external cochlear implant mainly includes a microphone for collecting sound signals and a speech processor for processing sound signals. Microphone is a kind of transducer for acoustic electric conversion. The external voice signal is converted into electrical signal through microphone. After amplification and filtering, the electrical signal is transmitted to the speech processor. The speech processor extracts the time-domain envelope and frequency-domain parameters of the signal. The speech processor sends signal parameters through an external modulation coil to send signals and energy. The internal receiving coil receives the signal and sends it to the corresponding electrode. Finally, the electrode array stimulates the auditory nerve at a certain rate and in a certain way, and produces the auditory perception similar to that of the normal human ear.

3   System Design

3.1   Hardware Circuit

The average cost of cochlear implant is about tens of thousands of dollars. The high price is not only the product cost of cochlear implant itself, but also the pre-operative evaluation, hospital costs, doctor costs, as well as the post-operative external debugging and regular maintenance costs. After the operation, there will be a series of follow-up costs. There is a huge demand for cochlear implant in every country in the world, but there is a lack of a cheap platform for cochlear signal acquisition simulation and algorithm research. The front-end signal acquisition and simulation system developed in this paper can make up for this gap.

This system includes two parts: hardware and software. The hardware consists of two ARM processors to form a dual channel acquisition system, which can be started at the same time by pressing the key, which is helpful to improve the portability and real-time of signal acquisition. At the same time, the two microphones are placed at adjustable distance. The two ARM processors collect and save the information of the two microphones at the same time, and accurately record the spatial orientation information of the two microphones, which can be used for the design of microphone array algorithm. The main modules of the system are described as follows.

Control and processor module: because the system is to collect dual channel signals and accurately record the differences between signals, the system uses two ARM processors to collect and process at the same time (STM32 chip is selected for the system). In order to accurately and synchronously start signal acquisition, the system uses a key switch to connect two STM32 pins at the same time, which can simultaneously start signal acquisition to reduce the time delay of two signal acquisition.

Voice signal acquisition module: the system uses the key switch to start two STM32 at the same time for signal acquisition, each STM32 controls the audio decoder, and two audio chips are connected with high-sensitivity acoustic and electrical sensors for signal acquisition.

Program download and online debugging module: the signal acquisition program, software interface and other programs of the system need to be downloaded through USB, and STM32 is connected through chip CH340G, so that the program can be downloaded to STM32 directly through USB, and serial communication can also be realized. On the other hand, the USB interface connected by CH340G chip also has the functions of power supply and serial communication. Another JTAG interface is used for online debugging.

Power module: the system provides 5 V power through power adapter, and converts the power into 3.3 V through power regulator chip, which is also provided to STM32 chip and flash chip.

Signal storage module: the system collects and controls the signal information of the two channels through two STM32 chips, and the information of the two channels is stored in two SD cards through the SD card interface. The SD card of this system adopts SPI communication mode. The SPI interface of SD card is connected to the corresponding pin of STM32 to realize SD communication and data storage.

3.2   Software GUI

The sound is collected by microphone, filtered and amplified by a pre-processing circuit, and finally connected to a computer. Through the development of voice simulation software GUI on the computer, after selecting and setting parameters on the GUI, the specific voice processing strategy is called, the collected voice signal is processed by the voice processing algorithm, then the corresponding analog voice in the synthesis algorithm is synthesized, and finally the synthetic voice is played through the speaker. The sound played by the speaker is based on the cochlear speech processing strategy and actual parameters. Therefore, the synthesized sound signal can simulate the hearing of cochlear users under the stimulation of electrodes. We use Matlab to develop the software GUI, as shown in Fig. 2.

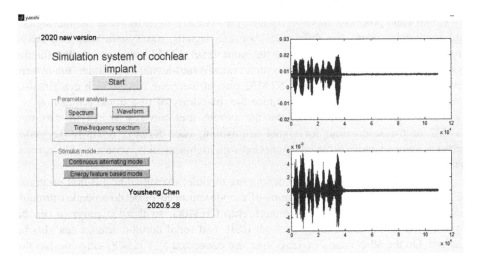

Fig. 2. Software GUI of the simulation system.

Besides speech synthesis and speech training, the GUI of the software can also extract and analyze parameters. For example, the spectrum parameters and time-frequency spectrum parameters of the signal can be extracted, as shown in Fig. 3 and Fig. 4:

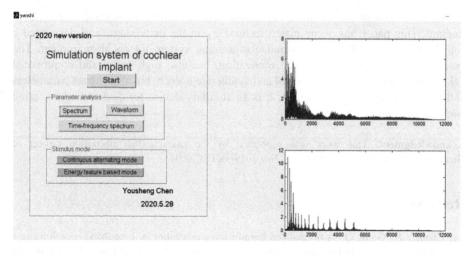

Fig. 3. Display of the spectrum parameter in the GUI.

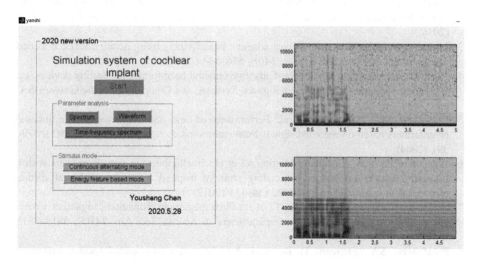

Fig. 4. Display of the time-frequency spectrum parameter in the GUI.

As can be seen from Fig. 3 and Fig. 4, the software GUI can analyze various effective speech parameters, which is helpful for speech training and system simulation of the cochlear implant.

4   Conclusion

There are a large number of hearing impaired patients in *Shenzhen* and other mega cities, which have great potential demand for cochlear implant, especially for obtaining high-quality hearing perception in noise environment. Improving speech recognition rate in noise environment is one of the final destination for the improvement of cochlear implant. This paper has accumulated technology in the early stage, and developed a sound simulation and deafness simulation training system for cochlear implant. The system has not only technological innovation, but also high social and commercial value. It can not only simulate signal and synthesize speech, but also extract parameters and train users of cochlear implant. It is an auxiliary device for deaf patients wearing cochlear implant.

Acknowledgment. This work was supported by the characteristic innovation project of Guangdong University in 2019 (Grant No. 2019GKTSCX094).

References

1. Chen, Y.S., Gong, Q.: A normalized beamforming algorithm for broadband speech using a continuous interleaved sampling strategy. IEEE Trans. Audio Speech Lan P **20**(3), 868–874 (2012)
2. Sanketha, M., Kashwan, K.R.: Implementation of cochlear implant for speech enhancement and timbre detection using fractional delay filter. In: ICRTIT 2016, Chennai, India, pp. 1–4 (2016)
3. Li, X.X., Wang, D.W., et al.: Robust adaptive beamforming using iterative variable loaded sample matrix inverse. IET J. Mag. **54**(9), 546–548 (2018)
4. Xiao, J.J., Luo, Z.Q., et al.: A robust adaptive binaural beamformer for hearing devices. In: 2017 51st Asilomar Conference on Signals, Systems, and Computers, Pacific Grove, USA, pp. 1885–1889 (2017)
5. Lockwood, M.E., Jones, D.L., et al.: Performance of time- and frequency-domain binaural beamformers based on recorded signals from real rooms. J. Acoust. Soc. Am. **115**(1), 379–391 (2004)
6. Lopez-Poveda, E.A., Eustaquio-Martin, A., et al.: Intelligibility in speech maskers with a binaural cochlear implant sound coding strategy inspired by the contralateral medial olivocochlear reflex. Hear. Res. **348**, 134–137 (2017)
7. Anderson, S.R., Kan, A., Thakkar, T., et al.: Pitch magnitude estimation can predict across-ear pitch comparisons in cochlear-implant users. J. Acoust. Soc. Am. **141**(5), 3815–3815 (2017)
8. Eyndhoven, S.V., Francart, T., Bertrand, A.: EEG-informed attended speaker extraction from recorded speech mixtures with application in neuro-steered hearing prostheses. IEEE Trans. Biomed. Eng. **64**(5), 1045–1056 (2017)
9. Guan, T., Yang, M., Wei, Z., et al.: Simulation of the optical stimulation mechanism of cochlear nerves. J. Tsinghua Univ. **57**(10), 1102–1105 (2017)
10. Jiang, B., Xia, N., Wang, X., et al.: Auditory responses to short-wavelength infrared neural stimulation of the rat cochlear nucleus. In: 39th Annual International Conference of the IEEE Engineering in Medicine and Biology Society (EMBC 2017), Seogwipo, South Korea, pp. 1942–1945. IEEE (2017)
11. Wang, J., Lu, J., Tian, L.: Effect of fiberoptic collimation technique on 808 nm wavelength laser stimulation of cochlear neurons. Photomed. Laser Surg. **34**(6), 1–6 (2016)

Intelligent Positioning and Navigation Systems

Assist GPS to Improve Accuracy Under Complex Road Conditions Using Sensors on Smart Phone

Li Sheng[ID], Rui Tian, and Haibo Ye[✉]

College of Computer Science and Technology, Nanjing University of Aeronautics
and Astronautics, Nanjing, China
{shengli,tian2018,yhb}@nuaa.edu.cn

Abstract. This paper presents the design and implementation of a new
vehicle tracking technology. It can assist GPS to achieve high precision
under special situations. For example, the situations when the road conditions are complex or the GPS signal strength is weak. In our method,
the barometer data and acceleration data are used to assist the GPS
data, and the Hidden Markov Model is used to assist the location tracking. We make two key technical contributions. The first is to propose
a Hidden Markov Model to combine the barometer and accelerometer
reading hints for estimating the location of the vehicle. The second is to
design some novel techniques for parameter estimation. The experiment
shows that the accuracy of our method is improved by 19.2% compared
with GPS under these special situations.

Keywords: Location tracking · Barometer · Hidden Markov Model

1 Introduction

Location tracking techniques are now widely used in many location based services, such as car navigation [9] and logistics management [13]. The GPS (Global
Positioning System) has high precision outdoors, making it the most used technology for location tracking. However, the GPS positioning accuracy will be
greatly affected in some scenarios. For example, there will have large error when
the GPS signal is bad, and the tracking accuracy will be affected in complex road
conditions. Also, when there are roads interlaced, the GPS tracking accuracy can
be influenced. More detail: 1) when the car is driving in a tunnel or under dense
tall buildings, the GPS signal will be very weak, and the tracking cannot be
precise. 2) when the car is passing the overpass, there may be several roads at
different altitudes but under the same GPS longitude and latitude. The altitude provided by GPS can have an error of tens of meters, which is not accurate
enough to know which road the car is driving on. A typical example is at car navigation, if the car goes to the wrong route when passing the overpass, the existing

© ICST Institute for Computer Sciences, Social Informatics and Telecommunications Engineering 2021
Published by Springer Nature Switzerland AG 2021. All Rights Reserved
M. Guan and Z. Na (Eds.): MLICOM 2020, LNICST 342, pp. 287–303, 2021.
https://doi.org/10.1007/978-3-030-66785-6_33

GPS based system cannot re-locate the car and recalculate the navigation route. Based on the above observations, an approach to improve the accuracy of GPS based vehicle tracking in such particular situations is desperately needed.

In order to improve the accuracy of GPS based vehicle tracking, the most common method is to utilize the accelerometer and compass for inertial navigation [4,5]. However, the sensors are noisy and the error of accelerometer and compass will accumulate [8] over time. Moreover, when it comes to complicated road conditions such as interlaced roads, even with the assistance of accelerometer, the GPS still can not realize precise tracking. Other techniques such as Wi-Fi [12] or cellular network [20] based positioning and tracking are not suitable here because they need infrastructure support and are not accurate enough [21].

In this paper, we believe that except for GPS, accelerometer and compass readings, there are also other information which can help us achieve more precise location tracking [6,7]. Take the barometer sensor on smart phone as an example, it can senses the precise altitude change of the car, which can help improve the tracking accuracy on the elevated roads and overpasses where the altitude changes along the road. Real-time traffic congestion and road conditions data can also help location tracking.

In this paper, we put forward a new solution to satisfy the need for accurately tracking a car in many situations. Our solution is to utilize the data collected from barometer and accelerometer to assist GPS. All of these sensors can be found in smart phones nowadays. We will feed the sensor data to a Hidden Markov Model (HMM) to derive the location list that the car is driving through. Generally, to solve this problem, we will face the following challenges: a) **The sensor data are noisy, they need to be preprocessed before use.** For example, the barometer reading will be affected by the weather, which should be handled carefully. b) **We will have to design some methods for initializing the parameters for HMM.**

In general, in this paper, we made the following contributions:

- We proposed an HMM based method to effectively combine different sensor readings to solve the problem.
- We designed some novel techniques for parameter estimation of the model.
- We improved GPS accuracy when tracking a moving car in particular situations by 19.2% compared to traditional GPS based method.

In the rest of this paper, we first discuss the problem definition and modeling in Sect. 2. Later we solve the model in Sect. 3. Section 4 shows the evaluation results of the proposed method. Section 5 shows the related work and finally Sect. 6 concludes this paper.

2   Problem Definition and Modeling

Figure 1 describes the overall structure of our method. First of all, the left part shows the application scenario of the method. Our method is designed to assist GPS in tracking the car under complex road conditions. The figure shows the

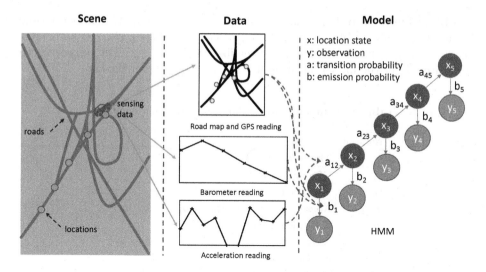

Fig. 1. Overview of our method.

scene of the car driving on the complex overpass. The locations in the figure are the real locations of the car passing by, but due to GPS error, we can not get the exact locations. The middle part of the figure shows the data obtained by mobile phone, they are road map, GPS data, barometer data and acceleration data. After preprocessing these data, we can convert them into the parameters needed by HMM. The part on the right shows the model we used. We use HMM to predict the most likely driving path of the car. We get the emission probability through GPS data and barometer data, and the transition probability through GPS data and acceleration data.

The following content of this section contains two parts. The first part gives some basic definitions and describes the problem that needs to be solved. The second part introduces how to solve this problem through HMM.

2.1 Problem Definition

First some notations will be defined in Table 1 to make our problem definition clearer.

In this paper, we will use barometer data and acceleration data to assist GPS to improve the tracking accuracy of GPS under special circumstances. Specifically, we solve the problem by using a probabilistic model called HMM. This model can help us get a sequence of unobserved states which is also called hidden states. In our solution, the hidden states are the passing-by locations of the car which we can not observe directly due to GPS error. Also, the observed readings of GPS, barometer and accelerometer depends on the hidden states. Based on the above observations, we define the problem as follows.

Problem Definition. For a moving car, given the road map M, number of time stamp T, and all the observation readings—GPS readings $\{g_t\}_{t=1:T}$, barometer readings $\{b_t\}_{t=1:T}$ and accelerometer readings $\{a_{t-1,t}\}_{t=1:T}$. The purpose is to accurately infer the hidden location list $Trace = \{l_t\}_{t=1:T}$ of the car.

Table 1. Notations and meanings for problem definition

Notation	Meaning
t	Time stamp
g_t	GPS reading at time t
b_t	Barometer reading at time t
$a_{t-1,t}$	Acceleration reading from time $t-1$ to time t
loc	A location point on the road
r	A road on the map, it can be represented as $r = \{loc_1, loc_2, ...\}$
M	Road map which contains a set of roads, represented as $M = \{r_1, r_2, ...\}$
l_t	Location of the car at time t
T	Number of time stamp
$Trace$	The trace of the car during T time stamps, represented as $Trace = \{l_1, l_2, ..., l_T\}$

2.2 Hidden Markov Model

Before introducing the model, some notations with their meanings are defined in Table 2.

Table 2. Notations and meanings for modeling

Notation	Meaning
N	Number of states in the state space
s_i	The ith state of state space, $i = 1 : N$
X	The state space, it can be represented as $X = \{s_1, s_2, ..., s_N\}$
M	Number of states in the observation space
o_i	The ith observation of observation space, $i = 1 : M$
Y	The observation space, it can be represented as $Y = \{o_1, o_2, ..., o_M\}$
A	State transition probability matrix
B	Emission probability matrix
Π	Initial state probability matrix
π_i	The initial probability of being in state $s_i, i = 1 : N$

In order to solve the problem, HMM is used in this paper. It is a probabilistic model and one of its applications is to get the hidden states based on the observed values. In this problem, the observed values are the GPS data, barometer data and acceleration data recorded by the mobile phone sensors in time series. The hidden states are the car's passing-by locations. There are two variables and three parameters of HMM, two variables are the state variable $(x_1, x_2, ..., x_t, ..., x_T)$, $x_t \in X$ and the observation variable $(y_1, y_2, ..., y_t, ..., y_T)$, $y_t \in Y$. State variable is also called hidden variable. Given a road map M, the state space X is all the location points on the map, and the state variable is the driving trace of the car. y_t in observation variable represents the observation value at time stamp t under hidden state x_t. Then three parameters of hidden Markov model are as follows.

Initial state probability matrix Π. The initial state probability matrix is actually the probability that the car may start from each state in the state space. The initial state probability matrix is represented as $\Pi = (\pi_1, \pi_2, ..., \pi_N)$. Each element $\pi_i = P(x_1 = s_i), 1 \leqslant i \leqslant N$ in Π denotes the probability that the car begins form location state s_i.

State transition probability matrix A. The state transition probability refers to the probability that every state in the state space is transferred to every other state. The size of the state transition probability matrix is $N * N$. Each value in the state transition matrix is denoted as $a_{ij} = P(x_{t+1} = s_j | x_t = s_i)$, $1 \leqslant i, j \leqslant N$. It represents the probability of transitioning from the location state at time t to the state at time $t + 1$.

Emission probability matrix B. The emission probability refers to the probability of observation value taking o_j at time stamp t, given the hidden state s_i. It can be represented as $b_{ij} = P(y_t = o_j | x_t = s_i), 1 \leqslant i \leqslant N, 1 \leqslant j \leqslant M$. Thus the size of emission probability matrix is $N * M$.

Now that we have got the three required parameters, we get the HMM $\lambda = (A, B, \Pi)$. Next we will get the most likely state sequence that produces the observations by using Viterbi algorithm. It is given by the following recurrence relations,

$$
\begin{aligned}
V_{1,k} &= P(y_1|k) \cdot \pi_k \\
V_{t,k} &= P(y_t|k) \cdot max_{x \in X}(e_{x,k} \cdot V_{t-1,x})
\end{aligned}
\tag{1}
$$

Here $V_{t,k}$ is the probability of the most probable state sequence responsible for the first t observations that have k as its final state. $e_{x,k}$ represents the probability of transitioning from state x to state k. The Viterbi path can be retrieved by saving back pointers that remember which state x was used in the second equation.

3 Solve the Model

This part will introduce how to solve the model proposed in the previous part, mainly introduce how to obtain the three parameters of HMM, and then use a modified Viterbi algorithm to solve our model to get the trace of the car.

Firstly, GPS data, barometer data and acceleration data can be acquired continuously in time series from sensors in mobile phone. After collecting these data, we pre-process these data using pre-processing method like [19]. Since the barometric pressure and altitude can be converted into each other, we convert the barometric pressure to altitude, and the conversion formula is as follows,

$$h = 44300 * (1 - (\frac{p}{p_0})^{\frac{1}{5.256}}) \tag{2}$$

In (2), h represents altitude, p represents barometric pressure and p_0 is the sea level standard atmospheric pressure. Next part of this section will introduce how to get the three parameters of HMM.

Get initial state probability matrix Π. The initial state probability is the probability that the car may start from each state of the state space. The state space X in our case refers to all the location points on the map, therefore N is very large, and it will cause too much calculation. However, as the initial state's GPS value is known, the probability of location points far from the GPS value is close to zero, and the number of these points is very large, so in order to reduce the complexity of calculation, we only consider the location points on the road within the error range of initial GPS value, and then calculate their probability according to the distance between them and the initial GPS location. We assume that the distance follows the normal distribution $N(0, \sigma_{gps}^2)$, where σ_{gps} is the error range of GPS, we give it a value of 10 m on normal road and 100 m when in tunnel. Figure 2 shows an example of getting the initial state probability, we map the longitude and latitude to a two-dimensional road map and divide each road into multiple location points. We get the probability density of each point through the normal distribution probability density function shown as follows.

$$f(g_{initial}) = \frac{1}{\sqrt{2\pi}\sigma_{gps}} exp(-\frac{g_{initial}^2}{2\sigma_{gps}^2}) \tag{3}$$

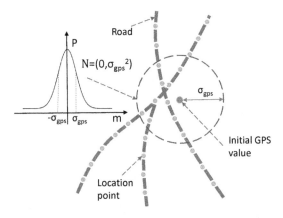

Fig. 2. Probability density function of initial location state.

In (3), $g_{initial}$ represents the distance between the first GPS point and its surrounding points within the error range σ_{gps}. Once we have got the probability density of each location state, next we can get the initial state probability matrix Π.

Get state transition probability matrix A. The state transition probability in our case refers to the probability that the car move from the previous location point at time t to the next location point at time $t+1$. The size of A is $N*N$ and N is very large, so it needs to be reduced properly to reduce the computational complexity. In our case, we only need to calculate the probability of points within the error range of the previous GPS point transfer to that of the next GPS point. The size of the state transition probability matrix can be reduced to $n*m$. n and m respectively refer to the number of location points within the error range of the two GPS points. Based on the above analysis, the size of state transition probability matrix changes dynamically between each two location states.

To estimate the transition probability for each location state, we utilize the accelerometer reading $\{a_{t-1,t}\}_{t=1:T}$ and the GPS reading $\{g_t\}_{t=1:T}$. Next part will introduce how to calculate the transition probability between each two location states.

First, the distances between all the location points within the error range of the previous GPS point and the next GPS point are calculated respectively and the results are represented as S_g. The size of S_g is $n*1$. Then we get the average speed of the car by dividing the duration time $v_g = S_g/t_{dur}$.

Then according to the acceleration reading, the car speed at the previous GPS sampling point and the sampling interval time, the displacement between the two GPS sampling points can be calculated by the displacement formula, the formula is as follows.

$$S_a = v_0 t_{dur} + \frac{1}{2} \sum_{i=1}^{t_{dur}} a_{i-1,i} \tag{4}$$

In (4), v_0 represents the car speed at the previous GPS sampling point, $a_{i-1,i}$ represents the acceleration reading of every second in a sampling time interval. t_{dur} is the interval time between each two sampling. Then we get the average speed of the car by $v_a = S_a/t_{dur}$.

Now that we have got the average speed of the car in two ways, respectively represented as v_g and v_a, Then we get the final average speed of the car by giving both of them a weight. It can be represented as

$$v_{avg} = a v_g + b v_a \quad (a+b=1) \tag{5}$$

We define $a = 0.4$ and $b = 0.6$ because the distance calculated from GPS data has relatively higher error than that of acceleration data.

Next we will calculate the distance matrix between all location points on the road map M within the error range of the former GPS point and that of the next GPS point, it is represented as S_l and the size of it is $n * m$. Then we get the average speed matrix by formula $v_l = S_l/t_{dur}$.

For each row of v_l, we assume that their values follow the normal distribution $N = (v_{avg}, \sigma_v^2)$, where v_{avg} is the expected value and the standard deviation σ_v is 10% of v_{avg}. The probability density function for average speed v_{avg} is as follows.

$$f(v_l) = \frac{1}{\sqrt{2\pi}\sigma_v} exp(-\frac{(v_l - v_{avg})^2}{2\sigma_v^2}) \tag{6}$$

In this way, we can get the state transition probability matrix A, the size of it is $n * m$.

Get emission probability matrix B. Finally we will estimate the emission probability for each observation. We use the combination of GPS reading $\{g_t\}_{t=1:T}$ and barometer reading $\{b_t\}_{t=1:T}$ as the observation. In the problem to be solved, emission probability refers to the probability of taking the GPS reading and the barometer reading under every hidden state. Similarly, the size of emission probability matrix is also reduced to reduce computational complexity.

We divide the computation of emission probability into two parts, one is the GPS emission probability, the other is the barometer emission probability, and then combine them to get the final emission probability. The specific steps are as follows.

Get GPS reading emission probability. According to the GPS value sampled at time t, the location points on the road map M within its error range are got. Assuming that the distance g_l between the GPS sampling point and these location points follow the normal distribution, the probability of these points is calculated. The following formula is the normal distribution probability density function for GPS reading.

$$f(g_l) = \frac{1}{\sqrt{2\pi}\sigma_g} exp(-\frac{g_l^2}{2\sigma_g^2}) \tag{7}$$

In (7), σ_g is the error expectation of GPS. And $f(g_l)$ is the probability density of g_l. Then we can get the emission probability P_g of GPS reading.

Get air pressure emission probability. According to the air pressure value sampled at time t, for the location points within the error range of GPS reading at time t, it is assumed that the air pressure values at these points also follow the normal distribution with respect to the sampled barometer reading. The following is the normal distribution probability density function for barometer reading.

$$f(b_l) = \frac{1}{\sqrt{2\pi}\sigma_b} exp(-\frac{(b_l - b_t)^2}{2\sigma_b^2}) \tag{8}$$

In (8), b_l represents the barometer reading of the surrounding location points, however actually we can not get the barometer value of location points from the map, we can only get the altitude information of every location point. Based on the above observation, we transfer the barometer reading b_t to altitude. We represent the altitude of hidden state at time t as h_t and transfer formula (6) as follows.

$$f(h_l) = \frac{1}{\sqrt{2\pi}\sigma_h} exp(-\frac{(h_l - h_t)^2}{2\sigma_h^2}) \tag{9}$$

In (9), h_l represents the altitude of one of the surrounding locations. σ_h is the error expectation of altitude. Here we set the value of σ_h to be 1 m. Finally, $f(h_l)$ is the probability density of parameter h_l. Then we can get the emission probability P_h of air pressure.

Now that we have got the probability of GPS reading and barometer reading, then we will combine them together to get the emission probability.

$$B = P_g * P_h \tag{10}$$

Finally, with the above three parameters of HMM, we maximize the probability with Viterbi algorithm and get the most probable trace of the car, thus we can determine which road on earth the car is driving on and then navigate it accurately.

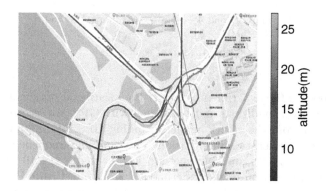

Fig. 3. Roads map for experiment.

4   Evaluation

In this part, we will analyse the results of experiment and evaluate the effect of our method. First, we will introduce our experimental environment. We choose Xinzhuang overpass and Xuanwu Lake Tunnel in Nanjing for experiment. Figure 3 shows the map of roads for our experiment. The color change on roads represents altitude change of road. The color bar on the right shows the color of altitude. We divide these roads into five parts as shown in Fig. 4, and carry out experiments on them respectively. The arrows on each map indicate the direction of the road. Road 1 has a diversion point, and one branch road turn around and pass under the main road. Road 2 has two diversion points and road 3 has a three-branch diversion point, they both contain changes in altitude. Road 4 has no fork but changes in altitude. Last the tunnel has almost no changes in altitude and no fork but GPS signal is very weak in it.

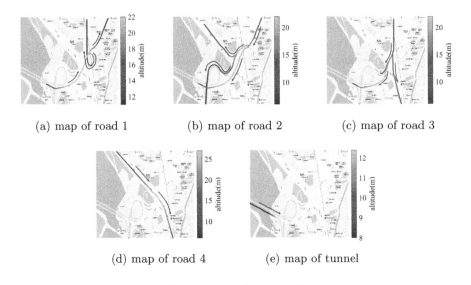

(a) map of road 1   (b) map of road 2   (c) map of road 3

(d) map of road 4   (e) map of tunnel

Fig. 4. Map of each road

The purpose of the experiment is to test the locating accuracy of our method under complex road conditions and compare it with GPS. We record a car's driving information from the smart phone, including GPS information, barometer information and acceleration information. The sampling frequency of the information is once every 2 s, and our method is executed every 10 s to track the car. The map information in the experiment was obtained from Baidu map, we divided each road into many location points, and the distance between each two points was 1 m. We only map the longitude and latitude of GPS reading to the map and don't use its altitude. We get altitude from barometer reading. Next, we will evaluate the experimental effect from several aspects.

4.1 Compare Our Method with GPS

The method proposed in this paper aims to assist GPS tracking in complex road conditions, so we need to compare it with GPS. Figure 5 shows the comprehensive locating accuracy of the two methods on all roads (excluding tunnel). As can be seen from the figure, the overall effect of our method is better than GPS. The locating accuracy of our method is 79.2% within 8 m, while that of GPS is 60%.

Next, we will separately compare the effects of the two methods on four roads. Figure 6 shows the comparison of the two methods on different roads. As

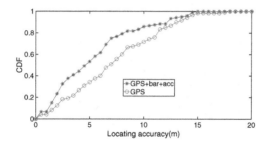

Fig. 5. The locating accuracy comparison between our method and GPS.

can be seen from Fig. 6, the effect of our method on each road is better than that of GPS. However, there are some places where the two curves intersect, and the difference is not big. This is because in some cases, for example, there are no interlaced roads, that is, there is no altitude difference, the method in this paper can not really play its advantages.

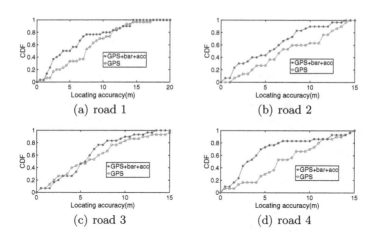

Fig. 6. Locating accuracy comparison of our method and GPS on each road.

4.2   Verify the Effect of Barometer Data on Accuracy

In order to verify the influence of air pressure data on locating accuracy, we will compare the method in this paper with that only using GPS and acceleration data. Figure 7 shows the comprehensive locating accuracy comparison of the two methods on all roads (excluding tunnel). It can be clearly seen from the figure that the effect of the method proposed in this paper is better. Therefore, we verify that the barometer data is helpful to improve the locating accuracy.

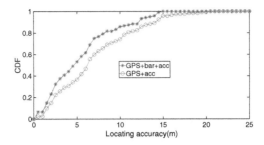

Fig. 7. Locating accuracy of our method and no barometer data method.

Next, we will analyze the four roads respectively to verify the impact of barometer data on locating accuracy, and the effect is shown in Fig. 8. In Fig. 8 (b)(c), the curve overlaps because the barometer data can not play its role fully without altitude difference, while some parts of road 2 and road 3 don't have obvious altitude change, so the effect of the two methods is almost the same under this situation.

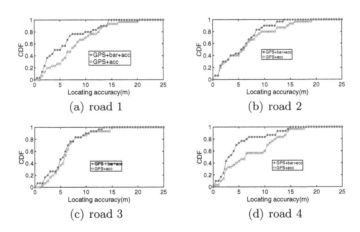

Fig. 8. Locating accuracy contrast on four roads.

4.3   Verify the Effect of Acceleration Data on Accuracy

In the method proposed in this paper, we use acceleration to calculate the transfer probability matrix in HMM. If we don't use acceleration data, we can't use HMM. Next, we will compare the method in this paper with the method using only GPS and barometric data.

Figure 9 shows a comparison of the locating accuracy of the two methods on all roads (except tunnel). It can be seen from the figure that the two curves have intersecting parts, and the difference between the two curves is relatively small

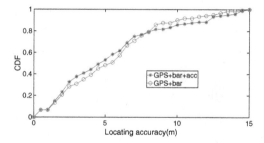

Fig. 9. Locating accuracy of our method and no acceleration data method.

when the abscissa is the same. It is because they all use the barometer data and this is very useful when there are altitude changes during driving the car. Although the effect of these two methods on overpasses is similar, their effect in tunnels is quite different. We will discuss the situation of tunnels separately later.

4.4   Comparison of the Effect of Four Methods on Overpass

The above three comparisons are actually the comparison between the three different methods and the method proposed in this paper. Next, we will compare the four methods together.

Figure 10 shows a comparison of the locating accuracy of the four methods together. Figure 11 uses a bar chart to compare the effects of the four methods. The abscissa represents the error range, and the ordinate represents the proportion of the error range. It can be seen from the figure that the method in this paper accounts for the highest proportion when the error is in the range of 0–5 m, while in the range of 10–15 m, the method in this paper accounts for a relatively low proportion, indicating that the method error is mainly concentrated in the low error area. We can clearly figure out that the method in this paper and the method using only GPS and barometer data are better than the other two methods without air pressure data on overpass.

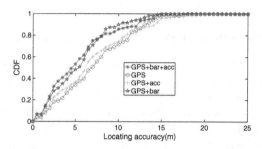

Fig. 10. Locating accuracy comparison of four methods on overpass.

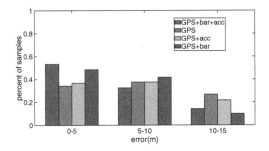

Fig. 11. Locating accuracy comparison of four methods on overpass.

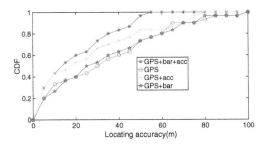

Fig. 12. Locating accuracy comparison of four methods in tunnel.

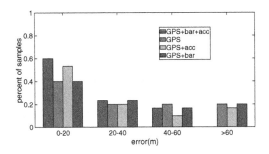

Fig. 13. Locating accuracy comparison of four methods in tunnel.

4.5   Compare the Effect of Four Methods in Tunnel

The above only evaluates the effect of these four methods on overpass, and next we will separately evaluate their effect in the tunnel. A comparison of their locating accuracy is shown in Fig. 12. It can be seen from the figure that in the tunnel, the effect of our method is obviously better than other methods and GPS works worst in tunnel.

Figure 13 analyses the proportion of several error ranges in detail. It can be seen from the figure that 60% of the error of our method is within 20 m, and the proportion of error over 60 m is zero. We can figure out that the effect of our method is better than other methods in tunnel.

5   Related Work

In recent years, there have been some methods proposed for vehicle tracking. The conventional way is to use GPS/INS integration system [4,5]. However, the error will accumulate over time. To solve the problem, authors in [8] introduced the development of a two-filter smoother (TFS) algorithm to improve the accuracy. Authors in [1] used a reduced inertial sensor system (RISS) instead of the full INS to improve the accuracy of the overall system. Authors in [11] proposed that extended Kalman filter (EKF) and Unscented Kalman Filter (UKF) be used to improve the accuracy. Authors in [18] design an adaptive dual-rate EKF estimator for fusing data from GPS and an INS in order to estimate the position.

Also, other sensors are used to assist GPS. Authors in [14] utilizes magnetometer and barometer to assist GPS/INS system. Authors in [10] proposed a method using odometer and barometer to integrate with GNSS/INS system. However, compared with our method, they need extra devices while our method only uses sensors on the smart phone, which is very portable.

In addition to GPS/INS integrated methods, some other methods have been proposed for location tracking. Authors in [2,22] employed a dead-reckoning algorithm for localization. Authors in [6] demonstrated how mobile devices can be used to accurately track driving patterns based solely on pressure data collected from the device's barometer. It only uses the barometer while our method is a combination of GPS, barometer and accelerator, which will have higher accuracy. Authors in [7] showed us how to use the barometer on the smart phone to improve vertical positioning accuracy. While our method can derive a track of the car instead of a single positioning point. Other techniques such as WheelLoc [15] only made use of low power sensors and cell tower information, but the accuracy was not good enough compared to our method. Authors in [3] extended the sensor management strategies of the EnTracked T system that intelligently determines when to sample different on-device sensors (e.g., accelerometer, compass and GPS) for trajectory tracking. Authors in [16,17] designed a mobile system that effectively captures significant journeys based solely on the embedded barometer sensor of a smart phone. However, it based on the analysis of a large amount of history data while our method is a real-time locating and tracking method.

As for the usage of HMM in tracking, authors in [19] proposed a HMM based method called BTrack. It can assist users to track their location on mountain roads. While our method in this paper focuses on track vehicle on the roads especially in situations such as tunnel and overpass where GPS error is large or GPS signal is weak.

6   Conclusion and Discussion

In this paper, we propose a novel method to assist GPS tracking. We use barometer data and acceleration data, combined with GPS data from the sensors on the smart phone, and use HMM to calculate the most likely driving path of the car. We only use the sensors on smart phones, do not need extra devices. We have carried out experiments on a complex overpass and in a tunnel. The experimental results show that the accuracy of our method is 19.2% higher than that of GPS. Also, the experiment results show that the comprehensive locating accuracy of our method is better than that of other methods. However, our method still has some defects, that is, it works better when there is obvious altitude change. In addition, our method uses HMM to calculate and the energy consumption is not considered. In our future work, we will consider improving the method to reduce the energy consumption and achieve higher accuracy.

References

1. Abosekeen, A., Noureldin, A., Korenberg, M.J.: Improving the RISS/GNSS land-vehicles integrated navigation system using magnetic azimuth updates. IEEE Trans. Intell. Transp. Syst. **21**(3), 1250–1263 (2019)
2. Aly, H., Basalamah, A., Youssef, M.: Accurate and energy-efficient GPS-less outdoor localization. ACM Trans. Spat. Algorithm. Syst. (TSAS) **3**(2), 4 (2017)
3. Bhattacharya, S., Blunck, H., Kjærgaard, M.B., Nurmi, P.: Robust and energy-efficient trajectory tracking for mobile devices. IEEE Trans. Mob. Comput. **14**(2), 430–443 (2014)
4. Godha, S., Cannon, M.: GPS/MEMS INS integrated system for navigation in urban areas. GPS Solut. **11**(3), 193–203 (2007)
5. Grewal, M.S., Weill, L.R., Andrews, A.P.: Global Positioning Systems, Inertial Navigation, and Integration. John Wiley & Sons, Hoboken (2007)
6. Ho, B.J., Martin, P., Swaminathan, P., Srivastava, M.: From pressure to path: barometer-based vehicle tracking. In: Proceedings of the 2nd ACM International Conference on Embedded Systems for Energy-Efficient Built Environments, pp. 65–74. ACM (2015)
7. Ho, P.F., Hsu, C.C., Chen, J.C., Zhang, T., et al.: Using barometer on smartphones to improve GPS navigation altitude accuracy. In: MOBICOM'18: Proceedings of the 24th Annual International Conference on Mobile Computing and Networking, pp. 741–743 (2018)
8. Liu, H., Nassar, S., El-Sheimy, N.: Two-filter smoothing for accurate INS/GPS land-vehicle navigation in urban centers. IEEE Trans. Veh. Technol. **59**(9), 4256–4267 (2010)
9. Maurya, K., Singh, M., Jain, N.: Real time vehicle tracking system using GSM and GPS technology-an anti-theft tracking system. Int. J. Electron. Comput. Sci. Eng. **1**(3), 1103–107 (2012)
10. Park, J., Lee, D., Park, C.: Implementation of vehicle navigation system using GNSS INS odometer and barometer. J. Position. Navig. Timing **4**(3), 141–150 (2015)
11. Ryu, J.H., Gankhuyag, G., Chong, K.T.: Navigation system heading and position accuracy improvement through GPS and INS data fusion. J. Sens. **2016**, 6 (2016)
12. Sapiezynski, P., Stopczynski, A., Gatej, R., Lehmann, S.: Tracking human mobility using WiFi signals. PLoS ONE **10**(7), e0130824 (2015)
13. Shamsuzzoha, A., Helo, P.T.: Real-time tracking and tracing system: potentials for the logistics network. In: Proceedings of the 2011 International Conference on Industrial Engineering and Operations Management, pp. 22–24 (2011)

14. Sokolovic, V.S., Dikic, G., Stancic, R.: Integration of INS, GPS, magnetometer and barometer for improving accuracy navigation of the vehicle. Def. Sci. J. **63**(5), 451–455 (2013)

15. Wang, H., Wang, Z., Shen, G., Li, F., Han, S., Zhao, F.: WheelLoc: enabling continuous location service on mobile phone for outdoor scenarios. In: 2013 Proceedings IEEE INFOCOM, pp. 2733–2741. IEEE (2013)

16. Won, M., Mishra, A., Son, S.H.: HybridBaro: mining driving routes using barometer sensor of smartphone. IEEE Sens. J. **17**(19), 6397–6408 (2017)

17. Won, M., Zhang, S., Chekuri, A., Son, S.H.: Enabling energy-efficient driving route detection using built-in smartphone barometer sensor. In: 2016 IEEE 19th International Conference on Intelligent Transportation Systems (ITSC), pp. 2378–2385. IEEE (2016)

18. Yan, W., Wang, L., Jin, Y., Shi, G.: High accuracy navigation system using GPS and INS system integration strategy. In: 2016 IEEE International Conference on Cyber Technology in Automation, Control, and Intelligent Systems (CYBER), pp. 365–369. IEEE (2016)

19. Ye, H., Yang, W., Yao, Y., Gu, T., Huang, Z.: Btrack: using barometer for energy efficient location tracking on mountain roads. IEEE Access **6**, 66998–67009 (2018)

20. Zaidi, Z.R., Mark, B.L.: Real-time mobility tracking algorithms for cellular networks based on Kalman filtering. IEEE Trans. Mob. Comput. **4**(2), 195–208 (2005)

21. Zandbergen, P.A.: Accuracy of iPhone locations: a comparison of assisted GPS, WiFi and cellular positioning. Trans. GIS **13**, 5–25 (2009)

22. Zhu, X., Li, Q., Chen, G.: APT: accurate outdoor pedestrian tracking with smartphones. In: 2013 Proceedings IEEE INFOCOM, pp. 2508–2516. IEEE (2013)

Indoor Localization Based on the LoRa Technology

Rui Tian, HaiBo Ye$^{(\boxtimes)}$, and Li Sheng

Department of Computer Science and Technology, NanJing University of Aeronautics
and Astronautics, Nanjing 210016, China
{tian2018,yhb,shengli}@nuaa.edu.cn

Abstract. In recent years, with the development of more advanced
mobile technologies and wider application requirements, many new technologies have been used for indoor localization. In this paper, we design
and implement an indoor localization system based on the LoRa wireless
communication technology. We proposed an improved KNN based algorithm which can greatly reduce the size of the fingerprint database. The
locating system is easy to deploy, it has good accuracy and low latency.
Our field study showed that it can locate a moving object or user with
the accuracy of 96.72%.

Keywords: Localization · Fingerprints · LoRa technology · KNN
algorithm

1 Introduction

The indoor localization technology is one of the most important research areas
of mobile computing. Especially in recent years, with the development of more
advanced mobile technologies and wider application requirements, many new
technologies have been used for indoor localization. The indoor localization technology can be used in many application scenarios, such as shopping malls, sub-
way stations, parking lots and large factories, in which better localization performance are required to provide useful services. For example, scholars [18] uses
Bluetooth devices to locate indoor shoppers, while scholars [6] uses WiFi devices
to locate indoor people. In these scenarios, localization will face many challenges,
such as the complex indoor structure and the effect of user movement. Different
applications have different performance requirements, such as the accuracy, low
latency, power efficiency and cost efficiency. Researchers are actively looking for
solutions suitable for locating requirements.

Most existing localization solutions can be grouped into the following categories. 1. Indoor localization based on WiFi signal strength [9,10]; 2. Indoor
localization based on Bluetooth [17,18,25]; 3. Indoor localization based on mobile
detection [4]. However, they can't satisfy our requirements for the following reasons. The energy consumption of WiFi devices is comparatively large and the

© ICST Institute for Computer Sciences, Social Informatics and Telecommunications Engineering 2021
Published by Springer Nature Switzerland AG 2021. All Rights Reserved
M. Guan and Z. Na (Eds.): MLICOM 2020, LNICST 342, pp. 304–319, 2021.
https://doi.org/10.1007/978-3-030-66785-6_34

communication radius of Bluetooth also is short, they need more devices to fully cover a certain area, which is not cost efficient. The solutions based on mobile activity detection is cost efficient. However, they need complex training process and the error may accumulate which will affect the localizaiton accuracy. None of the above methods can fully meet our needs. We hope to provide a better localization solution.

Recently, The NB-IOT and LoRa technologies have attracted a lot of interest in the research area. They are representative wireless communication technologies of the IoT(Internet of Things). The comparison between LoRa and NB-IoT [5] shown that LoRa works in ISM frequency band, no authorization is needed to use LoRa communication. Meanwhile, LoRa has the characteristics of long distance and low power consumption. With NB-IOT, you can achieve high communication quality by using public mobile communication infrastructure. However, it cost more and is more vulnerable to attack. Therefore, we try to study whether the LoRa technology can be a potential solution for indoor localization.

This paper focuses on designing and implementing an indoor localization system of locating the equipment or people in a certain area. The requirements of the localization system are as follows: 1. Easy to deploy, which means the system can be quickly deployed and ready to work in a certain area. 2. Reasonable accuracy which can meet the requirements of the application. 3. Low cost and low power consumption, effectively reduce the energy consumption and cost of the system.

We will face some challenges to achieve these requirements for building such a localization system. The first is the implementation of the localization system, how to use it simply and quickly to obtain the location information in the scene. Second, the wireless signal of LoRa devices is not stable, which can be easily interfered and influenced by the changing environment. The last challenge is how to use low-cost and low-power equipment to realize the localization function, while allowing the equipment to work for a long period.

In order to achieve these challenges, LoRa technology and related equipment are used to achieve an indoor localization system. The system build a wide range of coverage and achieve better indoor localization accuracy. In this system, according to the character of LoRa signal, we process the collected data and achieve a better localization accuracy. Our work mainly includes the following contributions. First of all, we design and implement a localization system based on LoRa technology. The system can provide real-time location information of objects which carry the localization equipment. Secondly, we propose a KNN algorithm based on down sampling, which greatly reduced the size of the fingerprint database. The system predict the location of objects at the same time and it's accuracy and precision are acceptable. Finally, we do experiments in the actual scene, the experimental results show that our system can achieve an average accuracy of about 96.72%.

2   System Design

Figure 1 shows the structure of the system, including the hardware part and software part. The hardware includes the LoRaWan device and the LoRa node device; The software includes the MQTT server, the LoRa node software and data processing module. The LoRa node transmit the data to the LoRaWan device using the wireless signal. Then the LoRaWan device report it to the server. In the system, we design and implement the node device data handler, the gateway handler and the related server-side program management to calculate the location information.

The hardware is responsible for data collection. The LoRa node starts data transmission. The received data is then uploaded from the LoRaWan device to the server by MQTT protocol for data analysis on the server. On the server side, the pre-established fingerprint database is used to classify and predict the observed data and realize the positioning function. The LoRa node device is connected with the gateway device respectively and sends data to the server in the network through the gateway.

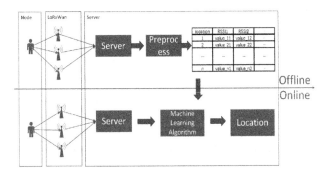

Fig. 1. System architecture

2.1   LoRa Technology

In free space, radio waves transmissions have no energy losses, but the energy density declines as space expands. The power of the receiver and sender has this characteristic and the formula is also known as the Friis free space equation.

$$P_R = P_T G_T G_R \left(\frac{\lambda}{4\pi d} \right)^2 \tag{1}$$

This equation describes the relationship between the transmitting power P_T (in dBw) of the wireless signal sender and the receiving power P_R (in dBw) of the wireless signal receiver in free space where G_T is the antenna gain of the transmitter, G_R is the antenna gain value of the receiver, λ is the working wavelength and d is the distance value [1].

The empirical model of path loss in indoor environment is presented by the existing research work [5].

$$PL(d) = PL(d_0) + 10nlog(\frac{d}{d_0}) + X_\delta \qquad (2)$$

The formula shows the power relationship between sender and receiver; N is the path loss coefficient, d (in dB) is the distance between sender and receiver, and X_δ (in dB) is a white noise which subject to Gaussian distribution.

The first formula introduces the energy density changes with distance in free space without loss, and the second formula introduces the path loss model in real scene. Based on the above two models, we can find that for the wireless signal sender, the receiving signal strength of the receiver is different when the distance d from the sender is different, and this is the theoretical basis of our work in this paper.

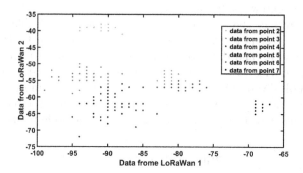

Fig. 2. RSSI values in different points

We use the LoRa equipment to test the variation of LoRa signal strength with distance in indoor environment. We collected a number of data at different points and plotted them. As can be seen from Fig. 2, the RSSI values fall in a zone for a certain point.

As mentioned in [6], the change of RSSI (Received Signal Strength Indication, RSSI) value can be divided into two types: temporal change (the value of RSSI at the fixed point may fluctuate) and spatial change (the value of RSSI changes with the change of equipment position). We can see the third and fourth points from Fig. 3 that the signal intensity is significantly lower than the model value. The reason is that the experimental site is located at the intersection of corridors. When the distance become larger than 50 m, the device begins to be affected by another corridor. In general, the signal strength of the device decreases with the increase of distance. In the indoor environment, RSSI value decreases with distance but the relationships are more complicated.

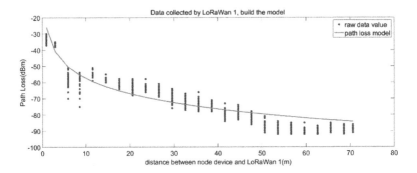

Fig. 3. RSSI value changes with different distance between LoRa node and LoRaWan

2.2 Generate the FingerPrints

The generation of fingerprint database refers to the establishment of fingerprint database in this area by collecting data in the offline stage and the signal intensity value of multiple gateways at each point.

First, we introduce the format of the data. As shown in Table 1 and Table 2, the data format 1 refers to the data transmission form from LoRa node device to LoRaWan device. The data format 2 refers to the data transmission form from LoRaWan device to the server. The node device first transmits the data signal to the LoRaWan. The LoRaWan records the node information and the received signal strength. After that, the LoRaWan reports the received data to the server. In this way, the system send data from the node to the server.

Table 1. Data format 1

Node Device ID	Node Device Time

Table 2. Data format 2

LoRaWan Device ID	LoRaWan Device Time	Node Device ID	Node Device Time	RSSI value

Secondly, we need to preprocess the data collected by the server. First, we try to do smoothing of the data from each gateway. The optional solutions are as follows: 1) the sliding average method, 2) the exponential sliding average method and 3) the SG filtering method. Here, we make use of the quadratic exponential smoothing. For a sequence X(1), X (2), ..., X (n), the formula for the first smoothing is

$$S^1(t+1) = aX(t) + (1-a)S^1(t) \tag{3}$$

where a is the smoothing coefficient. Then, the second smoothing is based on the first smoothing, as shown in the following formula:

$$S^2(t+1) = aS^1(t) + (1-a)S^2(t) \tag{4}$$

Based on the two formulas above, we can get X'(t+T), where

$$X'(t+T) = 2S^1(t) - S^2(t) + \left(\frac{a}{1-a}\right)(S^1(t) - S^2(t)) \tag{5}$$

After smoothing, we get more clean data.

Furthermore, the LoRa communications are unreliable. In the process of establishing fingerprint database, some error message exits. For example, some data is received by LoRaWan A but not by LoRaWan B. Easy to exist if the device does not transmit information continuously, then the device may be disconnected, this part of the data should be removed. For discontinuous data, a packet propagation error may result in data loss at a LoRaWan. In this case, we use a fitting method to fill in the missing value. In this way, we increase the volume of samples.

Algorithm 1. Smooth algorithm

Input: *collected*(RSSI_1, RSSI_2, RSSI_3, POINT)
Output: *smoothed*(RSSI_1', RSSI_2', RSSI_3', POINT)

1: let $s\_1 := \{\}$, $s\_2 := \{\}$
2: let $a := 0.6$
3: let $lenC :=$ the length of *collected*
4: **for** $i := 1$ to $lenC$ **do**
5:     $s\_1(1,i) := a * data(i,1) + (1-a) * data(i-1,1)$
6: **for** $i := 2$ to $lenC$ **do**
7:     $s\_2(1,i) := a * s\_1(i,1) + (1-a) * s\_1(i-1,1)$
8: let *smoothed* := $\{\}$
9: **for** $i := 2$ to $lenC$ **do**
10:     $smoothed(1,i) := 2s\_1(1,i) - s\_2(1,i) + a/(1-a) * (s\_1(1,i) - s\_2(1,i))$
     return *smoothed*

After processing the data, we get the RSSI values of three LoRaWan during the node device moving. Each LoRaWan Device give the observations of the node device. These observations comprise the fingerprint database. At a random moment, a record or an observation is composed of RSSI values from three LoRaWans. With the search and comparison of data in fingerprint database, the location of the device can be predicted (Fig. 4).

Some researchers have studied the method to dynamically adjustment fingerprint database [3]. Based on their conclusion, the dynamic adjustment algorithm

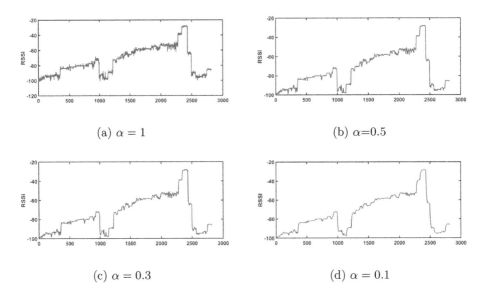

(a) $\alpha = 1$ (b) $\alpha = 0.5$

(c) $\alpha = 0.3$ (d) $\alpha = 0.1$

Fig. 4. Smoothed data

can improve the accuracy of the locating system. The initial setting of finger-print database may not be effective all the time, specially when the environment changed. Further more, during the locating process, a user can manually correct the location information by a mobile phone interface application.

2.3 Localization Algorithm

After data collection and data preprocession, the fingerprint database is created. On the basis of fingerprint database, KNN algorithm is used to realize the localization function.

To locate the objects, the first problem is the imbalanced data. The possible methods for the problem include: 1. Up-sampling, the way is to increase the number of samples of each class, let the amount of each class to be same; 2. Down-sample, which is to reduce the sample size of each class, let the amount of each class to be same; 3. Weight the data, it gives different weight to different sample. We choose the down-sample to solve the problem.

KNN algorithm have some drawbacks. When the number of sampling points is too huge, it will increase the calculation of KNN algorithm. It's also a huge work to do site survey in real scene. To deal with this problem, the system make use of the down-sample based method. According to the number of samples collected at each point (total of n points), we choose m samples in each point. Therefore $n * m$ records are obtained. These records constitute the fingerprint database.

Through the above process, we obtain a balanced data set, which is referred as the fingerprint database. Then KNN algorithm is used to do classification.

The theoretical basis of KNN algorithm is described below. Suppose we have a data set containing N points, C_k for category, with N_k, hence the $\sum N_i = N$. If a certain point needs to be predicted, K points closest to that point are obtained. If K points belong to C_k, there are

$$p(x|C_k) = \frac{K_k}{N_k} \qquad (6)$$

Similarly, in the unconditional case

$$p(x) = \frac{K}{N} \qquad (7)$$

The prior probability of the class is

$$p(C_k) = \frac{N_k}{N} \qquad (8)$$

Combining the above three equations, we get the posterior probability formula of the category according to bayes' law.

$$p(C_k|x) = \frac{p(x|C_k)p(C_k)}{p(x)} = \frac{K_k}{K} \qquad (9)$$

The pseudo code of KNN is shown below.

Algorithm 2. KNN algorithm
___
Input: labeled data $labd(data, label)$
data to be predicted $pred(data)$
Output: $pred(data, label)$
1: let $knn\_k := k$
2: **for** $i := 1$ to $labd.length$ **do**
3:     calculate the nearest knn_k points for $pred(i, :)$ in $labd(data, label)$
4:     count the knn_k points according to it's label, generate result
5:     label of $pred(i, :) :=$ the label of max num of result
6: **return** $pred(data, label)$

---

3 Experiment

3.1 Experiment Setting

First, we need to set the parameters of the wireless communication device before use. There are mainly the following five parameters: the spread spectrum factor, the transmitting power, the bandwidth, the coding rate and the wireless signal frequency.

1) The Spread spectrum factor. When other parameters are fixed, the bit rate of the device is fixed. The larger the spread-spectrum factor is, the lower the actual data transmission rate is.
2) Under the same conditions, the greater the transmitting power, the farther the transmission distance under the same conditions.
3) The smaller bandwidth, the longer transmission distance. However, when the bandwidth is too small, the probability that the device with low receiving sensitivity will not receive data increases.
4) The coding rate represents the proportion of useful information in the information.
5) The lower the wireless signal frequency, the better the signal penetration.

We choose the Arduino board as the basic platform and connect LoRa chip (SX1276/8) to the board to realize LoRa transmission. The system adopts Dragino LG-01s as LoRaWan Device. The device contains of Arduino Yun and LoRa chip. We set the same parameters in devices so that they can translate the message with each other.

3.2 Experiment Scenario

The LoRa network topology is a star shape. During the experiment, the process is to first send data from the LoRa node device to the LoRaWan device. The LoRaWan device get the received signal strength and some other important data. After that, the data will be transmitted to the server by the TCP/IP protocol. In our experiment, we totally set up three LoRaWan devices and one node device. The node device sends two data samples per second. The LoRaWan sends the data from the node device to the remote server. The layout of the experimental site is shown in Fig. 5. This is the first floor plan in a building. During the experiment, there may exist a small number of people walking by.

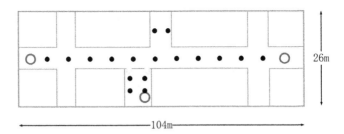

Fig. 5. The structure of the build

The node device can generate a device independent time. It is pushed to the MQTT server through the MQTT protocol. Then MQTT server saves and processes the data records.

3.3 Data Setting

By carrying the experiment and processing the collected data, we obtain the
most important part of the location algorithm: the fingerprint database. An
example of the fingerprint library is shown in Fig. 6. The first column is the
time of node device, the last column is the label of location and the rest are the
received signal strength of the LoRaWan devices.

1	2	3	4	5
262827	-100	-93	-32	1
265350	-100	-92	-31	1
266190	-99	-92	-32	1
267032	-99	-92	-32	1
269554	-96	-93	-32	1
272077	-100	-96	-32	1
282168	-99	-89	-32	1

Fig. 6. The collected data

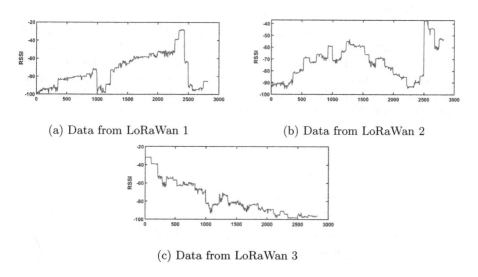

(a) Data from LoRaWan 1   (b) Data from LoRaWan 2

(c) Data from LoRaWan 3

Fig. 7. Smoothed data

Figure 7a, Fig. 7b and Fig. 7c show the RSSI value with the node device moving. It is worth noting that at the last four points, the RSSI values of LoRaWan
1 and LoRaWan 2 have changed significantly, but the RSSI value of LoRaWan
three devices has not changed much. This is because the LoRaWan device and
the node device are too far away, the RSSI values is attenuated, and the effect

of the movement of the location on the RSSI values begins to slow down. We use drawing tools to depict the collected data in three-dimensional coordinates. Each dimension represent a LoRaWan device. For different locations, the collected data are relatively independent to each other in Fig. 8.

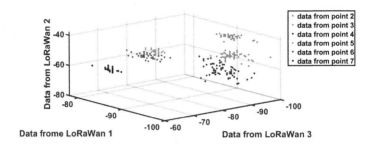

Fig. 8. Data in 3 dimension

4   Evaluation

4.1   Accuracy

In order to evaluate the accuracy of localization, we try using different machine learning algorithm for localization. We use SVM (Support Vector Machine, SVM), Cart decision tree, KNN (k nearest neighbor, KNN) and ensemble learning methods to train the model. In the initial state, using the data obtained from the measurement, the localization results are shown in the Table 3. Indoor localization using KNN methods can achieve promising accuracy.

Table 3. The accuracy of different methods.

Method	Wrong	Right	Accuracy
KNN (k = 13)	14	486	97.20%
SVM	19	481	96.20%
Cart Tree	32	468	93.60%
Ensemble	19	481	96.20%

Based on the existing data, the accuracy of the KNN localization results obtained under different k values is shown in Fig. 9. The KNN algorithm needs to calculate the distance from each point, so the calculation amount of the algorithm will increase with the increase of samples. In practical scenarios, the relationship between the amount of calculation and accuracy should be measured. Figure 10 show the CDF (cumulative distribution Function, CDF) curve of different methods.

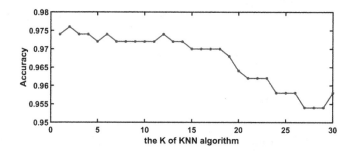

Fig. 9. Accuracy of different K values

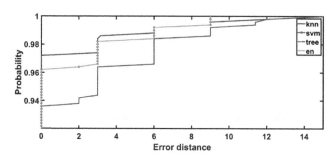

Fig. 10. CDF curve of different methods

4.2   System Deployment

During the deployment phase, we install the LoRaWan device and connect it to the Internet. Meanwhile, a server with public network IP is responsible for location calculation and recording. When the locator device appears in the system area, LoRaWan establishes a connection to the device, collects the signal strength information from the device and sends it to the server. The system supports a simple and quick deployment.

The system has two steps to achieve localization: offline pre-training and online prediction to achieve the localization function. The offline pre-training (fingerprint library method) is time-consuming which requires dividing the whole system area into grids and measuring the representative fingerprint within the grid. The online prediction is real-time. The system obtains the real-time records of the node device and use KNN algorithm to get the location point.

To test the location calculation delay of the algorithm under different data volumes, we used the collected data for evaluation. Suppose the initial data volume is t, where t_1 is the number of records in the fingerprint database and t_2 is the number of records to be predicted, satisfying $t = t_1 + t_2$. The following figure shows the time spent to complete the corresponding data volume ($t = 2817$). As can be seen from the Fig. 12, the Cart Decision Tree method takes less time, and the KNN algorithm is only as effective as the Cart Tree under the data volume of $10 * t$ (Fig. 11).

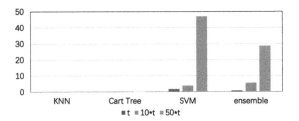

Fig. 11. Time of train and predict

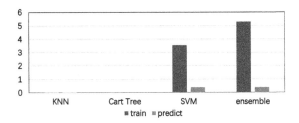

Fig. 12. Time consuming in same condition

We give the comparison of four methods under $10 * t$ data volume in Fig. 12. Where KNN algorithm doesn't need a learning process, it is meaningless to consider its model training. It can be seen that both SVM and ensemble methods require training classifier, and their training time is relatively long. Meanwhile, KNN and Cart Tree perform better in time.

5   Related Work

Indoor localization has been studied for several years. Here, we provide a brief introduction to related work in this field.

First is the emergence of Lora technology. Scholars began to study the characteristics of wireless communication technology Lora. Lora means long range and long distance. By using modulation and demodulation technology, long-distance data transmission is realized. Researchers [2,3] studied the distance characteristics of Lora in outdoor open space. [2] provides a simple introduction of Lora technology and how to establish an outdoor environment for experimental conditions. At the same time, it points out that when the Fresnel region between the transmitting device and the receiving device can have more than 60% of the visible region, the signal transmission is the best. [3] introduces some related contents of Lora protocol and the parameters of Lora equipment. The technical characteristics and reliability of Lora were studied [5,14,19].

The second is the field of indoor localization. There are classic radar localization system and Horus system to use WiFi for localization. The latter studies the change of RSSI signal in space and time, realized high-precision localization with WiFi device, deployed multiple gateway devices in the room, designed a system to locate the device, the effect is very good. The mobile air pressure sensor [14] is used to locate the mobile floor, and the signal characteristics of Lora enable it to locate the floor. A localization system is established by using WiFi device, and the fingerprint database is used to match the offline map for localization [9,10]. In addition, many researchers study the use of different detection methods for indoor localization, such as the use of low-power Bluetooth devices [17,18,25], light [23], sound [12] for indoor localization. Scholars [4] use multiple WiFi devices to study the data collection of heterogeneous devices and how to dynamically adjust the fingerprint database to achieve better accuracy and robustness. At present, the hot research in the field of location includes: using fingerprint signal to detect indoor and outdoor alternate areas [30,31], improving the accuracy of location by testing mobility [24] and using the combination of mobile phone sensor and GPS localization to realize localization and tracking in special scenes [16,25].

With the development of technology, there are many new application scenarios for localization, and many new requirements appear under these application scenarios. The research work of relevant aspects includes: 1. Using the changes of indoor environment signals to carry out indoor localization and action perception under the condition of non marking [7]; 2. Military applications, research on underwater and air localization technology; 3. Detection of human heart rate information using WiFi equipment [21]; localization between micro air vehicles [22].

6   Conclusion

In this paper, we proposed a new approach for indoor localizaiton based on the LoRa technology. We first study to signal characteristics of the LoRaWan in the indoor environment and find that it is possible to use the LoRa technology for indoor localizaiton. Then, we established the fingerprint database and proposed an improved KNN based algorithm which can greatly reduce the size of the fingerprint database. After that, we proposed our field study and the result show that the system performance is good enough for our requirements. We also find that the user movement in the indoor environment can affect the LoRa signal strength. Based on this feature, in the future work, we will focus on device free indoor localization based on the LoRa technology.

References

1. Aref, M., Sikora, A.: Free space range measurements with Semtech LoRa™ technology. In: 2014 2nd International Symposium on Wireless Systems within the Conferences on Intelligent Data Acquisition and Advanced Computing Systems, pp. 19–23. IEEE (2014)
2. Lavric, A., Popa, V.: Internet of things and LoRa™ low-power wide-area networks: a survey. In: 2017 International Symposium on Signals, Circuits and Systems (ISSCS), pp. 1–5. IEEE (2017)

3. Sinha, R.S., Wei, Y., Hwang, S.H.: A survey on LPWA technology: LoRa and NB-IoT. ICT Express **3**(1), 14–21 (2017)
4. Wang, H., Sen, S., Elgohary, A., et al.: No need to war-drive: unsupervised indoor localization. In: Proceedings of the 10th International Conference on Mobile Systems, Applications, and Services, pp. 197–210. ACM (2012)
5. Xu, W., Kim, J.Y., Huang, W., et al.: Measurement, characterization and modeling of LoRa technology in multi-floor buildings. IEEE Internet Things J. **7**(1), 298–310 (2019)
6. Youssef, M., Agrawala, A.: The Horus location determination system. Wireless Netw. **14**(3), 357–374 (2008)
7. Paul, A.S., Wan, E.A., Adenwala, F., et al.: MobileRF: a robust device-free tracking system based on a hybrid neural network HMM classifier. In: Proceedings of the 2014 ACM International Joint Conference on Pervasive and Ubiquitous Computing, pp. 159–170. ACM (2014)
8. Rai, A., Chintalapudi, K.K., Padmanabhan, V.N., et al.: Zee: zero-effort crowdsourcing for indoor localization. In: Proceedings of the 18th Annual International Conference on Mobile Computing and Networking, pp. 293–304. ACM (2012)
9. Wu, C., Yang, Z., Liu, Y.: Smartphones based crowdsourcing for indoor localization. IEEE Trans. Mob. Comput. **14**(2), 444–457 (2014)
10. Wu, C., Yang, Z., Liu, Y., et al.: WILL: wireless indoor localization without site survey. IEEE Trans. Parallel. Distrib. Syst. **24**(4), 839–848 (2012)
11. Yang, S., Dessai, P., Verma, M., et al.: FreeLoc: calibration-free crowdsourced indoor localization. In: 2013 Proceedings IEEE INFOCOM, pp. 2481–2489. IEEE (2013)
12. Machhamer, R., Dziubany, M., Czenkusch, L., et al.: Online offline learning for sound-based indoor localization using low-cost hardware. IEEE Access **7**, 155088–155106 (2019)
13. Yu, J., Na, Z., Liu, X., et al.: WiFi/PDR-integrated indoor localization using unconstrained smartphones. EURASIP J. Wireless Commun. Netw. **2019**(1), 41 (2019)
14. Ye, H., Gu, T., Tao, X., et al.: Scalable floor localization using barometer on smartphone. Wireless Commun. Mob. Comput. **16**(16), 2557–2571 (2016)
15. Liando, J.C., Gamage, A., Tengourtius, A.W., et al.: Known and unknown facts of LoRa: experiences from a large-scale measurement study. ACM Trans. Sens. Netw. (TOSN) **15**(2), 1–35 (2019)
16. Augustin, A., Yi, J., Clausen, T., et al.: A study of LoRa: long range & low power networks for the internet of things. Sensors **16**(9), 1466 (2016)
17. Hou, X., Arslan, T.: Monte Carlo localization algorithm for indoor positioning using Bluetooth low energy devices. In: 2017 International Conference on Localization and GNSS (ICL-GNSS), pp. 1–6. IEEE (2017)
18. Dickinson, P., Cielniak, G., Szymanezyk, O., et al.: Indoor positioning of shoppers using a network of Bluetooth low energy beacons. In: 2016 International Conference on Indoor Positioning and Indoor Navigation (IPIN), pp. 1–8. IEEE (2016)
19. Cattani, M., Boano, C.A., Römer, K.: An experimental evaluation of the reliability of LoRa long-range low-power wireless communication. J. Sens. Actuator Netw. **6**(2), 7 (2017)
20. Ye, H., Yang, W., Yao, Y., et al.: BTrack: using barometer for energy efficient location tracking on mountain roads. IEEE Access **6**, 66998–67009 (2018)

21. Khamis, A., Chou, C.T., Kusy, B., et al.: CardioFi: enabling heart rate monitoring on unmodified COTS WiFi devices. In: Proceedings of the 15th EAI International Conference on Mobile and Ubiquitous Systems: Computing, Networking and Services, pp. 97–106 (2018)
22. van der Helm, S., Coppola, M., McGuire, K.N., et al.: On-board range-based relative localization for micro air vehicles in indoor leader-follower flight. Auton. Robot. **44**, 1–27 (2019)
23. Zhang, H., Cui, J., Feng, L., et al.: High-precision indoor visible light positioning using deep neural network based on the Bayesian regularization with sparse training point. IEEE Photonics J. **11**(3), 1–10 (2019)
24. Carlino, L., Bandiera, F., Coluccia, A., et al.: Improving localization by testing mobility. IEEE Trans. Signal Process. **67**(13), 3412–3423 (2019)
25. Hou, X., Arslan, T., Juri, A., et al.: Indoor localization for Bluetooth low energy devices using weighted off-set triangulation algorithm. ION-GNSS **2016**, 2286–2292 (2016)
26. Chintalapudi, K., Padmanabha Iyer, A., Padmanabhan, V.N.: Indoor localization without the pain. In: Proceedings of the Sixteenth Annual International Conference on Mobile Computing and Networking, pp. 173–184. ACM (2010)
27. He, S., Chan, S.H.G.: INTRI: contour-based trilateration for indoor fingerprint-based localization. IEEE Trans. Mob. Comput. **16**(6), 1676–1690 (2016)
28. Jiang, Y., Li, Z., Wang, J.: PTrack: enhancing the applicability of pedestrian tracking with wearables. IEEE Trans. Mob. Comput. **18**(2), 431–443 (2018)
29. Zhang, L., Liu, J., Jiang, H., et al.: SensTrack: energy-efficient location tracking with smartphone sensors. IEEE Sens. J. **13**(10), 3775–3784 (2013)
30. Shtar, G., Shapira, B., Rokach, L.: Clustering Wi-Fi fingerprints for indoor-outdoor detection. Wireless Netw. **25**(3), 1341–1359 (2019)
31. Chow, K.H., He, S., Tan, J., et al.: Efficient locality classification for indoor fingerprint-based systems. IEEE Trans. Mob. Comput. **18**(2), 290–304 (2018)

Radar Target Detection Based on Information Theory

Chao Hu, Dazhuan Xu$^{(\boxtimes)}$, Deng Pan, and Boyu Hua$^{(\boxtimes)}$

College of Electronic and Information Engineering, Nanjing University of Aeronautics
and Astronautics, Nanjing 211106, China
{huchao,xudazhuan,pandeng,byhua}@nuaa.edu.cn

Abstract. In this paper, the information theory method (ITM) is
applied to radar detection system in the presence of complex additive white Gaussian noise (CAWGN). We introduce the target existence
parameter into the radar detection system, which realize the unification
of detection and estimation. We define the detection information in the
radar as the mutual information between the received signal and the existence state of the target, and then use the ITM to derive the theoretical
expression of target detection information. Meanwhile, we obtain corresponding expressions of the probability of false alarm and detection and
get the relationship between the two probabilities approximately. Detection information and the probability of detection probability and false
alarm are presented according to Neyman-Pearson (N-P) criterion based
on existing methods. The numerical simulation results show that the
theoretical detection performance of ITM can be obviously better than
that of N-P criterion, which confirms that it is effective to use mutual
information as a measure to evaluate the detection performance of the
system.

Keywords: Target detection · Information theory · Radar ·
Performance detection · Neyman-Pearson criterion

1 Introduction

The purpose of radar target detection is to obtain information about the distance, amplitude, phase and velocity of the target in the echo signal. However,
access to this information presupposes that the target must exist, so determining the existence of the target is particularly important in the field of radar
detection.

The traditional radar target detection needs to find the threshold value to
detect the presence of the target signal, but does not numerically describe the
information content of the target by information theory. Woodward and Davies
[1–3] applied information theory to radar detection system for the first time and
obtained the relationship between location information and SNR after information theory [4] published in 1948 by Shannon. Bell first studied the application of

© ICST Institute for Computer Sciences, Social Informatics and Telecommunications Engineering 2021
Published by Springer Nature Switzerland AG 2021. All Rights Reserved
M. Guan and Z. Na (Eds.): MLICOM 2020, LNICST 342, pp. 320–332, 2021.
https://doi.org/10.1007/978-3-030-66785-6_35

information theory in radar waveform design [5], giving the method of obtaining the best estimation waveform and the effect of energy distribution on the mutual information between the target and the receiving waveform.

Based on research of Woodward and Davies and Bell, some research-ers have studied [6] the relationship between information theory and parameter estimation in radar detection. Y. Yang and R.S. Blum [7] find that maximize the mutual information between the random target impulse response and the reflected waveforms and minimize the mean-square error (MSE) in estimating the target impulse response, which could lead to the same solution in optimum waveform design. Recently, Xu's team focus on research of targets' location infor-mation and amplitude-phase information in the field of radar and sensor radar based on information theory [8–10], and estimate the target parameters of inter-est by maximum likelihood estimation (MLE) [8] and MSE [9] and so on.

Most of the radar system utilize the N-P criterion to realize the detection mission [11], many researchers have a number of ways to detect targets, but none without the N-P criterion [12,13]. However, they only gave the judgment of the existence of the target and the relationship between false alarm rate and detection rate under their respective models. In [14], the presence or absence of a target is judged by the difference in the covariance matrix in the clutter envi-ronment. In [15], Michimasa Kondo maximizes the mutual information between the received signal and the estimated parameter, and the detection performance can be obtained roughly.

In [6–10,12–14], parameter estimation and target detection are studied sep-arately. In [16] and [17], a combination of Bayesian and N-P criterion methodol-ogy is developed, which could achieve the unification of detection and estimation. Although the two method is the best on their respective directions, their coalition does not result in optimal federation performance. Recently, some researches on performance, proposing new algorithms to achieve superior network throughput performance over existing schemes [18], proposing IRS-assisted secure strategy to significantly boost the secrecy rate performance [19].

In this paper, we introduce the target existence parameter into the radar detection system, which can use information theory to study both target detec-tion and parameter estimation. Firstly, on the basis of the previous research [5,6] on radar spatial information, the detection information under complex Gaussian scattering is discussed from the perspective of information theory. Then, the expressions of detection probability and false alarm probability are derived by using ITM under corresponding model, and the relationship between the two probabilities is obtained approximately. In addition, in order to evaluate the performance of information theory method, we also give the receiver operating characteristics (ROC) curves and detection information of N-P criterion, and conclude that the ITM is effective.

This paper is organized as follows. The system model of single target detec-tion system for single antenna radar is presented in Sect. 2. In Sect. 3, the expres-sion of target detection information is derived under complex Gaussian scattering model. Relation between false alarm probability and detection probability under information theory method and N-P criterion are derived in Sect. 4, respectively. In Sect. 5, on the basis of [15], the relationship between detection probability and falsealarm probability is deduced by using N-P criterion, and we got the corresponding detection information. In Sect. 6, the numerical results and analysis are presented, finally, in Sect. 7, the main results of this paper are discussed and concluded.

2 System Model

For the target detection in this paper, we focus on the existence of the target, so we introduce the target existence parameter into the radar detection system. In order to facilitate the analysis, we assume that if there is a target within the range of radar detection, it is a single target. To convert the received signal down to the baseband and passing through an ideal low-pass filter with a bandwidth of $B/2$, then the received signal is given by

$$z(t) = vys(t - \tau) + w(t), \tag{1}$$

where v denotes coefficient of existence, where $v \in \{0, 1\}$, $v = 0$ and $v = 1$ represent the target does not exists and target exist, respectively. $s(t)$ denotes baseband signal, y is scattering coefficient of target, which is modeled as

$$y = \alpha e^{j\varphi}, \tag{2}$$

where α is the amplitude of the scattering coefficient and φ is the phase of scattering coefficient. The scattering model of the target depends on the distribution of α and φ.

Assuming that d represents the distance between the rarget and receive, c denotes the signal propagation velocity, $\tau = 2d/c$ represent time delay of the target, $w(t)$ stand for the additive noise, which is modeled as a complex Gaussian zero-mean with noise power N_0. Suppose the reference point is at the detection interval and the detection range is $[-D/2, D/2)$, the time delay interval is $[-T/2, T/2)$, where $T = 2D/c$.

Given the radar transmitted signal is an ideal low-signal with bandwidth of $B/2$, i.e. the baseband signal is

$$s(t) = \sin c(Bt) = \frac{\sin(\pi Bt)}{\pi Bt}. \tag{3}$$

We sample the received signal $z(t)$ according to Shannon-Nyquist sampling theory, namely, $t = n/B$, the sampling sequence is

$$z(n/B) = v\alpha e^{j\varphi} s((n - B\tau)/B) + w(n/B). \tag{4}$$

Let $x = B\tau$ denotes the normalized time delay of target, we have

$$z(n) = v\alpha e^{j\varphi} s(n - x) + w(n), \tag{5}$$

where $n = -N/2, ..., N/2$, $N = TB$ is regard as the time bandwidth product. (5) notes that N points sequence $z(n)$ can completely reconstruct $z(t)$.

Concisely, (5) can be rewritten in vector form

$$\mathbf{Z} = VY\mathbf{U}(\mathbf{x}) + \mathbf{W},\tag{6}$$

where $\mathbf{Z} = \left[z\left(-\frac{N}{2}\right), ...z\left(\frac{N}{2}-1\right)\right]^T$, $Y = y = \alpha e^{j\varphi}$, $\mathbf{W} = \left[w\left(-\frac{N}{2}\right), ..., w\left(\frac{N}{2}-1\right)\right]^T$, $V = v \in \{0,1\}$ and $\mathbf{U}(\mathbf{x}) = \left[\sin c\left(-\frac{N}{2}-x\right), ..., \sin c\left(\frac{N}{2}-1-x\right)\right]^T$.

Assuming that target is uniformly distributed in the detection, the prior probability density of $\mathbf{X}$ is therefore given by

$$p(x) = \frac{1}{N}.\tag{7}$$

Here, we define the ratio of the power of useful signal to the noise power as SNR, namely

$$\rho^2 = \frac{E\left[\alpha^2\right]}{N_0}.\tag{8}$$

3   Detection Information

The mutual information between the received signal and the existence state of the target is called detection information. Let mutual information $I(\mathbf{Z};V)$ denotes existence information. According to the mutual information identity, we have

$$I(\mathbf{Z};V) = H(V) - H(V|\mathbf{Z}).\tag{9}$$

Note that $H(V)$ and $H(V|\mathbf{Z})$ denote the prior and the posterior entropy of V, respectively.

Where

$$H(V) = -p(1)\log_2 p(1) - p(0)\log_2 p(0)\tag{10}$$

and

$$H(V|\mathbf{Z}) = -E_{\mathbf{Z}}\left[\sum_v p(v|\mathbf{z})\log_2 p(v|\mathbf{z})\right].\tag{11}$$

The $p(1)$ and $p(0)$ is prior probability density of v, which represent the probability of target exist or not, respectively. $p(v|\mathbf{z})$ denotes the posterior probability density function of v.

Therefore, we can rewrite the existence information as

$$I(\mathbf{Z};V) = -p(1)\log_2 p(1) - p(0)\log_2 p(0)$$
$$+ E_{\mathbf{Z}}\left[\sum_v p(v|\mathbf{z})\log_2 p(v|\mathbf{z})\right].\tag{12}$$

Next, we study the calculation of complex Gaussian scattered target detection information.

3.1   Complex Gaussian Scattering

Complex Gaussian scattering means the y follows the complex Gaussian distribution, in which the α follows the Rayleigh distribution and the φ is uniformly distributed over the interval $[0, 2\pi]$, namely

$$p\left(\varphi\right) = \frac{1}{2\pi}. \tag{13}$$

As noted previously, $\mathbf{W}$ is the comples Gaussian noise vector whose elements are independent identically distributed (i.i.d) complex Gaussian variables with mean zero and variance N_0. Using (6), we can know the received vector $\mathbf{Z}$ is also complex Gaussian, and its covariance matrix $\mathbf{R}$, we have

$$
\begin{aligned}
\mathbf{R} &= E_{V,Y,\mathbf{W}} \left[\mathbf{Z}\mathbf{Z}^{\mathrm{H}}\right] \\
&= E\left[(VY\mathbf{U}(\mathbf{x}) + \mathbf{W})(VY\mathbf{U}(\mathbf{x}) + \mathbf{W})^{\mathrm{H}}\right] \\
&= \mathbf{U}\left(\mathbf{x}\right) E\left[VYY^{\mathrm{H}}V^{\mathrm{H}}\right]\mathbf{U}^{\mathrm{H}}\left(\mathbf{x}\right) + E\left[\mathbf{W}\mathbf{W}^{\mathrm{H}}\right] \\
&= N_0\mathbf{I} + Pv\mathbf{U}\left(\mathbf{x}\right)\mathbf{U}^{\mathrm{H}}\left(\mathbf{x}\right).
\end{aligned}
\tag{14}
$$

Where $P = E\left[\alpha^2\right]$ represents the power of target.

The determinant

$$|\mathbf{R}| = (N_0)^N \left(1 + v\rho^2\right) \tag{15}$$

doesn't matter the location of target. The inverse of the covariance matrix can be obtained by the matrix inverse formula

$$\mathbf{R}^{-1} = \frac{1}{N_0}\left(I - \frac{v\rho^2 \mathbf{U}(\mathbf{x})\mathbf{U}^H(\mathbf{x})}{1 + v\rho^2}\right). \tag{16}$$

The multi-dimensional probability density of $\mathbf{Z}$ conditioned on $\mathbf{X}$ and V is given by

$$p(\mathbf{Z}|v, x) = \frac{1}{\pi^N |\mathbf{R}|}\exp\left(-\mathbf{Z}^H \mathbf{R}^{-1}\mathbf{Z}\right). \tag{17}$$

Therefore

$$p(\mathbf{Z}|v, x) = \frac{1}{(\pi N_0)^N (1 + v\rho^2)}\exp\left(-\frac{1}{N_0}\mathbf{Z}^H\mathbf{Z}\right)\exp\left(\frac{1}{N_0}\frac{v\rho^2}{v\rho^2 + 1}\left|\mathbf{Z}^H\mathbf{U}(\mathbf{X})\right|^2\right). \tag{18}$$

Since the random variables $\mathbf{X}$ and V are independent of each other, we have

$$p\left(\mathbf{Z}, v\right) = \int_{-N/2}^{N/2} p\left(\mathbf{Z}|v, x\right)p\left(x\right)p\left(v\right)dx. \tag{19}$$

The posterior probability distribution $p\left(v|\mathbf{Z}\right)$ can be obtained by Bayes formula

$$p\left(v|\mathbf{Z}\right) = \frac{p(\mathbf{Z}, v)}{p(\mathbf{Z})}, \tag{20}$$

where

$$p(\mathbf{Z}) = p(\mathbf{Z}, v = 0) + p(\mathbf{Z}, v = 1). \tag{21}$$

Substituting (18), (19), (21) into (20),

$$p(v|\mathbf{Z}) = \frac{p(v)\frac{1}{N}\int_{-N/2}^{N/2} \frac{1}{1+v\rho^2} \exp\left\{\frac{1}{N_0}\frac{v\rho^2}{1+v\rho^2}\left|\mathbf{Z}^H\mathbf{U}(\mathbf{x})\right|^2\right\}dx}{p(0) + p(1)\frac{1}{N}\int_{-N/2}^{N/2} \frac{1}{1+\rho^2} \exp\left\{\frac{1}{N_0}\frac{\rho^2}{1+\rho^2}\left|\mathbf{Z}^H\mathbf{U}(\mathbf{x})\right|^2\right\}dx}. \tag{22}$$

Then, substituting (22) into (12), we can obtain detection information under complex Gaussian scattering model.

4 False Alarm and Detection

We can know that target signal exists or does not exist in received signal depends V from (6). There are two hypotheses to detect target's existence, H_0 corresponds to $V = 0$, target does not exist; and H_1 corresponds to $V = 1$, target exists. The received signal under the two hypotheses are given respectively as follows:

$$\begin{aligned} H_0 &: \mathbf{Z} = \mathbf{W} \\ H_1 &: \mathbf{Z} = Y\mathbf{U}(\mathbf{x}) + \mathbf{W}. \end{aligned} \tag{23}$$

Two probabilities of interes to evaluate detection performance. One is probability of detection P_D, that is, at hypothesis H_1, the probability having detected the target; the other probability of false alarm P_{FA}, the probability having detected the target at hypothesis H_0.

Next, we will discuss false alarm probability and detection probability from the perspective of information theory and N-P criterion respectively.

4.1 Information Theory Method

Two probabilities we interest are obtained from perspective of information theory, so we call this method studied in this paper information theory method (ITM).

For simplicity, following $\mathbf{Z}_1$ and $\mathbf{Z}_0$ represent the presence and absence of the target in the actual received signal, respectively.

Theorem 1. *If the observation interval is long enough, the probability of false alarm can be approximated as*

$$P_{FA} \approx p(1). \tag{24}$$

Proof. Under complex Gaussian scattering model, according to (22) and the definition of false alarm probability, we get false alarm probability as

$$P_{FA} = \frac{p(1)\frac{1}{N}\int_{-N/2}^{N/2} \frac{1}{1+\rho^2} \exp\left\{\frac{1}{N_0}\frac{\rho^2}{1+\rho^2}\left|\mathbf{Z}_0^H\mathbf{U}(\mathbf{x})\right|^2\right\}dx}{p(0) + p(1)\frac{1}{N}\int_{-N/2}^{N/2} \frac{1}{1+\rho^2} \exp\left\{\frac{1}{N_0}\frac{\rho^2}{1+\rho^2}\left|\mathbf{Z}_0^H\mathbf{U}(\mathbf{x})\right|^2\right\}dx}, \tag{25}$$

or

$$P_{FA} = \frac{p(1)\Upsilon(1, \mathbf{Z}_0)}{p(0) + p(1)\Upsilon(1, \mathbf{Z}_0)}, \tag{26}$$

where

$$\Upsilon(1, \mathbf{Z}_0) = \frac{1}{1+\rho^2} \frac{1}{N} \int_{-N/2}^{N/2} \exp\left(\frac{1}{N_0}\frac{\rho^2}{\rho^2+1}|w(x)|^2\right) dx. \tag{27}$$

It represents the time average of the exponential function of the white noise stochastic process in the observation interval. Assuming that the observation interval is long enough, the time average of the stationary process is equal to the ensemble average, then

$$\Upsilon(1, \mathbf{Z}_0) = E_w\left[\frac{1}{\rho^2+1} \exp\left(\frac{1}{N_0}\frac{\rho^2}{\rho^2+1}|w(x)|^2\right)\right]. \tag{28}$$

Given that $\xi = |w(x)|^2$ obeys the exponential distribution with parameter N_0, then

$$
\begin{aligned}
\Upsilon(1, \mathbf{Z}_0) &= \int_0^\infty \frac{1}{\rho^2+1} e^{\frac{1}{N_0}\frac{\rho^2}{\rho^2+1}\xi} \frac{1}{N_0} e^{-\xi/N_0} d\xi \\
&= \frac{1}{N_0}\frac{1}{\rho^2+1} \int_0^\infty e^{-\frac{1}{N_0}\frac{1}{\rho^2+1}\xi} d\xi \\
&= 1.
\end{aligned}
\tag{29}
$$

Consequently, substituting (26) into (29), then we obtain (24) which means that the probability of false alarm P_{FA} equals approximately to the probability that the target actually exists.

According to (22) and the definition of detection probability, we get detection probability as

$$P_D = \frac{p(1)\frac{1}{N}\int_{-N/2}^{N/2}\frac{1}{1+\rho^2}\exp\left\{\frac{1}{N_0}\frac{\rho^2}{1+\rho^2}|\mathbf{Z}_1^H\mathbf{U}(\mathbf{x})|^2\right\}dx}{p(0) + p(1)\frac{1}{N}\int_{-N/2}^{N/2}\frac{1}{1+\rho^2}\exp\left\{\frac{1}{N_0}\frac{\rho^2}{1+\rho^2}|\mathbf{Z}_1^H\mathbf{U}(\mathbf{x})|^2\right\}dx}. \tag{30}$$

It is obvious that P_D and $p(1)$ are related in (30). By substituting (24) into (30), we can easily obtain the relationship between detection probability P_D and false alarm probability P_{FA} as follow

$$P_D \approx \frac{P_{FA}\frac{1}{N}\int_{-N/2}^{N/2}\frac{1}{1+\rho^2}\exp\left\{\frac{1}{N_0}\frac{\rho^2}{1+\rho^2}|\mathbf{Z}_1^H\mathbf{U}(\mathbf{x})|^2\right\}dx}{1 - P_{FA} + P_{FA}\frac{1}{N}\int_{-N/2}^{N/2}\frac{1}{1+\rho^2}\exp\left\{\frac{1}{N_0}\frac{\rho^2}{1+\rho^2}|\mathbf{Z}_1^H\mathbf{U}(\mathbf{x})|^2\right\}dx}. \tag{31}$$

4.2 N-P Criterion

In radar detection, N-P criterion is often used. The purpose of N-P criterion is to optimize the detection performance under the condition that the probability of false alarm does not exceed the tolerance range.

Basing on (17) and (23), we can get the probability density function of $\mathbf{Z}$ under the two hypothesis as follows:

$$P(\mathbf{Z}|H_0) = \frac{1}{\pi^N N_0^N} \exp\left\{-\frac{1}{N_0}\mathbf{Z}^H\mathbf{Z}\right\}$$

$$P(\mathbf{Z}|H_1) = \frac{1}{\pi^N N_0^N (1+\rho^2)} \exp\left\{-\frac{1}{N_0}\left(\mathbf{Z}^H\mathbf{Z} - \frac{\rho^2}{1+\rho^2}|\mathbf{Z}^H\mathbf{U(x)}|^2\right)\right\},$$

(32)

The result of log-likelihood ratio test is

$$\gamma = |\mathbf{Z}^H\mathbf{U(x)}|^2 \underset{H_0}{\overset{H_1}{\underset{<}{>}}} \frac{1+\rho^2}{N_0\left(1+\rho^2\right)}\left(\ln\frac{1}{1+\rho^2} - ln(-\lambda)\right) = T,$$

(33)

where T denotes the threshold value, λ denotes the Lagrange multiplier, γ denotes sufficient statistics.

In order to get the maximum output SNR, assume that the baseband signal $\mathbf{U(x)}$ and the receive signal $\mathbf{Z}$ are completely matched, we can deduce that the relation expression between the probability of false alarm and detection

$$P_D = =P_{FA}{}^{\frac{1}{\rho^2+1}}$$

(34)

5   Detection Information Under N-P Criterion

When the target location is know, this paper adopts relationship between the detection information of the N-P detector and false alarm probability and the prior probability proposed in [15]

$$I\left(V;\hat{V}\right) = H\left(V\right) - H\left(V\Big|\hat{V}\right)$$
$$= H\left(V\right) - P_{\hat{V}}(0)H\left(A\right) - \left[1 - P_{\hat{V}}(0)\right]H\left(D\right),$$

(35)

where V indicates whether a source is really exist or not and $\hat{V}$ indicates receiving signal expressed in stochastic process. $P_{\hat{V}}(0)$ represents the probability that the target is detected as non-existent, then $1 - P_{\hat{V}}(0)$ represents the probability that the target is detected as existing,

$$P_{\hat{V}}(0) = p(1)P_D - p(1)P_{FA} + P_{FA}$$

(36)

A represents the actual existence probability of the target under the condition of the decision signal "target exists", D represents the probability of the target non-existence under the condition of the decision signal "target does not exist".
where

$$A = \frac{p(1)P_D}{P_{\hat{V}}(0)}$$

(37)

and

$$D = \frac{(1 - p(1))\left(1 - P_{FA}\right)}{1 - P_{\hat{V}}(0)}.$$

(38)

6   Numerical Results and Analysis

In this section, we present the simulation results about the detection information and ROC curves in the CAWGN environment using ITM and N-P criterion.

We assume that the sampling point N is 64, the detection internal is $[-N/2, N/2)$, and the noise power N_0 is set as 1. In addition, if the single target exists, it locates in the far-field with the true location $x = 0$.

6.1   Detection Information with Respect to SNR

In Fig. 1, the detection information is plotted with respect to SNR under complex Gaussian models. For convenience, the probability of target's real existence $p(1) = 0.5$ is used. As can be seen from Fig. 1, the solid curve represents the detection information curve of ITM, and the virtual curve represents the reachable region of detection information and SNR for any false alarm probability according to the detection information expression of N-P criterion. With the increase of SNR, the more information is obtained.

The detection information of ITM and N-P criterion increases from 0 to 1 with the increase of SNR, which verifies the correctness of the theoretical derivation. However, under the same SNR, the detection information of ITM is always greater than that of N-P criterion, which indicates that the detection performance of ITM is better than that of N-P criterion with the change of SNR.

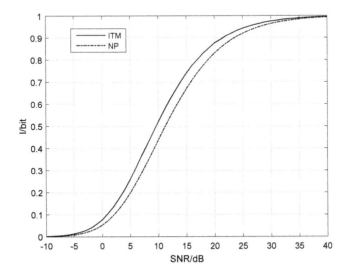

Fig. 1. Detection information with respect to SNR.

6.2   The ROC Curves Based on ITM and N-P Criterion

Figure 2 depicts the ROC curves based on ITM and N-P criterion under complex Gaussian scattering model, respectively, and the SNR is set as 0 dB, 5 dB. It can be seen that the probability of detection increases with the increase of probability of false alarm. On the condition of constant false alarm probability, the probability of detection increases with the increase of SNR. The probability of detection based on N-P criterion is always higher than that of ITM, which indicates that the performance of ITM is worse than that of N-P criterion from perspective of ROC.

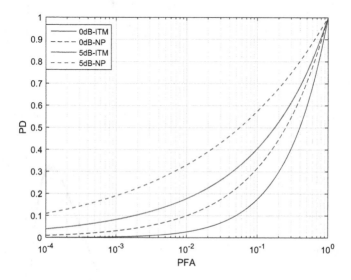

Fig. 2. The ROC curves based on ITM and N-P criterion.

6.3   Detection Information with Respect to Prior Probability

Figure 3 and Fig. 4 depict the relationship between detection information and prior probability. 0 dB and 5 dB respectively represent the low and medium SNR studied in this paper. The solid curve represents the detection information curve of ITM, and the virtual curve represents the reachable region of detection information and prior probability $p(1)$ for any false alarm probability P_{FA} according to the detection information expression of N-P criterion.

As we can see from the two figures, the detection information of ITM is aways much higher than that based on N-P criterion, which indicates that the detection performance of ITM is better than that of N-P criterion. The amount of detection information with respect to prior probability on the condition of a certain SNR could be see from Fig. 1, which further verifies its correctness.

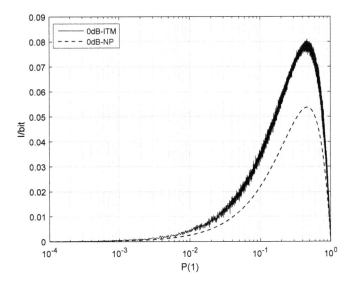

Fig. 3. 0 dB, detection Information with respect to prior probability.

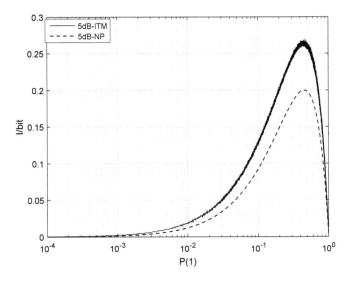

Fig. 4. 5 dB, detection Information with respect to prior probability.

7 Conclusion

In this paper, we introduce the target existence parameter into the radar detection system, which could use the same method for target detection and estimation. The detection information in radar is investigated, and the detection performance based on ITM and N-P criterion is discussed. In single target scenario, we derive the theoretical expression of detection information under complex Gaussian scattering model. Moreover, we find that the probability of false alarm is equal to the probability of target's real existence $p(1)$ by the approximation. And then we derive relational expression between the probability of detection and false alarm based on ITM and N-P criterion. Simulation results show that the detection information of ITM is better than that of N-P criterion from perspective of information theory, however, from the ROC curve, the result is opposite. At present, there is no final conclusion on which of the two criteria is the best, but our research work breaks the situation that N-P criterion dominates the whole country and opens up a new direction for the field of source detection. Finally, some issues such multi-target detection with interference are worthy of further investigations.

Acknowledgement. This work was supported by CEMEE State Key Laboratory fund under Grant 2020Z0207B, National Defense Science and Technology Key Laboratory fund under Grant 6142001190105.

References

1. Woodward, P.: Theory of radar information. Trans. IRE Prof. Group Inf. Theory **1**(1), 108–113 (1953)
2. Woodward, P.M.: Information theory and the design of radar receivers. Proc. IRE **39**(12), 1521–1524 (1951)
3. Woodward, P.M., Davies, I.L.: Information theory and inverse probability in telecommunication. Proc. IEE Part III Radio Commun. Eng. **99**(58) (1952)
4. Shannon, C.E.: IEEE xplore abstract - a mathematical theory of communication. Bell Syst. Tech. J. (1948)
5. Bell, M.R.: Information theory and radar waveform design. IEEE Trans. Inf. Theory **39**(5), 1578–1597 (1993)
6. Godrich, H., Haimovich, A.M., Blum, R.S.: Target localization accuracy gain in MIMO radar-based systems. IEEE Trans. Inf. Theory **56**(6), 2783–2803 (2010)
7. Yang, Y., Blum, R.S.: MIMO radar waveform design based on mutual information and minimum mean-square error estimation. IEEE Trans. Aerosp. Electron. Syst. **43**(1), 330–343 (2007)
8. Chen, Y., Xu, D., Luo, H., Xu, S., Chen, Y.: Maximum likelihood distance estimation algorithm for multi-carrier radar system. J. Eng. **2019**(21), 7432–7435 (2019)
9. Xu, D., Yan, X., Xu, S., Luo, H., Liu, J., Zhang, X.: Spatial information theory of sensor array and its application in performance evaluation. IET Commun. **13**(15), 2304–2312 (2019)
10. Shi, C., Xu, D., Zhou, Y., Tu, W.: Range-DOA information and scattering information in phased-array radar. In: 2019 IEEE 5th International Conference on Computer and Communications (ICCC), pp. 747–752 (2019)
11. McDonough, R.N., Whalen, A.D.: Detection of Signals in Noise, 2nd, vol. 16, no. 8, p. 1. Academic Press (1995)
12. Rohling, H.: Radar CFAR thresholding in clutter and multiple target situations. IEEE Trans. Aerosp. Electron. Syst. **AES-19**(4), 608–621 (1983)
13. Sevgi, L.: Hypothesis testing and decision making: constant-false-alarm-rate detection. IEEE Antennas Propag. Mag. **51**(3), 218–224 (2009)

14. Lin, F., Qiu, R.C., Browning, J.P., Wicks, M.C.: Target detection with function of covariance matrices under clutter environment. In: IET International Conference on Radar Systems (Radar 2012), pp. 1–6 (2012)
15. Kondo, M.: An evaluation and the optimum threshold for radar return signal applied for a mutual information. In: Record of the IEEE 2000 International Radar Conference [Cat. No. 00CH37037], pp. 226–230 (2000)
16. Tajer, A., Jajamovich, G.H., Wang, X., Moustakides, G.V.: Finite-sample optimal joint target detection and parameter estimation by MIMO radars. In: 2009 Conference Record of the Forty-Third Asilomar Conference on Signals, Systems and Computers (2009)
17. Moustakides, G.V.: Optimum joint detection and estimation. In: IEEE International Symposium on Information Theory (2011)
18. Tian, J., Zhang, H., Wu, D., Yuan, D.: QoS-constrained medium access probability optimization in wireless interference-limited networks. IEEE Trans. Commun. **66**(3), 1064–1077 (2018)
19. Qiao, J., Alouini, M.: Secure transmission for intelligent reflecting surface-assisted mmWave and terahertz systems. IEEE Wirel. Commun. Lett., 1 (2020)

Research on Source Detection and Its Performance Analysis in Sensor Array

Deng Pan, Dazhuan Xu$^{(\boxtimes)}$, Chao Hu, and Boyu Hua$^{(\boxtimes)}$

College of Electronic and Information Engineering, Nanjing University of Aeronautics
and Astronautics, Nanjing 211106, China
{pandeng,xudazhuang,huchao,byhua}@nuaa.edu.cn

Abstract. In this paper, the application of information theory to describe the existing problem of signal source in sensor array is investigated in the presence of complex additive white Gaussian noise (CAWGN). Firstly, We derive the theoretical formula of constant modulus scattering signal detection information under the condition of target matching in a single source scenario based on the information theory approach (ITA) and the theoretical expressions between detection probability and false alarm probability. Then, according to the Neyman-Pearson (N-P) criterion, the detection probability and false alarm probability of the constant modulus scattering signal are derived separately and derive the corresponding detection information through existing methods. Finally, the simulations of detection information and receiver operating characteristics (ROC), according to the presented expressions, are carried out to compare the detection performance based on information theory and N-P criterion. Our analysis indicates that the theoretical detection performance of ITA can be obviously better than that of N-P criterion, which also verifies the reliability and effectiveness of ITA.

Keywords: Sensor array · Source detection · Information theory · Detection information · N-P criterion · ROC

1 Introduction

Since Shannon founded the information theory [1], great achievements have been made in the field of communication, which laid a solid foundation for the rapid development of communication. Kondo has studied relationship between the optimum threshold and mutual information for radar return signal [2]. Some researchers have studied the relationship between information theory and parameter estimation in sensor array [3]. The Sensor Array system may make measurements of a source in order to determine its unknown characteristics.

In the work of Woodward and Davies [4–6], information theory was considered applicable to radar measurement problems for the first time. Woodward and Davies studied the range mutual information with respect to SNR in the single target radar detection. Shi and Xu [7] have investigated the application of

© ICST Institute for Computer Sciences, Social Informatics and Telecommunications Engineering 2021
Published by Springer Nature Switzerland AG 2021. All Rights Reserved
M. Guan and Z. Na (Eds.): MLICOM 2020, LNICST 342, pp. 333–345, 2021.
https://doi.org/10.1007/978-3-030-66785-6_36

information theory to describe radar measurement problems and the theoretical expressions and an asymptotic upper bound for the scattering information and the range-DOA information are presented in a single target scenario.

Single source detection is the basis of single source research, and is the precondition of resolution and tracking. It should be noted that detection here refers to the statistical judgment of the existence of single source. There are a lot of researches on the source detection at home and abroad. It includes multi-target detection under the condition of complex Gaussian clutter by using the maximum likelihood ratio test method [8], exploiting results from detection theory for deriving fundamental limitations on resolution and obtaining general resolution technology not based on any specific [9], proposing a polarization optimization method based on glowworm swarm optimization (GSO) algorithm to select the polarization waveforms of the transmit array to maximize detection probability [10], proposing new algorithms to achieve superior network throughput performance over existing schemes [11], proposing IRS-assisted secure strategy to significantly boost the secrecy rate performance [12], presenting an improved beamforming method to overcome this shortcoming [13] and proposing channel simulator and emulator that can get more accurate and realistic Doppler frequency than those of the existing models [14].

N-P criterion, a special case of Bayesian criterion, is to maximize the detection probability P_D under the condition of the false alarm probability P_{FA} limited within a specified constant range. Ma and Wang [15] have developed an efficient Bayesian approach to target detection in Cognitive radar. The approach, which uses the N-P criterion with priori probability, can improve the target detection effectively.

Few papers involve relating information theory with source detection, let alone comparing the detection performance of ITA with N-P criterion, which are the core content of this paper. In the remainder of this paper, we first construct the receiving signal model of sensor array in Sect. 2. In Sect. 3, based on the previous research of sensor array detection information, we further discuss the detection information in constant modulus scattering signal. In Sect. 4, the corresponding expressions of detection probability and false alarm probability in constant modulus scattering signal are derived based on ITA, and the relationship between detection probability and false alarm probability is obtained through different approximation methods. In Sect. 5, on the basis of reference [2,16], the relationship between detection probability and false alarm probability is deduced by using N-P criterion in constant modulus scattering signal, and we got the corresponding detection information. In Sect. 6, the numerical results are presented, the detection performance of ITA and N-P criterion is analyzed, which shows the superiority of each method. Finally, in Sect. 7, the main results of this paper are discussed and concluded.

2   System Model

Assuming that the uniform linear array model is shown in Fig. 1., a narrowband far-field source impinging on the antenna array and elements. The received signals at m-th (m = 0, 1, ..., M) array elements are expressed as

$$x_m(t) = s(t)ve^{j\omega_0 \tau_m(\theta)} + w_m(t). \tag{1}$$

In (1), $s(t)$ is the source signal, ω_0 is the angular frequency of the carrier signal. v equal to 0 or 1 indicates that the target does not exist or exists. $\tau_m(\theta) = md\sin\theta/c$ represents the time delay of the source signal at the direction angle with the m-th array element, where d is the distance between any two adjacent elements, c is the propagation speed of the signal, and $w_m(t)$ represents the additive Gaussian white noise with noise power N_0 at the m-th array element.

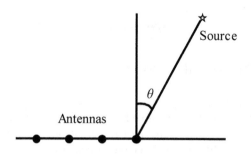

Fig. 1. System model.

Based on (1), a matrix equation is constructed as

$$\mathbf{x}(t) = v\mathbf{A}(\theta)s(t) + \mathbf{w}(t) \tag{2}$$

where $\mathbf{A}(\theta)$ is the transfer matrix between the source signal and the received signal

$$
\mathbf{A}(\theta) = [\mathbf{a}(\theta)]
$$
$$
= \begin{bmatrix} \exp(j\omega_0\tau_0(\theta)) \\ \exp(j\omega_0\tau_1(\theta)) \\ \vdots \\ \exp(j\omega_0\tau_{M-1}(\theta)) \end{bmatrix}. \tag{3}
$$

Concisely, omitting time t, we rewrite (2) as

$$\mathbf{x} = v\mathbf{A}(\theta)s + \mathbf{w} \tag{4}$$

The source signal is given by $s = \alpha e^{j\varphi}$, where the scattering coefficient α takes one distribution, namely, constant distribution. And the spatial phase φ is uniformly distributed in the interval $[0, 2\pi]$, then the prior probability density is $p(\varphi) = 1/2\pi$. Suppose the scattering coefficient α is a constant, $s = \alpha e^{j\varphi}$ is a constant modulus scattering signal.

Resultantly, we will provide the proof of the above case in the following sections.

Here, we define the SNR as

$$\rho^2 = \frac{E\left(\alpha^2\right)}{N_0}.$$ (5)

Note that the second moment of noise is given by $E\left[\mathbf{w}\mathbf{w}^H\right] = N_0 I$.

Next, we introduce a basic assumption on the system model about the direction of angle (DOA) Θ. The source is uniformly distributed in the observation interval $\left[-\frac{|\Theta|}{2}, \frac{|\Theta|}{2}\right]$, where $|\Theta|$ denotes the observation range, the priori probability of Θ is given by

$$p(\theta) = 1/|\Theta|.$$ (6)

3   Detection Information of Source

We can define the existence information as the mutual information between the spatial existence status and the received signal, i.e. $I(\mathbf{x}; v)$. According to information theory [1,17,18], the quantity of information obtainable from a sensor array observation is the difference of the entropies of the a priori and a posteriori probability distribution, that is

$$I(\mathbf{x}; v) = H(v) - H(v|\mathbf{x})$$ (7)

where

$$\begin{aligned} H(v) &= -E_v\left[\log_2 p\left(v\right)\right] \\ &= -p\left(0\right)\log_2 p\left(0\right) - p\left(1\right)\log_2 p\left(1\right) \end{aligned}$$ (8)

and

$$H(v|\mathbf{x}) = -E_{\mathbf{x}}\left[\sum p(v|\mathbf{x})\log_2 p(v|\mathbf{x})\right].$$ (9)

Note that $p\left(v\right)$ and $p(v|\mathbf{x})$ is the a priori and the a posteriori probability density function of, respectively.

Next, we will discuss existence information in constant modulus scattering signal.

3.1   Constant Modulus Scattering Signal

Constant modulus scattering means that the amplitude α of the scattering coefficient of the source is a constant, the phase φ of the scattering coefficient of the source is uniformly distributed over the interval $[0, 2\pi]$.

Under the given parameters Θ, V and Φ, the probability density function of the received signal $\mathbf{X}$ is expressed as

$$p\left(\mathbf{x}|\theta, \varphi, v\right) = \left(\frac{1}{\pi N_0}\right)^M \exp\left(-\frac{1}{N_0}(\mathbf{x} - v a\left(\theta\right) s)^H (\mathbf{x} - v a\left(\theta\right) s)\right).$$ (10)

The joint probability density of V and $\mathbf{X}$ is

$$p(\mathbf{x}, v) = \iint p(\mathbf{x}, \theta, \varphi, v) \, d\varphi d\theta$$

$$= \iint p(\mathbf{x} | \theta, \varphi, v) \, p(\theta) \, p(\varphi) \, p(v) \, d\varphi d\theta$$

$$= \frac{p(v)}{2\pi |\Theta|} \left(\frac{1}{\pi N_0} \right)^M \exp\left(-\frac{\left(\mathbf{x}^H \mathbf{x} + \alpha^2 v M \right)}{N_0} \right) \int_{-|\Theta|/2}^{|\Theta|/2} \int_0^{2\pi} \exp\left(\frac{2\alpha v}{N_0} \Re\left(e^{-j\varphi} \mathbf{a}^H(\theta) \mathbf{x} \right) \right) d\varphi d\theta$$

(11)

where $\Re(\bullet)$ denotes taking the real part of a complex number.

The conditional probability distribution $p(v|\mathbf{x})$ can be obtained by Bayes formula,

$$p(v|\mathbf{x}) = \frac{p(\mathbf{x}, v)}{p(\mathbf{x})}$$

$$= \frac{p(\mathbf{x}, v)}{p(\mathbf{x}, 0) + p(\mathbf{x}, 1)}$$

$$= \frac{p(v) \frac{1}{2\pi|\Theta|} \exp\left(-\frac{1}{N_0} \alpha^2 v M \right) \int_{-|\Theta|/2}^{|\Theta|/2} \int_0^{2\pi} \exp\left(\frac{2\alpha v}{N_0} \Re\left(e^{-j\varphi} \mathbf{a}^H(\theta) \mathbf{x} \right) \right) d\varphi d\theta}{p(0) + p(1) \frac{1}{2\pi|\Theta|} \exp\left(-\frac{1}{N_0} \alpha^2 M \right) \int_{-|\Theta|/2}^{|\Theta|/2} \int_0^{2\pi} \exp\left(\frac{2\alpha}{N_0} \Re\left(e^{-j\varphi} \mathbf{a}^H(\theta) \mathbf{x} \right) \right) d\varphi d\theta}$$

(12)

where (12) is a posterior probability distribution of the existence of the source when the received signal is known.

As shown in Fig. 1, substituting (12) into (7), we can simulate the detection information curve of constant modulus scattering signal.

4   The Relationship Between Detection Probability and False Alarm Probability Based on ITA

In this section, we derive the theoretical expressions between detection probability and false alarm probability in a single source scenario respectively based on ITA. For simplicity, following $\mathbf{x}_1$ and $\mathbf{x}_0$ represent the presence and absence of the source in the actual received signal, respectively.

Theorem 1. *In constant modulus scattering signal model, the false alarm probability P_{FA} can be approximated as*

$$P_{FA} \approx p(1).$$

(13)

Proof. In constant modulus scattering signal model, according to (12) and the definition of false alarm probability, we get false alarm probability as

$$P_{FA} = p(1|\mathbf{x}_0) = \frac{p(\mathbf{x}_0, 1)}{p(\mathbf{x}_0)}$$

$$= \frac{p(1)\frac{1}{2\pi|\Theta|}\exp\left(-\frac{M\alpha^2}{N_0}\right)\int_{-|\Theta|/2}^{|\Theta|/2}\int_0^{2\pi}\exp\left(\frac{2\alpha}{N_0}\Re\left(e^{-j\varphi}\mathbf{a}^H(\theta)\mathbf{w}\right)\right)d\varphi d\theta}{p(0) + p(1)\frac{1}{2\pi|\Theta|}\exp\left(-\frac{M\alpha^2}{N_0}\right)\int_{-|\Theta|/2}^{|\Theta|/2}\int_0^{2\pi}\exp\left(\frac{2\alpha}{N_0}\Re\left(e^{-j\varphi}\mathbf{a}^H(\theta)\mathbf{w}\right)\right)d\varphi d\theta}$$

$$= \frac{p(1)\frac{1}{2\pi|\Theta|}\exp\left(-\frac{M\alpha^2}{N_0}\right)\int_0^{2\pi}\int_{-|\Theta|/2}^{|\Theta|/2}\exp\left(\frac{2\alpha}{N_0}\Re\left(e^{-j\varphi}\mathbf{w}(\theta)\right)\right)d\theta d\varphi}{p(0) + p(1)\frac{1}{2\pi|\Theta|}\exp\left(-\frac{M\alpha^2}{N_0}\right)\int_0^{2\pi}\int_{-|\Theta|/2}^{|\Theta|/2}\exp\left(\frac{2\alpha}{N_0}\Re\left(e^{-j\varphi}\mathbf{w}(\theta)\right)\right)d\theta d\varphi}$$

$$\tag{14}$$

where $\mathbf{w}(\theta)$ equals $\mathbf{a}^H(\theta)\mathbf{w}$, $\mathbf{w}(\theta)$ is a scalar. And there is no source signal in received signal.

Then we can approximate the main part of (14) to

$$\frac{1}{|\Theta|}\int_{-|\Theta|/2}^{|\Theta|/2}\exp\left(\frac{2\alpha}{N_0}\Re\left(e^{-j\varphi}\mathbf{w}(\theta)\right)\right)d\theta$$

$$= \frac{1}{|\Theta|}\int_{-|\Theta|/2}^{|\Theta|/2}\exp\left(\frac{2\alpha}{N_0}\left(\mathbf{w}_R(\theta)\cos\varphi + \mathbf{w}_I(\theta)\sin\varphi\right)\right)d\theta$$

$$\approx \frac{1}{|\Theta|}\sum_{-|\Theta|/2}^{|\Theta|/2-1}\exp\left(\frac{2\alpha}{N_0}\left(\mathbf{w}_R(\theta)\cos\varphi + \mathbf{w}_I(\theta)\sin\varphi\right)\right) \tag{15}$$

$$\approx E\left[\exp\left(\frac{2\alpha}{N_0}\left(\mathbf{w}_R(\theta)\cos\varphi + \mathbf{w}_I(\theta)\sin\varphi\right)\right)\right]$$

where $\mathbf{w}_R(\theta)$ and $\mathbf{w}_I(\theta)$ denote the real and imaginary parts of $\mathbf{w}(\theta)$, respectively. $\mathbf{w}(\theta)$ obeys complex Gaussian distribution with zero mean and variance MN_0, so $\mathbf{w}_R(\theta)\cos\varphi + \mathbf{w}_I(\theta)\sin\varphi$ obeys complex Gaussian distribution with zero mean and variance $\frac{MN_0}{2}$. Then (15) can be further derived as

$$E\left[\exp\left(\frac{2\alpha}{N_0}\left(\mathbf{w}_R(\theta)\cos\varphi + \mathbf{w}_I(\theta)\sin\varphi\right)\right)\right]^{\mathbf{w}_R(\theta)\cos\varphi + \mathbf{w}_I(\theta)\sin\varphi = \lambda}$$

$$= \int_{-\infty}^{+\infty}e^{\frac{2\alpha}{N_0}\lambda}\frac{1}{\sqrt{\pi MN_0}}e^{-\frac{\lambda^2}{MN_0}}d\lambda \tag{16}$$

$$= e^{\frac{M\alpha^2}{N_0}}\int_{-\infty}^{+\infty}\frac{1}{\sqrt{\pi MN_0}}e^{-\frac{(\lambda - M\alpha)^2}{MN_0}}d\lambda$$

$$= e^{\frac{M\alpha^2}{N_0}}.$$

By substituting (16) into (14), we can easily obtain the result of (13).

In conclusion, we can obtain the expression of (13). And according to (13), we can find that the derivation of P_{FA} has nothing to do with whether the source signal exists or not in received signal $\mathbf{x}$.

Next, we will derive the theoretical expressions of detection probability and the approximate expressions of detection probability and false alarm probability in constant modulus scattering signal model.

According to above (12) and the definition of detection probability, we get detection probability as

$$P_D = p(1|\mathbf{x}_1)$$

$$= \frac{p(1)\frac{1}{2\pi|\Theta|}\exp\left(-\frac{M\alpha^2}{N_0}\right)\int_{-|\Theta|/2}^{|\Theta|/2}\int_0^{2\pi}\exp\left(\frac{2\alpha}{N_0}\Re\left(e^{-j\varphi}\mathbf{a}^H\left(\theta\right)\mathbf{x}_1\right)\right)d\varphi d\theta}{1-p(1)+p(1)\frac{1}{2\pi|\Theta|}\exp\left(-\frac{M\alpha^2}{N_0}\right)\int_{-|\Theta|/2}^{|\Theta|/2}\int_0^{2\pi}\exp\left(\frac{2\alpha}{N_0}\Re\left(e^{-j\varphi}\mathbf{a}^H\left(\theta\right)\mathbf{x}_1\right)\right)d\varphi d\theta}.$$
(17)

Substituting (13) into (17), we can obtain the relationship between detection probability P_D and false alarm probability P_{FA} as

$$P_D = \frac{P_{FA}\frac{1}{2\pi|\Theta|}\exp\left(-\frac{M\alpha^2}{N_0}\right)\int_{-|\Theta|/2}^{|\Theta|/2}\int_0^{2\pi}\exp\left(\frac{2\alpha}{N_0}\Re\left(e^{-j\varphi}\mathbf{a}^H\left(\theta\right)\mathbf{x}_1\right)\right)d\varphi d\theta}{1-P_{FA}+P_{FA}\frac{1}{2\pi|\Theta|}\exp\left(-\frac{M\alpha^2}{N_0}\right)\int_{-|\Theta|/2}^{|\Theta|/2}\int_0^{2\pi}\exp\left(\frac{2\alpha}{N_0}\Re\left(e^{-j\varphi}\mathbf{a}^H\left(\theta\right)\mathbf{x}_1\right)\right)d\varphi d\theta}.$$
(18)

Next, we will proceed to the derivation of N-P criterion in constant modulus scattering signal model.

5   The Relationship Between Detection Probability and False Alarm Probability Under N-P Criterion

According to reference [16] and system model, we have the following two hypotheses

$$\begin{aligned} H_0 &: \mathbf{x} = \mathbf{w} \\ H_1 &: \mathbf{x} = \mathbf{A}\left(\theta\right)s + \mathbf{w} \end{aligned}$$
(19)

where H_0 represents the hypothesis that the source does not exist and H_1 represents the hypothesis that the source does exist.

Next, we will derive the theoretical expressions of detection probability and false alarm probability of the two scattering coefficient signals under the N-P criterion.

According to reference [16] and (17), in the constant modulus model under the N-P criterion, we have false alarm probability as

$$P_{FA} = \int_{T'}^{+\infty} p(\Upsilon|H_0)d\Upsilon = \exp\left(-\frac{T'^2}{PN_0}\right).$$
(20)

From the above (20), we can get the detection threshold $T' = \sqrt{-PN_0\ln P_{FA}}$. Then we have detection probability

$$P_D = \int_{T'}^{+\infty} p(\Upsilon|H_1)d\Upsilon = Q_M\left(\sqrt{2M\rho^2}, \sqrt{-2\ln P_{FA}}\right)$$
(21)

where $Q_M\left(\cdot\right)$ represents the Q function of Marcum.

Equation (21) indicates the relationship between the detection probability and the false alarm probability of single source under the N-P criterion.

6   Detection Information Under N-P Criterion

When the source position is known, this paper adopts the relationship between the detection information of the NP detector and the false alarm probability and the prior probability proposed in the reference [2],

$$
\begin{aligned}
I\left(V;\hat{V}\right) &= H\left(V\right) - H\left(V\middle|\hat{V}\right) \\
&= -p\left(1\right)\log p\left(1\right) - \left(1 - p\left(1\right)\right)\log\left(1 - p\left(1\right)\right) \\
&\quad - \left(p\left(1\right)P_D - p\left(1\right)P_{FA} + P_{FA}\right)\left(-A\log A - \left(1 - A\right)\log\left(1 - A\right)\right) \\
&\quad - \left(1 - p\left(1\right)P_D + p\left(1\right)P_{FA} - P_{FA}\right)\left(-D\log D - \left(1 - D\right)\log\left(1 - D\right)\right)
\end{aligned}
\tag{22}
$$

where V indicates whether a source is really exist or not and $\hat{V}$ indicates a array receiving signal expressed in stochastic process,

$$
A = \frac{p\left(1\right)P_D}{p\left(1\right)P_D - p\left(1\right)P_{FA} + P_{FA}}
\tag{23}
$$

indicates source real existence probability under the decision signal "source existence" and

$$
D = \frac{\left(1 - p\left(1\right)\right)\left(1 - P_{FA}\right)}{1 - p\left(1\right)P_D + p\left(1\right)P_{FA} - P_{FA}}
\tag{24}
$$

indicates source non-existence probability under the decision signal "source non-existence".

In the next section, we will simulate the ROC curves and detection information curves under N-P criterion.

7   Numerical Results

The simulation parameters are set as follows: the actual value of DOA in a single source scenario is $\theta_0 = 0°$ (that is from the normal direction of the sensor arrays), and the observation internal is $\left[-\frac{\pi}{2}, \frac{\pi}{2}\right]$. The number of antenna M is set as 16 in the CAWGN environment. The value of the reflection coefficient is 1 when α is a constant.

7.1   Detection Information of Constant Modulus Scattering Signal

In Fig. 2, the prior probability of v is set equal and the detection information in a single source detection is illustrated, where s is a constant modulus scattering signal.

The blue solid curve represents the detection information curve of ITA. And the orange virtual curve represents the reachable region of detection information and SNR for any false alarm probability according to the detection information expression of N-P criterion. We can clearly observe the change trend of detection information in different SNR intervals obtained by sensor array under ITA and N-P criterion.

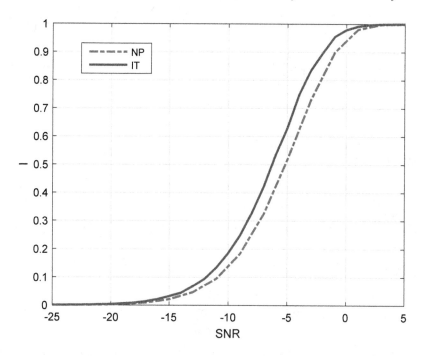

Fig. 2. Relationship between detection information of source and SNR

In the case of ITA, detection information quickly reaches the theoretical maximum value 1 from 0. And The blue curve is higher than the orange curve in the whole process of SNR change, which indicates that the detection performance of ITA is better than that of N-P criterion with the change of SNR.

7.2 The ROC Curves Under ITA and N-P Criterion for Constant Modulus Scattering Signal

According to the detection information curve of source in Fig. 2 and ROC simulation results, we take −20 dB to 0 dB as the observation interval, and select some representative curves to reflect the general trend of ROC curve.

– 20 dB and −10 dB represent low and medium SNR interval respectively.

Whether it is a blue curve or an orange curve, under the same false alarm probability P_{FA}, the value P_D of the dotted curve is higher than that of the solid curve under the same SNR, which indicates that the performance of ITA is worse than that of N-P criterion in terms of receiver operating characteristics in the midsole SNR range (Fig. 3).

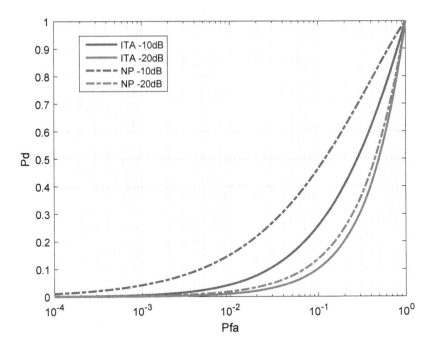

Fig. 3. ROC curves under ITA and N-P criterion for constant modulus scattering signal

7.3 The Relationship Between Detection Information and Prior Probability for Constant Modulus Scattering Signal

According to our previous research progress, combined with the research results of other researchers in related fields, we believe that the relationship between detection information and prior probability is more important than ROC.

In Fig. 2, the prior probability of v is set equal and the detection information in a single source detection is illustrated, where s is a constant modulus scattering signal.

According to the detection information curve of source in Fig. 2, we take -20 dB to 0 dB as the observation interval, and select some representative curves to reflect the general trend of detection information. Note that the prior probability is used as an independent variable instead of an equal probability distribution. Here, -20 dB and -10 dB represent low and medium SNR interval respectively.

The blue solid curve represents the detection information curve of ITA. And the orange virtual curve represents the reachable region of detection information and prior probability $p\,(1)$ for any false alarm probability P_{FA} according to the detection information expression of N-P criterion.

In Fig. 4 and Fig. 5, we can observe that the detection information value I of the blue solid curve is significantly greater than that of the orange dotted curve under the same prior probability $p(1)$ condition, which indicates that the detection performance of ITA is better than that of N-P criterion in the middle and low SNR range. This is predictable because the detection information is the theoretical value given by the information theory method.

Theoretical analysis shows that, even for small and weak sources, ITA has the possibility of detection, which is more beneficial to the detection of small and weak sources.

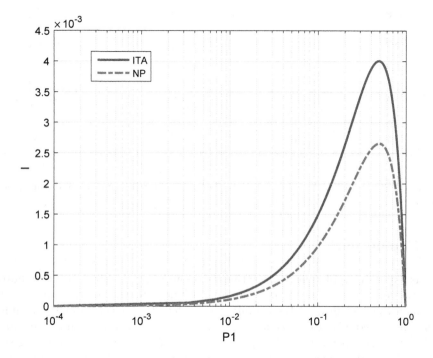

Fig. 4. SNR $= -20\,\mathrm{dB}$, the relationship between detection information and prior probability

The above comparative analyses further confirm the reliability and effectiveness of ITA in single source detection, and also provide important guiding significance for the selection of appropriate method for the detection of signals.

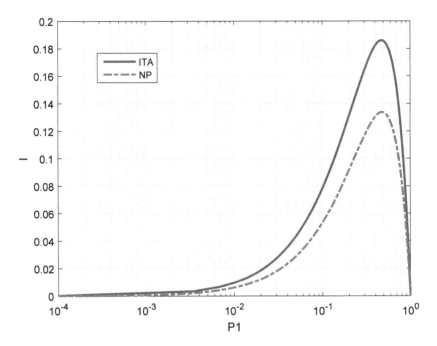

Fig. 5. SNR $= -10\,$dB, the relationship between detection information and prior probability

8 Conclusion

In this paper, we apply information theory to sensor array system in single source scenario, introduce the boolean variable v is to indicate whether the signal exists or not in the system model and unify source detection with parameter estimation. The closed form expressions between detection probability and false alarm probability have been derived respectively for constant modulus scattering signal. Theoretical analysis and numerical results are provided to corroborate that the detection information of ITA is better than N-P criterion, and the detection probability of N-P criterion is better than detection information criterion. At present, there is no final conclusion on which of the two criteria is the best, but our research work breaks the situation that N-P criterion dominates the whole country and opens up a new direction for the field of source detection. In addition, some issues such multi-sources detection with interference are worthy of further investigations.

Acknowledgement. This work was supported by CEMEE State Key Laboratory fund under Grant 2020Z0207B, National Defense Science and Technology Key Laboratory fund under Grant 6142001190105.

References

1. Shannon, C.E.: A mathematical theory of communication. Bell Syst. Tech. J. **27**(3), 379–423 (1948)
2. Kondo, M.: An evaluation and the optimum threshold for radar return signal applied for a mutual information. In: Record of the IEEE 2000 International Radar Conference [Cat. No. 00CH37037], pp. 226–230 (2000)
3. Xu, D., Yan, X., Xu, S., Luo, H., Liu, J., Zhang, X.: Spatial information theory of sensor array and its application in performance evaluation. IET Commun. **13**(15), 2304–2312 (2019)
4. Woodward, P.M., Davies, I.L.: Information theory and inverse probability in telecommunication. Proc. IEE Part III Radio Commun. Eng. **99**(58) (1952)
5. Woodward, P.M.: Information theory and the design of radar receivers. Proc. IRE **39**(12), 1521–1524 (1951)
6. Woodward, P.: Theory of radar information. Trans. IRE Prof. Group Inf. Theory **1**(1), 108–113 (1953)
7. Shi, C., Xu, D., Zhou, Y., Tu, W.: Range-DOA information and scattering information in phased-array radar. In: 2019 IEEE 5th International Conference on Computer and Communications (ICCC), pp. 747–752 (2019)
8. Doyuran, U.C., Tanik, Y.: Detection of multiple targets in non-gaussian clutter. In: 2008 IEEE Radar Conference, pp. 1–5 (2008)
9. Amar, A., Weiss, A.J.: Fundamental limitations on the resolution of deterministic signals. IEEE Trans. Signal Process. **56**(11), 5309–5318 (2008)
10. Jiang, H., Tang, X.: Polarimetric MIMO radar target detection based on glow-worm swarm optimization algorithm. In: 2014 IEEE International Conference on Acoustics, Speech and Signal Processing (ICASSP), pp. 805–809 (2014)
11. Tian, J., Zhang, H., Wu, D., Yuan, D.: QoS-constrained medium access probability optimization in wireless interference-limited networks. IEEE Trans. Commun. **66**(3), 1064–1077 (2018)
12. Qiao, J., Alouini, M.: Secure transmission for intelligent reflecting surface-assisted mmWave and terahertz systems. IEEE Wirel. Commun. Lett., 1 (2020)
13. Zhong, W., Xu, L., Zhu, Q., Chen, X., Zhou, J.: MmWave beamforming for UAV communications with unstable beam pointing. China Commun. **16**(1), 37–46 (2019)
14. Zhu, Q., et al.: A novel 3D non-stationary wireless MIMO channel simulator and hardware emulator. IEEE Trans. Commun. **66**(9), 3865–3878 (2018)
15. Ma, N., Wang, L., Tang, J., Liao, Q., Zhang, Y.: Cognitive target detection based on Bayesian approach in radar. J. Eng. **2019**(21), 7476–7479 (2019)
16. Richards, M.A.: Fundamentals of Radar Signal Processing, 2e (2005)
17. Jaynes, E.: Information theory and statistical mechanics. Phys. Rev. **106**(4), 620–630 (1957)
18. Johnson, O.: Information Theory and the Central Limit Theorem. Imperial College Press (2004)

A Novel Parking Lot Occupancy Detection System Based on LED Sensing

Dazhuang Sun[✉], Jing Chen, and Jie Hao

College of Computer Science and Technology,
Nanjing University of Aeronautics and Astronautics, Nanjing, China
{sundazhuang,cjcj81,haojie}@nuaa.edu.cn

Abstract. For the great market value, intelligent parking lot detection system has been studied extensively. Generally, additional sensors such as wide-angle lens cameras, ultrasonic detectors, pressure sensors and so on are required to be deployed in the parking lots, which incur high deployment cost. Considering the lighting infrastructures are widely deployed in the underground garage and the occupancy of a parking lot changes the ambient light intensity, in this paper we novelly reuse the existing lighting infrastructure and exploit the light sensing capacity of the light emitting diode (LED) to monitor the occupancy of the parking lots. The LED illuminators can be switched between light emitting and sensing state so that during sensing state, LED illuminators can work as light sensors. In our scheme, we feed the data collected by LED illuminators in a typical machine learning method, Support Vector Machine (SVM) algorithm to achieve accurate detection accuracy. We conduct simulative experiments and demonstrate the feasibility and effectiveness of the proposed LED sensing based parking lot occupancy detection system. The detection accuracy reaches 98.70%.

Keywords: Visible light technology · Machine learning · Intelligent parking system · Support Vector Machine · Automatic parking space detection

1 Introduction

The worldwide civilian vehicles maintain rapid growth in volume for decades. In China alone, the number of civilian vehicles in the past decade has reached an average of 140.63 million [1]. The rapid growth of civilian vehicles brings increasing demands of intelligent parking management system [2,3].

The essential issue in an intelligent parking management system is to detect accurately if the parking lots are occupied by vehicles. Existing parking management systems generally deploy cameras [3–5], ultrasonic detectors [6–8], pressure sensors [9], infrared detector [10] and so on for occupancy detection. These systems all require the deployment of extra equipment at the parking space.

© ICST Institute for Computer Sciences, Social Informatics and Telecommunications Engineering 2021
Published by Springer Nature Switzerland AG 2021. All Rights Reserved
M. Guan and Z. Na (Eds.): MLICOM 2020, LNICST 342, pp. 346–355, 2021.
https://doi.org/10.1007/978-3-030-66785-6_37

What's more, some systems (e.g. using the pressure sensors) even need ground reconstruction. Such as, the method proposed by the author of [3] is to pre-calculate the pixel value difference between the parking space and the registered space groove image. In this way, the occupancy of the parking space is detected. However, there are many difficulties in classifying parking spaces under many conditions in this design. Both natural light and headlamps can cause dramatic changes in image intensity. The wide-angle lens camera used in the design of [2] will cause a large image distortion, and the detection result will also be affected by vehicles, pedestrians or various obstacles.

Fortunately, lighting infrastructure is mandatory in most garages in which economic and energy efficient LED eliminators are mounted on the ceiling of the garages for illumination, particularly in the underground garages [11]. Besides illuminating, LED eliminators can also sense the ambient light intensity by biasing the LED driver and can be used as light sensors. As the occupancy of a parking lot will impact the light diffusion reflection, LED light sensor is an ideal candidate for occupancy estimation. Inputting the gathered data from LED light sensor into Machine learning algorithms yields an inference result for parking lot occupancy. Therefore, in the paper, we aim to design a parking lot occupancy detection system which reuses the existing lighting infrastructure without additional deployment cost for occupancy detection.

In the proposed system, we redesign the driver of the LED eliminators and switch them between the light illuminating state and light sensing state in a high frequency without incurring flicker. During the sensing state, the LED eliminators senses the ambient light diffusion reflection and then feed the sensing measurements to the occupancy inference algorithm to infer the occupancy results. This paper is organized as follows. Section 2 introduces how to design the LED sensing based system and employ Support Vector Machine algorithm to process collected data. In Sect. 3, we conduct simulative experiments to validate the proposed system. Section 4 concludes this paper.

Fig. 1. Underground garage

2   LED Sensing Based Parking Lot Detection System

In this section, we firstly illustrate how to drive the LED eliminators as the light sensors and then describe the parking lot occupancy inference algorithm.

2.1   LED as Parking Lot Occupancy Sensor

The target underground garage is shown in Fig. 1. When designing an underground garage intelligent parking system, we need to consider the standard dimension of vehicles which is shown in Table 1.

Table 1. Standard dimension of vehicles and parking space

	Minicar	Small car	Parking lot
Height (m)	1.8	2.0	≥ 2.2
Length (m)	3.8	4.8	2.5~2.7
Width (m)	1.6	1.8	5~6

The LED driver is redesigned in order to allow the LED to switch between light emitting state and light sensing state.

Due to the low SNR of a single LED bulb and also the illumination requirement, the LED illuminator mounted on the ceiling in the parking lot detection system is actually an LED array consisting of multiple LED bulbs. We refer to the LED illuminator as LED array hereafter. In order to enable the LED array to switch between the light emitting and sensing states, the LED array needs to connect to a Microcontroller Unit (MCU) by a bidirectional interface as shown in Fig. 2 and the specific connection method is shown in Table 2. Moreover, Fig. 3 re-designs the LED driving circuit as in [12,13]. When both switches SW1 and SW2 are turned on at the same time, the LED array works in the light emitting state. When only switch SW3 is turned on, the circuit is in the ready-to-light-sensing state and the remaining charge on the LED array is cleared. When both switches SW4 and SW5 are turned on, the LED array switches to the light sensing state. When the LED array senses the reflected light from a vehicle , it can generate a small photocurrent. To measure the generated photocurrent, we use resistor R2 greater than $10\,M\Omega$ to convert the weak photocurrent into a voltage signal that drives the amplifier to produce the sensing result.

2.2   LED Sensing Based Vehicle Detection

As shown in Fig. 4, when a vehicle enters the parking lot covered by an LED array, the LED array can capture the change of light diffusion caused by the vehicle movement. Figure 5 presents the LED reading caused by the occupancy of a vehicle. During the first 60 s, there is no car in the parking lot and the LED

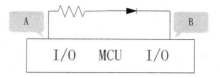

Fig. 2. Bidirectional interface between LED and MCU.

Table 2. The way the LED array connects to the I/O pins of the MCU

Working state	A–I/O	B–I/O	Description
Light emitting	VCC	GND	In the LED lighting status, the anode and cathode of the LED array are connected to VCC and GND through a simple I/O configuration
Ready-to-sense	GND	VCC	When the LED array is to be used for light sensing, the I/O configuration needs to be restored to the reverse bias mode, and the internal stray capacitance of the LED array needs to be charged
Light sensing	GND	IN	During the light sensing status, MCU reads the voltage change across the LED cathode and calculates the time it takes for the photocurrent to discharge the capacitor to the digital input threshold of the I/O pin and further the amount of incident light

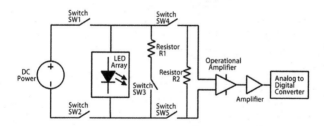

Fig. 3. LED array sensing circuit.

reading stays in a low level. Until 60 s, a vehicle enters the parking lot and the LED reading increases largely and stays in a high level afterwards. This implies that the occupancy detection can be realized by comparing the LED reading.

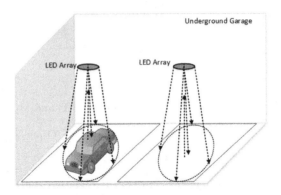

Fig. 4. Vehicles within the sensing range of the LED array.

We also explore the impact of the vehicle height on the LED reading. Figure 5(a) and Fig. 5(b) shows the LED reading when the distance between the vehicle roof and the LED array is 40 cm and 100 cm, respectively. In Fig. 5(a), due to the close proximity, the LED reading change resulted by the occupancy is high up to 0.15 V. In Fig. 5(b), the LED reading caused by the vehicle occupancy only increases by about 0.1 V, which is nevertheless can be detected easily. By comparison, we can conclude that the farther vehicle roof from the LED array, the more difficult it is to accurately infer the occupancy of the parking lot. The height of a vehicle is typically 1.6-1.8 m and the height of the garage is typically 2.2–2.8 m. Thus the distance of the vehicle roof and the LED array is roughly 0.4–1.2 m, which means the proposed LED sensing based occupancy detection is feasible in most cases.

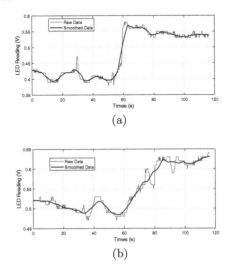

Fig. 5. Raw and smoothed LED readings.

Due to the raw voltage signals collected by LED array are subject to random noise and so on, we use a exponential moving average method to remove the noise from the raw LED reading.

$$v_t = k * v_{t-1} + (1 - k) * \alpha_t \tag{1}$$

where α_t is the raw voltage value at time t, v_t is the weight voltage value at time t, and k is the weight. The smoothed LED readings can be seen in Fig. 5. As the parking lot occupancy detection can be formulated as a binary classification, we feed the smoothed LED readings in Support Vector Machine (SVM) [14], as it is proven efficient in [12], and obtain the inference result.

3   Evaluation

In order to verify the proposed LED sensing based parking lot occupancy system, we conduct extensive simulative experiments. We use five paperboards in the most common colors, including black, white, red, frosting red, frosting black, to mimic the vehicles. Figure 6 shows the detailed experiment setup. The LED eliminator consists of the LED driver as shown in Fig. 6(a) and the LED array including 8 × 12 LED chips [15]. We use ultra-low-power microcontrollers MSP430F2418 as the MCU of the driver circuit [16]. The LED array take one sample every 1 ms the Fig. 6(c) shows the five paperboards in different colors. As measured, the field of view (FoV) of the LED eliminator is about 30 degree as shown in Fig. 6(d). According to the construction standard of the underground garage, the height of the garage is generally 2.2 m–3 m. It can be calculated that

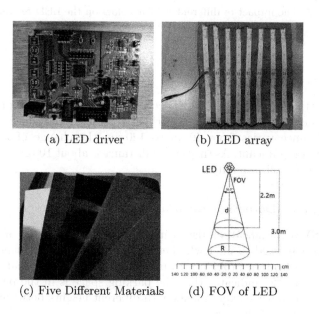

(a) LED driver   (b) LED array

(c) Five Different Materials   (d) FoV of LED

Fig. 6. Experimental setup.

the coverage area of one LED eliminator is much less than the area of one parking lot. Therefore, we can ignore the interference of the surrounding environment on the occupancy detection.

3.1 Impact of Vehicle Color

In this subsection, we explore the impact of vehicle colors on the LED readings. Figure 7 shows the LED reading change caused by the vehicle presence with different colors. When the vehicle is white, the change of LED reading is the most significant and black incurs the most trivial change. This conforms to our intuition since the white object reflects the light of all colors and on the contrary the black object absorbs all light. Also, we observed that frosted paperboards incurs less change too.

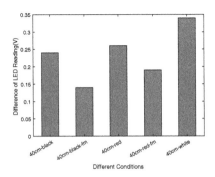

Fig. 7. The impact of different vehicle colors on the LED readings.

3.2 Impact of Distance

Figure 8 illustrates the change of LED reading caused by vehicle presence with varying distance between the white paperboard (vehicle roof) and the LED array. With the distance varies from 40 cm to 120 cm, the change of LED reading becomes more insignificant. As the typical distance is about 100 cm, the proposed system can work well in reality.

3.3 Occupancy Detection Accuracy

We use the SVM classification algorithm to infer the occupancy of the parking space. As we only need to infer whether the parking lot is occupancy or not, it is a binary classification problem. Assume that "1" indicates that the parking space is free, and "2" indicates that the parking space is in the parking space. We carried out extensive experiments with different heights between the vehicle roof and the ceiling of the garage.

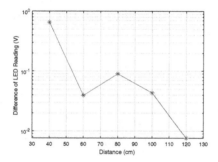

Fig. 8. The change of LED reading v.s. varying distances.

Table 3. Accuracy and precision of parking space detection

Distance	Accuracy	Precision
0.4 m	98.70%	98.07%
1.0 m	86.04%	78.27%

We move the paperboards of different colors into the coverage of LED array and move it out at vertical distance 1 m and 0.4 cm repeatedly, 20 times for each paperboard. Thus for each vertical distance about 3550×20 samples in total are collected and 70% samples are used as the training data. Accuracy and precision are used to evaluate the performance. The two metrics are defined as

$$accuracy = \frac{(TP + TN)}{(TP + FN + FP + TN)}, \tag{2}$$

$$precision = \frac{TP}{(TP + FP)}, \tag{3}$$

respectively, where TP denotes true positive, FN denotes false negative, FP denotes false positive, TN denotes true negative. The obtained occupancy detection accuracy and precision are shown in Table 3. The accuracy rate of the detection results of the SVM algorithm reaches 98.70% when the vertical distance is 0.4 m. The accuracy would stay above 86.04% as the vertical distance is generally below 1.0 m. The accuracy can be further improved by increasing the LED array size.

4 Conclusion

In this paper, we novelly reuse the existing lighting infrastructure and exploit the light sensing capacity of LED to detect the occupancy of the parking lots. The LED illuminators can be switched between light emitting and sensing states so that during sensing state, LED illuminators can work as light sensors. We conduct simulations and demonstrate the feasibility and effectiveness of the proposed LED sensing based parking lot occupancy detection system.

Currently, we only conduct simulative experiments and we plan to deploy a testbed in an underground garage and collect daily data to evaluate the practicality of the proposed system. Our system only considers the LED deployment that one LED eliminator is mounted on the top of one parking lot. In reality, in order to save costs, a single LED eliminator may cover multiple parking lots. Therefore, we plan to verify the feasibility of one LED eliminator monitoring multiple parking lots.

In this paper, we only use SVM to infer the occupancy. As the collected LED readings are of high temporal correlation, LSTM, Markov model and the other algorithms considering temporal correlation might improve the detection accuracy highly. Thus in the future work we aim to exploit more inference algorithms.

References

1. National data: National bureau of statistics of china. http://data.stats.gov.cn/easyquery.htm?cn=C01
2. Cho, W., et al.: Robust parking occupancy monitoring system using random forests. In: 2018 International Conference on Electronics, Information, and Communication (ICEIC), pp. 1–4, January 2018. https://doi.org/10.23919/ELINFOCOM.2018.8330608
3. Shih, S., Tsai, W.: A convenient vision-based system for automatic detection of parking spaces in indoor parking lots using wide-angle cameras. IEEE Trans. Veh. Technol. 63(6), 2521–2532 (2014). https://doi.org/10.1109/TVT.2013.2297331
4. Li, Q., Lin, C., Zhao, Y.: Geometric features-based parking slot detection. Sensors 18(9), 2821 (2018)
5. Jang, C., Sunwoo, M.: Semantic segmentation-based parking space detection with standalone around view monitoring system. Mach. Vis. Appl. 30(2), 309–319 (2018). https://doi.org/10.1007/s00138-018-0986-z
6. Shao, Y., Chen, P., Cao, T.: A grid projection method based on ultrasonic sensor for parking space detection. In: IGARSS 2018–2018 IEEE International Geoscience and Remote Sensing Symposium, pp. 3378–3381 (2018)
7. Suhr, J.K., Jung, H.G.: Automatic parking space detection and tracking for underground and indoor environments. IEEE Trans. Industr. Electron. 63(9), 5687–5698 (2016)
8. Suhr, J.K., Jung, H.G.: Sensor fusion-based vacant parking slot detection and tracking. IEEE Trans. Intell. Transp. Syst. 15(1), 21–36 (2014)
9. Mahdi, M.D., Anik, Z.H., Ahsan, R., Motahar, T.: EZ parking: smart parking space reservation using internet of things. In: 2018 International Conference on Advanced Computer Science and Information Systems (ICACSIS), pp. 113–118 (2018)
10. Yuan, C., Qian, L.: Design of intelligent parking lot system based on wireless network. In: 2017 29th Chinese Control And Decision Conference (CCDC), pp. 3596–3601, May 2017. https://doi.org/10.1109/CCDC.2017.7979129
11. Pérez-Gosende, P.A.: AHP-based approach for lighting system selection in an underground parking. In: The 17th LACCEI International Multi-Conference for Engineering, Education, and Technology: "Industry, Innovation, and Infrastructure for Sustainable Cities and Communities" (2019)

12. Yang, Y., Jie, H., Luo, J., Pan, S.J.: CeilingSee: device-free occupancy inference through lighting infrastructure based LED sensing. In: IEEE International Conference on Pervasive Computing and Communications (2017)
13. Xu, X., et al.: PassiveVLC: enabling practical visible light backscatter communication for battery-free IoT applications, pp. 180–192 (10 2017). https://doi.org/10.1145/3117811.3117843
14. Tax, D., Duin, R.: Support vector data description. Mach. Learn. **54**, 45–66 (01 2004). https://doi.org/10.1023/B:MACH.0000008084.60811.49
15. Luxeon xf-3535l. https://www.lumileds.com/uploads/487/DS142-pdf
16. Msp430f2418. http://www.ti.com/product/MSP430F2418

Intelligent Space and Terrestrial Integrated Networks

Outage Probability Analysis of UAV Assisted Satellite-Terrestrial Network

Tao Teng, Xiangbin Yu$^{(\boxtimes)}$, Xiaomin Chen, Kai Yu, and Guangying Wang

College of Electronic and Information Engineering,
Nanjing University of Aeronautics and Astronautics, Nanjing 211106, China
tengtaon@163.com, yxb_xwy@hotmail.com, chenxm402@nuaa.edu.cn,
yukai152163@163.com, wanggy2010@qq.com

Abstract. Satellite and UAV (unmanned aerial vehicle) communication are two vital techniques to support the upcoming 5G and beyond 5G network. Based on this, the paper considers a downlink UAV assisted hybrid satellite-terrestrial network under cognitive radio communication (HSTCN), a framework consisting of a hovering UAV and terrestrial distributed antenna system (DAS) is proposed, which is novel and complex. Our goal is to analyze the outage probability (OP) of satellite user under cognitive radio terrestrial network interference, in which the decode-and-forward UAV relay is applied to help signal transmission. The approximated closed-form outage probability is derived, experimental results are performed to demonstrate the correctness of the proposed OP results and reveal the impact of different system parameters on the satellite-terrestrial model.

Keywords: Distributed antenna system · Shadowed Rician fading · UAV · Cognitive radio · Outage probability

1 Introduction

In the age of 5G, more and more communication devices, accessed to terrestrial network, congest the communication [1,2]. Satellite and flying vehicles, such as unmanned aerial vehicles(UAV), airplanes, are applied to expanding terrestrial communication coverage, providing seamless connectivity and so on [3–6].

The idea of a hybrid satellite-terrestrial cognitive network (HSTCN) was established for satellite network integrating into terrestrial network, the satellite is licensed in air-to-ground network to operate in the same frequency band so that spectrum management works [7–12]. Yuhan Ruan et al. in [13] investigated the outage probability(OP) of an integral satellite-terrestrial network with intra-cell interference. Oluwatayo Y. Kolawole et al. in [14] studied the OP and the spectral efficiency of the proposed HSTCN where satellite network shares resources with terrestrial network. Kang An et al. in [15] researched the physical layer security of the proposed HSTCN, the optimal beamforming and

© ICST Institute for Computer Sciences, Social Informatics and Telecommunications Engineering 2021
Published by Springer Nature Switzerland AG 2021. All Rights Reserved
M. Guan and Z. Na (Eds.): MLICOM 2020, LNICST 342, pp. 359–370, 2021.
https://doi.org/10.1007/978-3-030-66785-6_38

power allocation algorithm was designed. Xingwang Li et al. in [16] proposed an unified framework for hybrid satellite/UAV terrestrial non orthogonal multiple access(NOMA) network, the approximate closed-form expression of the OP was obtained. Based on the approximate OP expression, the location optimization of UAV was analyzed. Xiaokai Zhang et al. in [17] investigated the OP and the ergodic capacity of NOMA based on the hybrid satellite-terrestrial network. The terrestrial network is used as relay cooperating with primary satellite network. Silin Xie et al. in [18] derived the closed-form expression of the OP with NOMA transmission. Imperfect channel state information was considered at all nodes.

The integration of the satellite and UAV could be applied to serve the remote areas as well as the disaster areas. UAV often acts as a relay to help satellite signal transmitting or terrestrial network transmitting. Research the architecture of [19–22] satellite-terrestrial network with the aid of the UAV. Xiaomin Chen et al. researched the multi-hop UAV assisted channel model establishment. With the proposed model, the OP, bit error rate and channel capacity are analyzed and derived [23, 24] . Optimization problems such as maximizing the system transmitting rate, finding the optimal UAV trajectory, power allocation of both the satellite and UAV groups are provided. It can be found that UAV fits well with the satellite-terrestrial network and the power allocation association is vital in the integration of satellite-UAV networks. Pankaj K. Sharma et al. in [25] investigated a hybrid satellite terrestrial network with decode-and-forward(DF) protocol and stochastic geometry. The outage probability under opportunistic UAV relay selection was provided, the secure outage probability of the proposed system model was analyzed in [26] either. Ting Qi et al. integrated NOMA into satellite-UAV network, both the outage probability and the power allocation algorithm were proposed to guarantee the fairness between two NOMA users [27].

Motivated by the aforementioned papers, in this paper, we construct a novel satellite-terrestrial network which consists of a UAV and a single cell DAS. Cognitive radio with underlay mode is applied to integrate the satellite with the terrestrial network. Outage probability is chosen to analyze the system performance. We make the following contributions: (1) A novel framework containing UAV and DAS is built for downlink performance analysis. (2) Cognitive radio is applied for satellite-terrestrial network integration, which makes the outage probability derivation difficult. (3) An approximated closed-form OP is derived, the related simulation is implemented to analyze the proposed model.

2   System Model

As shown in Fig. 1, we consider a downlink UAV assisted HSTCN which consists of one geosynchronous orbit(GEO) satellite s, one UAV relay g, N_t DA ports $b_1, \cdots, b_{N_t}$, one primary terrestrial user (PTU) pu, and one secondary satellite user (SSU) su. Satellite s communicates with SSU with the help of UAV by using DF protocol. At the same time, DA ports transmit signals to PTU, which causes interference to SSU under the same spectrum. For ease of analysis, all of the nodes are equipped with one antenna. Besides, by supposing a poor channel condition between satellite and SSU, the direct link is blocked.

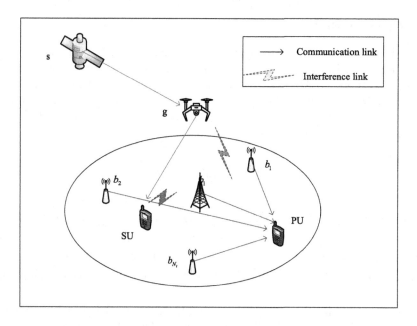

Fig. 1. System model

2.1 Signal Model

The communication between s and SSU takes place in a two-time phase. The received signal at UAV in the first phase can be given by

$$y_g = \sqrt{p_s}\sqrt{G_{s,g}}h_{s,g}x_s + n_g,\qquad(1)$$

At the second time slot, g decodes the received signal y_g and then retransmits to SSU. Thus, the received signal at SSU is written as

$$y_{su} = \sqrt{p_g}\sqrt{G_{g,su}}h_{g,su}x_s + \sum_{i=1}^{N_t}\sqrt{p_{bi}}\sqrt{G_{bi,su}}h_{bi,su}s_{bi} + n_{su}.\qquad(2)$$

where $n_g \sim CN\left(0,\sigma_g^2\right)$ and $n_{su} \sim CN\left(0,\sigma_{su}^2\right)$. To ensure the interference at PTU beyond to I_{th}, the transmitting power at UAV must satisfy

$$p_g = \min\left\{\frac{I_{th}}{\left|h_{g,pu}\right|^2}, p_{g\,\max}\right\},\qquad(3)$$

where I_{th} means interference-power threshold. By combining (2) with (3), the SINR at SSU can be formulated as

$$\gamma_{su} = \frac{\min\left\{\bar{\gamma}_s G_{s,g}\left|h_{s,g}\right|^2, G_{g,su}\left|h_{g,su}\right|^2\min\left\{\frac{\bar{\gamma}_{th}}{\left|h_{g,pu}\right|^2}, \bar{\gamma}_{g\,\max}\right\}\right\}}{\sum_{i=1}^{N_t}\bar{\gamma}_{bi}G_{bi,su}\left|h_{bi,su}\right|^2 + 1}.\qquad(4)$$

where $\bar{\gamma}_s = p_s/\sigma_g^2, \bar{\gamma}_{th} = I_{th}/\sigma_{su}^2, \bar{\gamma}_{bi} = p_{bi}/\sigma_{su}^2$.

2.2   Channel Model

The traditional satellite-terrestrial model includes the Loo model, Corazza model, etc. [28]. However, the theoretical probability density function(PDF) is complex. Authors Ali Abdi etc. in [29] proposed a simple model for Land Mobile Satellite(LMS) Channel named Shadowed Rician(SR) model with parameters (b_s, m_s, Ω_s). Under the situation of integer values m_s, references [30, 31] proposed a simple SR PDF expression, which can be written as

$$f(x) = \alpha \sum_{k=0}^{m_s-1} \zeta(k) x^k \exp\left(-(\beta - \delta) x\right). \tag{5}$$

where $\alpha = \left[(2b_s)^{m_s+1} m_s{}^{m_s}\right] / [(2b_s m_s + \Omega_s)^{m_s}]$, $\delta = \Omega_s / [2b_s (2b_s m_s + \Omega_s)]$. $\beta = 1/(2b_s)$, Ω_s is the average power of the shadow fading, $2b_s$ represents the average power of the multipath, $m_s \in (0, \infty)$ means the fading parameter of the shadow fading. $\zeta(k) = \left[(-1)^k (1 - m_s)_k \delta^k\right] / \left[(k!)^2\right]$, $(\cdot)_p$ is the Pochhammer symbol.

The channel fading between UAV and PTU/SSU is modelled as Rician fading. The PDF and cumulative distribution function(CDF) of the Rician channel can be written as

$$f(x) = (1 + K) \exp\left(-((1 + K) x + K)\right) I_0\left(\sqrt{4K(K+1) x}\right), \tag{6}$$

$$F(x) = 1 - Q_1\left(\sqrt{2K}, \sqrt{2(1+K) x}\right). \tag{7}$$

where K is Rician factor, $Q_M(a, b)$ means the Marcum Q function with order M. Besides, the channel between DA ports and SSU is assumed as Nakagami fading. Let $G_{s,g} = L_{s,g} G_s G_g \left(J_1(x)/(2x) + (36 J_3(x))/x^3\right)$ denote the propagation gain including free-space loss and antenna gain at both the satellite and the UAV, which can be described in [14]. Let $G_{g,su}$ and $G_{bi,su}$ be the antenna gain between the UAV/DA ports to SU, which has been described as $G_{g,su} = G_g G_{su} L_{g,su}$, $G_{bi,su} = G_{bi} G_{su} L_{bi,su}$ with $L_{\varsigma,su} = \left(h_{\varsigma,su}^2 + z_{\varsigma,su}^2\right)^{-\alpha/2}$, $\varsigma \in \{g, b_i\}$ respectively. $h_{\varsigma,su}$ is the difference in height between g/b_i and SSU, $z_{\varsigma,su}$ denotes the difference on the ground plane between SSU and the projection of ς. α means the path loss index. Based on the above definitions, the outage probability can be derived in the following section.

3   Outage Probability Analysis

Outage probability is defined as the probability that the transmitting link capacity falls below the needed user rate, which also can be written as:

$$F_1(x) = \Pr\left\{ \frac{\min\left\{ \bar{\gamma}_s G_{s,g}|h_{s,g}|^2, G_{g,su}|h_{g,su}|^2 \min\left\{ \frac{\bar{\gamma}_{th}}{|h_{g,pu}|^2}, \bar{\gamma}_{g\max} \right\} \right\}}{\sum_{i=1}^{N_t} \bar{\gamma}_{bi} G_{bi,su}|h_{bi,su}|^2 + 1} \le x \right\}$$

$$= \int_0^\infty F_2(xu) f_7(u)\, du. \tag{8}$$

where $F_2(x)$ denotes the probability that the numerator of (4) falls below x. To proceed further, $F_2(x)$ can be decomposed as:

$$F_2(x) = \Pr\left\{ \min\left\{ \bar{\gamma}_s G_{s,g}|h_{s,g}|^2, G_{g,su}|h_{g,su}|^2 \min\left\{ \frac{\bar{\gamma}_{th}}{|h_{g,pu}|^2}, \bar{\gamma}_{g\max} \right\} \right\} \le x \right\}$$

$$= F_3(x) + F_4(x) - F_3(x)F_4(x), \tag{9}$$

As is derived in [30], the closed-form expression of $F_3(x)$ is shown as:

$$F_3(x) = \Pr\left\{ \bar{\gamma}_s G_{s,g}|h_{s,g}|^2 \le x \right\}$$

$$= 1 - \alpha \sum_{k_5=0}^{m_s-1} \zeta(k) \sum_{p=0}^{k_5} \frac{k_5!}{p!}(\beta - \delta)^{-(k_5+1-p)}\left(\frac{x}{\bar{\gamma}_s G_{s,g}}\right)^p \exp\left(-\frac{x(\beta - \delta)}{\bar{\gamma}_s G_{s,g}}\right), \tag{10}$$

Moreover, $F_4(x)$ can be decomposed into two independent outage probability items, which gives the following equation:

$$F_4(x) = \Pr\left(\min\left\{ \frac{\bar{\gamma}_{th}}{|h_{g,pu}|^2}, \bar{\gamma}_{g\max} \right\} G_{g,su}|h_{g,su}|^2 \le x \right)$$

$$= \Pr\left\{ \frac{\bar{\gamma}_{th}}{|h_{g,pu}|^2} G_{g,su}|h_{g,su}|^2 \le x, \frac{\bar{\gamma}_{th}}{|h_{g,pu}|^2} < \bar{\gamma}_{g\max} \right\}$$

$$+ \Pr\left\{ \frac{\bar{\gamma}_{th}}{|h_{g,pu}|^2} > \bar{\gamma}_{g\max}, \bar{\gamma}_{g\max} G_{g,su}|h_{g,su}|^2 \le x \right\}, \tag{11}$$

By applying (6), (7) into (11) and utilizing [32] (Eq. 8), the closed-form expression of $F_4(x)$ is obtained. Then putting $F_4(x)$ together with $F_3(x)$ into $F_2(x)$, with variable substitution and simplification, the expression of $F_2(x)$ is written as:

$$F_2\left(x\right)=1-\sum_{k_1=0}^{\infty}\sum_{k_2=0}^{\infty}\sum_{k_5=0}^{m_s-1}\sum_{p=0}^{k_5}\Psi\left(k_1,k_2,k_5,p\right)\frac{x^{p+k_2}\exp\left(-\frac{x(\beta-\delta)}{\bar{\gamma}_s G_{s,g}}\right)}{\left[\frac{(1+K_{su})x}{G_{g,su}\bar{\gamma}_{th}}+(1+K_{pu})\right]^{k_2+k_1+1}}\times$$

$$\Gamma\left(k_2+k_1+1,\frac{(1+K_{su})x}{G_{g,su}\bar{\gamma}_{g\,max}}+\frac{(1+K_{pu})\bar{\gamma}_{th}}{\bar{\gamma}_{g\,max}}\right)-\sum_{k_4=0}^{\infty}\sum_{k_6=0}^{m_s-1}\sum_{p_1=0}^{k_6}\Psi\left(k_4,k_6,p_1\right)\times$$

$$x^{k_4+p_1}\exp\left(-\left(\frac{\beta-\delta}{\bar{\gamma}_s G_{s,g}}+\frac{1+K_{su}}{\bar{\gamma}_{g\,max}G_{g,su}}\right)x\right). \tag{12}$$

where K_{su} and K_{pu} denote the Rician fading parameters of $|h_{g,su}|^2$ and $|h_{g,pu}|^2$ respectively. $\Psi\left(k_1,k_2,k_5,p\right)$ and $\Psi\left(k_4,k_6,p_1\right)$ are given as follows:

$$\Psi\left(k_1,k_2,k_5,p\right)=\exp\left(-K_{su}-K_{pu}\right)\alpha\frac{\zeta\left(k_5\right)k_5!(\beta-\delta)^{-(k_5+1-p)}}{p!(\bar{\gamma}_s G_{s,g})^p}\times$$

$$\frac{(K_{pu}+1)^{k_1+1}(K_{pu})^{k_1}}{k_1!k_1 k_2!}\left(\frac{1+K_{su}}{G_{g,su}\bar{\gamma}_{th}}\right)^{k_2}\sum_{k_0=0}^{\infty}\frac{K_{su}^{k_0+k_2}}{(k_0+k_2)}, \tag{13}$$

$$\Psi\left(k_4,k_6,p_1\right)=\left[1-Q_1\left(\sqrt{2K_{pu}},\sqrt{\frac{2\left(1+K_{pu}\right)\bar{\gamma}_{th}}{\bar{\gamma}_{g\,max}}}\right)\right]\exp\left(-K_{su}\right)\times$$

$$\frac{\alpha\zeta\left(k_6\right)}{k_4!}\left(\frac{K_{su}\left(1+K_{su}\right)}{\bar{\gamma}_{g\,max}G_{g,su}}\right)^{k_4}\sum_{k_3=0}^{\infty}\frac{K_{su}^{k_3}}{(k_3+k_4)}\frac{k_6!(\beta-\delta)^{-(k_6+1-p_1)}}{p_1!(\bar{\gamma}_s G_{s,g})^{p_1}}. \tag{14}$$

As is discussed in [33], the PDF of the denominator in (4), denoted by $f_7\left(x\right)$, can be approximated as

$$f_7\left(x\right)=x^{m_b-1}\frac{e^{-x/\Omega_b}}{\Omega_b^{m_b}\Gamma\left(m_b\right)}. \tag{15}$$

where the shape parameter $m_b=\left(\sum_{i=1}^{N_t}\bar{\gamma}_{bi}G_{bi,su}\Omega_{su}\right)^2\Big/\left(\sum_{i=1}^{N_t}\bar{\gamma}_{bi}^2 G_{bi,su}^2\frac{\Omega_{su}^2}{m_{su}}\right)$,

the scale parameter $\Omega_b=\left(\sum_{i=1}^{N_t}\bar{\gamma}_{bi}^2 G_{bi,su}^2\frac{\Omega_{su}^2}{m_{su}}\right)\Big/\left(\sum_{i=1}^{N_t}\bar{\gamma}_{bi}G_{bi,su}\Omega_{su}\right)$ respectively. Thus, by substituting (12), (15) into (8) ,the OP of the SSU can be transformed as:

$$F_1\left(x\right)=I_1-I_2-I_3. \tag{16}$$

Here we need to calculate I_1, I_2, I_3 in turn. The closed-form expression of I_1 can be expressed as:

$$I_1=\int_0^{\infty}\frac{u^{m_b-1}e^{-u/\Omega_b}}{\Omega_b^{m_b}\Gamma\left(m_b\right)}du=1, \tag{17}$$

We now derive the analytical expression of I_2. First, the incomplete Gamma function $\Gamma(1 + n, x)$ can be transformed as the finite series expansion of polynomial expression [32] (Eq. 8.352.7), then $(1 + u)^k$ is approximated to u^k for ease of computational complexity. Finally, I_2 can be derived with the aid of [32] (Eq. 7.813.1).

$$
I_2 \approx \sum_{k_1=0}^{\infty} \sum_{k_2=0}^{\infty} \sum_{k_5=0}^{m_s-1} \sum_{p=0}^{k_5} \Psi(k_1, k_2, k_5, p) \frac{(k_2+k_1)!}{\Omega_b^{m_b} \Gamma(m_b)} \left(\frac{\bar{\gamma}_{th}}{\bar{\gamma}_{g\,\max}}\right)^{k_2+k_1+1} x^{p+k_2} \times
$$

$$
\exp\left(-[\omega_s x + \omega_{su} x + \omega_{pu}]\right) \sum_{m_q=0}^{k_2+k_1} \frac{[\omega_{su} x + \omega_{pu}]^{m_q - k_2 - k_1 - 1}}{m_q!} \frac{\left[\omega_{su} x + \omega_s x + \frac{1}{\Omega_b}\right]^{-(p+k_2+m_b)}}{\Gamma(k_2+k_1+1-m_q)} \times
$$

$$
G_{21}^{12}\left(\frac{\omega_{su} x}{[\omega_{su} x + \omega_{pu}]\left[\omega_{su} x + \omega_s x + \frac{1}{\Omega_b}\right]} \middle| \begin{matrix} 1 - p - k_2 - m_b, m_q - k_2 - k_1 \\ 0 \end{matrix}\right),
$$

$$(18)$$

By substituting the last term of (12) and the formula of (15) into (8), with the same operation like I_2, $(1 + u)^k$ is approximated to u^k, the integration of I_3 can be derived. Thus, the analytical closed form expression of I_3 is given by

$$
I_3 \approx \sum_{k_4=0}^{\infty} \sum_{k_6=0}^{m-1} \sum_{p_1=0}^{k_6} \Psi(k_4, k_6, p_1) x^{k_4+p_1} \frac{\exp\left(-\left(\frac{\beta-\delta}{\bar{\gamma}_s G_{s,g}} + \frac{1+K_{su}}{\bar{\gamma}_{g\,\max} G_{g,su}}\right)x\right)}{\Omega_b^{m_b} \Gamma(m_b)} \times
$$

$$
\frac{\Gamma(k_4 + p_1 + m_b)}{\left(\frac{\beta-\delta}{\bar{\gamma}_s G_{s,g}} + \frac{1+K_{su}}{\bar{\gamma}_{g\,\max} G_{g,su}}\right)^{k_4+p_1+m_b}}.
$$

$$(19)$$

where $\omega_{su} = (1 + K_{su})/(G_{g,su} \bar{\gamma}_{g\,\max})$, $\omega_{pu} = [(1 + K_{pu}) \bar{\gamma}_{th}]/\bar{\gamma}_{g\,\max}$ and $\omega_s = (\beta - \delta)/(\bar{\gamma}_s G_{s,g})$. From the above analysis, OP at SSU can be computed with (17), (18), and (19). To obtain more insights, the numerical results are provided for OP analysis in the next section.

4   Numerical Results

In the simulations, the concrete antenna gain parameters and the channel fading parameters are given in Table 1. Besides, the location of UAV, DA ports and terrestrial users are defined in Table 2. The theoretical curves are obtained using (16)–(19) with the substitution of finite terms(such as 15 terms) We found that the theoretical results agree well with Monte Carlo simulation. The polar coordinates of DA prots are set as $\{2R/3, [2\pi(j-1)]/(N_t-1)\}$, $j = 2, \cdots, N_t$, where one DA port is located in the center. Shadowed Rician parameters are set as $(b_s, m_s, \Omega_s) = (0.251, 5, 0.279)$, Rician factors at SSU/PTU are set as $2/1$ respectively. $\sigma_g^2 = \sigma_{su}^2 = N_0$, Nakagami fading parameters are $(m_{su}, \Omega_{su}) = (1, 1)/(2, 5)$ respectively.

Figure 2 shows the results of the OP versus $p_{g\,\max}$. The transmitting power of satellite and DA ports are set as its maximum transmitting power. It can be found that the value of OP decreases when $p_{g\,\max}$ increases, this is because increasing the value of $p_{g\,\max}$ can enlarge the SINR of the total system. The

Table 1. Simulation parameters

Notation	Value
Carrier bandwidth W	500 MHz
Carrier frequency f_c	20 GHz
The variance of AWGN N_0	-110 dBm
Antenna gain $G_s/G_g/G_u/G_{bi}$	53 dB/15 dB/4.8 dB/15 dB
3 dB angle of the UAV $\phi_{3\,dB}$	0.4°
Off axis angle of the UAV ϕ	0.6°
Maximum transmitting power $p_s/p_g/p_{bi}$(dB)	50 dB/40 dB/20 dB

Table 2. Terrestrial network parameters

Notation	Value
Node Height $h_g/h_{bi}/h_u$	200 m/30 m/0 m
Radius of the DAS R	1000 m
Pass loss index α	4
Projection location of the UAV/SU/PU	$(0,0)/(500,\pi/3)/(300,3\pi/2)$

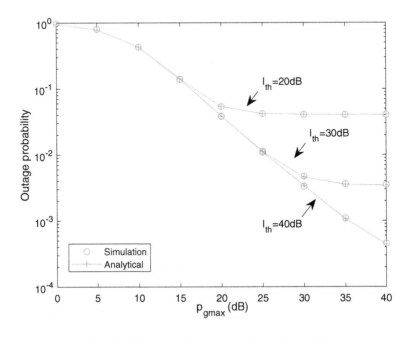

Fig. 2. OP with different cognitive threshold

curve of OP trends to be saturated eventually. It also can be found that when I_{th} increases, the value of OP decreases, when $I_{th} = 50$dB, the curve of OP decreases monotonically. Thus, when the interference power constraint is stricter, the OP of SSU is worse to protect the common communication between DAS and PTU.

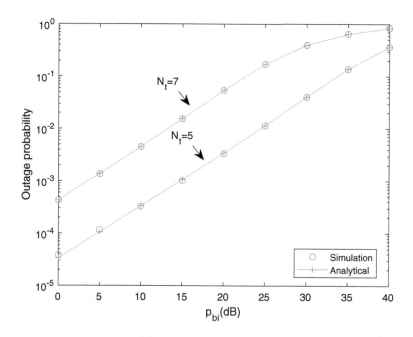

Fig. 3. OP with different number of DA ports

Figure 3 describes the OP for changing p_{bi} as well as the number of DA ports. It is obvious that when the transmitting power of DA port increases, the performance of OP decreases. This is because the transmitting signal of DA ports could cause interference to SSU. Moreover, if we increase the number of the DA ports, the OP at the SU will be worse. The reason for this phenomenon is that when the number of the DA ports increases, the condition of terrestrial communication becomes better, which causes the communication quality at SSU be worse. Besides, we can find that the approximated closed-form expression is still accurate despite of the approximation closed-form OP derivation in (18) and (19).

Finally, we investigate the outage probability performance based on the fixed satellite transmitting power and fixed UAV transmitting power(50 dB and 40 dB respectively)in Fig. 4. It is obvious that the value of the system OP increases when the transmitting power of the DAS increases. Moreover, when the transmitting channel at the terrestrial network become better, the system performance becomes worse than the previous. The main idea of Fig. 3 and Fig. 4 is

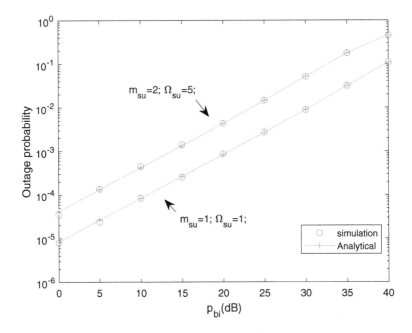

Fig. 4. OP with different values of m_{su}, Ω_{su}

illustrating the consequences of the terrestrial DAS network towards satellite communication. However, even if the proposed HSTCN needs to make a balance between satellite communication and the terrestrial network, air-ground integration did improve the total system transmission efficiency and expand the system coverage area. Several optimization problems for this model can be conducted to enhance system performance.

5 Conclusion

This paper presents a novel HSTCN model, where the framework containing UVA and DAS is set as terrestrial network. With mathematical derivation and integration operation, the closed-form OP expression of the satellite user is researched in this model. Compared with the existing work, our model is more complex and may contribute to the investigation of Satellite-UAV communication in the future. However, there are also some limitations in this paper, for example, the locations of the SSU, PTU, and the UAV are fixed, the asymptotic expression is also needed for OP performance analysis.

Acknowledgment. This work was supported in part by the National Key Scientific Instrument and Equipment Development Project under Grant No. 61827801 and in part by Aeronautical Science Foundation of China, No. 201901052001 and Postgraduate Research and Practice Innovation Program of Jiangsu Province (KYCX20-0202).

References

1. Tian, J., Zhang, H., Wu, D., Yuan, D.: QoS-constrained medium access probability optimization in wireless interference-limited networks. IEEE Trans. Commun. **66**(3), 1064–1077 (2017)
2. Qiao, J., Alouini, M.-S.: Secure transmission for intelligent reflecting surface-assisted mmwave and terahertz systems. arXiv preprint arXiv:2005.13451 (2020)
3. Vondra, M., Ozger, M., Schupke, D., Cavdar, C.: Integration of satellite and aerial communications for heterogeneous flying vehicles. IEEE Netw. **32**(5), 62–69 (2018)
4. Bai, L., et al.: Channel modeling for satellite communication channels at q-band in high latitude. IEEE Access **7**, 137691–137703 (2019)
5. Simunek, M., Font, F.P., Pechac, P.: The UAV low elevation propagation channel in urban areas: statistical analysis and time-series generator. IEEE Trans. Antennas Propag. **61**(7), 3850–3858 (2013)
6. Giambene, G., Kota, S., Pillai, P.: Satellite-5G integration: a network perspective. IEEE Network **32**(5), 25–31 (2018)
7. An, K., et al.: Performance analysis of multi-antenna hybrid satellite-terrestrial relay networks in the presence of interference. IEEE Trans. Commun. **63**(11), 4390–4404 (2015)
8. Lagunas, E., Sharma, S.K., Maleki, S., Chatzinotas, S., Ottersten, B.: Resource allocation for cognitive satellite communications with incumbent terrestrial networks. IEEE Trans. Cogn. Commun. Netw. **1**(3), 305–317 (2015)
9. Maleki, S., Chatzinotas, S., Krause, J., Liolis, K., Ottersten, B.: Cognitive zone for broadband satellite communications in 17.3c17.7 GHz band. IEEE Wireless Communications Letters **4**(3), 305–308 (2015)
10. Liang, T., An, K., Shi, S.: Statistical modeling-based deployment issue in cognitive satellite terrestrial networks. IEEE Wirel. Commun. Lett. **7**(2), 202–205 (2018)
11. Vassaki, S., Poulakis, M.I., Panagopoulos, A.D., Constantinou, P.: Power allocation in cognitive satellite terrestrial networks with QoS constraints. IEEE Commun. Lett. **17**(7), 1344–1347 (2013)
12. Wang, L., Li, F., Liu, X., Lam, K., Na, Z., Peng, H.: Spectrum optimization for cognitive satellite communications with cournot game model. IEEE Access **6**, 1624–1634 (2018)
13. Ruan, Y., Li, Y., Wang, C.-X., Zhang, R., Zhang, H.: Outage performance of integrated satellite-terrestrial networks with hybrid CCI. IEEE Commun. Lett. **21**(7), 1545–1548 (2017)
14. Kolawole, O.Y., Vuppala, S., Sellathurai, M., Ratnarajah, T.: On the performance of cognitive satellite-terrestrial networks. IEEE Trans. Cogn. Commun. Netw. **3**(4), 668–683 (2017)
15. An, K., Lin, M., Ouyang, J., Zhu, W.-P.: Secure transmission in cognitive satellite terrestrial networks. IEEE J. Sel. Areas Commun. **34**(11), 3025–3037 (2016)
16. Li, X., et al.: A unified framework for HS-UAV NOMA networks: performance analysis and location optimization. IEEE Access **8**, 13329–13340 (2020)
17. Zhang, X., et al.: Outage performance of NOMA-based cognitive hybrid satellite-terrestrial overlay networks by amplify-and-forward protocols. IEEE Access **7**, 85372–85381 (2019)
18. Xie, S., Zhang, B., Guo, D., Zhao, B.: Performance analysis and power allocation for NOMA-based hybrid satellite-terrestrial relay networks with imperfect channel state information. IEEE Access **7**, 136279–136289 (2019)

19. Zhu, Q., Wang, Y., Jiang, K., Chen, X., Zhong, W., Ahmed, N.: 3D non-stationary geometry-based multi-input multi-output channel model for UAV-ground communication systems. IET Microwaves Antennas Propag. **13**(8), 1104–1112 (2019)
20. Jiang, K., Chen, X., Zhu, Q., Chen, L., Xu, D., Chen, B.: A novel simulation model for nonstationary rice fading channels. Wirel. Commun. Mob. Comput. **2018**, 1–9 (2018)
21. Zhu, Q., et al.: A novel 3D non-stationary wireless MIMO channel simulator and hardware emulator. IEEE Trans. Commun. **66**(9), 3865–3878 (2018)
22. Zhu, Q., Liu, X., Yin, X., Chen, X., Xue, C.: A novel simulator of nonstationary random MIMO channels in Rayleigh fading scenarios. Int. J. Antennas Propag. **2016** 2016
23. Chen, X., Hu, X., Zhu, Q., Zhong, W., Chen, B.: Channel modeling and performance analysis for UAV relay systems. China Commun. **15**(12), 89–97 (2018)
24. Zhong, W., Xu, L., Zhu, Q., Chen, X., Zhou, J.: MmWave beamforming for UAV communications with unstable beam pointing. China Commun. **16**(1), 37–46 (2019)
25. Sharma, P.K., Deepthi, D., Kim, D.I.: Outage probability of 3-D mobile UAV relaying for hybrid satellite-terrestrial networks. IEEE Commun. Lett. **24**(2), 418–422 (2020)
26. Sharma, P.K., Kim, D.I.: Secure 3D mobile UAV relaying for hybrid satellite-terrestrial networks. IEEE Trans. Wirel. Commun. **19**(4), 2770–2784 (2020)
27. Qi, T., Feng, W., Wang, Y.: Outage performance of non-orthogonal multiple access based unmanned aerial vehicles satellite networks. China Commun. **15**(5), 1–8 (2018)
28. Loo, C.: A statistical model for a land mobile satellite link. IEEE Trans. Veh. Technol. **34**(3), 122–127 (1985)
29. Abdi, A., Lau, W.C., Alouini, M., Kaveh, M.: A new simple model for land mobile satellite channels: first- and second-order statistics. IEEE Trans. Wirel. Commun. **2**(3), 519–528 (2003)
30. Miridakis, N.I., Vergados, D.D., Michalas, A.: Dual-hop communication over a satellite relay and shadowed Rician channels. IEEE Trans. Veh. Technol. **64**(9), 4031–4040 (2015)
31. Upadhyay, P.K., Sharma, P.K.: Max-max user-relay selection scheme in multiuser and multirelay hybrid satellite-terrestrial relay systems. IEEE Commun. Lett. **20**(2), 268–271 (2016)
32. Gradshteyn, I.S., Ryzhik, I.M.: Table of Integrals, Series, and Products. Academic Press, Cambridge (2014)
33. Heath, R.W., Kountouris, M., Bai, T.: Modeling heterogeneous network interference using Poisson point processes. IEEE Trans. Signal Process. **61**(16), 4114–4126 (2013)

Design and Development of Intelligent Meter Data Acquisition Module Based on Bluetooth Technology

Xianyin Lai[✉]

University of Electronic Science and Technology of China, Zhongshan Institute,
Zhongshan 528400, China
Laixy081@163.com

Abstract. At present, the common communication interface ethernet, WIFI and so on can not meet the power requirement of the embedded device, but the Bluetooth device has the characteristics of low power consumption and strong anti-interference ability, and can meet the demand of intelligent meter wireless communication service. This design will focus on the practical application of wireless Bluetooth communication system in intelligent meter. Using the wireless Bluetooth communication system to connect the smart meter with the household appliances, the power information such as household appliances can be fed back to the power grid, which provides the possibility for the intelligent control of the smart grid.

Keywords: Bluetooth · Smart meter · Internet of things

1 Introduction

Foreign electronic meter development is very fast, Finland, Sweden, Norway and other Nordic countries and France, Britain, Germany, Spain, Belgium and Italy and other Western European countries, has completed the 100% electronic business user watt-hour meter. User tables are also making a gradual transition to electronic ones, such as those that have been discontinued in France since 2001 and those that have been updated in Italy since 2005 to automatic meter reading, while 80 per cent of British residents now use electronic meters.

Starting in 2010 as the era of smart grids, the number of smart meters installed worldwide will reach 220 million in 2015, and the main market for smart meters is expected to remain dominated by Europe and North America in the next five years, while Asian countries, driven by mainland China, will become potential markets. The following figure shows the intention of three-phase smart electricity:

This is a change in the way of collecting electricity information, but also a change in the development of science and technology and smart grid. In July 2009, China formulated a smart grid development plan, according to the plan, by 2020, China will be fully built a unified "strong smart grid". Moreover, China is expected to add 460 million smart meters during the 13th Five-Year Plan period, and the International Energy Agency estimates that the smart grid will cover 80° of the world's population by 2022.

M. Guan and Z. Na (Eds.): MLICOM 2020, LNICST 342, pp. 371–379, 2021.
https://doi.org/10.1007/978-3-030-66785-6_39

2 System Design

Intelligent meter data acquisition module system based on bluetooth technology consists of hardware part and software part, in which the hardware part includes bluetooth module, intelligent meter and collector. the software part includes the improved design of bluetooth protocol stack and the APP design of mobile phone. HT6015 intelligent ammeter is the main module of the main chip, processing the data transmitted through the Bluetooth module, forwarding the collector for data acquisition; after receiving the collector's response data, it is forwarded to the Bluetooth communication module.

(1) The function of the whole project is mainly composed of two parts:
(2) Data communication: through Bluetooth master-slave communication module;
(3) smart phone meter reading unit: using mobile phone smart operating system, and Bluetooth module to use Bluetooth to communicate, cooperate to complete the collection and setting of electric data of watt-hour meter, and have basic viewing data and parsing services.
(4) Smart phone meter reading unit: using the mobile phone smart operating system, and Bluetooth module to use Bluetooth to communicate, cooperate to complete the collection and setting of electricity data of watt-hour meter, and have basic viewing data and parsing services.

Considering the above system outline and the special communication mode of watt-hour meter, the characteristics of Bluetooth and smart phone, the technical scheme consists of three hardware parts: watt-hour meter, Bluetooth module and smart phone (Fig. 1).

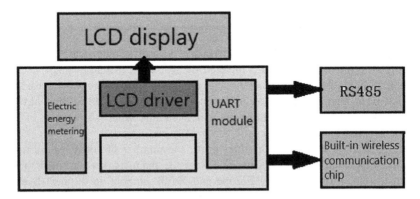

Fig. 1. System design block diagram

Bluetooth module, collector and smart phone meter reading software are the core part of the design, including hardware and software design and implementation. The hardware part includes the selection and application of the module, the layout of the circuit, the software part includes the design of the communication scheduling degree between the collector and the Bluetooth main module, and the design of the transmission code between the meter or the collector and the concentration. The communication protocol is to send and receive commands between the watt-hour meter and the Bluetooth module; the bluetooth communication between the bluetooth outer module and the smart phone transmits data.

3   System Hardware Design and Actualize

3.1   HT6015 Features

(1).   Introduction of modules

HT6x1x series is a mufti-function, high-performance, low-power single-phase intelligent meter dedicated 128k MCU chip, the internal integration of Cortex-M0 processor, clock management, power management, hardware automatic temperature compensation RTC, PLL, high-frequency RC, low-frequency RC, LCD drive and other units, as well as NVIC and DEBUG functions. The RTC unit which supports the compensation mechanism per second. the chip uses 32.768 Hz crystal oscillator clock source as the RTC clock source. through the clock automatic digital compensation unit integrated inside the chip, it helps the user to realize the RTC automatic compensation without software participation. HT6015 the basic features are as follows:

1) Use ARM Cortex-M0 CPU Core, 128 K Flash +8K SRAM
2) High Speed:CPU maximum operating frequency 22 M, program execution 0 wait.
3) Low Power Consumption: Minimum Power Consumption 3.3 µA in Hold Mode: Minimum Power Consumption 2.7µA in Sleep Mode.
4) RTC: Support per second compensation mechanism.
5) RTC Compensate: RTC Digital compensation for built-in curves, full temperature range RTC compensation without user software participation.
6) LCD: Support 4COM, 6COM, 8COM LCD show, SEG Interface supports up to 37 segments (80PIN) (Fig. 2).

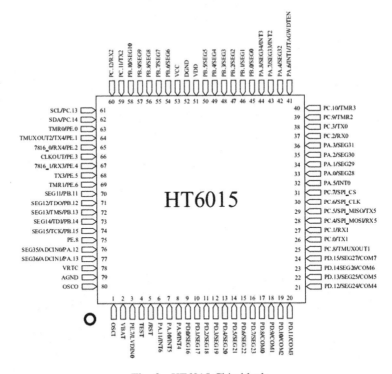

Fig. 2. HT6015 Chip block

3.2   Bluetooth Communication Module

nRF51802 is a universal ultra low power SoC, perfect fit Bluetooth low power consumption and 2.4 GHz proprietary wireless applications. It revolves around 32 bits arm Cortex-M0 CPU, have 256 KB Flash Memory +16 KB RAM. flexible 2.4 Ghz radio supports Bluetooth low power and 2.4 Ghz proprietary protocols such as Gazell.

The rich analog and digital peripherals are integrated, which can interact directly through a programmable peripheral interconnect (PPI) system without CPU intervention. The flexible GPIO enables you to connect SPI digital interfaces such as master/slave, TWI master device and UART to any of the 31 GPIO on the device (Fig. 3) (Table 1).

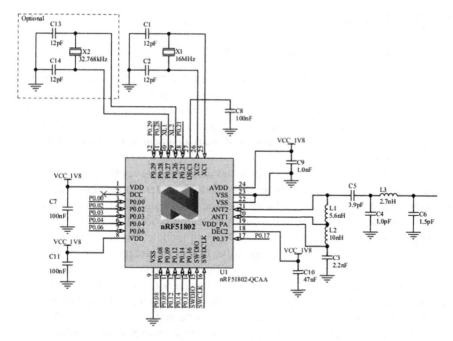

Fig. 3. nRF51802 module hardware circuit

Table 1. nRF51802 hardware connectivity of module

Designator	Value	Description
C1, C2, C13, C14	12 pF	Capacitor, NP0, ± 2%
C3	2.2 nF	Capacitor, X7R, ± 10%
C4	1.0 pF	Capacitor, NP0, ± 0.1pF
C5	3.9 pF	Capacitor, NP0, ± 0.1pF
C6	1.5 pF	Capacitor, NP0, ± 0.1pF
C7, C8, C11	100 nF	Capacitor, X7R, ± 10%
C9	1.0 nF	Capacitor, X7R, ± 10%
C10	47 nF	Capacitor, X7R, ± 10%
L1	5.6 nH	High frequency chip inductor ± 5%
L2	10 nH	High frequency chip inductor ± 5%
L3	2.7 nH	High frequency chip inductor ± 5%
U1	nRF51802-QCAA	Multi-protocol Bluetooth Low Energy and 2.4 GHz proprietary system-on-chip
X1	16 MHz	XTAL SMD 2520, 16 MHz, 8pF, ± 40 ppm
X2	32.768 kHz	XTAL SMD 3215, 32.768 kHz, 9pF, ± 20 ppm

4 System Software Design and Actualize

4.1 Design of Meter Reading Software

For testing whether Bluetooth module can interact effectively with users, it is necessary to develop a practical smart phone meter reading software, using the current common android mobile phone to collect and set the meter data. Along with the popularity of embedded systems, especially the rise of mobile phones arm chips and operating systems in recent years, the development of many practical software in mobile phones has become a reality.

Cell phone meter reading unit is installed meter reading application mobile phone, mobile phone meter reading software using android system to develop, meter reading program mainly contains several large modules: build communication channels, meter reading collection and setting, follow-up information processing.

At present, most smart phones have Bluetooth module, the first step of the mobile phone meter reading program to open the Bluetooth program, the mobile phone installed meter reading application and the Bluetooth module in the meter to connect, the second step to create a good transmission channel with Bluetooth serial device, and then according to the meter to generate a variety of command flow. The instruction stream is sent to the Bluetooth module and the returned information is collected, and the mobile phone program can also find the received and set log information or send them to the remote terminal, etc.

4.2 Function Declaration

① Meter setting: the previously well-set watt-hour meter will automatically display, after selecting the meter will display the table setting log;
② Automatic collection: the set of data items for automatic collection, if there is a preset collection method, can automatically collect the table address, automatically read the electricity information flowing through the meter; if the automatic collection of unavailable data will automatically re-collection;
③ Manual collection: according to the manual set of acquisition scheme for the collection of specific items.
④ Query acquisition: the interface gives priority to displaying the collected watt-hour meter, and the data collected by this meter will be displayed after selecting the meter;
⑤ Clear log: Clean up the collection log, first there will be a system display prompt, then confirm, after the log will be cleared;
⑥ Open Bluetooth: Bluetooth that can be started by the software, if the software does not have access, the access dialog will be displayed;
⑦ Connect Bluetooth: The software will automatically search for the available Bluetooth and then request a connection to the selected Bluetooth module, and the system will display a successful dialog after the connection is successful (Fig. 4).

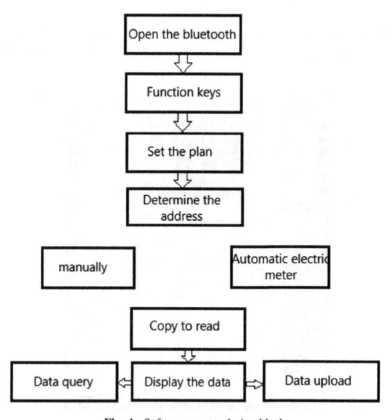

Fig. 4. Software master design block

5 System Debugging

As shown in Fig. 5: The burner is connected to the pc end and the Bluetooth module is connected with DuPont wire. After opening the serial port test assistant at the pc end, the baud rate, serial port number, data bit, stop bit and check bit are set.

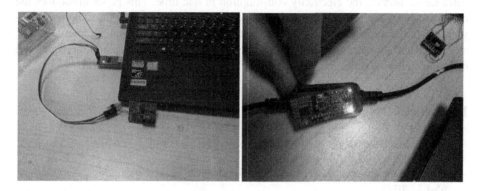

Fig. 5. System testing

Above shows the nRF51802 Bluetooth module used for this design, can be seen after the connection can normally send and receive data, signal lights also work normally. The diagram shows the watt-hour meter processing data, working properly (Fig. 6).

Fig. 6. System display effect

6   Conclusions

This paper collects the electricity demand data from the concentrator through Bluetooth module and displays it to the intelligent meter, and can also display it to the designed software to monitor the electricity consumption in real time. This paper introduces the performance of the t6015 chip and the nrf51802 module, designs the schematic diagram of the electric meter circuit part and draws pcb, designs and implements the system related driver, completes the splicing of the intelligent meter and the Bluetooth communication module, and the overall effect reaches the expected level.

References

1. Ma, S.: Internet of things communication technology and challenges based on 5G network. Mod. Inf. Technol. **9**, 195–196 (2018)
2. Guo, Q., Guo, J.: Application and development of smart meter in smart grid. Electr. Electr. **3**, 65–67 (2017)

3. Liu, Q., Cui, L., Chen, H.: Key technologies and applications of the Internet of Things. Comput. Sci. (2010)
4. Shihai, Y.: Electrical instrument and its application. China Electric Power Press, Beijing, pp. 42–43, September 2009
5. Yixiu Network: Electronic Power Technology Training Course, September 2014
6. Yunpeng, Z., Nanxing, Z.: Practical Electrician Manual. China Water Conservancy and Hydropower Press, Beijing, June 2008
7. Yunhao, L.: Introduction to the Internet of Things. Science Press, Beijing (2012)
8. Shenzhen Ruineng Microtechnology Co. Ltd., single-phase metering chip rn8207c user manual rev 1.1 [M]
9. Heng, Q.: Smart grid system analysis based on Internet of things technology. Jiangxi Building Materials, vol. 3 (2016)
10. Zhenhuan, Z.: Research and Implementation of Bluetooth-based Wireless Measurement System. Beijing University of Posts and Telecommunications (2008)
11. Ho, W.: The development of Bluetooth technology and its application prospects in the Internet of things. Appl. Energy Technol. (2016)

Multi Beam Forming Algorithms of LEO Constellation Satellite

Bingyu Xie$^{(\boxtimes)}$ and Mingchuan Yang

Communication Research Center, Harbin Institute of Technology,
1, 50001 Harbin, China
18742521283@163.com, mcyang@hit.edu.cn

Abstract. Since the 21st century, the development of mobile Internet and Internet of things technology has introduced new development opportunities for the field of communication satellites. A large number of researchers use multi beam technology in low earth orbit high-throughput satellite constellation to improve the performance of Internet of things services. In this paper, the development prospect of low orbit high-throughput communication satellite and the research significance of multibeam technology are summarized firstly, then some key technologies involved in the beamforming process are discussed, and the mathematical model of multibeam forming network is established with digital beamforming as the background. Then, the theory of beamforming criterion and algorithm is analyzed, and the least mean square algorithm and recursive least square algorithm are studied in detail. Finally, a variable step size least mean square algorithm is proposed and the simulation results are compared with those before the improvement, which can guide the selection of multi beam forming algorithm on the satellite.

Keywords: LEO satellite · Beamforming technology · Adaptive algorithm · LMS algorithm · Variable step-size

1 Introduction

Since the first international commercial communication satellite between North America and Europe, named "morning bird", was successfully launched by the United States in 1965, the satellite communication industry has experienced full development in recent decades. Since the 1990s, the rapid development of optical fiber and mobile cellular communication infrastructure on the ground has greatly squeezed the development space of commercial satellite communication industry. Although there is a certain momentum of growth, the development of its industrial scale is extremely difficult [1]. With the coming of the 21st century, the development of mobile Internet and Internet of things technology has brought new opportunities for the development of communication satellite industry, and a new development direction with multi-functional, comprehensive and Internet of things as the application goal has emerged.

The mobile broadband Internet satellite system based on LEO satellite constellation will realize the following services worldwide, including personal terminal wireless communication, global Internet access function, Internet of things access service,

M. Guan and Z. Na (Eds.): MLICOM 2020, LNICST 342, pp. 380–388, 2021.
https://doi.org/10.1007/978-3-030-66785-6_40

timely information flow push service, stronger navigation ability and navigation, aviation monitoring.

The multi beam antenna technology is indispensable in the realization of the above system and each sub beam is responsible for covering a certain range of target areas. Compared with the traditional single beam antenna, the multi beam antenna has many advantages (Fig. 1).

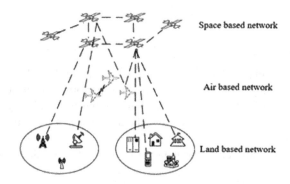

Fig. 1. The idea of the integration network of heaven and earth

2 Satellite Multi-beamforming Algorithm

2.1 Beamforming Based on Least Mean Square Algorithm

The least mean square (LMS) algorithm is an adaptive beamforming algorithm based on MMSE criteria in Table 3–1 above, which is the most widely used beamforming algorithm. It constructs a performance surface between the actual output and the desired signal through the square error under the condition that the desired signal D is known, and uses the random gradient method to minimize the error.

The basic principle of LMS algorithm is analyzed below:

At a specific time k, we sample the signal, and the error between the actual output of the array and the desired signal can be expressed as:

$$\varepsilon(k) = d(k) - w^H(k)x(k) \tag{1}$$

The expression of square error can be obtained by square it:

$$|\varepsilon(k)|^2 = |d(k) - w^H(k)x(k)|^2 \tag{2}$$

The cost function of LMS algorithm can be obtained by expanding the right expression of the above formula:

$$J(w) = D - 2w^H r + w^H R_{xx} w \tag{3}$$

Where, R_{xx} is the correlation matrix of antenna array, r is the correlation vector of the signal.

Because we don't know the statistical data of the signal, we can get the correlation matrix by sampling the snapshot data to estimate the signal. The estimated value is:

$$R_{xx}(k) = x(k)x^H(k) \tag{4}$$

$$r(k) = d^*(k)x(k) \tag{5}$$

The former formula is the cost function of the algorithm. The LMS algorithm approximates the optimal solution of the algorithm performance surface by finding its gradient and iterating in the opposite direction through the random gradient method. LMS algorithm is widely used in adaptive field because of its simple principle and small computation.

The following formula gives the iterative formula of LMS algorithm:

$$w_N(k+1) = w_N(k) - \frac{1}{2}\mu \nabla J(w_N(k)) \tag{6}$$

The updated formula of the weight vector is:

$$e_N(k) = d_N(k) - w_N^H(k)x_N(k) \tag{7}$$

$$w_N(k+1) = w_N(k) + \mu x_N(k)e_N^*(k) \quad 0 < \mu < Trace(R) \tag{8}$$

The parameter μ is called step factor, which is used to control the convergence rate and the stability of the algorithm.

How to choose the value of parameter μ will have a great influence on the convergence performance of LMS algorithm. If the step size factor is too small, the algorithm will appear over damping. If the step size factor is too large, the algorithm will not converge and will not get the optimal value. So the selection of parameter μ is very important.

The implementation steps of LMS algorithm are summarized as follows:

(1) Initialize the weight vector and record the weight vector of the array as $w(k)$;
(2) The sampling signal, $x(t)$, and $d(t)$, are recorded as $x(n)$, $d(n)$, respectively;
(3) Sampling time error estimation:

$$e(n) = d(n) - y(n) = d(n) - w^H x(n) \tag{9}$$

(4) Weight vector update:

$$w(n+1) = w(n) + \mu x(n)e^*(n) \tag{10}$$

LMS algorithm has the advantages of low computation complexity and small total computation. Each iteration of LMS algorithm only needs *4N* multiplication operations and *6N* addition operations. The main disadvantage of the algorithm is that it is difficult to choose a suitable step size to realize the trade-off between convergence speed and algorithm error.

The following is the implementation flow chart of LMS algorithm (Fig. 2).

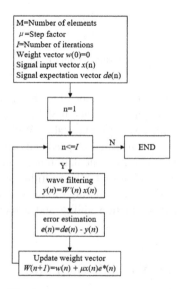

Fig. 2. LMS algorithm flow chart

2.2 Simulation Analysis of the LMS Algorithm

In the simulation stage, the number N of elements of the linear array is 8, the distance between elements is $\lambda/2$, the direction of the expected signal is $-20°$, the expected signal is cosine signal, and the direction of interference signal is $0°$. Set the noise as Gaussian white noise with power of 0dbW; the signal-to-noise ratio and dry noise ratio are both 10 dB. When the number of iterations is set to 500 and the step size is chosen as the gradient, it is found that when the step size is set to 0.001, an ideal result can be obtained (Fig. 3):

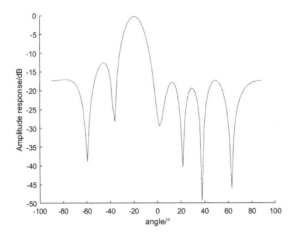

Fig. 3. LMS algorithm single beam forming

The LMS algorithm can form the main lobe of the beam in the desired direction, the algorithm achieves initial convergence after about 30 iterations, and the output signal of the array can roughly follow the desired signal stably. With the increase of the number of elements, it can achieve faster convergence speed and better stability of convergence error, but it will increase the amount of calculation accordingly.

Considering that the computation of LMS algorithm is very small and the complexity of the algorithm is low, using this algorithm on the satellite can reduce the demand for the satellite load calculation ability and achieve the purpose of saving hardware expenses.

3   LMS Algorithm with Variable Step Size

3.1   Sigmoid-based Variable Step-Size LMS

In the classical LMS algorithm, the step factor μ of the algorithm is constant, and the range of its error reaching the convergence requirement is $0 < \mu < Trace(R)$, Where, Trace(R) is the trace of the autocorrelation matrix of the signal received by the array antenna. The smaller the step size is, the smaller the error is, but the longer the convergence time constant is. Obviously, the fixed value of μ leads to the contradiction between the convergence speed and stability of LMS algorithm.

The LMS can be avoided to some extent by setting the convergence completion condition. The convergence speed and its steady-state performance should be considered at the same time. Therefore, the method of changing step factor with time in algorithm iteration is a simple and effective strategy. In order to achieve better steady-state performance in the later stage of the algorithm, the step factor of the algorithm should be reduced synchronously with the decrease of the mean square error. Therefore, it is an effective way to change the step factor of LMS algorithm to the dynamic value of error level with time.

Scholars at home and abroad do not have little research on variable step size LMS algorithm, among which the classical variable step size LMS algorithm is an algorithm proposed by Kwong. R. H. To dynamically change the step factor in the iterative process according to the instantaneous error of the algorithm. The expression of this algorithm can be written as:

$$\mu(n) = \alpha\mu(n-1) + be(n)^2 \tag{11}$$

Where: $0 < a < 1$, $b > 0$, and the step factor shall meet the following requirements:

$$\mu(n) = \begin{cases} \mu_{max}, \mu(n) > \mu_{max} \\ \mu_{min}, \mu(n) < \mu_{min} \\ \mu(n), others \end{cases} \tag{12}$$

Intuitively speaking, when the algorithm error increases, the step factor of the control algorithm is increased, so as to achieve faster return to the convergence error level. In the initial stage of the algorithm, the step factor can be preset to a larger value to achieve fast convergence, which is consistent with the control idea of the synchronous long factor. The parameters α and b in the algorithm are fixed values. In practice, a large number of experiments are needed to select the ideal α and b. similar to the fixed step size LMS algorithm, the step size is also obtained according to a large number of experimental experience, and the practicability is not improved obviously. Therefore, the algorithm has become a classic algorithm of variable step size LMS.

In the practical application scenario, another variable step-size lead mean square (SVSLMS) algorithm based on the sigmoid function has also been widely used. It is proposed by Qin Jingfan and others. The guiding idea is to map the error e(n) through the sigmoid function as the value of step factor μ(n):

$$\mu(n) = \beta\left(\frac{1}{1 + e^{-\alpha|e(n)|}} - 0.5\right) \tag{13}$$

The parameter α controls the shape of the sigmoid function and the rising speed of the curve, and the parameter β controls the value range of the sigmoid function.

Similarly, in the initial stage of the algorithm, due to the large instantaneous error, the algorithm step factor is at a relatively large level, and the algorithm can achieve a faster convergence speed in the early stage of the iteration. With the decrease of the error, the step factor will decrease rapidly to improve the stability of the algorithm.

Considering that the modulus $|e(n)|$ of error must be close to 0 when converging, we can increase the number of $|e(n)|$ terms in Eq. (4–3) to make the step factor curve more nonlinear in the region less than 1 and close to 0:

$$\mu(n) = \beta\left(\frac{1}{1 + e^{-\alpha|e(n)|^3}} - 0.5\right) \tag{14}$$

To sum up, the iterative process of the SVSLMS algorithm is summarized as follows:

(1) Initialize the weight vector, and record the weight vector of the array as $w(k)$;
(2) Signal sampling, sampling for element signal $x(t)$, expected signal $d(t)$, recorded as $x(n)$, $d(n)$;
(3) Sampling time error estimation:

$$e(n) = d(n) - y(n) = d(n) - w^H x(n) \qquad (15)$$

(4) Step factor update:

$$\mu(n) = \beta\left(\frac{1}{1 + e^{-\alpha|e(n)|^3}} - 0.5\right) \qquad (16)$$

(5) Weight vector update:

$$w(n+1) = w(n) + \mu x(n)e^*(n) \qquad (17)$$

3.2   Simulation Analysis of Variable Step Size LMS Algorithm and Classical Algorithm

Keep the simulation conditions of single beam forming unchanged, compare the effect of SVSLMS algorithm and classic LMS algorithm, and fix the number of iterations 200 times (Fig. 4):

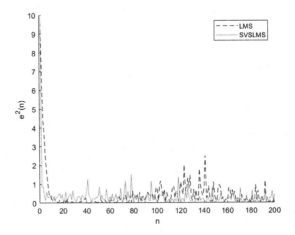

Fig. 4. Comparison of convergence error between SVSLMS and classical LMS

From the simulation results, it can be seen that after the initial convergence, the algorithm error of SVSLMS is generally more stable than that of classic LMS due to the reduction of step factor. At the same time, the convergence speed of SVSLMS algorithm in the early stage is also slightly improved compared with the classical algorithm.

However, the performance of SVSLMS algorithm in the graph still depends on the fixed values of α and β. How to continue to improve the flexibility of step factor adjustment and reduce the steady-state error at the same time will be an improvement direction worth studying.

Table 1 shows the calculation amount comparison of LMS, RLS and SVSLMS in each iteration when the array element number of array antenna is N:

Table 1. Complexity Comparison of LMS, RLS and SVSLMS

Algorithm name	Multiplication	Addition operation
LMS	$4N$	$6N$
RLS	$4N^2 + 7N$	$3N^2 + 4N$
SVSLMS	$4N + 6$	$6N + 2$

It can be seen from the table that the computational complexity of SVSLMS algorithm is slightly higher than that of classical LMS algorithm, and it is also much lower than RLS algorithm when the number of array elements N is large. Compared with the classical LMS algorithm, it has a significant advantage in improving the convergence stability. It can realize the relatively stable and fast convergence of the weight when the calculation complexity is not high, which makes the modified algorithm more applicable in the application scenario where the calculation complexity of the low orbit constellation satellite is not too high at the same time for the large-scale array antenna with many point beams.

4   Conclusion

The simulation model of the adaptive beamforming algorithm is established based on the mathematical model. The characteristics and advantages of different algorithms are compared from the convergence speed, convergence effect, steady-state error and so on. In view of the shortcomings of the convergence stability of the classical LMS algorithm, this paper explores the improvement feasibility of the variable step size LMS algorithm, and verifies the considerable improvement benefit and the acceptable increase cost of the operation amount through the simulation comparison. Based on the application requirements of multibeam in LEO constellation satellite, the factors of selecting the algorithm are compared.

References

1. Paulraj, A.J., Gore, D.A., Nabar, R.U., et al.: An overview of MIMO communications - a key to gigabit wireless. Proc. IEEE **92**(2), 198–218 (2004)
2. Zhou, M., Sorensen, S.B.: Multi-spot beam reflectarrays for satellite telecommunication applications in ka-band. In: Proceedings of the European Conference on Antennas and Propagation. IEEE, New York (2016)
3. De Sanctis, M., Cianca, E., Araniti, G., Bisio, I., Prasad, R.: Satellite communications supporting Internet of remote things. IEEE Internet Things J. **3**(1), 113–123 (2016)
4. Kwong, R.H., Johnston, E.W.: A variable step size LMS algorithm. IEEE Trans. Sign. Process. **40**(7), 1633–1642 (1992). https://doi.org/10.1109/78.143435

Mars Exploration Oriented Design and Simulation of Relay Communication

Yingzhe Dou, Xiaofeng Liu, and Mingchuan Yang[✉]

Communication Research Center, Harbin Institute of Technology, 1,
50001 Harbin, China
mcyang@hit.edu.cn

Abstract. In the deep space communication, traditional point-to-point communication system would no longer meet the requirements of long-distance information transmission and Mars exploration will mainly use the way of relay communication to transmit scientific exploratory data. On the basis of analyzing link visibility and link distance of on-orbit relay satellite, this paper proposes a new way of relay communication which can provide longer visible time and the capacity to cover Mars probe uniformly. The link visibility and link distance of the two relay communication way are simulated by STK, and the link performance of through link and the two relay way is simulated. The simulation results show that the relay constellation scheme which cover Mars probe uniformly reach higher performance in the link visibility and link coverage. Otherwise, the SNR of relay link can get 3 dB performance improvement. Compared with through link, relay constellation scheme that cover Mars probe uniformly can link performance based on obviously improving link visibility, which can be better applied to future Mars exploration.

Keywords: Deep communication · Mars exploration · Relay constellation · Link performance

1 Introduction

In the 21st century, with Mars Express, Mars Odyssey, Mars Scout Orbiter, Spirit and Opportunity, Phoenix and other Mars orbiters or Mars detectors successfully exploring Mars one after another, Mars exploration has gradually become the focus of global attention. During deep space exploration activities, a large amount of scientific exploration data needs to be returned to the earth. There are two main communication connection methods between the Mars target detector and the ground station: one is the point-to-point communication system, and the other is the relay communication system. The traditional point-to-point communication system has already been difficult to ensure the timely transmission of a large amount of detection data such as high-definition images and videos. Therefore, it will be a very advantageous choice to use the relay communication system to transmit various data and status information, and enhance the effectiveness of data transmission [2, 3].

With the increasing frequency of Mars exploration and exploration missions becoming more complex, the large amount of data transmission brought by the high-

© ICST Institute for Computer Sciences, Social Informatics and Telecommunications Engineering 2021
Published by Springer Nature Switzerland AG 2021. All Rights Reserved
M. Guan and Z. Na (Eds.): MLICOM 2020, LNICST 342, pp. 389–394, 2021.
https://doi.org/10.1007/978-3-030-66785-6_41

definition video and pictures in Mars exploration poses greater challenges to the relay satellites. Current Mars orbiter will not be able to meet the increasing demand for data transmission in the future, which requires longer relay transmission time and higher link reliability. Therefore, this paper studies a Mars relay system with longer visible time and higher link coverage.

2 Scene Construction and Simulation of On-Orbit Mars Orbiter

In order to analyze the relay communication performance of the Mars orbiter, a Mars relay network simulation scenario is built referring to the on-orbit Mars orbiter parameters. The parameters of the Mars orbiter in the simulation scenario refer to the Mars Global Prospector (MGS), Mars Odyssey and Mars Reconnaissance Orbiter (MRO); the Mars detector selects Curiosity as the reference, and the deep space station refers to China Kashi ground station. The parameters of Mars orbiter, Mars detectors and ground station are shown in Table 1 and Table 2.

Table 1. Orbital parameters of Mars orbiter.

Parameter	MGS	Odyssey	MRO
Track height (km)	400	400	Near Mars 255 Away from Mars 320
Track inclination (deg)	93	93.2	92.7
Ascension (deg)	210	75	225

Table 2. The parameters of Mars detector Curiosity and Kashi Station.

Name	Geographic location	Antenna elevation
Curiosity	5.45 °S, 137.8 °E, Mars	Min 10°
Kashi	39.5 °N, 75.9 °E, Earth	Min 10°

The Mars relay network simulation scenario of the Mars detector-Mars orbiter-ground station is built using STK. The link analysis module "Access" in STK was used to simulate the visible time and link distance of communication link. The start time of simulation is set to July 5, 2013, and the duration of simulation is 3 days. The visible time period of the link between Mars orbiter and Kashi station or Curiosity is shown in Fig. 1 and Fig. 2, where the horizontal continuous line segment indicates that the ground station or Curiosity and Mars orbiter are visible. The visible time and average distance of the link between Mars orbiter and Kashi station or Mars orbiter are summarized in Tables 3, 4 and 5.

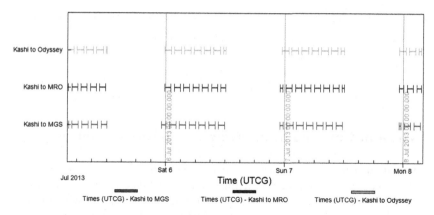

Fig. 1. Visible time period between MGS, Odyssey, MRO and Kashi Station

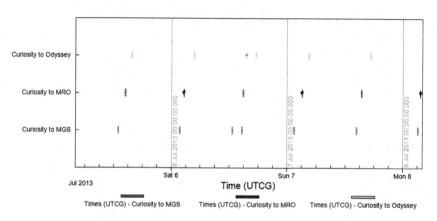

Fig. 2. Visible time periods between MGS, Odyssey, MRO and Curiosity

Table 3. Visible time and link coverage between MGS, Odyssey, MRO and Kashi stations.

Name	Min duration (s)	Max duration (s)	Mean duration (s)	Total duration (h)	Link coverage
MGS	1701	4662	4243	25.93	36.01%
Odyssey	90	4857	4061	25.95	36.04%
MRO	910	4266	3831	24.48	34%

Table 4. Link coverage in visible time between MGS, Odyssey, MRO and Kashi Station.

Name	Min duration (s)	Max duration (s)	Mean duration (s)	Total duration (h)	Link coverage
MGS	444	715	617	1.20	1.67%
Odyssey	230	710	589	0.98	1.36%
MRO	483	593	536	0.89	1.24%

Table 5. The average distance between Mars orbiter and Kashi station or Curiosity link.

Name	Kashi (km)	Curiosity (km)
MGS	3.66×10^8	886
Odyssey	3.66×10^8	882
MRO	3.66×10^8	654

3 System of Covering Mars Relay Constellation Uniformly

It is obvious that the link coverage of Mars orbiters to Mars detectors is low from Table 4. In order to increase the visible time of the target detector, a relay constellation system with covering time uniformly is designed. The relay constellation system consists of three satellites on an orbit plane, the three relay satellites are evenly distributed, with a phase interval of 120°. The constellation system consists of three evenly distributed satellites on an orbit plane with the orbital inclination of 115.567° and the satellite orbital height of 3590 km. Three satellites in the relay constellation system under uniformly covering are evenly distributed in an orbit plane. The specific orbit parameters of the three satellites in the constellation system are shown in Table 6. The Mars detector and deep space station still refer to the positions of Curiosity and Kashi station. Figure 3 and Fig. 4 show the visible time period of Mars orbiter and Kashi station or Curiosity respectively.

Table 6. Satellite orbit parameters of the relay constellation system under uniformly covering.

Name	Track inclination (deg)	Ascending intersection (deg)	True close angle (deg)
Mars-Sat1	115.567	145.113	0
Mars-Sat2	115.567	145.113	120
Mars-Sat3	115.567	145.113	240

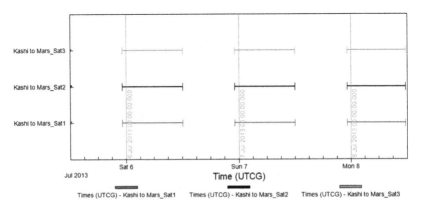

Fig. 3. Visible time period between Mars_sat1, Mars_sat2, Mars_sat3 and Kashi station

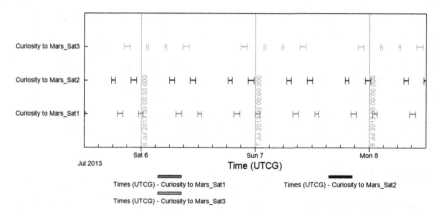

Fig. 4. Visible time period between Mars_sat1, Mars_sat2, Mars_sat3 and Curiosity

The visible time and average distance between Mars orbiter and Kashi station or Curiosity are shown in Tables 7, 8, and 9.

Table 7. Visible time and link coverage between Mars_sat1, Mars_sat2, Mars_sat3 and Kashi station.

Name	Min duration (s)	Max duration (s)	Mean duration (s)	Total duration (h)	Link coverage
Mars_Sat1	259	46413	34542	38.38	53.31%
Mars_Sat2	260	46143	34542	38.38	53.31%
Mars_Sat3	259	46414	34543	38.38	53.31%

Table 8. Visible time and link coverage between Mars_sat1, Mars_sat2, Mars_sat3 and Curiosity.

Name	Min duration (s)	Max duration (s)	Mean duration (s)	Total duration (h)	Link coverage
Mars_Sat1	349	4403	3522	11.74	16.31%
Mars_Sat2	1469	4385	3523	11.74	16.31%
Mars_Sat3	1288	4612	3020	10.07	13.99%

Table 9. Link average distance between Mars_sat1, Mars_sat2, Mars_sat3 and Kashi Station or Curiosity.

Name	Kashi (km)	Curiosity (km)
Mars_Sat1	3.659×10^8	4745
Mars_Sat2	3.659×10^8	4784
Mars_Sat3	3.659×10^8	4614

Comparing the data of the above three tables with Tables 3, 4, and 5, it can be seen that when the Mars orbiter increases orbit height, the link visible time and the coverage of the link of the Mars orbiter in the Mars relay constellation system under uniformly covering has been greatly improved, and the visible time of the Mars detector-Mars orbiter and Mars orbiter-ground station has been increased, which is conducive to the transmission of information and data in Mars exploration. In addition, in this relay communication system, the communication opportunities between the relay satellite and the target detector are equal, which is conducive to periodic planning.

4 Conclusion

This paper aims at the characteristics of deep space communication, especially the long distance and complicated communication environment in Mars exploration, uses STK to build a Mars relay network simulation scenario with reference to the orbit parameters of the on-orbit relay satellites of the United States and Europe, and analyzes link visibility and link distance of the mode. Then, a relay system with long visible time and uniformly covering the Mars detectors is proposed. The simulation results show that the link visibility and link coverage are significantly improved compared to the previous relay method.

References

1. The Global Exploration Roadmap. International Space Exploration Coordination Group, pp. 3–5 (2011)
2. Qiang, D., Shengyi, Z.: The status and development of Mars exploration relay communication orbiter. In: The Ninth Academic Annual Meeting of the Deep Space Exploration Technical Committee of the Chinese Aerospace Society, pp. 530–535 (2012)
3. Taylor, J., Makovsky, A., Barbieri, A., et al.: Mars Exploration Rover Telecommunications. Jet Propulsion Laboratory, California Institute of Technology, Pasadena, California, October 2005
4. Edwards, C.D.: Relay communications for mars exploration. Int. J. Satell. Commun. Netw. **25**(2), 111–145 (2007)
5. Reboud, O., et al.: An interplanetary and interagency network - lander communications at mars. In: AIAA International Conference on Spacecraft Operations, Heidelberg, Germany, May 2008

GEO and IGSO Based Hybrid Global Coverage Satellite Constellation Design

Xin Guan and Mingchuan Yang[(✉)]

Communication Research Center, Harbin Institute of Technology, 1,
50001 Harbin, China
mcyang@hit.edu.cn

Abstract. A hybrid global coverage satellite constellation is designed based on GEO and IGSO satellite considering that GEO satellite can provide favorable coverage performance to low latitude region while IGSO satellite can achieve high elevation angle to high latitude area. The designed satellite constellation can offer double-satellite coverage to the Chinese and nearby area, high elevation angle to high latitude area and seamless coverage to global area. The simulation results show that the Chinese and nearby area can achieve 100% single-satellite coverage and 87% double-satellite coverage. Besides, global area can reach more than 95% single-satellite coverage and north pole can get communication elevation angle over 30°.

Keywords: Satellite constellation design · Coverage · IGSO satellite · Communication elevation angle

1 Introduction

Building a satellite mobile communication system with global communication capabilities is one of the important issues to be solved in China's globalization strategy [1]. The low orbit, medium orbit or high orbit satellite constellation can be used to achieve the goal of seamless global coverage. For the design of the low-orbit global coverage satellite constellation, Rider proposed the best polar orbit design method [2], Walker et al. proposed the inclined circular orbit design method [3]. The Iridium is a typical polar orbit low-orbit constellation with a total of 66 satellites evenly distributed on six orbital planes. The inclination of the orbital planes is 90°, the altitude is 780 km, the eccentricity is 0, and the distance between adjacent track surfaces is 60°. It can achieve global continuous coverage in the case of communication elevation angle greater than 8°. Odyssey system is a typical mid-orbit constellation based on the design method of inclined circular orbit. It is composed of 12 stars and distributed on three orbital planes, each of which has 4 stars. The orbital height is 10354 km, which can provide a communication elevation of 22° [4]. Inmarsat is a typical high-orbit constellation system using GEO (Geostationary Orbit) satellites. It consists of 3 GEO satellites. High-orbit and low-orbit systems have distinct characteristics due to their different orbital heights, number of satellites and technical means. Considering the current development situation in China, choosing a GEO system with relatively low technical complexity and high cost performance is a good solution. However, relying on GEO

M. Guan and Z. Na (Eds.): MLICOM 2020, LNICST 342, pp. 395–400, 2021.
https://doi.org/10.1007/978-3-030-66785-6_42

satellites alone cannot provide an ideal communication elevation angle for high latitude areas, and there will also be coverage blindness for polar region. The IGSO (Inclined Geosynchronous Satellite Orbit) satellite has an orbital "8" shape due to its non-zero orbit inclination, which can provide high elevation angle coverage for high latitude areas. This paper designs a GEO + IGSO satellite constellation based on such considerations.

2   Features of the IGSO Satellite

The IGSO satellite orbits at the same altitude as the GEO satellite and has the same period of operation as the GEO satellite. It is also synchronized with the earth. However, the orbital inclination of the IGSO satellite is not zero, which determines that the ground track will not be a point like GEO, but an "8" shape, thus providing high elevation angle coverage for high latitude areas.

The orbital parameters of the IGSO satellite mainly include two orbital inclination angles and the longitude of the ground track when crossing the equator. Similar to the ground track of GEO satellite, the ground track of IGSO satellite will always pass through the same point on the equator. Therefore, the longitude of this point can be used for unique identification. The larger the orbital inclination is, the better the coverage of the polar and high latitudes will be, while the coverage of the middle and low latitudes will be reduced. When choosing the IGSO inclination, the influence of these two factors should be considered in a more specific target task.

In Ref. [5], the application of IGSO in the satellite mobile communication system is studied. The research results show that the use of IGSO satellites can significantly improve the low elevation angle problem of GEO satellites in high latitude areas. The constellation composed of two or three relatively small IGSO satellites could achieve better performance than a very large GEO satellite. The IGSO satellite constellation can be used to realize the continuous multi-star coverage of China, and the effective spatial diversity can be realized, which can obviously improve the anti-interference capability of the system. If the coverage of high latitude regions is required, three IGSO satellites are needed to ensure performance. In this paper, three IGSO satellites with common ground track are used to cover the Chinese and nearby area.

3   Hybrid Global Coverage Satellite Constellation Based on GEO + IGSO

3.1   Performance Indicators of Global Coverage Satellite Constellation Design

For a constellation with uninterrupted continuous coverage, the indicators to evaluate its coverage performance include the maximum (average, minimum) coverage weight and the maximum (average, minimum) elevation angle. This paper analyzes the coverage performance of the constellation based on STK (Satellite Tool Kit). The relevant parameters used in the analysis are as follows. The minimum communication elevation angle is 20°. Covered area includes global area, the Chinese and nearby area, Arctic area. Coverage performance and elevation angle statistical accuracy are regional resolutions with a latitude of 10° and a longitude of 1°.

3.2   Design Scheme Based on 2GEO + 3IGSO Hybrid Global Coverage Constellation

The constellation designed in this paper consists of 5 satellites, including 3 IGSO satellites and 2 GEO satellites. The two-dimensional map of the constellation and the coverage of each satellite are shown in Fig. 1, where different satellites are marked with different colors, and the coverage of satellites is represented by the corresponding border lines of the same color. The detailed parameters of each satellite are shown in Table 1.

It can be seen from Fig. 1 that the ground track of the IGSO satellite is an "8" shape. The goal of the constellation design in this paper is to provide multiple coverage of the Chinese and nearby area (70° E–150° E, 10° N–55° N), while taking into account the global coverage. In addition, it is necessary to ensure a high communication elevation angle for high latitude areas. Three IGSO satellites with common ground tracks and evenly distributed phases around the land can provide multiple coverage of the Chinese and nearby area and high elevation angle coverage in high latitude areas. It has better coverage performance than a GEO satellite. GEO1 and GEO2 mainly complete the coverage of low and middle latitudes in Africa and the Americas. In order to prevent coverage blindness, the coverage areas of GEO1 and GEO2 overlap, and the overlap point is located at N60°. This paper uses the IGSO satellite to cover the Chinese and nearby area, so the longitude when crossing the equator was selected near the land, which is E100°. In order to ensure the double-satellite coverage of the Chinese, and also to take into account that the high latitude areas have an ideal communication elevation angle, this paper chooses the inclination angle of IGSO as 45°. At this time, the double-satellite coverage rate of more than 80% can be guaranteed below the latitude of 60°. The average communication elevation angle can reach 55.1°, and the communication elevation angle at the North Pole can also reach nearly 30°.

Table 1. Satellite orbit parameters.

Name	Semi-major axis (km)	Longitude ascending node	Orbital inclination	Argument of perigee	True anomaly
GSO11	42164.2	199.1°	45°	0°	0°
IGSO21	42164.2	79.1°	45°	0°	120°
IGSO31	42164.2	319.1°	45°	0°	240°
GEO1	42164.2	59.1°	0°	0°	0°
GEO2	42164.2	0°	0°	0°	339.1°

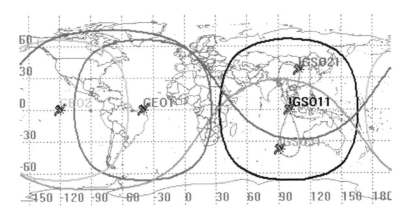

Fig. 1. 2GEO + 3IGSO constellation two-dimensional diagram

4   2GEO + 3IGSO Satellite Constellation Coverage Analysis

Based on the 2GEO + 3IGSO high-orbit hybrid satellite constellation designed above, this paper uses STK (Satellite Tool Kit) to perform coverage analysis. Figure 2 shows the global single-satellite coverage map of this constellation. Figure 3 shows the double-satellite coverage map of the constellation in the Chinese and nearby area. Since the constellation covers the northern and southern hemispheres symmetrically, Fig. 4 shows the coverage of the constellation in the Arctic region (60° N–90° N). The coverage of the Antarctic region is the same.

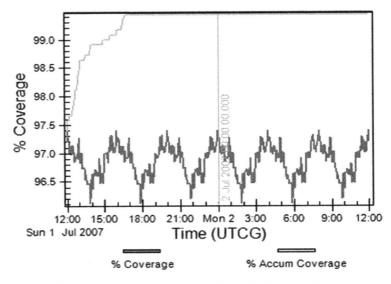

Fig. 2. Global single-satellite coverage of the 2GEO + 3IGSO constellation

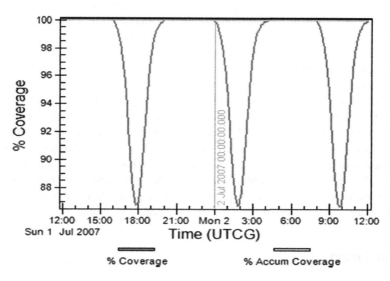

Fig. 3. 2GEO + 3IGSO constellation double-satellite coverage in the Chinese and nearby area

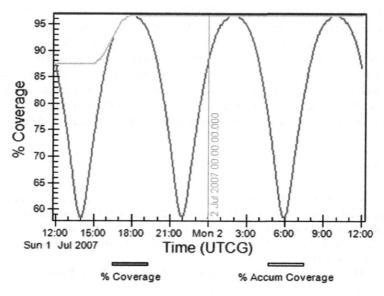

Fig. 4. 2GEO + 3IGSO constellation Arctic region coverage

It can be seen from Fig. 2 that the real-time single-satellite coverage of this constellation can reach more than 95%, and the highest can reach 97.4%. The cumulative coverage rate can reach 100%, indicating that the constellation can achieve seamless global coverage without covering blindness. As can be seen from Fig. 3, the real-time double-satellite coverage of this constellation on the Chinese and nearby area can reach more than 87%, and the highest can reach 100%. The double-satellite cumulative coverage can reach 100%, indicating that at least 2 satellites can be seen anywhere in the Chinese and nearby area within a day. It can also be found that within one day, there are three periods where the real-time double-satellite coverage rate is less than 90%, and each duration is about 1 h. In other words, the Chinese and nearby area can reach a double-satellite coverage rate of more than 90% within 21 h in a day. If the fading characteristics of the two satellite propagation paths can be statistically independent, the diversity technology can also be used to increase the system capacity.

As can be seen from Fig. 4, the real-time single-satellite coverage of this constellation in the polar region can reach more than 58%, and the maximum can reach 100%. Real-time double-satellite coverage can reach 100%, no coverage blind spot. There are three time periods in which a real-time single-satellite coverage rate is less than 80%, each of which is about 3 h. So 62.5% of the time during the day, more than 80% of single-satellite coverage rate can be obtained in the polar region.

5   Conclusion

This paper uses the advantages of IGSO satellites to provide high elevation angle coverage for high latitude areas, and solves the shortcomings that GEO satellites always have low elevation angles at high latitude areas and coverage blindness in the polar region. According to the goal of multiple coverage of the Chinese and nearby area and high elevation angle coverage of high latitude areas, an orbital inclination that can perform well multiple coverage of the target area and provide good communication elevation angles for high latitude areas is selected. The analysis results show that the constellation can provide double-satellite coverage for the Chinese and nearby area more than 80% of the day, the global real-time single-satellite coverage reaches more than 95%, and the communication elevation angle at the two poles reaches 30°.

References

1. Li, H., Liu, R., Han, F., Wang, J.: Development situation and countermeasures analyses for satellite communication. In: Virtual Operation and Cloud Computing-Proceedings of the 18th National Youth Communication Academic Annual Conference (Volume 1) (2013)
2. Rider, L.: Optimized polar orbit constellations for redundant earth coverage. J. Astronaut. Sci. 33(2), 147–161 (1985)
3. Walker, J.G.: Circular Orbit Patterns Providing Continuous Whole Earth Coverage. JBIS (1970). 24(1)
4. Feng, X., Peng, C.: Development progress and trends of foreign mobile satellite communications. Telecommun. Technol. 51(6), 156–161 (2011)
5. Zhang, G., Li, S., Gan, Z.: Study on the application of IGSO into mobile satellite communication. J. Commun. 27(8), 148–154 (2006)

Characteristics Analysis and Modeling of Satellite Mobile MIMO Channel

Yingzhe Dou and Mingchuan Yang[(✉)]

Communication Research Center, Harbin Institute of Technology, 1,
50001 Harbin, China
478561933@qq.com, mcyang@hit.edu.cn

Abstract. In recent years, with the rapid growth of satellite communication services, the spectral bandwidth needs to be increased urgently. In the face of the dilemma of limited orbit position and lack of spectrum resources, MIMO technology has been applied to satellite communications to improve the spectrum efficiency and channel capacity, which has become the main research direction, and the modeling of MIMO channel is an indispensable work. This paper firstly analyzes and summarizes the actual measurement work and channel characteristics of the satellite mobile MIMO channel, and on this basis, gives the concrete steps of using two-state Markov chain and taking C.Loo model as the subchannel to build the probability statistical model of satellite mobile MIMO channel. At the same time, according to the model established in this paper, the simulations are carried out in different environments, so as to study the effects of simulation parameters such as simulation environment, cross polarization discrimination and satellite elevation on the performance of satellite mobile MIMO systems.

Keywords: MIMO · Land mobile satellite · Channel model · Probability statistical model

1 Introduction

In recent years, with the rapid growth of satellite communication services, the spectral bandwidth needs to be increased urgently. In the face of the dilemma of limited orbit position and lack of spectrum resources, how to improve the spectrum efficiency and channel capacity of satellite communication systems has become the main research direction. Among them, the most remarkable technical achievement is MIMO (Multiple-Input Multiple-Output) technology, which has epoch-making significance in modern communication technology and is also the key technology of broadband wireless communication in the future [1].

For a satellite mobile MIMO communication system, the satellite mobile MIMO channel as its core is very important. The realization of any MIMO technology is closely related to the characteristics of its underlying MIMO channel. Satellite communication links are different from normal terrestrial MIMO communication systems, and their performance influence factors are also different. For the satellite system with a long communication link, the size of the satellite in the space segment itself is very

M. Guan and Z. Na (Eds.): MLICOM 2020, LNICST 342, pp. 401–409, 2021.
https://doi.org/10.1007/978-3-030-66785-6_43

small, and it is not easy to meet the condition that the distance between the antennas exceeds half of the wavelength of the signal. Compared with the terrestrial MIMO system, the distance between the satellite in the space segment and the mobile terminal on the ground is very long, so it is bound to have a strong correlation to place two or more antennas on a satellite [2].

It can be seen that only by establishing a satellite mobile communication channel model that can accurately and truly reflect the situation of masking and multipath that may be encountered in the actual signal transmission process, can we make a more in-depth study and analysis of the channel capacity and the factors affecting it. It is the premise of improving transmission efficiency and quality, and the basis of improving the performance of satellite mobile MIMO communication system. The research content of this paper also comes from this.

2   Measurement Activities and Characteristic Analysis of Satellite Mobile MIMO Channel

2.1   Representative Measurement Activities

The first and most representative measurement activity of satellite mobile MIMO channel characteristics was conducted by Peter R. king in Guildford, UK in the summer of 2005 [3]. He used antennas installed on an artificial platform at the top of a mountain to simulate the satellite antennas and installed them on a slope 6 meters above the ground to reduce local scattering. The main lobe of the antenna was far away from the terrain and was not blocked. The first side lobe of −20 dB was at the edge of the mountain covered by the grassland about 100 m away from the platform. The user terminal communicating with the antenna was simulated by a mobile van.

Three measurement environments were selected. The first environment is a tree-lined road with dense trees on both sides of the road, occasionally open space, and occasionally two-story houses outside the vegetation. The second environment is the suburb with dense two-story houses on both sides of the road and occasionally trees. The third environment is the city with dense two- to four-story houses and sporadic trees. The selection of these three environments is very representative, and the simulation environment assumptions and parameter selections later in this paper will also adopt these three environments, namely open rural, suburban, and urban environments.

Other representative measurement activities include the supplementary measurement activities conducted by Unwana M. Ekpe in Guildford, UK in 2009 and 2010 [4], and the ESA ARTES 5.1 MIMOSA [5], etc.

2.2   Characteristic Analysis of Satellite Mobile MIMO Channel

Based on the data collection, research and conclusion analysis of the above measurement activities, the channel characteristics which can be used for the subsequent modeling of MIMO channel are summarized as follows:

(1)   In the statistical sense, the probability density function of the signal envelope is studied. The experimental data is subjected to the kolmogoroff-smirnoff test to

know that the large-scale fading conforms to the lognormal distribution, and the small-scale fading conforms to the Rice distribution.

(2) In terms of the correlation between sub-channels, only the signals with short time interval in the large-scale fading have a close correlation in the time domain, and the small-scale fading is weakly correlated.

(3) Satellite mobile MIMO channel has the correlation between channels, which is the biggest difference between it and terrestrial MIMO channel. It is also an important part that cannot be ignored in modeling.

3 Modeling of Satellite Mobile MIMO Channel

3.1 Modeling Scenario and Channel Matrix

The modeling environment of this paper selects open rural, suburban, and urban, and the channel is a 2×2 MIMO LMS channel. That is to say, a single GEO satellite as the sending end and a single ground mobile terminal as the receiving end both use the dual circular polarization antenna with left and right circular polarization elements. The selected operating frequency is the S-band. Since the multipath echo has no significant time-domain extension, the resulting fading channel is assumed to be narrow-band, that is, frequency non-selective.

Under the above conditions, the MIMO LMS channel is modeled by a 2×2 MIMO channel matrix $H = |h_{ij}| (i, j = 1, 2)$. h_{ij} represents the fading component of SISO LMS subchannel formed between the transmitting side and the receiving side, where h_{11} and h_{22} represent the channel gain between antennas of the same polarization mode in the link, while h_{12} and h_{21} represent the channel gain between antennas of different polarization modes in the link. Since h_{ij} includes large-scale fading effect and small-scale fading effect, the channel matrix $\mathbf{H}$ can be expressed as the sum of two parts:

$$H = [h_{ij}] = [\bar{h}_{ij}] + [\tilde{h}_{ij}] = [\bar{H}] + [\tilde{H}](i, j = 1, 2) \tag{1}$$

Where each land mobile satellite subchannel follows the C. loo distribution:

$$h_{ij} = |h_{ij}| \exp(j\phi_{ij}) = |\bar{h}_{ij}| \exp(j\bar{\phi}_{ij}) + |\tilde{h}_{ij}| \exp(j\tilde{\phi}_{ij})(i, j = 1, 2) \tag{2}$$

$$p(|h_i|) = \frac{|h_i|}{b_0\sqrt{2\pi d_0}} \int_0^\infty \frac{1}{z} \exp\left[-\frac{(\ln z - \mu)^2}{2d_0} - \frac{(|h_i|^2 + z^2)}{2b_0}\right] I_0\left(\frac{|h_i|z}{b_0}\right) dz \tag{3}$$

Where ϕ_0 and ϕ are uniformly distributed over $[0, 2\pi)$. $|\bar{h}_i|$ represents the amplitude of large-scale fading, with (α, ψ) as the parameters, and it follows lognormal distribution. $|\tilde{h}_i|$ represents the amplitude of small-scale fading, with MP as the parameter, and it follows Rayleigh distribution.

$\alpha = 20\log_{10}(e^{\mu})$ and $\psi = 20\log_{10}\left(e^{\sqrt{d_0}}\right)$ are the mean and standard deviation, and $MP = 10\log_{10}(2b_0)$ is the average power. (α, ψ, MP) is called C.Loo statistical parameter triplet, and $I_0(.)$ is the modified Bessel function of first kind and zero order.

3.2 Generation of Large-Scale Fading in Satellite Mobile Polarized MIMO Channel

In the MIMO LMS channel based on the C.Loo model, large-scale fading is mainly caused by the shadow effect, and its influence on the signal changes slowly, which is also known as slow fading. The detailed modeling process of large-scale fading is as follows:

(1) First, in each state, generate 2×2 samples of Gaussian random sequence with zero mean, unit variance, and independent distribution.

(2) These four independent sequences are respectively passed through the lowpass infinite impulse response filter, so the large-scale fading has temporal correlation to some extent. The lowpass filter to simulate temporal correlation can be expressed as:

$$y_n = x_n + By_{n-1} \tag{4}$$

Where $B = \exp(-vT/r_c)$, T is the sampling time, v is the speed of the ground mobile terminal, and r_c is the coherent distance. By multiplying by $(1 - B^2)$, the samples after low-pass filtering can keep the statistical characteristics before filtering, so that the 2×2 channel matrix $\overline{H}_{uncorr}$ can be generated.

(3) Because of the large distance between the satellite and the earth and the small space between the antennas at the receiving end, the large-scale fading part experiences serious spatial correlation. Therefore, a 2×2 Gaussian matrix with zero mean and unit variance is introduced to simulate the joint correlation. The correlated channel characteristic matrix $\overline{H}_{uncorr}$ is represented by covariance matrix $\overline{H}_{corr}$ and uncorrelated channel characteristic matrix $\overline{C}$ as follows:

$$vec(\overline{H}_{corr}) = \overline{C}^{\frac{1}{2}}vec(\overline{H}_{uncorr}) \tag{5}$$

(4) In order to generate a lognormal channel matrix, the Gaussian matrix $\overline{H}_{corr}$ needs to be combined with the mean α and the standard deviation ψ, resulting in a large-scale fading channel matrix $\overline{H}$:

$$vec(\overline{H}) = 10^{\left[vec(\overline{H}_{corr})(\psi/20) + (\alpha/20)\right]} \tag{6}$$

(5) In addition to the change in signal amplitude, the Doppler shift will cause the linear change in the phase of the direct signal:

$$f = (v/\lambda) \cos \varphi \cos \theta \tag{7}$$

Where φ and θ are the azimuth and elevation angles of the user terminal, v is the moving speed of the user terminal, and λ is the signal wavelength. The constant phase increment is as follows:

$$\Delta\phi = 2\pi \frac{\cos \varphi \cos \theta}{F} \tag{8}$$

Where F is the reciprocal of the wavelength, and λ/F is the signal sampling interval.

(6) The influence of polarization diversity is described by the parameter cross polarization discrimination XPD_{ant}, which represents the ability of antennas to distinguish orthogonal polarization components. XPD_{ant} can be expressed as:

$$XPD_{ant} = 10 \log_{10}(\frac{E\left[\left|\bar{h}_{ij}^{j}\right|\right]}{E\left[\left|\bar{h}_{ij}^{k}\right|\right]}) = 10 log_{10}\left[\frac{(1 - \beta)}{\beta}\right] \tag{9}$$

Because the actual value of the XPD of the satellite antenna (i.e., the transmission side) is very large, it is assumed to be approximately ∞. XPD_{ant} here only represents the XPD of the receiving antenna that seriously affects the analysis. Generally, XPD_{ant} is known, so β can be inversely deduced with the above formula. Therefore, the influence of polarization on channel power can be expressed as follows:

$$\begin{bmatrix} E\left\{\left|\bar{h}_{11}^{k}\right|^{2}\right\} & E\left\{\left|\bar{h}_{12}^{k}\right|^{2}\right\} \\ E\left\{\left|\bar{h}_{21}^{k}\right|^{2}\right\} & E\left\{\left|\bar{h}_{22}^{k}\right|^{2}\right\} \end{bmatrix} = MP \begin{bmatrix} 1 - \beta & \beta \\ \beta & 1 - \beta \end{bmatrix} \tag{10}$$

3.3 Generation of Small-Scale Fading in Satellite Mobile Polarized MIMO Channel

In the process of radio wave propagation, in addition to large-scale fading caused by shadow effect, multipath effect and Doppler spread will also cause small-scale fading. Small-scale fading reflects the rapid fluctuation characteristics of received signals within a short distance and time, which is also known as fast fading. Due to the angular spread $\delta\theta$ caused by multipath and the multi-antenna cooperative localization of the user terminal, as well as the distance Δ between the antennas in the antenna array, the small-scale fading component $\tilde{h}_i$ is affected by the space-time correlation at the receiving end. The detailed modeling process is as follows:

(1) First, in each state, generate 2×2 samples of complex Gaussian random sequence with zero mean, unit variance, and independent distribution.
(2) Then, the samples are respectively passed through a lowpass U-shaped filter with unit energy, and the Butterworth filter will cause Doppler expansion. After Doppler shaping, the resulting complex sequence is multiplied by $\sqrt{b_0}$ to form a Rayleigh sequence. The elements in the sequence are arranged to form a matrix $\tilde{H}$ which is a 2×2 channel matrix with independent identically distributed zero mean circularly symmetric complex Gaussian elements of variance MP.
(3) Then, the correlation between the MIMO subchannels is generated to obtain a 2×2 MIMO small-scale fading channel matrix $\tilde{H}$. The formula used here is:

$$\tilde{H} = \tilde{R}_{rx}^{1/2} \cdot \tilde{H}_w \cdot \tilde{R}_{tx}^{1/2} \tag{11}$$

Where $\tilde{R}_{rx}$ and $\tilde{R}_{tx}$ are the covariance matrixes.

(4) Because the cross polarization discrimination of small-scale fading component $\tilde{h}_{ij}(i,j=1,2)$ is related to XPC of the propagation environment (expressed by XPC_{env}) and XPD_{ant}, the influence of polarization on channel power in small-scale fading can be expressed as follows:

$$\begin{bmatrix} E\left\{\left|\tilde{h}_{11}^k\right|^2\right\} & E\left\{\left|\tilde{h}_{12}^k\right|^2\right\} \\ E\left\{\left|\tilde{h}_{21}^k\right|^2\right\} & E\left\{\left|\tilde{h}_{22}^k\right|^2\right\} \end{bmatrix} = MP\begin{bmatrix} 1-\gamma & \gamma \\ \gamma & 1-\gamma \end{bmatrix} \tag{12}$$

Where the parameter γ is jointly determined by $XPC_{env} = 10\log_{10}[(1-\gamma_{env})/\gamma_{env}]$ and $\gamma = \beta(1-\gamma_{env}) + (1-\beta)\gamma_{env}$. β is the same as that of the large-scale fading part. MP represents the average power.

Using formula (1) to combine the large-scale fading part with the small-scale fading part, the final channel matrix $\mathbf{H}$ can be obtained. The complete satellite mobile MIMO channel modeling process is shown in Fig. 1.

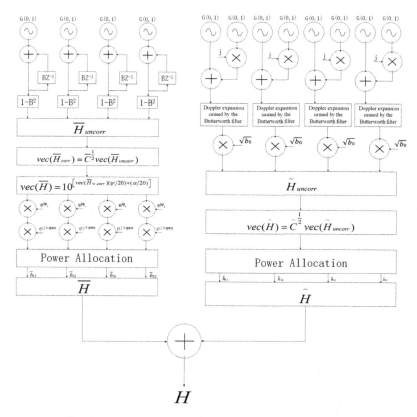

Fig. 1. Modeling process of satellite mobile MIMO channel

4   Simulation Analysis of Satellite Mobile MIMO Channel Model

Based on the established model, this chapter carries on the simulation analysis to the satellite mobile MIMO channel model.

In order to study the effect of different simulation parameters on the 1% outage capacity representing system performance, Fig. 2, Fig. 3 and Fig. 4 respectively simulate the influence of environment, antenna cross polarization discrimination and satellite elevation on system performance. It can be found that the performance of MIMO system is significantly better than that of SISO system, which is about double the improvement. Simulation environments will significantly affect the performance of the MIMO system, and open rural is the best while urban is the worst. What's more, larger cross polarization discrimination and satellite elevation can improve the system performance.

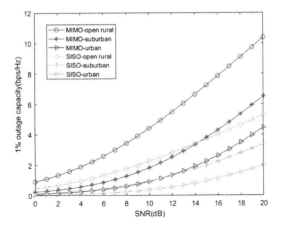

Fig. 2. 1% outage capacity of MIMO and SISO channel in different simulation environments

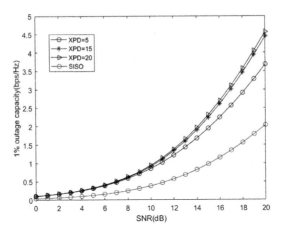

Fig. 3. 1% outage capacity of different cross polarization discriminations in urban environment

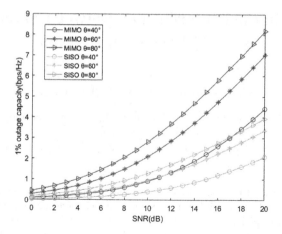

Fig. 4. 1% outage capacity of different satellite elevations in urban simulation environment

5   Conclusion

This paper summarizes the characteristics of the MIMO channel through the analysis of measurement activities and gives a modeling method of the narrow-band satellite mobile dual polarization 2×2 MIMO channel model based on two-state Markov chain. On this basis, the sub-channels' time series and the influence of different parameters on system performance is simulated. It is concluded that the performance of MIMO system is significantly better than that of SISO system; different simulation environments will significantly affect the performance of the MIMO system, and open rural is the best while urban is the worst; larger cross polarization discrimination and satellite elevation can improve the system performance. All of them provide theoretical support for the application of MIMO technology in satellite mobile communication system.

References

1. Pandey, P., Gandhiraj, R., Kirthiga, S., Jayakumar, M., Devi, N.M., Bera, S.C.: Emulation of channel model and estimation for MIMO based satellite land mobile system using software defined radio. Proc. Comput. Sci. **143**, 868–875 (2018)
2. Mhearáin, F.N., Fontán, F.P.: An enhanced statistical model for the dual polarised MIMO land mobile satellite channel. In: European Conference on Antennas and Propagation, Hague, pp. 3031–3039 (2014)
3. King, P.R., Stavrou, S.: Low elevation wideband land mobile satellite MIMO channel characteristics. IEEE Tran. Wireless Commun. **6**(7), 2712–2720 (2007)
4. Ekpe, U.M.: Modelling and measurement analysis of the satellite MIMO radio channel. Engineering and Physical Sciences University of Surrey, 75–92 (2012)
5. Chatzinotas, S., Ottersten, B., De Gaudenzi, R.: Cooperative and cognitive satellite systems, pp. 245–251 (2015)

Co-channel Interference Between Satellite and 5G System in C Band

Xinxin Miao$^{(\boxtimes)}$ and Mingchuan Yang

Communication Research Center, Harbin Institute of Technology, 1,
50001 Harbin, China
19S105149@stu.hit.edu.cn, mcyang@hit.edu.cn

Abstract. The 2019 World Radio Conference proposed to add 11 candidate frequency bands for the 5G system. Some of the C-bands are frequencies currently operated by the fixed-satellite service. When the 5G system and the fixed-satellite service share the same frequency band, the problem of co-frequency interference between systems is bound to occur. This paper studies the co-channel interference analysis from the 5G system to the FSS downlink in the 3400–3600 MHz frequency band. According to the specific interference scenario, antenna model and path loss model, Monte Carlo algorithm is used to evaluate the distribution of 5G interfering base stations, and the interference simulation analysis is carried out through link calculation, power control and system scheduling. The research results show that to meet the protection standards of the FSS system, the distance between the base station and the earth station needs to be at least 15 to 20 km. Moreover, the interference factors of the 5G system to the FSS mainly include angle between the main axis of the FSS earth station antenna and the direction of the base station interference signal, the number of 5G base stations, and the transmission power of 5G base stations.

Keywords: 5G · FSS earth station · Co-channel interference · Protection distance

1 Introduction

Communication technology is developing rapidly. Fifth generation mobile communication technology will support high-speed, low-latency and large- scale access services to enhance the overall performance of the system [1, 2]. World Radiocommunication Conference identifies millimeter wave bands as available frequency bands for 5G radio services [3]. For the sub 6 GHz frequency band, the World Radio Conference divided the 3400–3600 MHz frequency band as one of the candidate frequency bands for 5G systems [4]. However, this frequency band is also the frequency band where the fixed-satellite service operates. If the 5G system shares this frequency band with the satellite system, it will inevitably bring about interference problems between systems. Therefore, how to minimize the co-frequency interference between 5G systems and FSS is a prerequisite for large-scale deployment of 5G systems. Lots of research results show that when the FSS earth station (ES) is very close to the 5G system, the same channel deployment may become a big challenge. [5] analyzed in detail the three interference

M. Guan and Z. Na (Eds.): MLICOM 2020, LNICST 342, pp. 410–416, 2021.
https://doi.org/10.1007/978-3-030-66785-6_44

problems of C-band deployment of 5G systems and fixed-satellite services, and proposed measures to avoid interference based on the analysis results. For the problem of co-frequency interference, due to the limited site size of FSS earth stations, engineering measures and site-by-site coordination can be adopted to solve the problem of frequency coordination between operators and satellite operators. [6] studied the co-frequency interference between the 5G massive MIMO system and the FSS earth station on the 3.7–4.2 GHz, and analyzed the effect of the uplink and downlink transmissions of the 5G system on the satellite earth station. Lumped interference. Several interference mitigation techniques were identified and proposed, including protection distance, power control and frequency division.

In this paper, we mainly study the effect of interference from 5G system to the FSS earth stations in the downlink with 3400–3600 MHz band, where FES only works in the receiving mode. As the transmission power of 5G base station (BS) is far greater than that of 5G user equipment (UE), the interference from BSs to the FESs is larger than that of UEs to FESs. This paper focuses on the interference of 5G base stations to FSS earth stations. Through interference scenario simulation, system model assumptions, and interference simulation analysis, and finally determine the main interference factors of 5G BSs to FES.

2 Interference Scenarios and Analysis Methods

2.1 Interference Scenarios

The interference caused by 5G system to FSS earth stations mainly comes from 5G users and 5G base station [9]. However, because the transmission power of 5G base stations is much higher than that of 5G user equipment, the interference caused by base stations to FSS earth stations is much greater than that of 5G users. The following mainly studies the interference scenarios of 5G BSs to FSS ESs.

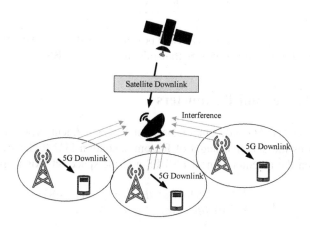

Fig. 1. Distribution topology of 5G BS and FSS ES

According to the current 5G network deployment, 5G base stations are numerous and densely distributed. When the strength of the base station interference signal received by the FSS ES is greater than its preset threshold, the low-noise module converter of the FSS ES is saturated with nonlinear distortion [5]. In this case, the FSS earth station will not work properly. This paper assumes that 5G base stations are evenly distributed around the FSS earth station in a ring. The distribution topology of 5G BS and FSS ES as shown in Fig. 1

2.2   Interference analysis

This paper uses the method in Recommendation ITU-R M.2101 to evaluate the interference of 5G BSs to FSS ESs. Since the user's position in the communication system is always changing, in order to approximate the operating state of the actual communication system, this paper uses the Monte Carlo algorithm to divide the entire system into multiple time segments for snapshot sampling. Then, the system simulation is completed according to the system's interference scenario, antenna model, path loss model, and propagation model.

If only the interference of a single 5G BS to the satellite ES is considered, the interference power received by the ES:

$$I_{5G} = \frac{P_{T,5G} G_{5G}(\theta_{BS,FES}) G_{FES}(\theta_{FES,BS})}{PL_{5G,FES}(d_{5G,FES})} \tag{1}$$

Where $P_{T,5G}$ is the transmission power of the 5G BS; G_{5G} is the antenna gain of the 5G BS; G_{FES} is the receiving antenna gain of the FSS ES; $PL_{5G,FES}$ is the path loss between the 5G base station and the FSS ES; $\theta_{BS,FES}$ is the angle between the direction of the BS to the user and the direction of the BS to the FSS ES; $\theta_{FES,BS}$ is the angle between the direction of the satellite to the FSS ES and the direction of the BS to the FSS ES.

Therefore, the interference power of 5G BS received by FSS ES is:

$$I_{agg} = 10 \log\left(\sum_{n=1}^{N} 10^{\frac{I_n}{10}}\right) \tag{2}$$

Where I_{agg} is the aggregate interference power of 5G BSs received by the FSS ES, and I_n is the $n-th$ interference power transmitted by the 5G BS.

3   System Model and Parameters

In the simulation, the 5G base station uses an 8×8 element array antenna model. The FSS ES uses the antenna model of Recommendation ITU-R S.465, in which the relation between the antenna gain of FSS ES and the space off-axis angle is:

$$G = \begin{cases} 32 - 25 \log(\varphi) \, dBi & \varphi_{\min} \leq \varphi \leq 48° \\ -10 \, dBi & 48° \leq \varphi \leq 180° \end{cases} \tag{3}$$

φ is the space the angle between the direction of the base station antenna and the main axis of the FSS ES antenna; φ_{min} is the minimum off-axis angle.

The propagation loss between 5G BS and FSS ES is mainly the link loss. This paper adopts the free space propagation model.

The main parameters determined by the 5G system and the FSS ES system according to the relevant recommendations of ITU-R are shown in Table 1:

Table 1. System parameters

Parameter	5G BS	UE	FSS earth station
Frequency band/MHz	3400–3600		3400–3600
Cell radius/m	300		–
Antenna model	ITU-R M.2101		ITU-R S. 465-6
Transmission power/dBm	50–60	23	–
Antenna height/m	20	1.5	22
Antenna downtilt	10°	–	
Antenna diameter/m	–	–	2.4
Antenna specification	64(8 × 8)	4(2 × 2)	–
Antenna array gain/dBi	5	5	20
Horizontal/vertical 3 dB width	65°	90°	–
Horizontal/vertical ratio	30	25	–
FSS noise factor/dB	5	9	–
Interference threshold/dB	–	–	I/N = −12.2 dB
Received noise level value	−118.6 dBm(10 lg KTB, T = 100 K, B = 1 MHz)		

4 System Simulation

In the actual operation of the communication system, the user's location plays a vital role, because the user's location determines the beamforming direction of the base station antenna it serves, which in turn affects the base station's interference to the FSS earth station direction. In the actual system, the user terminal changes all the time. In order to approximate the operating state of the actual system, the Monte Carlo method is used for static system-level simulation. Divide the entire system into multiple time segments, take snapshots and sample each time, and calculate the system status under the current snapshot. When the number of snapshots is sufficient, the system status in the real scene can be approximated.

According to the above system parameters, this paper mainly simulates co-channel interference of urban scenes. In the simulation, the transmission power of the 5G BS is 50–60 dBm, and the protection distance between the FSS ES and the 5G BS is initially set to 5 km. When the aggregate interference from the BS exceeds the specified interference threshold (I/N = −12.2 dB), the protection distance is gradually increased to 50 km. The relationship between the INR of 5G BSs to FSS ESs and the protection distance is shown in Fig. 2.

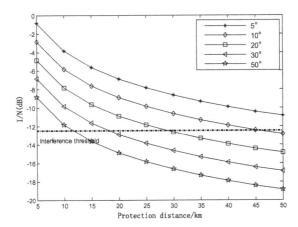

Fig. 2. Relationship between interference-to-noise ratio and protection distance received by FSS earth station

It can be seen from Fig. 2 that the larger the off-axis angle between the direction of the main beam of the FSS ES antenna and the interference signal of the BS, the smaller the protection distance required for coexistence between the satellite and the 5G system. If 95% interference threshold is considered. When the protection distance is 10 km, all the FSS earth stations except the ES with 50°off-axis angle cannot meet the conditions. Thus, increasing the angle between the main axis of the FSS ES antenna and the interference signal of the base station or increasing the protection distance can reduce the interference of the 5G BS to the FSS ES.

Figure 3 describes the relationship between the number of 5G base stations and the interference-to-noise ratio of FSS ES. The larger the angle, the greater number of base stations accommodated by FSS earth stations. But as the number of 5G base stations increases, the higher the interference-to-noise ratio, the greater the interference level of the FSS earth station. Thence, reasonable arrangement and control of the number of 5G base stations is one of the important means to reduce interference to FSS earth stations. Additionally, from the simulation results can be drawn, the higher the transmission power of the 5G BS, the stronger the interference level to the FSS ES, and the more difficult it is for the satellite to coexist with the 5G system. In order to minimize the impact of such situations on the FSS system, it is necessary to put forward higher requirements on the design of 5G base stations.

Figure 4 shows the relationship between the FSS earth station's received interference and noise ratio and the 5G base station and protection distance. When the 5G base station transmit power is 50 dBm, 53 dBm, 55 dBm, 57 dBm and 59 dBm, the required protection distance between the two systems is about 5 km, 7 km, 11 km, 16 km and 25 km respectively. The higher the transmit power of the 5G BS, the greater the protection distance required by the system, and the stronger the interference to the FSS ES, which is not conducive to the coexistence of satellites and 5G systems. In order to minimize the impact of such situations on the FSS system, it is necessary to put forward higher requirements for the design of 5G base stations.

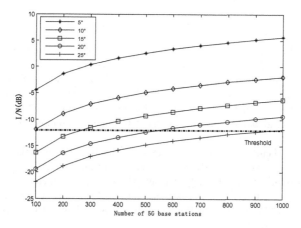

Fig. 3. The relationship between interference noise ratio and the number of BSs

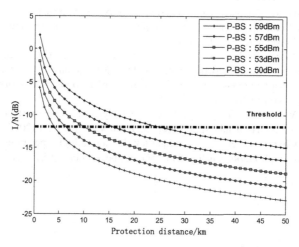

Fig. 4. The relationship between FSS interference to noise ratio and 5G base station transmit power

5   Conclusion

To solve the problem of interference coexistence between satellite and 5G system, this paper conducts interference analysis on the coexistence scenarios between 5G and FSS earth station. In the case of co-channel interference, we only consider the interference of 5G BS to FSS ES. Through the performance simulation of the interference-to-noise ratio of FSS receiver, it is concluded that to meet the interference threshold standard of FSS earth station, the protection distance between systems should be at least 15–20 km. Besides, the interference of 5G to the FSS system not only lies in the angle between the main axis of the FSS ES antenna and the interference signal of the 5G BS, but also depends on the number of 5G BSs and the transmission power.

References

1. ITU-R, IMT Vision-Framework and Overall Objectives of the Future Development of IMT for 2020 and Beyond, Recommendation M.2083-0, September 2015
2. IMT-2020 (5G) Promotion Group, White Paper on 5G Vision and Requirements, May 2014
3. Song, S.J., Chang, K.H., Yoon, C.H., Chung, J.M.: Special issue on 5G communications and experimental trials with heterogeneous and agile mobile networks. ETRI J. **40**(1), 7–9 (2018)
4. Li, Q.: Progress of global 5G spectrum licensing. Guangdong Commun. Technol **38**(10), 41–44 (2018)
5. Tan, H., Liu, Y., Feng, Z., Zhang, Q.: Coexistence analysis between 5G system and fixed-satellite service in 3400–3600 MHz. Sci. China Ser. F: Inf. Sci. **15**(11), 25–32 (2018)
6. Hattab, G., Moorut, P., Visotsky, E., Cudak, M., Ghosh, A.: Interference analysis of the coexistence of 5G cellular networks with satellite earth stations in 3.7–4.2 GHz. In: 2018 IEEE International Conference on Communications Workshops (ICC Workshops), Kansas City, MO, pp. 1–6 (2018)
7. Amendment of the Commission's Rules with Regard to Commercial Operations in the 3550–3650 MHz Band. April 2015
8. Son, H., Chong, Y.: Coexistence of 5G system with fixed satellite service Earth station in the 3.8 GHz Band. In: 2018 International Conference on Information and Communication Technology Convergence (ICTC), Jeju, pp. 1070–1073 (2018)
9. Hattab, G., Moorut, P., Visotsky, E., Cudak, M., Ghosh, A.: Interference analysis of the coexistence of 5G cellular networks with satellite earth stations in 3.7–4.2 GHz. In: 2018 IEEE International Conference on Communications Workshops (ICC Workshops), Kansas City, MO, pp. 1–6 (2018)
10. Li, K., Li, J., Wenhan, Y., Ying, X.: Interference analysis of FSS earth station by 5G system base station in 3.5 GHz band. Appl. Electron. Tech. **43**(08), 21–24 (2017)
11. Saha, R.K.: A hybrid system and technique for sharing multiple spectrums of satellite plus mobile systems with indoor small cells in 5G and beyond era. IEEE Access (2019)

Machine Learning Algorithm and Intelligent Networks

Energy PEC Enterprise Energy Management System Services

Yuyang Feng[✉]

Shenzhen Tuoyuan Energy Technology Co., Ltd., Shenzhen 518172, China
21503599@qq.com

Abstract. Energy PEC Enterprise provides enterprises with the function of energy visualization Kanban. Users can customize their energy-using devices by checking the box on the home page, and see the changes of energy consumption of the devices in real time, so as to achieve the overall energy-using macro data management of Zhen ding Technology.

Keywords: Visualization Kanban · Energy-using · Data management

1 Introduction

Demand management is mainly used for measurement management of transformer side demand, helping users to carry out basic capacity management and demand management charges. Users can choose whether to use demand charges or not based on the data, rather than the current basic capacity fee + actual consumption. The goal of this function module is to help users decide which charging method will reduce their actual electricity bill (Fig. 1).

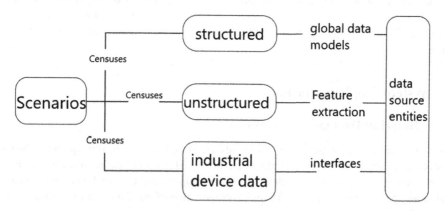

Fig. 1. Multi-source data aggregation

M. Guan and Z. Na (Eds.): MLICOM 2020, LNICST 342, pp. 419–423, 2021.
https://doi.org/10.1007/978-3-030-66785-6_45

2   System Design

Users can use in statistical analysis module calendar map function, energy consumption equipment energy consumption situation in a single month daily calendar display, energy consumption view in the form of macro energy consumption situation of the whole month, click on the figure in a single calendar can view the details of the data to a day, and can progress the data contrast of different calendar day (Fig. 2).

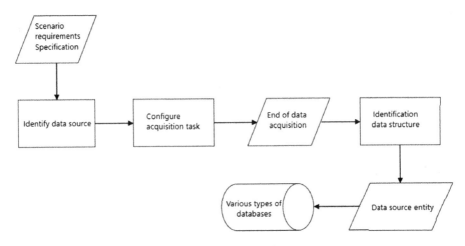

Fig. 2. Data flow chart

Users can directly view the historical energy consumption data of the equipment in the statistical analysis module, including the historical data of the equipment, such as electric energy, current, power, flow, pressure, temperature, etc., and can automatically calculate the maximum, minimum and average value of the data within a certain time range.

3   System Implementation

3.1   Historical Data Query Statistics

Users can directly view the historical energy consumption data of the equipment in the statistical analysis module, including the historical data of the equipment, such as electric energy, current, power, flow, pressure, temperature, etc., and can automatically calculate the maximum, minimum and average value of the data within a certain time range (Fig. 3).

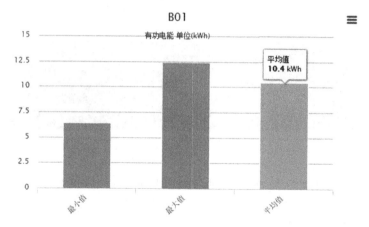

Fig. 3. Peak statistics

3.2 Energy Reference Line

Users can use the function of energy reference line in the statistical analysis module, set the energy reference line for each parameter of each equipment, define its assessment index, and achieve data quota management, which can be detailed to each workshop and each production line. Once the index exceeds the limit, the system will automatically alarm (Fig. 4).

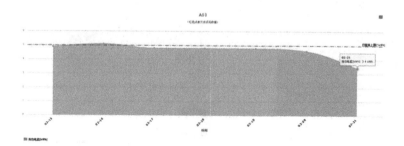

Fig. 4. Reference post

3.3 Comparison of Equipment Energy Consumption

Users can use the equipment energy consumption comparison function in the statistical analysis module to achieve the energy consumption comparison of the same type of equipment, the workshop and the factory. If Zhending Technology can dock with more systems in the future, it can achieve a fine comparison of equipment efficiency (Fig. 5).

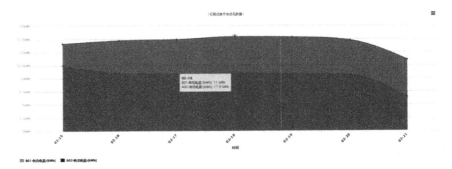

Fig. 5. Comparison of equipment energy consumption

3.4   Intelligence Reports

Energy PEC Enterprise provides smart reporting capabilities for enterprises, the ability to customize report templates, provide report design tools, and export, save, and print energy reports (Figs. 6 and 7).

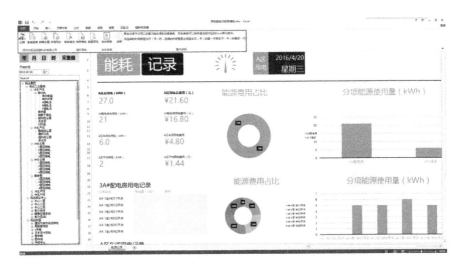

Fig. 6. Intelligence reports

Fig. 7. Compatible with computers, phones and tablets

4 Conclusions

A data acquisition module of intelligent meter based on WIFI is designed in this paper. Through analyzing the detailed data of HT6015 chip and ESP-7 WIFI module, the circuit schematic diagram of this module is designed and the code of related hardware is written, and the design and development of intelligent meter data acquisition module based on WIFI is realized.

References

1. Marinakis, V., et al.: From big data to smart energy services: an application for intelligent energy management. Future Gener. Comput. Syst. **110**, 572–586 (2020)
2. Samadi, E., Badri, A., Ebrahimpour, R.: Decentralized multi-agent based energy management of microgrid using reinforcement learning. Int. J. Electr. Power Energy Syst. **122**, 106211 (2020)
3. Wang, Y., et al.: Economic and efficient multi-objective operation optimization of integrated energy system considering electro-thermal demand response. Energy **205**, 118022 (2020)
4. Vivas, F.J., Segura, F., Andújar, J.M., Caparrós, J.J.: A suitable state-space model for renewable source-based microgrids with hydrogen as backup for the design of energy management systems. Energy Convers. Manag. **219**, 113053 (2020)
5. Oskouei, M.Z., Mohammadi-Ivatloo, B., Abapour, M., Anvari-Moghaddam, A., Mehrjerdi, H.: Practical implementation of residential load management system by considering vehicle-for-power transfer: profit analysis. Sustain. Cities Soc. **60**, 102144 (2020)
6. Sedighizadeh, M., Fazlhashemi, S.S., Javadi, H., Taghvaei, M.: Multi-objective day-ahead energy management of a microgrid considering responsive loads and uncertainty of the electric vehicles. J. Clean. Prod. **267**, 121562 (2020)
7. Fazlhashemi, S.S., Sedighizadeh, M., Khodayar, M.E.: Day-ahead energy management and feeder reconfiguration for microgrids with CCHP and energy storage systems. J. Energy Storage **29**, 101301 (2020)

Intelligent Water Scheme Design Based on Artificial Intelligence, Internet of Things and Big Data Technology

Tao Yang$^{(\boxtimes)}$ and Jinquan Ma

Shenzhen Koron Soft Co., Ltd., Shenzhen 518001, China
Yangtao0225@163.com

Abstract. The implementation of this project can effectively solve the problem of water shortage in urban economic development, change the single water supply pattern of Nansha District of Guangzhou drawing water from shawan waterway in the lower beijiang River and Shenzhen and Dongguan drawing water from Dongjiang river, and improve the water supply safety and emergency reserve capacity.

Keywords: Water supply · Safety · Informatization · Intelligent design

1 Introduction

In The Pearl River Delta project aims to optimize the allocation of water resources in the east and west of the Pearl River Delta, diverting water from the Xijiang River system in the west of the Pearl River Delta network to the east of the Pearl River Delta. The main water supply target is the water-deficient areas in Nansha District, Guangzhou, Shenzhen and Dongguan. Implementation of the project can effectively solve the water shortage problem in the development of urban economy, the change of guangzhou nansha district water from shawan waterway downstream beijiang river and shenzhen, dongguan city, from the single water supply pattern of dongjiang water, improve water supply safety and emergency support capability, improve downstream dongjiang river flow, water ecological environment, appropriate to the maintenance of nansha district, guangzhou, shenzhen and dongguan city water supply security and sustainable economic and social development plays an important role.After the completion of the project, the average water supply for many years was 1.708 billion cubic meters, including Nansha District 531 million cubic meters, 330 million cubic meters in Dongguan, and 847 million cubic meters in Shenzhen. The project also provides emergency back-up water supply to Hong Kong Special Administrative Region, Panyu District and Shunde District.

The project consists of one main line, two branch lines, a branch line, three pumping stations and a newly built regulating reservoir. The project draws water from Liushou of Xijiang River, pressurized by Grade 3 pumping stations of Liushou, Gaoxinsha and Luotian, and transports water to Gaoxinsha Reservoir, Dongguan Songmusshan Reservoir and Shenzhen Gongming Reservoir in Nansha District. The designed diversion flow rate is 80 cubic meters per second, and the total length of the

M. Guan and Z. Na (Eds.): MLICOM 2020, LNICST 342, pp. 424–428, 2021.
https://doi.org/10.1007/978-3-030-66785-6_46

water transmission line is 113.2 km, of which the trunk line is 90.3 km long, including the Dongguan sub-trunk line.

With a length of 3.6 km, shenzhen branch trunk line is 11.9 km long, nansha branch line is 7.4 km long, and gaoxinsha Reservoir is newly built.

The storage capacity is 4.82 million cubic meters. And don't for I, such as the project, project size is large (1) model.

Pearl river water resources allocation project investment in the history of guangdong province is the largest and longest water, the water area of the most widely water conservancy project, is a large bay area of guangdong water security strategic project, is the world's highest water pressure and shield tunnel is the longest water diversion project, is the pearl river delta core area long distance water conveyance project of deep tunnel, and the water distribution along the pearl river delta.

2 System Design

Overall plan with reference to the preliminary design review, follow the "wisdom water resources overall plan" and "water net letter level action plan for three years relevant requirements, the use of the Internet of things, cloud computing, big data, artificial intelligence, 5 g, such as a new generation of information technology, focusing on engineering construction, water regulation, project operation, emergency disposal, such as the core business, optimize the overall structure, optimize the platform construction, strengthen the construction of data, deepen the resources integration, expanding application of wisdom, provide scientific decision-making, fine management and comprehensive regulation of effective support, organization science, advanced technology, quality control, process can be traced back to the wisdom of the project objectives, as shown in Fig. 1:

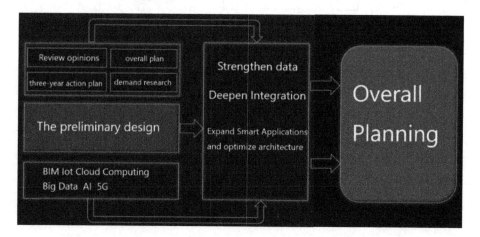

Fig. 1. Planning ideas

Combination of overall planning of the pearl river delta engineering actual demand, reference the advanced practice of related engineering experience, from the pearl river delta of engineering design, construction and whole life cycle of operations, focusing on senior management decision-making, combining various business management of engineering construction control, the safe operation of the project schedule, engineering science, engineering, emergency command, engineering intelligent maintenance and the actual need, provide a full range of intellectual support.

3 System Implementation

3.1 Overall Architecture

The pearl River Delta Intelligent Water Conservancy Project mainly includes a network, a brain and 7 intelligent applications. A network is mainly composed of the Internet of things and high-speed Internet connected information network connected with various monitoring devices; a brain is mainly composed of engineering cloud, big data and Taiwan in the project; seven intelligent applications mainly include intelligent construction and management, intelligent supervision, intelligent decision- making, intelligent scheduling, intelligent emergency response, intelligent operation and maintenance, and intelligent experience. See Fig. 2 for details:

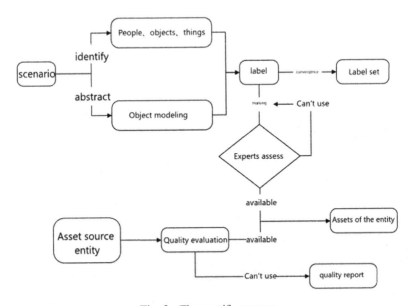

Fig. 2. The specific process

3.2 Data Resource Model System

Expression of engineering object model organization according to the data resources, reduce data redundancy, improve the ability of flexibility and easy connection between data structure, the object is divided into identity and attributes of object id only express ontology, the existence and uniqueness of the attribute is the ontology of possible related information, such as basic attributes, spatial and attribute, BIM properties, as well as logo or attributes are possible when phase characteristics, etc. As shown in the Fig. 3 below:

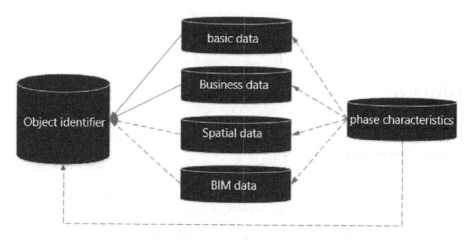

Fig. 3. Data resource model architecture diagram

4 Conclusions

In terms of time series, it covers all stages of the whole life cycle, such as project planning, construction, operation and maintenance, with a large time span. In terms of content composition, it covers IoT perception, automatic control, network communication, physical environment, basic hardware facilities, data center, intelligent platform, application system, etc. In terms of technology, IT includes monitoring technology, communication technology, industrial control technology, IT hardware network technology, physical environment construction technology, cloud computing/big data/artificial intelligence technology, BIM + GIS and other technologies, software development technology, water conservancy professional business and other technologies. In terms of system integration, it includes data integration among industrial control network, business network and Internet, data and process integration with Water Resources Department and Ministry of Water Resources, security authentication and process integration with provincial government affairs, data sharing and exchange with other departments, etc. From the point of construction units: including a number of different professional types, with different technical expertise, different section of the construction units.

How to ensure the home series, multiple unit construction technology, construction content to plan as a whole class for an organic whole, forming a joint collaborative community, can realize the seamless joint between each site content, several construction units to wrangling, harmonious coexistence, each other, to achieve high quality division of Labour cooperation, to ensure that the project, the Ministry of Water Resources and the provincial water resources bureau, the other part of the integration between integration, can guarantee the construction entity shall, according to the general technical requirements, the overall schedule, the overall goal all tasks efficiently and orderly organization work, must need to have a comprehensive ability to fall to the ground the total integration of units,Under the overall command of the owner, under the supervision of the supervisor, under the requirements of the design program and route, cooperate with all participating units to participate in the project construction.

References

1. Information Technology;Researchers at Zhejiang University Have Reported New Data on Information Technology (data-driven Solution for Optimal Units of Smart Water Conservancy). Internet WeeklyNews (2020)
2. Zhang, J., Liu, J., Jin, J.: Understanding and thinking on intelligent water conservancy. J. Water Cons. Water Transp. Eng. **2019**(06), 1–7 (2019)
3. Ge, Z.: Understanding and thinking of intelligent water conservancy construction in Shandong Province. Water Cons. Inf. **2019**(05), 6–8+19 (2019)
4. Sheng, X., Zuo, Z.: Application research of BIM technology in intelligent water conservancy of Hunan Province. Hunan Water Cons. Hydropower **2019**(05), 8–11 (2019)
5. Jiang, Y., Ye, Y., Zhao, H.: Research on the connotation characteristics, infrastructure and standard system of intelligent water conservancy big data. Water Cons. Inf. **2019**(04), 6–19 (2019)
6. Zhan, Q., Zhang, C.: Network security of intelligent water conservancy overall scheme. Water Cons. Inf. **2019**(04), 20–24+29 (2019)
7. Lu, X., Liu, S., Guo, X., Ma, Z.: Conception and thinking of intelligent water conservancy construction in Sichuan Province. Water Cons. Inf. **2019**(03), 4–9 (2019)

Energy + Cloud: A New Energy Management System

Tianyi Zheng[✉]

University of Electronic Science and Technology of China, Zhongshan Institute,
Zhongshan 528400, China
646640125@qq.com

Abstract. The main purpose of this project is to systematically monitor and analyze the power consumption in the industrial park of Skyworth Rock Base and give early warning of the equipment temperature.There are a total of 33 measurement monitoring points and temperature warning monitoring points in the Industrial park of Skyworth Rock Base, which monitor and control the electricity consumption in the research and development building, concentric building, complex building, water pump room and other areas in the industrial park.

Keywords: Analyze · Warning · Monitoring · Fine management

1 Introduction

Energy use is an essential part of all consumable businesses. Electricity, water, steam, etc. Rapid energy consumption increases the cost of production and management. How to save cost and manage effectively has always been a very difficult problem for enterprises.

At present, energy shortage and environmental degradation have become the biggest problems facing the world. In recent years, the global economy continues to high-speed growth and of mineral, the excessive use of water resources become the characteristics of global social development over the past couple of years, however, as the economic growth at the same time also triggered a global energy supplies and caused enormous pressure to environmental protection, the development of these problems require from individuals to the company must shoulder the responsibility of the social environment, take effective measures to reduce energy consumption.

The Chinese government attaches great importance to energy conservation and environmental protection and has made energy conservation and efficiency improvement part of its national strategy. By 2015, China's energy consumption per unit of GDP will be 16% lower than that of 2010. In industry, energy consumption per unit of industrial added value dropped by about 21%;The implementation rate of green building standards reached 15%.

M. Guan and Z. Na (Eds.): MLICOM 2020, LNICST 342, pp. 429–434, 2021.
https://doi.org/10.1007/978-3-030-66785-6_47

As a provider of high-quality energy information management system, Tuoyuan helps users to improve their business competitiveness by helping enterprises to effectively manage various enterprise equipment energy and continuously reduce energy consumption. Tuoyuan has 8 years of rich industry experience, service more than 100 enterprises, business involved in more than 30 industries. At every step of energy use, our solutions can help you save energy cost by 5%–30%/year, and reduce input cost by about 70% (Fig. 1).

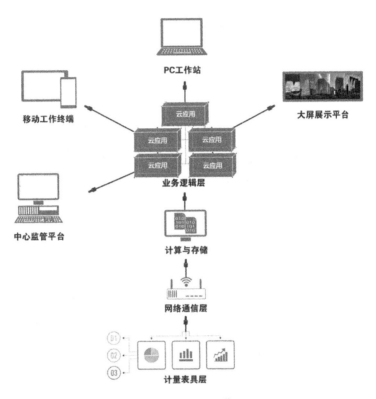

Fig. 1. The process diagram

2   System Design

The architecture of the energy management platform is shown in the following Fig. 2. The platform is mainly composed of three layers, namely the application layer, the data transmission layer and the data acquisition layer.

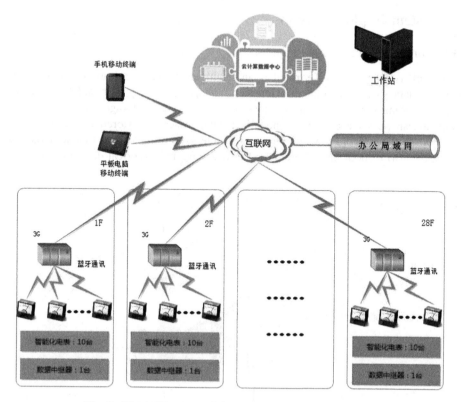

Fig. 2. The architecture of the energy management platform

1) Data acquisition layer: it is mainly composed of various measuring instruments, through which data acquisition of various energy or output (electricity, water, steam, compressed air, etc.) can be realized; The instrument is a direct acquisition equipment of energy consumption data, so its stability and accuracy are very important to the system.

2) Data transmission layer: Mainly composed of data repeater, it realizes data transmission from data acquisition layer to application layer through data transmission layer; The data repeater requires stable signal and strong anti-interference ability. The data repeater is responsible for the unified reception of the scattered transmitted information and serves as the summary gateway to transfer the information and data of each device to the cloud service platform.

3) Application layer: mainly composed of cloud service platform and clients, it realizes the final collection, storage, analysis and management of data; Cloud service platform is the core of the energy management platform, integrating collection, storage, analysis and management, while the user is the embodiment of the energy management platform, is to provide users with a variety of energy management data analysis tool, to help users achieve energy data analysis and management, provide clear data support, help enterprises to improve the efficiency of energy use. The user supports the use of multiple users and devices (mobile phones, tablets, work computers).

3   System Implementation

3.1   Jupiter Energy Data Terminal

The Jupiter Energy Data Terminal is an intelligent power monitoring terminal with built-in data storage. To measure current, voltage, power, power and so on many electric parameters, with a built-in clock and large capacity storage function, the time interval can be set according to historical data, frozen and stored in electric meter internal storage medium with wire and wireless communication function, can be convenient to readout instrument stored in real-time and historical data (Fig. 3).

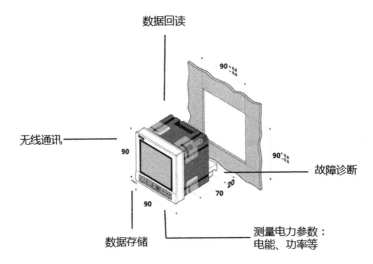

Fig. 3. Jupiter energy data terminal

3.2   Venus Intelligent Data Relay

Venus Intelligent Data Relay is an intelligent data repeater capable of collecting and forwarding energy data from Jupiter energy data terminal and Mercury Data Converter (Fig. 4).

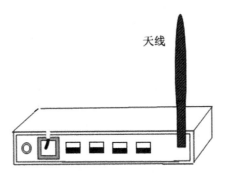

Fig. 4. Venus intelligent data relay

3.3   Mercury Intelligent Data Converter

Mercury Intelligent Data Converter is an intelligent data adapter that can transform Modbus protocol acquisition equipment. It is suitable for converting and storing data of data acquisition instruments with Modbus protocol, such as intelligent flow meter and existing intelligent electricity meter, to Mercury, and sending the data to the enterprise private cloud computing center through The Golden Star data repeater (Fig. 5).

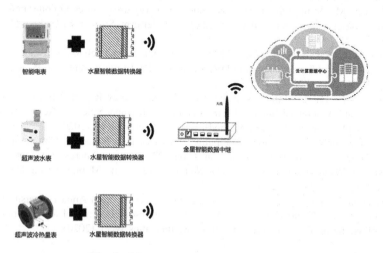

Fig. 5. Mercury intelligent data converter

4   Conclusions

From the perspective of enterprise management, Energy + cloud Energy management solutions provide enterprise managers with high visibility of Energy use and consumption, and assist enterprise decision makers in formulating and implementing Energy conservation and efficiency management strategies.

1) Rapid diagnosis of energy use problems and impacts to accelerate the promotion of energy conservation and efficiency;
2) Highly integrated equipment operation and energy consumption information;
3) Realize remote closed-loop energy management, optimize workflow, and maximize production efficiency;
4) Establish a high-quality and extensible energy management system, which lays a good foundation for enterprises to meet development and environmental challenges and establish digital management; Thus in the fierce competition of the market in favor of the unbeatable place.

References

1. Kumari, A., Gupta, R., Tanwar, S., Kumar, N.: Blockchain and AI amalgamation for energy cloud management: challenges, solutions, and future directions. J. Parallel Distrib. Comput. **143**, 148–166 (2020)
2. Ibrahim, G.J., Rashid, T.A., Akinsolu, M.O.: An energy efficient service composition mechanism using a hybrid meta-heuristic algorithm in a mobile cloud environment. J. Parallel Distrib. Comput. **143**, 77–87 (2020)
3. Lu, Y., Liu, M.: A simplified prediction model for energy use of air conditioner in residential buildings based on monitoring data from the cloud platform. Sustain. Cities Soc. **60**, 102194 (2020)
4. Hassan, H.A., Salem, S.A., Saad, E.M.: A smart energy and reliability aware scheduling algorithm for workflow execution in DVFS-enabled cloud environment. Fut. Gener. Comput. Syst. **112**, 431–448 (2020)
5. Energy - Solar Energy; Findings in the Area of Solar Energy Reported from University of Cadiz (Cloud Motion Estimation From Small-scale Irradiance Sensor Networks: General Analysis and Proposal of a New Method). Energy Weekly News (2020)
6. Information Technology - Cloud Computing; Researchers at School of Computing Science and Engineering Report New Data on Cloud Computing (Energy Efficient Resource Scheduling Using Optimization Based Neural Network in Mobile Cloud Computing). Technology News Focus (2020)
7. Information Technology - Cloud Computing; Study Results from Anna University Broaden Understanding of Cloud Computing (A novel energy estimation model for constraint based task offloading in mobile cloud computing). Mathematics Week (2020)

Smart Unmanned Vehicular Technology

Implementation of Non-stationary Channel Emulator Based on USRP

Dongyang Zhang, Kai Mao, Yang Yang, Benzhe Ning, and Qiuming Zhu[✉]

The Key Laboratory of Dynamic Cognitive System of Electromagnetic Spectrum Space, College of Electronic and Information Engineering, Nanjing University of Aeronautics and Astronautics, Nanjing 211106, China
{zhangdongyang,maokai,yangyang04,ningbenzhe,zhuqiuming}@nuaa.edu.cn

Abstract. Inspired by the modular design of virtual instruments, a discrete non-stationary channel model and a flexible hardware architecture are proposed in this paper. On this basis, a universal channel emulator is implemented on universal software radio peripheral (USRP) platform. Moreover, we proposed a sum of linear frequency modulation (SoLFM) method to accurately generate non-stationary channel fading with continuous phase, i.e., Rayleigh fading, Rice fading, and log-normal fading channels. In addition, hardware measurement results demonstrate that the measured statistical properties are well consistent with the corresponding theoretical ones.

Keywords: USRP · Virtual instrument · Non-stationary channel fading · SoLFM

1 Introduction

Wireless communication systems have played an important role in many important fields, such as satellite communication, telemedicine and mobile communication. In order to ensure the security and reliability of wireless communication systems, measurement campaigns should be taken into account under realistic conditions [1–3]. However, field tests are expensive and unrepeatable, which means large-scale test scenarios are limited. Alternatively, the channel emulator can reproduce the real channel in the laboratory for fast prototyping and performance evaluation of wireless communication systems under different conditions, which greatly reduces the research and development costs and production cycle [4–7].

There are several commercial channel emulators available, such as Elektrobit Propsim C8 and Spirent SR5500, which are extremely bulky and expensive. Moreover, they are mainly designed for standard channel models and inflexible to customize different functionality. In [8], the authors describe an improved scheme for Rayleigh fading channels based on field programmable gate array (FPGA), which achieved an improvement in resource consumption. In [9], a hardware correlated Lognormal distributed sequence generator based on FPGA was proposed.

© ICST Institute for Computer Sciences, Social Informatics and Telecommunications Engineering 2021
Published by Springer Nature Switzerland AG 2021. All Rights Reserved
M. Guan and Z. Na (Eds.): MLICOM 2020, LNICST 342, pp. 437–446, 2021.
https://doi.org/10.1007/978-3-030-66785-6_48

However, the hardware architecture of above researches mainly focused on the specific algorithm verification, which is not suitable for channel emulation of all kinds of fading. In [10], researchers developed an emulator to assess the bit error rate (BER) performance of multi-hop, multi-carrier communication systems on Universal Software Radio Peripheral (USRP). It should be noted that software-defined radio (SDR) are suitable options which offer flexibility and low cost in prototyping.

To the best of our knowledge, traditional emulators are designed for wide-sense stationary (WSS) [11]. However, a large number of researches [12–15] proved that the real channel has non-stationary characteristics. Although the study on non-stationary channel was carried out in [16], the parameter update was only a simple segment. Thus, the phase of the fading is not a smooth transition between adjacent channel states, which generates a deviation in the doppler frequency. This paper aims to overcome the problem. The major contributions and novelties of this paper are summarized as follows:

1) Considering the abrupt phase change characteristic between adjacent channel states, a sum of linear frequency modulation (SoLFM) method is proposed to generate non-stationary channel fading with continuous phase.
2) Based on the modular design of virtual instruments, we can focus on architectural and algorithmic issues which are of great significance for design. A low complexity universal hardware architecture is proposed and validated.
3) With the idea of SDR, a channel emulator is designed and implemented to efficiently reproduce multipath fading such as Rayleigh fading, Rice fading, and Lognormal fading, and reproduce the characteristics of the propagation in the laboratory.

The rest of this paper is organized as follows. Section 2 describes the system model and the system architecture of the emulator. Section 3 gives the design of the Non-Stationary Channel Emulation. Hardware test and validation are presented in Sect. 4. Finally, conclusions are drawn in Sect. 5.

2   Channel Emulator Design

Affected by the reflection and scattering of obstacles in the complex wireless communication environment, the signal reaching the receiver is made up of multiple paths with different power and delay [17]. In the condition of no obstacles between the transceivers, the signal travels in a straight line, which is called line-of-sight (LoS) path, otherwise it is a non-line-of-sight (NLoS) path [18]. Considering that FPGA has the characteristics of discretization and fixed-point operation, we propose a model which the discrete channel impulse response (CIR) can be expressed as

$$
\begin{aligned}
h(l,\varsigma) = {} & c^{\mathrm{LoS}}(l)h^{\mathrm{LoS}}(l)\delta(\varsigma - \left|\tau^{\mathrm{LoS}}(l)\right|_{T_s}) \\
& + \sum_{k=1}^{K(t)} c_k^{\mathrm{NLoS}}(l)h_k^{\mathrm{NLoS}}(l)\delta(\varsigma - \left|\tau_k^{\mathrm{NLoS}}(l)\right|_{T_s})
\end{aligned}
\tag{1}
$$

where l is the label of the discrete sequence obtained by sampling the time domain signal, ς denotes the label of the discrete sequence obtained by sampling the delay domain signal, T_s represents the sampling period, $\left|\tau_k^{\text{LoS}}(l)\right|_{T_s}$ and $\left|\tau_k^{\text{NLoS}}(l)\right|_{T_s}$ denote the rounding delay results of the LoS and NLoS paths, respectively. To carry out the real-time calculation of the output signal sample stream, the channel emulator convolves the discrete-time input signal with the discrete CIR in (1) as follows:

$$
\begin{aligned}
y(l) = {} & c^{\text{LoS}}(l)h^{\text{LoS}}(l)x(l)\delta(\varsigma - \left|\tau^{\text{LoS}}(l)\right|_{T_s}) \\
& + \sum_{k=1}^{K(t)} c_k^{\text{NLoS}}(l)h_k^{\text{NLoS}}(l)x(l)\delta(\varsigma - \left|\tau_k^{\text{NLoS}}(l)\right|_{T_s})
\end{aligned}
\tag{2}
$$

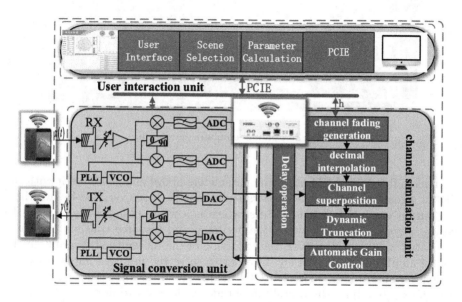

Fig. 1. Architecture of proposed channel emulator.

In order to accurately reproduce a wireless channel in a physical environment, this paper designs a flexible and reconfigurable channel emulator on the basis of (2). The emulator is designed by Labview FPGA module on the National Instrument USRP-Rio 2943R Software-Defined Radio platform which is equipped with a Xilinx Kintex-7 FPGA. As shown in Fig. 1 and Fig. 2, the channel emulator is made up of three units: user interaction unit, signal conversion unit and channel simulation unit. The user interaction unit provides a visual operation interface for users to configure associated parameters such as path delay, fading type, and spectrum shape. In the meanwhile, the RF input signals are down converted and sampled to digital complex baseband signals by the signal conversion unit. As the core part of the simulator, the channel simulation unit generates a non-stationary

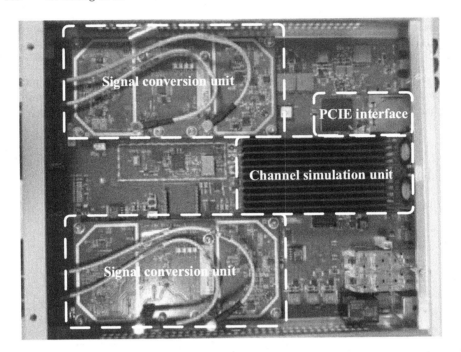

Fig. 2. Channel emulator hardware.

channel fading by SoLFM using the parameters above and combines it with the digital signals to produce a wireless environment. Moreover, the bit width of the output channel fading is 30 bits, which is a waste of hardware courses. To ensure a good tradeoff between the accuracy and resource consumption, it is truncated to 20 bits. However, the reduction of the bit width still results in the loss of amplitude and accuracy. In order to solve the negative impact of truncation, automatic gain control (AGC) module is added after truncation, which can effectively adjust the overall amplitude of the data to decrease the loss of accuracy.

3 Non-stationary Channel Fading Emulation

3.1 Principle of SoLFM Method

Traditional channel emulator often used sum of cisoids (SoC) method [19,20] to generate channel fading coefficients. The essence of the method is the sum of harmonics with different delays and power taking the place of the effects of direct radiation, scattering, reflection, and refraction during the wireless propagation,

$$\tilde{h}\left(t\right) = \lim_{N \to \infty} \sum_{n=1}^{N} e^{j\left(2\pi f_n t + \theta_n\right)} \tag{3}$$

where θ_n and f_n denote the initial phase and Doppler frequency of different branches. However, this method does not take into account the real-time changes of the channel parameters caused by the movement of the transceiver or scatterer. In other words, the channel does not meet the condition of wide sense stationary (WSS).

In order to solve this problem and reduce the complexity of hardware implementation, this article adopts the SoLFM method to generate non-stationary stochastic fading by upgrading $2\pi f_n(t)t$ to $2\pi \int_0^t f_n(\tau)d\tau$.

$$\tilde{h}(t) = \sum_{n=1}^{N} \sqrt{\frac{1}{N}} e^{j\left(2\pi \int_0^t f_n(\tau)d\tau + \theta_n\right)} \tag{4}$$

Meanwhile, due to the time-discrete characteristic of the hardware implementation, the model is further discretized as follows:

$$\tilde{h}(k) = \sum_{n=1}^{N} \sqrt{\frac{1}{N}} e^{j\left(2\pi \sum_{m=0}^{k} T_s f_n[m] + \theta_n\right)} \tag{5}$$

where m is the discrete time index, N is the number of sub-paths, T_s denotes the channel sampling period, $f_n[m]$ represents the discrete doppler frequency of sub-path, and θ_n is the random initial phase.

3.2   Hardware Implementation

The embedded Kintex-7 FPGA on the USRP Software-Defined Radio platform allows for the fast hardware implementation of the algorithm above. The hardware implementation with visual operations by Labview FPGA module include two key components. The embedded block RAM and ROM generate frequency control word and initial phase θ_n. Meanwhile, the look-up tables (LUT) combine the signals above to generate a time-varying fading with continuous phase based on the concept of direct digital synthesis (DDS). Instead of using existing Xilinx highly integrated intellectual property (IP), we design the prototype based on manual RTL-level design in HDL codes, which is tailored for our specific needs and costs less hardware sources.

As for implementation of the real-time delays in the tapped-delay line (TDL) Architecture, which is capable of performing the real-time convolution calculation by simple complex multiplication and additions, an embedded dual-port block RAM is adopted for parallel processing and real-time performance in Fig. 3. Limited to the sample rate of 100 MHz, the resolution of the delays is 10 ns, which satisfies the requirement of accuracy for most radio devices. Meanwhile, the maximum delay is decided by the depth of embedded block RAM available per path. Configuring the depth of 10000 can reach up to delay of 100 us, which is large enough for outdoor environment.

Just as depicted in formula (2), the path delay $\left|\tau_k^{\text{LoS}}(l)\right|_{T_s}$ denotes delayed signal and $h_k^{\text{NLoS}}(l)$ is realized by the non-stationary channel fading in the tapped-delay line architecture. Considering the fact that the sampling rate of the fading

is different from the delayed signal, they cannot perform multiplication operations directly. Consequently, a linear interpolator is needed before the TDL to
raise the low sampling rate of the fading in real time to complete the hardware
implement.

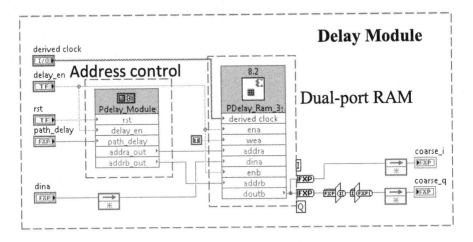

Fig. 3. Architecture of channel delay module.

Table 1. Resource consumption of FPGA.

Device Utilization	Used	Total	Percentage
Total Slices	17641	63550	27.8
Slice Registers	57792	508400	11.4
Slice LUTs	29657	254200	11.7
Block RAMs	133	795	16.7
DSP48s	302	1540	19.6

3.3   Resource Consumption

Following the above prototype design with the help of LabVIEW FPGA module,
the whole channel emulator has been successfully implemented on the USRP
Software-Defined Radio platform. It hosts an embedded Kintex-7 chip, which
consists of about 508400 Slice Registers, 254200 Slice LUTs, 795 Block RAMs
and 1540 DSP48. Taking one path for example, Table 1 summarizes the resource
consumption after synthesis and implementation at 100 MHz using LabVIEW
built-in local compiler. It can be seen from the table that DSP48s and Block

RAMs consume large amounts of resources, which occupy 19.6% and 16.7%, respectively. It mainly derived from the TDL, for multiplication and addition operations, and the channel delay for embedded block RAM. Considering the intrinsic consumption of the module, the embedded source is enough for 4 paths.

4   Measurements and Validations

In order to demonstrate the performance analysis and verify the effectiveness of the emulator intuitively, output waveform and amplitude distribution must be observed and calculated. Consequently, the testbed consists of a USRP as the channel emulator, a signal generator (Agilent E4438C) providing a 2 GHz carrier signal for testing, and an oscilloscope (Agilent N9340B) observing the measured waveform of channel emulator. Meanwhile, an industrial personal computer (IPC) running LabVIEW 2018 is connected to the USRP by the peripheral

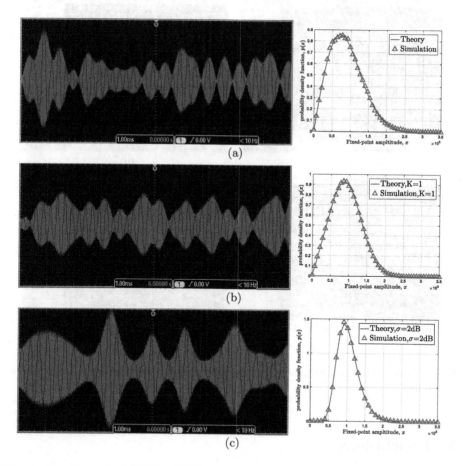

Fig. 4. Waveforms and PDFs of different channel fading (a) Rayleigh (b) Rice (c) Lognormal.

component interconnect express (PCIe) interface. At the beginning of the system, the host IPC downloads the compiled bitfiles into the FPGA and configures related channel parameters to be measured.

After the measurement, the output of waveform is shown in Fig. 4. Moreover, a large number of the measured waveform data are taken for statistical analysis of probability distribution function (PDF) by Matlab, which is shown in Fig. 4. It can be seen that the maximum distortion of the Rice distribution is 1.48% and the statistical Rician K-factor, K =1.02, is consistent with the input one, K = 1. The Rayleigh PDF deviation is 0.14 dB, and the maximum distortion of the lognormal distribution is 3.89%. In the meanwhile, the output of doppler power spectral density (DPSD) is shown in Fig. 5. The results show that the measured value is in good coincidence with the theoretical one and the emulator produces a physical channel which is similar to the natural one.

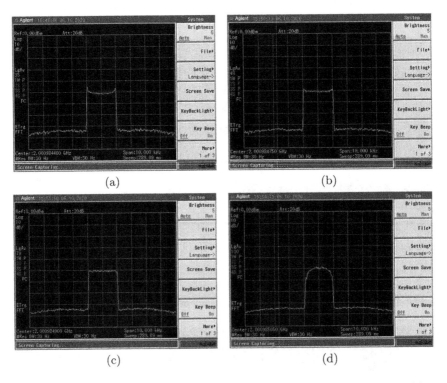

Fig. 5. Measured results of different DPSDs of (a) Jakes 6 dB (b) Jakes 3 dB (c) Flat (d) Round.

5 Conclusions

In this work, the design and prototypical implementation of a real-time channel emulator have been investigated based on the idea of virtual instrument and the USRP-RIO hardware implementation platform of National Instruments Corporation. The design allows to generate time-varying channel fading with continuous phase, such as Rayleigh fading, Rice fading and Lognormal fading in laboratory. It solves the problem that the wireless communication system cannot be quickly tested, and greatly reduces the research and development cost. Furthermore, hardware measurement results have demonstrated that the measured PDF agrees well with the theoretical ones, which verifies the feasibility of proposed scheme and implementation.

Acknowledgements. This work was supported in part by the National Key Scientific Instrument and Equipment Development Project under Grant No. 61827801, in part by Aeronautical Science Foundation of China, No. 201901052001, and in part by the Fundamental Research Funds for the Central Universities, No. NS2020026.

References

1. Zhang, J., Zhang, Y., Yu, Y., Xu, R., Zheng, Q., Zhang, P.: 3-D MIMO: how much does it meet our expectations observed from channel measurements? IEEE J. Sel. Areas Commun. **35**(8), 1887–1903 (2017)
2. Fan, W., et al.: A step toward 5G in 2020: low-cost OTA performance evaluation of massive MIMO base stations. IEEE Antennas Propag. Mag. **59**(1), 38–47 (2017)
3. Konishi, Y., Kim, M., Ghoraishi, M., Takada, J., Suyama, S., Suzuki, H.: Channel sounding technique using MIMO software radio architecture. In: Proceedings of EuCAP11, Rome, Italy, May 2011
4. Habib, B., Farhat, H., Zaharia, G., Zein, G.E.: Hardware simulator design for MIMO propagation channel on shipboard at 2.2 GHz. Wireless Pers. Commun. **71**(4), 2535–2561 (2013)
5. Joshi, G., Prasad, P.R., Singh, A.: FPGA implementation of channel emulator for testing of wireless air interface using VHDL. In: Proceedings of RTEICT16, Bangalore, India, May 2016
6. Jiang, K., Chen, X., Zhu, Q., Chen, L., Xu, D., Chen, B.: A novel simulation model for nonstationary rice fading channels. Wireless Commun. Mobile Comput. **2018**(1) (2018)
7. Patzold, M., Rafiq, G.: Performance evaluation of sum-of-cisoids Rice/Rayleigh fading channel simulators with respect to the bit error probability. Radio Sci. **49**(11), 997–1007 (2014)
8. Alimohammad, A., Fard, S.F., Cockburn, B.F., Schlegel, C.: An improved SOS-based fading channel emulator. In: Proceedings of VTC07, Baltimore, MD, USA, October 2007
9. Huang, D., Zeng, D.Z., Long, T., Yu, J.Y.: Design of a correlated Lognormal distributed sequence generator based on Virtex-IV series FPGA. In: Proceedings of ICCASM10, Taiyuan, Shanxi, China, October 2010
10. Merwaday, A., Rupasinghe, N., Gvenc, İ., Saad, W., Yuksel, M.: USRP-based indoor channel sounding for D2D and multi-hop communications. In: Proceedings of WAMICON14, Tampa, FL, USA, June 2014
11. Chen, B., Zhong, Z., Ai, B.: Stationarity intervals of time-variant channel in high speed railway scenario. China Commun. **9**(8), 64–70 (2012)

12. Eldowek, B.M., El-atty, S.M.A., El-Rabaie, E.M., El-Samie, F.E.A.: 3D non-stationary vehicle-to-vehicle MIMO channel model for 5G millimeter-wave communications. Digit. Signal Prog. **95**, 102580 (2019)

13. Gutibaierrez-Mena, J.T., Gutierrez, C.A., Luna-Rivera, J.M., Campos-Delgado, D.U., Vzquez-Castillo, J.: A novel geometrical model for non-stationary MIMO vehicle-to-vehicle channels. IETE Tech. Rev. **36**(1), 1–12 (2017)

14. Li, W., Chen, X., Zhu, Q., Zhong, W., Xu, D., Bai, F.: A novel segment-based model for non-stationary vehicle-to-vehicle channels with velocity variations. IEEE Access **7**, 133442–133451 (2019)

15. Zhu, Q., Wang, Y., Jiang, K., Chen, X., Zhong, W., Ahmed, N.: 3D non-stationary geometry-based multi-input multi-output channel model for UAV-ground communication systems. IET Microwaves Antennas Propag. **13**(8), 1104–1112 (2019)

16. Ispas, A., Ascheid, G., Schneider, C., Thoma, R.: Analysis of local quasi-stationarity regions in an urban macrocell scenario. In: Proceedings of VTC10, Taipei, Taiwan, China, May 2010

17. Zhu, Q., Li, H., Fu, Y., Wang, C.-X., Tan, Y., et al.: A novel 3D non-stationary wireless MIMO channel simulator and hardware emulator. IEEE Trans. Commun. **66**(9), 3865–3878 (2018)

18. Dhaka, A., Chauhan, S., Bhaskar, V.: Analysis and simulation of second-order statistics with modified characteristic function parameters in a multipath fading environment. Wireless Pers. Commun. **100**(3), 851–862 (2018)

19. Ghazal, A., Wang, C., Ai, B., Yuan, D., Haas, H.: A nonstationary wideband MIMO channel model for high-mobility intelligent transportation systems. IEEE Trans. Intell. Transp. Syst. **16**(2), 885–897 (2015)

20. Zhu, Q., Liu, X., Li, N., Chen, X.: An improved sum-of-sinusoids channel simulator based on Brownian motion. In: Proceedings of ISAP 2014, Kaohsiung, Taiwan, December 2014

21. Chen, Z., Wang, Q., Wu, D.O., Fan, P.: Two-dimensional evolutionary spectrum approach to nonstationary fading channel modeling. IEEE Trans. Veh. Technol. **65**(3), 1083–1097 (2016)

22. Ghiaasi, G., Ashury, M., Vlastaras, D., Hofer, M., Xu, Z., Zemen, T.: Real-time vehicular channel emulator for future conformance tests of wireless ITS modems. In: Proceedings of EuCAP16, Davos, Switzerland, April 2015

A V2V Channel Simulator for Velocity Variations in Non-isotropic Scattering Scenarios

Naeem Ahmed, Boyu Hua, Qiuming Zhu$^{(\boxtimes)}$, and Mao Kai

College of Electronic and Information Engineering, Nanjing University of Aeronautics and Astronautics, Nanjing 211106, China
{jubayar123,byhua,zhuqiuming,maokai}@nuaa.edu.cn

Abstract. Based on the consideration of variations in the velocity of both the mobile transmitter (MT) and the mobile receiver (MR), the method of vehicle-to-vehicle (V2V) channel simulation is mentioned in this letter. This method is able to simulate non-stationary fading channels under non-isotropic scattering scenarios. In which, the time variant parameters, i.e., complex channel coefficient, path power, and path delay are analyzed and derived. The proposed method can also be used for the real V2V communications by considering the effect of velocity variations on the channels. Besides, the analytical mathematical properties, i.e., probability density function (PDF), auto-correlation function (ACF), Doppler power spectral density (DPSD) are studied and executed under the Von Mises (VM) distribution. Simulation results show a well understanding between the analytical and emulated results, which ensures the efficiency of both the suggested method and derivations.

Keywords: Channel simulator · Non-isotropic scattering scenario · Statistical properties · V2V channel · Velocity variation

1 Introduction

V2V propagation channels have a great importance on the purpose and execution of novel communication protocols for vehicular ad hoc networks (VANETs) [1]. With consideration of a general design for non-stationary V2V channels with moving scatterers and terminal velocity variations [2] i.e., the mobile-to-mobile non-stationary (M2M) channel model introduced with dynamic velocities and trajectories [3]. Under multiple conditions, the channel model plays an essential role in designing, validation and optimization of communication system output [4]. The V2V communication is one of the most valuable communication systems, which can upgrade the security of life and resources by gathering and transferring information under sophisticated transportations [5]. In the meantime, fifth generation (5G) systems in [6] considered multiple-input multiple-output (MIMO) and V2V technologies for improving efficiency and develop the communication performance.

© ICST Institute for Computer Sciences, Social Informatics and Telecommunications Engineering 2021
Published by Springer Nature Switzerland AG 2021. All Rights Reserved
M. Guan and Z. Na (Eds.): MLICOM 2020, LNICST 342, pp. 447–458, 2021.
https://doi.org/10.1007/978-3-030-66785-6_49

The geometry-based stochastic model (GBSM) is a mainstream kind of modeling V2V channel in recent years due to its moderate accuracy and complexity. The channel is always changing constantly in the real world due to the moving objects and multiple-bounce scattering [3,7]. So, the assumption of the channel statistics does not change within a specific time and frequency [8]. The assumption of wide-sense stationary (WSS) modeling valid is only for very short time intervals, therefore in [9] a non-WSS V2V regular-shaped GBSM (RS-GBSM) is proposed. However, a large number of measured results show that the characteristics of V2V channel change with the scattering environment, i.e. the non-stationary feature of the V2V channel [10]. Besides, some existing models can be assorted as the movements in [11,12], imperfect receiver places in [13,14], and inadequate scatterers in [15,16] which investigated in channel modeling and statistical properties. Non-stationary V2V channel model is introduced in [17] which is much more accurate with real world GBSMs and also in [18] the model depicted the street scatterers, and supported for MIMO and wideband system. The non-stationary V2V channels allowed different velocities for both stable and moving scatterers. For both the LOS and NLOS cases, moving scatterers have an important contribution in the wideband V2V channels. In addition, increase and decrease tap powers, Doppler power spectral desity (PSD) and root-mean-square (rms) Doppler spread, reduce the rms delay spread in both LOS and NLOS scenarios. It can also increase the capacity for the LOS scenario, but for the NLOS scenario it has little impact [19]. In order to accord with non-isotropic scattering conditions, the sum-of-cisoids (SOC) simulation method was introduced in [20], which is better fitting with the measurements. By comparing the generalized method of equal areas (GMEA) with the Lp-norm method (LPNM) in [20,21] for designing SOC simulators has less time complexity and makes model parameters simpler while applying GMEA. The model in [22] V2V GBSM takes into account the variation in velocity of terminals along with moving scatterers, the measurement of real-time channel parameters and movements at different traffic conditions. The complex channel coefficient which is much more complicated comes to in consideration in this paper. The corresponding statistical properties i.e., PDF, ACF, and DPSD are also studied and executed under VM distribution scattering scenarios.

The remainder of the paper is structured according to this. Section 2 describes the reference model. Section 3 gives the proposed simulator and parameter computation method. The statistical properties of proposed method are executed in Sect. 4. The simulation and analyzed results are conducted in Sect. 5. At last, conclusions are drawn in Sect. 6.

2   Reference Model

Under a standard V2V communication scenario, the transmitter and receiver are moving with time-variant velocities, which can be denoted as v^T and v^R, accordingly. There are several propagation paths in the V2V communication system, and each path includes several sub-paths. The velocities of T and R are

in an initial distance, in which the angle between arrival signal with the direction of movements can be at the linear form of velocity variations [23].

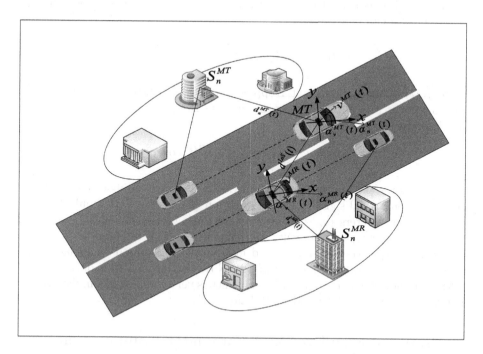

Fig. 1. A communication scenario of V2V channel model with velocity variations.

The time-variant channel impulse response (CIR) between the transmission and the receiver can be represented under non-stationary scattering scenarios as [24,25]

$$h(t,\tau) = \sum_{n=1}^{N(t)} \sqrt{P_n(t)} h_n(t) \delta(\tau - \tau_n(t)) \tag{1}$$

where $N(t)$ is the number of propagation paths distinguished by path delay $\tau n(t)$, path power $P_n(t)$ and channel coefficient $h_n(t)$. In (1) path delay $\tau_n(t)$ can be described as $\tau_n^T(t) + \tau_n^R(t) + \tilde{\tau}_n(t)$, where $\tau_n^T(t)$ and $\tau_n^R(t)$ explain the time delays of both the transmitter and receiver accordingly. And $\tilde{\tau}_n(t)$ describes the virtual link's equivalent pause. Additionally, it is also possible to model $h_n(t)$ by summing infinite sub-paths [24,26],

$$h_n(t) = \lim_{N \to \infty} \frac{1}{\sqrt{N}} \sum_{N=1}^{N} \exp\left\{ j\left(2\pi \int_0^t f_n(t)dt + \theta_n\right) \right\} \tag{2}$$

where N specifies the number of sub-paths, $f_n(t)$ is the time-variant Doppler frequency and the phase θ_n is periodic over $[\pi, -\pi)$ and can be represented as an independent, evenly distributed random variable over $[\pi, -\pi)$.

The channel impulse response (CIR) between T and R can be expressed as (1) under the general scattering environment, where N is the number of multipaths and sub-paths in each path, in (1) $h_n(t)$ represents the complex channel coefficient and can be expressed as

$$h_n(t) = \exp\left\{ j(2\pi \int_0^t f_n(t)dt + \theta_n) \right\} \tag{3}$$

where $f_n(t)$ is the time-variant Doppler frequency and the initial phase θ_n is periodical over $[\pi, -\pi)$. And f_n is the discrete Doppler frequencies and can be calculated by

$$f_n(t) = \frac{v^T(t)\cos\alpha_n^T(t) + v^R(t)\cos\alpha_n^R(t)}{\lambda} \tag{4}$$

where v denotes the amplitude of velocity, λ is the wave number, and α_n is the angle between arrival signal with the direction of movement. It should be mentioned that parameters $\{\theta_n, f_n\}$ are constant during each simulation trial under stationary scattering environments. In this paper $h_n(t)$ is modeled as an infinite sub-path superposition. Our proposed model can be acquired by replacing the current Doppler frequency model into (2). Note that our model is only designed for the complex channel coefficient $h_n(t)$ which is very complex to simulate rather than the power path $P_n(t)$ and path delay $\tau_n(t)$.

3   Proposed Simulator and Parameter Computation Methods

3.1   Proposed Simulation Method

The proposed method can be denoted as

$$\tilde{h}(t) = \frac{\sigma_\mu}{\sqrt{N}} \sum_{n=1}^{N} \exp\left\{ j\left(2\pi \tilde{f}_n t + \theta_n\right) \right\} \tag{5}$$

where N is the number of cissoids, θ_n is the initial phase of each path and can be developed by distinct random variables evenly distributed over $[-\pi, \pi)$. Doppler frequencies will be time-variant for the non-stationary situation due to changes of angles or velocities over time which can be modified as

$$\tilde{f}_n(t) = \frac{1}{\lambda}\left(v^T(t)\cos\alpha_n^T(t) + v^R(t)\cos\alpha_n^R(t)\right). \tag{6}$$

Most of existing non-stationary simulators or emulators use formula of $2\pi\tilde{f}_n(t)t$ directly to update the denoted model. In this case, the time-variant Doppler frequencies of generated fading channels would be

$$\int_0^t \tilde{f}_n(t)dt = \int_0^t \left(v^T(t)\cos\alpha_n^T(t) + v^R(t)\cos\alpha_n^R(t)\right)dt. \tag{7}$$

To overcome this shortcoming, submitting (7) into (5) which can be denoted as

$$
\hat{\mu}(t) = \frac{\sigma_\mu}{\sqrt{N}}
\sum_{n=1}^{N} \exp\left\{ j \left(\frac{2\pi}{\lambda} \int_0^t \left(\begin{array}{c} v^T(t) \cos\alpha_n^T(t) + \\ v^R(t) \cos\alpha_n^R(t) \end{array} \right) dt \right) + \theta_n \right) \right\}.
\tag{8}
$$

3.2   Computation of Time-Variant Doppler Frequencies

For the case of stationary scattering environments, i.e., isotropic scattering scenario, the angles follow a fixed distribution and can be approximated as independent with time instants or the locations of transceiver. Thus, the time-variant Doppler frequencies only depend on the amplitude of velocity. For a short time period, the speed can be approximated by a linear model [27],

$$
\begin{aligned}
v^T(t) &= v_0^T + a_0^T t \\
\alpha^T(t) &= \alpha_{n,0}^T + b_0^T t
\end{aligned}
\tag{9}
$$

$$
\begin{aligned}
v^R(t) &= v_0^R + a_0^R t \\
\alpha^R(t) &= \alpha_{n,0}^R + b_0^R t
\end{aligned}
\tag{10}
$$

where v_0, a_0 are constants describing the initial velocity and the rate-of-change of velocity. Submitting (9), (10) and (6) into (8), our simulation model can be simplified as

$$
\begin{aligned}
\hat{h}(t) &= \frac{\sigma_\mu}{\sqrt{N}} \sum_{n=1}^{N} e^{j\left\{ \frac{2\pi}{\lambda} \int_0^t \left(\begin{array}{c} (v_0^T + a_0^T t)\cos(\alpha_0^T + b_0^T t) \\ + (v_0^R + a_0^R t)\cos(\alpha_0^R + b_0^R t) \end{array} \right) dt + \theta_n \right\}} \\
&= \frac{\sigma_\mu}{\sqrt{N}} \sum_{n=1}^{N} e^{j\left\{ \frac{2\pi}{\lambda} \left(\begin{array}{c} (v_0^T \cos\alpha_{n,0}^T t + (a_0^T \alpha_{n,0}^T + b_0^T v_0^T)\frac{t^2}{2} \\ + a_0^T b_0^T \frac{t^3}{3}) + (v_0^R \cos\alpha_{n,0}^R t + \\ (a_0^R \alpha_{n,0}^R + b_0^R v_0^R)\frac{t^2}{2} + a_0^R b_0^R \frac{t^3}{3}) \end{array} \right) + \theta_n \right\}}.
\end{aligned}
\tag{11}
$$

It is noticed that this simplified model has been studied in [28–30]. In this case each path behaves like a chirp signal or a linear frequency modulation (LFM) signal, thus it is named as the sum-of-chirps model or the sum-of-LFM method in [28–30].

4   Stochastic Properties for Proposed Methods

4.1   Time-Variant PDF

For deriving the PDF of the proposed model here it can be described as

$$
\hat{\mu}_\xi(t, z) = (2\pi)^2 z \int_0^\infty \left\{ \begin{array}{c} j_0\left(2\pi \sqrt{\frac{\sigma_\mu(t)K(t)}{K(t)+1}} x\right) \cdot \\ \prod_{m=1}^{M} j_0\left(2\pi \sqrt{\frac{\sigma_\mu(t)}{N(K(t)+1)}} x\right) \cdot \\ j_0(2\pi z x) \cdot x \end{array} \right\} dx.
\tag{12}
$$

In (12) it shows that $\hat{h}_\xi(t,z)$ can entirely described by the variables of $N, \sigma_\mu(t)$ and $K(t)$, while the frequency variables have no impact. Thus, at every time period $\sigma_\mu(t)$ and $K(t)$ are stable. The PDF simulation model to obtain the output channels to the same components and quadrature components.

4.2   Time-Variant ACF

The ACF for non-isotropic scattering scenarios is a time-variant and corresponds both functions of time lag τ and time t. The time-variant ACF could be specified as

$$r_{hh}(\tau) = r_{mm}(\tau) + r_{\mu\mu}(\tau)$$
$$= E\{m^*(t)\,m(t+\tau)\} + E\{\mu^*(t)\,\mu(t+\tau)\} \tag{13}$$

where $r_{mm}(\tau)$ and $r_{\mu\mu}(\tau)$ denotes the path components respectively. Here $r_{mm}(\tau)$ can be approximately calculated by

$$r_{\tilde{m}\tilde{m}}(t,\tau) = \exp\left\{j2\pi \int_t^{t+\tau} \tilde{f}_n(\tau)d\tau\right\} =$$

$$\exp\left\{j\frac{2\pi\tau}{\lambda}\right\}\left[\left[\left(\begin{array}{c} v_0^T \cos \alpha_{n,0}^T(\tau) + \\ (a_0^T \alpha_{n,0}^T + v_0^T b_0^T) \\ (t\tau + \frac{\tau^2}{2}) + a_0^T b_0^T \\ (t^2\tau + t\tau^2 + \frac{\tau^3}{3}) \\ v_0^R \cos \alpha_{n,0}^R(\tau) + \\ (a_0^R \alpha_{n,0}^R + v_0^R b_0^R) \\ (t\tau + \frac{\tau^2}{2}) + a_0^R b_0^R \\ (t^2\tau + t\tau^2 + \frac{\tau^3}{3}) \end{array}\right) + \right]\right]. \tag{14}$$

The calculation of (14) shows the ACF changes over time-delay. The time-variant ACF with the VM distribution can be specified as

$$\tilde{r}_{\tilde{\mu}\tilde{\mu}}(\tau) = \sum_s^{\{1,2\}} \prod_i^{\{T,R\}} E\left\{\left(\tilde{\mu}_s^i(t)\right)^* \tilde{\mu}_s^i(t+\tau)\right\}. \tag{15}$$

Finally, the theoretical ACF in (13) of the proposed model can be obtained by substituting (13) and (14) into (15).

4.3   Time-Variant DPSD

The time-variant DPSD could be represented as

$$\tilde{S}_{\tilde{h}\tilde{h}}(f) = \int_{-\infty}^{\infty} \tilde{r}_{\tilde{h}\tilde{h}}(t,\tau)\exp\{-j2\pi f\tau\}\,d\tau. \tag{16}$$

For Doppler frequencies linear variation, we know

$$\mu(t) = \frac{\sigma}{\sqrt{N}} \sum_{n=1}^{N} \exp\left\{j\left[2\pi\left(f_n t + \frac{k_n}{2}t^2\right) + \theta_n\right]\right\}. \tag{17}$$

By the support of the Wigner-ville method the DPSD can be written as,

$$
\begin{aligned}
W_\mu(f,t) = \frac{\sigma^2}{N} \sum_{n=1}^{N} & \delta(f - f_n - k_n t) \\
+ 4 \sum_{n=1}^{N-1} \sum_{\substack{m=2 \\ m>n}}^{N} & \frac{\sigma^2}{\sqrt{\beta_{nm}}} \cos\left(\frac{\pi}{4} + \alpha_{nm} - \frac{4\pi\gamma_{nm}^2}{\beta_{nm}}\right)
\end{aligned}
\tag{18}
$$

where,

$$
f_n = \frac{v^T \cos\alpha_n^T + v^R \cos\alpha_n^R}{\lambda}
\tag{19a}
$$

$$
\alpha_{nm} = \theta_n - \theta_m + 2\pi \left(\frac{v^T \cos\alpha_n^T + v^R \cos\alpha_n^R}{\lambda}\right) t + \pi \left(k_n - k_m\right) t^2
\tag{19b}
$$

$$
\beta_{nm} = k_n - k_m
\tag{19c}
$$

$$
\gamma_{nm} = f - \left(\frac{v^T \cos\alpha_n^T + v^R \cos\alpha_n^R}{2\lambda} + \frac{k_n - k_m}{2} t\right).
\tag{19d}
$$

The initial phase is random and evenly spaced over $[0, 2\pi)$ hence the equation (18) could be withdrawn by building over the phases. Thus, the DPSD could be written as

$$
\begin{aligned}
S_\mu(f,t) &= W_\mu(f,t)|_{\bar{\theta}_n} \\
&= \frac{\sigma^2}{N} \sum_{n=1}^{N} \delta\left(f - (\frac{v^T \cos\alpha_n^T + v^R \cos\alpha_n^R}{\lambda}) - k_n t\right).
\end{aligned}
\tag{20}
$$

5   Simulated and Analyzed Results

The proposed model validated under typical V2V scenarios which is verified by computing both theoretical and simulated results. In this proposed simulation method different trajectories are considered for the different variations of MT and MR, i.e., the similar directions, the inverse directions. By considering those different scenarios the VM distribution with $\kappa = 1$ and the carrier frequency is 2.40 GHz. The movements of scatterers are evenly distributed around terminals and all the parameters also random with various scenarios. As for validating the simulation output along with the theoretical output we considered PDF, ACF and DPSDs at several time instants.

According to (12) in this method the output of PDFs at three different time periods where t = 0 s, 1 s and 2 s is differentiated with the analytical results in Fig. 2. Similarly, for comparing the analytical and emulated ACFs at three different time periods where t = 0 s, 1 s and 2 s is derived and established in

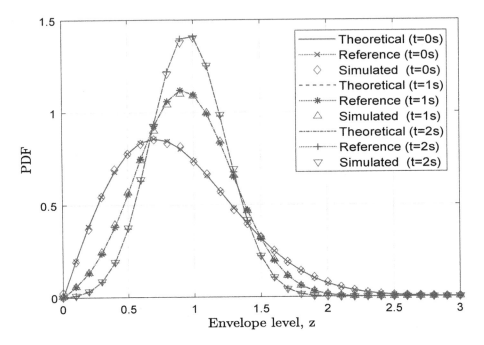

Fig. 2. Theoretical and simulated PDFs at different time instants.

Fig. 3. The simulation values generated by the improved method proposed in this paper are consistent with the analytical values of the reference model, and as the simulation time increases, both the PDFs and ACFs of the channel changes from Rayleigh distribution (t = 0 s) to Rice distribution (t = 1 s, 2 s). It should be noted that the larger the number of times the simulation, the closer the value of the simulation will be to the analytical value and the higher the accuracy of the simulation. As for the different time periods the simulated results of PDFs and ACFs showed a well matched results with the corresponding analytical results, which verifies simulated results with the analytical ones. Figures 2 and 3 shows a good agreement at different time instants.

Besides, the analytical DPSDs established by (16) are given in Figs. 4 and 5 which apparently shows the time divergence of the LOS components along with time path by the effect of velocity variations under different scenarios. Scatterers movements are considered to be evenly distributed across terminals. The T and R are shifting in two different scenarios along with different velocity patterns. Thus, the Doppler frequencies are computed and differentiate in Figs. 4 and 5 which shows that, the maximum Doppler shift in Scenario I and Scenario II are slightly changed from each other which also specifies the movements of scatterer. Those figures clearly show that the emulated Doppler frequencies of the designed method suited well with the analytical ones. As for the Doppler frequencies shifting overtime which can clearly be observed, means the velocity parameters v^T, v^R and also the acceleration parameters a^T, a^R are affecting the Doppler shifts

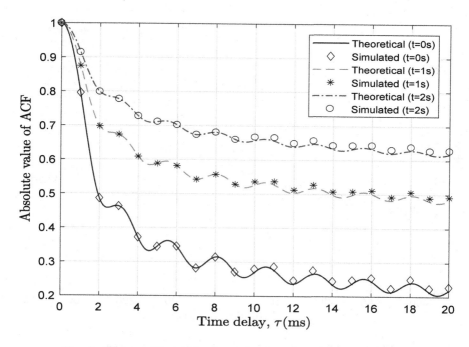

Fig. 3. Theoretical and simulated ACFs at different time instants.

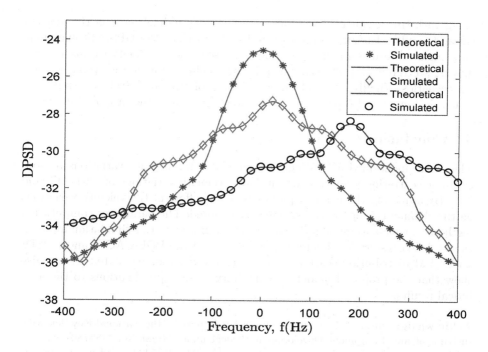

Fig. 4. DPSDs at different time instants under scenario I.

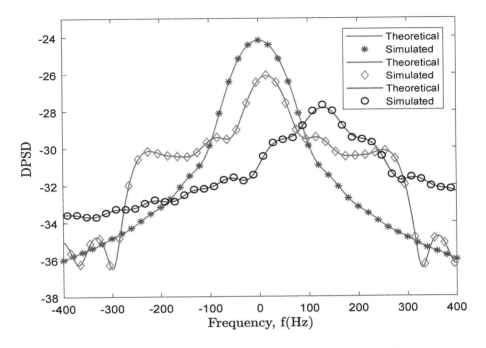

Fig. 5. DPSDs at different time instants under scenario II.

along with time, which proves the perfect understanding between the analytical and emulated results. Figures 4 and 5 shows that, the DPSD of analytical and emulated results for the first and second scenario of velocity variations with moving scatterers respectively, which is the results of the non-isotropic scattering scenarios. Finally, the well understanding of the analytical and simulated results in Figs. 4 and 5 confirms the accuracy, as well as the proposed model.

6   Conclusions

This letter mentioned a V2V channel simulator for velocity variations in non-isotropic scattering scenarios, which allows velocity variations of both MT and MR. By adjusting the channel parameters, the effort of the velocity variations on the channel characteristics specifically exposed. The parameter computation methods of time-variant simulations are given. Based on this simulation method, the analyzed results for different time instants of the PDFs, ACFs and DPSDs under VM distribution scattering scenarios are derived. Simulated results also show that the proposed model provides very close approximations to the analytical results.

Acknowledgments. This work was supported in part by the National Key Scientific Instrument and Equipment Development Project under Grant No. 61827801, in part by Aeronautical Science Foundation of China, No. 201901052001, and in part by the Fundamental Research Funds for the Central Universities, No. NS2020026.

References

1. Abbas, T., Sjöberg, K., Karedal, J., Tufvesson, F.: A measurement based shadow fading model for vehicle-to-vehicle network simulations. Int. J. Antennas Propag. 2015, Art. ID 190607, May 2015
2. Zhu, Q., Li, W., Wang, C.-X., Xu, D., Bian, J., et al.: Temporal correlations for a nonstationary vehicle-to-vehicle channel model allowing velocity variations. IEEE Commun. Lett. **23**(7), 1280–1284 (2019)
3. He, R., Ai, B., Stüber, G.L., Zhong, Z.: Mobility model-based nonstationary mobile-to-mobile channel modeling. IEEE Trans. Wireless Commun. **17**(7), 4388–4400 (2018)
4. Fei, D., He, R., Ai, B., Zhang, B., Guan, K., et al.: Massive MIMO channel measurements and analysis at 3.33 GHz. In: 10th International Conference on Communcation and Network in China (ChinaCom), pp. 194–198, August 2015
5. Wang, C.-X., Cheng, X., Laurenson, D.I.: Vehicle-to-vehicle channel modeling and measurements: recent advances and future challenges. IEEE Commun. Mag. **47**(11), 96–103 (2009)
6. Wang, C.-X., Bian, J., Sun, J., Zhang, W., Zhang, M.: A survey of 5G channel measurements and models. IEEE Commun. Surv. Tuts. **20**(4), 3142–3168 (2018)
7. Ghazal, A., Wang, C.-X., Ai, B., Yuan, D., Haas, H.: A nonstationary wideband MIMO channel model for high-mobility intelligent transportation systems. IEEE Trans. Intel. Trans. Sys. **16**(2), 885–897 (2015)
8. Herdin, M.: Non-stationary indoor MIMO radio channels, Ph.D. dissertation, Technische Universitat Wien, August 2004
9. Yuan, Y., Wang, C.-X., He, Y., Alwakeel, M.M., Aggoune, E.M.: 3D wideband non-stationary geometry-based stochastic models for nonisotropic MIMO vehicle-to-vehicle channels. IEEE Trans. Wireless Commun. **14**(12), 6883–6895 (2015)
10. Dahech, W., Pätzold, M., Gutiérrez, C.A., Youssef, N.: A non-stationary mobile-to-mobile channel model allowing for velocity and trajectory variations of the mobile stations. IEEE Trans. Wireless Commun. **16**(3), 1987–2000 (2017)
11. Guan, K., Ai, B., Nicolas, M.L., Geise, R., Moller, A., Zhong, Z., et al.: On the influence of scattering from traffic signs in vehicle-to-X communications. IEEE Trans. Veh. Technol. **65**(8), 5835–5849 (2016)
12. Cheng, X., Wang, C.-X., Ai, B., Aggoune, H.: Envelope level crossing rate and average fade duration of nonisotropic vehicle-to-vehicle ricean fading channels. IEEE Trans. Intell. Transp. Syst. **15**(1), 62–72 (2014)
13. Zhu, Q., Xue, C., Chen, X., Yang, Y.: A new MIMO channel model incorporating antenna effects. Prog. Electromagn. Res. M **50**, 129–140 (2016)
14. Zajic, A.G., Stuber, G.L.: Space-time correlated mobile-to mobile channels: modelling and simulation. IEEE Trans. Veh. Technol. **57**(2), 715–726 (2008)
15. Fan, W., de Lisbona, X.C.B., Sun, F., Nielsen, J.Ø., Knudsen, M.B., Pedersen, G.F.: Emulating spatial characteristics of MIMO channels for OTA testing. IEEE Trans. Antenna Propag. **61**(8), 4306–4314 (2013)
16. Zhang, J., Zhang, X., Yu, Y., Xu, R., Zheng, Q., et al.: 3D MIMO: how much does it meet our expectations observed from channel measurements. IEEE J. Sel. Areas Commun. **35**(8), 1887–1903 (2017)
17. Zhu, Q., Yang, Y., Chen, X., Tan, Y., Fu, Y., Wang, C.-X., et al.: A novel 3D non-stationary vehicle-to-vehicle channel model and its spatial-temporal correlation properties. IEEE Access **6**, 43633–43643 (2018)

18. Zhao, X., Liang, X., Li, S., Ai, B.: Two-cylinder and multi-ring GBSSM for realizing and modeling of vehicle-to-vehicle wideband MIMO channels. IEEE Trans. Intel. Trans. Sys. **17**(10), 2787–2799 (2016)
19. Liang, X., Zhao, X., Li, Y., Li, S., Wang, Q.: A non-stationary geometry-based street scattering model for vehicle-to-vehicle wideband MIMO channels. Wireless Pers. Commun. **90**(1), 325–338 (2016)
20. Gutiérrez, C.A., Pätzold, M.: The generalized method of equal areas for the design of sum-of-cisoids simulators for mobile Rayleigh fading channels with arbitrary Doppler spectra. Wirel. Commun. Mob. Comp. **13**(10), 951–966 (2013)
21. Gutiérrez, C.A.: Channel Simulation Models for Mobile Broadband Communication Systems. University of Agder, Kristiansand (2009)
22. Li, W., Chen, X., Zhu, Q., Zhong, W., Xu, D., et al.: A novel segment-based model for non-stationary vehicle-to-vehicle channels with velocity variations. IEEE Access **7**, 133442–133451 (2019)
23. Li, J., Jiang, D., Zhang, X.: DOA estimation based on combined unitary ESPRIT for coprime MIMO radar. IEEE Commun. Lett. **21**(1), 96–99 (2017)
24. Zhu, Q., Li, H., Fu, Y., Wang, C.-X., Tan, Y., Chen, X.: A novel 3D non-stationary wireless MIMO channel simulator and hardware emulator. IEEE Trans. on Commun. **66**(9), 3865–3878 (2018)
25. Wu, S., Wang, C.-X., Aggoune, H.M., Alwakeel, M.M., You, X.-H.: A general 3D non-stationary 5G wireless channel model. IEEE Trans. Commun. **66**(7), 3065–3078 (2018)
26. Patzold, M., Gutierrez, C.A.: Definition and analysis of quasi-stationary intervals of mobile radio channels Invited paper. In: Proc, pp. 1–6. IEEE VTC Spring, Porto, Portugal, June 2018
27. Pätzold, M.: Mobile Radio Channels, 2nd edn. Wiley (2012)
28. Pätzold, M., Gutierrez, C.A.: The Wigner distribution of sum-of-cisoids and sum-of-chirps processes for the modelling of stationary and non-stationary mobile channels. In: IEEE 83rd Veh. Tech. Conf. (VTC Spring), pp. 1–5, May 2016
29. Zhu, Q., Liu, X., Yin, X., Chen, X., Xue, C.: A novel simulator of non-stationary random MIMO channels in Rayleigh fading scenarios. Int. J. Antennas and Prop., 1–9 (2016). Art. ID 3492591
30. Jiang, K., Chen, X., Zhu, Q., Chen, L., Xu, D., Chen, B.: A novel simulation model for non-stationary rice fading channels. Wirel. Commun. Mobile Comput. **2018**(1), 1–9 (2018)

Ray Tracing Based Path Loss Modeling for UAV-to-Ground mmWave Channels in Campus Scenario

Mengtian Yao[1], Xiaomin Chen[1(✉)], Jian Wang[2], Boyu Hua[1], Weizhi Zhong[3], Qiuming Zhu[1(✉)], and Jingwen Yang[1]

[1] The Key Laboratory of Dynamic Cognitive System of Electromagnetic Spectrum Space, College of Electronic and Information Engineering, Nanjing University of Aeronautics and Astronautics, Nanjing 211106, China
{yaomengtian,chenxm402,byhua,zhuqiuming,yangjingwen}@nuaa.edu.cn
[2] China Institute of Radio Propagation, Qingdao 266107, China
wangjian@criep.com
[3] The Key Laboratory of Dynamic Cognitive System of Electromagnetic Spectrum Space, College of Astronautics, Nanjing University of Aeronautics and Astronautics, Nanjing 211106, China
zhongwz@nuaa.edu.cn

Abstract. In this paper, based on extensive ray tracing (RT) simulation data in campus scenario, a tailored path loss (PL) model for unmanned aerial vehicle (UAV) assisted air-to-ground (A2G) millimeter wave (mmWave) communications is proposed. The new model originates from the classic Close-in (CI) model, but takes the factor of UAV height into account with the help of extensive RT simulated data under the A2G campus scenario. The simulation and analysis results show that the proposed PL model matches better than the original CI model for certain trajectory at any UAV height. This modeling method can also be extended to any A2G scenarios by adjusting the parameters of model with RT simulated data.

Keywords: UAV-assisted mmWave communications · A2G channel · PL model · Large-scale fading · RT method

1 Introduction

Operating as the airborne base stations (BSs) or flying relays, the UAV-assisted communication has attracted great interests to expand the coverage in the fifth and beyond generation (5G/B5G) mobile communications. The mmWave technologies have also been adopted to meet the increasing demand of bandwidth, transmission rate, and massive connectivity. However, the mmWave communications involve very higher PL and have some new features compared with the conventional sub-6 GHz communications [1]. A thorough understanding of PL

M. Guan and Z. Na (Eds.): MLICOM 2020, LNICST 342, pp. 459–470, 2021.
https://doi.org/10.1007/978-3-030-66785-6_50

modeling and characteristics is essential for the system design and optimization of UAV-assisted communications.

Some channel models or measurements for the mmWave mobile communications have been done in [2–12] but only limited studies for the UAV scenarios can be found. The authors in [13] conducted field measurements by a UAV flying at five different altitudes in a rural environment and a PL regression curve was extracted. The authors in [14] presented an A2G model based on the measurements of over-water environments and analyzed the correlation of PL. In [15], the authors conducted measurements in the line-of-sight (LoS) and non-line-of-sight (NLoS) scenarios at 900 MHz, 1800 MHz, and 5 GHz and developed a log-distance PL model. Some other PL measurements of UAV channel with different carriers such as 1, 2.585, 4 and 4.3 GHz can be addressed in [17–19], but all of them are only for the sub-6 GHz band.

Note that the field measurement for mmWave UAV channels is difficult and costly. As an alternative option, some propagation models based on the RT simulations have been presented [20–22]. For example, the authors in [23] studied the PL in LoS and NLoS scenarios of mmWave A2G channels at 28 GHz by RT simulation. The authors in [24] proposed a prediction model for PL in A2G mmWave channels based on the machine learning method at 28 GHz and 73 GHz. In [25], a PL model including the factor of elevation angle at 28 GHz was proposed. In [26], an average PL considering LoS probability of mmWave A2G channels was proposed.

The RT simulation method is time consuming and sensitive to the map accuracy. It's more applicable to describe the PL model in a statistical way. However, the study of statistical modeling for the PL of A2G scenario is not sufficient. This paper intends to fill this gap. Based on the extensive RT simulation data in campus scenario, this paper develops a tailored PL model for UAV mmWave communications by considering the factor of UAV height. We compare the 3GPP model and our modified model at three different UAV heights, and validate the modified model by using RT method. This model can be generalized to any other scenes, but the parameter values need to be adjusted according to the RT simulation results.

This paper is organized as follows. Section 2 gives a basic stochastic PL model. In Sect. 3, the computation methods of LoS probability and path loss are developed and analyzed. In Sect. 4, the modified PL model of campus scenarios is evaluated by simulation method. Finally, some conclusions are given in Sect. 5.

2   Stochastic Path Loss Model

The measured-based PL model in a statistical way, i.e., stochastic model or empirical model is more popular. Note that the measured-based path loss modeling method is adopted in most of standardized mobile channel models, such as 3GPP, WINNER +, and ITU-R. A widely used model can be expressed by averaging the path loss in the LoS and NLoS scenarios as

$$L\,[\text{dB}] = P_{\text{LoS}} \cdot L_{\text{LoS}} + (1 - P_{\text{LoS}}) \cdot L_{\text{NLoS}} \tag{1}$$

where P_{LoS} denotes the LoS probability, L_{LoS} and L_{NLoS} are the path losses in the LoS and NLoS scenarios, respectively. It should be mentioned that the UAV propagation scenario is quite different with traditional mobile communications, i.e., three-dimensional (3D) propagation and valid scatterers only around the ground station. Thus, the model parameters provided in the standardized models cannot be used directly and this paper focuses on optimizing these parameters for the UAV mmWave scenarios. Beginning in 90's, the RT methods began to be widely used for the channel modelling, especially for small area and high frequency band [27]. Some well-known software tools based on the RT algorithms can also be found, e.g., Wireless Insite, Volcano, WaveSight, Winpro, and CloudRT. However, it's difficult to calculate all PL by huge number of rays in real-time.

3 Parameter Computation and Modification

3.1 LoS Probability

The UAV-assisted communications have a significant advantage on the mobile communications for having a much higher LoS probability. The LoS probability can be described by a statistical model of distance and environmental layout and it's usually frequency-independent for simplicity. The LoS probability model of rural environments in the 3GPP and ITU-R channel models originates from WINNER's exponential decay model. The NYU and 5GCM model update the parameters based on the 3GPP model. It should be mentioned that most of aforementioned methods are designed for the mobile communication environments. In order to set up a generic A2G PL model, the statistical ITU-R Rec. P.1410 model [28] is adopted in this paper. This model does not need precise information about buildings and is given as

$$P_{\text{LOS}} = \prod_{n=0}^{m} \left[1 - \exp \left(-\frac{\left(h_{\text{UAV}} - \frac{(n+0.5)(h_{\text{UAV}} - h_{\text{V}})}{m+1} \right)^2}{2\gamma^2} \right) \right] \qquad (2)$$

where $m = floor\left(d\sqrt{\alpha\beta} - 1 \right)$, d is the horizontal distance between the UAV and vehicle, h_{UAV} and h_{V} represent the height of the UAV and vehicle, respectively. α is the fraction of area with buildings to the total land area, β is the average buildings per square kilometer, and γ characterizes the height distribution of buildings.

The simulation results are given in Fig. 1. Different results of LoS probability can be found due to different propagation environments, where the suburban environment has the highest value and the high-rise urban environment has the lowest one. The reason is that the suburban environment is an open area while the high-rise urban environment has more obstacles. Moreover, the LoS probability of high-rise urban is below 40% with the distance over 100 m (Table 1).

Table 1. Parameters of different environments

Environment	α	β	γ
Suburban	0.1	750	8
Urban	0.3	500	15
Dense urban	0.5	300	20
High-rise urban	0.5	300	50

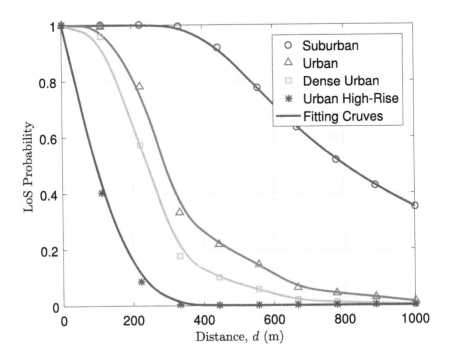

Fig. 1. LoS probabilities under different environments.

3.2 Modified Path Loss

For the mmWave communications, LoS and NLoS conditions are totally different and usually described separately. The PL model of 3GPP channel model and ITU-R model are similar and more suitable for the frequencies below 6 GHz. A well-known terrestrial log-distance PL model, namely CI model, has good parameter stability and is suitable for mmWave band [7]. The CI model bases on the free space path loss and the Friis' law, and accounts for the frequency and distance as

$$L^{\mathrm{CI}}\left(f_c, d\right)[\mathrm{dB}] = 32.4 + 20\log_{10}\left(f_c\right) + 10n\log_{10}\left(d\right) + \chi_\sigma \tag{3}$$

where χ_σ is a zero-mean Gaussian variable to represent the factor of shadow fading, d, f_c are the distance in m and carrier frequency in GHz at 1 m. In (3), n

is the path loss exponent (PLE) and it's recommended as 2.16 and 2.75 by the 3GPP standard in the case of LoS and NLoS.

Note that the factor of flying height is not considered in the above model. In order to make the model fit the UAV communications under the specific area, e.g., the campus scenario, we have conducted tremendous simulations and obtained lots of RT simulated data. In this simulation, we put a vehicle on the ground as a receiver and a UAV as a transmitter. The UAV's height starts from 30 m and increases every 20 m to 500 m, with a total of about 24 layers. For each layer, 1000 positions are selected and they are divided into LoS points and NLoS points. We calculate the path loss for the LoS point and NLoS point separately, and get the relevant data. By fitting these data, we introduce a new parameter with respect to the height of UAV, and upgrade the PL model under the LoS and NLoS scenarios, respectively, as

$$L_{\text{LOS}}\left(f_c, d, h_{\text{UAV}}\right)[\text{dB}] = 32.4 + 20\log_{10}\left(f_c\right) \qquad (4)$$
$$+ 10\left(2.16 + 0.0001h_{\text{UAV}}\right) \cdot \log_{10}\left(d\right) + \chi_{\sigma\text{LOS}}$$

$$L_{\text{NLOS}}\left(f_c, d, h_{\text{UAV}}\right)[\text{dB}] = 32.4 + 20\log_{10}\left(f_c\right) \qquad (5)$$
$$+ 10\left(2.75 - 0.0001h_{\text{UAV}}\right) \cdot \log_{10}\left(d\right) + \chi_{\sigma\text{NLOS}}$$

where $\chi_{\sigma\text{LoS}}$ and $\chi_{\sigma\text{NLoS}}$ denote the shadowing in LoS and NLoS scenarios, respectively. In practice, $\sigma_{\text{LoS}} = 5.9\,\text{dB}$ and $\sigma_{\text{NLoS}} = 8.2\,\text{dB}$ is desirable.

In order to compare the difference between the 3GPP model, the CI model, and our modified model, we assume $h_{\text{UAV}} = 100, 500$ m, $h_{\text{V}} = 1.5$ m and $f_c = 28\,\text{GHz}$. It is clearly shown that the results of our modified PL model matches the model used in the 3GPP standard, in which the PL increases as the distance increases. The PL is more severe in the NLoS scenario due to the obstacles, and is 30 dB higher than in the LoS scenario when the distance between UAV and vehicle is 5000 m. Moreover, when the UAV height is higher, the difference becomes more obvious, which also means our modified model will be more adapted to different UAV heights (Fig. 2).

4   Simulation and Validation

4.1   Scenario Setup

In this section, we'll analyze the campus tailed PL model in the NUAA campus, which contains 66 buildings with an average height of about 30 m. The surface of buildings is concrete, and the open ground of campus is mostly wet soil. The dimensions of modeled terrain are 1590 m by 1100 m. All the trees, roads, and lake are included in the database. We set six UAV trajectories, each trajectory is simulated at altitudes of 30, 50, 100, 150, 300, and 500 m, and the rest parameters are given in Table 2. Direct, reflection and diffraction are also considered in the simulation (Fig. 3).

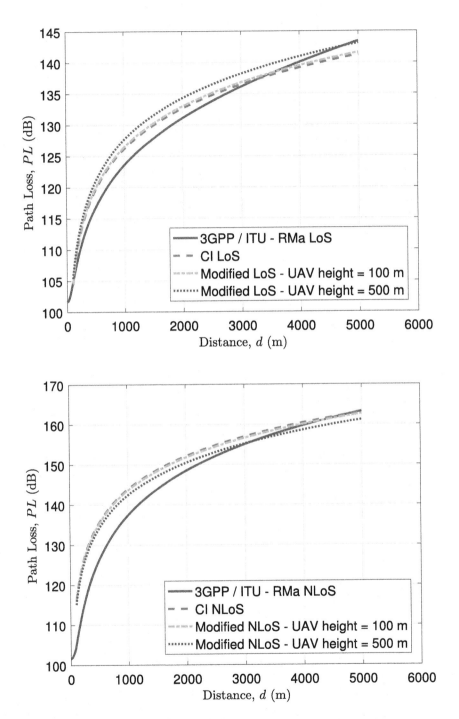

Fig. 2. Comparison of different methods under (a) LoS scenario, (b) NLoS scenario.

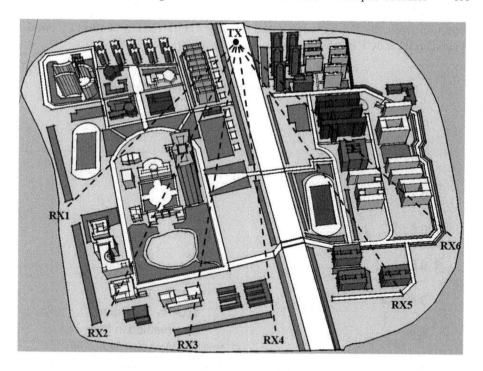

Fig. 3. 3D geographical database of NUAA campus.

Table 2. Simulation parameters

Parameters	Values
Vehicle height	2 m
UAV height	30 m, 50 m, 100 m, 150 m, 300 m, 500 m
Carrier frequency	28 GHz
System bandwidth	500 MHz
Antenna	Omnidirectional antenna
Polarization	Vertical polarization

4.2   Validation and Analysis

Instead of measurement campaign, another way to validate the LoS probability model is by using extensive RT simulations. Actually, a sufficiently large area and enough simulations can ensure that the result is not dependent on the randomly selected cases. In order to compare and analyze the LoS probability, we set $h_{UAV} = 100$ m, $h_V = 1.5$ m. The simulation results of different methods are given in Fig. 4. As we can see that the LoS probability increases as the elevation angle increases due to the decrease of obstacles. Although they all have a certain deviation from the RT model, we can see that the deviation of the ITU model is smaller than 3GPP model and the method in [29].

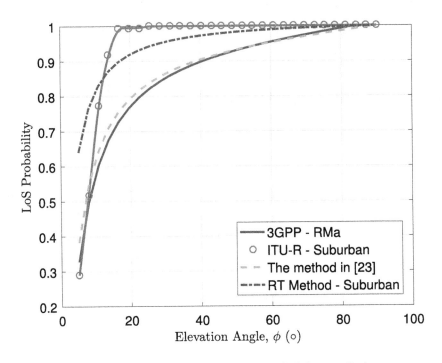

Fig. 4. Comparison of different LoS probability methods.

Then, we use the simulated result by RT method to validate the proposed PL model. Note that the RT method is related to the specific environment and fluctuates greatly. During the simulation, 6 typical trajectories are selected and each trajectory takes six different heights of 30 m, 50 m, 100 m, 150 m, 300 m, and 500 m. Figure 5 shows the path loss results of one typical trajectory, and the UAV height is 50 m. As we can see in the figure, our modified method can fit the path loss trend generated by the RT method and produce reasonable statistics in Table 3 and Table 4.

Moreover, Table 3 shows that in all cases the standard deviation between the PL model and the RT method is lower than 3.5402 dB and the median path loss exponent (PLE) is 2.17. It can be seen that the accuracy of our modified model under the LoS scenario is very high. Table 4 illustrates that the PLE under the NLoS scenario ranges from 2.7000 for the highest height, to 2.7470 for the lowest height and the median path loss exponent is 2.74. The standard deviation between the PL model and the RT method ranges from 6.0998 dB to 10.6271 dB. It is reasonable because the lower the flight altitude, the more the path loss is affected by the obstacle, and the RT method is more accurate.

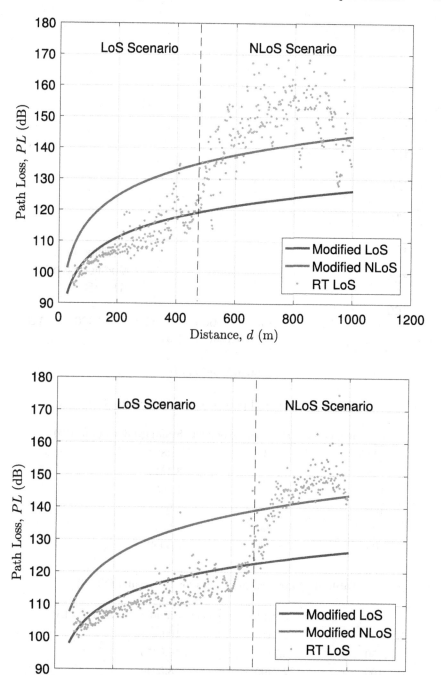

Fig. 5. Path loss results of one typical trajectory (a) UAV height = 30 m, (b) UAV height = 50 m, (c) UAV height = 100 m.

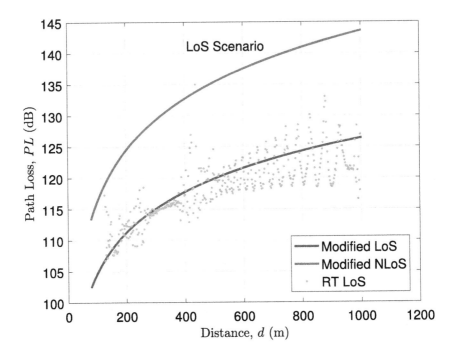

Fig. 5. (*continued*)

Table 3. Statistical properties for RT results (LoS)

UAV height (m)	Path loss exponent	Standard deviation (dB)
30	2.1630	3.4822
50	2.1670	3.4313
100	2.1700	1.4655
150	2.1750	2.0913
300	2.1900	2.9649
500	2.2100	3.5402

Table 4. Statistical properties for RT results (NLoS)

UAV height (m)	Path loss exponent	Standard deviation (dB)
30	2.7470	10.6271
50	2.7450	10.0353
100	2.7400	8.5940
150	2.7350	7.9383
300	2.7200	7.3789
500	2.7000	6.0998

5   Conclusions

In this paper, we have developed a new PL model for UAV mmWave communications by considering the factor of UAV height. For the campus scene, we have obtained extensive RT simulation data and got the tailored parameter value of the new factor by fitting these data. The simulation results have shown that our modified match well with RT method at any UAV height. Moreover, this model is generic for any A2G scene, as long as we adjust the parameter value according to the scene and this's our future work.

Acknowledgements. This work was supported by the National Key Scientific Instrument and Equipment Development Project under Grant No. 61827801, the Fundamental Research Funds for the Central Universities under Grant No. NS2020026 and Open Foundation for Graduate Innovation of NUAA under Grant No. KFJJ 20190418.

References

1. Rappaport, T.S., MacCartney, G.R., Samimi, M.K., Sun, S.: Wideband millimeter-wave propagation measurements and channel models for future wireless communication system design. IEEE Trans. Commun. Syst. **63**(9), 3029–3056 (2015)
2. Majed, M.B., Rahman, T.A., Aziz, O.A.: Propagation path loss modeling and outdoor coverage measurements review in millimeter wave bands for 5G cellular communications. Int. J. Electron. Comput. Eng. **8**(4), 2254–2269 (2018)
3. Fan, W., Carton, I., Kyosti, P., Karstensen, A., Jamsa, T., et al.: A step toward 5G in 2020: low-cost OTA performance evaluation of massive MIMO base stations. IEEE Antennas Propag. Mag. **59**(1), 38–47 (2017)
4. Zhang, J., Shafi, M., Molisch, A., Tufvesson, F., Wu, S., et al.: Channel models and measurements for 5G. IEEE Commun. Mag. **56**(12), 12–13 (2018)
5. Wang, C.-X., Bian, J., Sun, J., Zhang, W., Zhang, M.: A survey of 5G channel measurements and models. IEEE Commun. Surv. Tuts. **20**(4), 3142–3168 (2018)
6. Hindia, M.N., I-Samman, A.M.A., Rahman, T.A., Yazdani, T.M.: Outdoor large-scale path loss characterization in an urban environment at 26, 28, 36, and 38 GHz. Phys. Commun. **27**(1), 150–160 (2018)
7. Rappaport, T.S., Xing, Y., MacCartney, G.R., Molisch, A.F., Mellios, E., Zhang, J.: Overview of millimeter wave communications for fifth-generation (5G) wireless networks-with a focus on propagation models. IEEE Trans. Antennas Propag. **65**(12), 6213–6230 (2017)
8. Zhou, A., Huang, J., Sun, J., Zhu, Q., Wang, C.X., Yang, Y.: 60 GHz channel measurements and ray tracing modeling in an indoor environment. In: Proceedings of the WCSP 2017, Nanjing, China, December 2017
9. Ji, W., Liu, Y.J., Li, S.D.: Study on the propagation characteristics of indoor millimeter-wave at 37.2 GHz by SBR method. In: Proceedings of the ISAPE, Hangzhou, China, December 2018
10. Zhong, W., Xu, L., Zhu, Q., Chen, X., Zhou, J.: MmWave beamforming for UAV communications with unstable beam pointing. China Commun. **16**(1), 37–46 (2019)
11. Zhu, Q., et al.: A novel 3D non-stationary wireless MIMO channel simulator and hardware emulator. IEEE Trans. Commun. **66**(9), 3865–3878 (2018)

12. Zhu, Q., Wang, Y., Jiang, K., Chen, X., Zhong, W., Ahmed, N.: 3D non-stationary geometry-based multi-input multi-output channel model for UAV-ground communication systems. IET Microw. Antennas Propag. **13**(8), 1104–1112 (2019)
13. Galkin, B., Kibilda, J., DaSilva, L.A.: Backhaul for low-altitude UAVs in urban environments. In: Proceedings of the ICC 2018, Kansas City, MO, USA, July 2018
14. Matolak, D.W., Sun, R.: Air-ground channel characterization for unmanned aircraft systems-Part I: methods, measurements, and models for over-water settings. IEEE Trans. Veh. Technol. **66**(1), 26–44 (2016)
15. Shi, Y., Enami, R., Wensowitch, J., Camp, J.: Measurement-based characterization of LOS and NLOS drone-to-ground channels. In: Proceedings of the WCNC 2018, Barcelona, Spain, April 2018
16. Zhu, Q., et al.: Spatial correlations of a 3-D non-stationary MIMO channel model with 3-D antenna arrays and 3-D arbitrary trajectories. IEEE Wireless Commun. Lett. **8**(2), 512–515 (2019)
17. Cai, X., et al.: An empirical air-to-ground channel model based on passive measurements in LTE. IEEE Trans. Veh. Technol. **68**(2), 1140–1154 (2019)
18. Chen, J., Raye, D., Khawaja, W., Sinha, P., Guvenc, I.: Impact of 3D UWB antenna radiation pattern on air-to-ground drone connectivity. In: Proceedings of the VTC 2018, Chicago, IL, USA, April 2019
19. Cui, Z., Briso-Rodrguez, C., Guan, K., Calvo-Ramrez, C., Ai, B., Zhong, Z.: Measurement-based modeling and analysis of UAV air-ground channels at 1 and 4 GHz. IEEE Antennas Wireless Propag. Lett. **18**(9), 1804–1808 (2019)
20. Chu, X., Briso, C., He, D., Yin, X., Dou, J.: Channel modeling for low-altitude UAV in suburban environments based on ray tracer. In: Proceedings of the EuCAP 2018, London, UK, April 2018
21. Cui, Z., et al.: Analytical modeling of UAV-to-vehicle propagation channels in built-up areas. IEEE Wireless Commun. Lett. (2019)
22. Khawaja, W., Ozdemir, O., Guvenc, I.: UAV air-to-ground channel characterization for mmWave systems. In: Proceedings of the VTC 2017, Toronto, ON, Canada, September 2017
23. Wang, X., Gursoy, M.C.: Coverage analysis for energy-harvesting UAV-assisted mmWave cellular networks. IEEE J. Sel. Areas Commun. **37**(12), 2832–2850 (2019)
24. Yang, G., Zhang, Y., He, Z., Wen, J., Ji, Z., Li, Y.: Machine-learning-based prediction methods for path loss and delay spread in air-to-ground millimetre-wave channels. IET Micro. Antennas Propag. **13**(8), 1113–1121 (2019)
25. Dutta, S., Hsieh, F., Vook, F.W.: HAPS based communication using mmWave bands. In: Proceedings of the ICC 2019, Shanghai, China, July 2019
26. Meng, S., Su, X., Wen, Z., Dai, X., Zhou, Y., Yang, W.: Robust drones formation control in 5G wireless sensor network using mmWave. Wireless Commun. Mob. Comput. **18**(1), 1–7 (2018)
27. Hu, S., Guo, L.X., Liu, Z.Y.: A fast ray-tracing algorithm for rugged terrain. In: Proceedings of the CSQRWC 2019, Taiyuan, China, July 2019
28. ITU-R: Rec. P.1410-2 Propagation data and prediction methods for the design of terrestrial troadband millimetric radio access systems. P Series, Radiowave propagation (2003)
29. Cheng, L., Zhu, Q., Wang, C.-X., Zhong, W., Hua, B., Jiang, S.: Modeling and simulation for UAV air-to-ground mmWave channels. In: Proceedings of the EuCAP20, Copenhagen, pp. 1–5, March 2020

A Novel Non-stationary Channel Model for UAV-to-Vehicle mmWave Beam Communications

Kai Mao[1], Qiuming Zhu[1(✉)], Maozhong Song[1(✉)], Benzhe Ning[1], Boyu Hua[1],
Weizhi Zhong[2], and Xiaomin Chen[1]

[1] The Key Laboratory of Dynamic Cognitive System of Electromagnetic Spectrum
Space, College of Electronic and Information Engineering, Nanjing University
of Aeronautics and Astronautics, Nanjing 211106, China
{maokai,zhuqiuming,smz108,ningbenzhe,byhua,chenxm402}@nuaa.edu.cn
[2] The Key Laboratory of Dynamic Cognitive System of Electromagnetic Spectrum
Space, College of Astronautics, Nanjing University of Aeronautics and Astronautics,
Nanjing 211106, China
zhongwz@nuaa.edu.cn

Abstract. Taking into account of three dimensional (3D) trajectory, 3D
antenna array, and 3D directional beam, a new unmanned aerial vehicle
(UAV) to vehicle (U2V) millimeter wave (mmWave) channel model is
proposed. Based on the propagation theory and ray tracing (RT) simulation results, the proposed U2V channel model is composed of a line-
of-sight (LoS) path and three strongest non-line-of-sight (NLoS) paths
or single-bounce (SB) paths. Meanwhile, considering the time-variant
velocity and beam direction, the computation method of time-variant
channel parameters, i.e., angles, delays, and powers, are also given and
analyzed. The simulation results show that the statistical properties of
proposed channel model, i.e., power delay profile (PDP) and power angle
profile (PAP), are time-variant due to the non-stationarity of U2V propagation environment. Moreover, the simulated autocorrelation function
(ACF) fits well with the theoretical one as well as the measured one,
which validates the correctness of proposed model.

Keywords: U2V mmWave channel · Non-stationary channel ·
Channel model · 3D trajectory · 3D beam

1 Introduction

The fifth-generation (5G) or beyond 5G (B5G) mobile communication system is
expected to provide high transmission rate and connect everything, where the
UAV has been considered a promising component as the flying base station or
flexible relay [1,2]. However, different with traditional mobile communication
scenarios, the UAV flies in the 3D space with 3D trajectory and 3D-shaped

© ICST Institute for Computer Sciences, Social Informatics and Telecommunications Engineering 2021
Published by Springer Nature Switzerland AG 2021. All Rights Reserved
M. Guan and Z. Na (Eds.): MLICOM 2020, LNICST 342, pp. 471–484, 2021.
https://doi.org/10.1007/978-3-030-66785-6_51

antenna array. Moreover, to compensate the high path loss caused by mmWave band, the 3D beam-forming technologies are usually adopted in UAV mmWave communications [3,4]. These new features would affect channel characteristics significantly and make the traditional mobile channel models unsuitable [5,6]. Therefore, it is vital to deeply understand the UAV mmWave beam channel for the system design, algorithm optimization, and performance evaluation of U2V communication systems.

Several UAV channel models for sub-mmWave can be addressed in [7–13]. These models have considered part of new features, e.g., 3D scattering environment or 3D trajectory by upgrading the traditional deterministic channel models (DCMs) or geometry-based stochastic models (GBSMs), but they were not applicable for the mmWave band. For the existing mmWave channel models, most of them focused on the land mobile communication scenarios [14–22], and only a few involved the UAV mmWave scenario [23–26].

The authors in [23,24] used the RT method to simulate huge amount data of UAV mmWave channel and analyzed the characteristics of channel parameters, i.e., received power, path delay and propagation angle. However, the basic channel model was 2D in [23] and the ground station was fixed in [24]. The authors in [25] analyzed the 2D UAV mmWave channel characteristics by field test in an anechoic chamber. In [26], the authors proposed a 3D UAV-to-ground mmWave channel based on the GBSM method, but the velocity of UAV was constant and the ground station is also fixed. Recently, a 3D mmWave UAV channel model allowing time-variant arbitrary trajectory was proposed in [27], but the authors ignored the factor of 3D-shaped antenna rotation and beam-forming. This paper aims to fill this gap. The major contributions and novelties are summarized as follows:

1) A 3D U2V mmWave beam channel model considering the 3D arbitrary trajectory, 3D antenna array, and 3D directional beam is proposed. Based on the RT data and directional beam characteristics, the new model consists of a LoS path and three strongest NLoS paths to achieve the tradeoff between complexity and precision.

2) A deterministic and stochastic mixed computation method of channel parameters for the proposed model is developed. The deterministic channel parameters, e.g., powers, angles, and delays, are calculated by the time-variant geometric relationship, and the stochastic channel parameters, e.g., the angles and delays of rays are generated randomly based on the distribution obtained by the RT method.

3) Considering a typical U2V mmWave communication scenario, the channel parameters, i.e., angles, delays, and powers, are simulated and analyzed. Moreover, the statistical properties of ACF and Doppler power spectral density (DPSD) are also simulated and validated by theoretical and measured ones.

The rest paper is organized as follows. In Sect. 2, a 3D U2V mmWave beam channel model is proposed. Section 3 gives the hybrid computation method of channel parameters. The simulation and analytical results of channel parameters and statistical properties are conducted in Sect. 4. Finally, conclusions are drawn in Sect. 5.

2   U2V mmWave Beam Channel Model

Let us consider the down link of U2V communication system, where the UAV adopts the 3D beam-forming to compensate the high path loss and the vehicle is equipped with omnidirectional antennas as shown in Fig. 1. In the figure, there are two local coordinate systems denoted as the UAV coordinate system and vehicle coordinate system with their origins at the central position of UAV and vehicle, respectively. Under the realistic condition, the UAV and vehicle travel with 3D arbitrary velocities as

$$\mathbf{v}_{\text{rx/tx}}(t) = \left\| \mathbf{v}_{\text{rx/tx}}(t) \right\| \begin{bmatrix} \cos \beta^v_{\text{rx/tx}}(t) \cos \alpha^v_{\text{rx/tx}}(t) \\ \cos \beta^v_{\text{rx/tx}}(t) \sin \alpha^v_{\text{rx/tx}}(t) \\ \sin \beta^v_{\text{rx/tx}}(t) \end{bmatrix} \tag{1}$$

where $\left\| \mathbf{v}_{\text{tx/rx}}(t) \right\|$ is the amplitude of $\mathbf{v}_{\text{tx/rx}}(t)$, $\alpha^v_{\text{tx/rx}}(t)$ and $\beta^v_{\text{tx/rx}}(t)$ are the travel direction of UAV and vehicle on the azimuth and elevation plane, respectively. Moreover, the location vectors of UAV transmitting antenna and vehicle receiving antenna in their own coordinate systems can be denoted as $\mathbf{d}_{\text{tx/rx}}(t) = [d^x_{\text{tx/rx}}(t), d^y_{\text{tx/rx}}(t), d^z_{\text{tx/rx}}(t)]$. During the movement of UAV and vehicle, the location of each antenna may change and this paper introduces a rotation matrix $\mathbf{R}_{\text{tx/rx}}(t)$ to take this factor into account

$$\mathbf{R}_{\text{tx/rx}}(t) = \begin{bmatrix} \cos \beta^v_{\text{tx/rx}}(t) \cos \alpha^v_{\text{tx/rx}}(t) & -\sin \alpha^v_{\text{tx/rx}}(t) & -\sin \beta^v_{\text{tx/rx}}(t) \cos \alpha^v_{\text{tx/rx}}(t) \\ \cos \beta^v_{\text{tx/rx}}(t) \sin \alpha^v_{\text{tx/rx}}(t) & \cos \alpha^v_{\text{tx/rx}}(t) & -\sin \beta^v_{\text{tx/rx}}(t) \sin \alpha^v_{\text{tx/rx}}(t) \\ \sin \beta^v_{\text{tx/rx}}(t) & 0 & \cos \beta^v_{\text{tx/rx}}(t) \end{bmatrix}. \tag{2}$$

Considering the U2V communication, the propagation channel can be modeled as the combination of LoS part $H^{\text{LoS}}(\tau, t)$ and NLoS part $H^{\text{NLoS}}(\tau, t)$. The LoS part contains one direct path while the NLoS part contains several non-direct paths with different delays, e.g., SB, double bounce, etc. Thus, the total channel impulse response (CIR) between the pth UAV antenna and qth vehicle antenna scaled by the K-factor K_R can be expressed as

$$H_{p,q}(\tau, t) = \sqrt{\frac{K_R(t)}{K_R(t) + 1}} H^{\text{LoS}}(t) + \sqrt{\frac{1}{K_R(t) + 1}} H^{\text{NLoS}}(\tau, t). \tag{3}$$

In order to achieve the tradeoff between complexity and precision, we have performed huge number of simulations by RT method on the U2V mmWave channel under different scenarios. The simulated results show that the LoS path and ground specular (GS) path usually exist, and the powers of GS path and 1st SB path are 20–30 dB below the one of LoS path. Moreover, the power of 2st SB path has much lower power, e.g., below 60 dB, comparing with the one of 1st

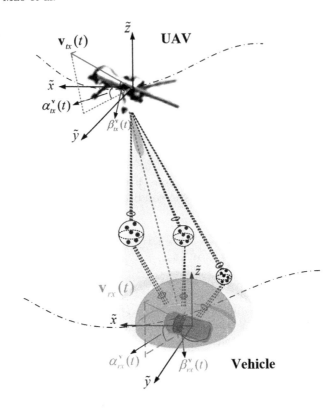

Fig. 1. Typical U2V communication scenario.

SB path. Based on these results, this paper only takes the GS and two strongest SB paths into the NLoS part as

$$H^{\text{NLoS}}(\tau,t) = \underbrace{H^{\text{GS}}(\tau,t)}_{ground\ specular} + \underbrace{H^{\text{SB}_1}(\tau,t)+H^{\text{SB}_2}(\tau,t)}_{Single\ bounce} \tag{4}$$

$$= \sum_{j=1}^{3}\sum_{m=1}^{M} h_m^j(t)\delta(t-\tau_m^j(t)),\ j = \{GS,\ SB_1, SB_2\}$$

where M is the valid ray number of each path, $h_m^j(t)$ and $\tau_m^j(t)$ are the channel coefficient and delay of mth ray within the GS and SB paths, respectively. Furthermore, the channel coefficient is modeled by the summation of several rays (or sub-paths) as

$$h_m^j(t) = \exp(j\Phi_m)\exp\left(j2\pi\frac{\mathbf{r}_{\text{rx},m}^j(t)\cdot\mathbf{R}_{\text{rx}}(t)\cdot\mathbf{d}_{\text{rx}}(t)}{\lambda}\right) \tag{5}$$

$$\cdot \exp\left(j2\pi\frac{\mathbf{r}_{\text{tx},m}^j(t)\cdot\mathbf{R}_{\text{tx}}(t)\cdot\mathbf{d}_{\text{tx}}(t)}{\lambda}\right)\exp\left(\frac{j2\pi}{\lambda}\int_0^t f_m^j(t')\mathrm{d}t'\right)$$

where Φ_m represents the random initial phase distributed uniformly over $[0, 2\pi)$, λ is the wavelength, and $\mathbf{r}_{\mathrm{tx/rx},m}^{j}(t)$ and f_m^j denote the spherical unit vectors and Doppler frequency of mth ray, respectively, and can be further expressed as

$$\mathbf{r}_{\mathrm{tx/rx},m}^{j}(t) = \begin{bmatrix} \cos \beta_{\mathrm{tx/rx},m}^{j}(t) \cos \alpha_{\mathrm{tx/rx},m}^{j}(t) \\ \cos \beta_{\mathrm{tx/rx},m}^{j}(t) \sin \alpha_{\mathrm{tx/rx},m}^{j}(t) \\ \sin \beta_{\mathrm{tx/rx},m}^{j}(t) \end{bmatrix} \tag{6}$$

$$f_m^j(t) = \frac{\mathbf{v}_{\mathrm{tx}}(t) \cdot \mathbf{r}_{\mathrm{tx},m}^{j}(t) + \mathbf{v}_{\mathrm{rx}}(t) \cdot \mathbf{r}_{\mathrm{rx},m}^{j}(t)}{\lambda} \tag{7}$$

where $\alpha_{\mathrm{tx/rx},m}^{j}$ is the azimuth angle of departure (AAoD) or arrival (AAoA), and $\beta_{\mathrm{tx/rx},m}^{j}$ is the elevation angle of departure (EAoD) or arrival (EAoA).

The LoS path between UAV antenna and vehicle antenna can be viewed as a special case of NLoS path and can be expressed as

$$H^{\mathrm{LoS}}(t) = \exp\left(-j2\pi \frac{D_{\mathrm{LoS}}(t)}{\lambda}\right) \exp\left(j2\pi \frac{\mathbf{r}_{\mathrm{rx}}^{\mathrm{LoS}}(t) \cdot \mathbf{R}_{\mathrm{rx}}(t) \cdot \mathbf{d}_{\mathrm{rx}}(t)}{\lambda}\right)$$
$$\cdot \exp\left(j2\pi \frac{\mathbf{r}_{\mathrm{tx}}^{\mathrm{LoS}}(t) \cdot \mathbf{R}_{\mathrm{tx}}(t) \cdot \mathbf{d}_{\mathrm{tx}}(t)}{\lambda}\right) \exp\left(\frac{j2\pi}{\lambda} \int_0^t f^{\mathrm{LoS}}(t') dt'\right) \delta(t - \tau^{\mathrm{LoS}}(t)) \tag{8}$$

where $D_{\mathrm{LoS}}(t)$ is the distance between the UAV and vehicle, $\mathbf{r}_{\mathrm{tx/rx}}^{\mathrm{LoS}}(t)$ and f^{LoS} denote the spherical unit vectors and Doppler frequency of LoS path, respectively. In (8), $\mathbf{r}_{\mathrm{tx/rx}}^{\mathrm{LoS}}(t)$ is determined by $\alpha_{\mathrm{tx/rx}}^{\mathrm{LoS}}$ and $\beta_{\mathrm{tx/rx}}^{\mathrm{LoS}}$ according to (6), and f^{LoS} can be obtained by $\mathbf{r}_{\mathrm{tx/rx}}^{\mathrm{LoS}}(t)$ according to (7).

3   Computation of Channel Parameters

3.1   Time-Variant Geometric Parameters

Since the UAV and vehicle move with 3D arbitrary trajectories, the time-variant location vector of UAV (or vehicle) can be expressed as

$$\mathbf{L}_{\mathrm{tx/rx}}(t) = \mathbf{L}_{\mathrm{tx/rx}}(t_0) + \int_{t_0}^{t} \mathbf{v}_{\mathrm{tx/rx}}(t) dt \tag{9}$$

where $\mathbf{L}_{\mathrm{tx/rx}}(t_0)$ denotes the initial location vector of UAV (or vehicle) at $t = t_0$. Thus, the distance vector between the UAV and vehicle denoted as $\mathbf{D}_{\mathrm{LoS}}(t)$ or between UAV/vehicle and jth scatters denoted as $\mathbf{D}_{\mathrm{tx/rx},j}(t)$ can be expressed as

$$\mathbf{D}_{\mathrm{tx/rx,LoS}}(t) = \mathbf{L}_{\mathrm{tx/rx}}(t) - \mathbf{L}_{\mathrm{rx/tx}}(t) = D_{\mathrm{tx/rx,LoS}}(t_0)\mathbf{r}_{\mathrm{tx/rx}}^{\mathrm{LoS}}(t) + \int_{t_0}^{t} \mathbf{v}_{\mathrm{tx,rx}}(t) dt \tag{10}$$

$$\mathbf{D}_{\mathrm{tx/rx},j}(t) = \mathbf{L}_{\mathrm{tx/rx}}(t) - \mathbf{L}_j(t) = D_{\mathrm{tx/rx},j}(t_0)\mathbf{r}_{\mathrm{tx/rx}}^{j}(t) + \int_{t_0}^{t} \mathbf{v}_{\mathrm{tx/rx}}(t) dt \tag{11}$$

where $\mathbf{v}_{tx,rx}(t)$ denotes the relative velocity between the UAV and vehicle, and $\mathbf{r}_{tx/rx}^j(t)$ is the spherical unit vectors of each NLoS path, which can be obtained by the mean angle parameters $\bar{\alpha}_{tx/rx}^j$ and $\bar{\beta}_{tx/rx}^j$ according to (6). Thus, the distance between UAV and vehicle in LoS scenario and the one between the UAV (or vehicle) and jth scatterer can be calculated by

$$D_{\mathrm{LoS}}(t) = \sqrt{ \begin{array}{l} \left(\begin{array}{l} D_{tx/rx,\mathrm{LoS}}(t_0) \cos(\alpha_{tx/rx}^{\mathrm{LoS}}(t_0)) \cos(\beta_{tx/rx}^{\mathrm{LoS}}(t_0)) \\ + \int_{t_0}^t (v_{tx,rx}(t)) \cos(\alpha_{tx,rx}^v(t)) \cos(\beta_{tx,rx}^v(t)) dt \end{array} \right)^2 \\ + \left(\begin{array}{l} D_{tx/rx,\mathrm{LoS}}(t_0) \cos(\beta_{tx/rx}^{\mathrm{LoS}}(t_0)) \sin(\alpha_{tx/rx}^{\mathrm{LoS}}(t_0)) \\ + \int_{t_0}^t (v_{tx,rx}(t)) \sin(\alpha_{tx,rx}^v(t)) \cos(\beta_{tx,rx}^v(t)) dt \end{array} \right)^2 \\ + \left(\begin{array}{l} D_{tx/rx,\mathrm{LoS}}(t_0) \sin(\beta_{tx/rx}^{\mathrm{LoS}}(t_0)) \\ + \int_{t_0}^t (v_{tx,rx}(t)) \sin(\beta_{tx,rx}^v(t)) dt \end{array} \right)^2 \end{array} } \tag{12}$$

$$D_{tx/rx,j}(t) = \sqrt{ \begin{array}{l} \left(\begin{array}{l} D_{tx/rx,j}(t_0) \cos(\bar{\alpha}_{tx/rx}^j(t_0)) \cos(\bar{\beta}_{tx/rx}^j(t_0)) \\ - \int_{t_0}^t (v_{tx/rx}(t)) \cos(\alpha_{tx/rx}^v(t)) \cos(\beta_{tx/rx}^v(t)) dt \end{array} \right)^2 \\ + \left(\begin{array}{l} D_{tx/rx,j}(t_0) \cos(\bar{\beta}_{tx/rx}^j(t_0)) \sin(\bar{\alpha}_{tx/rx}^j(t_0)) \\ - \int_{t_0}^t (v_{tx/rx}(t)) \sin(\alpha_{tx/rx}^v(t)) \cos(\beta_{tx/rx}^v(t)) dt \end{array} \right)^2 \\ + \left(\begin{array}{l} D_{tx/rx,j}(t_0) \sin(\bar{\beta}_{tx/rx}^j(t_0)) \\ - \int_{t_0}^t (v_{tx/rx}(t)) \sin(\beta_{tx/rx}^v(t)) dt \end{array} \right)^2 \end{array} } \tag{13}$$

where $\alpha_{tx,rx}^v(t)$ and $\beta_{tx,rx}^v(t)$ denote the relative travel direction between the UAV and vehicle on the azimuth and elevation plane, respectively.

3.2   Time-Variant Angle Parameters

Based on the geometric relationships, the time-variant angles such as the EAoD, AAoD, EAoA, and AAoA of LoS path under dynamic scattering scenarios can be expressed, respectively, as

$$\alpha_{tx/rx}^{\mathrm{LoS}}(t) = \begin{cases} \arccos(\frac{\|\mathbf{D}_{tx/rx,\mathrm{LoS}}^x(t)\|}{D_{\mathrm{LoS}}(t)}), & \mathbf{D}_{tx/rx,\mathrm{LoS}}^x(t) \geq 0 \\ \pi - \arccos(\frac{\|\mathbf{D}_{tx/rx,\mathrm{LoS}}^x(t)\|}{D_{\mathrm{LoS}}(t)}), & \mathbf{D}_{tx/rx,\mathrm{LoS}}^x(t) < 0 \end{cases} \tag{14}$$

$$\beta_{tx/rx}^{\mathrm{LoS}}(t) = \arcsin(\frac{\|\mathbf{D}_{tx/rx,\mathrm{LoS}}^z(t)\|}{D_{\mathrm{LoS}}(t)}) \tag{15}$$

where $\mathbf{D}_{tx/rx,\mathrm{LoS}}^x(t)$ denotes the x component of $\mathbf{D}_{tx/rx,\mathrm{LoS}}(t)$. Similarly, the mean angles of time-variant EAoD, AAoD or EAoA, AAoA for the NLoS paths can be calculated respectively by

$$\bar{\alpha}_{tx/rx}^j(t) = \begin{cases} \arccos(\frac{\|\mathbf{D}_{tx/rx,j}^x(t)\|}{D_{tx/rx,j}(t)}), & \mathbf{D}_{tx/rx,j}^x(t) \geq 0 \\ \pi - \arccos(\frac{\|\mathbf{D}_{tx,rx,j}^x(t)\|}{D_{tx/rx,j}(t)}), & \mathbf{D}_{tx/rx,j}^x(t) < 0 \end{cases} \tag{16}$$

$$\bar{\beta}^j_{\text{tx/rx}}(t) = \arcsin\left(\frac{\left\| \mathbf{D}^z_{\text{tx/rx},j}(t) \right\|}{D_{\text{tx/rx},j}(t)}\right). \tag{17}$$

It should be mentioned that the angle of each ray within the NLoS path is random and cannot be calculated in a deterministic way. In this paper, we take the random factor into account and model them as the summation of a random offset angle and the mean angle of each path,

$$\alpha^j_{\text{tx/rx},m}(t) = \bar{\alpha}^j_{\text{tx/rx}}(t) + \Delta\alpha_m \tag{18}$$

$$\beta^j_{\text{tx/rx},m}(t) = \bar{\beta}^j_{\text{tx/rx}}(t) + \Delta\beta_m. \tag{19}$$

Based on the RT simulation results and measurement results in the 3GPP channel model, the offset angles $\Delta\alpha_m$, $\Delta\beta_m$ in this paper are obtained by generating a normal random variable with zero mean value and a Laplace distributed random variable, respectively.

3.3 Time-Variant Delays and Powers

The time-variant delays of LoS and NLoS paths are determined by the transmission distance and they can be calculated respectively by

$$\tau^{\text{LoS}}(t) = \frac{D_{\text{LoS}}(t)}{c} \tag{20}$$

$$\bar{\tau}^j(t) = \frac{D_{\text{tx},j}(t) + D_{\text{rx},j}(t)}{c} \tag{21}$$

where c is the speed of light. Furthermore, the delay of each ray within the NLoS path can be obtained by adding a random delay offset $\Delta\tau_m$ on the mean value of path delay as

$$\tau^j_m(t) = \bar{\tau}^j(t) + \Delta\tau_m. \tag{22}$$

The random delay offset $\Delta\tau_m$ is assumed to follow the exponential distribution and the corresponding power of each ray can be calculated by

$$P^j_m(t) = \exp\left(-\tau^j_m(t)\frac{1 - r_\tau}{r_\tau \sigma_\tau}\right) 10^{-\frac{Z_m}{10}} \tag{23}$$

where r_τ and σ_τ are the delay scalar and delay spread, respectively, and Z_m follows a Gaussian distribution $N(0,3)$. When the LoS power is normalized to be 0 dB, the ray powers can be normalized as

$$\tilde{P}^j_m(t) = \frac{P^j_m(t)}{K_R(t) \cdot \sum\limits_{m=1}^{M} P^j_m(t)} \tag{24}$$

Thus, the total power of NLoS paths should be $1/(K_R(t) + 1)$ as shown in (3).

4   Simulation Results and Analysis

In this section, we simulate the proposed U2V channel model and compare the simulated results with the analytical and measured ones. In the simulation, the 3D time-variant velocities and directions of both terminals and 3D beam forming are considered. The detailed simulation parameters are given in Table 1. It should be mentioned that the effect of beam tracking error is not included. The beam width of UAV antenna array is assumed to be 30° while the one of vehicle antenna array is 180°.

Table 1. Simulation parameters.

Definition	Value	Definition	Value
$\|\mathbf{v}_{\mathrm{tx}}(t)\|$	$10 + 0.5t \text{ m/s}$	$\|\mathbf{v}_{\mathrm{rx}}(t)\|$	$2 + t \text{ m/s}$
$\alpha_{\mathrm{tx}}^{v}(t)$	$120 - 2t°$	$\beta_{\mathrm{tx}}^{v}(t)$	$6 + 5t°$
$\alpha_{\mathrm{rx}}^{v}(t)$	$-120 + 2t°$	$\beta_{\mathrm{rx}}^{v}(t)$	$0°$
f_0	28 GHz	K	7 dB
$\|\mathbf{L}_{\mathrm{tx}}(t_0)\|$	400 m	$\|\mathbf{L}_{\mathrm{rx}}(t_0)\|$	100 m

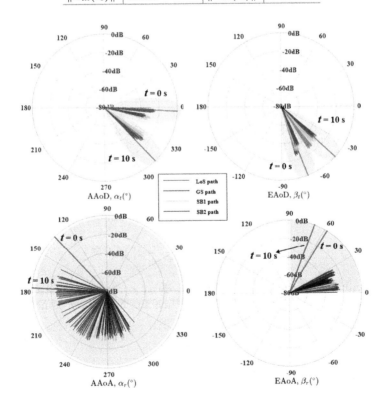

Fig. 2. The time-variant PAPs of LoS path and NLoS paths.

For the U2V mmWave beam channel, the angle parameters are more complicated and related with both the scattering scenario and beam width. Figure 2 gives the time-variant PAPs of LoS path and rays within three NLoS paths at two different time instants $t_1 = 0\,\text{s}$ and $t_2 = 10\,\text{s}$. As we can see, the AAoD and EAoD are limited within the beam and the beam changes to the desired direction at different time instants. In addition, the vehicle antenna is usually close to the ground and thus the EAoA ranges from $[0°\ 90°]$.

Based on the parameter computation method of (20)–(24), the delays and powers are calculated. The time-variant PDPs of proposed channel model are simulated and given in Fig. 3. In the figure, the delay and power of LoS path are both normalized and the number of intra-path rays is set as 32. As we can see that the power of each NLoS path and each intra-path rays show the trend of exponential decay with the increasement of relative delay.

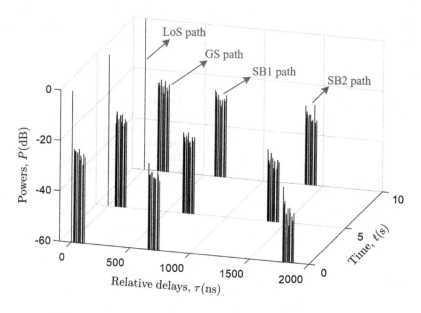

Fig. 3. The time-variant PDPs of proposed U2V channel.

In order to verify the correctness of proposed mmWave channel model, this paper focuses on analyzing and verifying two typical second order statistical properties, i.e., ACF and DPSD. The time-variant theoretical ACF of proposed model can be derived by substituting (3) into the ACF definition,

$$\rho\left(\Delta t; t\right) = E\left[H^*(t)H(t+\Delta t)\right] = \rho^{\text{LoS}}\left(\Delta t; t\right) + \rho^{\text{NLoS}}\left(\Delta t; t\right). \qquad (25)$$

Considering the similar characteristic of each NLoS path, we only take the first one into account. The theoretical and simulated results of ACFs including the LoS path and first NLoS path are shown in Fig. 4. It shows that the ACFs change over time due to the time-variant channel parameters. Furthermore, we can get the time-variant DPSD by using the Fourier transform on the ACF. The simulated results are shown in Fig. 5, which also demonstrate that the Doppler frequency changes in a complicated way under the U2V communication scenario.

Finally, to further verify the consistency of proposed channel model with the realistic channel, the simulated ACFs are compared with the field-measured ones in [28]. To the best of our knowledge, there are very few literatures involving UAV mmWave channel measurement [25,29,30] and none of them so far analyzed the measured ACFs. Since the proposed model is compatible for the sub-mmWave channel by adjust some channel parameters. The measured ACF of sub-mmWave channel in [28] is chose. The beam width is ignored and some simulation parameters are configured as $f_0 = 2\,\mathrm{GHz}$, $\|\mathbf{L}_{\mathrm{tx}}(t_0)\| = 300\,\mathrm{m}$, and $\|\mathbf{v}_{\mathrm{rx}}(t)\| = 1.2\,\mathrm{m/s}$. The comparison result is given in Fig. 6 which shows a good agreement between the simulated result and the measured one.

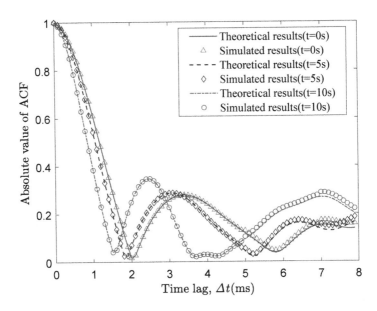

Fig. 4. The simulated and theoretical time-variant ACFs at three time instants.

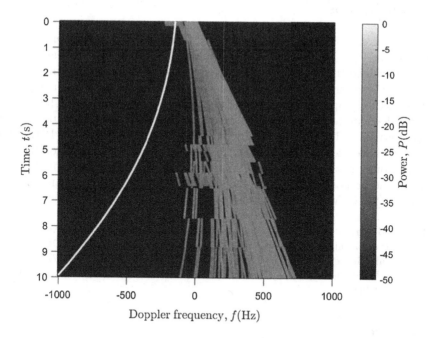

Fig. 5. The simulated time-variant DPSDs.

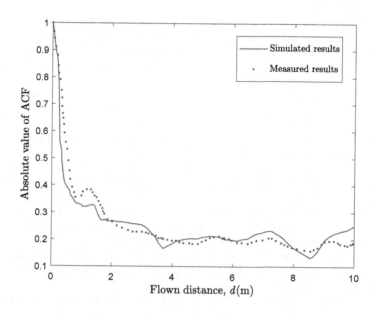

Fig. 6. The simulated and measured ACFs.

5 Conclusions

This paper has proposed a U2V mmWave channel model by considering the 3D trajectory of UAV and vehicle, 3D antenna array, and 3D directional beam. In order to achieve the tradeoff between complexity and precision, only the LoS path and three strongest NLoS paths have been included in the new model. Moreover, the computation method of channel parameters have also been given. It is divided into a deterministic part and a stochastic part to guarantee both the correctness and efficiency. Finally, the statistical characteristic of PDP, ACF, and DPSD have been simulated, analyzed and compared with the theoretical and measured ones. In the future, we will perform more channel measurements as well as apply the proposed model to the optimization of beam-forming and tracking algorithms for UAV mmWave communications.

Acknowledgements. This work was supported in part by the National Key Scientific Instrument and Equipment Development Project under Grant No. 61827801, in part by Aeronautical Science Foundation of China, No. 201901052001 and No. 2017ZC52021, in part by the Fundamental Research Funds for the Central Universities, No. NS2020026 and No. NS2020063.

References

1. Zhang, L., Zhao, H., Hou, S., Zhao, Z., Xu, H., et al.: A survey on 5G millimeter wave communications for UAV-assisted wireless networks. IEEE Access **7**, 117460–117504 (2019)
2. Li, B., Fei, Z., Zhang, Y.: UAV communications for 5G and beyond: recent advances and future trends. IEEE Internet Things J. **6**(2), 2241–2263 (2018)
3. Zhong, W., Xu, L., Zhu, Q., Chen, X., Zhou, J.: MmWave beamforming for UAV communications with unstable beam pointing. China Commun. **16**(1), 37–46 (2019)
4. Zhong, W., Xu, L., Liu, X., Zhu, Q., Zhou, J.: Adaptive beam design for UAV network with uniform plane array. Phys. Commun. **34**(2), 58–65 (2019)
5. Khawaja, W., Guvenc, I., Matolak, D.W., Fiebig, U., Schneckenburger, N.: A survey of air-to-ground propagation channel modeling for unmanned aerial vehicles. IEEE Commun. Surv. Tuts. **21**(3), 2361–2391 (2019)
6. Zhang, C., Zhang, W., Wang, W., Yang, L., Zhang, W.: Research challenges and opportunities of UAV millimeter-wave communications. IEEE Wireless Commun. **26**(1), 58–62 (2019)
7. Cui, Z., Briso-Rodrguez, C., Guan, K., Calvo-Ramrez, C., Ai, B., Zhong, Z.: Measurement-based modeling and analysis of UAV air-ground channels at 1 and 4 GHz. IEEE Antennas Wirel. Propag. Lett. **18**(9), 1804–1808 (2019)
8. Chu, X., Briso, C., He, D., Yin, X., Dou, J.: Channel modeling for low-altitude UAV in suburban environments based on ray tracer. In: Proceedings of the EuCAP 2018, London, UK, pp. 1–4, April 2018
9. Zhu, Q., Wang, Y., Jiang, K., Chen, X., Zhong, W., Ahmed, N.: 3D non-stationary geometry-based multi-input multi-output channel model for UAV-ground communication systems. IET Microw. Antennas Propag. **13**(8), 1104–1112 (2019)

10. Chang, H., Bian, J., Wang, C.-X., Aggoune, E.M.: A 3D non-stationary wide-band GBSM for low-altitude UAV-to-ground V2V MIMO channels. IEEE Access **7**, 70719–70732 (2019)

11. Zhang, X., Cheng, X.: Three-dimensional non-stationary geometry-based stochas-tic model for UAV-MIMO Ricean fading channels. IET Commun. **13**(16), 2617–2627 (2019)

12. Zhu, Q., Jiang, K., Chen, X., Zhong, W., Yang, Y.: A novel 3D non-stationary UAV-MIMO channel model and its statistical properties. China Commun. **15**(12), 147–158 (2018)

13. Chen, X., Hu, X., Zhu, Q., Zhong, W., Chen, B.: Channel modeling and perfor-mance analysis for UAV relay systems. China Commun. **15**(12), 89–97 (2018)

14. Huang, J., Liu, Y., Wang, C.-X., Sun, J., Xiao, H.: 5G millimeter wave channel sounders, measurements, and models: recent developments and future challenges. IEEE Commun. Mag. **57**(1), 138–145 (2019)

15. Gonzlez-Plaza, A., Calvo-Ramrez, C., Briso-Rodrguez, C., Garca-Loygorri, J.M., Oliva, D., Alonso, J.I.: Propagation at mmW band in metropolitan railway tunnels. Wireless Commun. Mobile Computing **2018**, 1–10 (2017)

16. Liu, X., Yin, X., Zheng, G.: Experimental investigation of millimeter-wave MIMO channel characteristics in tunnel. IEEE Access **7**, 108395–108399 (2019)

17. He, R., Ai, B., Stber, G.L., Wang, G., Zhong, Z.: Geometrical-based modeling for millimeter-wave MIMO mobile-to-mobile channels. IEEE Trans. Veh. Technol. **67**(4), 2848–2863 (2018)

18. Bas, C.U., Wang, R., Sangodoyin, S., Hur, S., Whang, K., et al.: 28 GHz propa-gation channel measurements for 5G microcellular environments. In: Proceedings of the ACES 2018, Denver, CO, pp. 1–2 (2018)

19. Wang, C.-X., Bian, J., Sun, J., Zhang, W., Zhang, M.: A survey of 5G channel measurements and models. IEEE Commun. Surv. Tuts. **20**(4), 3142–3168 (2018)

20. Fan, W., Carton, I., Kyosti, P., Karstensen, A., Jamsa, T., et al.: A step toward 5G in 2020: low-cost OTA performance evaluation of massive MIMO base stations. IEEE Antennas Propag. Mag. **59**(1), 38–47 (2017)

21. Zhang, J., Shafi, M., Molisch, A., Tufvesson, F., Wu, S., et al.: Channel models and measurements for 5G. IEEE Commun. Mag. **56**(12), 12–13 (2018)

22. Fu, Z., Cui, H., Geng, S., Zhao, X.: 5G millimeter wave channel modeling and sim-ulations for a high-voltage substation. In: Proceedings of the iSPEC 2019, Beijing, China, pp. 1822–1826 (2019)

23. Yang, G., Zhang, Y., He, Z., Wen, J., Ji, Z., Li, Y.: Machine-learning-based pre-diction methods for path loss and delay spread in air-to-ground millimetre-wave channels. IET Microw. Antennas Propag. **13**(8), 1113–1121 (2019)

24. Khawaja, W., Ozdemir, O., Guvenc, I.: Temporal and spatial characteristics of mm wave propagation channels for UAVs. In: Proceedings of the GSMM 2018, Boulder, CO, USA, pp. 1–6, May 2018

25. Geise, R., Weiss, A., Neubauer, B.: Modulating features of field measurements with a UAV at millimeter wave frequencies. In: Proceedings of the CAMA 2018, Vasteras, Sweden, pp. 1–4, September 2018

26. Michailidis, E.T., Nomikos, N., Trakadas, P., Kanatas, A.G.: Three-dimensional modeling of mmWave doubly massive MIMO aerial fading channels. IEEE Trans. Veh. Technol. **69**(2), 1190–1202 (2020)

27. Cheng, L., Zhu, Q., Wang, C.-X., Zhong, W., Hua, B., Jiang, S.: Modeling and sim-ulation for UAV air-to-ground mmWave channels. In: Proceedings of the EuCAP 2020, Copenhagen, pp. 1–5, March 2020

28. Simunek, M., Fontn, F.P., Pechac, P.: The UAV low elevation propagation channel in urban areas: statistical analysis and time-series generator. IEEE Trans. Antennas Propag. **61**(7), 3850–3858 (2013)
29. Lemos Cid, E., Alejos, A.V., Garcia Sanchez, M.: Signaling through scattered vegetation: empirical loss modeling for low elevation angle satellite paths obstructed by isolated thin trees. IEEE Veh. Technol. Mag. **11**(3), 22–28 (2016)
30. Khawaja, W., Ozdemir, O., Guvenc, I.: UAV air-to-ground channel characterization for mmWave systems. In: Proceedings of the VTC 2017, Toronto, ON, pp. 1–5 (2017)

Energy Efficient Communication of Fuel-Powered UAV Relay, Design of Positions and Power Allocation

Tong Zhang$^{(\boxtimes)}$, Gang Wang, Ruofei Zhou, Yikun Zou, and Mingchuan Yang

Harbin Institute of Technology, Harbin 150001, China
18b905025@stu.hit.edu.cn

Abstract. In this paper, we study the energy efficient communication of a fuel-powered UAV relay. Since the fuel-power UAV has separate power supply for communication and operation, and the fuel can support hours' flight, we focus on the energy efficient communication of the UAV. We study two scenarios as a comparison, including the UAV working as a one-way relay and a two-way relay. The non-convex optimization problem is solved using successive convex approximation (SCA) method and difference of convex functions (DC) programming. The upper bounds and lower bounds of the data rates are proposed to transform the problem to an equivalent convex optimization problem. Numerical results show that the proposed upper bounds and lower bounds of the data rates converges to the same value. And the convergence of the objective function is also shown. The differences of the UAV's placement and power allocation as a one-way relay and a two-way relay are compared in the discussion.

Keywords: Energy efficient communication · Fuel-powered UAVs · One-way relay · Two-way relay

1 Introduction

In recent years, the application of unmanned aerial vehicles (UAVs) on communication networks has drawn wide attention [1,2,4]. Related studies focused on the UAV-assisted communication networks and UAVs in cellular networks [3,7,10]. Benefit from their high mobility, UAVs have bright prospect of working as relays or temporary base stations to build provisional communication networks for disaster recovery and wilderness exploration.

Unlike electric UAVs, which have short flight endurance, and fuel-cell UAVs, which requires high budget and long start-up time [5,6], fuel-powered UAVs have mature technologies, long endurance of flight and are adaptable to different environments. Fuel-powered UAVs are driven by internal combustion engines (ICEs) [8]. Although they also have drawbacks, such as noise and relatively

---

This work is supported in part by National Natural Science Foundation of China (No. 61671184, No. 61901137).

M. Guan and Z. Na (Eds.): MLICOM 2020, LNICST 342, pp. 485–491, 2021.
https://doi.org/10.1007/978-3-030-66785-6_52

lower efficiencies, they are still irreplaceable when high load, long endurance and low budget are required.

There are two categories of energy efficiencies related to UAV relays or base stations, energy efficient operation and energy efficiency communication [11]. When it comes to electric UAVs, the energy efficient operation is quite important because the communication module and operation are powered jointly by electric, and the operation consumes much more energy than the communication. As for fuel-powered UAVs, the energy efficient communication should be also considered, since the communication module is powered by batteries separately. The mission time is related to both the communication and the operation.

As for studies considering the problems of energy efficiency of UAVs, most of the studies focused on electricity-powered UAVs, of which the communication power and mechanical power are jointly provided by batteries [1,9]. The influence of the UAV's positions and communication power to the energy efficient of communication module on fuel-powered UAV relays has been left as unexplored questions. In this paper, we focus on the energy efficiency communication, related to the UAV positions. The UAV, working as a one-way relay and a two-way relay, are both studied, as a comparison.

2   System Model

We consider a three node communication system, consisting of a UAV and two ground nodes. The UAV flies at a fixed altitude as a relay. Denote the ground nodes as Node 1 and 2, and the UAV as A. Use k to denote the number of ground users, $k = 1, 2$. The positions of the ground users are $(x_k, y_k, 0)$. The UAV's position is (x_A, y_A, H). The power from the ground nodes is denoted as p_k. The power from the UAV to the two ground nodes is denoted as $p_{A,k}$. Suppose the UAV and the ground nodes have line of sight (LoS) channels, the channel gains between Node 1 and Node 2 and the UAV are $|h_{A,k}|^2 = C\sqrt{(x_A - x_k)^2 + (y_A - y_k)^2 + H^2}^{-\alpha}$, where C and α are the path loss at the reference distance, and path loss exponent, respectively. Then the data rate of from Node k to the UAV and the data rate from the UAV to the Node k are

$$R_{k,A} = \log_2\left(1 + \frac{p_k|h_{A,k}|^2}{\sigma^2}\right), R_{A,k} = \log_2\left(1 + \frac{p_A|h_{A,k}|^2}{\sigma^2}\right), \quad (1)$$

where σ^2 is the power of Gaussian white noise.

The energy efficiency of the one-way UAV relay can be formulated as

$$EE_o = \frac{R_{A,k}}{p_{A_k} + p_0}, \quad (2)$$

where p_0 is the circuit power of the communication module. Considering the information causality constraint, we have

$$R_{up} \leq R_{down}, \quad (3)$$

which means the information transmitted from UAV should be less than the information received by the UAV. We consider the constraints of communication power for the ground nodes and the UAV. The maximum power for a ground node is denoted as P_G, while the maximum power for the UAV is denoted as P_A. Then we have

$$p_1 \leq P_G, p_{A,2} \leq P_A. \tag{4}$$

The problem for power allocation and UAV's position is formulated as

$$\max_{p_1, p_A, x_A, y_A} EE_o \tag{5}$$

$$s.t. (3), (4)$$

The energy efficient problem of two-way relay is similar to the one way relay situation:

$$EE_t = \frac{1}{2} \sum_{k=1}^{2} \frac{R_{A,k}}{p_A + p_0} \tag{6}$$

$$s.t. (3),$$

$$p_k \leq P_G, \sum_{k=1}^{K} p_{A,k} \leq P_A \tag{7}$$

3 The Position and Power of the UAV

The energy-efficient problems are non-convex because of the non-concave objective functions and the constraint (3). To find the optimal power allocation scheme and the UAV's position, we refer to the successive convex approximation (SCA) method and difference of convex functions (DC) programming method.

We introduce the slake variables $\breve{\eta}_k$ for the energy efficiency. According to the SCA method, we consider the convex constraints

$$\ln \breve{\eta}_k^{(j-1)} + \frac{1}{\breve{\eta}_k^{(j-1)}} \delta_{\eta_k} + \ln \left(p_{A,k}^{(j-1)} + p_0 \right) + \frac{1}{p_{A,k}^{(j-1)} + p_0} \delta_{p_{A,k}} \leq \ln \left(\bar{R}_{A,k} \right), \tag{8}$$

$$\bar{R}_{A,k} \leq \check{R}_{A,k}, \tag{9}$$

where $\check{R}_{A,k}$, is the lower bound of $R_{A,k}$, we have

$$\check{R}_{A,k} = \log_2 \left(1 + \gamma_{A,k}^{(j)} \right), \check{R}_{k,A} = \log_2 \left(1 + \gamma_{k,A}^{(j)} \right), \tag{10}$$

where

$$\ln \gamma_{A,k}^{(j-1)} + \frac{\delta_{\gamma A,k}}{\gamma_{A,k}^{(j-1)}} + f \left(\delta_{x_A}, \delta_{y_A} \right) \leq \ln \left[\left(p_{A,k}^{(j-1)} + \delta_{p_{A,k}} \right) C \right]. \tag{11}$$

$$\ln \gamma_{k,A}^{(j-1)} + \frac{\delta_{\gamma_{k,A}}}{\gamma_{k,A}^{(j-1)}} + f \left(\delta_{x_A}, \delta_{y_A} \right) \leq \ln \left[\left(p_k^{(j-1)} + \delta_{p_k} \right) C \right], \tag{12}$$

$$f\left(\delta_{xA}, \delta_{yA}\right) = \ln \sigma^2 + \frac{\alpha}{2} \ln \left[\left(x_A^{(j-1)} - x_k\right)^2 + \left(y_A^{(j-1)} - y_k\right)^2 + H^2\right]$$

$$+ \frac{\alpha}{2} \frac{\left[\delta_{xA}^2 + \delta_{yA}^2 + 2\left(x_A^{(j-1)} - x_k\right)\delta_{xA} + 2\left(y_A^{(j-1)} - y_k\right)\delta_{yA}\right]}{\left(x_A^{(j-1)} - x_k\right)^2 + \left(y_A^{(j-1)} - y_k\right)^2 + H^2}, \quad (13)$$

Then we derive an upper bound of $R_{A,k}$ as

$$\widehat{R}_{A,k} = \log_2\left(1 + \phi_{A,k}^{(j-1)}\right) + \frac{\delta_{\phi A,k}}{\ln 2\left(1 + \phi_{A,k}^{(j-1)}\right)}, \quad (14)$$

where

$$\ln\left(\phi_{A,k}^{(j-1)} + \delta_{\phi A,k}\right) + \ln\left(\beta_k\right) \geq \ln\left(\frac{p_{A,k}^{(j-1)} C}{\sigma^2}\right) + \frac{1}{p_{A,k}^{(j-1)}}\delta_{p A,k}, \quad (15)$$

$$\beta_k \leq X^{\frac{\alpha}{2}} + \frac{\alpha}{2}X^{\frac{\alpha}{2}-1}\Delta_X, \quad (16)$$

$$X = \left(x_A^{(j-1)} - x_k\right)^2 + \left(y_A^{(j-1)} - y_k\right)^2 + H^2, \quad (17)$$

$$\Delta_X = \delta_{xA}^2 + \delta_{yA}^2 + 2\left(x_A^{(j-1)} - x_k\right)\delta_{xA} + 2\left(y_A^{(j-1)} - y_k\right)\delta_{yA}. \quad (18)$$

According to SCA method, as for the one-way relay, in the jth iteration, $\check{\eta}_2^{(j)}$, $p_{A,2}^{(j)}$, $p_1^{(j)}$, $\gamma_{A,2}^{(j)}$, $\gamma_{1,A}^{(j)}$, $x_A^{(j)}$, $y_A^{(j)}$, and $\phi_{A,k}^{(j)}$ are updated. The update increment $\delta_1 = \left\{\delta_{\check{\eta}_2}, \delta_{p A,2}, \delta_{p 1}, \delta_{\gamma A,2}, \delta_{\gamma 1,A}, \delta_{xA}, \delta_{yA}, \delta_{\phi,k}\right\}$ are given by solving (P1)

$$\max_{\delta_1, \bar{R}_{A,k}} \check{\eta}_2^{(j-1)} + \delta_{\check{\eta}_2} \quad (P1)$$

$$s.t.(8), (9), (11), (12), (15), (16)$$

$$\widehat{R}_{A,2} \leq \check{R}_{1,A} \quad (19)$$

$$p_1^{(j-1)} + \delta_{p 1} \leq P_G \quad (20)$$

$$p_{A,2}^{(j-1)} + \delta_{p A,2} \leq P_A. \quad (21)$$

The algorithm to solve the UAV's position and power allocation is given in Algorithm 1. In each iteration, (P1) is solved. With the algorithm converges, the solution converges to the optimal solution of the energy efficient problem. The way to solve the energy efficient problem of two-way relay is similar, thus is omitted for simplicity.

Algorithm 1. Trajectory and Power Solution for One-way UAV Relay

---

1: Initialize the iteration number j=0, and $\check{\eta}_2^{(0)}$, $p_{A,2}^{(0)}$, $p_1^{(0)}$, $\gamma_{A,2}^{(0)}$, $\gamma_{1,A}^{(0)}$, $x_A^{(0)}$, $y_A^{(0)}$, and $\phi_{A,k}^{(0)}$;

2: **repeat**

3:   Solve the convex optimization problem (P1) to obtain $\boldsymbol{\delta}_1$;.

4:   Update the variables $\check{\eta}_2^{(j)}$, $p_{A,2}^{(j)}$, $p_1^{(j)}$, $\gamma_{A,2}^{(j)}$, $\gamma_{1,A}^{(j)}$, $x_A^{(j)}$, $y_A^{(j)}$, and $\phi_{A,k}^{(j)}$.

5:   Update the iteration number $j = j + 1$.

6: **until** The value of the objective function reaches a convergence

---

4 Numerical Results and Discussion

In this section, we show the numerical results of the proposed algorithms. The ground nodes are fixed at $(0,0,0)$ and $(2000,0,0)$. The height of the UAV is set to be $H = 100$ m. The communication system's bandwidth is 20 MHz, and works at 5 GHz. The parameter of LoS path-loss at reference distance is -46 dB, the path-loss exponent is set to be 2. The noise spectrum density is -169 dBm/Hz [10]. The circuit power is set to be 0.02 Watt.

Figure 1 shows the convergence of the proposed algorithms. Figure 2 shows the influence of available power for the ground nodes and the UAV. The results imply that with more power available, the energy efficiency of the one-way relay increases, while for the two-way relay, the energy efficiency increases first and then keeps stable.

The upper bounds and the lower bounds of the data rates are shown in Fig. 3 and Fig. 4. With the algorithms converges, the upper bound of data rates, $\hat{R}_{A,k}$ and the lower bounds of the data rates $\check{R}_{A,k}$, as well as the slake variables $\bar{R}_{A,k}$ converges to the same value. In fact, since we only focus on the energy efficiency of the UAV, the power from the ground nodes is not specially considered. When the available power for the ground nodes is limited, $\check{R}_{k,A}$ and the upper bound of $R_{A,k}$ converge to the same value. But if the ground nodes have superfluous power, the results of $\check{R}_{k,A}$ may be higher than what is needed. This is because we did not focus on the energy efficiency of the users, thus as long as it dose not violate the information causality constraints, $\check{R}_{k,A}$ is not specially minimized. This part will be discussed in the future work.

The communication power from the UAV can be seen in Fig. 5. The communication power of the one-way relay decreases when more power is available, because the UAV is near Node 2 to maintain better channel conditions. In Fig. 6 that with more power available, the UAV, as a one-way relay, moves to near Node 2, while the two-way relay stays in the center between the two ground nodes. This is because for the one-way relay, with more power available, Node 1 can transmit with higher power to the UAV to maintain the information causality, the UAV can move near to the destination node for better channel so as to save its communication power. But as for the two-way relay, UAV needs to communicate with both of the two ground nodes, thus neither moving to Node 1 nor moving to Node 2 helps to save energy.

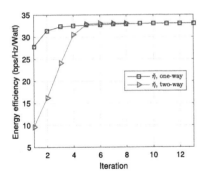

Fig. 1. The convergence of the proposed algorithms.

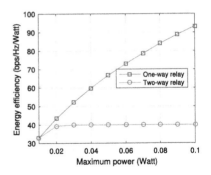

Fig. 2. The influence of the communication power on energy efficiencies.

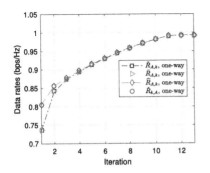

Fig. 3. Convergence of $\check{R}_{A,k}$, $\bar{R}_{A,k}$, $\widehat{R}_{A,k}$ and $\check{R}_{k,A}$ of one-way relay.

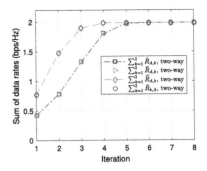

Fig. 4. Convergence of $\check{R}_{A,k}$, $\bar{R}_{A,k}$, $\widehat{R}_{A,k}$ and $\check{R}_{k,A}$ of two-way relay.

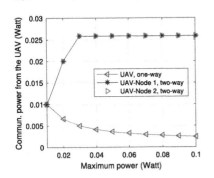

Fig. 5. The influence of the maximum power on the UAV's communication power.

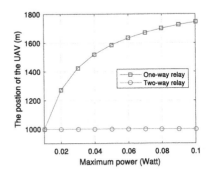

Fig. 6. The influence of the communication power on the UAV's positions.

5   Conclusion

In this paper, we studied the communication systems with fuel-powered UAV working as a one-way relay and a two-way relay, as a comparison. To maximize the energy efficiency of the communication for the UAV relay, we solve the non-convex problem by referring to SCA method and DC programming. Results show the convergence of the proposed algorithms and the efficiency of the upper bounds and lower bounds of the data rates. The positions and communication power of the UAV working as a one-way relay and a two-way relay are different when the communication power supply increases. The future work will be extended to the energy-efficient UAV trajectory design and power allocation for multi-users, and multiplexing techniques will be also taken into consideration.

References

1. Ahmed, S., Chowdhury, M.Z., Jang, Y.M.: Energy-efficient uav relaying communications to serve ground nodes. IEEE Commun. Lett. **24**(4), 849–852 (2020). https://doi.org/10.1109/LCOMM.2020.2965120
2. Ahmed, S., Chowdhury, M.Z., Jang, Y.M.: Energy-efficient uav-to-user scheduling to maximize throughput in wireless networks. IEEE Access **8**, 21215–21225 (2020). https://doi.org/10.1109/ACCESS.2020.2969357
3. Eom, S., Lee, H., Park, J., Lee, I.: UAV-aided two-way mobile relaying systems. IEEE Commun. Lett. **24**(2), 438–442 (2020)
4. Jiang, H., Zhang, Z., Wu, L., Dang, J.: Three-dimensional geometry-based uav-mimo channel modeling for A2G communication environments. IEEE Commun. Lett. **22**(7), 1438–1441 (2018)
5. Kaya, K., Hames, Y.: A study on fuel cell electric unmanned aerial vehicle. In: 2019 4th International Conference on Power Electronics and their Applications (ICPEA), pp. 1–6 (2019)
6. Savvaris, A., Xie, Y., Malandrakis, K., Lopez, M., Tsourdos, A.: Development of a fuel cell hybrid-powered unmanned aerial vehicle. In: 2016 24th Mediterranean Conference on Control and Automation (MED), pp. 1242–1247 (2016)
7. Wang, H., Wang, J., Chen, J., Gong, Y., Ding, G.: Network-connected uav communications: potentials and challenges. China Commun. **15**(12), 111–121 (2018)
8. Wang, Y., Shi, Y., Cai, M., Xu, W., Pan, T., Yu, Q.: Study of fuel-controlled aircraft engine for fuel-powered unmanned aerial vehicle: energy conversion analysis and optimization. IEEE Access **7**, 109246–109258 (2019)
9. Zeng, Y., Zhang, R.: Energy-efficient UAV communication with trajectory optimization. IEEE Trans. Wirel. Commun. **16**(6), 3747–3760 (2017). https://doi.org/10.1109/TWC.2017.2688328
10. Zeng, Y., Zhang, R., Lim, T.J.: Throughput maximization for UAV-enabled mobile relaying systems. IEEE Trans. Commun. **64**(12), 4983–4996 (2016)
11. Zeng, Y., Zhang, R., Lim, T.J.: Wireless communications with unmanned aerial vehicles: opportunities and challenges. IEEE Commun. Mag. **54**(5), 36–42 (2016)

Throughput Maximization for the System of UAV as Mobile Relay Between Moving Vehicles

Yue Li[1,2(✉)], Demin Li[1,2], Wei Hu[1,2], and Xiaoyang Tang[1,2]

[1] College of Information Science and Technology, Donghua University,
Shanghai 201620, China
[2] Engineering Research Center of Digitized Textile and Apparel Technology,
Ministry of Education, Shanghai 201620, China
2181305@mail.dhu.edu.cn, deminli@dhu.edu.cn

Abstract. In recent years, due to the strong mobility and maneuverability of unmanned aerial vehicle (UAV), many scholars began to pay attention to the research of UAV as mobile relay auxiliary vehicle network. However, how to improve the throughput of the vehicle network which UAV as mobile relay is always an urgent problem. In this paper, we use the UAV as a mobile relay between two disconnected mobile vehicles to establish a new communication link to carry and forward traffic information. Firstly, we propose a throughput optimization model of UAV as inter-vehicle mobile relay under the limits of the propulsion power and the amount of data successfully transmitted by the UAV. Then, the objective function is proved to be convex, and the optimization model is solved by using Lagrange multiplier method with Karush-Kuhn-Tucker (KKT) condition. Finally, numerical simulation is carried out, we can see that the throughput of the information transmission system of the UAV as a mobile relay decreases with the increase of the amount of data required to be successfully transmitted, and it can be proved that the proposed optimization method is superior to other mobile relay methods under sufficient propulsion energy.

Keywords: UAV · Relay · Throughput

1 Introduction

UAVs have been widely used to assist the Internet of vehicles (IOV) in collecting real-time road traffic information, and have been proved to be effective in reducing the delay and loss of information [1,2]. With the addition of UAV, the

Supported by NSF of China under Grant No. 61772130, No. 71171045 and No. 61772130; the Innovation Program of Shanghai Municipal Education Commission under Grant No. 14YZ130; and the International S&T Cooperation Program of Shanghai Science and Technology Commission under Grant No. 15220710600.

M. Guan and Z. Na (Eds.): MLICOM 2020, LNICST 342, pp. 492–504, 2021.
https://doi.org/10.1007/978-3-030-66785-6_53

communication connectivity between vehicles with disconnected or weak communication connection is enhanced, which can increase the stability of vehicle network. The traditional IOV is a network that vehicles collects and shares real-time information through wireless communication between vehicles and road side units (V2R), wired communication between road side units (R2R), single-hop and multi-hop communication between vehicles (V2V) in [3]. However, in some road networks, there may be insufficient RSU deployment and sparse vehicles on the road, disconnection of communication may occur during information transmission, and this will leads to delay and loss of information. The addition of UAV is equivalent to the addition of a new sensor node, which can act as a mobile relay when there is a lack of RSU or a long distance between vehicles on the road, assist vehicles to carry and forward road traffic information, and realize the sharing of information between vehicles.

Scholars have previously proposed the use of ferries in mobile ad-hoc networks to assist the information transfer between nodes, often referred to as data ferrying. Ferries collect information from the source node and forward it to the destination node, which improves the transmission performance and reduces energy consumption of the system in [4]. Then with the development of UAV technology, UAV as mobile relay is widely used in various mobile ad-hoc networks, and in order to improve the performance of the relay system has done a lot of research. UAV is used as mobile relay between two fixed sensors on the ground in literature [5,6], with different transmission modes, but both maximize the throughput of the system by optimizing UAV flight paths, UAV transmission power and source nodes transmission power. In addition, the authors in [7] use the UAV as a mobile relay between a fixed base station (BS) and multiple mobile users, and then maximizes the total data transmission rate of all users by optimizing the flight path of the UAV and the transmission power of the UAV to each mobile user. However, in the above research on UAV as mobile relay, the propulsion energy consumption of UAV was not considered in the optimization of UAV flight path. Regarding the energy consumption of UAV as a mobile relay, both calculation energy consumption and propulsion energy consumption are considered in literature [8]. UAV as the mobile relay between the fixed user on the ground and the moving edge computing access point (AP), under the bandwidth limitation, the trajectory movement limitation of the UAV and the limitation of computing tasks, so as to minimize the weighted energy consumption of the UAV and the user of completing the computing task. In fact, for UAV, the communication energy consumption is often ignored because it is far less than the propulsion energy consumption. In literature [9] and [10], the propulsion energy of UAV is also considered. Literature [9] is that when upward communication is carried out between UAV and multiple fixed nodes on the ground, the maximum energy efficiency of UAV can be obtained by optimizing the flight path of UAV. Then in literature [10], the UAV still acts as a mobile relay between two fixed nodes, but the UAV flies along the circular trajectory between two nodes, and maximizes the energy efficiency of the UAV by optimizing the radius of the circular trajectory, power distribution and the flight speed of UAV. However, we can find that the above literatures do not consider that the communication range of the source nodes is limited so that the nodes cannot communicate with each other, and do not consider the amount of successful data transmission required by the UAV in the relay process, after all, the purpose of UAV as relay is to ensure the transmission of information.

In this paper, we use the UAV as a mobile relay to establish new communication between two vehicles which cannot communicate because of the long distance, such application scenarios are rarely analyzed. Here, because the driving direction of the vehicle is fixed along the road, the flight direction of the UAV as a mobile relay auxiliary vehicle is also fixed, so there is no need to optimize the flight path of the UAV. In addition, in order to ensure sufficient information transmission time and efficient communication between vehicles and UAV, we use maximum power for both vehicles and UAV. What's more, we considered not only the limitation of the propulsion power of the UAV but also the amount of data that the UAV needs to successfully transmit as a relay. The main contributions in this paper are as follows:

Firstly, we propose a throughput optimization model of UAV as a mobile relay between moving vehicles, which consider the constraints of UAV propulsion energy, the limits of vehicle communication range and the amount of data needs to successfully transmit in the progress of UAV as a relay.

Secondly, the convexity of the objective function is proved, and the objective function is solved by Lagrange multiplier method with KKT condition.

Thirdly, according to the actual vehicle movement and UAV flight restrictions, we set reasonable parameters and conducted numerical simulation to verify the accuracy of our model. Compared with other methods of UAV as mobile relay, it is verified that the optimization method proposed by us is obviously superior to other methods.

The structure of this paper is as follows: Sect. 2 is the process of establishing the system model; Sect. 3 is the problem formulation and solution of the model; Sect. 4 is the result analysis of the simulation; Sect. 5 is the summary of the paper.

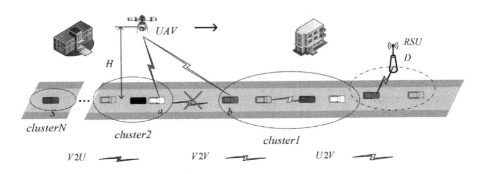

Fig. 1. UAV relay between moving vehicles on the road

2 System Model

As shown in Fig. 1, we consider a scenario where there is an RSU at one end of the road, single lane and the length of the road is L_{SD}, vehicles on the road need to send data packets to the RSU by means of carry and forward (packages contains information about the vehicle's speed, location, and destination, etc.). Here, we randomly divided the vehicles into clusters according to the communication range of the vehicles. The vehicles in the cluster can communicate through multiple hops, but vehicles between clusters, such as vehicle a in cluster 2 and vehicle b in cluster 1, cannot communicate because the distance between them is beyond the communication range of vehicles. Moreover, if the speed of vehicle a is always less than the speed of vehicle b, vehicle a cannot send its own package until it reaches the range of RSU, which may cause a huge delay. Therefore, we take advantage of the strong mobility of the UAV to make it act as a mobile relay between the cluster head vehicles of the clusters to establish a new information transmission link.

We take the disconnect between cluster 1 and cluster 2 as an example, and assume that vehicle a and vehicle b are the cluster head vehicles of cluster 2 and cluster 1 respectively. Here, we assume that the speed of vehicle a is V_a, the speed of vehicle b is V_b, $V_a \leq V_b$ and we assume that their speed will not change for the duration of the UAV as relay. The initial distance between vehicle a and vehicle b is set as L_{ab}, all vehicle has the same communication range and set as R_v, and $L_{ab} > 2R_v$. The UAV cruised above the road at the height of H, and as shown in the figure1, it forwarded the data of vehicle a to vehicle b. The vehicle's communication range is R_v, so when the distance between the UAV's projection point on the ground and vehicle a is $R_a = \sqrt{R_v^2 - H^2}$, vehicle a can communicate with the UAV. Once vehicle a can upload packets to the UAV, the three-dimensional coordinate system is established. At this time, the coordinates of UAV, vehicle a and vehicle b are set as $(0, 0, H)$, $(R_a, 0, 0)$ and $(L_{ab} + R_a, 0, 0)$ respectively. We assume that the UAV flies at a speed of V_U in the process of acting as a relay, there are two ways to collect data when UAV receives data uploaded by vehicle a, so there are two ways for UAV to act as mobile relay between vehicles.

2.1 Relay During Flying Forward

The UAV flies over the communication range of vehicle a at a speed of V_U, $V_a < V_U \leq V_{max}$. As soon as the UAV enters the communication range of vehicle a, vehicle a uploads data to the UAV. Therefore, the instantaneous transmission rate when vehicle a sends data to the UAV is:

$$R_a(t) = B_v \log_2(1 + \frac{P_v \cdot \gamma_0}{(H^2 + (R_a + V_a t - V_U t)^2)^{\frac{\alpha}{2}}}) \tag{1}$$

Here, B_v is the bandwidth of the vehicle a, P_v is the transmitting power of the vehicle a and we assume that the transmitting power of all vehicles are the same. $\alpha(\alpha \geq 2)$ is the path loss exponent and we set $\alpha = 2$ in this paper, γ_0 is the signal-to-noise ratio (SNR) when the reference distance is 1.

We assume that the UAV immediately forwards the data uploaded by vehicle a to vehicle b. Therefore, when the UAV forwards the packet to vehicle b, the instantaneous transmission rate can be expressed as:

$$R_U(t) = B_U \log_2(1 + \frac{P_{Umax} \cdot \gamma_0}{(H^2 + (L_{ab} + R_a + V_b t - V_U t)^2)^{\frac{\alpha}{2}}}) \tag{2}$$

Here, B_U is the bandwidth of the UAV, P_{Umax} is the maximum transmission power of the UAV to ensure that the UAV can maintain communication with vehicle b.

In addition, the upload time of data packet sent by vehicle a to UAV can be expressed as:

$$t_u = \frac{2 \cdot R_a}{V_U - V_a} \tag{3}$$

Therefore, the total amount of data uploaded by vehicle a during the upload time can be expressed as:

$$Q_a = \int_0^{t_u} R_a(t) dt \tag{4}$$

And in the process transmitting information by UAV, the amount of data required to be successfully forwarded is greater than Q. Then the total amount of data forwarded from the UAV to vehicle b can be expressed as: We all know that when the UAV flies in the air as a mobile relay, it needs to consume communication energy and propulsion energy to maintain the UAV's communication capability and flight status in the air. And the actual communication energy consumption is much less than the propulsion energy, so it is often ignored. According to literature [11], the energy consumption of maintaining the flight state of UAV in the air can be written as:

$$E_{fly} = t_u \cdot (c_1 V_U^3 + \frac{c_2}{V_U}) \tag{5}$$

Where c_1 and c_2 are two parameters related to the weight of the aircraft, air density, wing area, etc. What's more, the energy of the UAV is very limited, and some energy needs to be reserved for recall. Therefore, the UAV propulsion energy in the relay process required to keep the UAV in the air must not be greater than E_{max}.

2.2   Relay When Relative Hovering

The UAV flies directly above vehicle a at maximum speed, and then receives data uploaded by vehicle a at the same speed as vehicle a, that is $V_U = V_a$. In fact, at this time, vehicle a and the UAV remain relatively stationary. Assume that the time that the UAV stays in relative hover is t_h, then the total amount of data transmitted from vehicle a to UAV can be expressed as:

$$Q_{ah} = t_h \cdot B_v \log_2(1 + \frac{P_v \cdot \gamma_0}{H^\alpha}) \tag{6}$$

When the UAV reaches the top of vehicle a, the distance between vehicle a and vehicle b increases to $L = L_{ab} + \frac{(V_b - V_a) \cdot R_a}{V_{max} - V_a}$. Then, when the UAV forwards data to vehicle b, the instantaneous transmission rate can be expressed as:

$$R_{Uh}(t) = B_U \log_2(1 + \frac{P_{Umax} \cdot \gamma_0}{(H^2 + (V_U t - L - V_b t)^2)^{\frac{\alpha}{2}}}) \tag{7}$$

And the data forwarded by the UAV to vehicle b can be expressed as:

$$Q_{Uh} = \int_0^{t_h} R_{Uh}(t)dt \geq Q \tag{8}$$

The propulsion energy consumption of UAV in the relay process can be expressed as:

$$E_{fh} = t_h \cdot (c_1 V_U^3 + \frac{c_2}{V_U}) \leq E_{max} \tag{9}$$

3   Problem Formulation and Analysis

The purpose of the UAV as a relay is to forward the traffic information of vehicle a in cluster 2 to vehicle b in cluster 1 in this paper, so as to establish communication between random clusters of vehicles on the road. In this paper, our goal is to maximize the throughput of the UAV as a mobile relay system by optimizing the speed of the UAV while meeting the data requirements for successful transmission of the UAV and the constraints of propulsion energy. Therefore, the objective function can be expressed as follows:

$$\max_{V_U} \quad \frac{Q_{U_{total}}}{t} \tag{10a}$$

$$s.t. \quad V_a \leq V_U \leq V_{max} \tag{10b}$$

$$E_f = t \cdot (c_1 V_U^3 + \frac{c_2}{V_U}) \leq E_{max} \tag{10c}$$

$$Q \leq Q_{U_{total}} \leq Q_{a_{total}} \tag{10d}$$

Where $t = t_u \cdot I_{(V_U > V_a)} + t_h \cdot I_{(V_U = V_a)}$, $Q_{U_{total}} = Q_U \cdot I_{(V_U > V_a)} + Q_{Uh} \cdot I_{(V_U = V_a)}$ and $Q_{a_{total}} = Q_a \cdot I_{(V_U > V_a)} + Q_{ah}(t) \cdot I_{(V_U = V_a)}$. $I_{condition}$ is an indicator function, which is 1 when the condition is true, or 0 otherwise. And because the data forwarded by the UAV to vehicle b must be not greater than the data uploaded by vehicle a, so here we set $Q_{U_{total}} \leq Q_{a_{total}}$.

The above problems can be divided into the following two sub-problems to solve. For the problem of the UAV acting as a relay during relative hover:

$t_h \leq \frac{E_{max}}{c_1 V_U^3 + \frac{c_2}{V_U}}$, and Q_{Uh} is a monotonically decreasing function of t_h, therefore

$Q \leq Q_{Uh} \leq \int_0^{\frac{E_{max}}{c_1 V_U^3 + \frac{c_2}{V_U}}} R_{Uh}(t)dt$.

We define the system throughput of UAV maintaining relative hover is:

$$T_h = \frac{Q_{Uh}}{t_h} \tag{11}$$

Theorem 1. T_h is monotonically decreasing function of t_h.

Proof.

$$\frac{dT_{Uh}}{dt_h} = \frac{t_h R_{Uh}(t_h) - Q_{Uh}}{t_h^2} \tag{12}$$

Where $Q_{Uh} = \frac{B_U}{(V_b - V_a)} \cdot \{s_2 \log_2(1 + \frac{P_{Umax}\gamma_0}{H^2 + s_2^2}) - s_1 \log_2(1 + \frac{P_{Umax}\gamma_0}{H^2 + s_1^2}) + \frac{2}{\ln 2} \cdot$
$[\frac{(H^2 + P_{Umax}\gamma_0)^{\frac{3}{2}}}{H^2 + P_{Umax}\gamma_0 + s_1 \cdot s_2} \arctan(\frac{s_2 - s_1}{\sqrt{H^2 + P_{Umax}\gamma_0}}) - \frac{H^3}{H^2 + s_1 \cdot s_2} \arctan(\frac{s_2 - s_1}{H})]\} > 0$, $s_2 = -L$ and $s_1 = (V_a - V_b)t_h - L$. And $R_{Uh}(t_h) = B_U \log_2(1 + \frac{P_{Umax}\gamma_0}{H^2 + s_1^2})$, so we can get that $R_{Uh}(t_h) - Q_{Uh} \leq 0$, T_h is monotonically decreasing function of t_h.

When $Q_{Uh} = \int_0^{t_h} R_{Uh}(t)dt = Q$ and $t_h \leq \frac{E_{max}}{c_1 V_U^3 + \frac{c_2}{V_U}}$ is satisfied, the throughput T_h reaches the maximum value.

And the problem of the UAV acting as a relay only when flying forward can be rephrased as:

$$\max_{V_U} \frac{Q_U}{t_u} \tag{13a}$$

$$s.t. \quad V_a < V_U \leq V_{max} \tag{13b}$$

$$Q \leq Q_U \leq Q_a \tag{13c}$$

$$E_{fly} \leq E_{max} \tag{13d}$$

Theorem 2. The function 13(a) is convex.

Proof. Let $f_0(V_U) = \frac{Q_U}{t_u}$, and we can calculate that $Q_U = \frac{A}{(V_U - V_b) \ln 2}$. Here, $A = \{Z_1 \ln(1 + \frac{P_{Umax} \cdot \gamma_0}{H^2 + Z_1^2}) - Z_2 \ln(1 + \frac{P_{Umax} \cdot \gamma_0}{H^2 + Z_2^2}) + \frac{2(H^2 + P_{Umax}\gamma_0)^{\frac{3}{2}} \arctan(\frac{Z_1 - Z_2}{\sqrt{H^2 + P_{Umax}\gamma_0}})}{H^2 + P_{Umax}\gamma_0 + Z_1 \cdot Z_2} - \frac{2H^3 \arctan(\frac{Z_1 - Z_2}{H})}{H^2 + Z_1 \cdot Z_2}\}$, $Z_1 = L + R_a$, $Z_2 = L + R_a + \frac{2R_a \cdot (V_b - V_U)}{V_U - V_a}$. The first derivative of Q_U can be obtained as follows:

$$Q'_U = \frac{-A}{(V_U - V_b)^2 \ln 2} + \frac{2R_a(V_b - V_a) \ln(1 + \frac{P_{Umax}\gamma_0}{H^2 + (Z_2)^2})}{(V_U - V_b)(V_U - V_a)^2 \ln 2} \tag{14}$$

And the second derivative of Q_U is:

$$Q''_U = \frac{2A}{(V_U - V_b)^3 \ln 2} - \frac{4R_a(V_b - V_a) \ln(1 + \frac{P_{Umax}\gamma_0}{H^2 + (z_2)^2})}{(V_U - V_b)(V_U - V_a)^3 \ln 2}$$

$$+ \frac{8P_U \gamma_0 Z_2 R_a^2 (V_b - V_a)^2}{(V_U - V_a)^4 (V_U - V_b)(H^2 + Z_2^2)(H^2 + P_U \gamma_0 + Z_2^2)} \tag{15}$$

Then, the first derivative of $f(V_U)$ can be obtained as follows:

$$f_0'(V_U) = \frac{Q_U}{2R_a} + \frac{(V_U - V_a)Q_U'}{2R_a} \tag{16}$$

The second derivative of $f(V_U)$ is:

$$f_0''(V_U) = \frac{Q_U'}{R_a} + \frac{(V_U - V_a)Q_U''}{2R_a} \geq 0 \tag{17}$$

According to the convex function theorem, we prove that the problem $13(a)$ is a convex function.

For the constraint $13(b)$, here are two affine functions with respect to V_U. For constraint $13(c)$, Q_U is a function that decreases monotonically as the V_U increases, if we want satisfy $Q_U \geq Q$, the speed of the UAV should be less than or equal to a certain speed value, and here we set as V_Q. And for constraint $13(d)$, when $V_a < V_U \leq V_{max}$, E_{fly} is a function that decreases monotonically as the V_U increases. So when satisfy $E_{fly} \leq E_{max}$, the speed of the UAV as a relay should be greater than a certain speed, and here we set as V_{fly}. From the above discussion, we can find that the feasible region of solution exists only when $V_{fly} \leq V_Q$. However, if $V_{fly} > V_Q$, it indicates that the flight energy of the UAV is insufficient. At this time, the UAV maintains the same speed of vehicle a collects and forwards information directly above vehicle a, that is, the UAV remains in relative hover as a relay.

We construct the Lagrangian function as follows:

$$\begin{aligned}
\ell(V_U, \lambda_1, \lambda_2, \lambda_3, \lambda_4, \lambda_5) = {} & f(V_U) + \lambda_1(Q_U - Q_a) + \lambda_2(Q - Q_U) \\
& + \lambda_3(V_a - V_U) + \lambda_4(V_U - V_{max}) + \lambda_5(E_{fly} - E_{max})
\end{aligned} \tag{18}$$

Suppose $(V_U^*, \lambda_1^*, \lambda_2^*, \lambda_3^*, \lambda_4^*, \lambda_5^*)$ is the set of optimal solutions with a maximum value of $f(V_U)$, that satisfies the KKT condition:

$$\frac{\partial \ell}{\partial V_U}|_{V_U = V_U^*} = 0 \tag{19a}$$

$$f_1(V_U^*) = (Q_U - Q_a) \leq 0 \tag{19b}$$

$$f_2(V_U^*) = (Q - Q_U) \leq 0 \tag{19c}$$

$$f_3(V_U^*) = (V_a - V_U^*) \leq 0 \tag{19d}$$

$$f_4(V_U^*) = (V_U^* - V_{max}) \leq 0 \tag{19e}$$

$$f_5(V_U^*) = (E_{fly} - E_{max}) \leq 0 \tag{19f}$$

$$\lambda_i^* \geq 0, i = 1 \sim 5 \tag{19g}$$

$$\lambda_i^* \cdot f_i(V_U^*) = 0, i = 1 \sim 5 \tag{19h}$$

$19(a)$ is a necessary condition for obtaining feasible solution by Lagrange multiplier method, $19(b)$–$19(f)$ are the initial constraints, $19(g)$ is the condition that the inequality Lagrange multiplier has to satisfy, and $19(h)$ is the relaxed complementary constraint. Under the constraints in $19(a)$–$19(f)$ above, the maximum throughput value that satisfies the constraints can be calculated.

4   Simulation

In this section, we verify the effectiveness of our optimization algorithm by numerical experiments. We assume that the UAV altitude is $H = 100\,\text{m}$, the vehicle's communication radius $R_v = 150\,\text{m}$, therefore, $R_a = \sqrt{150^2 - 100^2} = 50\sqrt{5}\,\text{m}$. And we assume that the maximum speed of the UAV is $V_{max} = 50\,\text{m/s}$, the bandwidth $B_v = B_U = 500\,\text{Khz}$, and when the reference distance is 1, the SNR $\gamma_0 = 80\,\text{dB}$. The transmission power of the vehicle is $P_v = 3\,\text{dBm}$, and the maximum transmission power of the UAV is $P_{Umax} = 20\,\text{dBm}$ to ensure that the UAV can always communicate with vehicle b in the relay process.

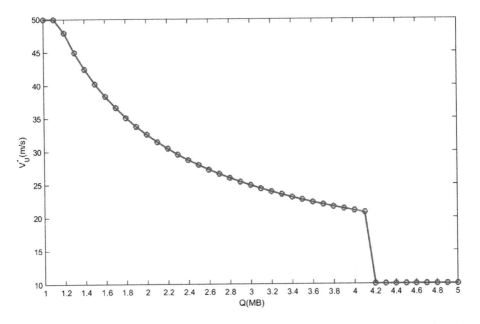

Fig. 2. Optimal flight speed V_U^* versus Q with $E_{max} = 2500\,\text{J}$, $V_a = 10\,\text{m/s}$ and $V_b = 15\,\text{m/s}$.

The optimal speed V_U^* of UAV changes with the limit of uploaded data Q can be seen in Fig. 2, and here we set $V_a = 10\,\text{m/s}$, $V_b = 15\,\text{m/s}$, $L_{ab} = 1000\,\text{m}$ and $E_{max} = 2500\,\text{J}$. As shown in Fig. 2, when the amount of data successfully transferred $Q \leq 1.2\,\text{MB}$, the UAV can fly at maximum speed. However, when $Q > 1.2\,\text{MB}$, V_U^* decreases with the increase of Q. And when $Q > 4.1\,\text{MB}$, the velocity of V_U^* plummets to $10\,\text{m/s}$, this is due to insufficient propulsion energy.

Then, we simulated the influence of flight energy constraint on the optimal speed of UAV. Here, we set $V_a = 10\,\text{m/s}$, $V_b = 15\,\text{m/s}$, $L_{ab} = 1000\,\text{m}$ and $Q = 5\,\text{MB}$. See Fig. 3, when the UAV flight energy $E_{max} \leq 3500\,\text{J}$, the UAV and vehicle a remain in relative hover mode. But when $E_{max} > 3500\,\text{J}$, the UAV can fly at optimized speed. We can conclude that when UAV flight energy is

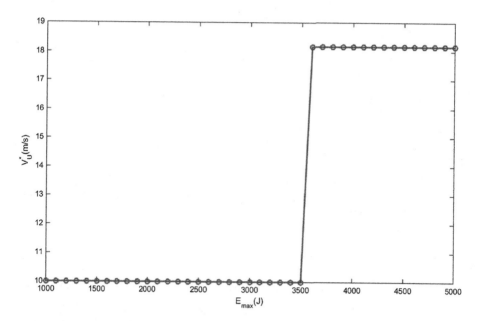

Fig. 3. Optimal flight speed V_U^* versus E_{max} with $Q = 5\,\text{MB}$, $V_a = 10\,\text{m/s}$ and $V_b = 15\,\text{m/s}$.

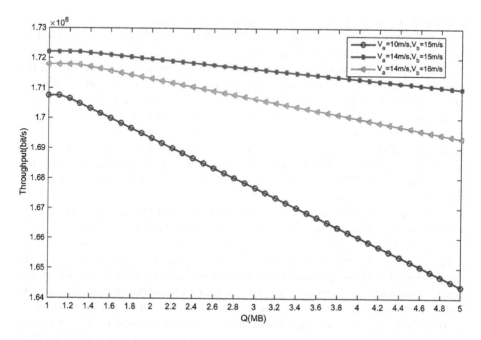

Fig. 4. Throughput of the system versus Q with random V_a and V_b.

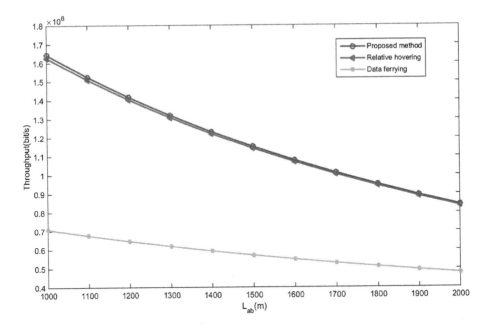

Fig. 5. Performance comparison of UAV operating in different modes of mobile relay with $V_a = 10\,\text{m/s}$, $V_b = 15\,\text{m/s}$.

insufficient, UAV needs to keep hovering relative to vehicle a for relay. However, when UAV flight energy is sufficient, UAV flight speed can be optimized to maximize the relay throughput of UAV.

In Fig. 4, we compare the throughput of the system with the increase of the data Q for successful transmission at different vehicle speeds under sufficient energy. Here we set $E_{max} = 5 \times 10^4\,\text{J}$, and it can be found that the throughput of the system is decreasing with the increase of Q. Moreover, when the speed of vehicle b is the same, the greater the speed of vehicle a, the greater the throughput of the system. When the speed of vehicle a is the same, the greater the speed of vehicle b, the smaller the throughput of the system. That is, the smaller the speed difference between vehicle b and vehicle a, the greater the throughput of the system.

In the case of sufficient flight energy, we compared the throughput changes of UAV as a mobile relay in relative hover mode, data ferrying mode in [4] and our proposed optimization method with $V_a = 10\,\text{m/s}$, $V_b = 15\,\text{m/s}$. As shown in Fig. 5, it can be found that as the distance between vehicles increases, the throughput of UAV as a mobile relay in the three modes all shows a decreasing trend. In addition, the throughput of the proposed optimization method is always better than that of the relative hover method and the data ferrying method.

What's more, we also compared the throughput changes of UAV as a mobile relay in relative hover mode, data ferrying mode, power optimization method in [5] and our proposed optimization method with $V_a = V_b = 10\,\text{m/s}$. The power optimization method is to optimize the transmission power of UAV and vehicle a after the flight path of UAV is fixed. When vehicle a and vehicle b are at the same speed, vehicle a and vehicle b are stationary relative to each other. As shown in Fig. 6, it can be found that as the distance between vehicles increases, the throughput of UAV as a mobile relay in the four modes all shows a decreasing trend. The communication distance between the UAV and the vehicle does not change with time, therefore, the throughput of the relay mode of UAV maintaining relative hover is as close as the throughput of the proposed method. And in this case, the proposed optimization method is superior to the throughput of other UAV as mobile relays.

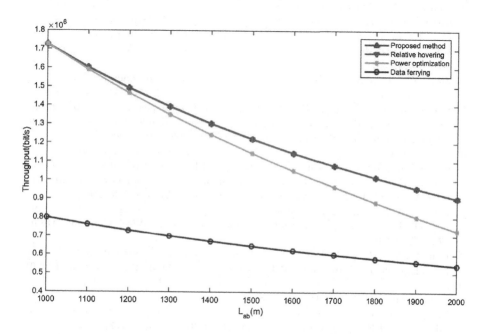

Fig. 6. Performance comparison of UAV operating in different modes of mobile relay with $V_a = V_b = 10\,\text{m/s}$.

5   Conclusion

In this paper, we use the UAV as a mobile relay between moving vehicles on the road. Under the limits of UAV flight energy and the amount of data successfully transferred, we optimize the speed of the UAV in the relay process to maximize the throughput of the UAV as a mobile relay system. Contrast with other system of UAV as mobile relay, our scenario was not considered, and we considered the requirements for the amount of data successfully transferred during the relay, the communication range of the source node, and the propulsion energy requirements of the UAV. However, we only consider the case that there is no communication between one cluster and another on the road. For the actual road, there may be a broken connection between multiple clusters. At this time, we need to consider the dynamic change due to the movement of vehicles, which is also the direction of our future work.

References

1. Fawaz, W., Atallah, R., Assi, C., Khabbaz, M.: Unmanned aerial vehicles as store-carry-forward nodes for vehicular networks. IEEE Access **5**, 23710–23718 (2017)
2. Khabbaz, M., Antoun, J., Assi, C.: Modeling and performance analysis of UAV-assisted vehicular networks. IEEE Trans. Veh. Technol. **68**(9), 8384–8396 (2019)
3. Guo, C., Li, D., Zhang, G., Zhai, M.: Real-time path planning in urban area via VANET-assisted traffic information sharing. IEEE Trans. Veh. Technol. **67**(7), 5635–5649 (2018)
4. Zhao, W., Ammar, M., Zegura, E.: A message ferrying approach for data delivery in sparse mobile ad hoc networks. In: Proceedings of the 5th ACM International Symposium on Mobile Ad Hoc Networking and Computing, pp. 187–198 (2014)
5. Zeng, Y., Zhang, R., Lim, T.J.: Throughput maximization for UAV-enabled mobile relaying systems. IEEE Trans. Commun. **64**(12), 4983–4996 (2016)
6. Jiang, X., Wu, Z., Yin, Z., Yang, Z.: Power and trajectory optimization for UAV-enabled amplify-and-forward relay networks. IEEE Access **6**, 48688–48696 (2018)
7. Xue, Z., Wang, J., Ding, G., Wu, Q.: Joint 3D location and power optimization for UAV-enabled relaying systems. IEEE Access **6**, 43113–43124 (2018)
8. Hu, X., Wong, K., Yang, K., Zheng, Z.: UAV-assisted relaying and edge computing: scheduling and trajectory optimization. IEEE Trans. Wirel. Commun. **18**(10), 4738–4752 (2019)
9. Eom, S., Lee, H., Park, J., Lee, I.: UAV-aided wireless communication designs with propulsion energy limitations. IEEE Trans. Veh. Technol. **69**(1), 651–662 (2020)
10. Song, Q., Zheng, F.: Energy efficient multi-antenna UAV-enabled mobile relay. China Commun. **15**(5), 41–50 (2018)
11. Zeng, Y., Zhang, R.: Energy-efficient UAV communication with trajectory optimization. IEEE Trans. Wirel. Commun. **16**(6), 3747–3760 (2017)

Energy Optimization with Adaptive Transmit Power Control for UAV-Assisted Data Transmission in VANETs

Wei Hu[1,2(✉)], Demin Li[1,2], Xingxing Hu[1,2], and Yue Li[1,2]

[1] College of Information Science and Technology, Donghua University, Shanghai, China

[2] Engineering Research Center of Digitized Textile and Apparel Technology, Ministry of Education, Shanghai 201620, China
WeiHu@mail.dhu.edu.cn, deminli@dhu.edu.cn

Abstract. Time for unmanned aerial vehicle (UAV) assisted vehicular ad hoc networks (VANETs) to promote the efficient data transmission is limited. To this end, improving the endurance of UAV has become a crucial issue. In this paper, we first propose an energy optimization model to improve the endurance of UAV, which consider not only the flying energy, but also communication energy. By considering the relative position between UAV and vehicle, adaptive transmission power is applied to communication energy consumption. Second, in order to verify the existence of the solution, we use Rolle's theorem and the monotonicity of the function to prove the objective function, and obtain the approximate solution of the objective function by using the principle of inequality. Finally, compare with optimized algorithm and algorithm without optimized communication energy, and our proposed algorithm which performance is better than the existing energy optimization algorithms.

Keywords: Adaptive transmit power control · Relative position · Energy optimization

1 Introduction

With the process of urbanization, social problems and contradictions related to vehicle have gradually become prominent. However, due to some features such as intermittent network connectivity [13] and small network coverage, there will causing road traffic accidents by lack of information interaction between vehicles.

Supported by NSF of China under Grant No. 61772130, No. 71171045, No. 61772130 and No. 61901104; the Innovation Program of Shanghai Municipal Education Commission under Grant No. 14YZ130; and the International S&T Cooperation Program of Shanghai Science and Technology Commission under Grant No. 15220710600.

M. Guan and Z. Na (Eds.): MLICOM 2020, LNICST 342, pp. 505–516, 2021.
https://doi.org/10.1007/978-3-030-66785-6_54

To deal with these issues, UAV can be utilized to cooperate with VANETs which flexible, fast moving, and low cost [7]. Additionally, the energy of UAV is limited. Therefore, energy optimization of UAV should be developed to extend the endurance of UAV and reduce the service time [1].

Energy optimization of UAV is different from traditional base stations, which need extra energy to maintain flight. Simultaneously, different trajectories will affect energy consumption. In [8], Optimize the trajectory of the UAV by considering the relationship between the communication throughput and the propulsion energy of the UAV, the energy efficiency of maximizing the data transmission rate and minimizing the energy has been studied. Mozaffari M. and Saad W deploy multiple UAVs as mobile base stations to meet the user's rate requirements, a transmission method is proposed to minimize the transmit power in [5]. To this end, in [9], the derivation of the propulsion power consumption model of the UAV, joint optimization of the trajectory and allocate communication time. Consequently, special single-fly-hover energy optimization is studied. In [3,10,11], energy optimization by optimizing location deployment and performance of UAV. In addition, some studies consider the UAV are employed as mobile relays by optimize the trajectories to get better communication performance [15,16]. These methods are not consider dynamic sensor nodes, it seems more significance to consider the energy optimization under dynamic nodes.

Adaptive transmit power control means that the transmit power has the ability to adapt autonomously, which environmental conditions of communication between sensor nodes has change in a wireless sensor network. In [2], proposed that the relationship between transmitted power and received power in one clear line of sight (LoS) path. In [6], the authors used to control the transmit power by controlling the network topology. In [17], the differences of power consumption and data rate between fixed transmit power and adaptive transmit power are analyzed and shows that FTP has a positive impact on the data rate and power consumption performance. Amir Haider and Seung-Hoon Hwang [12] proposed A-TPC algorithm with SB-SPS, the algorithm is better in packet reception ratio. In the UAV-assisted wireless communication network, Kendeepan et al. in [4] considered that there would be a certain amount of communication energy consumption, proposed a real-time adaptive cooperative transmission scheme for dynamic selection between direct links and cooperative links to improve energy use efficiency.

However, all the above presented works assumes nodes are stationary, consider dynamic nodes, such as vehicles and the model which considering the UAV's adaptive transmit power and relative position at the same time is rarely discussed. More importantly, our model can greatly reduce the energy consumption and enhance service performance. Specifically, the contributions and motivations of this paper are as follows:

– First, We systematically studied the correlation between the relative position and the adaptive transmission power, and propose an energy optimization model that can improve UAV broadcast vehicle information and meet certain communication service requirements.

– Second, the feasibility and effectiveness of the model are verified by the proof
of the objective function by Roll's theorem and the inequality theorem.

The remainder of this paper is organized as follows: In Sect. 1, it presents the
system model of adaptive transmit power improvement and explains in detail.
In Sect. 2, we describes the implementation method of the algorithm. In Sect. 3
demonstrates our proposed energy performance based on adaptive power, and
presents analysis followed by simulation results. Finally, Sect. 4 summarizes the
final results.

2   System Model

In this paper, we design a scenario in which the front and rear ends of the
road deployed road side unit (RSU) that collect information on road traffic
conditions, as shown in Fig. 1, by deploying multiple UAVs in three-dimensional
space to consist UAV network, besides we consider a segment with unidirectional
traffic flow, UAV can provide higher coverage in instance and broadcast traffic
information to other vehicles instantly. We assume that all vehicles can be served
by stationary and mobile units, and the strong mobility of UAV can provide
better information services for the entire road network.

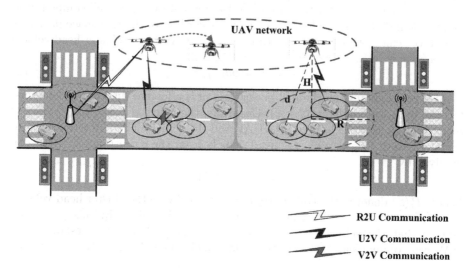

Fig. 1. Overview of UAV assisted vehicular in areas not covered by RSU

In addition, We assume that a section of RSU that is not covered is divided
into a series of subsegments, and each road section is provided with a UAV
to provide network services. When the UAV is flying in the road section with
communicates with cluster head vehicle, speed remains the same. Assume that
the minimum service time of UAV is T, the speed of UAV is ν, and the coverage

radius is R. Because the height of UAV is stable and large, therefore the width of the road can be ignored, compared with the transmission range between vehicle and UAV. That is we does not consider the left and right movement of UAV and cluster head vehicle.

Due to the limitation of the range of communication for all vehicles, several clusters are automatically formed, and a UAV only communicates with the one cluster head vehicle. We assume the vehicle's position information and speed are already known by the UAV and the vehicle's arrival rate in the road subsection satisfies the Poisson distribution, the vehicle travels at different speeds in different directions and speed of vehicle satisfies $\nu_0 \in [\nu_{min}, \nu_{max}]$, moreover speed of the cluster head vehicle in the subsegment remains the same, and driving forward direction remains the same. Similarity, timing starts when vehicle entering the coverage of UAV, the relative position between the cluster head vehicle and the UAV's vertical projection is x. We assume that there is only one clear Los path between the transmitter and receiver in the free space propagation model, so the distance between the UAV and the cluster vehicle can be expressed as

$$d(x) = \sqrt{x^2 + H^2} \tag{1}$$

For ease of exposition, we ignore the effects of ground reflection models. Note that in practice, the distance between the UAV and the cluster head vehicle affect on the channel quality. Furthermore, the Doppler effect is also well compensated due to the mobility of the UAV. Therefore, according to the free-space path loss model, the channel gain in service time from the UAV to the cluster head vehicle can be expressed as

$$h(x) = \beta d(x)^{-\xi} \tag{2}$$

Where β denotes the channel power gain at a reference distance of 1 meters. ξ is the path loss exponent($\xi \geq 2$). Generally, the received power of a vehicle is related to the distance between the UAV and the vehicle, Therefore, the received signal strength [14] at a cluster head vehicle from the corresponding UAV can be given by

$$P_r(x) = P_t(x)h(x) \tag{3}$$

Where $P_t(x)$ denoted the transmitted power of UAV to the cluster head vehicle. $P_r(x)$ denoted the received power of cluster head vehicle. In this paper, we assume that the vehicle's received power is greater than the threshold α, so UAV can communicate with cluster head vehicle. Therefore, we have

$$P_r(x) \geq \alpha \tag{4}$$

Obviously, given threshold α, we can get the minimum transmitting power of the UAV varies with relative position x as

$$P_t(x) = \frac{\alpha}{h(x)} = \frac{\alpha}{\beta}(H^2 + x^2)^{\xi} \tag{5}$$

Besides, we know the energy consumption of UAV has two main aspects. On the one hand, energy consumed by the UAV to maintain flight and attitude propulsion, on the other hand, communication energy which used to communicate with sensor nodes on the ground, such as vehicle, base station etc.

Generally speaking, the propulsion energy of a UAV is mainly determined by the speed and acceleration of the UAV and the time of acceleration is short, in order to easy to analyze the speed of the UAV, we ignore the energy consumed by the UAV for acceleration and deceleration. Obviously, the left and right trajectory of the UAV is uncertain. Thus, the propulsion energy of the UAV can be expressed as

$$E_f = \frac{MR\nu^2}{\nu - \nu_0} \qquad (6)$$

Where M denotes the weight of UAV. It can be seen that the greater the mass of the UAV, the more energy it takes to overcome gravity to do work, and the energy consumption of UAV increases rapidly with speed. In practice, although the communication energy consumed by UAV is very small, it is important for calculating energy. In this paper, we consider the coverage is large, in order to maintain such a large communication range, a large amount of communication energy will be consumed. In addition, the height of UAV is certain, the communication energy of UAV only decided by the distance between the UAV and the cluster head vehicle which actually related to the size of the relative position x between the UAV projection and the cluster head vehicle. We observed that there is no influence of the ground objection, so the vehicle's received power can be expressed as

$$E_o = \int_R^0 P_t(x) \frac{R - x}{\nu - \nu_0} dx + \int_0^R P_t(x) \frac{R + x}{\nu - \nu_0} dx$$
$$= \int_0^R P_t(x) \frac{2x}{\nu - \nu_0} dx = \int_0^R \frac{\alpha}{\beta} (H^2 + x^2)^{\frac{\xi}{2}} \frac{2x}{\nu - \nu_0} dx \qquad (7)$$

Based on the above, we can get the total energy consumption of the UAV as

$$E = E_f + E_o \qquad (8)$$

The UAV needs to chase with the vehicle ahead and provide the real time traffic information, and the communication time between the UAV and the vehicle greater than T, which the interaction of information is considered complete. Besides UAV have a maximum speed limit, and other constraint conditions are satisfied as

$$\nu > \nu_0 \qquad (9)$$

$$\frac{2R}{\nu - \nu_0} \geq T \qquad (10)$$

$$\nu \leq \nu_{max} \qquad (11)$$

It can be seen from the limiting conditions that if the speed of UAV is greater, the communication time will be shorter. We assume that the maximum speed of the UAV is large, and the optimal speed of the UAV is always less than the maximum speed of the UAV, therefore we have

$$\nu \leq \frac{2R}{T} + \nu_0 \qquad (12)$$

Because the energy of the UAV is limited, and exceed a certain amount of energy consumption and need to be charged in time. Here we set the total energy of the UAV is ϵ, and the energy constraints are

$$E \leq \epsilon \qquad (13)$$

3   Analysis

3.1   Problem Formulation

Based on the above discussions, we formulate the UAV energy minimization problem to service one cluster head vehicle as

$$\min_{\nu} \quad \{\frac{MR\nu^2}{\nu - \nu_0} + \int_0^R \frac{\alpha}{\beta}(H^2 + x^2)^{\frac{\xi}{2}} \frac{2x}{\nu - \nu_0} dx\} \qquad (14a)$$

$$s.t. \quad E \leq \epsilon \qquad (14b)$$

$$\nu_0 < \nu \leq \frac{2R}{T} + \nu_0 \qquad (14c)$$

Note that the constraint (14c) is a non-convex constraint, therefore, the problem is hard to solved. For ease of presentation, we use B denote these values, that is $B = \frac{\alpha}{\beta}\int_0^R(H^2 + x^2)^{\frac{\xi}{2}}2xdx$, and use $V = \frac{2R}{T} + \nu_0$. Thus, our model can be simplified as

$$\min_{\nu} \quad \{\frac{MR\nu^2}{\nu - \nu_0} + \frac{B}{\nu - \nu_0}\} \qquad (15a)$$

$$s.t. \quad E \leq \epsilon \qquad (15b)$$

$$\nu_0 < \nu \leq V \qquad (15c)$$

3.2   Problem Decomposition

In this section, in order to consider easiest one case, we omit constraint to easy to solve, A generic function is defined as follow:

$$E(\nu) = \frac{MR\nu^2}{\nu - \nu_0} + \frac{B}{\nu - \nu_0} \qquad (16)$$

The image of the objective function resembles a check mark function. The difference in the value of T will affect the optimal solution. Therefore, we classify and discuss the objective function.

Theorem 1. *if $\nu > \nu_0$, the optimal solution to energy-minimization problem is*

$$\nu^* = \sqrt{\frac{B + MR\nu_0^2}{MR}} + \nu_0 \tag{17}$$

correspondingly, the minimum energy consumption of the UAV is

$$E(\nu^*) = \frac{B + MR\nu^{*2}}{\nu^* - \nu_0} \tag{18}$$

Proof. See Appendix A

By considering that the maximum speed V of the UAV is greater than or less than the optimal speed ν^*, that will cause different energy levels. Therefore, we divide the maximum speed V of the UAV into two parts.

In part one, the speed V of the UAV cannot reach the optimal speed ν^* of the UAV, that is $V < \nu^*$. According Theorem 1, the optimal value is unique. And the interval of speed is $\nu_0 < \nu \leq V < \nu^*$, The reciprocal of the $E'(\nu)$ is less than 0, that is $E'(\nu) < 0$, indicating that the $E(\nu)$ monotonically decreasing. So the energy consumption of UAV decreases as ν increases.

In the interval $\nu_0 < \nu \leq V$, the optimal solution to energy-minimization can be express as

$$\nu^* = V \tag{19}$$

correspondingly, the minimum energy consumption of the UAV is

$$E(\nu^*) = \frac{B + MRV^2}{V - \nu_0} \tag{20}$$

In part two, the speed V of the UAV great than the optimal speed ν^* of the UAV, that is $V > \nu^*$. And the optimal value ν^* at this time is $\nu^* \in (\nu_0, V)$. the optimal solution to energy-minimization can be obtain as

$$\nu^* = \sqrt{\frac{B + MR\nu_0^2}{MR}} + \nu_0 \tag{21}$$

Similarly, the optimal energy consumption of UAV is

$$E(\nu^*) = \frac{B + MR\nu^{*2}}{\nu^* - \nu_0} \tag{22}$$

4   Performance Evaluation and Results

In this section provides numerical results to validate the proposed design. The speed of the cluster head vehicle $\nu_0 = 20$ m/s, and the threshold value of the cluster head vehicle's received power is set $P_r = 10$ dBm. Set the communication time T and $\xi = 2$. Without loss of generality, we assume that when the UAV communicates with the cluster head vehicle, the speed of the UAV remains unchanged and only serves one cluster head vehicles within range.

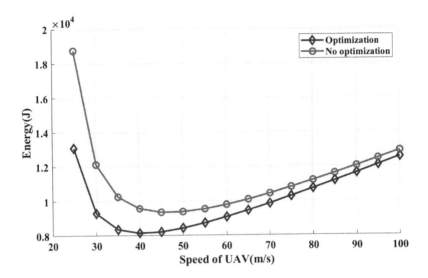

Fig. 2. Energy consumption of UAV at different speeds

To verify the theoretical analysis, we first plotted the trend of UAV energy as a function of UAV speed. As shown in Fig. 2, we can clearly see that as the speed of the UAV increases, the energy consumption continues to increase. In addition, since the speed of the vehicle is set to 20 m/s, it can be found that when the speed of the UAV communicates with the vehicle, the closer it is to the speed of the vehicle, the longer it takes to service the vehicle, and the more energy consumption during data transmission. And in order to verify the advantages of our algorithm in energy optimization, we compare it with algorithms that have not been optimized in communication energy. We observed that the greater the UAV speed, the shorter the data transmission time, and the closer the optimization algorithm is to the energy without the optimization algorithm in energy consumption. On the whole, the optimized algorithm will save a certain amount of energy.

Next, we consider that the size of the UAV's coverage radius is related to the UAV's transmit power which affects the energy consumption. In Fig. 3, we plotted the changes in the energy of the two algorithms with the UAV's coverage radius. It can be seen that as the radius R increases, the energy consumption of the UAV also increases accordingly. Because of the large range of implementation. The coverage of the UAV needs a lot of power, which will consume a lot of communication energy. Because this paper uses adaptive transmit power, as long as it guarantees a certain communication time, it is considered that the energy under the optimization algorithm is completed and the performance is improved compared with the algorithm without optimization.

Similarly, we plotted the energy consumption trends at different altitudes. We found that the energy consumption under the optimized algorithm is more energy-efficient than the optimized algorithm in Fig. 4, the optimized algorithm

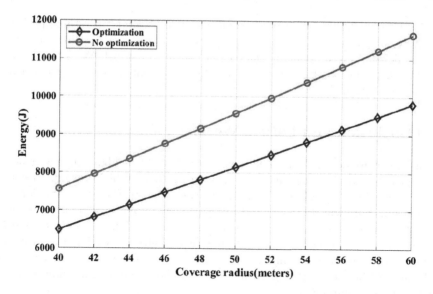

Fig. 3. Energy consumption of UAV at different coverage radius

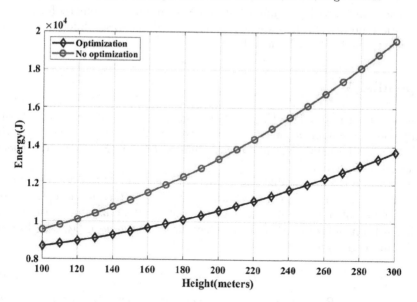

Fig. 4. Energy consumption of UAV at different heights

improves the endurance of the UAV when the distance between the UAV and the cluster head vehicle is increased. And the threshold value of receive power set by the vehicle is not changed, the energy consumption is also increased as the altitude is increased. We further found that this effect is greater with increasing altitude.

We observe that the energy consumption of UAV under the same path loss exponent, and choose the optimal speed according to the speed of different cluster head vehicles, thereby reducing the energy consumption of UAV. Thus we have not included those results of different path loss exponent and analysis because of space limitation in this paper.

5   Conclusion and Future Work

In this paper, we design and evaluate energy optimization algorithms with adaptive transmit power. In the area not covered by RSU, vehicles are divided into multiple clusters through V2V communication. Due to the carry and forward mechanism, there will be a certain delay. UAVs are deployed to assist in wireless communication, which reduces the delay and reduce traffic accident caused by untimely access to information. Our numerical results show that the proposed energy optimization algorithm reduces the energy consumption to compared with the traditional energy algorithm, and can guarantee the minimum communication time requirements.

In the future, we would like to consider the multiple cluster head vehicle into the model, which provide communication between multiple vehicles for real-time information interaction. In addition, we also would like to set different directions of vehicle to deploy UAV rationally.

Appendix A

When $\nu > \nu_0$, the problem $E(\nu)$ is differentiable on the interval (ν_0, ∞), there is only one stable point $\nu^{\sharp}$, and $\nu^{\sharp}$ is the extreme value of $E(\nu)$ at (ν_0, ∞), when $E(\nu^{\sharp})$ is extreme value, the minimum value of $E(\nu)$ is $E(\nu^{\sharp})$. So the energy-minimization is $E(\nu^{\sharp})$.

Due to $\nu^{\sharp}$ is the only stable point of $E(\nu)$ in the interval (ν_0, ∞), thus for any point of $\nu \in (\nu_0, \nu^{\sharp}) \bigcup (\nu^{\sharp}, \infty)$, there will be $E'(\nu) \neq 0$. Furthermore, we confirm that $E'(\nu)$ is different symbol at both ends of $\nu^{\sharp}$. If we assume $E'(\nu)$ is same symbol at both ends of $\nu^{\sharp}$, there will be have two point $\nu_1, \nu_2 \in (\nu_0, \nu^{\sharp}) \bigcup (\nu^{\sharp}, \infty)$, which can be given as

$$E'(\nu_1)E'(\nu_2) < 0 \tag{23}$$

According to the Rolle theorem, we can get the existence a point $\nu_e \in (\nu_1, \nu_2)$, which make

$$E'(\nu_e) = 0 \tag{24}$$

From the above formula, which is contradicts the existence of only one stable point. Obviously, $E(\nu)$ is strictly monotone in these two intervals. Therefore, $E(\nu^{\sharp})$ is minimum value of UAV's energy, and $\nu^{\sharp}$ is the optimal solution to energy-minimization.

By simplifying the problem, we can get the following formula

$$E(\nu) = MR(\nu - \nu_0) + \frac{B + MR\nu_0^2}{\nu - \nu_0} + 2MR\nu_0 \tag{25}$$

Looking closely at the above formula, we found that the shape is like a check function. In order to further visualize the mathematical characteristics of the expression, we use $k = \nu - \nu_0$ to change the element. Through method of passing the mean inequality to address the problem.

$$MRk + \frac{B + MR\nu_0^2}{k} + 2MR\nu_0 \geq 2\sqrt{MRk \cdot \frac{B + MR\nu_0^2}{k}} + 2MR\nu_0 \tag{26}$$

When $MRk = \frac{B + MR\nu_0^2}{k}$, take the equal sign. So the energy of UAV is the minimum.

$$k = \sqrt{\frac{B + MR\nu_0^2}{MR}} \tag{27}$$

Therefore, the optimal solution to energy-minimization is

$$\nu^* = k + \nu_0 = \sqrt{\frac{B + MR\nu_0^2}{MR}} + \nu_0 \tag{28}$$

References

1. Zeng, Y., Zhang, R., Lim, T.J.: Wireless communications with unmanned aerial vehicles: opportunities and challenges. IEEE Commun. Mag. **54**(5), 36–42 (2016)
2. Friis, H.T.: A note on a simple transmission formula. Proc. IRE **34**(5), 254–256 (1946)
3. Mozaffari, M., Saad, W., Bennis, M., Debbah, M.: Efficient deployment of multiple unmanned aerial vehicles for optimal wireless coverage. IEEE Commun. Lett. **20**(8), 1647–1650 (2016)
4. Kandeepan, S., Gomez, K., Reynaud, L., et al.: Aerial-terrestrial communications: terrestrial cooperation and energy-efficient transmissions to aerial base stations. IEEE Trans. Aerosp. Electron. Syst. **50**(4), 2715–2735 (2014)
5. Mozaffari, M., Saad, W., Bennis, M., et al.: Optimal transport theory for power-efficient deployment of unmanned aerial vehicles, pp. 1–6 (2016)
6. Zheng, L., Wang, W., Mathewson, A., O'Flynn, B., Hayes, M.: An adaptive transmission power control method for wireless sensor networks. In: IET Irish Signals and Systems Conference (ISSC 2010), Cork, pp. 261–265 (2010)
7. Xiang, H., Tian, L.: Development of a low-cost agricultural remote sensing system based on an autonomous unmanned aerial vehicle (UAV). Biosyst. Eng. **108**, 174–190 (2011)
8. Zeng, Y., Zhang, R.: Energy-efficient UAV communication with trajectory optimization. IEEE Trans. Wirel. Commun. **16**(6), 3747–3760 (2017)
9. Zeng, Y., Xu, J., Zhang, R.: Energy minimization for wireless communication with rotary-wing UAV. IEEE Trans. Wirel. Commun. **18**(4), 2329–2345 (2019)
10. Alzenad, M., El-keyi, A., Lagum, F., Yanikomeroglu, H.: 3-D placement of an unmanned aerial vehicle base station (UAV-BS) for energy-efficient maximal coverage. IEEE Wirel. Commun. Lett. **6**(4), 434–437 (2017)

11. Al-Hourani, A., Chandrasekharan, S., Kaandorp, G., Glenn, W., Jamalipour, A., Kandeepan, S.: Coverage and rate analysis of aerial base stations. IEEE Trans. Aerosp. Electron. Syst. **52**(6), 3077–3081 (2016)
12. Haider, A., Hwang, S.-H.: Adaptive transmit power control algorithm for sensing-based semi-persistent scheduling in C-V2X mode 4 communication, July 2019
13. Fan, X., Huang, C., Fu, B., Wen, S., Chen, X.: UAV-assisted data dissemination in delay-constrained VANETs. Mobile Inf. Syst. (2018)
14. Liu, J., Nishiyama, H., Kato, N., Guo, J.: On the outage probability of device-to-device-communication-enabled multi channel cellular networks: an RSS-threshold-based perspective. IEEE J. Sel. Areas Commun. **34**(1), 163–175 (2016)
15. Zhan, C., Zeng, Y., Zhang, R.: Energy-efficient data collection in UAV enabled wireless sensor network. IEEE Wirel. Commun. Lett. **7**(3), 328–331 (2018)
16. Lyu, J., Zeng, Y., Zhang, R.: Cyclical multiple access in UAV-aided communications: a throughput-delay tradeoff. IEEE Wirel. Commun. Lett. **5**(6), 600–603 (2016)
17. Hakim, H., Boujemaa, H., Ajib, W.: Performance comparison between adaptive and fixed transmit power in underlay cognitive radio networks. IEEE Trans. Commun. **61**(12), 4836–4846 (2013)

Late Track

Secure and Reliable D2D Communications with Active Attackers: A Game-Theoretic Perspective and Machine Learning Approaches

Yijie Luo[✉], Yang Yang, Sixuan An, and Zhibin Feng

Army Engineering University of PLA, Nanjing, China
yijieluo@sina.com, sheep_1009@163.com,
1102719288@qq.com, fengzb1995@163.com

Abstract. Frequent communications among massive terminal devices are ubiquitous in forthcoming 5G Internet of Thing (IoT) networks. It strengthens links of massive machine-type-communication (MMTC), pushes forward the process of Internet of everything. However, due to continual interactions among different devices and the broadcast characteristic of wireless channels, it also brings new security challenges. Recently, physical layer security launches a new solution to guarantee information theoretic security. To enhance the physical layer security performance of massive intelligent devices, especially in D2D communications, the game theory and machine learning methods are introduced. In this paper, we first review physical layer security problems on D2D communications under different attack scenarios. Game theory is proposed to describe hierarchical and heterogeneous interactions among legitimate users and active attackers in 5G IoT networks, then some distributed machine learning methods are proposed to obtain equilibrium states among different agents. Moreover, numerical results are provided to verify availability and efficiency of proposed game-theoretic learning approaches. Finally, we discuss open issues and future research directions in term of anti-eavesdropping and anti-jamming problems in D2D communications when facing active attackers.

Keywords: D2D communications · Full-duplex active eavesdropper · Physical layer security · Hierarchical game · Distributed machine learning

1 Introduction

The fifth generation (5G) mobile communication system is being quickly deployed at the present, and studies on key technologies of the next generation 5G and 6G networks are opening up. We can see that the future mobile communications focus on applications of artificial intelligence (AI) from the published literature, not simple superposition of them, but deep integration of huge application and intelligent networks [1–3]. AI [1, 2], edge computing [3] and Internet of Thing (IoT) technologies will drive important innovations of mobile communications, ever change the actual world in the future [4]. Frequent interactions among lots of devices will exist everywhere in the

© ICST Institute for Computer Sciences, Social Informatics and Telecommunications Engineering 2021
Published by Springer Nature Switzerland AG 2021. All Rights Reserved
M. Guan and Z. Na (Eds.): MLICOM 2020, LNICST 342, pp. 519–533, 2021.
https://doi.org/10.1007/978-3-030-66785-6_55

future, diverse communication requirements of different users face huge challenges, and AI technology, such as machine learning [5], will act an important part in it.

In the next 5G mobile communications or IoT networks, since communications between device to device (D2D) or machine to machine (M2M) will be frequent, it is difficult to guarantee communication security. Physical layer security will be a valid supplement and enhancement for communication network security. Adopting transmission technologies (artificial jamming [6], full-duplex receiving [7], multiple antenna [8] and relay cooperation [9]) to make transmission rates larger than eavesdropping rates, perfect physical layer security can be achieved. However, due to the existence of massive users and information asymmetric of different users, it is difficult to obtain perfect physical layer security. Moreover, when attackers become more active and intelligent, that is to say, they can launch different attacks flexibly, secure and reliable communications among a lot of devices in 5G IoT networks can be hardly ensured.

Game theory is a valid mathematic tool, which can analyze competition and cooperation among multi-users, it is suitable to model physical layer security and anti-jamming problem of legitimate users against active attacks. Furthermore, intelligent devices can achieve better communication performance through machine learning methods. Therefore, by way of combination of game theory and machine learning methods, not only joint physical layer security and anti-jamming problem can be solved in theory, but also robust anti-eavesdropping and anti-jamming strategies can be obtained in reality. At the present, game theory and machine learning methods have been extensively studied on resource management, power control in cellular networks and dynamic spectrum access in cognitive radio networks. Moreover, they have been already used under active eavesdropping and intelligent jamming scenarios [10–12].

D2D communication is the direct communication between cellular users without forward by the base station. In the underlay way, D2D users have the opportunity to share the same spectrum of cellular users to transmit messages directly between them. In the future 5G IoT networks, D2D communications will extensively exist. In D2D communications, on one hand, strategies-making of distributed D2D users is asynchronous. On the other hand, there exists a natural hierarchical structure between cellular users and D2D users. Therefore, it is very suitable to use hierarchical and heterogeneous game-theoretic learning methods to combat active attackers in D2D communications.

In the following sections, we first review security threats in D2D communications with different active attacks, then illustrate applications of the game theory and machine learning methods for physical layer security and anti-jamming in D2D communications, finally we propose the future research directions and open issues in D2D communications with active attacks from the game theory perspective.

2 Review of Anti-eavesdropping and Anti-jamming in D2D Communications

Physical layer security problems are always studied with the assumption that eavesdroppers are passive. That is to say, when they wiretap confidential messages of legitimate users, they always keep silent. Compared with passive eavesdroppers, active attackers will do much more harm to legitimate users. On one hand, active attackers can launch active jamming attack to destroy reliable communications among legitimate users. On the other hand, active attackers can switch different attack types due to different attack aims, and they can adaptively adjust their attack strategies to bring more destruction for legitimate users.

We can divide active attackers into active eavesdroppers and active jammers according to attack types of them. Due to the duplex mode, active eavesdroppers can be further divided into half-duplex active eavesdroppers and full-duplex active eavesdroppers. The former ones only launch eavesdropping or jamming at different time slots, while the last ones can use two attack modes simultaneously. Active jammers are also called smart jammers, who can intelligently adjust their jamming power or channels to destroy reliable communications among legitimate users. Figure 1, 2 and 3 illustrate the scenarios of secure and reliable D2D communications with different active attackers. We analyze technology challenges in D2D communications with these kinds of active attackers in this section.

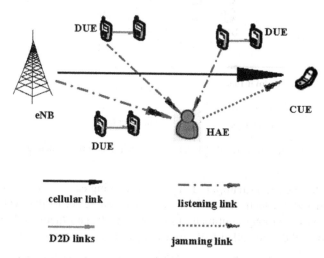

Fig. 1. Illustration of secure D2D communications with a half-duplex active eavesdropper.

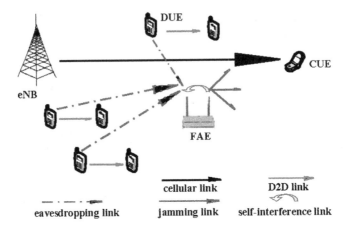

Fig. 2. Illustration of secure D2D communications with a full-duplex active eavesdropper.

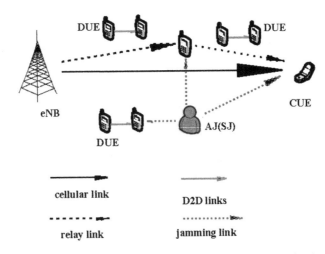

Fig. 3. Illustration of reliable D2D communications with an active jammer.

Half-Duplex Active Eavesdropper (HAE): Considering eavesdroppers become more intelligent and more selective, that is to say, they can select to passively eavesdrop private transmission among legitimate users, or actively jam them to destroy reliable communications, they are called half-duplex active eavesdroppers.

Full-Duplex Active Eavesdropper (FAE): If active eavesdroppers are of more hardware resources, they can launch eavesdropping and jamming attacks simultaneously, they are called full-duplex active eavesdroppers.

Active (Smart) Jammer (AJ/SJ): Active or smart jammers can adaptively adjust their jamming power or channels, and finally to decrease transmission rate and communication reliability of legitimate users.

If eavesdroppers can select passive eavesdropping or active jamming, legitimate users want to optimize their achievable secrecy rates or transmission rates accordingly. In [15], power allocation optimization was studied to improve the average achievable secrecy rate of legitimate users with a half-duplex active eavesdropper. When this kind of eavesdroppers intrude into D2D communications, not only the cooperation between cellular users and D2D users, but also the countermeasure between legitimate users and the half-duplex active eavesdropper should be joint considered. In [16], with the help of D2D cooperative relay and friendly jammers, the average achievable secrecy rate of the cellular user was enhanced with a half-duplex active eavesdropper.

Compared with the half-duplex active eavesdropper, it does much more harm to legitimate users when the active eavesdropper works on the full duplex mode. Firstly, the full-duplex active eavesdropper can carry out wiretapping and jamming attacks at the same time, anti-eavesdropping and anti-jamming demands of legitimate users should be jointly considered. Secondly, not only the inner interference between cellular users and D2D users should be considered, but also the outer jamming brought by the full-duplex eavesdropper should be referred to. In [10], transmission power of legitimate users or jamming power of the full-duplex active eavesdropper was hierarchically optimized to combat each other. The active eavesdropper was regarded as a jamming-aided eavesdropper in this works, where jamming attacks were launched to facilitate the eavesdropping, and the goal was to maximize the wiretap rate. While in [17], transmission rate of the cellular user and achievable secrecy rate of D2D users were joint optimized, while the full-duplex active eavesdropper carried out eavesdropping and jamming attacks at the same time to pursue the completely opposite goal.

Smart jammers can adaptively modify jamming channel strategy or jamming power to maximize jamming effects on legitimate users. Some researches considering that under smart jamming scheme, how to combat smart jammers through channel allocation and power control [18–24]. In [23], based on the spectrum waterfall, a recursive convolutional neural network was designed and a deep learning algorithm was proposed to combat dynamic and intelligent jammers. In [24], to combat a smart jammer, power control of the transmitter and relay were jointly optimized. In D2D communications, when smart jammers intrude, the inner interference should be avoided as soon as possible, and the outer jamming should be reduced to maintain robust transmission.

3 Game-Theoretic Learning Methods for Secure and Reliable D2D Communications

In the above section, we have analyzed new challenges for maintaining secure and reliable D2D communications when facing with active attackers. Then in this section, we study how multiple intelligent devices to enhance their anti-eavesdropping and anti-jamming performance by means of mutual cooperation and self-learning with game-theoretic learning methods. On one hand, in the future mobile communication networks or IoT networks, different intelligent devices are of different priorities, and their spectrum access or power control decisions are made asynchronously, so it is appropriate to use game theory to model complex interactions among them. On the other hand, not only the information exists in different distributed D2D (M2M) users, but also the one between legitimate users and vicious attackers are asymmetrical. Moreover, they don't want to interact with their information, machine-learning based methods can be applied to improve physical layer security and anti-jamming performance in D2D communications.

Now we discuss how to apply game theory and machine learning methods under different active attack scenarios in D2D communications.

3.1 Game-Theoretic Learning Methods Against Half-Duplex Active Eavesdroppers

When eavesdroppers become active and intelligent, it means that they can select different attack types, passive eavesdropping or active jamming. If they work on the half-duplex mode, they can switch between the two attack types. Therefore, the cooperation among legitimate users and the confrontation between legitimate users and half-duplex active eavesdroppers can be formulated as a non-cooperative game or hierarchical game. In [15], the scenario was considered that the transmitter can allocate power to transmit data and broadcasting artificial interference, while the active eavesdropper can select to work as a passive eavesdropper or an active jammer under the half-duplex constraint. The strategic and extensive wiretap games were proposed and the pure-strategy and mix-strategy equilibrium were proved.

In D2D communications, when half-duplex active eavesdroppers intrude, cooperative relay or friendly jammer selection of D2D users and attack type selection of active eavesdroppers can be studied under the game framework. In [28], the cooperative D2D node selection problem of the base station and the attack type selection problem of the active eavesdropper were jointly modeled as a non-cooperative game. A learning algorithm based on fictitious-play was proposed and the mixed-strategy Nash equilibrium of the proposed game was reached. In [16], a Stackelberg game was proposed to formulate the competition between legitimate users and active eavesdropper, and a Q-learning based algorithm was proposed to obtain the mixed-strategy Stackelberg equilibrium.

In the above researches, we can find that as attackers becoming more and more intelligent. To combat them, some machine learning approaches were gradually employed to solve the physical layer security and anti-jamming problem. Not only legitimate users, but also active eavesdroppers have learning abilities to a certain degree. When active eavesdroppers can work on the full duplex mode, and can adaptively modify their jamming power, some more complex learning algorithms should be proposed to update power or spectrum strategies of legitimate users against them.

3.2 Game-Theoretic Learning Methods Against Full-Duplex Active Eavesdroppers

In general wireless networks, some game models have been utilized to model the confrontation between legitimate uses and full-duplex active eavesdroppers. In [10, 29], the power decision processes between legitimate users and the full-duplex active eavesdropper were studied at a Stackelberg game framework, the existence of the

Stackelberg equilibrium was proved, and heuristic legitimate power and jamming power allocation algorithms were proposed. In [30], the jamming power optimization of the full-duplex active eavesdropper and the transmission power optimization of the legitimate transmitter were formulated as a non-cooperative game, the sufficient conditions for the existence of the pure-strategy Nash equilibrium was derived, and the mixed-strategy Nash equilibrium was obtained by a fictitious-play based algorithm. Furthermore, in consideration of the cooperation among legitimate users and the confrontation between legitimate users and active eavesdroppers in a uniform framework, [31] proposed a three-stage Stackelberg game scheme among the transmitter, multiple relays and the full-duplex active eavesdropper, achieved cooperative communication, decreased the wiretapping probability and improved the secrecy performance.

We introduced the full-duplex active eavesdroppers into D2D communications. In [18], we formulated sequential power strategies of the base station, multiple D2D users and the full-duplex active eavesdropper to be a multi-layer Stackelberg game. Moreover, we proposed a hierarchical power control algorithm joint based on best response (BR) and stochastic learning automata (SLA) to enhance achievable secrecy rates of all D2D users and the transmission rate of the cellular user. And furthermore, in [32], we joint considered D2D relay selection, power control of the cellular user, and jamming power optimization of the active eavesdropper in a three-tier Stackelberg game, and a hierarchical and heterogeneous algorithm based on SLA and Q-learning was proposed to achieve the mixed-strategy Stackelberg equilibrium.

From the researches above, we can find hierarchical game have been applied to study the joint anti-jamming and physical layer security problem when facing with full-duplex active eavesdroppers. Moreover, we combine multi-tier hierarchical game and distributed machine learning methods to analyze and study the complex interactions among cellular users, D2D users and full-duplex active eavesdroppers.

3.3 Game-Theoretic Learning Methods Against Smart Jammers

When facing with smart jammers, hierarchical game can be also applied to describe dynamic interactions between legitimate users and smart jammers. Some researches considering that under smart jamming scheme, how to combat smart jammers through power control and channel allocation. Authors in [18] formulated the anti-jamming problem as a Stackelberg game, in which legitimate user was regarded as the leader, smart jammer as the follower, both changed their power strategies to maximize their utility. In [33], a Bayesian Stackelberg game was proposed to model anti-jamming scheme with the uncertainty of channel state and transmission cost. In [34], authors proposed an anti-jamming Stackelberg game in wireless networks, in which relay nodes were introduced and worked as the vice leader in the proposed game. And in [35], the discrete power control problem on anti-jamming was modeled as a Stackelberg game, and a hierarchical learning algorithm was proposed.

In [36], we formulated the hierarchical competitive relationship between a user and jammer as a Stackelberg game, and proposed a hybrid learning algorithm based on Q-learning and multi-armed bandit (MAB) for combating smart jamming. In D2D communications, when smart jammers intrude, the inner interference should be avoided as soon as possible, and the outer jamming should be reduced to maintain robust transmission. Therefore, not only the competition and cooperation between cellular users and D2D users should be considered, but also the dynamic confrontation between legitimate users and smart jammers should be studied.

4 Numerical Results and Discussions

In this section, we will provide some numerical results with different active attackers and demonstrate the availability and efficiency of hierarchical game learning methods proposed in the former section.

4.1 Half-Duplex Active Eavesdropping Scenario

Under the system model in Fig. 1, we set up a cellular cell, where an evolved Node B (eNB) located on the center of a square area of 1 km * 1 km, and a cellular user and N D2D users are randomly located on the square area of 0.5 km * 0.5 km centered by the eNB, while the active eavesdropper is randomly located between the square area of 0.5 km * 0.5 km and 1 km * 1 km around the eNB. For our simulations, suppose that the transmit power of the eNB, all D2D users and the half-duplex active eavesdropper are 1 W, 0.1 W, and 0.1 W respectively. Considering that the half-duplex active eavesdropper can select passive eavesdropping or active jamming attack pattern, legitimate users cooperative with each other to combat it.

Firstly, considering that the hierarchical structure between the cellular user and all D2D users, we formulate their hierarchical interactions as a Stackelberg game to combat the half-duplex active eavesdropper. Furthermore, the cooperative power control problem among all D2D users is modeled as an exact potential game and a learning algorithm based on SLA is proposed to converge to the mixed-strategy Nash equilibrium of the lower-tier game, finally the Stackelberg equilibrium is received. The performance comparison of the proposed algorithm with selfish D2D power control algorithm (SDPCA) and the random selection algorithm (RSA) is presented in Fig. 4. We can see that the sum utility, which describes the tradeoff between secure requirements and power costs of all D2D users, decreases with the active jamming probability of the active eavesdropper, and the proposed algorithm outperforms other two algorithms.

Secondly, in consideration of the adaptive strategy selection of the half-duplex active eavesdropper, joint relay selection and friendly jamming power control of legitimate users and attack pattern selection of the active eavesdropper is formulated as a non-cooperative game. In the proposed game, a "best" D2D user is chosen to relay the confidential message of the cellular user, and other $N - 1$ D2D users working as friendly jammers to improve the average secrecy rate of the cellular user together. Then we propose a fictitious-play based algorithm to obtain the mixed-strategy Nash equilibrium of the proposed game. Figure 5 shows the performance advantage of the proposed algorithm compared with the nearest neighbor relay selecting algorithm with the increasing number of D2D users.

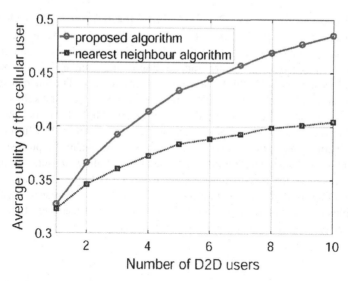

Fig. 4. Utility of the cellular user versus number of D2D users with a half-duplex active eavesdropper

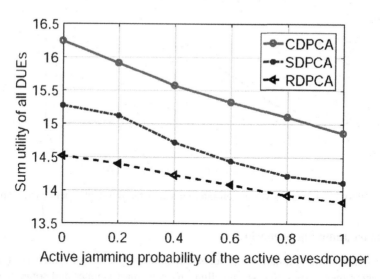

Fig. 5. Utility of all D2D users versus jamming probability of a half-duplex active eavesdropper

4.2   Full-Duplex Active Eavesdropping Scenario

The simulation under the full-duplex active eavesdropping scenario is made under the system model in Fig. 2. We first let the eNB on the origin of coordinates, the coordinates of the cellular user is (200 m, 200 m), 5 D2D users are randomly located in the square area of 300 m, 300 m, and the full-duplex active eavesdropper is located at 500 m, 500 m. Suppose that transmission power sets of the cellular user and the full-duplex active eavesdropper are $\mathcal{P}_C = \mathcal{P}_A = \{0.2, 0.4, 0.6, 0.8, 1\}$ W, and the transmission power set $\mathcal{P}_D = \{0.02, 0.04, 0.06, 0.08, 0.1\}$ W is shared by all D2D users. In this situation, we consider that the full-duplex active eavesdropper can modify its jamming power to destroy the secure transmission of the cellular link and the reliable communication of D2D links, while the cellular user and all D2D users can select their suitable power level to combat it. We formulate a three-layer Stackelberg game to express the cooperation between the cellular user and all D2D users, and the confrontation between legitimate users and the active eavesdropper. We further propose two hybrid learning algorithms based on BR and SLA to obtain the pure-strategy and the mixed-strategy Stackelberg equilibrium. The utility of all D2D users versus the self-interference factor of the active eavesdropper is shown is Fig. 5. We can see that the utility of all D2D users decreases with the increasing of the self-interference factor of the full-duplex active eavesdropper and the proposed hybrid learning algorithms both present better performance than the RSA algorithm (Fig. 6).

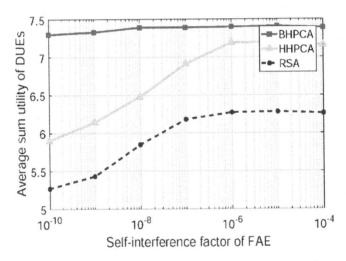

Fig. 6. Utility of D2D users versus self-interference of the full-duplex active eavesdropper

4.3   Smart Jamming Scenario

We also make some simulations under smart jamming scenario, which is shown in Fig. 3, where there exists an eNB, a cellular user, a smart jammer and some candidate D2D relay users. The coordinates of eNB and the cellular user are $(0\,\text{km}, 10\,\text{km})$ and $(10\,\text{km}, 0\,\text{km})$. The smart jammer is located in $(10\,\text{km}, 10\,\text{km})$. There are 4 D2D users, which are located in $(2.5\,\text{km}, 2.5\,\text{km})$, $(5\,\text{km}, 2.5\,\text{km})$, $(5\,\text{km}, 5\,\text{km})$, $(7.5\,\text{km}, 5\,\text{km})$ respectively. Considering that the smart jammer can select its jamming strategy according to listening messages, the legitimate transmitter and the selected relay can intelligently modify their transmission power to anti-smart jamming of this kind. The hierarchical interactions among different users is formulated as a Stackelberg game, and a hybrid learning algorithm based on Q learning and multi-armed bandit (MAB) is proposed, and the performance of legitimate users is compared with the random selecting algorithm with different eavesdropping errors is shown in Fig. 7.

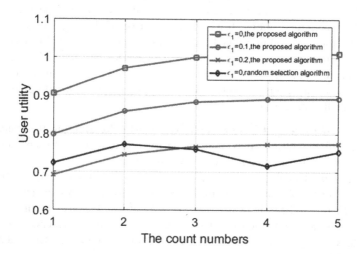

Fig. 7. Utility of legitimate users versus time slots with eavesdropping error of an active jammer

From all numerical results shown above, the game-theoretic learning approaches are available for legitimate users to improve the physical layer security and anti-jamming performance under active attacks.

5 Future Research Directions

We have discussed the physical layer security and anti-jamming problems in D2D communications under different attacking scenarios in previous sections. It has been verified that game-theoretic learning methods were feasible and effective to combat active attackers, and some research results have been achieved to improve anti-eavesdropping and anti-jamming performance of legitimate users. However, in view of complex interactions among different agents and information uncertainty of electro-magnetic environment, there are a lot of open issues to be solved. Then we analyze the future research directions on secure and reliable D2D communications when facing with active attackers.

Practical Cooperation Mechanisms and Technologies of Legitimate Users: To confront active attackers, necessary cooperation among legitimate users is needed, not only among D2D users, but also between cellular users and D2D users. Some researches have introduced social relationship into D2D communications, how to employ social relationship among D2D users to further improve security performance and transmission reliability with intelligent attackers is worth to study. Moreover, considering the hierarchical characteristic between cellular users and D2D users, how to design the hierarchical cooperation mechanism is a future research direction. Due to emerging technologies of 5G, such as non-orthogonal multiple access (NOMA), multiple antenna technology, millimeter-wave (mmWave) communications and unmanned aerial vehicle (UAV) enabled communications, transmission efficiency and security of wireless communications can be enhanced accordingly. Take the example of UAV enabled communications, from the perspective of the physical layer security, UAVs can work as mobile relays or friendly jammers to help improve anti-eavesdropping performance of massive machine-type devices. Recently, there are few works on secure and reliable communications by the aid of these emerging technologies against active attackers. Therefore, it will be an open issue to introduce them into combating intelligent attackers.

Tradeoff of Offensive and Defensive of Active Attackers: From the standpoint of active attackers, they want to maximize the destruction to legitimate users and unlikely to be discovered. On one hand, when they work as passive eavesdroppers, they can only wiretap confidential information and hard to be discovered. On the other hand, they can do much more harm to legitimate users when they work as active jammers, while can be easier to be found since they need to transmit vicious jamming signals. So there exists a tradeoff of offensive and defensive of active attackers, how to apply flexible attack strategies to maximize their destruction to legitimate users and hide their positions will be an open issue.

Massive D2D Communications Modeling and Multi-tier and Heterogeneous Game Formulation: At the present, the scheme that legitimate users cooperate with each other to maximize their utilities have been studied under game theory frameworks. But when the number of active eavesdroppers or legitimate users becomes very large, how to model their interactions using game theory and how to obtain the stationary or optimal equilibrium solutions will be a huge challenge. On one hand, the mean field game, which is a kind of differential game, can be applied to model group behavior of a huge number of players and describe the influence of crowd behavior on the individual agent. While due to dynamic changes of attacking strategies, how to quickly obtain stationary states of the mean field game will be a new challenge. On the other hand, considering complex interactions among cellular users, D2D users and intelligent attackers, multi-tier Stackelberg game should be formulated to improve security and reliability of legitimate users. Whether the equilibrium of multi-tier game exists should be discussed and the existence condition should be further analyzed.

Optimization with Incomplete Information and Applications of Deep Reinforcement Learning: Since the positions of legitimate users and intelligent attackers are competitive, there are no information exchanges between them. They only make their decisions based on imperfect information for each other. There have been some researches on the physical layer security or anti-jamming problem based on limited observations, while with no information on the opposite side, how to maximize their utilities based on machine learning methods is an issue worthy of studying. The deep reinforcement learning methods are suitable for solving the problem under such situation and don't need to apply under a special game framework. Based on deep reinforcement learning methods, intelligent users can update their power and channel selections according to training data without any information on attackers' utilities and strategy sets. Deep reinforcement learning methods have just been used to confront smart jammers, while how to accelerate convergence of deep reinforcement learning methods are really an open issue.

6 Conclusion

In this paper, we have analyzed security threats in D2D underlaying cellular networks under different attacking scenarios. Based on hierarchical game framework, we expound the optimization objective description, utilities design and strategies selection of cellular users and D2D users. Furthermore, we have illustrated kinds of machine learning methods, such as fictitious play, MAB, Q-learning and SLA, to optimize transmission power, relay selection and other strategies to improve the physical layer security and anti-smart jamming performance. Finally, the future directions and challenges were discussed.

References

1. Ahmed, K.-I., Tabassum, H., Hossain, E.: Deep learning for radio resource allocation in multi-cell networks. IEEE Network Early Access 33(6), 188–195 (2019)
2. Nawaz, S.-J., Sharma, S.-K., Wyne, S., Patwary, M.-N., Asaduzzaman, M.: Quantum machine learning for 6G communication networks: state-of-the-art and vision for the future. IEEE Access 7, 46317–46350 (2019)
3. Alrowaily, M., Lu, Z.: Secure edge computing in IoT systems: review and case studies. In: 2018 IEEE/ACM Symposium on Edge Computing (SEC), Seattle, WA, pp. 440–444 (2018)
4. Zhang, P., Niu, K., Tian, H., Nie, G.-F., Qi, Q., Zhang, J.: Technology prospect of 6G mobile communications. J. Commun. 40(1), 141–148 (2019)
5. Sim, G.-H., Klos, S., Asadi, A., Klein, A., Hollick, M.: An online context-aware machine learning algorithm for 5G mmWave vehicular communications. IEEE/ACM Trans. Networking 26(6), 2487–2500 (2018)
6. Hamamreh, J.-M., Arslan, H.: Joint PHY/MAC layer security design using ARQ with MRC and null-space independent, PAPR-aware artificial noise in SISO systems. IEEE Trans. Wireless Communications 17(9), 6190–6204 (2018)
7. Zheng, G., Krikidis, I., Li, J., Petropulu, A.P., Ottersten, B.: Improving physical layer secrecy using full-duplex jamming receivers. IEEE Trans. Signal Process. 61(20), 4962–4974 (2013)
8. Geraci, G., Egan, M., Yuan, J., Razi, A., Collings, I.-B.: Secrecy sum-rates for multi-user MIMO regularized channel inversion precoding. IEEE Trans. Commun. 60(11), 3472–3482 (2012)
9. Zou, Y.-L., Champagne, B., Zhu, W.-P., Hanzo, L.: Relay-selection improves the security-reliability tradeoff in cognitive radio systems. IEEE Trans. Commun. 63(1), 215–228 (2015)
10. Tang, X., Ren, P.-R., Wang, Y.-C., Han, Z.: Combating full-duplex active eavesdropper: a hierarchical game perspective. IEEE Trans. Commun. 65(3), 1379–1395 (2017)
11. Abedi, M.-R., Mokari, N., Saeedi, H., Yanikomeroglu, H.: Robust resource allocation to enhance physical layer security in systems with full-duplex receivers: active adversary. IEEE Trans. Wireless Commun. 16(2), 885–899 (2017)

12. Li, L., Petropulu, A.-P., Chen, Z.: MIMO secret communications against an active eavesdropper. IEEE Trans. Inf. Forensics Secur. **12**(10), 2387–2401 (2017)

13. Qu, J., Cai, Y., Zheng, J., Yang, W., Wu, D., Hu, Y.: Power allocation for device-to-device communication underlaying cellular networks under a probabilistic eavesdropping scenario. Ann. Telecommun. **71**(7), 389–398 (2016). https://doi.org/10.1007/s12243-016-0515-x

14. Mei, W.-D., Chen, Z., Fang, J., Fu, B.: Secure D2D-enabled cellular communication against selective eavesdropping. In: IEEE ICC 2017 Communication and Information System Security Symposium, pp. 1–6 (2017)

15. Mukherjee, A., Swindlehurst, A.-L.: Jamming games in the MIMO wiretap channel with an active eavesdropper. IEEE Trans. Signal Process. **61**(1), 82–91 (2013)

16. Luo, Y., Yang, Y., Duan, Y., Yang, Z.: Joint D2D cooperative relaying and friendly jamming selection for physical layer security. In: Meng, L., Zhang, Y. (eds.) MLICOM 2018. LNICST, vol. 251, pp. 115–126. Springer, Cham (2018). https://doi.org/10.1007/978-3-030-00557-3_12

17. Luo, Y.-L., Feng, Z., Jiang, H., Yang, Y., Huang, Y., Yao, J.: Game-theoretic learning approaches for secure D2D communications against full-duplex active eavesdropper. IEEE Access **7**, 41324–41335 (2019)

18. Yang, D., Xue, G., Zhang, J., Richa, A., Fang, X.: Coping with a smart jammer in wireless networks: a Stackelberg game approach. IEEE Trans. Wireless Commun. **12**(8), 4038–4047 (2013)

19. Xu, Y., et al.: A one-leader multi-follower Bayesian-Stackelberg game for anti-jamming transmission in UAV communication networks. IEEE Access **6**, 21697–21709 (2018)

20. Yu, L., Wu, Q., Xu, Y., Ding, G., Jia, L.: Power control games for multi-user anti-jamming communications. Wireless Netw. **25**(5), 2365–2374 (2018). https://doi.org/10.1007/s11276-018-1664-9

21. Tang, X., Ren, P., Wang, Y., Du, Q., Sun, L.: Securing wireless transmission against reactive jamming: a Stackelberg game framework. In: Proceeding of IEEE GLOBECOM, pp. 1–6 (2015)

22. Wu, Y., Wang, B., Liu, K.J.R., Clancy, T.C.: Anti-jamming games in multi-channel cognitive radio networks. IEEE J. Sel. Areas Commun. **30**(1), 4–15 (2012)

23. Liu, X., Xu, Y., Jia, L., Wu, Q., Anpalagan, A.: Anti-jamming communications using spectrum waterfall: a deep reinforcement learning approach. IEEE Commun. Lett. **22**(5), 998–1001 (2018)

24. Feng, Z.-B., et al.: Power control in relay-assisted anti-Jamming systems: a Bayesian three-layer Stackelberg game approach. IEEE Access **7**, 14623–14636 (2019)

25. Song, L., Niyato, D., Han, Z., Hossain, E.: Game-theoretic resource allocation methods for device-to-device communication. IEEE Commun. Mag. **21**(3), 136–144 (2014)

26. Wang, F., Song, L., Han, Z., Zhao, Q., Wang, X.: Joint scheduling and resource allocation for device-to-device underlay communication. In: IEEE Wireless Communication and Networking Conference (WCNC), pp. 1–6 (2013)

27. Chu, Z., et al.: Game theory based secure wireless powered D2D communications with cooperative jamming. In: Wireless Days, pp. 95–98 (2017)

28. Luo, Y.-J., Yang, Y., Cui, L.: Research on physical layer security in D2D enabled cellular networks with an active eavesdropper. Sig. Process. **34**(1), 119–125 (2018)

29. Tang, X., Ren, P., Han, Z.: Power-efficient secure transmission against full-duplex active eavesdropper: a game-theoretic framework. IEEE Access **5**, 24632–24645 (2017)

30. Huang, W., Chen, W., Bai, B., Han, Z.: Wiretap channel with full-duplex proactive eavesdropper: a game theoretic approach. IEEE Trans. Veh. Technol. **67**(8), 7658–7663 (2018)

31. Fang, H., Xu, L., Zou, Y., Wang, X., Choo, K.R.: Three-stage Stackelberg game for defending against full-duplex active eavesdropping attacks in cooperative communication. IEEE Trans. Veh. Technol. **67**(11), 10788–10799 (2018)
32. Luo, Y.-J., Yang, Y.: D2D friendly jamming and cooperative relaying for combating a full-duplex active eavesdropper. In: ICCT 2019, pp. 1–6 (2019)
33. Jia, L., Yao, F., Sun, Y., et al.: Bayesian Stackelberg game for anti-jamming transmission with incomplete information. IEEE Commun. Lett. **20**(10), 1991–1994 (2016)
34. Li, Y., Xiao, L., Liu, J., et al.: Power control Stackelberg game in cooperative anti-jamming communications. In: International Conference on Game Theory for Networks, pp. 1–6 (2015)
35. Jia, L., Yao, F., Sun, Y., et al.: A hierarchical learning solution for anti-jamming Stackelberg game with discrete power strategies. IEEE Wirel. Commun. Lett. **6**(6), 818–821 (2017)
36. Feng, Z., et al.: An anti-Jamming hierarchical optimization approach in relay communication system via Stackelberg game. Appl. Sci. **9**, 1–14 (2019)

Author Index

Printed in the United States
By Bookmasters